American Foreign Policy and the Blessings of Liberty
and Other Essays

AMERICAN FOREIGN POLICY

AND THE BLESSINGS OF LIBERTY

AND OTHER ESSAYS

by Samuel Flagg Bemis

New Haven and London, Yale University Press, 1962

Library of Congress catalog card number: 62-16561

Acknowledgment is made, for
kind permissions to reprint,
to the following: American
Antiquarian Society, *American
Historical Review, Canadian Historical Review,
Daughters of the American Revolution
Magazine,* Indiana University
Press, Massachusetts Historical
Society, *Pacific Review,
U.S. News and World Report,
Virginia Quarterly Review.*

Preface

THESE ESSAYS AND ADDRESSES are selected from the bibliography appended to this volume and extend over nearly a half-century of interest in the history of American foreign policy and diplomacy. Each essay is printed exactly as it originally appeared except for minor corrections and for changes in the titles of Chapters 9 and 17. The author prefers to let them stand thus, for better or worse. Stylistically, the text and notes, however, have been edited according to the rules of the Yale University Press. Grateful acknowledgment for permission to reprint these articles is made to their original publishers, who are fully identified above. I am indebted to Mrs. Marian Neal Ash, Miss Helen C. Boatfield, and Mrs. Elizabeth F. Hailey for seeing the book through the press, and finally to the Mature Scholars Fund of Yale University for enabling publication.

Samuel Flagg Bemis

New Haven, Conn.
March 1962

Contents

Contents

Key to Abbreviations in Footnotes

A.H.A   American Historical Association.

A.H.R.   *American Historical Review.*

Arch. Aff. Etrang.   Archives du Ministère des Affaires Étrangères, Paris.

A.G.N.   Archivo General de la Nación, Buenos Aires.

A.H.N.   Archivo Histórico Nacional, Madrid.

A.S.P., C.N.   *American State Papers, Commerce and Navigation.*

A.S.P., F.R.   *American State Papers, Foreign Relations.*

A.S.P., I.A.   *American State Papers, Indian Affairs.*

C.A.   Canadian Archives. Series letter, volume number, and pages follow consecutively, e.g.: C.A., Q, 41, 15 indicates Canadian Archives, Series Q, Volume 41, page 15. Sometimes a volume is in two parts, as C.A., Q, 41–2, 15.

D.S.   Department of State Records, Washington.

M.H.S.   Massachusetts Historical Society.

M.P.C.   *Michigan Pioneer and Historical Collections.*

P.R.O.   Public Record Office, London.

P.R.O., C.O.   Public Record Office, Colonial Office Papers, followed consecutively by series number and volume number as in P.R.O., F.O.

P.R.O., F.O.   Public Record Office, Foreign Office Papers, followed consecutively by series number and volume number, e.g.: P.R.O., F.O., 115, 8 indicating Series 115, Volume 8, the pagination to bound volumes of MSS not being given in this instance. The enumeration of series and volume follows the official *List of Foreign Office Records to 1837 Preserved in the Public Record Office.*

1. American Foreign Policy and the Blessings of Liberty

As HISTORIANS DEBATE about the philosophy of history, and philosophers reason about the meaning of history, and even the meaning of meaning, cannot most of us agree that history, among its other great attributes, has a certain usefulness? A principal service of history is that, by extending our experience, individually and universally, back beyond the touch of our own lifetime, it fortifies our judgment in dealing with problems of the present and measuring our hopes for the future—I will not say in shaping the future. Of course our historical experience must be validated by critical scholarship. The experience must also be appraised and reappraised in relation to the ever-changing present as we move along toward the future. Like all social processes, the evolution and practice of foreign policy takes place in space and time. In the case of the United States it would seem to be in widening space and shortening time. It takes place in space and time, but it must also be measured in terms of human values.

Can the diplomatic history of the United States strengthen our judgment in facing the problems of today which include nothing less than the survival of our nation and the principles we have stood for in the world? Only if we relate our historical experience to the successive stages of world politics and power in which American diplomacy has operated for better or worse for nearly two centuries. And only if we measure the history of American foreign policy in terms of the fundamental purposes and values of our life as a nation and our determination as a people to preserve them.

We have been hearing much these days about the necessity of a national purpose and the formulation of national goals for the good life.

Delivered as the presidential address at the December 1961 meeting of the American Historical Association. Published in *American Historical Review, 67,* no. 2, 1962.

An address later at the same meeting by Secretary of State Dean Rusk, replying to some of the points made by Professor Bemis, was published under the title "Some Issues of Contemporary History" in the *Department of State Bulletin, 46,* no. 1177, Jan. 16, 1962.

As if the national purpose had not long since been stated in the principles of our Declaration of Independence, "life, liberty, and the pursuit of happiness"; and in the preamble to our Constitution, "to form a more perfect Union, establish Justice, insure domestic Tranquility, promote the general Welfare, and secure the Blessings of Liberty to ourselves and our Posterity."

This basic statement describes the original *raison d'être* of our nation. "In every period," to quote Leonard Krieger on Karl Marx, "the kind of activity with which men are most concerned—which they consider the most important—gives tone and color to the rest." [1] It was liberty which set the tone and gave color to the activities of our countrymen at the beginning of our nation. The Blessings of Liberty were the fundamental "rights of Englishmen" stemming from colonial charters and evolving through the seventeenth and eighteenth centuries by American constitutional custom which appropriated for itself the British parliamentary Bill of Rights of 1688. These freedoms of the individual are the values for which the United States has stood throughout its history in the shifting configurations of power and politics in the world of nations. They are the values which we invoke today, now, for all our citizens. They are also in varying degree the values of the remaining free peoples of the world. "With us, and throughout all history," wrote Albert Camus shortly before his death, "they deny servitude, falsehood and terror." [2] These values are our birthright of liberty, "laws, freedom, faith in God," as sounds the old hymn, "out of ages richly poured."

We have not lacked a clear purpose as a nation. What we seem to have been lacking is a continued consciousness of that purpose, of these congenital Blessings of Liberty. What we seem to have been losing is the hardened will to make them prevail at all costs in the historically shifted strategy of American defense and diplomacy. As far as goals for the good life are envisioned, they depend on the survival of liberty.

As through the long ages of geology, movements of the earth's land masses have wrought compelling changes in the number and configuration of the continents, in their identity, in their climate, and in the creatures living on them, so throughout the history of international relations, changes in the balance of power have affected the configuration, number, identity, and policy of nations and their peoples in the shorter period of human history. Governments have had to adapt

1. Leonard Krieger, "The Use of Marx for History," *Political Science Quarterly*, 75 (Sept. 1960), 360.
2. Albert Camus, *The Rebel* (New York, 1959), p. 283.

themselves to such geopolitical alterations or sink amid the strife of nations. These shifts, sometimes gradual, sometimes sudden and revolutionary as in the history of geology, have hitherto served the diplomatic historian as landmarks, helping him, as the strata of the earth's crust assist the geologist, to tell where we as a nation came from, where we have been, where we are now, and perhaps, but only perhaps, the direction in which we may be moving from here.

May I suggest that in the history of American foreign policy there are five major stages or shifts presenting themselves slowly, or suddenly, that can engage our attention here: the three long centuries that produced the European state system before the American Revolution; the quick era of revolution and emancipation, 1776–1823; the century after 1815 of isolation and security; the new picture of power and politics that appeared at the end of the nineteenth century as a prelude to the world wars of the twentieth century; and the present cold war at the beginning of our swiftly moving atomic age.

The first great geopolitical shift with which the historian of American foreign policy need concern himself, but which merely requires mention here, was from the Mediterranean to the Atlantic. It led to the discovery and colonization of the New World coincidentally with the appearance of the national states of Portugal, Spain, Holland, France, and England on the Atlantic fringe of the new European system. We may bracket with the years 1492–1776 the age of European dynastic and colonial wars, toward the end of which emerged the independence of the United States in revolt against British sovereignty with the aid of the French alliance.

Our national independence introduced a second major alteration in the configuration of power. The era of emancipation embraced three violent political revolutions in the Western world and their sequela of wars: the North American Revolution, the French Revolution, and the Latin American revolutions.

Thanks to the necessities of Great Britain and Spain in the wars of the French Revolution, President Washington, that wise, patriotic leader with far-seeing vision and sound judgment, slow thinking, perhaps, but by no means a "bewildered" or senile statesman as some would picture him, was able to preserve American neutrality and to liberate American territory in the Old Northwest from British occupation by his treaty of 1794 with Great Britain, and to open the Mississippi to the sea and free the Old Southwest from Spanish occupation by his treaty of 1795 with Spain. These were the first two treaties negotiated by the new national government—that was George Washington's constant word for it, "national."

There were other large windfalls for the United States coming out of the European cyclone. Thanks to immediate concerns in Europe during Jefferson's presidency, Napoleon Bonaparte had to abandon his plans for re-establishment of a French colonial empire in the Mississippi Valley. The resulting Louisiana Procurement—to use Edward Channing's fitting phrase—doubled the territory of the United States overnight within little more than a quarter century after the Declaration of Independence.

Napoleon's usurpation in Spain furnished the pretext for the Latin American revolutions. To preserve the neutrality of the United States in Spain's colonial war and in the vain hope of keeping the republic of the north from recognizing the independence of the new states of the south, Ferdinand VII's restored monarchy signed the so-called Transcontinental Treaty of 1819, placing Florida under the American flag and explicitly recognizing, for the first time by a foreign power, the sovereign position of the United States on the Pacific Coast. Soon thereafter, out of Anglo-American concerns over the possibility of European intervention in Latin America, came the independent pronouncement of President Monroe—behind the wooden wall of the British navy to be sure, but with what Dexter Perkins calls a "bold republican tone."

These great and happy successes did not come to pass within the neutrality desired by the fathers of American foreign policy. Neutrality in the general wars of Europe we have never been able perfectly to enjoy. Somehow when these wars extended to the oceans, they ceased to be "ordinary" wars confined strictly to their own continent such as George Washington envisioned in his Farewell Address. The neutrality of the United States broke down twice in the first half-century of its independence, as it has collapsed twice again during the last half-century.

Even during the two wars that signalized the first two collapses of American neutrality, the United States did not seek to make an alliance with its enemy's enemy: with Great Britain against France during the "quasi war" of 1798–1800, or with Napoleon in the second war with Great Britain of 1812–15. Experience of the fathers with the entanglements of the life-saving French alliance of the Revolution confirmed their aversion, and the distrust of their sons, to any more entangling alliances. This distrust dominated American foreign policy in the next hundred years of world politics.

On the whole the newly established policy had responded tolerably well, under the leadership of natural statesmen, to the international politics of the era of emancipation.

The peace settlements at Ghent and at Vienna presaged another shift in our geopolitical center of gravity: across the continent, from the Atlantic to the Mississippi Valley and on to the Pacific Ocean. During the century of isolation that followed, the security of an expanding nation was maintained with the smallest of standing armies, little more than a force for pacification and domination of the Indian tribes, and with a correspondingly small navy, armed forces less than those of even the smallest European powers. Of course, I do not speak of the improvisations of armies and navies during the war with Mexico or during the sectional War for Southern Independence, forces promptly demobilized after the conflicts were over.

Granted the preservation of the Union, the greatest achievement of American nationality during the nineteenth century was expansion of the nation across the empty continent to the shore of the "other ocean." It established the territorial basis of the United States as a world power and a bastion of freedom today. Thanks to the European wars and their aftermath in the Old World and the New, and the continued collisions of European friendships and enmities, the United States was able to redouble its national territory within scarcely a half century after the treaties of Ghent and Vienna. This continental consummation occurred during a period of what Professor C. Vann Woodward so nicely calls "free security." It was during the long period of comparative peace on the great oceans that the high objectives of American foreign policy were carried forward and largely achieved.

One international war did feature the rounding out of the Transcontinental Republic, otherwise expansively perfected by peaceful diplomacy between 1783 and 1867. It would be generally agreed, I suppose, on both sides of the Rio Grande, that the War of 1846–48 between the United States and Mexico—not the only war between two American countries fought during this period—might have been avoided if the two nations had been pledged to the Mexican-American, inter-American, and United Nations peace machinery of the twentieth century. Historians and statesmen in the United States from John Quincy Adams, William Jay, and Abraham Lincoln to Woodrow Wilson, Justin Smith, and Eugene Barker have debated the justice of the war with Mexico, none with perfect objectivity. But I have not been able to find any American today who would wish to repudiate President

Polk's foreign policy and the Civil War that followed by handing back to Mexico the territory purchased by the Treaty of Guadalupe Hidalgo and the succeeding Gadsden Purchase. What an excitement such a suggestion stirred up in 1917 when the Zimmerman telegram proposed officially that Germany, Japan, and Mexico unite to take back the "lost provinces"!

The reasons for the easy successes of the United States during the eighteenth and nineteenth centuries were: our "detached and distant position," to use the familiar words of Washington's Farewell Address; Europe's distresses America's advantage, certainly sensed by our early statesmen, more clearly realized by the historian today; and the position of Canada, at first in effect a hostage—if such were needed—for Anglo-American peace during the British century, in our later times a friendly accouplement of Anglo-American solidarity and alliance in the turbulent twentieth century. There were other, more irenic factors that benignly colored the geopolitical position of Canada. Cultural sympathies, demographical affinities, and economic relationships bonded the peoples of the United States and Canada increasingly to peace. And there was the ever-peaceful disposition of the Canadian people and their own unpreparedness for war. Certainly no war with the United States would ever have arisen from them, or from any significant segment of them.

So American foreign policy adapted itself with easy instinct to the immensely favorable configuration of world politics during the last three quarters of the nineteenth century. We were so safe and foolproof that we did not need much of a policy. Some wiseacres thought we did not even need diplomatic representation abroad. Oh, wondrous century, so fortuitously fortunate for our nation! Oh, happy, golden, bygone years of safety, in lucky innocence, apart from the world around us!

During the nineteenth century, that is, after 1815, the danger to our nation was from within. Is it not a demonstration of the foolproof position of the United States that we were able uniquely to indulge in a great civil war without any permanent lesion to our foreign policy? But does the diplomatic experience of that century fortify our judgment in dealing with the problems of this century and measuring our hopes for the future?

The happy age of isolation and continental contentment approached its end over the historical "watershed" of the 1890s. The fourth great geopolitical shift in the axis of American foreign policy and diplomacy was from east-west to north-south: to the isthmus of Central America and its outlying island citadels in both oceans.

An unprecedented phenomenon in world politics set the shift in motion toward the end of the century: the sudden appearance of three new world powers—Germany, the United States, and Japan. The advent of two of these powers, each with a first-class army and building toward a first-class navy, was of great portent for the third power, the United States, as well as for the British Empire at its apogee.

Neither Germany nor Japan had a friendly hostage, like Canada, for peaceful relations with the United States; on the contrary, the United States had presented Japan with a future hostage when it acquired Alaska in 1867 and with an immediate one when it took over the Philippine Islands in 1898. Japan could threaten Alaska and the Philippines; Germany conceivably could threaten our Atlantic coast and the Caribbean. Against these possibilities the United States depended on its new one-ocean navy to meet Germany in the Atlantic (in case of British neutrality), or Japan in the Pacific. An American canal under American control against all comers became more imperative than ever as a waterway through which to pass the navy from one ocean to the other as circumstances might require. No one at the turn of the century, not even Alfred Thayer Mahan, dreamed of a simultaneous two-ocean war.

One may feel that it was the isthmian question that animated the Expansionists of 1898. They found the popular hysteria over Cuba convenient to their "large policy" of securing control of the strategic radius of the future canal. Strategic designs, public opinion, and the pressure of party politics combined to push the reluctant President McKinley into the Cuban-Spanish-American War which resulted in the liberation of Cuba and the ejection of Spain from the New World. It also led to the utterly unanticipated acquisition of the Philippine Islands and all the then uncharted complications for the United States that followed in the Far East. In various essays published during the first decade of the present century Captain Mahan laid down his famous dicta for the policy of the United States as a world power, which one is tempted to put into capsule form: in America, predominance; in Asia, cooperation; in Europe and Africa, abstention. So great was the weight of tradition that Mahan did not, nor did any other student of strategy that I know of, venture to combine these three separate concepts into a global strategy. So heavy were the precepts of an age of successful isolation that only a handful of political thinkers on this side of the water, such as Mahan, Theodore Roosevelt, the young diplomat Lewis Einstein, and perhaps Colonel E. M. House, could take in the implications for the United States of an upset in the world balance of power from a German victory in any war with Great Britain. Even Theodore

Roosevelt turned his attention altogether to domestic reform by 1912. In the presidential campaign of that year neither Roosevelt's New Nationalism nor Wilson's New Freedom said much about foreign policy or military preparedness. When war unexpectedly broke out in the Old World only two years later, it did not alarm our people very much at first; it seemed so remote, like a fiery collision between two distant stars of another system. Woodrow Wilson enjoined his countrymen to be neutral in thought as well as deed.

One thing might have been obvious as this war developed: if Germany won, the United States had much to lose from the altered balance of power, as weighed in terms of the future security of the Republic and the values it stood for in the world; if Great Britain and its allies won, there was nothing to fear, at least in the Atlantic world—this indeed was proven by the event.

One would like to believe that Wilson perceived this geopolitical problem clearly—as did Theodore Roosevelt begin to see it when in 1915 he turned again to foreign policy as a better issue in domestic politics than internal reform. One would like to conclude that Wilson weighed alternatives and determined to throw in the weight of the United States on the side of national security and basic Anglo-American freedoms. Instead, Wilson, with the support of a majority of his countrymen, clung during three years to the old formulas of previous decades. All within the realm of neutrality he adopted a choice of neutral policy which insisted on holding Germany to "strict accountability"—rather than later adjudication—for damage to neutral American lives and property caused by illegal attacks by German submarines on belligerent merchant ships, whether unarmed or armed, and finally on neutral American unarmed merchant ships. That choice is what eventually precipitated a combination of other well-known factors—economic, psychological, and political—into the third breakdown of American neutrality when Wilson proved unable to bring about a negotiated peace between the opposing belligerents.

German unrestricted submarine warfare finally torpedoed Wilson's policy of neutrality. The captured German archives have clarified the now waning controversy raised by the disillusioned revisionists of 1929–38. The recent studies from those archives by Karl E. Birnbaum and by Ernest R. May have reinforced the conclusions presented by Charles Seymour a generation ago based on the findings of the committee of the German *Reichstag* investigating the causes of the first war and the first defeat, which investigation used the same documents. In the last analysis international law, and the reaction of the United

States, played no role in the decision of the German high command to resort to unrestricted submarine warfare against belligerent and neutral shipping alike; the only way—so they were fatally persuaded—to bring Britain to her knees within three months was to cut off her overseas carriage, no matter how.

For the United States the real and surpassing value of the victory over Germany in 1918 was temporary preservation of the Blessings of Liberty behind a safe balance of power in the Atlantic world, followed by a diplomatic adjustment with Japan that at least promised to preserve a balance in the Pacific.

After Versailles and after the Washington treaties of 1922, when the New World again seemed secure from danger overseas, east or west, the United States during the Republican Restoration reverted to the traditional Washingtonian, Adamsonian, and Monrovian foreign policy that had worked so successfully in a bygone geopolitical age. The thoughts and plans of our military strategists came to regard the intervention of 1917–18 in Europe as an accident—this conclusion notwithstanding realization by the same thinkers that the balance of power and America's security had hinged on events across the Atlantic.[3]

Thus the United States, out of traditions going back to another age only temporarily interrupted by the First World War, of its own free will helped to jettison the victory of 1918. It demobilized its army; it limited its naval forces by treaty, and by example. This reversion to isolation was an instinctive adaptation to a deceptive picture of peace soon to disappear as foreign dictators rose to challenge the balance of power in a new and even more terrible war. Our teachers and our preachers, our statesmen and our legislators, even our military planners, and some of our own historians, had taken a mistaken measure of American foreign policy. The resulting neutrality legislation only served, so to speak, to keep us out of the First World War. American neutrality broke down again—the fourth breakdown in our history—within two or three years after the neutrality legislation of 1935–37.

Scarcely had the Second World War been fought and won in a desperate trial of heroism and arms by the victorious Allies, when a new historical revisionism in the United States raised its head over the disaster of Pearl Harbor to gainsay the foreign policy of Franklin D. Roosevelt, even as revisionists in the previous generation had repudiated Wilson's policy.

Since 1945 historical writers have pursued the subject of the United

3. Fred Greene, "The Military View of American National Policy, 1904–1940," *A.H.R.*, 66 (Jan. 1961), 354–77.

States and the Second World War, pursued it not without polemics, oppugnation, prejudice, passion, and personal pain. In surveying these historiographical battles, we must remember that again, in 1939, there was much to lose, perhaps everything to lose, in case of a victory of the Axis Powers. It is difficult to see how there can be any doubt but that the United States and the whole Western Hemisphere would have been in great peril, whether immediate or proximate, had President Roosevelt stood by with arms folded around the new neutrality laws and permitted Hitler, Mussolini, and Japan to have overturned the balance of power by a defeat of Great Britain and the Commonwealth whether in the Atlantic or the Pacific, Southeast Asia, India, or Australia.

The new revisionists, notably Charles A. Beard, did not fail to point out that after waging the Second World War at a terrible cost we now face a greater danger than ever. Who would deny this fearsome fact? But the presence of new danger, as Professor Eugene C. Murdock has reminded us—along with the Germans [4]—is no argument against the liquidation of the old. Could we have lived on as a free nation preserving the Blessings of Liberty, with allies to join our effort, if Nazi Germany and Imperial Japan (not to mention Mussolini's Italy) had won the Second World War?

Our great miscalculation, if one may so presume to say, in the diplomacy of the Second World War came not from Roosevelt's courageous —however disingenuous to the voters—departure from neutrality to preserve the birthright of our forefathers at the risk of a global war, but from his misjudgment of the nature and forces of Soviet policy, from his naive assumption that he could cooperate with Russian revolutionary power once the Soviet Union no longer had need for such cooperation, once it stood victoriously on the World Island of Eurasia. The hunchful and hopeful President relied on the policy of Teheran and Cairo, already antiquated by the rush of events in Europe and Asia. After Yalta, traditional American foreign policy toward China collapsed on the continent of Asia. Where is the Open Door now?

Once again, after the complete defeat and surrender of the Axis Powers in 1945, the New World seemed safe, as it had seemed so safe after the First World War, and there was again a disposition to withdraw our forces from Europe and Asia and this time to trust our destiny to a new league of nations. The United States pinned its hopes to the flag of the United Nations—to quote President Truman. This illusion of safety was short-lived. To use the words of James B. Conant: "The

4. Eugene C. Murdock, "Zum Eintritt der Vereinigten Staaten in der Zweiten Weltkrieg," *Vierteljahrshefte für Zeitgeschichte, 4* (Jan. 1956), 100.

coup d'état in Prague, the Berlin Blockade, the Korean War demonstrated the kind of world in which we lived, a divided world; and the division was broad and deep. The issue was freedom." 5

The Soviet Harvest—apt phrase of Langer and Gleason—at the end of the Second World War introduced the latest and most sudden new configuration of power. Accompanying this latest geopolitical shift, the most revolutionary change for the strategy of American defense and diplomacy, is the following complex of phenomena completely altering the position of the United States in the world:

1. The scientific and technological revolution of our times which mushroomed into the atomic age at Alamagordo at 5:30 A.M. on July 16, 1945.

2. Disintegration of the old empires of the nineteenth and twentieth centuries—German, Japanese, Italian, British, French, Dutch, and Belgian—and replacement of their colonies by many new nations with Western ideas and desires but also weak enough to produce a widening vacuum of power.

3. Substitution of a new Red imperialism controlling and oppressing adjacent satellites even more imperiously than the Western empires ever ruled their overseas colonies in Asia and Africa. It is a new and bitter system of colonization, now spreading to the Western Hemisphere in defiance of the Monroe Doctrine.

4. The risen tide of color.

5. Regrouping of the former world powers subsidiary to two opposing superpowers that face each other and each other's allies on three fronts: at the hither rim of the two great oceans at each end of a new geopolitical axis bending over the North Pole.

6. Potential military supremacy of Soviet Russia, allied with Communist China, on the World Island.

7. The end of the freedom of the seas, and the threatened naval supremacy of Russia sallying forth from her land mass to the great oceans with a powerful fleet of submarines and all the implications of offshore nuclear bombardment of our cities on both coasts as well as destruction of surface vessels, whether obsolete navies or helpless merchant marine.

8. A balance of terror in the air and in space beyond the atmosphere which still preserves a precarious balance between freedom and slavery in the world.

Beyond these revolutionary factors in the shifting international configuration of our times is another even more dynamic factor of

5. *The Defense of Freedom* (Stamford, Conn., 1960).

incalculable implications: the great population explosion of the pullulating peoples of this globe.

To meet the rapidly developing picture of the atomic age, the United States after the Second World War embarked on a diplomatic revolution. It repledged itself, within the newly chartered Organization of American States, against intervention by any one state, directly or indirectly, within the internal or external affairs of another American state, or by any group of states except in accordance with existing treaties, one of which was the Inter-American Treaty of Reciprocal Assistance of 1947. At astronomical expense it lavished upon friend and foe, for their rehabilitation beyond the standards of 1939 and for their armament or rearmament, a sum of billions of dollars greater than the total ever extracted in all former wars from the vanquished by the victors—and the stream flows on and on toward over a hundred billion dollars. It developed disparate and subtly qualified regional, and bilateral, defensive alliances with at least forty-four nations within the United Nations, based on the putative historical lessons of past world wars.

History taught, so the argument ran, that if the Imperial German government had realized that the United States would become identified with Great Britain and her allies, there would have been no war in 1914; that if the United States had been a member of the first League of Nations there would not have been any Second World War. However all that may or may not have been, history also argued, so it was urged, that Hitler certainly would not have ventured war in 1939 if he had known that Germany would have to fight the United States and Great Britain firmly leagued with the Western nations in a revived system of collective security. Therefore Stalin and his successors—men did not yet think of Mao Tse-tung and his successors—would know better, from the lessons of the German and Japanese catastrophes, than to start a third world war.

This conclusion based on might-have-beens from the two world wars proves by no means to be a conclusive lesson of history. It is not at all certain that what might—or might not—have stayed Imperial Germany in 1914, or given pause to Hitler's Germany in 1939, will now stay Khrushchev and/or Red China from setting off another world war, or from winning the global fruits of victory undamaged by another war, simply by softening up the Western nations and peacefully overbuilding them in armed power until the victims, frightened and nerveless, accept the coils of tyranny in order to avoid a nuclear war.

How has our foreign policy and diplomacy adapted itself to this last and most momentous shift of all? It is too early to measure the success of our diplomacy in the cold war, much as one might be tempted to do so. Certainly there are steps that we would not take if we had the opportunity to do things over again. Certainly we have neglected to take some steps that manifestly we should have taken. But so far as one can gauge the present, it would seem that the American diplomatic revolution—most striking in all the history of diplomacy—was at least a nonpartisan response to the new requirements of the "prolonged and complex struggle" which President Eisenhower in his farewell telecast so soberly and poignantly bequeathed to his successor.

Whether our new alliances marshal united power at home and abroad and morale sufficient to stop the new aggressors is indeed a vital question. Whether by these commitments we have overextended our military power beyond the capacity of our allies and ourselves to deploy on exterior lines to all the danger spots is for our military authorities to answer. But would not history since ancient times lead its votaries to question whether money, however massively, helpfully, and generously bestowed, can be substituted for foresight, for work, pride, sacrifice, courage, or valor, either in the giver or the taker? And does not a policy of containment by its very nature yield the initiative to the revolutionary aggressor? Really it has not contained all around the World Island of Eurasia. Meanwhile, time has been on the side of the Communists. They have crushed Hungary, with impunity. They have pushed into Laos, despite SEATO. They have jumped the Near East over NATO and CENTO and reached into Africa to compound chaos in the Congo. They have leaped the Atlantic over OAS to establish another Communist front in Cuba, a fourth front for the United States to defend at our very doorstep. In Eastern Asia the Open Door has closed. In the Western Hemisphere, is the Monroe Doctrine dead, as Khrushchev said?

Surely the history of our foreign policy in relation to the successive postures of power in the world shows that during the eighteenth and nineteenth centuries the United States profited adventitiously from the highly favorable circumstances of a secure and prosperous isolation. Surely this fortunate age cannot recur. America no longer enjoys a detached and distant position—on the contrary. Europe's distresses and those of Asia and Africa are no longer America's advantage; they are now America's distresses, too. Canada no longer is the hostage but rather the indispensable linchpin of Anglo-American solidarity.

Nor do the great wars of the first half of the twentieth century afford a wholly reliable experience for the global compass of our foreign policy during the second half of the century in which we are now so unpropitiously projected. "We fail to see the world in perspective," Dean Acheson has suggested, "because we regard it through eyes which we have inherited from our grandparents and great grandparents." [6] From our parents, too, he might have said, and from our own yesterdays.

For the world has changed much since Mr. Acheson wrote these words only a couple of years ago—witness Cuba. "The world into which we were born is gone," declared President Julius A. Stratton as the Massachusetts Institute of Technology reached its centenary last spring; "we have little or no idea of the world into which our children may grow to maturity. It is this rate of change, even more than change itself that is the dominant fact of our time." Things are changing so rapidly— just look at the moon!—that I have been worried lest they should change to stultify these remarks since they were submitted to the *American Historical Review*, in September, for publication in the January 1962 issue.

In this rapidly changing world does liberty, does freedom still set the tone and give color to our major activities, as it did in the days of our nation's founders when they bequeathed its blessings to us? Take the tone of the academic world. Have not our social studies been tending overmuch to self-study—to what is the matter with us rather than to perils and strengths that test our liberty? Too much self-study, too much self-criticism is weakening to a people as it is to an individual. There is such a thing as a national neurosis. A great people's culture, Alfred North Whitehead reminded us, begins to decay when it commences to examine itself.

A great and virile people, Theodore Roosevelt's characterization of the American people, can also waste itself away when it turns to massive self-indulgence. In self-study and self-indulgence we have been losing sight of our national purpose rather than failing to have one. During the letdown of the last fifteen years we have been experiencing the world crisis from soft seats of comfort, debauched by mass media of sight and sound, pandering for selfish profit to the lowest level of our easy appetites, fed full of toys and gewgaws, our military preparedness held back by insidious strikes for less work and more pay, our manpower softened in will and body in a climate of amusement. Massive self-indulgence and massive responsibility do not go together. A great nation cannot work less and get more, with fun for all, in today's stern posture of power.

6. Dean Acheson, "The Premises of American Policy," *Orbis, 3* (Fall 1959), 268.

How can our lazy social dalliance and crooning softness compete with the stern discipline and tyrannical compulsion of subject peoples that strengthen the aggressive sinews of our malignant antagonist? Only if we can freely sacrifice for the Blessings of Liberty what they are forced to sacrifice for the compulsions of tyranny.

If the measurement of American foreign policy in space and time throughout our history offers little precedent for meeting the challenge of revolutionary changes in today's global picture, there is one thing sure in this crisis of our national life: the unchanging value of our inheritance of freedom, as we confront the dilemma of our times.

The dilemma of our times, in this latest and fateful *Gestalt* of world power, is whether to stand firmly in defense of the Blessings of Liberty at the risk of a third world war that may destroy civilization and with it all human freedom and dignity, or to accept Communist revolution and slavery that would also destroy those same precious freedoms and leave the world materially intact under new masters. We still pray that there may be a middle way for freedom. But in the face of the two extremes of this dilemma Bertrand Russell advocates, and too many with him on both sides of the Atlantic, even after the lessons of Hungary, Tibet, and Cuba, accepting Soviet mastery rather than standing fast for the Rights of Englishmen and the Rights of Man, that is, for the Blessings of Liberty. This is a counsel of defeatism for all we hold dear.

For if we stand, to quote a book review of September last year, "committed in every fiber of our being not merely to protect our nation but also to struggle for the cause of freedom on the world scene," [7] we may win, and win without a final Armageddon of the globe. To quote an utterance of the same author four months later: "proud of our ancient heritage—we shall pay any price, bear any burden, meet any hardship, support any friend or oppose any foe in order to assure the survival and success of liberty."

The historian of the future, if there is to be such, will have to decide, in taking the historical measure of American foreign policy, whether the people in this government of the people, by the people, and for the people, and also the peoples of other allied governments, had, as well as the power and unity, the social discipline, the spirit of sacrifice, the nerve and the courage to guard for themselves and their posterity the Blessings of Liberty.

7. John F. Kennedy, in review of B. H. Liddell Hart's book, *Deterrent or Defense,* in *Saturday Review*, Sept. 3, 1960, pp. 17–18.

2. *British Secret Service and the French-American Alliance*

IT LIES in the very nature of his trade that the international spy should, whenever he can, obliterate the traces of his work; nevertheless, despite his efforts, his story will sometimes leave material for the sober historian, to be used when, decades after the events, confidential archives are opened. In them may be found two principal classes of sources, which have served for the preparation of this narrative: reports of operatives and spies to their superior officers, which in turn were digested and summarized for perusal by high executives, and petitions and memorials for reward for past services rendered. From such material one can reconstruct a hitherto untold chapter of the diplomatic history of the American Revolution that should awe the genius of Mr. E. Phillips Oppenheim himself.

The British intelligence service during the early years of the American Revolution was under the direction of William Eden, then an ambitious undersecretary of state, who later as Lord Auckland was one of that group of brilliant diplomatists who developed their talent during the long struggle against the forces of the French Revolution and the brains and battalions of Bonaparte. He recruited his well-paid informants from among American-born British subjects who found themselves in England at the beginning of the war, men who could easily pose as patriots or at least as friendly to the Revolutionary cause. His right-hand man was Paul Wentworth, of the famous New Hampshire family of that name but otherwise biographically obscure.[1] It was he who helped to digest the great mass of informative matter arriving from numerous secret correspondents in Europe and America, and who continually made rapid and hazardous trips back and forth across the Channel in the prosecution of his enterprises. At first con-

1. Francis Wharton, *The Revolutionary Diplomatic Correspondence of the United States* (6 vols. Washington, 1889), *1*, 661, gives the few references.

Read at the 1923 meeting of the American Historical Association. Published in *American Historical Review*, 29, no. 3, 1924.

sidered by the Continental Congress as a loyal American and made one of its confidential correspondents in London in 1774, he soon attached himself rather abjectly to the party in power in England and to the particular political fortunes of Eden, in whose future he justly placed great confidence. He had a salary of £200 a year, with liberal expense accounts and a vague promise of a baronetcy, a seat in Parliament, and a sinecure on one of the administrative boards of government in case of marked success.[2] His bargain with the ministry is characteristic of the place-hunter and spy of the time, though Wentworth was a very able man who was willing to work hard for his reward. His dispatches and those of others of this gentry reveal no more than conventional expressions of patriotism and sacrifice. They were working their jobs for the main chance.

Wentworth at the beginning of his career had submitted some historical and geographical memoirs on the colonial controversy. The geographical and economic information contained in them came from his personal experience. For the historical background so profusely employed to illustrate political points he drew from Dr. Edward Bancroft's *Remarks on a Review of the Controversy between Great Britain and her Colonies*,[3] an argument for a constitutional adjustment to reconcile the colonies within the empire. Wentworth had helped the author in the preparation of the manuscript.[4] Bancroft, a native of Westfield, Massachusetts, was educated in England as a physician. A widely traveled man, he was more than a dabbler in that field of general scientific curiosity which then passed for "philosophy." With this versatility he combined a tolerable gift for writing and a well-concealed but unrivaled genius for intrigue. His essays had won him the friendship of Franklin during the latter's long sojourn in London. When Silas Deane appeared in France as the first diplomatic representative of the United States abroad, he carried not only his instructions written

2. See Wentworth to Eden, Dec. 12, 1777, Jan. 1 and 4, 1778, Apr. 3, 1778, in Auckland MSS, as preserved in photographic copies in B. F. Stevens's Facsimiles of Manuscripts in European Archives relating to America, 1773–1783 (London, 1889–98), nos. 315, 328, 768, 343. Hereinafter we shall refer to the facsimiles as SF.

A note of John Robinson, Secretary of the Treasury, to General Sir William Howe, Mar. 8, 1777, suggests that Wentworth may have enjoyed this salary in addition to an allowance of £500 a year made to Governor Wentworth, "to be paid to his relation Mr. Wentworth." The Lords of the Treasury expected the latter would not draw any more bills on his salary, as a consequence. See Hist. MSS Commission, *Report on American Manuscripts in the Royal Institution of Great Britain* (4 vols. 1904–09), *1*, 94.

3. London, 1769.

4. Wentworth to Eden, Dec. 17, 1777, Auckland MSS (SF 231).

by Benjamin Franklin but letters of introduction to Bancroft. These brought the essay writer over from England to become Deane's intimate associate. When Franklin himself and a little later the proud and jealous Arthur Lee joined Deane to make a joint commission, Bancroft continued to be the confidant of the American representatives, with the exception of Lee. Lee expressed suspicions of Bancroft's loyalty. Bancroft boldly and successfully challenged the accusation as an insult to his integrity. No proof could be produced, and Lee's querulous and quarrelsome conduct soon lost him the confidence of his own colleagues as well as that of the French Foreign Office.[5] Despite several nerve-shaking escapes from detection, Bancroft maintained his confidential position. After the dissolution of the commission he remained the friend and adviser of Franklin, "assisting" him throughout the war and during the peace negotiations of 1782–83.[6]

While engaged as secretary and adviser to the commissioners Bancroft made mysterious trips back and forth to London. In the course of one of these he engaged himself, through Wentworth, to supply the ministry with information of the secret activities of the commissioners.[7] The immunity with which he passed back and forth to enemy territory ought to have opened the eyes of all three of the American agents, but he allayed any suspicions that might have arisen by furnishing them with what purported to be secret information obtained in London. While really faithful to the British side, which paid him the most money, he posed as an American spy. From the commissioners he drew a secretary's salary and even cleverly complained and threatened to quit when his pay was delayed. Franklin and Deane to the end believed him a sacrificing American patriot and an honorable gentleman. His strange career for a long time misled historians of the Revolution. Dr. Wharton in his edition of the *Revolutionary Diplomatic Correspondence of the United States*,[8] after analyzing the question of the man's

5. P. L. Ford, *Edward Bancroft's Narrative of the Objects and Proceedings of Silas Deane, as Commissioner of the United Colonies to France; Made to the British Government in 1776* (Brooklyn, N.Y., Historical Printing Club, 1891); Bancroft's "Memorial" to Carmarthen, Sept. 16, 1784, P.R.O., F.O., 4, 3, printed at the end of this article.

6. See the Memorial referred to in the preceding footnote.

7. Wentworth to Suffolk, Nov. 16, 1777, Auckland MSS (SF 218), speaks of the "£200 due next quarter" to Bancroft. For exact state of Bancroft's emoluments at various times, see his Memorial of Sept. 16, 1784, to Carmarthen, below.

8. *1*, 640–41. Bancroft's true identity was pointed out by P. L. Ford, after an examination of a part of the Stevens facsimiles. Ford printed in that year a typical report of the agent, together with a short biography. The historian George Bancroft guessed

loyalty, concludes that he was one hundred per cent American. He thus laughs away the accusations against him:

> It may hereafter appear, on the unearthing of the secret-service papers of the British foreign office, that this [that of a spy] was really Bancroft's position. But if it be so, he presents a case of which history affords no parallel. To believe him guilty of such atrocious and yet exquisitely subtle perfidy we must believe that, ingenuous, simple-hearted, and credulous as he appeared to the general observer, occupying to Franklin and to America a position not unlike what Boswell did to Johnson and Corsica, though with certain scientific aptitudes to which Boswell laid no claim and with an apparent occasional heroism of which Boswell was incapable, he was, nevertheless, a dissembler so artful as to defy the scrutiny of Franklin, with whom he was in constant intercourse; an intriguer so skillful as, without money or power, to deceive Vergennes and the multitudinous police with which Vergennes encircled him; a villain so profoundly wary as to win the confidence of Paul Jones, professedly aiding him in desperate secret raids on the British coast, and yet, by an art almost unfathomable, reserving the disclosure of these secrets to British officials until a future day which never came; a double traitor, whose duplicity was so masterly as to be unsuspected by the British court, which held him to be a rebel; and by such men as LaFayette, as John Adams, as Jefferson, who regarded him as a true friend. This amusing combination of apparently absolutely inconsistent characteristics may exist in bewildering harmony in the character of Edward Bancroft; but such a phenomenon should not be believed to exist without strong proof.

We quote all this because we cannot improve on it as an eloquent description of Bancroft's perfidy. For the secret service papers are now unearthed, so far as Bancroft is concerned, and have long been adequately available in the Stevens photographic facsimiles of the private papers of Lord Auckland.

In December 1776 Bancroft entered into a written engagement, through Wentworth, to correspond with him and Lord Stormont, in return for a payment of £500 down and £400 per annum.[9] His corre-

---

E. Bancroft's real character as early as 1866; *History of the United States* (10 vols. Boston, 1834–75), *9*, 62, 64. It is apparently to George Bancroft's undocumented but reliable statement that Dr. Wharton was directing the above passage.

9. See Ford, p. 9, and "Engagement of Dr. Edwards" in the hand of Paul Wentworth, Auckland MSS (SF 235). Bancroft's loyalty to the ministry did not pass

spondence, under the fictitious name of "Dr. Edwards," was to be left regularly in a sealed bottle in the hole of a tree on the south side of the Tuileries. He also had frequent clandestine interviews with Wentworth. It was stipulated that he should supply "his knowledge" of the following subjects:

The progress of the Treaty with France, and of the assistance expected, or commerce carryed on or in any of the ports of that Kingdom.

The same with Spain, and of every other Court in Europe.

The agents in the foreign islands in America, and the means of carrying on the Commerce with the Northern Colonys.

The means of obtaining credit—effects and money; and the channells and agents used to apply them; the secret moves about the Courts of France and Spain, and the Congress agents, and tracing the lines from one to the other.

Franklin's and Deane's correspondence with the Congress, and their agents; and the secret, as well as the ostensible letters from the Congress to them. Copys of any transactions, committed to papers, and an exact account of all intercourse and the subject matter treated of, between the Courts of Versailles and Madrid, and the agents from Congress.

Subjects to be communicated to Lord Stormont.

Names of the two Carolina ships, masters both English and French, description of the ships, and cargoes; the time of sailing, and the port bound to.

The same circumstances respecting all equipments in any port in Europe together with the names of the agents imployed.

The intelligence that may arrive from America, the captures made by their privateers, and the instructions they receive from the deputys.

How the captures are disposed of.

The serviceable communications of the double-dealing doctor, enabling the ministry to read the innermost secrets of the American commissioners and to place their cruisers across the track of munition cargoes to Washington's army, as well as to supply the British ambassador

---

unsuspected by his employers, but it stood the test of opening up his private correspondence in the post office, and of various other checks which we shall see were put on him. Compare this with Bancroft's Memorial of Sept. 16, 1784, to Carmarthen, below.

at Paris (Lord Stormont) with material for protesting French violations of neutrality, were only a part of Eden's abundant American intelligence. A scheme was devised to get hold of a large number of the original dispatches of the commissioners, for Bancroft's secretarial duties left him time to copy only the more important documents and to make digests of the rest of the information that passed under his attention. Eden doubtless also wished the satisfaction of checking his spy's copies by comparison with the originals. The plan, referred to in the Auckland papers as the "Hynson business," may now be set forth.

Deane had in France with him as personal secretary one William Carmichael of Maryland, a young man of some independent means, plausible parts, and a large but not very shrewd liking for backstairs work.[10] A sojourn in England had brought him into touch with the radical politics of the day. He had also been a seeker after the lower pleasures of London resorts and, perhaps in that channel, had made the acquaintance of a number of American sea captains who plied the transatlantic trade in the days before the Prohibitory Acts. His taste for such companionship did not improve his personal morals but brought him acquaintance, which later proved useful to the American cause, with the very men who might be recruited to command privateers and munition ships clandestinely fitting out in France. Carmichael was deputed by the commissioners to the task of enlisting such services.[11] One of the persons thus approached was a certain Joseph Hynson, a fellow Marylander. According to the intelligence of Eden the two men, Carmichael and Hynson, showed considerable affection for each other and had mistresses who inhabited the same house in London. Hynson was an experienced seaman of the adventurous sort well adapted to the work in hand. Out of employment and funds, he was anxious, he professed, to return to America. It was arranged that a cutter should be surreptitiously purchased at Dover and cleared ostensibly on an innocent voyage. Hynson was then to take her to France to be fitted out as

10. Carmichael sums up his career in France in a letter to Franklin, dated Feb. 1, 1778, preserved in manuscript among the Franklin Papers, *8*, 82, in the collections of the American Philosophical Society, in Philadelphia. See also his letter to the Committee of Correspondence, Wharton, *2*, 184–89. He was appointed secretary to the commissioners by Congress, Nov. 28, 1777, but was sent home by the commissioners before his commission reached France. I. M. Hays, ed., *Calendar of Franklin Papers in the Library of the American Philosophical Society* (5 vols. Philadelphia, 1908), *4*, 244.

11. "Statement concerning the Employment of Lieut. Col. Edward Smith with regard to Captain Hynson and a Sketch of the Information obtained," March 1777, Auckland MSS (SF 248).

a swift-sailing, armed packet-boat to serve as a means of regular transmission of the commissioners' dispatches to Congress. He was to command her on the first voyage and thus advantageously achieve his desire of returning to his native land.

To his close friends, Hynson let it be known that he was off in the service of the Americans on some such adventure, mysteriously hinted at but never wholly explained. A certain Reverend John Vardill, a Tory in Eden's employ (who had for his wages the promise of a professorship in "the college at New York" when the rebellion should have been suppressed), was known by these friends to have held out to Hynson a profitable offer to betray his American connections. The valiant sea captain in vigorous terms let it be understood that he had indignantly repulsed such overtures. Actually he accepted them. It was fixed that he should take the packet out of Dover without hindrance from the Admiralty, which was made cognizant of the whole plot. After leaving a French port with the American dispatches he was to sail the ship into a trap set by British cruisers. A long correspondence on this subject, in which appear an intelligence officer named Lieutenant Colonel Edward Smith and elaborate signals concerted with the navy, is preserved among Eden's papers.[12]

Hynson took the ship across the Channel as desired by both parties. While she was being refitted with some delay he spent his time at Paris in close touch with the commissioners and in intimacy with his friend Carmichael. With their errands he passed back and forth to the French ports and was able to get much marine information highly desirable to the British embassy and ministry, to which it was promptly relayed through Smith, whom Hynson regarded as his superior officer. Carmichael was not unaware of Hynson's connections with Smith. The commissioners' agent appears in the role of such an intimate friend as not to have divulged his knowledge. He not only continued to be intimate with the spy but himself actually went to the verge, if not over the edge, of treason. Smith had hopes, through Hynson, of contaminating Carmichael, and reported to Eden that the American had gone so far as to promise if necessary to steal from the commissioners such papers as Hynson might require.[13] But the investigator is puzzled in determining Carmichael's precise status—if indeed it can be precisely

12. The numerous documents may be found by consulting the index to the Stevens Facsimiles, vol. 25, under the heads of Hynson, Smith, etc.

13. "Information obtained by Lt. Col. Smith during the six weeks of his intercourse with Capt. Hynson, in February and March, 1777," Mar. 27–28, 1777, Auckland MSS (SF 670).

defined—by a memorial of his written at about this time,[14] for Vergennes's eye, in which he urged that France should come into an American alliance as the one way of abasing Britain before she should have
successfully offered peace terms to the sorely tried revolted colonies.

For various reasons, none of which shows any distrust of Hynson's
perfect loyalty, Franklin and Deane decided to send out the dispatches
on an earlier boat under the command of one Captain Folger. They
were forwarded to Folger in Hynson's care at Havre. Hynson delivered
the dispatch pouch, but the contents which Folger received and unsus-
pectingly carried to America proved when opened by the Committee
of Correspondence of the Continental Congress to be a wad of blank
paper.[15] Long before the abstraction could be known by the commissioners, even before the rifled pouch could have reached America, Hynson had personally delivered the dispatches to Smith in England, and
Eden had the satisfaction of carefully arranging about six months'
accumulation of them for the private perusal of George III, who sometimes had doubted the loyalty of the various British operatives working in France.[16] "Hynson has by this conduct fully discharged his
promises made some months ago," wrote Eden to the king. "Lord North
gave him at my desire £200, and the promise of £200 a year. He was an
honest rascal, and no fool though apparently stupid." [17]

The honest rascal now hurried back to France, but found himself
mistrusted. Deane refused to have anything to do with him.[18] His "old
friends" the Americans, with the exception of Carmichael, deserted
him. The miserable wretch, who thought the milk of human kindness

14. Carmichael to the Count ———, 1777, SF 647. This long memoir, and a
translation by the Count d'Estaing, is preserved in the French archives. What appears to be an obliterated month date after the "1777" might be "1 Jan'y," "1 July,"
or less likely "1 June." The memorial also speaks of the "ensuing winter." Because
of this internal evidence, and the probability that the first letter of the month of
the date begins with a "J," I conclude the memorial to have been written by
Carmichael at some time during the first six weeks of 1777, and not during the
November and December negotiations.

15. Lt. Col. Edward Smith to Eden, Oct. 20, 1777, Auckland MSS (SF 205); Wharton,
2, 664.

16. Wrapper with Eden's endorsement on which is added a Note by the King,
Apr. 6, 1777, Auckland MSS (SF 249).

17. William Eden to George III, Oct. 20, 1777, Auckland MSS (SF 275).

18. "I do not write you to reproach you for the ungrateful and treacherous part
you have acted:—I leave this to your own reflections, but as you have had the
assurance to write to me, and to propose the betraying your new patrons, in the
manner you have wickedly but in vain attempted to betray your former, and with
them your Country, I must tell you that no letters from you will hereafter be received by—DEANE." Deane to Hynson, Paris, Oct. 26, 1777, Auckland MSS (SF 208).

should cause a little thing like the possibility of treason to be overlooked by the friends he studied to betray, was quite unhappy. He
remained hidden in his room, only occasionally slipping out to send a
dispatch by Lord Stormont's couriers to Smith. He urged that officer
to come to Paris and explain things to the commissioners, to assure
them that he, Hynson, had not unduly "expanded himself." He thought
that a reassuring word from Smith might smooth over his ruptured
friendship with them!

The day after his arrival at Paris Hynson breakfasted with Carmichael, who gave him a message from the commissioners asking
whether Smith would soon be in Paris. Apparently they regarded the
latter as a reputable British agent with whom some sort of honest
negotiations might be possible. Hynson replied that he expected him
soon. In a letter to Smith, Hynson says that the commissioners desired
him to keep low until Smith's arrival. "They at the same time said that
the French Court had knowledge of my going to England and that
they [i.e., the commissioners] were accused of sending me there, which
was the reason they could not agree to see me at present." Soon Hynson
reported that even Carmichael was now forbidden to visit him.[19] Carmichael nevertheless made such visits clandestinely (at least Hynson
believed they were clandestine). During one of them occurred this
interesting conversation, as reported in Hynson's own grammar and
spelling to Smith:

> [Carmichael] was expressing a great desire that you come to Paris.
> I asked him what end he thought it would answer. He said a very
> great one, that the gentln was [were?] wishing to have some con-
> versation with you, I told him there was one thing, that the Com-
> missioners would harken to nothing but independance, and that
> was what England would never allow them. He said if there was
> to be a meeting we might talk high at first. I told him that would
> answer no end, did he think the Gentlemen would expect any
> other terms, than that of independance. He said there was a di-
> vision about giving up their independance, but he said you would
> be surprised to hear Dr. Franklin says that whenever Great Britain
> would shew a disposn for peace he would be the first to give up
> this independance. Mr. Deane he said had made the same declara-
> tion. But Dr. Franklin said he knew they had no mind for peace.
> He said Mr. Lee lived in a higher stile than he had ever done, and

19. J. Hynson to Nicholas Noel [Smith], Nov. 23, 1777, Auckland MSS (SF 308);
Hynson to Smith, Nov. 25, ibid. (SF 309).

had a great deal of pride, he dare say he would wish to continue as he was, therefore he was the only one that would be against giving up independance but declared it would be given up immediately upon England's showing a disposn for *peace*. This was before any of the accounts [that is, of Burgoyne's surrender, news of which reached the port of Nantes on November 30, 1777].

On December 10, after that news had arrived at Paris, Carmichael came again. "When I asked him what the Gentlemen seemed to talk of at present he said of nothing but their success. He believed it was too late to think of anything now. I therefore at present will not urge your coming to Paris." [20]

Even Carmichael's visits now stopped. Suspected by the Comte de Vergennes, he was ordered back to America, with dispatches. At first there was question of his being entrusted with these, but somebody broke into his room and found his correspondence innocent; Franklin and Deane therefore insisted on his bearing the papers as a mark of their esteem and respect; [21] at least this is Wentworth's account of it, though it is likely that what reached him was a distorted version of the plundering of Lee's papers by Carmichael, at Deane's instigation.[22] Hynson, humanly lonely and in despair, begged to be relieved of his service and given employment in America.[23] He was no longer able to get anything out of the commissioners and he had been told that if he continued in Paris he was likely to be arrested as a spy. "It is a carracter I heartily despise," he wrote, "I had rather you would send me to Amerrica as a common soldier, where I might be of some use." [24] Despite the previous largesses of the ministry he again asked for money. Eden wrote Smith that "the trifling sum [£40] would readily be reim-

20. Hynson to Smith, Paris, Dec. 10, 1777, Auckland MSS (SF 314).

21. Wentworth to Eden, Jan. 6, 1778, Auckland MSS (SF 332).

22. "At a meeting of the Commissioners for the United States, held at Passi Jan. 7 1778 Mr. Deane informed Mr. Lee that he did not open Mr. Lee's Dispatches. That Mr. Carmichael did open them. That Mr. Carmichael was now in possession of the Book in which they were written; which Mr. Deane believed he intended to carry to America with him. That Mr. Deane had written for and expected a Copy of them. That they contained a Libel on two of the best men in America; for which Mr. Deane knew one of them to be a man of such spirit, that if he knew it, he would come over on purpose to call Mr. Lee to account for it." Silas Deane to the American commissioners. Memorandum, Jan. 1778. See *Calendar of Franklin Papers, 1,* 358, referring to volume 8, 85a, of the manuscripts, in American Philosophical Society.

23. Hynson to Smith, Dec. 10, 1777, Auckland MSS (SF 314).

24. Hynson to Smith, Dec. 17, 1777, Auckland MSS (SF 316).

bursed, and with pleasure if Mr. Hynson would either catch Mr. Deane or Mr. Carmichael who have departed with despatches in different ships." [25]

Carmichael as early as November 1, 1777, had written to an unidentified English correspondent, presumably a publicisit of the Opposition, a letter which was intercepted in the English post office and delivered over to Eden. In it was mentioned a peace without victory. "It might well be imagined that some scheme of accommodation might be hit upon which would make us good friends. If we could on one side lose the idea of supremacy and on the other that of dependence we might be friends by treaty, never by confederation." He represented "our leading man" as trembling for fear lest his propositions to France should be accepted. "He wishes no European connection. He despises France and hates England." Carmichael professed to be eager to secure the interests of his constituents (whoever they were). "I would implicitly follow every instruction that meant their ease, their success and their present happiness, though the mode should be contrary to what I should chuse of doing it. I wish you would busy yourself with paragraphs on the folly of the war." [26]

Carmichael's letter, and his later interviews with Hynson, professed to indicate that there was—at least before Burgoyne's surrender—some division on the question of independence among the American commissioners and that they, with the exception of Arthur Lee, might have been willing to arrange a peace by compromise. The dispatches intercepted by Hynson also revealed these dissensions and supported the same idea. Similar information was furnished by the communications of another British spy, one Thornton, who served as Arthur Lee's personal secretary and whose information is less important than that of Bancroft only because Lee lacked the confidence of the other two commissioners and of the French court.[27] Lee's papers, too, had been stolen from him that summer in Berlin by the British minister to that court, Hugh Elliot, whom a grateful ministry rewarded with a gentle reprimand and £1,000 cash.[28] All this news agreed with and neatly supple-

25. Eden to Suffolk, Dec. 1777 (precise date not given), Auckland MSS (SF 312). The allusion is to Simeon Deane, a brother of the commissioner.

26. William Carmichael to "Monsieur Jean Trouville," Nov. 1, 1777, Auckland MSS (SF 288).

27. See Wharton, *1*, 659. After Lee signed the French treaties Thornton was able to send a draft to London. His most dangerous activities were in his representations of himself to Lee as an American spy and his furnishing false military information, which Lee trustfully sent over to the Congress. Ibid., *1*, 208.

28. Elliot had estimated his expenses in this job to be £500: the correspondence

mented that of the agile Bancroft. Only a fortnight after the successful completion of the Hynson business one of Bancroft's personal letters to an English correspondent was opened in the mails by other agents of the argus-eyed Eden. To a correspondent in the City who was his partner in stocks and insurance speculations and also one of his friends in the Opposition party, Bancroft revealed information not sent in to Wentworth, news to the effect that Burgoyne's invasion from Canada had been stopped and that his army, after severe losses, was in retreat.[29] By this news Bancroft and his partners were able to anticipate the great drop in the value of British funds that followed the announcement. He must have made a "killing" on the London 'Change. Wentworth a few weeks later reported him to be very flush with money.[30]

If the well-informed Bancroft was willing to gamble on his information, the ministry had its forebodings. Ministers who had just been expressing to each other in exuberant terms the fine mettle of their health and indulging in long weekends in the country actually began to lose sleep and really to worry over the outcome of the campaign in America. A victory by the Americans might invite the open acceptance of their cause by France and Spain. It boded nothing less than a possible break-up of the empire. The military situation made a peace maneuver desirable, particularly when the several sources of intelligence from Paris indicated division of opinion among the American commissioners and an apparent willingness of Franklin and Deane to accept a reconciliation within the empire. Eden began to formulate propositions of peace which were eventually adopted by Lord North. In order to give any overtures a bigger chance of success he resolved to sound out the American commissioners to learn whether they would agree to any peace short of actual independence.

The Paris intrigues were now taken out of the hands of Hynson and Smith and placed under the more expert management of Wentworth, the emissary usually employed on the most important and delicate business.[31] He was hurriedly ordered to France with a written com-

---

relating to the dishonorable business is preserved in the Auckland MSS (SF 1451–1481).

29. Bancroft to Thomas Walpole, undated, received Nov. 7, 1777, Auckland MSS (SF 289). The letter quoted information received by a vessel which left Portsmouth on Sept. 4. It spoke of a loss of 600 to 800 men in one engagement (probably that at Bennington, Aug. 15).

30. Wentworth to Eden, end of 1777, Auckland MSS (SF 324).

31. Beaumarchais's agents shadowed Wentworth in Paris, as of course did the police. On Dec. 17 Beaumarchais warned Vergennes: "He is related to the Marquis

mission dated December 6, 1777, directing him to ascertain the commissioners' idea of a peace, to secure full information of their relations with France, Spain, and the other powers of Europe, the naval preparations under way in the two Bourbon monarchies, and in general everything of significance as to the rapidly developing European crisis, which it was hoped to prevent by interesting the Americans in a peace negotiation before they could conclude an alliance with France. Wentworth carried no actual powers to treat of peace; all he had was a letter from Eden full of amiable expressions of conciliation and respect for Franklin, written shortly after the news of Burgoyne's actual surrender was announced in London. This he might read to Deane and Franklin. The gist is well stated in its last paragraphs:

> We have often been asked here, "Do you mean anything short of unconditional surrender?" I wish to answer that question by putting another to those who are in the confidence of the colonies; "do you mean anything short of unqalified independence?" If they answer in the negative I have only to tell them that nothing less than a ten years' unsuccessful war can prepare this country for such an ultimatum. But if they answer: "We are indeed at this moment independent de facto, yet we cannot wish any peace to leave us in that state, which, every circumstance considered, might end in a wild anarchy and confusion; still less can we wish to place the qualified controul, which should rest somewhere, in the hands of nations who are strangers to our blood, language, and constitutional principles of Government." In reply to such an answer (and such an answer I should expect from wise and good men) I would request them to proceed and tell me frankly and seriously their sentiments both as to the grounds of an accommodation and the mode of negotiating it.
>
> Well, but how shall all this and the various matters connected with it be negotiated? How will the voice of peace be heard in the midst of such a war?
>
> I shall shortly and in the fewest words add, that if I knew any

---

of Rockingham; is a particular friend of Lord Suffolk, is employed by the Ministers in difficult matters, keeping in touch with the Opposition as much as with the Royalists. . . . This Mr. Wentworth speaks French like you, and better than I do; he is one of the cleverest men in England. So early as last year he made efforts in Paris with the same object.

"I also know that two Americans, one of whom is Carmichael, are about to leave for America with very important despatches. Now these would give us information!" Arch. Aff. Etrang., Angleterre, vol. 526, f. 270 (SF 1781).

clear or indeed plausible answers to these questions, and the others which they obviously imply, I am cordially disposed and fortunately situated to turn such knowledge to the most immediate, and most benevolent purposes. I hope to hear from you.[32]

In Paris Wentworth met further details of the smashing defeat of Burgoyne and news to the effect that Howe appeared to be hemmed in at Philadelphia by Washington's troops.[33] He found that Bancroft had gone "on the wing" to London, there to collect some sort of insurance "which may affect Deane and Company." Actually Bancroft's journey was, we think, to collect his recent winnings, and perhaps in a maneuver of confidence to the commissioners to sound out the British Opposition as to its strength and peace attitude after Saratoga. On December 17, Wentworth managed to have a "secret and confidential" interview with Deane. He suggested that the war had been forced on the British ministry by circumstances not under its control, that they were now anxious to undo a mistaken policy, and that they rather than any Opposition party coming into power were the persons who could best negotiate such a devoutly-to-be-wished-for consummation. He prefaced his peace proposals with a long historical disquisition, illustrated by quotations from Bancroft's essay of 1769, and frequently interrupted by rejoinders from Deane. He then broached a program for which, he said, he was solely responsible, namely a reversion to the colonial status of 1763 with a repeal of the obnoxious acts passed since that date. Deane stood out for absolute independence as necessary for any possible negotiations. After several hours' animated discussion both men, exhausted, adjourned till later in the day. They then went over the ground again and Wentworth proposed an armistice with cessation of hostilities by sea and land, British troops to be withdrawn from everywhere except "New York Island," Long Island, Governor's Island, Staten Island, and Shelter Island. Long Island was to continue permanently in the possession of the king's forces, in a situation which he compared to the barrier fortresses of the Netherlands, while the smaller islands mentioned were to be neutralized for the sake of safe barriers to Long Island. As a precedent for this he cited the Dunkirk humiliation imposed by Great Britain on France in the peace of 1763! Confidence and security thus established, continued Wentworth, commissioners might then be appointed

32. Eden to Wentworth, Dec. 5, 1777, Auckland MSS (SF 483). For Eden's instructions to Wentworth see "Minutes arranged with Mr. Wentworth," Dec. 6, 1777, ibid. (SF 484).

33. Wentworth to Eden, Paris, Dec. 11, 1777, Auckland MSS (SF 225).

by Great Britain to work out the details of a peace based on a commercial union and the "grand basis of the Navigation Acts." He then took Deane up into a high mountain and turned his vision to a panorama of honors and emoluments for the leaders who might be successful in effecting such a reconciliation: governors general, privy seals, great seals, treasurers, secretaries, councilors in the general governments (Wentworth conceived of three such general governments for the colonies), local barons, and knights. This he left to work on the minds of the commissioners. Deane is not recorded as having offered any comment in this connection. Wentworth ended by developing a grand scheme for agricultural education and the development of American lands after a reconciliation should have been achieved.[34]

Two anxious weeks passed before the British agent could arrange another interview. Meanwhile rumors spread that the French court had declared itself in favor of open recognition of the United States and a treaty of amity and commerce—which it actually did on December 6 —rumors which in the absence of Bancroft he could not with certainty confirm. Carmichael, with Deane's brother, was leaving for America with important dispatches. This made Wentworth all the more suspicious. By December 25 Bancroft had returned from London. Through him Wentworth attempted again to arrange a meeting with the commissioners. They instructed Bancroft to wait until the next Monday before replying to the Englishman and then to endeavor to amuse him with hopes and difficulties until the dispatches were well on their way. Bancroft of course told this to Wentworth. The latter grew nervous and harassed in spirit. In such a great and critical moment, he wrote his chief, he could not rely entirely on Bancroft. The latter had been in conference with the Opposition and admitted having brought back a packet—he did not believe him when he said it was sealed—for the commissioners. Other unofficial peacemakers were suspected of approaching the Americans at this time, in anticipation of the opening of Parliament on January 20.

> Take care that America and the West Indies don't glide through our fingers [Wentworth wrote], while we by inefficient means try to prevent alarm, and hush up a perilous situation, perhaps only so because we shrink from it. . . . I have determined to amuse the agents by hopes of all they wish—it can do no harm—and if you are alert the business can be done in America either way [i.e.,

34. Wentworth to Eden, Paris, Dec. 17, 1777, Auckland MSS (SF 231).

by peace or war]—by peace the safest—before these insidious people throw poison there. . . . Ambitious as I am to be an [English peace] Commissioner—while I am here, I can't be elsewhere, yet I see so strong the necessity to despatch privately—if possible in England—and wait the approbation of Parliament, that I urge it against my own hopes. Ed—— [Bancroft] is not all that he should be. He offered to repay all that he had received. That cursed journey to London has spoiled all.[35]

Finally, on January 6, 1778, an interview was arranged, through Bancroft, with Franklin. It occurred under the express condition that Arthur Lee should not be present, a stipulation by Wentworth which was agreeable for both Franklin and Deane to accept. Ostensibly the meeting occurred on the score of old acquaintanceship. Franklin made a condition that there should be not the remotest allusion to personal emoluments such as had been mentioned to Deane. At the outset he let it be known that the Americans would consent to no peace without independence, that he had no powers to treat, and that he could not have anything more than a polite conversation with anyone who had no powers on the part of Great Britain. Wentworth then read Eden's letter without revealing the author. Franklin said it was "interesting," but straightway he launched out into a discursive and lively harangue on British barbarism and military atrocities in America. Wentworth tried to "moderate" him, and repeatedly endeavored to bring him back to the point, and to demonstrate the advantages of maintaining an imperial union. "I never knew him to be so eccentric," he reported, "nobody says less generally and keeps a point more closely in view, but he was diffuse and unmethodical to-day." Wentworth suggested, too, that Franklin and Deane be given protection for a journey to negotiate in England—which would have separated them from Vergennes at a critical moment. To all these remarks Franklin replied loosely and indefinitely. Finally in Deane's presence he declared "that if the [British] Commissioners were appointed to meet them properly authorized he would treat of Peace—I say Peace—I am ready and I am sure my colleagues are so on the broad bottom of reciprocal advantage." [36]

With this equivocal answer Wentworth set out for London on Janu-

35. See letters of Wentworth to Eden, Dec. 17, 18, 22, 25, 28, 29, 1777, Jan. 1, 1778, Auckland MSS (SF 231, 317, 234, 233, 321, 322, 722, 327).

36. Wentworth to Eden, Jan. 7, 1778, Auckland MSS (SF 489). See also Wentworth's other dispatches during the first week in January, ibid. (SF 324, 325, 329, and 769).

ary 15, carrying the additional discomforting information from Bancroft that the commissioners hoped soon to negotiate a treaty of independence with a government made up of the Opposition.[37]

The most significant and interesting part of this chapter of secret diplomacy is the use Franklin made of it. Surrounded by spies in his own household, himself provided with no secret service other than that furnished him by British agents who affected to be American patriots, the shrewd and unassuming old man, outranking them all in acumen, profited prodigiously from these backstairs dealings. He took no pains to conceal from Vergennes that he had received peace approaches. Though he said nothing of the Wentworth interview, Wentworth's presence and purpose were known to the French foreign minister and to his police.[38] Bancroft had received from an unidentified correspondent in England on December 17 a letter requesting him, in view of his close connection with the commissioners, to discover what terms would be acceptable to them. He was told that the government intended to make through Parliament an offer of peace as soon as the recess was over. The writer hoped that something "a little short of independence" might be acceptable.[39] Bancroft gave this to the commissioners and Franklin turned it over to Vergennes. France a week previously had declared for open aid and a recognition of independence. A treaty was actually in negotiation, but the final signature depended on whether Spain, the ally of the Bourbon Family Compact, would join France. On December 31 it was known that Spain would not. Should France go in alone? Now or never was the time for Vergennes to decide. If he waited longer for the policy of Spain to change, might not the dreaded reconciliation take place and the whole object of French policy—the abasement of Britain—be lost? [40] There is no doubt that Franklin allowed these thoughts to ferment in the minister's mind,[41] nor is there

37. Wentworth to Eden, Paris, Jan. 10, 1778, Auckland MSS (SF 335). A Sir Philip Gibbes, who seems to have represented the Opposition, was approaching Franklin at this time. See Wentworth to Eden, Jan. 7, 1778, ibid. (SF 489), and Gibbes to Franklin, Paris, Jan. 5, 1778, Franklin Papers, *8*, 15, in American Philosophical Society. This letter asked for an appointment to consider peace on the basis of "constitutional principles." I have found no answer to it by Franklin.

38. Beaumarchais to Vergennes, Dec. 17, 1778, Arch. Aff. Etrang., Angleterre, vol. 526, f. 270 (SF 1781).

39. SF 1787.

40. Henri Doniol, *Histoire de la participation de la France à l'établissement des États-Unis d'Amérique* (5 vols. Paris, 1886–99), *2*, 104–06.

41. See Van Tyne, "Influences which determined the French Government To Make the Treaty with America, 1778," in *A.H.R.*, *21* (1916), 539. He cites correspondence of the French ambassador in London.

any doubt that at this juncture Vergennes was glad to have good representations of an alarmist nature to make to the King of France.[42] A royal council was held on January 7 at which it was decided unanimously to negotiate, without the concurrence of Spain, an offensive and defensive alliance as well as a treaty of commerce and amity with the United States.[43] The next day a French emissary, Gérard, appeared before the commissioners and put them a question which unlocks the significance of the whole episode. Both question and answer are preserved in the French archives in Franklin's own handwriting.

Question, What is necessary to be done to give such satisfaction to the American Commissioners as to engage them not to listen to any propositions from England for a new connection with that country?

Answer, The Commissioners have long since proposed a treaty of Amity and Commerce, which is not yet concluded: the immediate conclusion of that treaty will remove the uncertainty they are under with regard to it, and give them such a reliance on the friendship of France as to reject firmly all propositions made to them of peace from England, which have not for their basis the entire freedom and independence of America, both in matters of Government and commerce.

On the sixth of February the alliance was signed. The pledge of Franklin, repeated in different terms by Deane,[44] held good thereafter. The secret overtures of Eden's agents in Paris proved to be the preliminaries of the well-known peace commission to America, authorized by the British Parliament in February 1778, offering to the Americans the olive branch in one hand or the sword in the other, a peace without victory on the terms, roughly, of the *status quo* of 1763.[45] Eden, it

42. On this point the evidence adduced by Professor E. S. Corwin in *French Policy and the American Alliance* (Princeton University Press, 1916), see especially p. 128, is quite conclusive. See Vergennes to Montmorin, Dec. 27, 1777, in which Vergennes makes use of the letter to Bancroft as an argument for immediate action by Spain. Arch. Aff. Etrang., Espagne, vol. 587, f. 307 (SF 1805). See also Doniol, 2, 704–09, 771–73.

43. Doniol, 2, 707.

44. Arch. Aff. Etrang., États Unis, vol. 3, nos. 4 and 8 (SF 774 and 776), for statements of Franklin and Deane, respectively. For Gérard's narrative see SF 1831, quoted by Corwin, p. 153.

45. 18 George III, c. 13. The royal instructions to the peace commission sent to America are conveniently printed in S. E. Morison, *Sources and Documents Illus-*

should be recalled, was a member, indeed the mainspring, of this commission. Before the negotiations could gather any headway in America the terms of the French alliance arrived at Philadelphia. The hopes which the North ministry had indulged of dividing American patriots by such offers were doomed when it became known that the strongest military and naval power in Europe had clasped hands with the United States. That alliance meant in the end complete victory. The part played by the British spies of William Eden therefore was no small contribution to the achievement of American independence.

It remains to be stated that Bancroft continued true to his British employers. On January 22 he wrote Wentworth a letter outlining the terms of the prospective treaties. A careful summary of the treaties actually signed between the two parties followed on March 4. The terms of the treaty of commerce and amity were known in England before they were straightway announced there by the French ambassador; the terms of the secret alliance, though not announced by the ambassador, were known there at the same time, long before they were known in America.[46] Bancroft claimed that by a special messenger he achieved the unprecedented (and, we think, unbelievable) feat of getting the treaty to Whitehall within *forty-two hours* after it was signed at Versailles.[47]

During the hostilities between England and France Bancroft remained at his post in Paris, receiving a salary of £500 per annum, which in 1780 was increased to £1,000. After the fall of the North ministry the stipend was continued by Shelburne during the peace negotiations and at least one quarter's payment was made by Fox, the secretary who instructed David Hartley to negotiate "fairly and ingenuously with Franklin." Though both Shelburne and Fox availed themselves of Bancroft's services as unblushingly as did Lord North, there is no evidence in the Oswald or Hartley correspondence to show that these ingenuous personalities were aware that the same tool had been employed by their principals. Fitzherbert and Strachey, trained diplomatists of the Foreign Office school, made good use of him. Fitzherbert

trating the American Revolution, 1764–1783 (Oxford University Press, 1923), pp. 186–203.

46. Bancroft to Wentworth, Jan. 22–28, 1778, Auckland MSS (SF 492). Wentworth, "Intelligence from Mr. Edwards," with abstract of the treaties of commerce and alliance signed Feb. 6, 1778, between France and America; dated Paris, Mar. 4, 1777, ibid. (SF 1881).

47. The ordinary time for the journey by the king's couriers was five days. A quiet passage would be made in four. For Bancroft's statement see his Memorial to Carmarthen, Sept. 16, 1784, below.

praised him as "a valuable treasure to government both as a source of intelligence of all sorts and as an instrument to be employed in guiding indirectly . . . the views and conduct of the American Commissioners." In June 1783, Bancroft went to America on a trip of several months, during which he tried to make himself useful to Great Britain by propaganda and the supplying of information. We find him back in London in September 1784, soliciting for the prompt payment of his stipend and a promised pension. His remarkable memoir of September 17, one of the most startling documents in early American diplomatic history, is printed at the end of this chapter.[48]

Hynson, disgusted with his adventures in Paris, left for England and took passage on the man-of-war *Centaur* on a voyage in which he was instrumental in betraying an American munition ship into the hands of the Admiralty. This is the last we hear of him, in what he wrote to be a new and happier life.[49] Wentworth's further doings, however interesting they may be, must await the future biographer of him and Eden. The enigmatic Carmichael returned safely to Maryland. He served his state during the year 1779 in the Continental Congress. In the latter part of that year he accompanied John Jay to Spain, and served there as secretary to the unrecognized American legation until Jay's departure from Madrid in 1782. During these years he continued a friendly and intimate correspondent of Franklin, who recommended him as Jay's successor.[50] It was Carmichael who in 1783 was recognized as the first official American representative to the Spanish court. He served until his recall in 1794 as a highly unsuccessful minister of the United States.[51] He died in Madrid, February 9, 1795, on the eve of his intended departure for the United States.

48. See private and confidential letters of Fitzherbert to Shelburne, Dec. 14 and 18, 1782, Stevens Transcripts of Shelburne Papers in Lansdowne House; Edwards to Strachey, Dec. 4, 1782, P.R.O., C.O. 5, 8, p. 376 (Stevens Transcripts). For Dr. Bancroft's perspicuous observations on political conditions in America in 1783–84, see George Bancroft, *History of the Formation of the Constitution of the United States* (2 vols. New York, 1882), *1*, 331, 367, 380, 403.

49. Hynson to Smith, Jan 4, 1778, Auckland MSS (SF 330); Donatien Le Ray de Chaumont, Anecdote Intéressante, Apr. 18, 1778. Arch. Aff. Étrang., États Unis, vol. III, no. 92, f. 205 (SF 810). Hynson's voyage *may* have been intended to intercept Carmichael and Simeon Deane.

50. E. E. Hale and E. E. Hale, Jr., *Franklin in France* (2 vols. Boston, 1887), *1*, for this correspondence.

51. Another British agent in Paris then was a miserable character by the name of George Lupton. He was an American by birth who enlisted in the service of Eden for such occasional money rewards as he could secure from that employer. Lupton succeeded in ingratiating himself with Carmichael and the sea captains who

EDWARD BANCROFT'S MEMORIAL TO THE MARQUIS OF CARMARTHEN [52]

My Lord

I had some days since, the honor of seeing, and Conversing with Mr. Pitt, concerning the Business mentioned in the enclosed Paper, to which he appeared very favourably disposed, and very obliging promised to take the first opportunity, after his return from the Country (where he was then going) to settle it with your Lordship; desiring in the meantime, that I would wait on and explain the matter to you. As I have not hitherto found the opportunity of a verbal Explanation, I beg that your Lordship will be pleased, to peruse the inclosed *very exact State of Facts,* and afterwards, have the goodness to Communicate it, to Mr. Pitt, and such others of the King's Ministers, as your Lordship may think proper; flattering my self, that it will effectually remove every difficulty that may exist in the Business relative to it.

I had also the honor of acquainting Mr. Pitt of something respecting Ireland, which he will doubtless mention, as I intended doing, to your Lordship and it being expedient for me to return to Paris in about ten days I hope your Lordship will allow me the honor of a few minutes Conversation some time in the ensuing week. I have that of being with great Respect

    My Lord

                        Your Lordships most Humble
                        and most devoted Servant
                                EDW'D BANCROFT

DUKE STREET
   17th Sept 1784
     Most Hon'ble Marquis of Carmarthen

In the month of June 1776, Mr. Silas Deane arrived in France, and pursuant to an instruction given him by the Secret Committee of Congress, wrote to me in London, requesting an interview in Paris, where I accordingly went, early in July, and was made acquainted with the purposes of his Mission, and with every thing which passed between him, and the French Ministry. After staying two or three weeks there, I returned to England,

---

served the commissioners. He posed as an American willing to undertake small speculations in supplying the army with munitions and clothing. He wrote copious letters to Eden which added nothing very new to the information supplied by Bancroft, Wentworth, and Hynson, but they were doubtless useful in checking the accuracy and trustworthiness of other informers. Lupton was not aware of the activities of the other agents. When Bancroft threatened to leave the American commission because his salary had not been paid, Lupton had hopes of getting a place as his successor, thus putting himself in a position in which (he wrote) he would be able to gather information of the most vital character. Lupton's debauches in Paris ruined him as a successful agent. His reports cease at the beginning of 1778. Reference to them may be had, under the name, in the index to the Stevens Facsimiles.

52. P.R.O., F.O. 4, 3. Carmarthen was Foreign Secretary in 1784.

convinced, that the Government of France would endeavour to Promote an Absolute Separation, of the then United Colonies, from Great Britain; unless a speedy termination of the Revolt, by reconciliation, or Conquest, should frustrate this project. I had then resided near ten years, and expected to reside the rest of my Life, in England; and all my views, interests and inclinations were adverse to the independancy of the Colonies, though I had advocated some of their Claims, from a persuasion, of their being founded in Justice. I therefore wished, that the Government of this Country, might be informed, of the Danger of French interference, though I could not resolve to become the informant. But Mr. Paul Wentworth, having gained some general Knowledge of my Journey to France, and of my intercourse with Mr. Deane, and having induced me to believe, that the British Ministry were likewise informed on this Subject, I at length Consented to meet the then Secretaries of State, Lords Weymouth and Suffolk, and give them all the information in my power; which I did, with the most disinterested views; for I not only, did not ask, but expressly rejected, every Idea of, any reward. The Declaration of Independancy, was not then known in Europe, and I hoped, that Government, thus informed of the Danger, would prevent it, by some accomodation with the Colonies, or by other means. It had been my original intention to stop after this first Communication; but having given the first notice of a beginning intercourse, between France and the United Colonies, I was urged on, to watch and disclose the progress of it; for which purpose, I made several Journeys to Paris, and maintained a regular Correspondence with Mr. Deane, through the Couriers of the French Government. And in this way, I became *entangled* and obliged to proceed in a kind of Business, as repugnant to my feelings, as it had been to my original intentions. Being thus devoted to the Service of Government, I consented like others, to accept such Emoluments, as my situation indeed required. And in Feb'y 1777, Lord Suffolk, to whom by Ld Weymouths Consent, my Communications were then made, formally promised me, in the King's Name, a Pension for Life of £200 pr an. to Commence from the Christmas preceeding. This was for Services *then rendered;* and as an inducemnt for me to go over and reside in France, and continue my services there, until the Revolt should terminate, or an Open rupture with that nation ensue, his Lordship farther promised, that when either of these Events should happen, my permanent pension of £200 pr an. should be increased to £500 *at least.* Confiding in this promise, I went to Paris, and during the first year, resided in the same House with Dr. Franklin, Mr. Deane etc., and regularly informed this Government of every transaction of the American Commissioners; of every Step and Vessel taken to supply the revolted Colonies, with Artillery, Arms etc.; of every part of their intercourse with the French and other European Courts; of the Powers and instructions given by Congress to the Commissioners, and of their correspondence with the Secret Committees etc. and when the Government of France at length determined *openly* to support the Revolted Colonies, I gave notice of this determination, and of the progress made in forming the two Treaties of Alliance and Commerce, and when these were signed, on the Evening of the 6th of Feb'y, I at my own Expence, by a special Messenger, and with unexampled dispatch, conveyed this intelligence to this City, and to the King's Ministers, within 42 hours, from the instant of their Signature, a piece of information, for which many individuals here, would, for purposes of Speculation, have given me more than all that I have received from Government. Afterwards, when that decisive measure, of sending Count D'Estaign with the fleet from Toulon, to Commence Hostilities at the Delaware and New York, was adopted, I sent intelligence of the direct object and Plan of the Expedition. I had originally explained to Lord Suffolk my Determination to quit this business, whenever an Open War with France, should destroy, what had been my principal inducement to meddle with it; I mean, the hope of preventing a Separation of the revolted Colonies: And as this war now appeared unavoidable, I requested that the King's Ministers would, as soon as practicable, provide other Sources of information, and permit me to withdraw myself. This request however was never granted. But to fullfill the promise made by my Lord Suffolk my permanent Pension was increased to 500 £ per an. and regularly entered, in Book Letter A. payable to Mr. P. Wentworth for the use of Edwd. Edwards; the name, by which, for greater Secrecy, it had been long before agreed to distinguish me. In June 1780, the King's Ministers, reflecting that this Pension had been given as the reward of *Antecedent* Services, and that it would be unreasonable, to require a longer Continuance of them, without a farther recompense, agreed to allow me an additional yearly sum of £500, *so long as I should reside in France;* and they encouraged me to expect that this last Sum, or at least a Considerable part of it, would be ultimately added to my permanent pension, in case Government should be satisfied with my future services. I accordingly received from his Majesties Treasury the Stipulated annual allowance of £1000, until the month of April 1782; when the Change of Ministers, with Mr. Burkes Bill, created some difficulty on this Subject. But the matter being Explained to my Lord Shelburne, he took care, before his resignation, to secure and pay me through the then Secretary of State, for foreign Affairs, (my Lord Grantham), a full years Sallary, though the last quarter was not then due. In June 1783, I came to London, and informed Lord North (to whom my latter information had by particular direction been addressed) of my intention of going to America, where I offered my Services, in promoting measures and dispositions, favourable to the interests of this Country, as well as in giving information of the State of things there, and of the views and proceedings of Congress etc. I likewise reminded him, of the Encouragement which I had received to expect that the second 500 £ pr. an. or at least a part of it would be made permanent like the first, adding, that if my services in America, were accepted, it would as I presumed, in any case, be thought reasonable, to Continue to me, at least while there, the same allowance as had been made me in France. With this Proposition, his Lordship appeared to be satisfied, but at a subsequent interview, he referred me to Mr. Fox for a decision respecting it, as well as for the payment of a quarter Sallary, then due, alledging, that Mr. Burke's Bill, had made it absolutely necessary, to provide for me, through that Department. I accordingly saw and conversed with Mr. Fox respecting my situation and propositions, which he promised to consider of; but as I had not foreseen any difficulty, or delay, and had already agreed, and Paid for, my Passage to Philadelphia, I was obliged to follow the Ship to the Downs, on the 12th of August 1783, before any decision was made, and indeed, whilst Mr. Fox was out of Town. I however informed him, by Letter, on the evening of my departure, that he might expect the Continuation of my Services to Government whilst in America, and requested that the quarters Salary, then due, might be paid to Mrs. Bancroft. She accordingly soon after received £250 for that Quarter; since which nothing has been paid for my account. On my part, I have endeavoured, as far as practicable, whilst absent, in America, to render myself useful to the British nation and Government. Great Events indeed did not occur for Communication, and the ill temper produced in America by the Proclamation, respecting the intercourse from thence to the West Indies, did not allow me to do all I had hoped, in promoting sentiments and dispositions favourable to this Country; though I endeavoured it, and I think with some little Success, in particular Channels and Connections; and I have endeavoured, occasionally, to vindicate the late measures of this Government, in Newspapers, particularly under the Signature of Cincinnatus, against the Publications of Common Sense.

One years Salary was due to me at midsummer last, which I request the payment of: what it shall be, must depend on the Kings pleasure, and that of his Ministers: I make no Claim beyond the permanent pension of £500 pr an. for which the Faith of Government has been often pledged; and for which, I have sacrificed near eight years of my Life, and my pursuits in it; always avoiding any Kind of appointment, or emolument from, as well as any sort of Engagement to, any Government in the United States; in the full determination, of remaining to the end of my Life, a faithful Subject to my natural, and most Gracious Sovereign.

In Dr. Bancroft's Sept. 17, 1784.

Sᴛ. Jᴀᴍᴇs's 16th Sept'r 1784.

Note. Since the publication of this article in 1924, research has brought out much detail of the operation of the British secret service during the American Revolution. Significant studies are: Lewis Einstein, *Divided Loyalties* (London, 1933); T. P. Abernethy, "Commercial Activities of Silas Deane in France," *A.H.R.*, *39* (1934); Carl Van Doren, *Secret History of the American Revolution* (New York, 1941); Julian P. Boyd, "Silas Deane: Death by a Kindly Teacher of Treason?" *William and Mary Quarterly*, 3d ser. *16* (1959).

3. The Rayneval Memoranda of 1782 on Western Boundaries and Some Comments on the French Historian Doniol

SO OBVIOUSLY vital to the history of this nation was the treaty of peace and independence of 1783 that every piece of documentary evidence pertaining to its negotiation is of enduring value to the historian and to the student of American history. The purpose of this paper is to present some hitherto unused and unprinted memoranda relating to the western boundary settlement in that negotiation, to attempt a critical examination of these documents, and to suggest some implications arising from them. The documents I have called the Rayneval Memoranda.

We recall that an important turning point in the peace negotiations at Paris and Versailles in 1782 was the decision of John Jay on his own responsibility and secretly, secretly both to France and to his own colleague, Franklin, to send a personal agent, actually a British subject and hanger-on of the British peace mission, one Benjamin Vaughan, to England. The object of this mission was to persuade Lord Shelburne, the Prime Minister, that he had better alter the commission of his official peace plenipotentiary, Richard Oswald, so as to enable him to treat with representatives of the independent United States of America instead of with any commissioner or commissioners of the colonies or plantations, or any one of them, or "any description of men"—the wording of Oswald's original commission.

Jay was persuaded to take this step, we remember, because of his doubt of the good faith and full loyalty of the ally of the United States, France. Every serious writer on this chapter of American diplomatic history has properly stressed Jay's reasons for doubting French loyalty in these negotiations that were so vitally important to the United States, namely: (1) the suspicion of French straightforwardness engendered in his mind by his diplomatic experiences in Spain, culminating in his dis-

---

Published in a paperbound volume by the American Antiquarian Society, 1938. Reprinted from *Proceedings of the American Antiquarian Society, 47,* April 1937.

putations at Paris with the Count de Aranda, Spanish ambassador to France, as to the western boundaries of the United States; (2) the intercepted dispatch from the French *chargé d'affaires* at Philadelphia, Barbé-Marbois, which the British astutely placed in Jay's hands in Paris, a dispatch in which Marbois stressed to Vergennes, the French Minister of Foreign Affairs, the weakness of the American claim to fisheries in British territorial waters; (3) the memorandum delivered to Jay on September 6 by Rayneval, private secretary to Vergennes, in which Rayneval suggested the territorial compromise—so well-known to students of the negotiations—that would, to use Franklin's later words, have cooped up the United States between the Appalachian Mountains and the Atlantic seaboard.[1]

It was the Rayneval memorandum of September 6, together with the postscript in Rayneval's covering letter, announcing that he would be absent from Versailles for some days, which finally spurred Jay to independent action. He instantly and correctly divined that Rayneval had gone on a secret and confidential visit to England, to talk peace behind the backs of the regular negotiators who then represented the various belligerents in Paris.

> The perusal of this memoir [records Jay] convinced me—
> 1st. That this court [France] would, at a peace, oppose our extension to the Mississippi.
> 2dly. That they would oppose our claims to the free navigation of that river.
> 3dly. That they would *probably* support the *British* claims to all the country above the thirty-first degree of latitude, and *certainly* to all the country north of the Ohio.
> 4thly. That in case we should not agree to divide with Spain in the manner proposed, that then this court would aid Spain in negociating with Britain for the territory she wanted, and would agree that the residue should remain to Britain.[2]

Jay felt that Vergennes would rather "postpone the acknowledgment of our independence by Britain to the conclusion of a general peace than aid us in procuring it at present." With this alarm in his

1. An interesting long memorandum on the approaching peace, by an unidentified French military officer, proposed exactly this and even "exciting" the English to constrict the American boundaries. Whether Vergennes or Rayneval were influenced by this memoir is impossible to say. The document is in Arch. Aff. Etrang., Correspondance Politique, Angleterre, vol. 53F., f. 111–31.

2. Jay to Livingston, Paris, Nov. 17, 1782, Wharton, *The Revolutionary Diplomatic Correspondence of the United States, 6,* 27.

mind he sent Vaughan to England on the secret mission above-mentioned, to countercheck Rayneval's secret mission to London, to say to Lord Shelburne that it "appeared to be the obvious interest of Britain immediately to cut the cords which tied us to France, for that, though we were determined faithfully to fulfill our treaty and engagements with this court, *yet it was a different thing to be guided by their or our construction of it.*" [3]

Historians, I repeat, have stressed Jay's reasons for suspicion of perfect French loyalty, but they have been by no means agreed that those reasons were justified. A study of the memoranda about to be presented may help to arrive at a more secure judgment on this point. The Rayneval memorandum as addressed to Jay on September 6, 1782, has long been familiar from the translation printed by Sparks, Wharton, and others. The French text,[4] here printed, retaining its imperfections in spelling and punctuation, with Rayneval's covering letter to Jay, shows that the translation (presumably by Jay) is substantially correct.[5]

Versailles le 6 septembre [1782].

J'ai l'hr., M., de vous envoyer, comme vous l'avez desiré, mes idées personnelles sur la manière de terminer vos discutions de limites avec l'Espagne; je desire qu'elles vous paroissent dignes d'être prises en considération.

J'ai fait réflexion, M., sur ce que vous m'avez dit hier du défaut de pouvoirs de M. l'ambeur. d'Espagne. Vous ne sauriez, selon moi, mettre cette raison en avant pour vous dispenser de traiter avec cet l'ambeur. sans l'offenser et sans contredire les premières démarches que vous avez faites vis-à-vis

3. It may be said, incidentally, that the alteration of Oswald's commission enabling him to treat with representatives of the United States was not a clean-cut recognition of American independence, which was in fact deferred through negotiation to the final peace, exactly as Vergennes preferred it to be. But it did result in an acceleration of the Anglo-American negotiations and (in combination with other factors) the relinquishment of the American ambitions for the cession of Canada, which Franklin had carefully nursed along up to this point.

4. The documents are reproduced *verbatim et literatim* from the MS copies in Arch. Aff. Etrang., Correspondance Politique, États Unis, vol. 22, 197–204. Except for minor differences in spelling and punctuation they correspond with the copies in the Papers of the Continental Congress, 110, 2, 185–91. The covering letter only is printed by H. Doniol, *Histoire de la participation de la France à l'établissement des États-Unis d'Amérique, 5,* 159–60. Wharton, *6,* 25–27, prints both in English translation.

5. The first sentence could better be translated: "There is question between Spain and the United States and America how to regulate their respective limits toward the Ohio and the Mississippi River," rather than "The question . . . is . . . etc." This slight correction of translation is of historical importance because it shows that the memoir had been composed since the issue arose between Jay and Aranda in Paris.

de lui. Cette réflexion me conduit à vous conseiller, M., de revoir M. le Cte d'Aranda, et de lui faire une proposition quelconque sur l'objet dont il est question: celle qui résulte de mon mémoire me semble la plus propre à effectüer une conciliation raisonnable, mais c'est à vous à juger si je me trompe, parceque vous seul avez connoissance des titres que les États-Unis peuvent avoir pour étendre leurs possessions aux dépens des nations que l'Añgre elle-même a reconnues pour indépendantes. Au reste, M., quel que soit l'usage que vous croirez devoir faire de mon mémoire, je vous prie de le regarder au moins comme une preuve de mon zèle et de mon désir d'être utile à la cause de votre patrie.

J'ai l'h^r. d'etre avec une parfaite considération, eta.

Rayneval

P.S. Comme je serai absent pendant quelques jours, je vous prie d'adresser votre réponse à M. Henin.[6]

Idée

Sur la maniere de determiner et fixer les limites entre l'Espagne et les Etats Unis du côté de l'Ohio et vers le Mississippi.

Il est question entre l'Espagne et les Etats Unis de l'Amérique Septentrionale de regler les limites respectives vers l'Ohio & le Mississippi. Les Americains prétendent que leur domaine s'etend jusqu'au Mississippi, et l'Espagne soutient le contraire.

Il est evident que les Américains ne peuvent emprunter que de l'Ang^re. le droit qu'ils pretendent avoir de s'etendre jusqu'au Mississippi. Ainsi pour determiner ce droit il convenient d'examiner ce qu'a pensé et fait à cet égard la Cour de Londres.

On sait qu'avant le traité de Paris la france possédoit la Louisiane et le Canada, et qu'elle a regardé les peuples sauvages situés à l'Est du Mississippi où comme indépendants ou comme étant sous sa protection.

Cette prétension n'a causé aucune querelle. L'Ang^re. n'a imaginé d'en faire que pour les terreins situés vers la source de l'Ohio dans la partie où elle a donné à ce fleuve le nom d'Allegany.

Il s'est ensuivi de là une discution de limites entre les Cours de Versailles et de Londres: mais il seroit superflu d'en suivre les details, il sufit d'observer qu'en 1755 l'Angleterre a proposé la délimitation suivante. Elle est parti du point où la rivière des Boeufs se jette dans l'Ohio à l'endroit appellé Venango; elle a remonté cette rivière vers le lac Erié jusqu'à la distance de 20 lieues;

---

6. In the English translation appended to the French copy of Rayneval's letter in Papers of the Continental Congress, 110, 2, 185, appears this additional paragraph, for which there is no counterpart in the French copy there given: "I must desire you not to let the perusal of the following Memoir make you forget the Postscript of the above Letter for, in the sequel, you will find it of some importance." Wharton prints this.

Henin was another secretary in the Foreign Office.

et reprenant au dit endroit de Venango, elle a tiré une ligne droite jusqu'aux dernieres montagnes de la Virginie qui ont leur versant à l'ocean. Quant aux Peuplades sauvages situés entre la ligne qui vient d'être indiquée et le Mississippi le Ministere Anglois les regarda comme independantes. Il resulte de là que d'après les propositions mêmes de la Cour de Londres, prèsque tout le Cours de l'Ohio apartenoit à la france, et que les contrées situées à l'ouest des montagnes etoient régardées comme n'aiant rien de commun avec les Colonies.

Lorsqu'en 1761, on négocia la paix, la France offroit à l'Ang^{re}. la cession du Canada. Il fût question de régler les limites de cette Colonie, et celles de la Louisiane. La France pretendit que presque tout le cours de l'Ohio faisoit partie de la Louisiane, et la Cour de Londres pour prouver que ce fleuve apartenoit au Canada produisit plusieurs pieces probantes, entr'autres la carte que M. de Vaudreuil remit au Commandant anglois en abandonnant le Canada. Le Ministère de Londres soutint en même tems qu'une partie de ces sauvages situés à l'Est du Mississippi etoit indépendante, l'autre sous sa protection, et qu'elle en avoit acheté une partie des 5. Nations Iroquoises. Les malheurs de la France coupêrent court à cette discution: le Trainté de Paris assigna le Mississippi pour limites entre les possessions de la France et cettes de la grande Bretagne.

Voyons les dispositions que la Cour de Londres a faites en conséquence du Traite de Paris.

Si Elle eût regardé les vastes terreins situés à l'Est du Mississippi comme faisant partie de ses anciennes Colonies, elle l'auroit déclaré, et auroit fait des dispositions en conséquence: Loin de là, le Roi d'Ang^{re}. dans une proclamation du mois d'Octobre 1763 fait connoître d'une maniere précise et positive que les terreins en question sont situés entre le Mississippi & *les anciens etablissemens anglois*. Il est donc de la derniere évidence que la Cour de Londre Elle même, lorsqu' Elle etoit encore souveraine des 13 Colonies, ne regardoit pas les terreins susmentionnés comme faisant partie de ces mêmes Colonies; et il resulte de là de la manière la plus demonstrative, qu'elles n'ont aujourdhui aucun droit sur ces terreins; pour soutenir le contraire il faudroit détruire tous les principes du droit, de la nature et des gens.

Les Principes qui viennent d'être etablis sont aplicables à l'Espagne comme aux Etats Unis: cette puissance ne peut pas étendre sa proprieté au delà de ce qu'elle a conquis: or on soit qu'elle n'a pas dépassé le fort de Natches, situé vers le 31 dégré de latitude; ainsi ses droits se bornent à ce dégré: ce qui est au delà est ou indépendant ou appartenant à l'Ang^{re}., ni l'Espagne ni les Americains n'ont rien à y pretendre le futur traité de paix pourra seul regler les droits respectifs.

La conséquence de tout ce qui vient d'etre dit est: que ni l'Espagne ni les Etats Unis n'ont aucun droit de souveraineté sur les sauvages dont il est question, et que la transaction qu'ils feroient sur ce Pays seroient sans objet.

Mais l'avenir peut amener de nouvelles circonstances; et cette réflexion porte à croire qu'il seroit utile que la Cour de Madrid et les Etats Unis fissent un arrangement eventuel.

Cette arrangement pourroit être fait de la manière suivante. On tireroit une ligne droite depuis l'angle oriental du Golfe du Mexique qui fait la section entre les deux Florides jusqu'au fort Toulouse situé dans le Pais des Alibamous; dela on remonteroit la rivière de Locushatchi depuis l'embouchure de laquelle on tireroit une ligne droit jusqu'au fort où comptoir Quenassée; depuis ce dernier endroit on suivroit le cours de la rivière Euphasée jusqu'à l'endroit où elle se jette dans celle de Cheraqués: on suivroit le cours de cette dernière jusqu'à l'endroit où elle reçoit celle de Pelisippi; on suivroit celle ci jusqu'à sa Source, d'où l'on tireroit une ligne droite jusqu'à la riviere de Cumberland, dont on suivroit le cours jusqu'à son embouchure dans l'Ohio. Les sauvages à l'oüest de la ligne qui vient d'être indiquée seroient libres sous la protection de l'Espagne; ceux situés à l'Est seroient libres et sous la protection des Etats-Unis, ou bien les Américians s'arrangeroient avec Eux comme ils l'entendroient; le commerce seroit libre avec les uns et les autres.

En jettant les yeux sur la carte on verra que l'Espagne perdroit presque tout le cours de l'Ohio, et que les établissements que les Americains peuvent avoir sur cette rivière démeureroient intactes et même qu'ils auroient une espace très etendue pour en former de nouveaux.

Quant au cours et à la navigation du Mississippi ils suivent le sort de la propriété; ils apartiendront donc à la nation à qui appartiendront les deux rives. Si donc par le futur traité de paix l'Espagne conserve la florida occidentale, elle sera seule propriétaire du cours du Mississippi depuis le 31 degré de latitude, jusqu'à l'embouchure de ce fleuve: quelque soit le sort de ce qui est audelà de ce point vers le Nord, les Etats Unis n'y sauroient prétendre, faute d'être maitres de l'une ou de l'autre rive du fleuve.

Pour ce qui est des terreins situés au Nord de l'Ohio, il y a lieu de présumer que l'Espagne n'y formera aucune pretention; leur fort devra être reglé avec la Cour de Londres.

Now, the thought of this important document is based, in abridged and modified character, on an earlier and longer memorandum on the same subject which Rayneval had recently composed during the progress of the discussion between Aranda and Jay over the western boundaries of the United States. The earlier memorandum enables us to pierce a little further behind the veil of French policy and to see to what extent all of Jay's fears of French loyalty were justified. For convenience, we shall refer to this earlier and longer document as Rayneval's Historical Memorandum, to be distinguished from Rayneval's Compromise Memorandum delivered to Jay on September 6 and above presented to the reader in the original. The history of this Historical Memorandum we can trace quite readily in at least three archival copies, below printed for the first time, in parallel columns. We can follow its origin, with more particulars, in the dispatches of Jay and of Aranda to their respective governments recording their discussions with each other. Of these dispatches, those of Aranda are the closest and best source, and are accompanied by a day-to-day diary [7] in which he sets down his conversations with Jay, Vergennes, and Rayneval with great detail, so great a detail that I have been tempted to turn the narrated conversations with Jay into direct discourse. Jay's long dispatch, on the other hand, is summary, not precise as to dates of interviews, and was written several weeks afterward, under date of November 17, 1782.[8] Before presenting the Historical Memorandum, in its three versions, a brief description of these diplomatic discussions is in order.

Jay had been in Spain from January 1780, to May 1782, trying to secure a treaty which would bring recognition of the United States and if possible an alliance. For such a recognition he had finally offered, upon instructions from Congress, a reciprocal guaranty of the territories of each party in North America, together with a relinquishment by the United States of the navigation of the Mississippi River below 31° North Latitude (the old boundary of West Florida before 1764, when the British moved the line north to the latitude of the mouth of the Yazoo). It was a remarkable concession. We recall that Jay realized its significance and that he carefully made it contingent upon immediate acceptance. In making this contingent offer he appended to it this anomalous commentary:

> Nor can Mr. Jay omit mentioning the Hopes and Expectations of Congress that his Majesty's Generosity and Greathness of Mind, will prompt him to alleviate as much as possible the Disadvantages to which this Proposition subjects the United States, by either granting them a free port under certain Restrictions, in the vicinity, or by such other marks of his Liberality and Justice, as may give him additional claims to the affection and attachment of the United States.[9]

If Spain had accepted this offer, even subject to some discussion and possible rectification of the line of 31° North Latitude, she could have avoided much later dispute with the United States, while having

7. Printed by J. F. Yela Utrilla, *España ante la independencia de los Estados Unidos* (2d ed. 2 vols. Lérida, 1925), 2, 355–64.

8. See Wharton, *6*, 11–51.

9. Yela, 2, 347–48.

the new republic pledged to a guaranty of Spain's possessions. The Mississippi question would have been shelved at least for some years—for how long no man can say; the proposed relinquishment was "for the future," without time limit. It was indeed fortunate for the United States that Spain did not accept this proposed treaty.[10] It would have been an embarrassment to future western expansion. Jay personally was opposed to the offer which he presented only in obedience to his instructions. Immediately Spain refused it, he prudently withdrew it. Spain rejected it because her principal minister, Floridablanca, was determined not to set a bad example to her own American colonies by recognizing the independence of English colonies revolting against their mother country. In this conviction he overrode the advice of the able Count de Aranda, Spanish ambassador in Paris, who had counseled a treaty of mutual territorial guaranty and even alliance as a protection to those very Spanish colonies which he correctly feared would be menaced by future "Anglo-American" western expansion.[11]

When Jay arrived in Paris in June 1782, from Spain, he renewed his discussions for a Spanish treaty with Aranda, to whom he had been referred informally by Floridablanca. Despite the favorable prospects for recognition of independence by Great Britain herself in the peace negotiations then under way in France, Aranda refused to have any official or formal diplomatic conversations with Jay. In fact he had no powers to treat with a plenipotentiary of the United States, and he was most cautious not to take any step which could be construed as a recognition of the independent status of the United States before Great Britain should do so.[12] He nevertheless felt himself authorized by his

10. The essential features of the same treaty appeared later in 1786 when Jay, as Secretary for Foreign Affairs of the Continental Congress, initialed similar articles with Diego de Gardoqui, Spanish minister in the United States. This time Spain was eager for the treaty, but it failed because of the opposition of the southern states to forbear even for a stipulated term of twenty-five years to use the navigation of the Mississippi, the highway from their western lands to the outside world. The danger of such a treaty being ratified by a majority of the thirteen states was the principal reason for the clause in the federal Constitution of 1787 requiring a two-thirds majority of the senators present for the ratification of a treaty.

11. Richard Konetzke, *Die Politik des Grafen Aranda; ein Beitrag zur Geschichte des spanisch-englischen Weltgegensatzes im 18. Jahrhundert* (Berlin, 1929).

12. Aranda in his no. 2207 to Floridablanca of June 1, 1782, anticipating the arrival of Jay from Spain, thus recapitulates Floridablanca's instructions: "His Majesty authorizes me to listen to Jay, or whatever other American deputy, the same as I would to the English emissaries; but without concluding anything to communicate to His Majesty the results of the conferences, and to receive the royal orders." See also Aranda to Floridablanca, no. 2295, Paris, Sept. 8, 1782; no. 2301, Paris, Sept. 15, 1782; no. 2314, Paris, Oct. 4, 1782. A.H.N., Estado, legajo 6609.

instructions to hold informal discussions with Jay that might lay the basis—*ad referendum*—for a future relationship. For this purpose he indulged in talk with Jay, as between two private gentlemen.[13] In these confabulations Aranda tried to feel Jay out and discover the terms and position of the United States. Jay himself was looking for a real treaty with Spain, which would have been a diplomatic triumph for his country, and for himself. Consequently he engaged in discussions which lasted from August 3 until September 10, 1782, when Jay broke them off because of Aranda's manifest lack of powers. The record of these discussions [14] has not been exploited in the detail [15] which is desirable to illustrate the Rayneval Memoranda. Let us review it.

Jay presented himself at Aranda's residence, on Saturday, August 3, 1782, at half past ten in the morning, after soliciting an appointment.[16] Aranda exhibited a copy of Mitchell's Map [17] of North America of 1755 —a map destined to be the most important single map in the diplomatic history of the United States and of North America, and an atlas which remains unidentified.

Jay mentioned other smaller and provincial maps. "We can look at them later on," remarked Aranda, "but first let us get a general idea of things as a whole for a demarcation line between the dominions which might remain to Spain and to the Thirteeen United States.[18] In my opinion the way to do this would be by major well-known and indelible landmarks, without bothering over a matter of a hundred leagues more or less. In any event such a dividing line would have to

13. Aranda to Floridablanca, no. 2241, July 6, 1782. Ibid.

14. I take the conversations from Aranda's *Diario* enclosed with Aranda's no. 2266 of Aug. 10, 1782, and 2290 of Sept. 3, 1782, A.H.N., Estado, legajo 6609, printed with many minor inaccuracies, by Yela, 2, 355–64. A photocopy of the original is in the Library of Congress. This is supplemented, as indicated in footnotes, by Jay's dispatch of Nov. 17, 1782, Wharton, 6, 11–51.

15. In a more summary way I have touched upon it in my *Pinckney's Treaty* (Johns Hopkins Press, 1926; rev. ed. Yale University Press, 1960), pp. 38–43; and *The Diplomacy of the American Revolution* (New York, 1935), pp. 216–20.

16. In this exchange of *billets* Aranda was careful to avoid using his own official title or to address Jay in any official capacity which might imply thereby a recognition of the United States.

17. Aranda notes the precise edition: *Amerique septentrionale avec les routes, distances en milles, villages, et establissements—les 8 feuilles francois et anglois— par le Dr. Mitchel traduit de l'Anglois par le Rouge Ingenieur Geographe du Roy ruë des grands augustins 1756* [with a supplementary title:] *North America so Doctor Mitchel zu London in 1755 ten jahr ausgegeben jetzaber in das franzosische ubersetzet.*" From Library of Congress photocopy of the *Diario*.

18. Here Aranda slipped into the new terminology. He usually spoke of the "Colonies."

fall more or less in the Indian country and the Indians would have to be domesticated by each party, so as to make of them tranquil barriers between the two realms."

The two seemed to be agreed on this principle, thought Aranda.

"Now, where would you draw the boundary?" he asked Jay.

"By a well-marked division," said Jay, putting his finger on the source of the Mississippi and following the river down to New Orleans.

"Then you wouldn't leave us West Florida?" asked Aranda. "Not only did that used to be ours, but we have reconquered it from the English."

"Since the Colonies take by subrogation the rights of England," observed Jay, "and the latter had those well-known boundaries, these same cannot be gainsaid from the source of the Mississippi to where the real boundary of West Florida begins."

"Quite so," agreed Aranda. "For this reason, Spain having reconquered West Florida, the boundaries of the whole Mississippi are established by the Treaty of Paris. To Spain are subrogated the rights of this treaty by virtue of her reconquest of the province."

"The provinces have their title by charter grants from the British Crown," said Jay, "to indefinite hinterlands. The part of the Mississippi which is not the boundary of Florida alone, should not belong to Spanish reconquest, but to England, and in default of the latter to the United States [19] in her place."

"Any Prince has just as good a right [20] to make grants with expansive imaginary boundary lines as did the British Crown to its establishments," countered Aranda. "Spain could draw hers from both extremes of Louisiana and the Florida coast in parallel lines way to the most unknown and frozen north countries. The boundaries would intersect each other and the maps would be nothing but a crosswork of rival claims of equal value. It is more probable to suppose that he who holds the mouth of the Mississippi, together with a long stretch of its lower course, would have the right to go all the way up it, always as his own. We must get away from such pretensions based on the indefinite lines of these English maps, like this one here. I have never considered them to mean anything. By this map and the other provincial maps all the region beyond the main boundary lines of the

19. Aranda, recounting the conversation, uses the word "Colonies." Jay, we may presume, would certainly have said "United States."

20. Spain, of course, had claimed for herself, nothing less than the New World west of the demarcation line, in 1493 and after.

colonies [21] is savage country, to which both of us parties have equally good, or indeed equally unreasonable rights. Let us remember this in marking out for ourselves the major landmarks; then each of us may clothe the naked body as best he can. My idea of a dividing line is one to keep the lower part of the river courses, at least, under one owner."

"Please let me see just where you would put that on the map," invited Jay.

"Right here," said Aranda, trying to indicate a line which might serve at least as a basis of argument. "Let us start at the western end of Lake Superior and follow the lake shores along as far as the end of Lake Erie or Oswego. These are positions which cannot leave lands back of them in dispute."

As he said this Aranda had the thought that if Spain could put forts in certain strategic points she could then control the interior region vis-à-vis her rival.

"Now we will drop the line down to the confluence of the Grand Kanawha with the Ohio," he continued, "thence to the apex of the innermost [i.e. westernmost] angle of South Carolina, so as to continue the demarcation toward some outstanding point, say a lake,[22] in the Apalache country, or the river George,[23] without however going all the way, simply marking the beginning of the line so as to indicate it would go that way. We would have to stop before we get to the boundary of Georgia or of Florida until we know what their real boundaries are."

"Why do you go as far as that, without going down to the lake?" asked Jay.

"Since East Florida is still English, we ought not to draw lines into the interior."

To this last Jay agreed.

Aranda marked his proposed line in red on a Mitchell and sent it to his chief, Floridablanca, in Madrid, promising to send him any further refinements of boundary discussion and suggestions.

Jay at no time—or Franklin either, at any time—either in this first discussion or in subsequent conversations during these negotiations,[24]

21. *La linea magistral de limites de las Colonias.* Presumably he meant the line of the Proclamation of 1763.

22. On the Mitchell's Map used by the negotiators there is a single lake near the boundary of East Florida, about 83° West Longitude.

23. The Altamaha River.

24. In the negotiations of 1786 in New York with the Spanish minister to the United States, Diego de Gardoqui, Jay was prepared rather "to yield a few acres than to part in ill humour," also to "forbear" to use the navigation of the Mississippi

receded an inch from the Mississippi River in the west, or the line of 31° North Latitude in the south. Nothing less than the whole eastern watershed of the Mississippi Valley was thus in dispute from the first conversation. Jay and Franklin were its staunch defenders in 1782.

The two American commissioners left the Mitchell's Map, marked with Aranda's boundary suggestion, at Vergennes's office, on August 10. "Dr. Franklin joined with me," recorded Jay at a later date, "in pointing out the extravagance of this line; and I must do him the justice to say, that in all his letters to me, and in all his conversations with me respecting our western extent, he has invariably declared it to be his opinion that we should insist upon the Mississippi as our western boundary, and that we ought not, by any means, to part with our rights to the free navigation of it.

"The Count de Vergennes was very cautious and reserved; but M. Rayneval, his principal secretary, who was present, thought we claimed more than we had a right to." [25]

Not long after,[26] Jay had another interview with Rayneval, who asked him whether he had made any progress in his negotiations with Aranda. Jay explained that Aranda had no actual powers to treat—which was, of course, true. Rayneval expressed surprise at any difficulties on that head, considering the public as well as the private character of that "nobleman." Neither his public nor his private character, however respectable, had empowered him to treat with the United States of America, replied Jay; consequently his Court could easily disavow anything he said—a perfectly appropriate observation.

When the Spanish ambassador, on Wednesday, August 21, made his regular call at Vergennes's office, he expressed to the minister his satisfaction that Jay had opened up with Vergennes the subject of the boundaries. He said that he would like to talk it over with his Excellency another day soon, when Vergennes had more time.

On Friday, August 23, Aranga came back to Vergennes, "to sound out his thought and to instruct him well on what might be suitable [*de lo que conviniese*]." Vergennes thought Jay's boundary claims rather extraordinary. He pronounced as quite in order the arguments which Aranda had made in his discussions with the American. Aranda ex-

---

for a period of twenty-five years, in return for a commercial treaty and a mutual guaranty of the territory of each party in America; but Congress would not allow these concessions. General Washington privately approved of them. See my *Pinckney's Treaty.*

25. Wharton, *6*, 23.

26. Probably Monday the 19th of August.

plained his motives in making such an expansive claim, the same motives which we have noted already. Vergennes remarked that Jay had said that there were actual American settlements far beyond Aranda's red line.[27] Aranda said he would be willing to take these into consideration if Jay would specify them; but that he could not, under his instructions, consent to the line of the Mississippi—this would be unsuitable for many reasons—; but a few leagues more or less would make little difference. "If His Excellency wish to take the trouble to intervene, I would be grateful to him for it, but let him begin by explaining things concretely to Jay."

Vergennes showed himself disposed to do so. He asked Aranda to have a talk with Rayneval, the minister's first secretary, a person very well informed on the region in question, indeed the only one who could readily argue with Jay, because he was having more to do with him and because he spoke English. According to Aranda, Jay spoke Spanish and French very imperfectly. Aranda agreed. Vergennes sent for Rayneval. The minister then turned to other business. Aranda and Rayneval went upstairs to the latter's office, taking the Mitchell's Map along with them.

Aranda started in by reviewing what had already passed between him and Jay. He declared that Jay's claims were all the more extraordinary, since those English possessions were composed of two parts: the one that could be called colonies, which might contain a known population; the other crown territory, conquered from other countries: that was to say, Canada, and the Floridas.

The theoretical extension of these regions, in back of the colonies, declared Rayneval, not only had nothing to do with them, but also the English government itself, which once had allowed the colonies [28] to

27. For the various lines referred to in these discussions see Charles O. Paullin and John K. Wright, *Atlas of the Historical Geography of the United States* (Carnegie Institution of Washington and the American Geographical Society of New York, 1932).

28. The reader does not need to be reminded that the colonies had not drawn their own boundaries. If they had done so they might have been in a more secure constitutional position against later amputations by treaty, royal proclamation, and act of Parliament, viz.: treaty of Paris of 1763 (which recognized the Mississippi River as the boundary between French Louisiana [except the "island" of New Orleans] and British territories); proclamation of Oct. 7, 1763 (creating the three new colonies of Quebec, East Florida, and West Florida, and setting aside the trans-Appalachian West and Great Lakes country as an Indian reservation); the royal commission to the governor of Georgia, June 6, 1764 (moving the boundary of West Florida from 31° North Latitude to the latitude of the mouth of the Yazoo River); and the Quebec Act of June 22, 1774 (extending the boundary of Quebec south to the Ohio River

draw their boundaries indefinitely from east to west, could not now countenance them, but would have to cut them off by north and south lines from Canada to Florida, considering these two possessions as the patrimony of the crown, because conquered by it. It was in the middle of this territory that lived various Indian nations which had not yet submitted to anybody.

Notwithstanding all this, complained Aranda, Jay wanted to push on regardless right up to the Mississippi.

Rayneval said Aranda's remarks were just, and Jay's stand too visionary [*ideal*]. To prove this he went on to observe that when Louisiana and Canada had belonged to France, the latter had always considered all this intermediary region, including even the Great Lakes, as her own, all under the same master, without stopping to draw a dividing line between Canada and Louisiana.

"But he still had something stronger against Jay," Aranda reports Rayneval to have declared.

> That was that when France lost Canada, and it came to treating of the boundary of Louisiana which remained to her, the English argued that the boundaries of Canada came down to the line of the Ohio and that of the Mississippi, because M. de Vaudreuil, French governor of Canada, had so declared in a provisional explanation which had taken place between the commanders of both nations when the English conquered it. By virtue of this argument it was this boundary which prevailed, so far as the Mississippi, and along that river to the sea, because of their conquest from France of the region of Mobile and from Spain of Florida. Under this supposition the Americans on the right bank of the Ohio could not extend their claims since they had not made themselves masters of Canada, which belonged to England. Similarly they had no right to the left bank because the same British crown claimed that the Floridas extended up back of Georgia, the Carolinas and Virginia as far as the Ohio River.

Looking on the map for Fort Toulouse on the Alabama River, Rayneval said that when France possessed the Mobile region on the other [that is, east] side of the Mississippi between it and Spanish Florida, she had established that fort as a base and a boundary between the English and the Spanish, and that from the mouth of the river

---

and west to the Mississippi). It was the King who had granted the colonial boundaries in the charters. It was the King (and in 1774, Parliament) who later modified them.

upwards it had always been considered under the generic name, and as such it united with Canada "above."

"Seeing Rayneval was so far from thinking like Jay, and so well informed about those parts," noted Aranda, "I told him that he might restore the map to Jay, and dissuade him from his intentions so that he would moderate his claims, beginning with a designation of those settlements which are supposed to be included beyond the line [*los establecimientos que suponía internados*], and since I had an abundance of such maps I would deliver one with the same demarcation to the Count de Vergennes for his use; and that we would go along marking up the maps with lines for discussion; after fixing them, we would make fair copies on other similar maps. M. de Rayneval acquiesced, and even assured me *he would work out a memorandum* [29] that would be useful under the circumstances, for which I thanked him. M. de Vergennes then came in; we told him what we had said; he seemed to agree; and on this our talk ended."

Aranda sent the promised map to Vergennes the next day (Saturday, August 24).

Before Rayneval's memorandum was completely drafted, Aranda had a conference with Vergennes himself, on Sunday, August 25. Vergennes asked him if he insisted on his red line. Aranda said no, providing Spain retained a boundary which would keep the "Colonists" well away from the Mississippi and would be fixed by indelible landmarks. Vergennes then said that if Jay "wouldn't listen to reason there would be a way of agreeing that the intervening savage nations should remain neutral, open to traffic with both Spaniards and Colonists." Aranda feared that this would furnish the "Colonists" a pretext for encroaching on the Indian territory under the guise of redressing grievances; it would be better to fix a real boundary for the proposed neutral Indian nations.

Vergennes then took the map which Jay had left and they went over it together. Vergennes said that "to content" the Americans it would be necessary to show them some consideration for their hinterlands. He suggested that, in the territory above the Ohio, Aranda might move his line back west as far as the Wabash River and the western end of Lake Erie. Aranda agreed to swing the lower end of this line west to the "Beaver Ponds" (close to the Ohio River, between the Great Miami and Little Miami, not far from the present Cincinnati). This was in effect "splitting the difference" (for the territory north of the Ohio) between Aranda's original line and Vergennes's proposed

29. Italics inserted.

compromise. Vergennes said he would not oppose this, but that, since the American way of internal commerce was by river courses, he thought they would hold out against losing the Wabash; whereas keeping to it as a dividing line to the Ohio, this boundary, together with that of the Great Kanawha, south of the Ohio, would give them room enough to calm and moderate their claims. Aranda, taking his text from Rayneval's previous explanations, observed that France and England had both admitted that Canada came down to the Ohio, so that Spain and the Americans were treating about territory which, though said to belong to England, had not actually been taken possession by either of them.[30] Because of this an agreement should be so fixed that if either party should expand beyond its own boundaries, whether as a result of wars with the Indians or of depopulated areas, it would come up against a definitely marked "preventive line," now to be fixed, beyond which it could not pass. If Jay would not be reasonable about giving up the Mississippi, he would have to bend (*tendría que plegarse*) before the objection that Spain could treat of that only with the English, not with the Americans; at all events any dividing line would always have to be a suitable distance away from the Mississippi.

Vergennes observed that the Americans could not refuse a line start-ing from Fort Toulouse, on the Alabama, the terminus of ancient French claims. Aranda did not neglect to note that this line should be extended to include not only the portion of the old French Mobile region, but also all the portions of West Florida recently conquered by Spain from Great Britain.

Rayneval now came in. He vouchsafed that he was working out a clear statement of the whole question. In Vergennes's presence Aranda begged him to do so according to his lights.

The next day, Monday, August 26, at half-past one in the afternoon, Jay appeared at Aranda's residence.

"Are you satisfied with my maps?" asked Aranda.

"I like the Atlas very much," replied Jay, "but not so much the big map [Mitchell's], because it is not exact." [31]

30. In this Aranda passed over the Spanish raid on Fort St. Joseph, Michigan, in 1781. But Jay in his briefer account of these conversations says that in the first discussion Aranda claimed title to British (formerly French) territory "by the con-quest of West Florida and certain posts on the Mississippi and Illinois."

For the negligible diplomatic effect of George Rogers Clark's temporary occupa-tion of Vincennes, Kaskaskia and Cahokia, see my *Diplomacy of the American Revo-lution*, p. 219.

31. For a representation of Mitchell's Map in relation to modern geography, illustrated by superimposing the principal features of Mitchell's Map over a modern

"Well, you also have the general map in the Atlas," responded Aranda, affecting a tone of natural frankness. "It is all the same with me which one we use—there doesn't seem to be any better. It doesn't matter what map you take if you stick to your first proposition of the Mississippi boundary. All you need for that is not a map but a pen to write it down."

"When I left my country," [32] retorted Jay, "I had very positive instructions which allow me no latitude."

Aranda remembered that Jay's full powers, a copy of which he had forwarded to his Court on August 10, gave him express authority for a treaty of amity and commerce, but had said nothing about boundaries. He thought it better not to mention this lest it confirm Jay in his refusal to retreat from the Mississippi. So the ambassador changed his tactics.

"Oh! Instructions are one thing. Authority [33] is another," he insinuated. "To treat about boundaries all one does is to say what one wants. But before one negotiates one has to discuss how to go about a thing, without putting it down as if it were already settled. *Prius est esse, quam operari.* Your Congress is too eminent a body to allow one to think they would impute to you any such intent [of disobeying his positive instructions]. I must bear in mind, however, that each side has its claims. A totally new establishment like your own, treating at a distance of a thousand leagues, with a long and uncertain navigation intervening, would not send a plenipotentiary without leaving him some leeway of authority, to take the reasoning of others and to agree to things in a form that is satisfactory all around. Much less could you do so yourself, Mr. Jay, who have been its President, a man esteemed and respected in your nation. We all take you for a plenipotentiary. If you, a plenipotentiary, say that you have a course laid out from which you can't make any deviation, all these conferences, geographical maps and persuasive arguments are pretty useless."

"Few ministers plenipotentiary," stated Jay, "have discretionary powers to transfer and cede to others the country of their sovereigns." [34]

"But, it isn't your country," insisted Aranda. "What right have you to the territory of the free and independent Indians?"

---

map, a scheme devised by S. W. Boggs, see my *Diplomatic History of the United States,* map 8.

32. Aranda puts it: *"Respondióme, que a su partida de las Colonias. . . ."*

33. *"Facultades"* is Aranda's word.

34. This sentence is taken from Jay's account as set down three months later. See Wharton, *6,* 24.

"The right of pre-emption over them, and of sovereignty over them in respect to other nations, the same as His Catholic Majesty in Mexico and Peru," Jay answered.[35]

"On the Mississippi," Jay persisted, "they have not said anything else to me, nor left me any discretion."

"Then what did you do in Madrid when you talked about boundaries?" asked Aranda, who was aware of Jay's earlier, contingent offer to Floridablanca.

"Once only," said Jay, "when I explained them generally by the Mississippi, I was told roundly without any reasons, that this just couldn't be. Things remained that way. There was no point in going further."

"My Court made a natural reply to such an unheard-of claim," Aranda declared. "When you saw how admissible it was, it was up to you to ask what Spain wanted, then to refute her claims and support those of Congress. If you lacked power to make any agreement, at least you could have set forth the respective claims, and thus in time you could have informed your principals of the aspect and status of the subject, so that you could have ascertained their final intentions completing the agreement. You would have them by now to explain and talk over with me."

"Since they didn't say anything more about it in Madrid," remarked Jay sententiously, "the matter remained so."

"According to what has been said," Aranda said reproachfully, "we are right back where we were. I have not only denied the Mississippi but I have also drawn a line which has a better *right* to fundamental support than you have for the Mississippi."

"Your line forces me into a discussion," stated Jay, "because it suggests to me various arguments that neither Congress, nor I for that matter, had imagined. If I had known this when I left my country, I could have explained to the United States the existing difficulties."

Aranda asked if Franklin had equal powers to treat jointly with Jay in regard to Spain. Jay said no. Aranda again urged the difficulty for anybody without discretionary powers to negotiate so far away from home.

"Do you have confidence enough," Aranda then asked Jay, "in the French Ministry to confide your situation to them and listen to what they have to say on it?"

"Yes," Jay replied.

Aranda notes that he then persuaded him to do so.

35. Wharton, *6*, 24.

"If, in view of your papers, you find you are not authorized to discuss boundaries, nor to regulate them, let me know so in writing, so that I shall be under no illusions about your not being able to do so."

"I will not delay to do so," said Jay.

During the conversation the two men had indulged in some talk about the value to the United States of Spain's entry into the war. Aranda averred that his nation, by secret succors, by actual declaration of war, by drawing off the forces of the enemy, had aided the "Colonies."

"In some of the expenses, yes," Jay admitted rather coldly, "but as to making war, they entertained me in Madrid with the idea of aid by force of arms, but at the most we see that all this was dedicated to the conquest of Florida for Spain herself. This did not help us at all in Charlestown or New York."

When Aranda remonstrated at this, Jay complained that Spain had not prohibited the British garrison, which surrendered at Pensacola, from reinforcing British forces at New York. Aranda explained that this was just British bad faith.

Jay, close-mouthed as usual (noted Aranda), took his leave with the noncommittal remark that now he saw things much differently than upon his arrival, that he desired that his mission might be well carried out.

The following Friday, August 30, at Versailles again, Aranda told Vergennes and Rayneval of his last interview with Jay. Both Frenchmen doubted that Jay's papers empowered him to make more than a treaty of amity and commerce with Spain. So Aranda showed them "a bit" of Jay's powers,[36] at which they marveled. They then observed that, according to the correspondence of La Luzerne,[37] the Court of Spain had begun a discussion of the boundary question in the "Colonies" themselves, through Don Juan de Miralles.[38] This, offered Aranda, was doubtless why nothing had gone any farther in Madrid.

36. Jay's full powers of Sept. 29, 1779, named him Minister Plenipotentiary, "giving him full power, general and special, to act in that quality, to confer, treat, agree and conclude with the ambassador or plenipotentiary of his catholick majesty vested with equal powers, of and concerning a treaty of amity and commerce, and of alliance." *Journals of the Continental Congress, 1774–1789* (Library of Congress edition, Washington, 1904–38), *15*, 1121. A copy of these powers delivered to Aranda, August 3, 1782, is in Aranda's no. 2266 to Floridablanca of Aug. 10, 1782. A.H.N., Estado, legajo 6609.

37. French minister in the United States, 1779 to 1784.

38. Spanish informal "observer" in the United States, Jan. 9, 1778—April 28, 1780.

Vergennes was obliged at this point to attend a committee meeting. He left Rayneval with Aranda to discuss boundaries.

Again the two bent over the map. First they drew a line from Fort Toulouse to what they supposed to be the borders of East Florida so as to include the recent Spanish conquest of West Florida. This line appears on the Rayneval Historical Memorandum as a line from the point where the 31st degree North Latitude crosses the Perdido River, to Fort Toulouse.[39] Then, to get to the Ohio River from Fort Toulouse, Rayneval drew a line running up the Toulouse (*Tolosa*) River, from there to the Cherakee or Hogohegee (Tennessee) and down that to the Ohio. When Aranda observed how close this came to the Mississippi, at the mouth of the Tennessee, they changed the line so as to leave the Tennessee at the confluence of the Pelisipi, then going up the latter to its source, thence to the source of the Cumberland and down that to the Ohio [40] "as far as its entrance into the Mississippi, so that the Americans would remain far away from the latter, though it is true that the English would remain masters all along the Mississippi, and north of the Ohio, because it could not be denied to them that this region had been a dependency of Canada and so recognized by France."

Rayneval then read to Aranda the memorandum on which he was working, illustrating the whole territorial question in those regions on the basis of whether England had considered them to be her own, or as independent nations, or as neutral. Aranda asked for a copy. Rayneval gave him one.

"From the discourses which have intervened," Aranda noted in his diary, "I deduce that Jay has shown himself little content with the Court of Madrid, that nevertheless he is beginning to be undeceived about his claim to the River Mississippi, that he doesn't have the rights, nor the support, that he had figured on." [41]

Rayneval arranged an interview with Jay on the 5th of September

39. On Rayneval's holograph draft of the Historical Memorandum this is part of a marginal emendation, laying down a proper boundary, which suggests that he inserted the boundary into his first draft only after discussion with Aranda.

40. On Mitchell's Map the Cumberland appears much farther away from the Mississippi than it actually is.

41. To Floridablanca, Aranda reported: "The memorandum on which Mr. de Rayneval is working doesn't leave any doubt that England, as the possessor of Canada, is mistress of the St. Lawrence River as far as the Ohio, so recognized by France even when she possessed Louisiana; thus we could not and should not treat with the Colonies over that part." No. 2290, Sept. 1, 1782. A.H.N., Estado, legajo 6609.

in which he labored at length to effect a compromise. He urged Jay to continue his conversations with Aranda. I have discovered no detailed record of this interview, which was the last Jay had with either French or Spanish spokesmen on the subject of western boundaries—he was henceforth to confine his talk to England. Jay notes that the interview is sufficiently recorded in Rayneval's letter of September 6, containing the Compromise Memorandum. We may assume that this written memorandum was received on either the 6th or 7th. On the 9th Jay learned that Rayneval had actually gone to England. On the 10th he heard that, on the eve of Rayneval's departure, Aranda had had a three-hour conference with him at Versailles.[42] The same day, the 10th, the British put into Jay's hand a copy of Marbois's intercepted dispatch from Philadelphia arguing down the American fishery claims. Jay immediately had a long talk with Vaughan on the 11th of September. Vaughan straightway left for England to get Oswald's commission changed, to enable the British envoy to treat with plenipotentiaries of the United States—something that Aranda could not yet do.

The commission was changed as Oswald himself had already importuned his superiors to change it. The turning point of the negotiations was passed. Vaughan returned to Paris on the 27th with Oswald's new commission. From then on negotiations proceeded steadily to the signature on November 30th of the Anglo-American preliminary and conditional articles of peace, which recognized the boundaries desired by the Continental Congress. Rather than let Spain clinch her claim to the Mississippi country, Jay—and Franklin, so it proved—preferred to let go Canada in turn for British acknowledgment of the American boundaries of 31° North Latitude on the south, the Mississippi on the west, and the familiar river and lakes line on the north. On this territorial basis the preliminary articles were finally signed.

It has seemed necessary to detail at length these boundary discussions because they show the exact origin of the Historical Memorandum of Rayneval.[43] There are extant at least three copies of the Rayneval Historical Memorandum. One is his own holograph copy, with marginal addenda also in his own hand. This copy is in the files États

42. This long conference did not apparently touch the question of the United States. It was occasioned by Aranda's delivery to Vergennes of a memorandum embodying Spain's observations on the heads of propositions of peace attributed by de Grasse to Shelburne. It was to verify these propositions that Rayneval was going to England. See Aranda to Floridablanca, no. 2294 (draft) of Sept. 8, 1782. A.H.N., Estado, legajo 4062.

43. As noted below this had been carelessly attributed in archival endorsements to July 1782.

Unis of the series Correspondance Politique in the Archives of the
French Foreign Office. Another copy, in a clerk's hand, is in the same
archives, same series, in the Angleterre files. A third copy, sent to Spain
on September 8th by Aranda, is in the papers of the Spanish embassy
at Paris, now preserved in Archivo Histórico Nacional, Estado Series,
(Legajo 6609) in Madrid.[44] I reproduce below in parallel columns, with
annotations, these three copies. I do this because only careful comparison of internal (for example, the corrections copied from one copy to
another, left to right, as explained in my footnotes) and external evidence demonstrates that: the holograph memorandum, obviously the
first, was composed by Rayneval sometime between August 23 and 30,
and modified (as to boundaries) in the conference between him and
Aranda on the 30th. The Angleterre copy was made sometime after
August 30, and before September 7 when Rayneval left for England,
presumably soon after August 30. The Aranda copy was made from the
Angleterre copy sometime before September 8, when Aranda sent it
to Spain, presumably before Rayneval left for England on the 7th;
perhaps Aranda secured it in the long interview he had with Rayneval
on the eve of the latter's departure; perhaps even it was given to Aranda
on the 30th of August, the day he asked for it.

44. B. F. Stevens in a note on his transcript of the États Unis copy (transcript now
in the Library of Congress) states that there is a duplicate copy of what I call the
Aranda copy, in the Archivo de Simancas. Presumably this is the copy sent by Aranda
to Spain, as distinct from the one kept in his own files of embassy papers (later removed to Spain and now in the Archivo Histórico Nacional) which copy I here
reproduce.

Memoire.

Concernant les terreins situés à l'Est du Mississippi, depuis la floride occidentale j'usqu'aux frontières du Canada.[a]

Il s'est établi une négociation entre la Cour de Madrid et les Etats-unis de l'Amérique Sept.te relativement aux terreins qui font l'objet de ce mémoire: La Cour de Madrid les reclame soit à titre de conquête, soit comme des dépendances de la Louisiane; les Etats-unis, de leur côté,

a. From Arch. Aff. Etrang., Correspondance Politique, États Unis, vol. 22, 309–17. Apparently in handwriting of Rayneval. I have tried to preserve the irregular punctuations and accents.

This document is endorsed, "1782. On a lieu de croire que ce mémoire a été rédigé dans le courant du mois de J.ᵗ 1782." This endorsement is in another hand, presumably that of an archivist. As explained in the narrative of this article, the *mémoire* was actually written during the latter part of August and first of September, 1782.

MÉMOIRE

concernant les Terreins situés à l'Est du Mississipi, depuis la Floride Occidentale jusqu'aux frontières du Canada.[a]

Il s'est établi une négociation entre la Cour de Madrid et les Etats-unis de l'Amérique Septentionale relativement aux terreins qui font l'objet de ce Mémoire: La Cour de Madrid les reclame, soit à titre de conquête, soit comme des dépendances de la Louisiane; les Etats-Unis de leur côté

a. Arch. Aff. Etrang., Correspondance Politique, Angleterre, vol. 537, pp. 389–99, 385–88. In a French clerk's handwriting.

MÉMOIRE concernant les Terreins

situés à l'Est du Mississipi, depuis la Floride Occidentale jusqu'aux frontières du Canada.[a]

Il s'est établi une négociation entre la Cour de Madrid et les Etats-unis de l'Amérique Septentionale relativement aux terreins qui font l'objet de ce Mémoire: La Cour de Madrid les reclame, soit à titre de conquête, soit comme des dépendances de la Louisiane; les Etats-Unis de leur côté

a. Enclosed in Aranda's no. 2295, to Floridablanca, Paris, Sept. 7, 1782. A.H.N., Estado, legajo 6609. In a Spanish clerk's handwriting.

This document is endorsed in Spanish: "Received at Versailles, September 7, 1782, and drawn up by Mr. Rayneval, under-secretary [*primer oficial*] of State [*de Estado*]."

les reclament comme appartenants aux Colonies respectives dans la parallèle desquelles ils sont situés.

Pour pouvoir prononcer avec connoisance de cause sur des prétentions aussi opposées, il est nécessaire de fixer l'état des lieux tel qu'il étoit avant le traité de Paris de 1763; ce n'est que d'après cet état que l'on pourra déterminer et concilier les droits respectifs des Espagnols et les [sic] Etats-unis.

Il est notoire que les établissements connus sous le nom de Louisiane, formés vers le commencement de ce siècle ne devinrent considérables que lors du fameux système de Laws: on sait que cet administrateur des finances, pour donner de la valeur au papier qu'il avoit crée et qui perdoit déja 50% imagina la compagnie dite

les reclament comme appartenants aux Colonies respectives dans la parallèle desquelles ils sont situés.

Pour pouvoir prononcer avec connoisance de cause sur des prétentions aussi opposées, il est nécessaire de fixer l'état des lieux tel qu'il étoit avant le Traité de Paris de 1763; ce n'est que d'après cet état que l'on pourra déterminer et concilier les droits respectifs des Espagnols et des Etats-unis.

Il est notoire que les établissements connus sous le nom de Louisiane, formés vers le commencement de ce siècle ne devinrent considérables que lors du fameux système de Laws: on sait que cet administrateur des finances, pour donner de la valeur au papier qu'il avoit crée et qui perdoit déja 50% imagina la Compagnie dite

les reclament comme appartenants aux Colonies respectives dans la parallèle desquelles ils sont situés.

Pour pouvoir prononcer avec connoisance de cause sur des prétentions aussi opposées, il est nécessaire de fixer l'état des lieux tel qu'il étoit avant le Traité de Paris de 1763; ce n'est que d'après cet état que l'on pourra déterminer et concilier les droits respectifs des Espagnols et des Etats-unis.

Il est notoire que les établissements connus sous le nom de Louisiane, formés vers le commencement de ce siècle ne devinrent considérables que lors du fameux système de Laws: on sait que cet administrateur des finances, pour donner de la valeur au papier qu'il avoit crée et qui perdoit déja 50%, imagina la Compie dite

Memoire.

du Mississipi. On ne suivra
pas cette compagnie dans ses
opérations on se contentera
d'observer qu'elle n'eût qu'une
existence éphemère: mais que
les Colonies qu'elle avoit
vivifiées furent maintenües;—
qu'elles s'étendirent vers l'Est
en conquérant entr'autres
le pays des Natchez, et qu'elles
se portèrent au nord jusqu'au pays
des Illinois. La Colonie avoit
pour bornes à l'Est un assez
grand nombre de peuplades
sauvages, tels que les Alibamous,
les Creeks, etc. une partie de
ces sauvages étoient amis
et protégés de la france;
d'autres étoient attachés à
la grande Bretagne. La france
étoit maitresse du cours de
l'Ohio, lequel servoit pour
la communication entre la
Louisiane et le Canada.

La

MÉMOIRE

du Mississipi. On ne suivra
pas cette compagnie dans ses
opérations; on se contentera
d'observer qu'elle n'eût qu'une
existence éphemère: mais que
les Colonies qu'elle avoit
vivifiées, furent maintenües;—
qu'elles s'étendirent vers l'Est
en conquérant entr'autres
le Pays des Natchez, et qu'elles
se portèrent au nord jusqu'au Pays
des Illinois. La Colonie avoit
pour bornes à l'Est un assez
grand nombre de peuplades
sauvages, tels que les Alibamous,
les Creeks, etc. une partie de
ces sauvages étoient amis
et protégés de la France;
d'autres étoient attachés à
la grande-Bretagne. La France
étoit maitresse du cours de
l'Ohio, lequel servoit pour la
communication entre la
Louisiane et le Canada.

Les évenements de [a] la

a. The words "Les évenements de" are inserted in this copy in a handwriting that resembles Rayneval's.

MÉMOIRE concernant les Terreins

du Mississipi. On ne suivra
pas cette Comp.ie dans ses
opérations; on se contentera
d'observer, qu'elle n'eût qu'une
existence éphemère: mais que
les Colonies qu'Elle avoit
vivifiées, furent maintenues,
qu'elles s'étendirent vers l'Est
en conquérant entr'autres
le Pais de Natchez, et qu'elles
se portèrent au nord jusqu'au Pays
des Illinois. La Colonie avoit
pour borne à l'Est un assez
grand nombre de peuplades
sauvages, tels que les Alibamous,
les Creeks, etc. une partie de
ces sauvages étoient amis
et protégés de la France;
d'autres étoient attachés à
la grande-Bretagne. La France
étoit maitresse du cours de
l'Ohio, lequel servoit pour
la communication entre la
Louisiane et le Canada.

Les évenements de la

guerre de 1756 ayant forcé
la france de faire des
sacrifices, Elle offrit à Langre.
l'anbandon de tout
le canada. Cette offre engagea
une discution sur les limites
de cette contrée. Le Ministère
de Versailles soutint que tout
ce qui n'étoit pas Canada
étoit Louisiane, et tout ce
qui n'étoit pas Louisiane
étoit Canada; cela vouloit
dire qu'il nexistoit aucune
possession intermédiaire
entre ces deux Colonies.
il s'agissoit donc de
déterminer ce qui formoit
la Louisiane, que la France
conservoit, et ce qu'appartenoit
au Canada, qu'elle étoit
disposé disposée à abandonner.
Le ministère de france
proposa de partir de la
rivière perdido située
entre la Mobile et Pensacola;
de remonter jusqu'au fort
Toulouse placé dans le

guerre de 1756 aiant forcé
la France de faire des
sacrifices, Elle offrit à
l'Angre. l'abandon de tout
le Canada. Cette offre engagea
une discution sur les limites
de cette Contrée. Le Ministère
de Versailles soutint que tout
ce qui n'étoit pas Canada
étoit Louisiane, et que tout ce
qui n'étoit pas Louisiane
étoit Canada; cela vouloit
dire qu'il n'existoit aucune
possession intermédiaire
entre ces deux Colonies.
Il s'agissoit donc de
déterminer ce qui formoit
la Louisiane, que la France
conservoit, et ce qui appartenoit
au Canada, qu'elle étoit
disposée à abandonner.
Le Ministère de France
proposa de partir de la
Rivière Perdido située
entre la mobile et Pensacola,
de remonter jusqu'au Fort
Toulouse placé dans le

guerre de 1756 aiant forcé
la France de faire des
sacrifices, Elle offrit à
l'Angleterre l'abandon de tout
le Canada. Cette offre engagea
une discution sur les limites
de cette Contrée. Le Ministère
de Versailles soutint que tout
ce qui n'étoit pas Canada
étoit Louisiane, et que tout ce
qui n'étoit pas Louisiane
étoit Canada: cela vouloit
dire qu'il n'existoit aucune
possession intermédiaire
entre ces deux Colonies.
Il s'agissoit donc de
déterminer ce qui formoit
la Louisiane, que la France
conservoit, et ce qui apartenoit
au Canada, qu'elle étoit
disposée à abandonner.
Le Ministère de France
proposa de partir de la
Rivière de Perdido située
entre la mobile et Pensacola;
de remonter jusqu'au fort
Toulouse placé dans le

Memoire.

pays des Alibamous; de
prendra la pointe
occidentale du Lac Erié,
d'aboutir de là à la
pointe orientale du lac Huron;
de remonter vers le nord
et se perdre dans les
terres vers la Baye de
Hudson. En jettant les
yeux sur la carte on
remarquera que par cette
delimitation la france
conservoit presque tout
l'Ohio, ainsi que les lacs
à l'exception de ceux
d'Erié et d'Ontario.

    La Cour de Londres
fut eloignée d'adopter
la ligne qui vient d'etre
indiquée; Elle prétendit
que selon un mémoire
de 1755, signé par
M. de Mirepoix, un écrit
signé de M. de Silhouette,
et la carte remise par
M. de Vaudreuil lors de
la redition du Canada,

MÉMOIRE

Pays des Alibamous, de
prendre la pointe
Occidentale du Lac Erié;
d'aboutir de là à la
pointe Orientale du Lac Huron;
de remonter vers le Nord
et se perdre dans les
terres vers la Baye de
Hudson. En jettant les
yeux sur la carte, on
remarquera que par cette
délimitation la France
conservoit présque tout
l'Ohio, ainsi que les Lacs,
à l'exception de celle
d'Erié et d'Ontario.

    La Cour de Londres
fût bien éloingée d'adopter
la ligne qui vient d'être
indiquée; Elle prétendit
que selon un Mémoire
de 1755 signé par
M. de Mirepoix, un écrit
signé de M. de Silhoüette,
et la carte remise par
M. de Vaudreuil lors de
la remise du Canada

MÉMOIRE concernant les Terreins

Pais des Alibamous; de
prendre la pointe
Occidentale du Lac Erié;—
d'aboutir de là à la
pointe Orientale du Lac Huron,
de remonter vers le Nord
et se perdre dans les
Terres vers la Baye de
Hudson. En jettant les
yeux sur la carte, on
remarquera que par cette
délimitation la France
conservoit présque tout
l'Ohio, ainsi que les lacs,
à l'exception de celui
d'Erié et d'Ontario.

    La Cour de Londres
fût bien éloignée d'adopter
la ligne qui vient d'être
indiquée; Elle prétendit
que selon un Mémoire
de 1755 signé par
M. de Mirepoix, un écrit
signé de M. de Silhouette
et la carte remise par
M. de Vaudreuil lors de
la memise du Canada,

cette Colonie comprenoit
les lacs ontario, Erié,
Huron, Michigan et Supérieur
et même les outrepassoit,
et que les françois avoient
toujours regardé l'Ohio comme
une dépendance du Canada;
que les territoires des deux
côtés de cette rivière ont
été vendus à l'Angre.
par les sauvages des six
nations; que les mêmes
nations lui ont vendu le
pays de Cheraquis en
1729; que les Chicachas
étoient sujets de la Grande-
Bretagne; qu'il y avoit
des établissements anglois
dans leur pays; que
les anglois avoient des
factories et des des [sic]
établissements chez les
Creeks, à l'exception du
fort Toulouse usurpé
par les françois sur
l'angre. qui l'avoit
fait construire; que

cette Colonie comprenoit
les Lacs Ontario, Erié,
Huron, Michigan et Supérieur
et même les outrepassoit,
et que les François avoient
toujours régardé l'Ohio comme
une dépendance du Canada;
que les Territoires des deux
côtés de cette revière ont
été vendus à l'Angleterre
par les sauvages des six
nations; que les mêmes
nations lui ont vendu le
Pais des Cheraquis en
1729, que les Chicachas
étoient sujets de la grande-
Bretange; qu'il y avoit
des établissements Anglois
dans leur Pays; que
les Anglois avoient des
factories et des
établissements chez les
Creeks, à l'éxception du
Fort Toulouse ursurpé
par les François sur
l'Angre. qui l'avoit
fait construire; que

cette Colonie comprenoit
les Lacs Ontario, Erié,
Huron, Michigan et Supérieur
et même les outrepassoit,
et que les François avoient
toujours regardé l'Ohio comme
une dépendence du Canada;
que les Territoires des deux
côtés de cette Rivierè ont
été vendus à l'Angre.
par les sauvages des six
nations; que les mêmes
nations lui ont vendu le
Pais des Cheraquis en
1729; que les Chicachas
étoient sujets de la grande-
Bretagne; qu'il y avoit
des établissements Anglois
dans leur Pays; que
les Anglois avoient des
factories et des
établissements chez les
Creeks, à l'exception du
Fort Toulouse usurpé
par les François sur
l'Angleterre qui l'avoit
fait construire; que

Memoire.

les 6 nations ont
subjugué les Miamis et
les Illinois, et qu'elles
ont fait vente de tous
ces pays aux anglois.
 Pour ce qui est des limites
de la Louisiane (c'est toujours
la Cour de Londres qui parle).
elles ne sauroient être
admises selon la ligne
tracée par la france,
parcequ'elles comprendroient
du côté des Carolines
des régions très-étendües
et des nations nombreuses
qui ont toujours été
censées être sous la
protection du Roi d'angre;
protection à laquelle ce
Pe. n'étoit pas dans l'intention
de renoncer, et que
S. Mte. uniquement pour
le bien de la paix,
consentoit à laisser
sous la protection de
la grande Bretagne les
peuples intermédiares

MÉMOIRE

les six nations ont
subjugué les Miamis, et
les Illinois, et qu'elles
ont fait vente de tous
ces Pais aux Anglois.
 Pour ce qui est des limites
de la Louisiane (c'est toujours
la Cour de Londres qui parle).
elles ne sauroient être
admises selon la ligne
tracée par la France,
parcequ'elles comprendroient
du côté des Carolines
des régions très-étendües
et des nations nombreuses
qui ont toujours été
censées être sous la
protection du Roi d'Angre;
protection à laquelle ce
Prince n'étoit pas dans l'intention
de renoncer, et que
Sa Mte. uniquement pour
le bien de la paix
consentoit à laisser
sous la protection de
la grande-Bretagne les
peuples intermédiares

MÉMOIRE concernant les Terreins

les six nations ont
subjugué les Miamis, et
les Illinois, et qu'elles
ont fait vente de tous
ces Pais aux Anglois,
 Pour ce qui est des limites
de la Louisiane (c'est toujours
la Cour de Londres qui parle)
elles ne sauroient être
admis selon la ligne
tracée par la France,
parcequ'elles comprendroient
du côté des Carolines
des régions très-étendues
et des nations nombreuses
qui ont toujours été
censées être sous la
protection du Roi d'Angleterre,
protection à laquelle ce
Prince n'étoit pas dans l'intention
de renoncer, et que
sa Majesté uniquement pour
le bien de la paix,
consentoit à laisser
sous la protection de
la grande-Bretagne les
peuples intermédiares

dont il s'agit et
particulièrement les
Cherokées, les Creeks, les
Chicavas [a] [sic], les Cháctaws, et
d'autres situés entres les
*établissements britanniques
et le Mississippi.*
  Tous les détails
ci-dessus ont été consignés
ministeriellement lors de
la négotiation entamée
en 1761. On sait que,
quoique 'elle ait été
interrompue, le système
de la Cour de Londres
fût consacré par le traité
de Paris, lequel donne [a]
à la Louisiane pour limite
le Cours du Mississippi
depuis son embouchure
jusqu'à sa source.
  En résumant les détails

a. Both the Aranda copy and the Angleterre copy take over the eccentric spelling of this word.

dont il s'agit, et
particulièrement les
Cherokées, les Creeks, les
Chicavas, les Chactaws, et
d'autres, situés *entres les
établissements Britanniques
et le Mississippi.*
  Tous les détails
ci-dessus ont été consignés
ministériellement lors de
la négotiation entamée
en 1761. On sait que
quoiqu'elle ait été
interrompue, le système
de la Cour de Londres
fût consacré par le Traité
de Paris, lequel donna [a]
à la Louisiane pour limite
le cours du Mississippi
depuis son embouchure
jusqu'à sa source.
  En resumant les détails

a. At first written *donne*, as in **Rayne**val's holograph, but then corrected to *donna (sic)* by the copyist.

dont il s'agit, et
particulièrement les
Cherokées, les Creeks, les
Chicavas, les Choctaws et
d'autres situés *entre les
établissements Britanniques
et le Mississippi.*
  Tout les détails
ci-dessus ont été consignés
ministériellement lors de
la négotiation entamée
en 1761. On sait que
quoiqu'elle ait été
interrompue, le système
de la Cour de Londres
fût consacré par le Traité
de Paris, lequel donna [a]
à la Louisiane pour limite
le cours du Mississippi
depuis son embouchure
jusqu'à sa source.
  En resumant les détails

a. In Rayneval's holograph the verb is *donne*. This is corrected in the past absolute tense in the Angleterre copy. The Aranda copy follows this correction, thus suggesting that it was made from the Angleterre copy.

Mémoire.

dans lesquels on vient
d'entrer il paroit
évident: primo, que la
france possédoit autrefois
des terreins quelconques
à l'Est du Mississipi
comme dépendants de
la Louisiane; 2ᵈᵒ que

la Cours de Londres,
tout en contestant ces
terreins, avoïe, qu'une
partie étoit independante,
que l'autre étoit seulement
sous sa protection; et
que tous étoient situés
entre le Mississippi et
les etablissements
britanniques.

Il resulte de ces
deux propositions, qu'en
aucum tems les pays dont
il s'agit n'ont été
considérés comme faisant

MÉMOIRE

dans les quels on vient
d'entrer, il paroit
évident: primo, que la
france possédoit autrefois
des Terreins quelconques
à l'Est du Mississipi
comme dépendants de
la Louisiane.
    2ᵈᵒ. que la
Cour de Londres,
tout en contestant ces
terreins, avoüe, qu'une
partie étoit indépendante,
que l'autre étoit seulement
sous sa protection; et
que tous étoient situés
entre le Mississippi et
les établissements
Britanniques.[a]

Il resulte de ces
deux propositions, qu'en
aucun tems les Pais dont
il s'agit n'ont été
considérés comme faisant

a. The italics are here introduced. They
do not occur in the Rayneval holograph.

MÉMOIRE concernant les Terreins

dans les quels on vient
d'entrer, il paroit
évident: 1°., que la
France possédoit autrefois
des Terreins quelconques
à l'Est du Mississipi
comme dépendants de
la Louisiane; 2°. que

la Cour de Londres,
tout en contestant ces
Terreins, avoue, qu'une
partie étoit indépendante,
que l'autre étoit seulement
sous sa protection; et
que tous étoient situés
entre le Mississippi et
les etablissements
Britanniques.[a]

Il résulte de ces
deux propositions, qu'en
aucun tems les Pais dont
il s'agit n'ont été
considérés comme faisant

a. The italics here do not occur in the
Rayneval holograph. They correspond with
those in the Angleterre copy.

partie des ci-devant
Colonies Angloises, et que
ces mêmes Colonies,
devenues indépendantes,
ne peuvent déduire
aucun droit de propriété
de celui de la Cour de
Londres. Si les Américains
prétendent trouver ce
droit dans leurs chartres,
il faut (en admettant le
principe que la Cour de
Londres a pû disposer
des peuplades dont il
est question), il faut
que ces chartres soient
bien claires et bien
précises, et, surtout,
qu'elles soient postérieures
au Traité de Paris. Mais
dans le cas même où
ces chartres seroient de
la plus grande précision
sur l'objet dont il s'agit,
elles seroient sans force
et sans valeur faute d'être
etaiées par une possession

partie des ci-devant
Colonies Angloises, et que
ces mêmes Colonies,
devenues indépendantes,
ne peuvent déduire
aucun droit de propriété
de celui de la Cour de
Londres. Si les Américains
prétendent trouver ce
droit dans leurs chartres,
il faut (en admettant le
principe que la Cour de
Londres a pû disposer
des peuplades dont il
est question), il faut
que ces chartres soient
bien claires et bien
précises, et, surtout,
qu'elles soient postérieures
au Traité de Paris. Mais
dans le cas même où
ces chartres seroient de
la plus grande précision
sur l'objet dont il s'agit,
elles seroient sans force
et sans valeur faute d'être
etaiées par une possession

partie des ci-devant
Colonies angloises, et que
ces mêmes Colonies,
devenues indépendantes,
ne peuvent déduire
aucun droit de propriété
de celui de la Cour de
Londres. Si les Américains
prétendent trouver ce
droit dans leurs chartres,
il faut (en admettant le
principe que la Cour de
Londres a pû disposer
des peuplades dont il
est question), il faut
que ces chartres soient
bien claires et bien
précises, et, surtout,
qu'elles soient postérieures
au traité de Paris. Mais
dans le cas-même où
ces chartres seroient de
la plus grande précision
sur l'objet dont il s'agit,
elles seroient sans force
et sans valeur faute d'être
étayées par une possession

Memoire.

paisible: cette vérité peut se démontrer. Les pays occupés par les sauvages nommés ci-dessus n'ont jamais été abandonnés, ils ne pouvoient donc être, comme on dit, primo-occupanti. La Cour de Londres a elle même rendu hommage à cette verité, en avançant qu'elle en a acheté une partie et que le surplus étoit sous sa protection, et que le tout étoit situé entre ses établissements et le Mississipi il resulte de cette dernière assertion, que le prétendu droit de propriété et de protection de l'Anglre. n'a jamais été incorporé aux Colonies;—ainsi ces Colonies navoient point ce double droit lorsqu'elles ont secoué le jong de leur mère-patrie.

MÉMOIRE

paisible. Cette vérité peut se démontrer. Les Païs occupés par les Sauvages nommés ci-dessus n'ont jamais été abandonnés, ils ne pouvoient donc être, comme on dit, primo occupanti. La Cour de Londres a Elle-même rendu homage à cette vérité, en avançant qu'Elle en a acheté une partie, et que le surplus étoit sous sa protection, et que le tout étoit situé entres ses établissements et le Mississipi.   Il resulte de cette dernière assertion, que le prétendu droit de propriété et de protection de l'Angleterre n'a jamais été incorporé aux Colonies; ainsi ces Colonies n'avoient point ce double droit lorsqu'Elles ont secoué le jong de leur Mère-Patrie.

MÉMOIRE concernant les Terreins

paisible. Cette vérité peut se démontrer. Les Païs occupés par les sauvages nommés ci-dessus n'ont jamais été abandonnes, il ne pouvoient donc être, comme on dit, primo occupanti. La Cour de Londres a Elle-même rendu homage à cette vérité, en avançant qu'Elle en a acheté une partie, et que le surplus étoit sous sa protection, et que le tout étoit situé entre ses établissements et le Mississipi. Il resulte de cette dernière assertion, que le prétendu droit de propriété et de protection de l'Angre. n'a jamais été incorporé aux Colonies; ainsi ces Colonies n'avoient point ce double droit lorsqu'Elles ont secoué le jong de leur Mère-Patrie.

L'ont elles acquis
depuis? C'est une question
de fait à laquelle on
ne risque rien de
répondre négativement:
on ose croire que les
américains ne citeront
pas comme une preuve
de conquête et de propriété
l'excursion ephemère
qu'un Colonel Clark a doit
avoir faite en 1779 [sic]
jusqu'au dela du Mississippi:
ce n'est point ainsi que

a. This is the only mention I have ever seen of the exploits of George Rogers Clark in the diplomatic correspondence relating to the negotiation of the peace. It does not seem to me enough to attribute to Clark any influence on the peace terms, far from supporting the exaggerated claims that his "conquest" enabled the United States to win the Northwest in the peace negotiations. As a matter of fact Clark had withdrawn to the line of the Ohio before 1782 and the British exerted, from their Lake posts, more effective influence over this "no man's land" than did the United States. See my *Diplomacy of the American Revolution*, p. 219. There is of course a voluminous secondary literature on the subject.

L'ont-elles acquis
depuis? C'est une question
de fait à laquelle on
ne risque rien de
répondre négativement:
on ose croire que les
Américains ne présenteront
pas comme une preuve
de conquête et de propriété
l'excursion éphémère
qu'un Colonel Clark a doit
avoir faite en 1779 [sic]
jusqu'au delà du Mississippi:
ce n'est point ainsi que

a. See footnote at this place in the Aranda copy.

L'ont elles acquis
depuis? C'est une question
de fait à laquelle on
ne risque rien de
répondre négativement:
on ose croire que les
Américains ne présenteront
pas comme une preuve
de conquête et de propriété
l'excursion éphémère
qu'un Colonel Clark doit
avoir faite en 1779
jusqu'au delà du Mississippi:
ce n'est point ainsi que

Memoire.

l'on acquiert de nation
à nation.[a]

a. It is at this point that the long addendum marked "a." on the Angleterre copy and on the Aranda copy was inserted. It does not occur in the Rayneval holograph.

MÉMOIRE

l'on acquiert de Nation
à Nation. (a) [a]

    Les Américains citent
des chartres; des faits
propres à l'administration
Britannique et une
proclamation du Roi
d'Angre. de 1763,
et surtout la possession,
pour prouver que leurs
domaines s'étendent
à l'Oüest jusqu'au
Mississipi.

    Ou ne peut rien
dire du contenu des
chartres faute de les
connôitre; il en est
de même des faits
imputés à l'administration
Britannique: mais on
peut assûrer que la
proclamation invoquée
ne favorise point la

a. The long addendum "a," not to be found in the Rayneval holograph, was inserted here, as in the Aranda copy. I have indicated it by indenting it.

MÉMOIRE concernant les Terreins

l'on acquiert de Nation
à Nation. (a) [a]

    Les Américains citent
des chartres; des faits
propres à l'administration
Britannique et une
proclamation du Roi
d'Angleterre de 1763,
et surtout la possession
pour prouver que leurs
domaines s'étendent
à l'Ouest jusqu'au
Mississipi.

    On ne peut rien
dire du contenu des
chartres faute de les
connôitre; il en est
de même des faits
imputés à l'administration
Britannique: mais on
peut assûrer que la
proclamation invoquée
ne favorise point la

a. It is at this point that the extensive addendum was inserted in this copy, after the Angleterre copy. It does not occur in the Rayneval holograph. I have indicated the addendum by indentation.

prétention Américaine.

Cette pièce est du mois d'Octobre 1763. Elle a pour objet principal de distribüer en 4 gouvernments les conquêtes qui ont été assûrées à la Couronne Britannique par le Traité de Paris dans l'Amérique Septentrionale. Cet acte borne les limites de la Floride Occidentale au 31 degré de latitude; il ne renferme aucune disposition soit directe, soit indirecte, concernant les limites des anciennes Colonies Angloises, et elle renferme, relativement aux Indiens le passage suivant:

"Et comme il est
"juste et raisonable
"et essentiel à l'intérêt

prétention Américaine.

Cette pièce est du mois d'Octobre 1763. Elle a pour objet principal de distribüer en 4 gouvernments les conquêtes qui ont été assûrées à la Couronne Britannique par le Traité de Paris dans l'Amérique Septentrionale. Cet acte borne les limites de la Floride Occidentale au 31 degré de latitude; il ne renferme aucune disposition soit directe, soit indirecte, concernant les limites des anciennes Colonies Angloises, et elle renferme, relativement aux Indiens le passage suivant:

"Et comme il est
"juste et raisonable
"et essentiel à l'intérêt

Mémoire.

"de nos Colonies que
"les differentes nations
"ou Tribus d'Indiens
"avec lesquelles nous
"sommes liés et qui
"vivent sous notre
"protection, ne soient
"point molestées et
"détruites dans les
"parties de notre
"Domination qui n'ont
"point été cédées ou
"achetées a notre avantage,
"mais qui leur ont été
"reservées pour leurs
"chasses. Nous avons donc
"de l'avis de notre
"conseil privé, déclaré
"que notre volonté
"royale et plaisir,
"est qu'aucune
"Gouverneur ou
"Commandant-en-chef
"dans nos Colonies
"de Quebec, Est, et
"Ouest Floride ne
"s'arroge, sous quelque

MÉMOIRE

"de nos Colonies que
"les differentes nations
"ou tribus d'Indiens
"avec lesquelles nous
"sommes liés et qui
"vivent sous notre
"protection, ne soient
"point molestées et
"détruites dans les
"parties de notre
"Domination que n'ont
"point été cedées ou
"achetées à notre avantage,
"mais qui leur ont été
"reservées, pour leurs
"chasses. Nous avons donc,
"de l'avis de notre
"Conseil privé, déclaré
"que notre volonté
"royale et plaisir,
"est qu'aucun
"Gouverneur ou
"Commandant-en-chef
"dans nos Colonies
"de Quebec Est et
"Ouest Floride ne
"s'arroge, sous quelque

"prétexte que ce soit,
"d'accorder aucune
"concession ou aucune
"patente pour les
"Terres situées au delà
"de leur Gouvernment,
"et aussi qu'aucun
"Gouverneur ou
"Commandant-en-chef
"dans aucune de nos
"Colonies ou plantations
"en Amérique n'accorde
"aucune concession ou
"passe aucune patente
"pour aucune des
"Terres situées au delà
"des sources des Rivières
"qui tombent dans
"l'Ocean atlantique
"à l'Est et au nord
"Ouest; et que toutes
"les Terres qui ne
"nous ont pas été
"cédées ou achetées
"par nous, soient
"réservées aux susdte.
"Indiens ou à quelqu'uns

"pretexte que ce soit,
"d'accorder aucune
"concession ou aucune
"patente pour les
"terres situées au delà
"de leur Gouvernment,
"et aussi qu'aucun
"Gouverneur ou
"Commandant-en-chef
"dans aucune de nos
"Colonies ou plantations
"en Amérique n'accorde
"aucune concession ou
"passe aucune patente
"pour aucune des
"Terres situées au delà
"des sources des rivieres
"qui tombent dans
"l'ocean atlantique
"à l'Est et au nord
"Ouest; et que toutes
"les terres qui ne
"nous ont pas été
"cédées ou achetées
"par nous, soit
"reservées aux susdtes
"Indiens ou à quelqu'uns

Memoire.

MÉMOIRE

"*d'Eux.*
"Nous déclarons
"de plus qu'il est
"de notre volonté
"royale et de notre
"plaisir pour le
"present, ainsi qu'il
"a été dit ci-dessus,
"de reserver sous
"notre souveraineté,
"protection et Domination
"pour l'usage des dites
"Indiens toutes les terres
"ou Territoires qui ne
"sont pas renfermées
"dans les limites de
"nos dits trois nouveaux
"Gouvernments ou dans
"les limites du Territoire
"accordé à la Compagnie
"de la Baye d'Hudson,
"de même que toutes
"les Terres ou Territoires
"placées à l'Ouest
"des sources des rivières
"qui tombent dans la
"mer, à l'Est ou au

MÉMOIRE concernant les Terreins

"*d'Eux.*
"Nous déclarons
"de plus qu'il est
"de notre volonté
"royale et de notre
"plaisir pour le
"present, ainsi qu'il
"a été dit ci-dessus,
"de reserver sous
"notre souveraineté,
"protection et Domination
"pour l'usage des dites
"Indiens toutes les terres
"ou Territoires qui ne
"sont pas renfermées
"dans les limites de
"nos dits trois nouveaux
"Gouvernements ou dans
"les limites du Territoire
"accordé à la Compagnie
"de la Baye d'Hudson,
"de même que toutes
"les Terres ou Territoires
"placées à l'Ouest
"des sources des Rivières
"qui tombent dans la
"mer, à l'Est ou au

"Nord Ouest, comme
"il est dit ci-dessus.
Les dispositions
qui viennent d'etre
raporteés, prouvent
invinciblement que les
sauvages situées à
l'Ouest des Etats-unis
n'y étoient pas
incorporés avant le
Traité de Paris et
que l'intention du Roi
d'Angre. qui supose
en être devenu
propriétaire par ce
Traité, n'étoit en
aucune manière de
faire cette incorporation:
on peut même dire
que ce Prince a
déterminé d'une
manière assez précise,
quoiqu'indirecte, les
limites des Colonies
en leur défendant
d'aquerir au delà
des sources des

"nord Ouest, comme
"il est dit ci-dessus.
Les dispositions
qui viennent d'être
raporteés, prouvent
invinciblement que les
sauvages situées à
l'Ouest des Etats-unis
n'y étoient pas
incorporés avant le
Traité de Paris et
que l'intention du Roi
d'Angre. qui supose
en être devenu
propriétaire par ce
Traité, n'étoit en
aucune manière de
faire cette incorporation:
on peut même dire
que ce Prince a
déterminé d'une
manière assez précise,
quoiqu'indirecte, les
limites des Colonies
en leur défendant
d'aquerir au delà
des sources des

Memoire.

MÉMOIRE concernant les Terreins

Rivières qui se jettent
dans la Mer atlantique:
En examinant la
carte on voit clairement
que moiennant
cette indication les
frontières des Etats-unis
touchent aux nations
sauvages qui se
trouvent entr'eux et
le Misissipi. Les versants
sont une limite naturelle
et commode; et il
étoit d'autant plus
simple de l'assigner
aux Colonies que leur
établissement a etî
pour objet primitif
le Commerce, et que
toute relation de
Commerce entre
l'atlantique et le
Golfe du Mexique
est impossible par
l'intérieur des Terres,
parcequ'il faudroit
avoir recours à

MÉMOIRE

Rivières qui se jettent
dans la Mer Atlantique:
En examinant la
carte ou voit clairement
que moiennant
cette indication les
frontières des Etats-unis
touchent aux nations
sauvages qui se
trouvent entr'eux et
le Misissipi. Les versants
sont une limite naturelle
et commode; et il
étoit d'autant plus
simple de l'assigner
aux Colonies que leur
établissements a etî
pour objet primitiff
la Commerce et que
toute relation de
Commerce entre
l'Atlantique et le
Golfe du Mexique
est impossible par
l'intérieur des terres,
parcequ'il faudroit
avoir recours à

80

des partages qui
seroient ou
impracticables ou trop
dispendieux; on sait
l'encombrement qui
forment toutes les
marchandises que
fournissent toutes les
contrées de l'Amérique.
Au surplus on ignore
si postérieurement à
la proclamation qui
vient d'être raportée,
la Cour de Londres
a changé le régime
des ses Colonies: il y a
lieu de présumer
que non, et que si les
Américains se sont
étendus, ce ne peut
être que du côté de
l'Ohio: il paroit, en
effet, que ce sont les
Virginiens et les
Marylandois qui
reclament le plus le
maintien des possessions

des partages qui
seroient ou
impraticable ou trop
dispendieux; on sait
l'encombrement que
forment toutes les
marchandises que
fournissent toutes les
contrées de l'Amérique.
Au surplus on ignore
si postérieurement à
la proclamation qui
vient d'être raportée,
la Cour de Londres
a changé le régime
de ses Colonies: il y a
lieu de presumer
que non, et que si les
Américains se sont
étendus, ce ne peut
être que du côté de
l'Ohio: il paroit, en
effet, que ce sont les
Virginiens et les
Marylandois qui
reclament le plus le
maintien des possessions

Memoire.

MÉMOIRE

que les Etats-unis
prétendent avoir à
l'Oüest. Dans ce
dernier cas, il ne
sauroit y avoir de
difficulté avec l'Espagne,
si cette Puissance
adopte la ligne de
démarcation indiquée
dans le present
Mémoire: la discution
ne pourra avoir lieu
qu'entre les Américains
et la Cour de Londres,
parceque cette Cour
soutiendra que les
deux rives de l'Ohio
avec les terreins
circonvoisins lui
appartiennent comme
dépendances du Canada.
Mais cette question
n'a rien de commun
avec ce qui fait
l'objet de ce Mémoire.
Quant à l'Espagne, Elle
n'avoit, en vertu du Traité

MÉMOIRE concernant les Terreins

que les Etats-unis
prétendent avoir à
l'Ouest. Dans ce
dernier cas il ne
sauroit y avoir de
difficulté avec l'Espagne,
si cette Puissance
adopte la ligne de
démarcation indiquée
dans le presente
Mémoire: la discution
ne pourra avoir lieu
qu'entre les Américains
et la Cour de Londres,
parceque cette Cour
soutiendra que les
deux rives de l'Ohio
avec les Terreins
circonvoisins lui
appartiennent comme
dépendances du Canada.
Mais cette question
n'a rien de commun
avec ce qui fait
l'objet de ce Mémoire.
Quant à l'Espagne, Elle
n'avoit, en vertu du Traité

Quant à l'Espagne elle
n'avoit, en vertu du traité

par lequel la france lui a cédé la Louisiane, pas plus de droit que les Américains aux pays dont il est question: elle n'avoit aquis cette contrée que telle qu'elle se trouvoit réduite par le traité de Paris. Mais des que le Roi d'Espagne s'est trouvé en guerre avec l'Angre. il a pû conquérir tout ce qui appartenoit à cette puissance à l'Est du Mississippi: son droit à cet égard étoit égal à celui des Etats-unis. Ainsi S. Mte. Cque. peut opposer aux Américains un droit exclusif non seulement sur la floride occidentale, mais aussi sur les terreins situés plus au nord que ses armes occupent actuellement. Le Roi d'Espagne n'a aucunement à compter de ces conquêtes avec les Etats-unis; la possession incommutable ne peut en

par lequel la France lui a cédé la Louisiane, pas plus de droit que les Américains aux Pais dont il est question: Elle n'avoit acquis cette Contrée que telle qu'elle se trouvoit réduite par le Traité de Paris. Mais des que le Roi d'Espagne s'est trouvé en guerre avec l'Angre. il a pû conquérir tout ce qui appartenoit à cette Puissance a l'Est du Mississippi: son droit à cet égard étoit égal à celui des Etats-unis. Ainsi Sa Mté. Cathque. peut opposer aux Américains un droit exclusif non seulement sur la floride-occidentale mais aussi sur les terreins situés plus au nord que ses armes occupent actuellement. Le Roi d'Espagne n'a aucunement à compter de ces conquêtes avec les Etats-unis; la possession incommutable ne peut

par lequel la France lui a cédé la Louisiane, pas plus de droit que les Américains aux Pais dont il est question: Elle n'avoit acquis cette Contrée que telle qu'elle se trouvoit réduite par le Traité de Paris. Mais dés que le Roi d'Espagne s'est trouvé en guerre avec l'Angleterre, il a pû conquerir tout ce qui appartenoit à cette Puissance à l'Est du Mississipi: son droit à cet égard étoit égal à celui des Etats-unis. Ainsi Sa Mté. Cathe. peut opposer aux Américains un droit exclusif non seulement sur la Floride-Occidentale, mais aussi sur les Terreins situés plus au nord que ses armes occupent actuellement. Le Roi d'Espagne n'a aucunement à compter de ses conquêtes avec les Etats-unis; la possession incommutable ne peut

Mémoire.

être discutée qu'avec la
Cour de Londres.

Au reste, les droits de
l'Espagne ne sauroient
s'étendre au dela de ses
conquêtes: le droit de la
guerre ne donne que ce
que l'on tient réellement,
il ne connoit point les
aquisitions des conquêtes
idéales: il résulte de là,
que pour que l'Espagne
puisse reclamer avec
justice les terreins situés
sur le Mississippi, jusqu'à
l'embouchure de l'Ohio,
aussi bien que ceux situés
le long de cette dernière
rivière,[a] il faut qu'elle les
ait fait occuper par ses
troupes: dans le cas
contraire elle n'y a aucun
titre; ils appartiennent encore

a. The words between commas are a marginalium inserted at this point in the same handwriting. It is incorporated in both the Angleterre copy and the Aranda copy.

MÉMOIRE

être discutée qu'avec la
Cour de Londres.

Au reste, les droits
de l'Espagne ne sauroient
s'étendre au delà de ses
conquêtes: le droit de la
guerre ne donne que ce
que l'on tient réellement;
il ne connôit point les
acquisitions, les conquêtes
idéales: Il résulte de là,
que pour que l'Espagne
puisse réclamer avec
justice les terreins situés
sur le Mississippi jusqu'à
l'embouchure de l'Ohio,
aussi bien que ceux situés
le long de cetter d'ère.
Rivière, il faut qu'Elle les
ait fait occuper par ses
troupes: dans le cas
contraire, Elle n'y a aucun
titre; ils appartiennent encore

MÉMOIRE concernant les Terreins

être discutée qu'avec la
Cour de Londres.

Au reste les droits
de l'Espagne ne sauroient
s'étendre au delà de ses
conquêtes: le droit de la
guerre ne donne que ce
que l'on tient réellement;
il ne connôit point les
acquisitions, les conquêtes
idéales: il resulte de là,
que pour que l'Espagne
puisse réclamer avec
justice les Terreins situés
sur le Mississippi jusqu'à
l'embouchure de l'Ohio,
aussi bien que ceux situés
le long de cette dernière
Rivière, il faut qu'Elle les
ait fait occuper par ses
troupes: dans le cas
contraire, Elle n'y a aucun
titre; ils appartiennent encore

a la grande-Bretange.
 Les Américains soutiennent
qu'ils ont des établissements
sur l'Ohio. Si le fait est
vraye, ils ont la possession
pour Eux, et l'Espagne
est sans qualité pour la leur
contester. Mais on ne sauroit
regarder comme une possession
les ventes de terreins faites
inconsidérément par l'Etat
de Virginie: ces ventes
sont un être de raison
si elles n'ont pas étés
suivies par des prises
de possession effectives:
et dans ce dernier cas
leur validité ne pourra
être discutée qu'avec
l'Angre. qui se trouve
être le possesseur a dépouillé.
 De tout ce qui vient
d'être dit il semble resulter

a. In the Angleterre copy this word is
corrected to *propriétaire*. The Aranda
copy follows the correction.

à la Grande-Bretagne.
 Les Américains soutiennent
qu'ils ont des Etablissements
sur l'Ohio. Si le fait est
vrai, ils ont la possession
pour eux, et l'Espagne
est sans qualité pour la leur
contester. Mais on ne sauroit
regarder comme une possession
les ventes de terreins faites
inconsidérément par l'Etat
de Virginie: ces ventes
sont un être de raison,
si elles n'ont pas été
suivies par des prises
de possession effectives:
et dans ce d^{er}. cas
leur validité ne pourra
être discutée qu'avec
l'Angleterre qui se trouve
être propriétaire a dépouillé.
 De tout ce qui vient
d'être dit, il semble résulter

a. In the Rayneval holograph original
the word was *possesseur*. Here it is corrected, in Rayneval's handwriting, to *propriétaire*. The correction is copied in the
Aranda copy.

à la grande-Bretagne.
 Les Américains soutiennent
qu'ils ont des établissements
sur l'Ohio. Si le fait et
vrai, ils ont la possession
pour eux, et l'Espagne
est sans qualité pour la leur
contester. Mais on ne sauroit
regarder comme une possession
les ventes de Terreins faites
inconsidérément par l'Etat
de Virginie: ces ventes
sont un être de raison,
si elles n'ont pas été
suivies par des prises
de possession effectives:
et dans ce dernier cas
leur validité ne pourra
être discutée qu'avec
l'Angleterre, qui se trouve
être le propriétaire a dépouillé.
 De tout ce qui vient
d'être dit, il semble resulter

a. Here the Aranda copy follows Rayneval's correction from the word *possesseur* in the Angleterre copy of his holograph original.

Memoire.

avec la plus grande évidence,
que la négotiation entamée
entre la Cour de Madrid
et les Etats-unis
relativement aux terreins
situés sur le Mississippi
et l'Ohio, est sans objet;
que cette négotiation porte
sur des Pays dont la
plus grande partie[a]
n'appartient ni aux uns ni
aux autres, et que les deux
parties ne se doivent aucun
compte de ce qu'elles peuvent
posseder actuellement dans
les contrées en question.

Comme néanmoins il
peut arriver que l'Espagne
aquît, par le futur traité
de paix une portion quel-
conque des terreins situés
à l'Est du Mississippi, et
que les Américains

a. The words *dont la plus grande partie*
are introduced as a marginalium in the
same (Rayneval's) handwriting. They are
followed in the Angleterre and Aranda
copies.

MÉMOIRE

avec la plus grande évidence,
que les négotiations entramées
entre la Cour de Madrid
et les Etats-unis
relativement aux terreins
situés sur le Mississippi
et l'Ohio, du moins quant
à présent,[a] est sans objet; que
cette négotiation porte sur les Pais
dont la plus grande partie
n'appartient ni aux uns ni
aux autres, et que les deux
parties ne se doivent aucun
compte de ce qu'Elles peuvent
posséder actuellement dans
les Contrées en question.

Comme néanmoins il
peut arriver que l'Espagne
aquît par le futur Traité
de paix une portion quel-
conque des terreins situés
à l'Est du Mississippi, et
que les Américains

a. The words *du moins quant à présent*
are introduced in a marginalium in Rayneval's handwriting and are taken over in
the Aranda copy.

MÉMOIRE concernant les Terreins

avec le plus grande évidence,
que les négotiations entramées
entre la Cour de Madrid
et les Etats-unis
relativement aux terreins
situés sur le Mississippi
et l'Ohio est, dumoins quant
à présent,[a] sans objet; que cette
négotiation porte sur des Pais
dont la plus grande partie
n'appartient ni aux uns ni
aux autres, et que les deux
parties ne se doivent aucun
compte de ce qu'Elles peuvent
posséder actuellement dans
les contrées en question.

Comme néanmoins il
peut arriver que l'Espagne
aquît par le futur Traité
de paix une portion quel-
quonque des Terreins situés
à l'Est du Mississippi, et
que les Américains

a. The words between commas are
copied from Rayneval's marginal addendum in the Angleterre copy of his holograph original, in which last mentioned
draft they do not appear.

conservassent leurs populations vraies ou idéales sur l'Ohio, la prudence veut qu'il soit fait un réglement éventuel entre les deux Etats, afin de prévenir d'avance les discutions et querrelles qui pourroient facilement survenir.

Dans cette suposition il s'agiroit de convenir de deux choses:

1°. de la navigation du Mississipi; 2do. de la limite qu'auroient les possessions espagnoles et celles des Etats-unis.

Ad primum. Le cours des rivières appartient de droit au Souverain des deux rives; le cours entraine de droit la navigation. Ainsi le Mississippi apartiendra à l'Espagne seule partout où elle sera maitresse des deux rives de ce fleuve: tel est le droit rigoureux: les exceptions ne peuvent être

---

conservassent leurs possessions vraies ou idéales sur l'Ohio, la prudence veut qu'il soit fait un Réglement éventuel entre les deux Etats, afin de prévenir d'avance les discutions et les querelles qui pourroient facilement survenir.

Dans cette suposition il s'agiroit de convenir de deux choses:

1°. de la navigation du Mississippi; 2do. de la limite qu'auroient les possessions espagnoles et celles des Etats-unis.

Ad primum. Le cours des rivières appartient de droit au Souverain des deux rives: le cours entraine de droit la navigation. Ainsi le Mississippi apartiendra à l'Espagne seule partout où Elle sera maitresse des deux rives de ce fleuve: tel est le droit rigoureux: les exceptions ne peuvent être

---

conservassent leurs possessions vraies ou idéales sur l'Ohio, la prudence veut qu'il soit fait un Réglement éventuel entre les deux Etats, afin de prévenir d'avance les discutions et les querelles qui pourroient facilement survenir.

Dans cette suposition il s'agiroit de convenir de deux choses:

1°. de la navigation du Mississipi; 2°. de la limite qu'auroient les possessions Espagnols et celles des Etats-unis.

Ad primum. Les cours des Rivières apartient de droit au Souverain des deux rives: le cours entraine de droit la navigation. Ainsi le Mississippi apartiendra à l'Espagne seule partout où Elle sera maitresse des deux rives de ce fleuve: Tel est le droit rigoureux: les exceptions ne peuvent être

Memoire.

établies que par des conventions expresses: ces vérités sont constatées par autant d'exemples qu'il y a de fleuves qui arrosent pleusieurs pays.

Mais, dans la suposition que les Américains ont des établissement sur l'Ohio, il sera de leur grande convenance d'avoir un débouché par le Mississipi: ce cera le seul moyen de les vivifier. Mais l'Espagne repugne à accorder cette faveur, parce qu'elle craindroit d'avoir par là la porte à la contrebande. Les Américains sentent la force de ces réflexions; ils se contentent d'avoir ou un entrepôt où un port franc vers l'embouchure du Mississipi; et à cette condition ils sont prêts à renoncer à leurs prétentions sur les terreins situés sur

MÉMOIRE

établies que par des Conventions expresses ces vérités sont constatées par autant d'exemples qu'il y a de fleuves qui arrosent plusieurs Pais.

Mais dans la suposition que les américains ont des Etablissements sur l'Ohio, il sera de leur grande convenance d'avoir un débouché par le Mississippi: ce cera le seul moyen de les vivifier. Mais l'Espagne repugne à accorder cette faveur, parcequ'Elle craindroit d'ouvrir par là la porte à la contrebande. Les Américains sentent la force de ces réfléxions; ils se contentent d'avoir, ou un entrepôt ou un port-franc vers l'embouchûre du Mississippi; et à cette condition, ils sont prêts à renoncer à leurs prétentions sur les terreins situés

MÉMOIRE concernant les Terreins

établies que par des Conventions expresses: ces vérités sont constatées par autant d'exemples qu'il y a de fleuves qui arrosent plusieurs Pais.

Mais dans la suposition que les Américains ont des établissements sur l'Ohio, il sera de leur grande convenance d'avoir un débouché par le Mississippi: ce sera le seul moien de les vivifier. Mais l'Espagne repugne à accorder cette faveur, parcequ'Elle craindroit d'ouvrir par là la porte à la contrebande. Les Américains sentent la force de ces réfléxions; ils se contentent d'avoir, ou un entrepôt, ou un port-franc vers l'embouchure du Mississippi; et à cette condition, ils sont prêts à renoncer à leurs prétentions sur les Terreins situés le bord oriental de ce fleuve.

Il est à observer que jusqu'au commencement **des hostilités entre l'Espagne** et l'Angre, cette dernière puissance avoit l'usage libre et illimité de la navigation du Mississippi; les anglois ne payoient aucun droit; n'étoient sujets à aucune visite, et pouvoient naviguer depuis le fond du Mississippi et de l'Ohio jusqu'en Angre. L'Espagne gagnera beaucoup si les Américains prennent la place des Anglois; puisque ceux-là ne commenceront point avec l'Europe par le Golfe du Méxique, que par conséquent ils ne pourront point verser

sur le bord occidental [a] **de ce** fleuve.

Il est à observer que jusqu'au commencement **des** hostilités entre l'Espagne et l'Angleterre, cette dᵉʳᵉ. Puissance avoit l'usage libre et illimité de la navigation du Mississippi; les Anglois ne payoient aucun droit, n'étoient sujets à aucune visite, et pouvoient naviguer depuis le fond du Mississippi et de l'Ohio jusqu'en Angleterre. L'Espagne gagnera beaucoup si les Américains prennent la place des Anglois, puisque ceux-là ne commenceront point avec l'Europe pour le Golfe du Méxique, que par conséquent ils ne pourront point verser

sur le bord Occidental de ce fleuve.

Il est à observer que jusqu'au commencement des hostilités entre l'Espagne et l'Angleterre, cette dernière Puissance avoit l'usage libre et illimité de la navigation du Mississippi; les Anglois ne paioient aucun droit, n'étoient sujets à aucune visite, et pouvoient naviguer depuis le fond du Mississippi et de l'Ohio jusqu'en Angre. L'Espagne gagnera beaucoup si les Américains prennent la place de Anglois; puisque ceux-là ne commenceront point avec l'Europe par le Golfe du Mexique, que par conséquent ils ne pourront point verser

a. *Occidental* is obviously a copyist's mistake. In the original Rayneval holograph the word is *oriental*. Rayneval in reading over the copy (which he corrected in other respects) did not catch this error. The copyist of the Aranda copy faithfully copies this uncorrected error.

Memoire.

de contrebande sur les côtés de ce Golfe: d'un autre côté la nouvelle-orleans, ou toute autre endroit à sa place, devenant l'entrepôt des Américains, il en résultera un grande mouvement de commerce dont la principal bénéfice sera pour les Espagnols, qui feront seuls la navigation de l'Europe en Amérique, soit comme propriétaires, soit comme simples commissionnaires.

Il paroit donc, que la Cours de Madrid peut, sans inconvénient, accorder aux Américains ou un entrepôt ou un port franc au bas du Mississippi. cette Puissance pourroit établir quelques droits légers sur les importations et les exportations sous le non de droit d'entrepôt; elle pourra aussi éxiger que tout ce qui entreroit dans le port seroit visité, et

MÉMOIRE

de contrebande sur les côtés de ce golphe: d'un autre côté la Nouvelle-Orléans, ou tout autre endroit à sa place, devenant l'Entrepôt des Américains, il en résultera un grand mouvement de commerce dont la principal bénéfice sera pour les Espagnols, qui feront seuls la navigation d'Europe en Amérique, soit comme propriétaires, soit comme simples Commissionnaires.

Il paroît donc que la Cour de Madrid peut, sans inconvénient, accorder aux Américains, ou un Entrepôt, ou un port-franc au bas du Mississippi. Cette Puissance pourroit établir quelques droits légers sur les importations et les exportations sous le nom de droit d'Entrepôt; Elle pourra aussi éxiger que tout ce qui entreroit dans le port seroit visité, et

MÉMOIRE concernant les Terreins

de contrebande sur les côtés de ce Golfe: D'un autre côté la nouvelle-Orleans, ou tout autre endroit à sa place, devenant l'entrepôt des Américains, il en résultera un grand mouvement de commerce dont le principal benêfice, sera pour les Espagnols, qui feront seuls la navigation d'Europe en Amérique, soit comme propriétaires, soit comme simples Commissionnaires.

Il paroît donc que le Cour de Madrid peut, sans inconvénient, accorder aux Américains, ou un Entrepôt, ou un port franc au bas du Mississippi. Cette Puissance pourroit établir quelques droits légers sur les importations et les exportations sous le nom de droit d'Entrepôt; Elle pourra aussi exiger que tout ce qui entreroit dans le Port seroit visité, et

convenir des formes
nécessaires pour que les
visites ne soient pas illusoires.
Si pour se soustraire à l'un
ou à l'autre les américains
citent l'exemple de l'Angre,,
ou pourra leur répondre
que cette Puissance avoit
des possessions à l'Est
du Mississippi; qu'à ce
titre la moitié de ce fleuve
lui appartenoit de droit,
et que la navigation étoit une
suite immédiate de sa
propriété territoriale.ᵃ

a. Fortunately for Spain, **this memoir was not published, nor made known to the United States. It would have put an argument in the mouths of American diplomatists later.**

convenir des formes
nécessaires pour que les
visites ne soient pas illusoires.
Si pour se soustraire à l'un
ou à l'autre les Américains
citent l'exemple de l'Angleterre,,
on pourra leur répondre
que cette Puissance avoit
des possessions à l'Est
du Mississippi; qu'à ce
titre le moitié de ce fleuve
lui appartenoit de droit,
et que la navigation étoit une
suite immédiate de sa
propriété territoriale.ᵃ (b)
    Si les anglois
    conservent les rives de
    l'Ohio comme dépendantes
    du Canada, ils demanderont
    peut-être à être maintenue
    dans la jouissance de
    la navigation libre sur

a. **The sentence following the (b) was introduced as a marginal addendum in** Rayneval's handwriting. It does not occur in the original Rayneval holograph. I have indented it here.

convenir des formes
nécessaires pour que les
visites ne soient pas illusoires.
Si pour se soustraire à l'un
ou à l'autre les Américains
citent l'exemple de l'Angleterre,
on pourra leur répondre
que cette Puissance avoit
des possessions à l'Est
du Mississippi; qu'a ce
titre la moitié de ce fleuve
lui appartenoit de droit,
et que la navigation étoit
une suite immédiate de sa
propriété Territoriale. (b.) ᵃ
    Si les Anglois
    conservent les rives de
    l'Ohio comme dépendantes
    du Canada, il demanderont
    peut-être à être maintenue
    dans la jouissance de
    la navigation libre dans

a. The designation "(b.)" refers to a marginal addendum, here represented by indenting, copied on the margin from an identical addendum which Rayneval introduced in the Angleterre copy. Unlike other marginal additions by Rayneval to the Angleterre copy, this addendum was not copied into the main text of the Aranda copy.

Quant ᵃ aux limites des
terreins contentieux, dans le
cas où le Congrès persisteroit
dans sas prétentions, on
pourroit les déterminer
de la manière suivante.
En supposant que l'Espagne
conservera la floride
occidentale et que cette
province s'étend vers le
nord jusqu'au 31 degre
de latitude, on partiorit,

a. The indented matter here is in the form of a marginal addendum added to the paper as a result of discussions with Aranda on August 30. See Aranda's *Diario,* Yela, 2, 364. The Angleterre copy follows this addendum.

le Mississippi; ce
n'est pas ici le lieu
d'examiner ce que
l'Espagne pourra ou
devra faire à cet égard.
Quant aux limites des
terreins contentieux, dans le
cas où le Congrès persisteroit
dans ses prétentions, on
pourroit les déterminer
de la manière suivante:
En supposant que l'Espagne
conservera la Floride—
Occidentale, et que cette
province s'étend vers le
nord jusqu'au 31 ᵉᵐᵉ dégré
de ~~latitude~~ (c) ᵃ on partiroit,

a. A marginal addendum is inserted at this place in Rayneval's hand, and then later stricken out. This was done apparently after constructing with Aranda the changes in boundaries added to the original holograph on August 30, for the matter stricken out occurs in the marginal addendum to the original Rayneval holograph document [q.v.] viz:
(c.) "C'est la limite que lui donne la Cour de Londres."
The boundary as finally corrected is introduced into paragraph 8 of the *Résumé* in the Aranda [q.v.].

le Mississippi; ce
n'est pas ici le lieu
d'examiner ce que
l'Espagne pourra ou
devra faire à cet égard.
Quant aux limites des
Terreins contentieux, dans le
cas où le Congrès persisteroit
dans ses prétentions, on
pourroit les déterminer
de la manière suivante.
ᵃOn partiroit de
l'angle du golfe du
Mexique où les deux
Florides se touchent;

a. The boundary line which is introduced here, indented, is copied from the marginal revisions of Rayneval's holograph copy, revisions made by Rayneval when reading over the Angleterre copy [q.v.].

à cette latitude, de point parallele au Rio perdido situé entre la Mobile et Pensacola;

on tireroit une
ligne droite sur le fort
Toulouse situé dans le
pays des Alibamous;
de ce fort on remonteroit
la rivière d'Alabama
ou Coussa jusqu'à
l'endroit où elle recoit
celle de Locushatchi; on
suivroit cette dernière
jusqu'à sa source, et
de là on tireroit une
ligne droite sur le

à cette latitude, du point parallèle au Rio perdido situé entre la Mobile et Pensacola,
de l'angle du golfe du Mexique où les deux Florides se touchent; a
on tireroit de là une
ligne droite sur le fort
Toulouse situé dans le
Pais des Alibamous,
de ce fort on remonteroit
la rivière d'Alabama
ou Coussa jusqu'à
l'endroit où elle reçoit
celle de Locushatchi; on
suivroit cette dère.
jusqu'à sa source, et
de là on tireroit une
ligne droite sur le

on tireroit de là une
ligne droite sur le fort
Toulouse, situé dans le
Pais des Alibamous;
de ce fort en remonteroit
la Rivière d'Alabama
ou Coussa jusqu'à
l'endroit où elle reçoit
celle de Locushatchi; on
suivroit cette derniere
jusqu'à sa source, et
de là on tireroit une
ligne droite sur le

a. The words *"de l'angle . . . se touchent"* are a marginalium inserted here by Rayneval, and taken over in the Aranda copy, which excludes Rayneval's deletions (here reproduced) from the Angleterre copy.

MÉMOIRE concernant les Terreins

comptoir apellé Kanassée
ou Tanassée; de cet endroit
on suivroit la rivière
Euphasée, et ensuite
celle des Chéroquées
ou Hogohegées j'usqu'à

l'endroit où elle reçoit celle
de Pelisipi: on remonteroit
cette dernière par sa branche
occidentale jusquà sa source;
de là on tireroit une ligne
droite jusqu'à la source
de la rivière Cumberland, et
l'on suivroit le cours
de cette Rivière jusqu'à
son embouchure dans
l'Ohio.

MÉMOIRE

Comptoir appellé Kanassée [a]
ou Tanassée; de cet endroit
on suivroit la rivière
Euphasée, et ensuite
celle des Chéroquées
ou Hogohegées jusqu'à l'embouchure de l'Ohio
l'endroit où elle reçoit celle
de Pelesipi: ou remonteroit
cette dernière par sa branche
occidentale jusqu'à sa source;
de là on tireroit une ligne
droit [sic] jusqu'à la source
de la rivière de Cumberland,
et l'on suivroit le cours
de cette rivière jusqu'à son
embouchure dans l'Ohio.[b]

a. The word Kanassee, omitted by the copyist is written in by Rayneval's hand. It is followed in one Aranda copy.

b. The words between the phrase *l'embouchure de l'Ohio*, stricken out above, and the words between it and this footnote were inserted in Rayneval's hand to take the place of those stricken out by him in this copy.

Memoire.

comptoire appellé Kanessée
ou Tanassée; de cet endroit
on suivroit la rivière
Euphasée, et ensuite
celle des Cheroquées
ou Hogohegée juscequ'à
son embouchure dans
l'Ohio.

Les sauvages
situés entre la ligne
qui vient d'etre tracée
et les frontières des
Etats-unis demeureroient
libres et neutres, et les Espagnols
comme les Américains
auroient également la
faculté de commercer
avec Eux. Dans le cas
où les Américains auroient
avec ces sauvages des
discutions résultantes
de l'incertitude des
limites, ils s'arrangeroient
comme ils le jugeroient
à propos: L'Espagne ne
s'opposera point aux
extensions de Terrein
qu'ils pourront obtenir.

Resumé du présent Mémoire
1°. Les Américains n'ont

Les Sauvages
situés entre la ligne
qui vient d'etre tracée
et les frontières des
Etats-unis demeureroient
libres [a] et neûtres et les **Espagnols**
comme les Américains
auroient également la
faculté de commercer
avec Eux. Dans le cas
où les Américains auroient
avec ces Sauvages des
discutions résultantes
de l'incertitude des
limites, ils s'arrangeroient
comme ils le jugeroient
à propos: l'Espagne ne
s'opposera point aux
extensions de terrein
qu'ils pourront obtenir.

Résumé du présent Mémoire
1°. Les Américains n'ont

a. The word *libres* is inserted over a caret by Rayneval in this copy. It is followed in the Aranda copy.

Les sauvages
situés entre la ligne
qui vient d'etre tracée
et les frontières des
Etats-unis demeureroient
neutres, et les **Espagnols**
comme les Américains
auroient également la
faculté de commercer
avec Eux: **Dans le cas**
où les Américains auroient
avec **des sauvages des**
discutions résultantes
de l'incertitude des
limites, ils s'arrangeront
comme ils le jugeront
à propos: l'Espagne ne
s'opposera point aux
extentions des terrens
qu'ils pourront obtenir.

Résume du présent mémoire
1°. Les américains n'ont

Memoire.

aucun droit aquis sur les terreins situés à l'Est du Mississipi au sud de l'Ohio.

2do. Que le droit de propriéte de l'Espagne à l'Est du même fleuve, ne s'étend pas au delà de ses conquêtes.

3. Que la propriété incommutable des uns et des autres ne peut être traitée qu'avec la Cour de Londres

4°. Que les pays non-occupés, c'est à dire, les peuplades sauvages situés entre le Mississipi, l'Ohio et les Colonies angloises, sont indéppendantes tant de l'Espagne que des Etats-unis; que par conséquent

MÉMOIRE

aucun droit aquit sur les terreins situés à l'Est du Mississipi au sud de l'Ohio.

2°. le droit de propriéte de l'Espagne, à l'Est du même fleuve, ne s'étend pas au delà de ses conquêtes.

3°. la propriété incommutable des uns et des autres ne peut etre traitée qu'avec la Cour de Londres

4°.[a] les Pais non-occupés, c'est-à-dire, les peuplades sauvages situées entre le Mississippi, l'Ohio et les Colonies Angloises, sont indéppendantes tant de l'Espagne que des Etats-Unis; par conséquent elles

a. See note a. in right column opposite.

MÉMOIRE concernant les Terreins

aucun droit acquit sur les Terreins situés à l'Est du Mississipi au sud de l'Ohio.

2°.[a] Le droit de propriété de l'Espagne, à l'Est du même fleuve, ne s'étend pas au delà de ses conquêtes.

3°.[a] La propriété incommutable des uns et des autres ne peut être traitée qu'avec la Cour de Londres.

4°.[a] Les Pais non occupés, c'est-à-dire, les peuplades sauvages situées entre le Mississippi, l'Ohio et les Colonies Angloises, sont indéppendantes tant de l'Espagne que des Etats-unis; par conséquent elles

a. In the Angleterre copy, as in the Rayneval holograph original, the word *que* introduced these paragraphs. Rayneval struck it out when reading over the Angleterre copy. The Aranda copy follows these corrections, thus proving, with other corrections, that it is copied from the Angleterre copy, which in turn is copied from the holograph copy.

ne sont pas matière à transaction entre ces deux Puissances.

5°. Dans l'incertitude du sort des Terreins appartenants à l'Angleterre, la prudence veut qu'il soit fait une Convention éventuelle entre la Cour de Madrid et les Etats-unis tant sur la navigation du Mississippi que sur les limites des possessions Espagnols dans cette partie.

6°. L'Espagne répugne à accorder la navigation de crainte de la contrebande; les Américains renoncent aux Terreins s'ils obtiennent un port-franc ou un entrepôt vers l'embouchûre du Mississippi.

7°. La demande des Américains ne présente aucun inconvénient pour l'Espagne noiennant les

---

ne sont point matière à transaction entre ces deux Puissances.

5°. dans l'incertitude du sort des terreins appartenants à l'Angleterre, la prudence veut qu'il soit fait une Convention éventuelle entre la Cour de Madrid et les Etats-unis tant sur la navigation du Mississippi que sur les limites des possessions espagnols dans cette partie.

6°. L'Espagne répugne à accorder la navigation de crainte de la contrebande; les Américains renoncent aux terreins s'ils obtiennent un port-franc ou une Entrepôt vers l'Embouchûre du Mississippi.

7°. La demande des Américains ne présente aucun inconvénient pour l'Espagne moyennant les

---

elles ne sont point matière à transaction entre ces deux Puissances.

5. Que dans l'incertitude du sort des terreins appartenants à l'angre. la prudence veut qu'il soit fait une convention éventuelle entre la Cour de Madrid et les Etats-unis tant sur la navigation du Mississipi que sur les limites des possessions espagnoles dans une partie.

6. L'Espagne répugne à accorder la navigation de crainte de la contrebande; les Américains renoncent aux terreins s'ils obtiennent un port-franc ou un entrepôt vers l'embouchure du Mississippi.

7. Que le demande des Américains ne presente aucun inconvénient pour l'Espagne.

Memoire.

8. Les limites de possession
espagnoles pourroient être
fixés de la manière suivante:
on suivroit le Rio perdido;
de là en ligne droite sur
le font Toulouse; on remontoit
la rivière d'Alabama ou
Coussa et ensuite celle de
Locushatchi; de là on tireroit
une ligne droite sur Kanessée;
on suivroit la riviére
Euphasée, ensuite celle de
Cherokée, jusqu'à son
embouchure dans l'Ohio.

MÉMOIRE

precautions indiquées.[a]
8º. Les limites des possessions
espagnoles pourroient être
fixées de la manière suivante:
~~en~~ suivroit la Rio-perdido;
de là en ligne droit sur
le fort Toulouse; on remonteroit
la rivière d'Albama ou
Coussa et ensuite celle de
Locushatchi; de là on tireroit
une ligne droite sur Kanessée;
on suivroit la rivière
Euphasée, ensuite celle de
Cheroquées jusqu'à son
embouchûre dans l'Ohio.[b]

a. The words *moyenant les précautions
indiquées* are added in Rayneval's handwriting. They are followed in the Aranda
copy.

b. On reading over this copy Rayneval
struck out the passages indicated. The
Aranda copy leaves these out and substi-
tutes the corrected boundary proposals on
pages 93–94 above, in this document.

MÉMOIRE concernant les Terreins

précautions indiquées.
8º. Les limites des possessions
Espagnoles pourroient être
fixées de la manière suivante:
[a]On partiroit de l'Angle
du Golfe du Mexique où les
deux Florides se touchent;
on tireroit de là une ligne
droit sur le fort Toulouse,
situé dans le Pais des
Alibamous; de ce fort on
remonteroit la Rivière
d'Alabama ou Coussa
jusqu'à l'endroit où elle
reçoit celle de Locushatchi;
on suivroit cette dernière
jusqu'à sa source, et de
là on tireroit une ligne
droit sur le comptoire
apellé Kanassée ou
Tanassée; de cet endroit

a. Here are inserted the corrections
[q.v.] made by Rayneval in the Angleterre
copy of the original boundary suggestions
written on the margin [q.v.] of the original holograph memorandum.

on suivroit la Rivière Euphasée, et ensuite celle des Cheroquées ou Hogohegées jusqu'à l'endroit ou elle reçoit celle de Pelisipi: on remonteroit cette dernière par sa branche occidentale jusqu'à sa source; de là on tireroit une ligne droite jusqu'à la source de la Rivière de Cumberland, et l'on suivroit le cours de cette Rivière jusqu'à son embouchure dans l'Ohio.

9°. Les peuplades sauvages situées à l'Est de cette ligne demeurent libres, et les Espagnols comme les Américains pourront commercer avec eux.

10°. Les Américains arrangeront leurs limites avec les sauvages comme ils l'entendront, et pourront acquérir des extensions de Terrein.

9. Les peuplades sauvages situés à l'Est de cette ligne demeurent libres; et les espagnols commes les Américains pourront commercer avec Eux.

10. Les américains arrangeront leurs limites avec les sauvages comme ils l'entendendront et pourront aquérir des extensions de terreins.

What conclusions may we draw from a close study of the records of these boundary discussions, the text of the Compromise Memorandum, printed above on pages 43–45, and the texts of the Historical Memorandum, printed just above on pages 62–99? I suggest:

1. The Historical Memorandum, as compared with the Compromise Memorandum, shows more fully (but probably not completely) details of policy of the French Foreign Office. In the Historical Memorandum certain policy is displayed to Spain which Rayneval and his chief did not then see fit to exhibit to the United States in the Compromise Memorandum, which varies very considerably from the Historical Memorandum.

The principal variations are as follows:

  a. The historical argument is much condensed in the Compromise Memorandum, and even altered.
  b. The Compromise Memorandum omits historical discussion of ancient boundaries south of the Ohio, although the compromise boundary is drawn off from such.
  c. The Compromise Memorandum inserts more historical argument to sustain continuing British sovereignty north of the Ohio.
  d. The Compromise Memorandum omits discussion of the crown charters to the Colonies, also of the "ephemeral incursions" of Colonel George Rogers Clark into the region north of the Ohio.
  e. In the matter of the navigation of the Mississippi the Compromise Memorandum merely states the principle that such is controlled by the Power which owns both banks. It does not make the proposal, suggested to Spain in the Historical Memorandum, that Spain grant the navigation of the Mississippi, with a free port or at least an entrepôt, in return for the acceptance by the United States of the compromise boundary suggested in both memoranda.
  f. The Compromise Memorandum introduces the statement, for American consumption, that by the proposed compromise boundary "Spain will lose almost the whole course of the Ohio." (It does not mention that the United States, on its part, would lose the whole course of the Mississippi.)

There are other variations between the two memoranda, which careful reading will discover. The purpose in printing them here is to afford such close study.

I have suggested that the Historical Memorandum explains more details of French policy than does the Compromise Memorandum. It shows, for example, that *the boundary proposals of Rayneval's Compromise Memorandum were worked out in close cooperation with Aranda, the Spanish ambassador, and were obviously designed to favor Spain as against the United States.* It shows that for some reason Rayneval did not see fit to introduce the proposal that the United States accept the compromise boundary in return for Spain granting the navigation of the Mississippi—a suggestion which had been a feature of the treaty settlement proposed for Spain and the United States in the Historical Memorandum. Whether this modification was due to Aranda [45] may only be guessed, pending further researches in the Spanish archives; in fact it may never be known.

2. The Historical Memorandum, read in connection with the Compromise Memorandum, helps us to judge to what extent Jay's suspicions of French loyalty are to be justified:

a. Jay was convinced by the Compromise Memorandum that France, in the peace negotiations, would oppose the extension of the United States to the Mississippi.

The Historical Memorandum, and the circumstances of its preparation, only strengthen his justification for this conviction.

b. Jay was convinced by the Compromise Memorandum that France would oppose the claim of the United States to the free navigation of the Mississippi.

The fact that Rayneval suggested this in the Historical Memorandum, known only to Aranda, but suppressed it in the Compromise Memorandum presented to Jay, shows that France was not inclined to champion, at least, this important interest of her American ally. In fact, Rayneval definitely opposes this American desire for the navigation by stressing in the Compromise Memorandum that the navigation of the Mississippi belongs solely to those powers which possess the banks of the river. Thus Jay's suspicions on this score were not unjustified.

---

45. In communications later to Floridablanca, Aranda seemed to favor extending to the United States the privilege of navigation, with a place at New Orleans for the sale of produce, but no right to go in or out of the Mississippi from or to the sea. Aranda's no. 2362 to Floridablanca, Paris, Jan. 1, 1783. A.H.N., Estado, legajo 6609. He felt that French proposals for a free port at New Orleans—which we perceived incorporated in Rayneval's Historical Memorandum—were designed to secure French entrance there. Aranda's no. 2414 of April 3, 1783. Ibid. Note that these views were expressed considerably later than the composition of Rayneval's Memoranda, in fact after the Anglo-American preliminaries had been announced.

   c. The Compromise Memorandum convinced Jay that France would "probably support the British claims to all the country above the thirty-first degree of latitude, and certainly to all the country north of the Ohio."

     The Historical Memorandum abundantly fortifies this.

   d. Jay was certain, from the Compromise Memorandum, that in case the United States would not divide the western territory with Spain in the manner proposed, then France would aid Spain in negotiating for the territory she wanted, and would agree that the residue should remain to Britain.

     There is nothing in the Historical Memorandum which undoes the basis for this belief. Further, the Historical Memorandum, considered in reference of Rayneval's mission to England, strengthens the grounds for Jay's suspicion.

It is a curious fact that one copy of the Historical Memorandum, the copy which we have designated here as the Angleterre Copy, is found in the files Angleterre, along with miscellaneous papers relating to England and the peace negotiations, including Rayneval's instructions and reports from London.[46] Why is a copy filed in that series? Presumably because it was interesting in connection with the negotiations then going on between France and Great Britain. We may even venture the conjecture that Rayneval may have taken it to England with him on his celebrated secret visit to Lord Shelburne.[47] It is even not inconceivable that he showed it to the British Prime Minister. About this we can only wonder.

In his dispatches to Vergennes reporting his mission to England, Rayneval makes only the briefest allusions to American affairs in his conversations with Shelburne. These almost incidental remarks are highly suggestive. While it has long been clear (since Doniol's publication) that the purpose of Rayneval's trip to London was to verify

   46. Arch. Aff. Etrang., Correspondance Politique, Angleterre, vols. 537, 538.

   47. In his dispatch no. 2294 of Sept. 8, 1782, referred to above (p. 60, note 42) Aranda, after commenting on the ostensibly unexceptionable character of Rayneval's mission to London, reported: "But underneath such a good pretext, I am inclined to believe there is hidden more than meets the eye. . . . I noticed when I entered [Vergennes's office] that M. de Vergennes and Rayneval had their hands full of other papers which looked as though they had recently been copied, and not yet even folded; which left me no doubt that they are material for Rayneval's governance . . . my conception is that Rayneval is going to treat provisionally France's interests, in order that, these being assured in agreement with England, France may align herself more or less, according to the obstacles that may be presented by the other interested parties [*otros comprometidos*]."

the peace offers ascribed to Shelburne by the paroled prisoner of war, the Count de Grasse—including the British cession of Gibraltar—it is certain that at least incidental talk took place between Rayneval and Shelburne about the United States and the peace. Rayneval went out of his way to say that the Americans had no real claim to fishery rights anywhere outside their own territorial waters, except on the high seas. This he had already told the British envoy in Paris. On the subject of boundaries, reported Rayneval to Vergennes: "I merely said that the English Ministry ought to find in the negotiations of 1754 relative to the Ohio the limits which England, then sovereign of the thirteen United States, thought she ought to assign them." It was, of course, one of the principal arguments of the Historical Memorandum as well as of the Compromise Memorandum, that Great Britain had admitted, during the negotiations attendant upon the Seven Years' War, that French territory came down as far south as the Ohio, thus cutting off the colonies at least at that river. The Historical Memorandum adduced further arguments from history to show that the colonies were also cut off south of the Ohio from the western watershed of the Appalachians.

"He [Rayneval] appears rather Jealous than partial to the Americans upon other points, as well as that of the Fishery," noted Shelburne for the King's eye, after talking with the French agent. "We spoke about observing secrecy in case we should succeed in establishing preliminaries," reported Rayneval to Vergennes. "I assured him it would be most faithfully guarded on our part. My Lord fears gamblers in the public funds and would be extremely desirous to frustrate their endeavors. I said we could arrange to conclude in the greatest secrecy so as to throw the curious off the scent. My Lord fears the Americans and Dutch: I repeated that there would be a way to put them off the track principally by keeping them ignorant of the negotiation between France, Spain and England. Lord Shelburne has this article infinitely at heart." [48] It is significant that after these conferences with Rayneval, Shelburne made another try for the line of the Ohio before closing with the American on the line of the Great Lakes—the Mississippi and 31° North Latitude.

The Franco-American Alliance of February 6, 1778, declared that

48. These quotations are reproduced from my *Diplomacy of the American Revolution*, pp. 221–22, notes 16–18, where the original sources are indicated, in British Public Record Office; Arch. Aff. Etrang.; Wharton; and Sir. J. Fortescue, *The Correspondence of King George the Third, from 1760 to December, 1783* (6 vols. London, 1927–28).

"neither of the two parties shall conclude either peace or truce with Great Britain without the formal consent of the other first obtained." It did not preclude separate negotiations, or preliminary articles of peace by either party, so long as no peace or truce was *concluded* without the consent of the other party. It guaranteed American independence, and the boundaries of the United States as they should be fixed in the final peace. There was nothing in it to prevent France from deprecating to the enemy American boundary claims and refusing to support them before peace was made. On the other hand, such would be the last thing to expect a loyal ally to say to a common enemy. It cannot be said that Rayneval's conversations, either with Aranda, or with Shelburne, were violations of that alliance. But when one notes these French animadversions at London against American claims and interests, and, above all, the suggestion for a separate and secret preliminary peace, the Americans (and Dutch) to be kept meanwhile off the track; when one realizes, as we now know, that the Secretary for Foreign Affairs in the Continental Congress owed his office to the French minister at Philadelphia, La Luzerne; when we recall that the instructions of the Continental Congress to its plenipotentiaries, to negotiate hand in hand with the French Ministry and not to undertake anything without its knowledge, were insinuated by the French minister in Philadelphia, La Luzerne, at Vergennes's orders; [49] when we think of all this, and that the French Court itself was secretly planning and conjuring preliminary articles of peace with England inimical to the vital interests of an indispensable ally; then, I say, we can only applaud the action taken by the American commissioners in violating their instructions and in signing, without consulting France, the preliminary and conditional articles of November 30, 1782.[50]

In violating the instructions of Congress, their sovereign, the commissioners were really violating the instructions of the patron, Vergennes. If only half of Jay's suspicions had been well founded, he was abundantly justified in urging his colleagues (who needed no urging) to carry on the remainder of their negotiations without the privity of the French Court. Whether Jay's suspicions justified him in going behind Franklin's back in sending Vaughan to England is another

49. *Diplomacy of the American Revolution*, pp. 184–90.

50. I have suggested elsewhere that Vergennes found this separate signature not unacceptable, because of the pressure it put on Spain to make peace without getting Gibraltar. *Diplomacy of the American Revolution*, p. 241.

matter. The Doctor had been just as willing as Jay to steer a course independent from France, though never disloyal to France; in fact, Franklin already had had his confidential communications with Shelburne, through Oswald, all unknown to Vergennes, about Canada, for example, and other things.

We will not follow here Livingston's pained expostulations to the commissioners for their "unnecessary distrust" of France. Nor will we pause to describe the debate in the Continental Congress which failed to pass a resolution of censure.[51] We will only join in applause of their countrymen for Franklin, Jay, Adams, and Laurens, in winning this, the greatest diplomatic victory in the history of our nation.

In so closing I wish to append a querulous and disingenuous dispatch of Vergennes to La Luzerne, the French minister in the United States, dispatch no. 40 of July 21, 1782. It is taken from a draft copy presumably by Rayneval[52] in the files États-Unis, vol. 25, pp. 63–71, of the series Correspondance Politique in the Archives of the Ministry of Foreign Affairs at Paris. Remember that, though Vergennes signed the dispatch, and perhaps dictated part of it, Rayneval drafted it. Observe in the passages relating to American boundaries the similarity of phrases here and there to similar ones found in Rayneval's Historical Memorandum and Compromise Memorandum of the year before. This dispatch is a noteworthy illustration of the caution with which Vergennes's dispatches—so copiously, but still so imperfectly published by the historian, Doniol—must be used. Doniol relies on the validity of the content of Vergennes's dispatches, that part of them which he selects for publication. For him it is enough if his statements can be backed, chapter and verse, by a citation of the dispatch concerned. Of this particular dispatch, he says: "The Minister's explanations reflect, as calmly and precisely as they do incontestably, the course he had followed." "They will remain," adds Doniol "without appeal in history."

Will they?

Historians have almost without exception accepted Doniol's state-

51. On this question see the remarks of E. C. Burnett, in the preface of vol. 7 of *Letters of Members of the Continental Congress* (Carnegie Institution of Washington, 1934), viii-ix.

52. Published in part by Doniol, *Histoire de la participation de la France à l'établissement des Étas-Unis d'Amérique*, 5, 293–96: that part beginning with *"Les limites"* and ending *"l'occasion s'en présentera naturellement."* I have indented slightly those portions omitted by Doniol. The original spelling, accents, and punctuation are here precisely reproduced.

ments. Because of this uncritical acceptance of statements faithfully [53]
documented, an over-idealistic interpretation of the motives of the
great French diplomat for a long time permeated the historiography
of the American Revolution. Actually, it is not enough to support a
statement by an authentic reference to Vergennes's dispatches unquestionably accepted as a contemporary source of a most direct nature.
Actually Vergennes put into these dispatches what he wanted his
diplomatic agents to say. Skilled by long experience—an experience
shared by such a skillful aid as Rayneval—he selected, he dressed, he
colored, he even invented the facts and arguments which he wished
to instill, according to circumstances, for the solution of his immediate problems, problems which arose from his one constant, unswerving,
and altogether praiseworthy aim: to enhance the power, the prestige,
and the glory of his sovereign. Doniol's statements are often supported
only by the historical residue left by a critical analysis of Vergennes's
dispatches. This paper has attempted such an analysis for a small, but
not inconspicuous, phase of the justly celebrated peace negotiations
of 1782. Vergennes's complete dispatch follows.

VERGENNES TO LA LUZERNE, JULY 21, 1783

A V^{lles}. le 21 Juillet 1783

J'ai reçu successivement, M, les dépêches que vous m'avez fait l'h^r. de
m'ecrire depuis le n°. 299 jusqu'au n°. 331 inclusivement.

Les representations que vous avez faites à M^r. Morris pour l'empêcher de
nous demander de nouveaux fonds, ont été infructueuses; ce sur-intendant des
finances abusant les facilités qu'il a éprouvées jusqu'à présent de notre part,
a tellement multiplié ses traites, qu'elles surpassent de près de 2,000,000. les
six que le Roi a accordés pour l'année courante. M^{rs}. Franklin et Jay m'ont
passé une office pour demander 1900# à compte des 3 millions énoncées dans
la resolution du congrès; j'ai mis cette demande sous les yeux du Roi; mais
SM^{té}. s'est trouvée dans l'impossibilité absolüe de la prendre en considération,
et c'est pour en instruire M^{rs}. franklin et Jai que je leur ai adressé les 2
lettres dont vous trouverez la copie ci-jointe. Il eût certainement été fort
agréable au Roi de soulager par de nouveaux secours les finances des Etats-
unis: mais S. M^{té}. ne sauroit aggraver le poids des charges qui pesent sur ses
peuples pour une nation qui rejette avec une obsténation sans exemple tous
les expédients qui ont été proposés jusqu'à present pour faire cesser sa
détresse; d'ailleurs la guerre qui vient de finir a couté des sommes énormes à
la france; l'année courrante est plus couteuse qu'une année de guerre, parce

---

53. For an instance where Doniol omitted a vital part of a document which part
dulled the edge of French idealism and even loyalty, see my *Hussey-Cumberland
Mission and American Independence* (Princeton University Press, 1931), pp. 119,
185–92.

qu'il faut desarmer et solder tous les comptes; et il n'est malheureusement que trop évident que tout cela ne peut se faire que moyennant des emprunts. Vous avez M. trés lumineusement expliqué les verités à M^r. Morris, et ce surintendant verra par l'expérience, que vous ne l'avez point trompée. On murmurera probablement en amèrique, les partisants de L'ang^{re}. s'efforceront de nous d'écrier: mais c'est un mal auquel nous ne saurions remédier; d'ailleurs nous n'avons jamais fondé notre politique à l'égard des Etats-unis sur leur reconnaissance: ce sentiment est infiniment rare entre souverains, et les républiques ne le connoissent point. Ainsi, M. tout ce que nous avons à faire à l'égard des Amèricains, est, comme vous l'observez très bien, de laisser les choses suivre leur mouvement naturel; de ne point nous écarter de la marche noble, franche et desintéressée que nous avons tenüe jusqua present à l'égard des américains; de les bien observer dans toutes leurs demarchés, et, si nous ne pouvons les dériger d'apres les grands principes qui ont servi de base à notre alliance avec eux, de prendre à tems les mesures nécessaires pour n'etre point les duppes de leur ingratitude et de leur fausse politique.

L'existence future du Congres, M, presente d'importantes question à discuter, et je prévois qu'il se passera quelque tems avant qu'elles soient décidées. je pense comme vous, que le conservation du Congrès nous conviendroit; mais ce qui nous convient peut être davantage est que les Etats-unis ne prennent point la consistance politique dont ils sont susceptibles, parceque tout me persuade que leurs vües et leurs affections seront bien versatiles, et que nous ne pourrons point compter sur eux si jamais il nous survient de nouvelles distractions avec l'ang^{re}. Du reste, M, ce que je viens de dire n'est qu'un aperçu qui m'est personnel: j'ai d'autant moins aprofondi la matière, que tel que puisse être le resulte des reflexions les plus mûres, je juge que quand même nous le voudrions nous sommes sans moyen pour influer sur les arrangements domestiques des Etats-unis, et qu'en tout état de cause nous ne pourrons qu'etre spectateurs tranquils de comotions que leur constitution et leur raports intérieurs pourront éprouver.

Les limites, M, auxquelles l'ang^{re}. a consenti du côté du Mississippi, ont dû causer quelquétonnement en Amérique; car on ne s'etoit sûrement pas flatté que le ministère anglais iroit au delà des versants [54] de la chaine de montagnes qui borde les Etats unis pour ainsi dire depuis l'ohio jusqu'à la georgie. quoiqu'il en soit l'avantage qui resulte de là pour la Rep. américaine est plus idéal que réel; en effet la plûpart des peuples indiens placés entre les Etats-unis et le Mississippi sont des sauvages indépendants et sur lesquels la cour de Londres n'avoit que des prétentions très illusoires ou au moins très équivoques; d'ailleurs, l'ang^{re}. en cedant la navigation du Mississippi, a donné ce qui ne lui appartenoit plus: il est de principe que les rivières appartiennent à ceux à qui appartiennent les bords; or l'Espagne étoit, à l'epoque du 30 9bre maîtresse des bords du Mississippi au moins depuis Natchès jusqu'à son embouchure dans le golfe du Mexique, et S. M. C. a été maintenüe incommutablement dans cette propriété par les préliminaires

54. The words *des versants* are omitted by Doniol.

signés le 20 Janv. il resulte de là, M, que l'angre. a cédé aux Américains un etre de raison ou plutôt une source de querelles avec l'Espagne, et qu'ils ne pourront point, malgré leur traité, naviguer dans les parties inférieures du Mississippi sans le consentement de la Cour de Madrid.

Je ne sais pas, M, comment on a pû imaginer que les limites accordées aux américains du côté de l'ouest, nous avoient donné de l'humeur, et que nous avons tâché d'engager le ministère Bque. à les restreindre. Ce qu'il y a de très certain est que j'ai constamment ignoré l'état de la négotiation entre les commissaires anglais et américains; que dans un entretien que j'ai eu avec M. Adams, si je ne me trompe, au commencement de 9bre ce plénipre ne m'a dit que des choses très vagues sur les limites du côté du nord sans faire mention de celles de l'ouest et que je n'ai été instruit que par la lecture des articles provisionales.

Il est vrai que M. Jai ayant entamé une négociation avec M. le Cte d'Aranda relativement aux limites des Etats-unis du côté du Mississippi, et ne pouvant tomber d'accord avec cet ambassadeur, invita Mr. de Rayneval d'aplanir les difficultés qu'il rencontroit, et que celui ci lui addressa, au moment de son départ pour l'angre., un mémoire qui démontroit que ni les amèricains ni les Espagnols navoient de droits sur les peuplades qui habitent entre les apalaches et le Mississippi; mais cet écrit n'exprimoit que l'opinion personnelle de Mr. de Rayneval comme il en a prevenu Mr. Jay, ainsi il ne pouvoit être considéré que comme non existant relativement au ministère du Roi. J'entre dans ce detail, M, parceque j'ai lieu de regarder Mr. Jay comme l'auteur des insinuations qui doivent avoir été faites au Congres pour nous rendre suspects, et que je juge devoir, à tout événement, vous mettre en état de les détruire: pour vous fournir toutes les armes dont vous pourrez avoir besoin pour remplir cette tàche, je vous envoye copie du mémoire de Mr. de Rayneval, ainsi que de la lettre dont il l'a accompagné en l'envoyant à Mr. Jay.

Quant à l'article des pêcheries nous en avons toujours dit notre sentiment avec la plus grande franchise: vous pourrez, M, vous en convaincre si vous voulez bien reprendre la correspondance de M. Gerard. Il y a une diférence entre établir des principes et exprimer des voeux: nos voeux ont de tout tems été pour les américains, mais nos principes ont condamné leurs prétentions; au surplus en quel tems les avons nous manifestés? c'etoit lorsque nous avons vû l'etat de Massachusset disposé à mettre la paix et l'indépendance au prix du droit de pêcher sur les côtes de Terre-neuve, Mais notre opinion ne pouvoit pas influer sur les négociations, puisque nous n'en connoissions point les détails, et qu'elles ont été terminées de la manière la plus brusque, la plus inopinée et, je puis le dire, la plus extraordinaire.

Cette derniére circonstance, M, a dû nous affecter vivement, parcequ'elle étoit un manquement de procedé et d'egards dont il existe peu d'exemples, et nous n'avons jamais douté que le Congrès ne partageât notre opinion à cet égard. L'intention où cette assemblée a été de servir contre ses representants a paru au Roi la satisfaction la plus complete, et S. Mte. contente de cette démonstration, a fort aprouvé les soins que vous avez pris pour empêcher que ses plaintes n'eussent des suites fâcheuses pour les plénip^res^ américains: il faut croire que l'admonition qu'ils auront probablement recüe leur fcra sentir la nécessité de mettre dorénavant plus de mesure et d'égards dans leur demarches. Je puis même vous dire que j'ai depuis quelques tems lieu d'etre satisfait de leur conduite. Mais je suis fort en doute sur les principes de M^r^. Adams et Jay; il me revient à leur égard des notions qui confirment ce que vous m'avez mandé du contenu de leurs dépêches. Leur jalousie contre M^r^. Franklin est leur principal mobile; elle les irrite et les aveugle au point qu'ils ne rougissent point de dénoncer ce ministre comme vendu à la france et de rendre notre politique suspecte. Mais j'ai trop bonne opinion de la pénétration et de la sagesse de Congrès pour supposer que malgré l'ostracisme qui y règne, il ne soutiendra pas un homme qui a rendu les services les plus importants à sa patrie, et qu'il ne rejettera pas avec mépris les insinuations que l'on pourra lui faire contre les principes et les sentiments de S. M^té^. J'aprends que M^r^. Franklin a demandé son rapel, mais que le Congrès n'a pas encore prononcé sur sa demande. Je desire qu'il la rejette du moins quant à présent, parcequ'il seroit impossible de donner M^r^. Franklin un successeur aussi sage et aussi conciliant que lui; d'aileurs je craindrois qu'on ne nous laissât M. Jay, et c'est l'homme avec qui j'aimerais le moins traiter d'affaires; il est égoiste, et pas trop accessible aux préventions, et à l'humeur. Au reste, M, tous ces détails sont pour vous seul; vous n'aurez aucun usage à en faire, parcequ'en voulant servir M^r^. Franklin nous courrions le risque de lui nuire en donnant un lüeur de vraisemblance aux insinuations mensongères de ses collegues; cependant la reserve que je vous recommande, ne doit pas vous empêcher de rendre justice à sa loyauté et à la constante sagesse de sa conduite lorsque l'occasion s'en presentera naturellement.

Je suis étonné, M, que le Congrès ait revoqué en doute la nécessité de ratiffier le traité provisionel fait avec le Cour de Londres: cet acte seul peut corroborer la signature des plenip^res^. et donner au traité le forcee exécutoire. J'ignore si ceux ci l'ont reçu: leur silence me fait présumer qu'il ne leur est pas encore parvenu. Ils sont occupés de leur traité définitif; mais la négociation est, par le fait du plenip^re^. anglais, dans un etat de langueur qui va incessament nous causer beaucoup d'embarras; en effet, nous sommes, aussi bien que l'Espagne, d'accord sur tous nos faits, de manière que nous sommes en état de signer: les hollandais vont incessament être dans la même position; aussi nous sommes arrêtés uniquement par le traité amirician. Si ce cas arrive nous aviserons aux moyens de parer à cet inconvénient, le Roi persistant à ne vouloir terminer que conjointement avec ses amis.

Les plénip^res^. américains m'ont consulté relativement à la médiation des deux Cours ip^les^: je leur ai observé que ces deux Cours n'ayant jamais offert leur médiation au Congrès il pouvoit ou reclamer ou s'en passer. Je ne sais pas encore à quel parti ils jugeront à propos de s'arrêter: selon moi la plus simple sera de traiter sans aucune intervention étrangère.

Vous êtes porté à croire, M, que c'est la cour de Londres qui a préparé le raprochement qui vient de s'opérer entre celle de Lisbonne et les Etats-unis, mais je n'ai aucune notion propre à étayer votre opinion à cet égard et je suis persuadé que les seules circonstances ont determinés le Ministère Portugaise à rechercher les Américains.

Nous sommes fort occupés, M, de tout ce qui est relatif à notre commerce avec l'amérique, et nous sentons plus que jamais la nécessité de lui accorder des encouragements et des faveurs. Le Roi vient d'ordonner une diminution de droits sur les sels de Marenne, et j'ai lieu de croire que la même opération aura lieu à l'egard des eaux de vie. D'un autre côte S. M^te. a déclaré l'Orient port-franc: c'est l'endroit que les américains ont toujours desiré de préférence à tous les autres. Le point le plus dificile à fixer ce sont les longs crédits dont les negt^s. américains ont besoin: l'administration n'y peut rien: la confiance seul pourra déterminer nos negt^s à se livrer à ceux d'amérique.

4. Canada and the Peace Settlement of 1782-83

IN VERSAILLES a century and a half ago they put pens to the most important diplomatic document in the history of Canada and of the United States.[1] The peace settlement of a hundred and fifty years ago was a major European disposition, nay, it was a global arrangement of which the Anglo-American relations, however important for Canada and the United States, were only a part. A study of the treaty of peace between Great Britain and the United States cannot be complete without relating it to the diplomacy of the other belligerents, France, Spain, and the Netherlands; and the armed neutrals, who included the mediating neutrals, Russia and the emperor. Practically all of Europe, except Turkey and some of the small Italian states, was thus concerned. To summarize much of these diplomatic complications in one sentence,[2] without further analyzing them here, we may say that French

1. The preliminary articles of the peace between the United States and Great Britain, recognizing American independence and setting the boundaries between that republic and the remaining British dominions in North America, were signed on Nov. 30, 1782, to go into effect only when articles of peace should be agreed upon between France and Great Britain. On Jan. 20, 1783, French and Spanish plenipotentiaries agreed to preliminary articles of peace between those allied belligerents respectively and Great Britain. Hostilities ceased on that date. Then the American articles automatically took effect. The war was over, although negotiations between British and Dutch delayed the signature of the definitive articles of the general peace until Sept. 3, 1783.

Historians have already devoted so much attention to the Anglo-American phases of this peace settlement that it may require some hardihood again to review a subject which has elicited so much erudition. But despite the microscopic treatment which these negotiations have received, new material is now available. In addition to the well-known sources, the recently published *Correspondence of King George the Third,* ed. Sir John Fortescue, the Spanish archives, examination of the records of the French Foreign Office without relying too much on the selections presented by Doniol, another perusal of the Shelburne Papers in the William L. Clements Library, Ann Arbor, Mich., and some study of the vast mass of various original pieces, transcripts, and facsimiles now collected in the Clements Library and the Library of Congress have provoked this attempt to deal afresh with a subject of persistent interest.

2. A complete documentary history of these peace negotiations and their ramifica-

Read at the 1932 meeting of the American Historical Association. Published in *Canadian Historical Review, 14,* no. 3, 1933.

approval of the terms of peace rested on France's rather incompatible obligations to her two separate allies: independence for the United States, Gibraltar for Spain. Independence, which meant splitting apart the rival British Empire, revenge for 1763, was the principal French objective; but Spanish aid in the war had been extravagantly purchased with the promise of at least Gibraltar and Minorca for Spain, and if possible Florida, even Jamaica. Spain had captured Florida and raided British territory as far north as Michigan. In 1782 Spain wanted to perfect her title from Florida to the Great Lakes. She had also captured Minorca, but notwithstanding a formidable siege she had not been able to possess herself of Gibraltar.

Must Gibraltar go to Spain, according to the letter of the secret Franco-Spanish alliance, before the war could end? What were to be the boundaries of the independent United States to the north, and to the west? The questions became delicately interrelated, not only to themselves, but to the significance of Canada in the peace settlement.

To divorce these two questions as much as possible and to play the one ally against the other, Vergennes adroitly turned the Anglo-American negotiation into a channel of its own. It was British strategy to seduce the Americans into a separate peace, and a consequent violation of their French alliance, by playing on their fears that, with independence accomplished in fact, France might keep them in the war indefinitely in pursuit of exorbitant demands of Spain and France in Europe, Asia, and Africa.[3] Vergennes, we repeat, shrewdly divined this, and met it by deflecting the Americans into separate discussions with England—to which they took quite willingly—where France would not be present openly to discountenance their demands. At the same time it was his plan to keep the United States tied up with the general negotiations, and to have any settlement go hand in hand with a general European settlement and be dependent upon it.[4] He had already caused the American Congress to put its peace envoys under his advice and control.[5] In the final negotiations the only *sine*

---

tions would require at least a dozen stout printed volumes of the type of F. Wharton's *Revolutionary Diplomatic Correspondence of the United States*. The mere compilation of it would be the work of years which should absorb the exclusive attention of a trained scholar with assistants.

3. *Correspondence of George the Third, 5,* 448.

4. Lord John Russell, *Memorials and Correspondence of Charles James Fox* (4 vols. London, 1853–57), *1,* 360; Arch. Aff. Etrang., Espagne, vol. 607, f. 135 (Stevens transcripts), Vergennes to Montmorin, May 31, 1782.

5. Arch. Aff. Etrang., Correspondance Politique, États Unis, vol. 15, Vergennes to La Luzerne, no. 14, March 9, 1781; ibid., vol. 17, La Luzerne to Vergennes, no. 147, June 11, 1781.

qua non of their instructions of June 15, 1781,[6] was absolute independence, and specific injunction to follow the advice of the French court on other points of the peace. For desirable boundaries Congress referred them to previous instructions to John Adams of August 14, 1779, which had indicated: on the south the northern boundary of Florida based on the parallel of 31 degrees; on the west the Mississippi; on the north a line from the intersection of the northern boundary of New York at the St. Lawrence straight to Lake Nipissing and thence to the source of the Mississippi. "Although it is of the utmost importance to the peace and Commerce of the United States that Canada and Nova Scotia should be ceded," these first instructions read, "and more particularly that their equal common right to the Fisheries should be guarantied to them, yet a desire of terminating the war hath induced us not to make the acquisition of these objects an ultimatum on the present occasion."[7] If the American commissioners, Franklin, Jay, Adams, and Laurens should obey the letter of their instructions, Vergennes thus had the Americans under his thumb, a predicament against which Jay and Adams protested manfully to Congress.[8] And he might make intimations to Spain, even to the enemy Great Britain, as to how far he would support American demands over and above the bare independence guaranteed by the Franco-American alliance.

In these negotiations between Great Britain and her former colonies the principal issue turned out to be the boundary of the independent United States. The French alliance had stipulated that the boundaries were to be fixed *at the peace,* no peace to be made without the consent of both allies. For the future of their new nation the Americans were eager to make good the claim to as much territory as possible, certainly the maximum prescribed by Congress. The boundary question, then, made Canada a great stake in the negotiations. If Canada had been included within the territory of the United States, the other questions which assumed importance after the American commissioners lost sight of Canada would never have existed. Presumably there would have been left no fishery question, no Mississippi question, no question of indemnities either way. The problem of peace would have reduced itself to a simple recognition of the independence of the United States (including Canada) with removal of British troops from the continent, repatriation of prisoners, and the payment of pre-war civil debts.

Such a simple solution was, of course, a great dream. With the attitudes which we now so positively know that Spain and France enter-

6. *Journals of the Continental Congress, 20,* 651–52.
7. Ibid., Aug. 14, 1779, *14,* 959–60.
8. Wharton, *Revolutionary Diplomatic Correspondence, 4,* 716; *5,* 373, 703, 838.

tained toward American expansion in the West, it is difficult to imagine that Great Britain would actually relinquish her hold on that continent, particularly if she knew that not even her European enemies favored such a withdrawal. The Mississippi Valley was also a stake, and that fertile basin was more important to the new republic than the more northern stretches of Canada. Here, indeed, is a reason which caused the American plenipotentiaries to abandon their earlier ambitions for Canada.

Three of the four American commissioners for making peace looked forward at the beginning of the diplomatic contacts to the acquisition of Canada. John Adams had Canada in mind when Lord Shelburne released Henry Laurens from the Tower and sent him to The Hague to sound out his colleague on terms of peace.[9] The idea had also struck Laurens as something possible of attainment; Adams reported to Franklin that Laurens believed that many people in England favored it. Canada had been an interesting subject and favorite object to Franklin since 1776. In his early conversations with the agent of Lord Shelburne, Richard Oswald, Franklin had confidentially suggested its cession. So far as records remain to show, he did not reveal to his colleagues that fact. Nor are we able to state that he divulged to them, or to Vergennes, the outline of terms of peace which he disclosed secretly to Oswald as late as July, after John Jay had arrived at Paris on June 23, and while an attack of influenza prevented him from taking his part in the negotiations. Franklin's terms, orally delivered in response to Oswald's repeated importunities for them, and never mentioned in Franklin's dispatches, were: as "necessary" articles—independence, boundary settlement with Canada restricted to its limits before the Quebec Act of 1774, freedom to fish on the grand banks of Newfoundland and elsewhere; as "desirable" articles—indemnification to the American people for private property destroyed by British forces, a public acknowledgment of the wrong done to America, equal trading privileges for American and British and Irish ships in each other's ports, and finally, "the giving up of every part of Canada." [10] Franklin urged that the cession of Canada would make a perfect peace of "sweet reconciliation."

It has often been related how the unambitious Oswald was immediately impressed with the idea of giving up every part of Canada. He was willing to pay that price to be able to make a separate peace with

9. Ibid., 5, 543.

10. Russell, *Memorials and Correspondence of Charles James Fox, 4,* 239–41: Oswald to Shelburne, Paris, July 10, 1782.

the "colonies." He relayed Franklin's suggestions sympathetically to Shelburne.

Would it be necessary for British statesmen to offer this extravagant price to cut off the United States, as they wished to do, with a separate peace? If any responsible British statesman, in the secret chamber of his mind, ever considered this mighty sacrifice of all of North America to save the rest of the empire in both Indies, there has been left no record. It became unnecessary. Before British victories at Gibraltar had decided the fate of the Franco-Spanish negotiations, the bitter exigencies of which only could have pressed for the relinquishment of Canada to seduce America, John Jay recovered from the influenza and took his active part in the discussions at Paris with Oswald. Jay's reaction to the apparition of Spanish territorial designs in the Mississippi Valley, and his suspicions that France supported those designs and secretly undermined other cherished American objectives, wiped out of the diplomatic picture even any putative chance which historians may have felt that Franklin had, in the earlier phases of the negotiation, to get all of Canada.

From the day he first set foot on European soil, Jay had developed a distrust of European diplomacy. The inquisitiveness of Conrad Alexandre Gérard, the French diplomatist who was returning from America on the ship that bore Jay from his homeland to Spain, about the content of his fellow-traveler's instructions; the equivocal attitude of Spain during Jay's unsuccessful mission there; her refusal to recognize American independence; the secret Spanish treaty that had bound France to stay in the war until Gibraltar should be retrieved by Spain, the terms of which Jay either positively knew or accurately surmised—all this made him fear that France would try to make American independence wait for, and depend on, non-American objects. After Jay's arrival at Paris other grounds for these suspicions confirmed them.

The first of these was the studious avoidance by the Shelburne Cabinet, in contrast to the policy of Charles James Fox, secretary in charge of foreign affairs in the preceding Rockingham Cabinet, of any act or phrase which might imply a recognition of the American colonies as an independent nation. The first instructions of the Continental Congress had very pointedly forbidden any negotiation with Great Britain without a preliminary recognition of the United States as sovereign, free, and independent.[11] Concerning the point of independence Frank-

11. In the instructions to the first peace plenipotentiary, John Adams, dated Aug. 14, 1779, Congress had laid down this principle in those words. In the revised instructions of June 15, 1781, which controlled the actual negotiations, independence

lin, in his confabulations with British agents, had insisted that there must be a recognition by Great Britain of the United States preliminary to any negotiation of a treaty. Shelburne from the beginning had been well aware of this American condition. Upon Laurens's return from The Hague, Shelburne, while still what we may call Home and Colonial Secretary in Rockingham's Cabinet, noted in a letter to the King that the American prisoner had come back from Holland "changed, touchy and conceited, and vulgarly so. . . . An acknowledgment of independence must be a preliminary and no proceeding without France." [12] At this time Charles James Fox was openly advocating such a preliminary recognition. Fox's peace commissioner to treat with France and Spain, Thomas Grenville, had given Franklin assurance to this effect. But it was Shelburne, whose agent was Oswald. When Rockingham died, Shelburne became Prime Minister. Fox resigned. Shelburne significantly continued to keep the American negotiation of Oswald under the control of the new Home Secretary (who also administered what was left of the Colonial Department), Thomas Townshend. With the change of ministry Franklin scented a change in policy on independence. He immediately repudiated any points of peace that he had suggested in confidence to Oswald. "I did understand from him [Grenville]," Franklin now took care to state in writing to Oswald, July 12, without any reference to the memorandum of "necessary" and "desirable" terms which he had recently read to the anxious Scot, "that such an acknowledgment [of independence] was intended before the commencement of the treaty; and until it is made and the treaty formally begun, propositions, and discussions, seem, on consideration, to be untimely, nor can I enter into particulars without Mr. Jay, who is now ill with the influenza." [13] There is no record of his having again broached the subject of Canada, or, indeed, having outlined any further program of peace.

In view of much historical discussion about Franklin later having been overpersuaded by the advice of his colleagues, Jay and Adams, to negotiate the preliminary terms of the treaty somewhat independently of French advice, it behooves us at this point to note that: (1) Franklin had confidentially suggested the cession of Canada without any con-

---

remained a *sine qua non*, everything else, even boundaries, being left subject to modification upon advice of the French court. See *Journals of the Continental Congress*, at relevant dates.

12. *Correspondence of George the Third*, 5, 487: Shelburne to the king, April 24, 1782.

13. Russell, *Memorials and Correspondence of Charles James Fox, 4*, 253.

sultation with Vergennes; (2) Franklin himself mentioned the detailed American terms of peace to Oswald quite independently of Vergennes, and carefully covered up his own responsibility for them, so that the only record we have is Oswald's report of what he could remember of the memorandum as it was read to him; (3) Franklin made it plain that there must be a preliminary acknowledgement of American independence before the treaty; (4) he reserved any commitment pending conference with Jay (whom Oswald had not yet seen). Is it not plain that the Sage of Passy, whom historians have unanimously represented as overpersuaded by his more youthful and downright colleagues, had been the first to take the path, which all presently trod, to a violation of their instructions to proceed only under the full confidence and advice of the French minister?

Shelburne's stratagem in avoiding any recognition of the United States was quite apparent when a copy of Oswald's intended commission arrived on August 8. It betrayed the phraseology of the actual document, which still had to await the official signatures and seals to be imposed by certain British dignitaries loitering in the country.[14] By this advance text of a still unsigned commission, Oswald was to be empowered to treat, agree, and conclude with "any commissioner or commissioners, named or to be named by the said colonies or plantations, or with any body or bodies, corporate or politic, or any assembly or assemblies, or description of men, or any person or persons whatsoever, a peace or truce with the said colonies or plantations, or any of them, or any part or parts thereof." [15] This commission, so carefully worded as not to recognize any plenipotentiaries of the United States, and even to divide the "colonies" among themselves, was a sufficient explanation that the Shelburne ministry was not yet ready to recognize independence before the treaty should be signed. Oswald's accompanying instructions confirm this construction.[16] In case no treaty should result, having employed such cautious powers as these the British government would have acknowledged nothing.

Franklin, Jay, and Vergennes discussed the text of Oswald's commission on August 10. Vergennes, very anxious to have the several peace

14. Wharton, *Revolutionary Diplomatic Correspondence*, 5, 651: Franklin to Vergennes, Aug. 8, 1782.

15. It was actually the text of an order from the king to the attorney general, directing that a commission be made out in the phraseology therein laid down. It is printed in ibid., 5, 613.

16. A draft is in Shelburne Papers, *71*, 1–18. Lord Fitzmaurice in his *Life of William, Earl of Shelburne* (London, 1875–76) fixes date of instructions as July 31, 1782.

negotiations "tied together," [17] though proceeding separately and slowly (for Spain's sake), advised accepting the commission as soon as the authenticated document should arrive. So long as independence was made an article of the final treaty, he said, the form of the commission was unimportant.

He turned to Franklin and asked what he thought about it. The doctor said he thought it "would do." Jay said that he did not like it. He thought it best to proceed cautiously.[18] When presently the two Americans were alone after the interview, he argued vigorously with Franklin, pointing out that it was the interest of France to postpone any British recognition of American independence until French views and the objectives of Spain could be gratified by a peace. This explained Vergennes's advice, he said. Jay thought that the French minister was trying to slow up the Anglo-American negotiations on that ground. Franklin believed on the other hand that he was trying to hasten them, professed confidence in Vergennes's loyalty, and—may we be permitted to smile at this—Franklin cited the instructions of Congress to take French advice! [19]

Jay now worked on Oswald. He convinced the English plenipotentiary of the utter impossibility of ever treating with Great Britain on any other than an equal footing.[20] He made him understand that this meant a preliminary recognition of independence irrespective of the treaty, as Grenville had promised in May—indeed, we may add, as Franklin had been careful to require.

When all this was reported to London, the Cabinet, on August 29,

17. Arch. Aff. Etrang., Correspondance Politique, États Unis, vol. 21, f. 145: "Réflexions sur l'Acte du 25 Juillet, 1782."

18. Vergennes concluded after this interview that it was agreed that the Americans should deliver a copy of their full powers to the English commissioner, and that notwithstanding his solicitations they should defer entering into the subject until he produced the original of his commission. See Hale, *Franklin in France*, 2, 155: Vergennes to La Luzerne, Versailles, Aug. 12, 1782. In the Franklin Papers, no. 2594, in the Library of Congress is a formula to this effect conveyed from Vergennes in Lafayette's handwriting, with provision for complete renunciation of independence by the first article of the treaty.

19. This is taken from Jay's account of the interview in Wharton, *Revolutionary Diplomatic Correspondence, 6*, 15.

20. "I told him plainly that I would have no concern in any negociation in which we were not considered as an independent people" (ibid., *6*, 16: Jay to Livingston, Nov. 17, 1782). Oswald describes these interviews with Jay and Franklin in great detail in his letters, with attached minutes, from August 7 to 21. See transcript of "Oswald's Journal" in Franklin Papers.

agreed in principle to such a preliminary recognition as the two Americans had demanded, that is, if such should prove to be unavoidable and provided the Americans would agree at the same time to make peace on the basis of the four "necessary" articles of Franklin's proposed terms.[21] This was rather a neat surrender. If Franklin and Jay had stood firm and promptly followed up the advantage they had gained, by the former's subtle suggestions and the latter's firm insistence, an advance recognition of independence would have been wrung from George III and preliminaries of peace could have been signed before news reached England, on September 30,[22] of the failure of the great assault on Gibraltar, an event which naturally raised British hopes and heightened British tone. Such preliminaries would have given the United States all that it secured under the articles of November 30—if we assume that Franklin's overlooking of fish-drying privileges on shore in Newfoundland would have been caught up—and these without mention of the status of private debts to British creditors, or of British Loyalists in America; all these, of course, without Canada and Nova Scotia. All of Canada was not one of the "necessary" terms. But Canada before the Quebec Act of 1774, as envisaged in those "necessary" terms, would have restricted Britain to the lower St. Lawrence valley and the then wild regions north and west of Lake Nipissing. Some curious delays now veiled this possibility to the American commissioners, so that they never knew of it.

The dispatches containing the new British offer reached Paris on September 4. In the accompanying instructions [23] Townshend bade Oswald, before showing his hand and agreeing to independence preliminary to any treaty, at least to make an effort to persuade the Americans to accept independence as the first article in the treaty, offering as an inducement peace on the basis of Franklin's "necessary" articles pure and simple.

The fact that Oswald consumed a few days with this preliminary sparring delayed matters just enough for the appearance of a memorable conjuncture of circumstances which gave the negotiation quite another turn and prolonged it two months more. If the Americans, particularly Jay, had known of the August 29 decision of the Cabinet, they

21. *Correspondence of George the Third, 6,* 118.

22. Ibid., 138.

23. P.R.O., F.O., 95, 511 (Stevens transcripts), Memorandum, enclosed in Townshend to Oswald of Sept. 1, 1782; Shelburne Papers, 70, f. 188, Townshend to R. Oswald, Sept. 1, 1782.

need not have had another worry. To the advantage of Great Britain, it was never revealed to them because of this delay and what happened during it.

This group of new developments afforded more grounds for Jay's mounting suspicions. He had been holding informal discussions with Aranda, the Spanish ambassador at Paris, looking toward a possible treaty with the United States. Jay presently broke off these conversations when it became apparent that Aranda had no power to treat with him or even formally to recognize him as a plenipotentiary of the United States. Aranda had revealed Spain's intention of claiming a wide domain east of the Mississippi, and north to the Great Lakes. Further, Rayneval, Vergennes's confidential secretary, had supported, with the sanction of Vergennes, the Spanish pretentions. Vergennes now dictated to Rayneval to submit to Jay a written memorandum, long since so notorious, dated September 6, suggesting a compromise boundary which would have dropped British territory down to the Ohio (the boundary of the Quebec Act) and have pushed the limits of the United States far east from the Mississippi.[24]

Rayneval's sinister boundary compromise, vouchsafed as his "personal ideas," further fired Jay's suspicions of French straightforwardness. At this very time the British succeeded in putting into his hands the translated copy of a dispatch intercepted from Barbé Marbois, secretary of the French legation at Philadelphia, to Vergennes. It argued against support to the American fishery claims and boundary pretentions. We may dismiss the doubts which have been expressed as to the authenticity of this dispatch by saying that a copy of the original exists in the archives of the French Foreign Office. And then Jay learned, on September 9, that Rayneval, shortly after delivering to him the memorandum on boundaries, had left on an unannounced and unexplained trip to England, where no French diplomatist had set foot since hostilities began. In concealing this mission Vergennes was keeping as much from the Americans as they were presently to hide from his knowledge. Jay concluded that Vergennes was working with France's

24. There is a threefold record of these conversations. Jay's account is printed in Wharton, *Revolutionary Diplomatic Correspondence, 6,* 28–31. Aranda's account is set forth in great detail in his dispatches to Floridablanca, nos. 2207, June 1; 2241, July 6; 2266, Aug. 10; 2274, Aug. 18; 2290, Sept. 1; 2301, Sept. 15; 2314, Oct. 4, 1782; with enclosures of billets (as Aranda studiously called his notes with Jay arranging for interviews), and a lengthy diary of the conversations (now printed by F. Yela Utrilla, *España ante la independencia de los Estados Unidos.* The evolution of this compromise suggestion is illustrated by an historical memorandum composed by Rayneval which has been discussed in Chap. 3 of this volume, pp. 40–110.

Spanish ally and the common enemy to talk down the American claims as to boundaries and fisheries. He was now positive that the French wanted to postpone any recognition of American independence until the final articles of a general peace among all the belligerents, which would include a settlement of the question of Gibraltar and other non-American affairs. The historian, today privileged to consult without restriction the full diplomatic correspondence of Great Britain, France, Spain, and the United States, the private papers of Lord Shelburne, and the recently printed *Correspondence of King George the Third,* cannot dispute the accuracy of Jay's conclusions.[25]

To block these French designs Jay hastily made a countermove which he revealed neither to the French Court nor to his own colleague Franklin. He dispatched a messenger—none other than one of Shelburne's confidential informants in Paris, a Benjamin Vaughan, who had connections by marriage with Henry Laurens—to say to the British ministry what he and Franklin already had given Oswald to understand:

25. Floridablanca had urged France that it was important to defer recognition of American independence until the general peace, lest the colonies, being satisfied, might drop out of the war before Gibraltar was secured for Spain. Vergennes assured the Spanish minister that he was delaying the negotiation with England until the fate of Gibraltar should be determined. He did not pledge himself to block any premature recognition of American independence—that he could not guarantee—but it is significant that he argued with the Americans that it was proper to include actual recognition by Great Britain in the final peace, rather than to insist upon a preliminary recognition. See Arch. Aff. Etrang., Correspondance Politique, Espagne, vol. 608, ff. 15, 113, 119 (Stevens transcripts), Montmorin to Vergennes, July 8, Aug. 12, 1782, Vergennes to Montmorin, Aug. 10, 1782; and Wharton, *Revolutionary Diplomatic Correspondence, 6,* 17, Jay to Livingston, Nov. 17, 1782. It is vastly more significant that he revealed to the British peace commissioner at Versailles, Fitzherbert, that he had so advised the Americans! This, reported Fitzherbert to the Secretary for Foreign Affairs, Lord Grantham, "certainly evinces clearly that Your Lordship was founded in your suspicion that the granting Independency to America as a previous measure is a point which the French have by no means at heart, and perhaps are entirely averse from." See P.R.O., F.O., France, vol. 558, 165, and 257 (Stevens transcripts): Fitzherbert to Grantham, nos. 54 and 55, Aug. 29 and Sept. 11, 1782.

The French archives show that the real reason for Rayneval's sudden unannounced trip to London was to confirm the accuracy of a set of British peace proposals which the paroled prisoner of war, the Comte de Grasse, brought from Lord Shelburne, representing (inaccurately) that statesman as willing to cede Gibraltar to Spain. Rayneval's own report, printed by Doniol in *Revue d'histoire diplomatique, 6* (1892), 62–89, and the printed *Correspondence of George the Third, 6,* 125, show that he took occasion to deprecate American pretentions to fisheries and western boundaries.

Later Vergennes importuned John Adams to do something for the British Loyalists. Wharton, *Revolutionary Diplomatic Correspondence, 5,* 872.

that there could be no treaty without a commission to Oswald empowering him to treat with commissioners of the United States of America; that as Great Britain could not conquer the United States it was to her interest to conciliate them; that it was the interest of France, but not of England, to postpone the recognition of American independence to the final treaty. It followed that "it was the obvious interest of Britain immediately to cut the cords which tied us to France, for that, though we were determined faithfully to fulfil our treaty and engagements with this court, *yet it was a different thing to be guided by their or our construction of it*"; that the United States would not stay in the war to satisfy the demands of Spain; that America would not make peace without the fisheries—such a settlement would irritate and inflame, and lead to resentment and consequent restraints on British commerce; that it was to the advantage of Great Britain to see the United States extend to the Mississippi, because by arranging free commerce by the St. Lawrence and Mississippi Great Britain would have as a market for her manufactures the multiplying populations of American citizens who would take up these hinterlands.[26]

One consistent effort of British diplomacy had been to bring the Americans to a separate peace, or at least to separate preliminaries. It was now apparent that the latter was distinctly possible.

Oswald's earnest letters and Vaughan's reports convinced Shelburne that it would be desirable to alter the commission as Franklin and Jay required [27] if the negotiation with them were to go forward. Shelburne's Cabinet already on August 29 had voted *if necessary* to recognize American independence unconditionally before the treaty and irrespective of further negotiations. It was easy to vote the lesser concession now that the Americans had failed to insist on the more radical recognition. Immediately it was resolved, on September 19, "that a new Commission be made out under Your Majesty's Great Seal for enabling Mr. Oswald

26. Ibid., *6*, 17: Jay to Livingston, Nov. 17, 1782.

27. Hale, *Franklin in France*, 2, 131–44: Oswald to Shelburne, Sept. 10, 11, 1782, enclosing draft of a letter by Jay of Sept. 10, representing that the Americans could not treat except on equal terms, etc. See also F. Wharton, *Digest of the International Law of the United States* (Washington, 1887), *3*, 945–49; *Correspondence of George the Third*, *6*, 128. Doubt that Vaughan had anything to do with influencing the decision disappears after reading the Townshend Papers in the Clements Library. See particularly Ashburton to Shelburne, Spitchwell Park, Sept. 16, 1782; and Shelburne to Townshend mentioning important "private letters from Paris" presumably by Vaughan, dated Wycombe, "Monday." The inquisitive reader might also consult P.R.O., F.O., France, vol. 558, f. 257 (Stevens transcripts), Fitzherbert to Grantham, no. 55, Sept. 11, 1782, received Sept. 14; and Franklin Papers, transcript of "Oswald's Journal," Oswald to Shelburne, Sept. 10, 1782.

to treat with the Commissioners appointed by the Colonys, under the title of Thirteen United States, inasmuch as the Commissioners have offered under that condition to accept the Independence of America as the First Article of the Treaty." [28] This curious language, still dragging in the word "colonies," was by no means a clear-cut recognition of American independence. It is doubtful whether even Oswald's new commission [29] to treat with the commissioners of the United States of America constituted such a recognition beyond recall. Though Europe generally took it as a recognition, the British government (with the possible exception of the lord chancellor) did not so admit,[30] and it is quite probable that, if the ensuing negotiations had broken down, Great Britain would have maintained obstinately that she had never recognized the independence of the United States.[31] In demanding and accepting Oswald's new commission Jay and Franklin deserted that irreproachable high ground on which they had previously stood for an explicit and unequivocal preliminary recognition of American independence, as the first instructions to Adams had required, a recognition which on August 29 the Cabinet had been willing to vote. Into this concession they had been hastened by their reaction to Rayneval's conduct. If it had not been for their quite understandable suspicions, the American commissioners might have forced Oswald's hand, under his instructions of September 1, before the first good news from Gibraltar reached London on September 30. In that case they could have had their preliminaries two months earlier and without mention of Loyalists or debts and on the basis at least of Franklin's "necessary" articles. These articles would have limited Canada to the Nipissing line

28. *Correspondence of George the Third, 6,* 131.

29. Text in Wharton, *Revolutionary Diplomatic Correspondence, 5,* 748.

30. "They came unanimously and without hesitation to the resolution which is contained in the minute which I enclose to your Lordship; it not appearing to them that the making such an alteration in the commission was of importance enough to put a stop to the negotiation or that it by any means amounted to a final acknowledgment of Independence, it only giving them during the negotiation the title which they wished to assume" (Townshend Papers: Draft of letter of Townshend to the lord chancellor, Sept. 20, 1782). Like the lord chancellor, Lord Ashburton was also distant in the country and could not attend; but in a letter of Sept. 16, to Shelburne from Spitchwell Park, he expressed some doubt whether the altered commission would not constitute an express recognition; and further doubt whether it were right for the executive to acknowledge independence without a treaty (ibid.).

31. George III warmly expressed himself against William Pitt's speech on the American preliminaries, in which he assumed that independence was now irrevocable, even though the present treaty proved abortive (*Correspondence of George the Third, 6,* 175).

—that is, present Quebec and northward, and Canada north of a line from the southernmost corner of Lake Nipissing to the source of the Mississippi. As it was, the negotiations were delayed unfruitfully and Franklin and Jay had by no means secured even what they thought they were getting—an advance recognition of American independence.

Vaughan returned to Paris, on September 27, with the courier who brought the new commission for Oswald.[32] The negotiations now proceeded in regular form at a lively pace. On October 5, they took shape in a set of preliminary articles of peace, drafted by Jay with Franklin's approval, to take effect only upon the signature of preliminary articles between Great Britain and France.

This draft [33] consisted of Franklin's "necessary" articles, plus a new article stipulating freedom of navigation and commerce by both parties on the Mississippi River, *and elsewhere throughout all their dominions on the terms of nationals.* They laid down this boundary for the United States: on the north, what we shall call the Nipissing line; on the west, the Mississippi; on the south, the line along the 31st parallel; on the east, the Atlantic Ocean including for the United States all islands lying within twenty leagues of the coast; on the northeast, Oswald prevailed finally on Jay and Franklin to leave this boundary open to be fixed by a joint commission after the war. Except for this concession on the northeast, this line of October 5 conforms precisely to the original instructions issued on August 14, 1779, by the Continental Congress to John Adams.[34]

Jay correctly divined that if the British could be sure of commercial vestibules to the American western country,[35] they would accept these boundaries. Quebec would be one of these side-door entries; Florida could be another. He therefore urged on Oswald that England instead of Spain ought to retain West Florida at the final peace, and might well

32. Wharton, *Revolutionary Diplomatic Correspondence, 6,* 11–49, Jay to Livingston, Paris, Nov. 17, 1782; Fitzmaurice, *Life of Shelburne, 3,* 183.

33. It is printed under date of October 8 in Wharton, *5,* 805. Fitzmaurice dates it October 5. It was conveyed by Oswald to Townshend on October 7. An endorsed addendum concerning a possible joint commission for the northeast boundary seems to have been added on the seventh.

34. The various boundary proposals have been worked out with great care and thoroughness on Mitchell's *Map of North America* of 1755 (the map actually used by the negotiators) by C. O. Paullin, *Atlas of the Historical Geography of the United States,* published jointly by the Carnegie Institution of Washington and the American Geographical Society of New York (Baltimore, 1932), 52–54, plates 89, 90.

35. Dr. Gerald S. Graham has emphasized the value of this inland trade in the views of the Shelburne ministry, in his scholarly essay, *British Policy and Canada, 1774–1791, a Study in 18th Century Trade Policy* (London, 1930), pp. 46 ff.

remove her troops from New York and other American ports, still occupied, in order to reconquer that province. He argued to Vaughan [36] what he had persistently said to Oswald: that the United States, by consenting to the mutually free navigation of its several lakes and rivers, would afford for Great Britain an inland navigation to a great free market—in a way, a monopoly—for the sale of European manufactures to the anticipated millions of English-speaking settlers in the western hinterlands of the new American republic. By luring the British into West Florida as an easy entrance to the trade of the American West, Jay hoped to keep the Spanish away from the east bank of the Mississippi above West Florida. Incidentally he saw a means of enticing the British garrison away from the still occupied Atlantic seaports. Here, too, is the explanation of the separate article in regard to West Florida in the actual preliminaries.[37]

It is fortunate for the United States that Jay's preference for Great Britain instead of Spain as a neighbor in West Florida—a preference which apparently commended itself to Franklin [38] also—came to naught in the final peace. As Vaughan shrewdly pointed out to Shelburne, West Florida would have been a focus of expansion into the interior territory to the north and, in the circumstances of its possession by Great Britain, "the River St. Lawrence, the Lakes, the Ohio, and the Mississippi will form a trading coast at the back of the American Colonies, somewhat as the Atlantic does at the front." [39] Anyone familiar with the process of American territorial expansion since 1783 will realize the estoppel which Jay's invitation and Franklin's complaisance in regard to Florida signified. Luckily this particular provision of the projected preliminaries presently dropped out because the provision for mutual free navigation and commerce *everywhere,* on the basis of nationals in each other's dominions, collided with the British navigation laws. Meanwhile Jay had practically won his point of ejecting Spain from the West by committing Great Britain to the Mississippi as a boundary.

But where was Canada now? Historians have wondered whether John

36. Wharton, *6*, 31; Hale, *Franklin in France*, *2*, 170. G. W. Brown has a cogent analysis of a phase of this point in "The St. Lawrence in the Boundary Settlement of 1783," *Canadian Historical Review*, *9* (Sept. 1928), 223–28.

37. Lord Shelburne later expressed himself to this effect to Rufus King, United States minister to Great Britain, in 1802. See C. R. King, ed., *Life and Correspondence of Rufus King* (New York, 1894–1900), *4*, 93.

38. M.H.S., *Proceedings*, 2nd series, *17*, 421: Vaughan to Shelburne, Paris, Dec. 4, 1782.

39. Ibid., 409: Vaughan to Shelburne, Paris, Oct. 3, 1782.

Jay, by insisting on a revision of Oswald's commission, delayed affairs
until the news of the successful defense of Gibraltar had raised the
tone and stiffened the terms of the British. They have asked whether
by this insistence John Jay upset the American applecart in which
Franklin had been so patiently and so gently trundling Canada. The
answer is that Canada tumbled out of that vehicle when Jay was wheel-
ing it singlehanded during Franklin's indisposition, sometime between
the arrival of Oswald's revised commission, on September 27, and October 5 when Jay and Oswald agreed on the draft of preliminary articles.
Though favorable, but not conclusive, news from Gibraltar had reached
London as early as September 30,[40] there is no indication that Oswald
availed himself of it as an argument to exclude Canada from the treaty.
Oswald and Jay discussed Canada,[41] but it was not included in Jay's
draft of October 5, except insofar as it was delimited by the Nipissing
line. Jay had become so frightened at Spain's claims to the east bank
of the Mississippi and France's apparent support of them that he let
Canada go and promised free navigation and trade into the American
West from the Mississippi River and from the St. Lawrence–Great
Lakes system. He did this in order to use Great Britain as an aid in
pushing Spain out of the West and, to make sure at least of the minimum boundary which Congress had instructed the commissioners to
get. Learning of Spain's territorial pretensions in the Mississippi Valley,
and France's attitude toward them, Jay was anxious to secure a title
from Great Britain which would help protect the American West.
Leaving Canada and Florida in British possession was to him a cheap
price to pay for this. After the Jay draft of October 5, which Oswald reported [42] had the approval of Franklin, we hear no more of Canada.[43]

40. *Correspondence of George the Third, 6,* 138. This must be news of the failure
on September 13 of the great bombardment by the Chevalier d'Arçon's floating
batteries, which marked the climax of the besieging efforts. Lord Howe's fleet definitely relieved Gibraltar on Oct. 13, 1782. See C. Fernandez Duro, *Armada Española*
(Madrid, 1901), 7, 319, 331.

41. Hale, *Franklin in France,* 2, 169: Oswald to Townshend, Paris, Oct. 2, 1782.
In a postscript to this letter Oswald says: "I hope to get clear of the advisable articles
[i.e., Franklin's "advisable" articles, as distinguished from his "necessary" articles],
but as to some of those in my instructions I doubt I shall not [sic] succeed."

42. P.R.O., F.O., France, vol. 557, f. 665 (Stevens transcripts): Oswald to Townshend, Oct. 8, 1782.

43. When Adams, Franklin, Jay, and Laurens dispatched to Livingston the signed
preliminary articles, on Dec. 14, 1782, they reveal the motive for relinquishing
Canada: "We knew this court and Spain to be against our claims to the western
country, and having no reason to think that line more favorable could ever have
been obtained, we finally agreed to those described in this article; indeed they appear

The British, on their part, and despite French hints, were willing to yield to the American demand for the Mississippi, because it meant separate provisional preliminary articles of peace with the United States which might be an entering wedge in the Franco-American alliance.

It is not within our compass to follow closely the remainder of the negotiations. The British victory at Gibraltar stiffened the tone of British diplomacy everywhere. Shelburne sent over Strachey, an undersecretary in the Home Office, to bolster Oswald's front. It is a familiar chapter of history, how they finally succeeded in changing the Nipissing line to the actual boundary of today; and how they moved the boundary of Nova Scotia from the cartographically definite St. John to the uncertain St. Croix. Certainly Strachey deserves well of Canada for that; but back of him Canada owes her actual boundary to John Jay and to Sir George Eliott, the doughty defender of Gibraltar. The Americans finally offered to Oswald and Strachey a choice between the 45th parallel from the St. Lawrence to the Mississippi and the present peaceful boundary of river and lake. Shelburne took the river-and-lake line.

The American commissioners did so well with boundaries in these historic negotiations, they secured so much more than their government would have accepted had it been pushed on that point,[44] that the astonished twentieth-century student is almost ready to believe they might have secured anything miraculous in the shape of a continental domain. But, seriously, was there ever a chance of their getting all of Canada not to mention Nova Scotia?

I believe not. The American plenipotentiaries dreamed of it. Franklin tried for it. Oswald himself, had it been within his power, might have yielded it. But Shelburne never approved such a cession, so far as we know, though he did read some of Oswald's statements without comment. He apparently knew less about Canada than about any other portion of the British Empire. He was certainly prodigal of boundary lines. He might have accepted readily enough the Nipissing line, before the relief of Gibraltar. Even after that he might have accepted the line of 45 degrees which the Americans offered as alternate to the river-and-lake line: 45 degrees from the St. Lawrence all the way west, which would have left southern Ontario within the United States. Perhaps it is only accidental that he did not choose that interesting

to leave us little to complain of and not much to desire" (Wharton, *Revolutionary Diplomatic Correspondence, 6,* 132).

44. See note at end of this chapter.

line, which would have brought within the future Dominion of Canada in exchange for southern Ontario: northern Michigan, the northern third of Wisconsin, the northern two-thirds of Minnesota; and, perhaps, in the future course of western expansion, North Dakota with a strip of South Dakota, Montana, northern Idaho, Washington, and Puget's Sound, and even a slice of Oregon, including the whole Columbia River, profoundly altering, perhaps removing entirely, the whole Oregon question. But there is no evidence that Shelburne ever considered giving up all of Canada, or Nova Scotia. England, beleaguered as she was, was never pressed as far as that. After Rodney's great victory, known in London on May 18, 1782,[45] Great Britain could have had a general peace at any time by the relinquishment of Gibraltar and the recognition of the independence of the United States. There was talk now and then of yielding the rocky fortress, and the Cabinet was somewhat divided on the question, but I have found no evidence of any intention to lighten the sledge by throwing Canada to the wolves. Jay's prudent caution undoubtedly delayed the Anglo-American negotiations until after Gibraltar was saved, and his fear of Spain in the Mississippi Valley caused him never to try to get all of Canada, which had been in the minds of Adams and Franklin. But if Jay had thought of it, as had the other plenipotentiaries, we cannot believe that the United States could have got it. Had a choice been necessary, we may be permitted to guess that Britain would have sacrificed Gibraltar first.[46]

45. *Annual Register, 1782* (London, 1783), 25.

46. The fact that Congress repeatedly refused to adopt motions to modify the instructions to the commissioners, which stopped short of a boundary ultimatum, is pretty good proof that it would have accepted less expansive territories. La Luzerne, the French minister, successfully opposed a strong movement headed by Samuel Adams and James Lovell to alter the instructions which made the king of France *"maître de la négociation."* Though Congress never placed itself on record any more than to refuse to make boundaries or fisheries *sine qua non*, or to relieve the commissioners from French control, we have at least some significant hints that if required it would have accepted as a minimum boundary the watershed of the Appalachians (south of Pennsylvania). Gouverneur Morris (who subsequently turned out to be a notorious opponent of western expansion), although he was chairman of the committee which drafted the instructions of Aug. 14, 1779, to John Adams, has left two undated drafts in his handwriting which laid down much more meagre boundaries. The editors of the *Journals of the Continental Congress* mention one of them, found in the papers of the Continental Congress, in connection with the boundary discussions of 1779 (*Journals, 13,* 341). It indicates a western boundary which departs from the Mississippi at the Illinois to follow viâ that river to Lake Michigan and the "northern shore of the waters of Lakes Superior and Huron" thence to the Nipissing line at Lake Nipissing; this would have lopped off a big and valuable

triangle of the northwest region from the instructions finally agreed to on Aug. 14, 1779. The other draft by interior evidence was written after Oct. 18, 1780, when Gouverneur Morris was no longer a member of Congress. Sparks thought it was written in 1781. This would have accepted, if required by France, the crest of the Appalachian Mountains south of Pennsylvania and continuing along the watershed to the southern boundary of Georgia, with the back country established *if possible* as an independent Indian territory. Sparks identified the draft in Morris's handwriting and sent it to Secretary of State Daniel Webster in 1842 along with information about the celebrated "red-line map." See H. B. Adams, *The Life and Writings of Jared Sparks*, 2, 397. We print it (for Adams did not reproduce the enclosure) from Sparks's transcript found with the original letter in the archives of the Department of State by Dr. Hunter Miller:

Your knowledge of our true interests, and the instructions given to Mr. John Adams, bearing date the 14th Augt. 1779 & 18*th* Oct. 1780, will point out those things which you must endeavor to obtain in a Treaty of peace. But since circumstances may require some Alteration with respect to our Boundaries, we have thought it proper more fully to communicate to you our sentiments upon that subject.

There can be no doubt but that the territory contained within the following lines is also within the limits of the United States. Beginning at the Atlantic Ocean at the eastern boundary of the province of Maine, and running thence along the said Eastern boundary to the high grounds which divide the waters falling into the Atlantic from those which fall into the River St Lawrence thence along the said high grounds to the Head of Connecticut River—thence down the same to the latitude of forty five degrees north—thence westerly in that latitude to the river of St Lawrence—thence along the said river & lake Ontario to the mouth of Oswego or Onandaga River—thence up the same river southwardly to the latitude of forty-three degrees North—thence in that latitude along the northern Boundary of Pensilvania to the western Boundary thereof—thence along the same to the southern boundary thereof, and along that boundary Easterly to the Western boundary line of Maryland—thence to Lord Fairfax's Line—thence southwardly along that line to the high grounds which divide the waters falling into the Atlantic from those which fall into the Mississippi—thence along those grounds to the southern boundary of Georgia as settled by the proclamation in 1763—and thence along that boundary to the Atlantic.

With respect however to the Eastern boundary of the Province of Maine, as that has never yet been ascertained, we conceive it to be open to negotiation; but not so as to be carried westward farther than the river of Kennebeck.

You will perceive that the above lines exclude the fort of Niagara, and also a great part of the countries ceded by the Indians at Fort Stanwix on the fifth of November 1768, although the former was long considered to be within the bounds of New York, and much of the latter has been granted to subjects of these States by authority derived from the King of Great Britain. Our Instructions before mentioned, of the fourteenth of August, contain an extent which ought if possible to be obtained. Admitting it however to be impracticable, the next object will be to extend our boundary along the Lakes Ontario and Erie to the northern boundary of Pensilvania, so as to include the above mentioned Indian Grant, or at least so much thereof as may be contained within the following line.

Beginning where the western boundary line of Pensilvania crosses the Ohio—thence down along the Ohio to the mouth of the Great Kenhawa—thence up the Kenhawa south eastwardly to the head thereof in the Alegany Mountains. These points must be strongly contended for, and not departed from without the most evident necessity.

You must also endeavor to obtain an admission that the countries eastward of the Mississippi, and not included within the bounds of the United States, those of Nova Scotia, the Floridas or the antient boundary of Quebec, are subject to the free and independent Indian Nations—or at least as much of them as possible. This you must adjust in the best and most extensive manner which you can; but you must insist that all Fortresses on our Frontiers be demolished, and that no new ones be erected—in consideration of which you may make reciprocal stipulations. This latter point also you must not recede from, but in the last necessity.

Notwithstanding the clear rights and equitable claims of the United States, yet from a sincere desire of peace, from a thorough attachment to the principles of the alliance with his most Christian Majesty, and to evince to the whole world the moderation by which our councils are directed,—although we have every reason to hope the most favorable events from a continuance of the War, yet we will ultimately consent that the boundaries of the United States be restricted within the limits first described, provided the same shall be expressly required by our good ally the King of France, in whose friendship we have the greatest confidence. And as we are desirous on all occasions to manifest our good faith, we therefore direct you to act entirely in concert with the ministers of his most Christian Majesty—not at all doubting that you will meet with an equal return of Confidence on their part. We confide also that from the known equity of the high mediating powers, our claims will be heard examined and judged with the utmost impartiality.

Finally we most strictly command and enjoin you not to swerve from the principles of our said Alliance in any possible case.

Robert R. Livingston, elected Secretary for Foreign Affairs, on Aug. 10, 1781, over whom La Luzerne claimed a commanding influence (Arch. Aff. Etrang., Correspondance Politique, États Unis, vol. 19, f. 66, Library of Congress transcripts: La Luzerne to Vergennes, no. 191, Nov. 1, 1781), in an official dispatch to Franklin written on Jan. 7, 1782, *after Yorktown*, communicated as his personal views that great concessions if necessary might be made on boundaries. His language was loose but suggests the proposal of Morris's draft above quoted:

There is some reason to believe [said Livingston] that Great Britain considered their [British] rights in many instances as extending no further than their rights of pre-emption and protection, as may be inferred from passages in the negociations for a peace with France in the year 1761, referred to in the margin. [Wharton (*Revolutionary Diplomatic Correspondence, 6*, 89) explains here that the marginal reference is to the answer of the king to the ultimatum of France, received in September 1761, second section of eleventh article.] This suggests a new idea, which, however, I am not warranted by act of Congress in mentioning, and therefore you will only consider it as the sentiment of an individual. If the mediators should not incline to admit our claim, but determine on restricting our limits, either by the extent of our grants [state grants of land beyond the

Appalachians], the course of the mountains, the sources of the rivers, or any other of those arbitrary rules that must be sought for when solid principles are relinquished, perhaps it would not be difficult to bring them to agree that the country beyond those limits belongs to the nations who inhabit it; that it should enjoy its independence under the guarantee of France, Spain, Great Britain and America, and be open to the trade of those whose lands border upon them.

I suspect that La Luzerne may have facilitated Livingston's researches into the diplomacy of the Seven Years' War.

It should be noted that at the very time that Livingston was getting off this dispatch a committee of Congress, composed of James Lovell, Daniel Carroll, and James Madison, was drawing up a report vindicating in great detail the title of the United States to the Mississippi Valley and to the fisheries (Wharton, *Revolutionary Diplomatic Correspondence*, 5, 667; *Journals of the Continental Congress*, 23, 472–523) which report they presented to Congress on Jan. 8, 1782, where it was debated but kept in committee, rather than turned over to the Secretary for Foreign Affairs for transmission to the commissioners, as some members desired. On Aug. 20, 1782, it was resolved that "the report be committed." It was thus buried in committee never to be resurrected.

5. The London Mission of Thomas Pinckney, 1792-96[1]

THOMAS PINCKNEY, of Charleston, South Carolina, was the first minister of the United States, under the present federal government, to the court of St. James's. His appointment, in November 1791, was largely a matter of form then necessary to complete a full exchange of diplomatic representatives which had been initiated in the summer of that year by the establishment of George Hammond as first British minister in the United States. The impressive strength manifested by the government under the new Constitution destroyed the contempt with which George III's advisers had regarded the American Union ever since independence, and put an end to their refusal to lodge a representative at the American capital. The presence of George Hammond as British minister at Philadelphia in 1791 was, in fact, the first marked success of Washington's new administration in the field of foreign affairs. It had been understood that if a minister should

1. This paper is based on Pinckney's official dispatches and instructions in the archives of the Department of State. These have been studied in the light of contemporary correspondence of the British Foreign Office and of the various sources for the history of the Jay Treaty, supplementary source material which is indispensable for any thorough understanding of the Pinckney mission. I am indebted to the Carnegie Institution of Washington, Department of Historical Research, for copies and digests of the papers in the archives of the Department of State. These were made by Dr. Newton D. Mereness. For remarks on the importance of the Pinckney papers in the archives of the Department of State see A. C. McLaughlin, *Report on the Diplomatic Archives in the Department of State, 1789-1840* (Washington, Carnegie Institution, 1906), p. 11. Thomas Pinckney's letterbooks, now preserved in the collections of the South Carolina Historical Society, I have not been able to examine personally, but the librarian of the society, Miss Mabel L. Webber, has obligingly examined them for me in respect to certain points. These papers were used by Trescot for his *Diplomatic History of the Administrations of Washington and Adams,* and also by the Rev. Dr. C. C. Pinckney for his biography of his grandfather, *Life of General Thomas Pinckney,* which contains a certain number of pieces from the family papers. The biography, not the work of a professional scholar, is discursive, and written with little attention to other sources than the family papers.

Published in *American Historical Review, 28,* no. 2, 1923.

be sent to the United States an American representative would be dispatched at once to London. It was after Hammond had specifically notified the Secretary of State of this expectation [2] that Pinckney was notified of his appointment. [3]

The President's selection was an expedient one and the appointment was acceptable to Pinckney personally. [4] It gave the extreme South

2. Hammond to Grenville, Philadelphia, Oct. 28, Nov. 1, 16, 1791, P.R.O., F.O., America, 4, 11.

3. Jefferson to Pinckney, draft, Nov. 6, 1791, Jefferson MSS, Library of Congress, printed as letter sent in H. A. Washington, ed., *The Writings of Thomas Jefferson* (9 vols. New York, 1854–56), *3*, 298; but the letter actually sent was of Nov. 9. Among the Jefferson MSS is a letter of that date from the President, amiable but decided, of which the whole text is, "Enclosed is the letter to Majr. Pinckney. For the reasons mentioned to you yesterday, I prefer London to Paris for his Mission. Yrs. affect'ly." Apparently Jefferson had suggested Paris. The offer was enclosed in a letter to the postmaster at Charleston, who was requested to forward it quickly, and sent thither by sea by the hands of the young Lord Wycombe, eldest son of the Marquis of Lansdowne (Shelburne), who after visiting the northern and eastern states was now sailing for Charleston, armed with introductions from the President to the chief men of South Carolina; Jefferson MSS, Washington MSS, and Washington's letterbook, Library of Congress. Pinckney to Edward Rutledge, Nov. 24, 1791, in Charles C. Pinckney, *Life of General Thomas Pinckney* (Boston and New York, 1895), pp. 99–101; to Jefferson, accepting, Nov. 29, D.S., Dispatches, England, *3;* to Washington, do., Washington MSS.

4. According to Alexander Hamilton (J. C. Hamilton, ed., *The Works of Alexander Hamilton* [7 vols. New York, 1850–51], 7, 700), Pinckney's appointment originated in the President's own mind. This statement receives corroboration from a letter which Jefferson wrote in cipher to Short Nov. 9, 1791, secretly informing him of the offer to Pinckney, and adding, "There was never a symptom by which I could form a guess on this subject till 3 days ago," i.e., till Nov. 6, the date of the draft mentioned in the preceding note; P. L. Ford, ed., *The Writings of Thomas Jefferson* (10 vols. New York, 1892–99), *5*, 389. Washington may have seen Major Pinckney at Yorktown, though he had never met him before that (Washington to Gates, May 12, 1781, Washington MSS, B XIII), and he must have seen something of him during his fortnight's visit to South Carolina in the spring of this same year 1791. Jefferson had no personal acquaintance with him; *Writings* (ed. Washington), *3*, 298. Hammond reports to Grenville, Nov. 1, 1791, that he had been informed, through a private channel, that the President was in "some degree of indecision with respect to two of his personal friends, whom he would wish to bring forward upon this occasion"; no. 2, P.R.O., F.O., 4, 11. On Nov. 16, no. 4, ibid., he wrote that most probably the post in London had been offered to "a Mr. Rutledge of South Carolina," but the joint letter of May 24, 1791, by which Edward Rutledge and C. C. Pinckney decline Washington's offer of a seat in the Supreme Court (W. C. Ford, ed., *The Writings of George Washington* [14 vols. New York, 1889–93], *12*, 43), puts that notion out of the question. James Bowdoin the younger, afterward minister to Spain, applied for the appointment Dec. 3, too late; see his letter in Gaillard Hunt, *Calendar of Applications and Recommendations for Office during the Presidency of George*

the most important post in the diplomatic service and it sent to the British court a man who was highly *persona grata*. Pinckney was a lawyer of forty, a planter, with a good military record and one term as governor of his state to his credit. Absolutely devoid of any diplomatic experience, he was a staunch supporter of the new Constitution and had used his official influence in South Carolina to secure its ratification. As much as any American patriot could be who had nearly died of wounds received on the field of battle against the troops of George III, Pinckney was a friend of England. When his father had been colonial agent for South Carolina in London the young boy had been entered at the fashionable Westminster School, and his educational career did not end until, after his course at Oxford and year's sojourn in France, he had finished his studies at the Temple.[5] If his intellectual training and eighteen years in England did not leave him with a pleasing style, it endowed him with an appreciation of literary merit and a devotion to the classical culture which the best English minds of that day were so content to indulge. Contact with the European world, too, had served to polish the natural urbanity, social balance, and dignity which were the birthright of his name.

Pinckney accepting the offer, the nomination was laid before the Senate, with others, on December 22, and confirmed on January 12, 1792. The delay was not due to any opposition to Pinckney's name, but to a prolonged consideration of the whole matter of appointments to diplomatic service abroad.[6] He arrived in Philadelphia at the end of April and embarked at New York for his post June 18.[7]

Hammond, the new British minister, had been quick to sound out the political temper of American personalities. Because of the political intimacy which he had cultivated with Alexander Hamilton and

---

Washington (Washington, 1901), p. iv. Before Pinckney replied to Jefferson or had said anything about his appointment, some one in Charleston knew of it and, much to his vexation, gave the information to the press (Pinckney to Jefferson, Dec. 1, 1791, D.S., Dispatches, Eng., *3*). There is nothing to substantiate John Adams's capricious charge, which he later withdrew after it had been the cause of much embarrassment in the presidential campaign of 1800, that the appointment was the result of a successful intrigue of the Pinckney brothers for the place (see Pinckney's *Pinckney*, pp. 150–76).

    5. Pinckney's *Pinckney*. He returned to America in 1774, just in time to participate vigorously in the Revolution against the crown.

    6. *Writings of Washington* (ed. Ford), *12*, 96–97, 99–100; *Jefferson* (ed. Ford). *5*, 417, 421, 423, 433; Jefferson MSS; John Marshall, *The Life of George Washington* (5 vols. Philadelphia, 1804), *5*, 370 n.

    7. *Writings of Jefferson*, *5*, 512. Hammond to Grenville, July 3, 1792, no. 28, P.R.O., F.O., *4*, 16; Ternant to Dumouriez, June 20, A.H.A., *Annual Report*, 1903, *2*, 133.

other leading Federalists he had exceptional facilities for this. It should be remembered that in 1792 Hamilton was Anglophile enough to propose in cabinet meeting an Anglo-American alliance, one of the purposes of which would be to secure from Spain the opening of the Mississippi River to the joint navigation of Americans and Canadians.[8] Hammond soon became confident that Pinckney could be counted among the "party of the British interest," i.e., those who opposed any specific discriminations on British commerce and who advocated generally closer relationships between the two countries on the basis of the status quo.

> Those persons of this country who are desirous of promoting and preserving a good understanding with Great Britain are extremely well satisfied with Mr. Pinckney's appointment, as they consider the circumstance of his education at Westminster School, and of his having passed a great part of his life in England, as having a natural tendency to inspire him with a predilection for the country, and a desire of rendering his conduct satisfactory.

This was Hammond's information privately conveyed to Grenville soon after he learned of the new appointee.[9] "A man of mild and liberal manners and perfectly untinctured with any sort of prejudices," [10] was his judgment after meeting Pinckney just before the latter sailed for England.[11]

In the paucity of specific duties prescribed for the minister, Jefferson's instructions indicate readily enough what the student of the period knows, that all the matters of major importance were then being handled by the Secretary of State personally in his negotiations with Hammond. Pinckney's chief duty was that of expressing "that spirit of sincere friendship which we bear to the English nation." In all transactions with the Foreign Secretary he was directed to conciliate that official's good disposition by whatever in language or attentions might tend to that effect. He was particularly recommended to seek

8. A.H.R., 27, 423.

9. Hammond to Grenville, private, Philadelphia, Jan. 9, 1792, Hist. MSS Com., *The Manuscripts of J. B. Fortescue, Esq., Preserved at Dropmore*, cited as *Dropmore Papers*, 2, 250.

10. Same to same, June 8, 1792, no. 21, P.R.O., F.O., 4, 15.

11. "We have a new American Minister, Mr. Pinckney, an old friend and brother-Westminster of mine, whose manners and temper exactly qualify him for the place he has taken. I have known him above thirty years, and do not know a more worthy and excellent man." J. B. Burges, undersecretary for foreign affairs, to Lord Auckland, British minister at The Hague, private, Whitehall, Aug. 10, 1792. Robert Eden, ed., *The Journal and Correspondence of William, Lord Auckland* (4 vols. London, 1861–62), 2, 431.

the liberation of American commerce from restrictions imposed on it within British dominions, especially the West Indies, and to seek the adoption of some arrangement for the protection of American seamen from the press-gangs of British ports.[12]

The first of these subjects was soon absorbed by the Hammond-Jefferson negotiations in the United States and does not appear to have been touched by Pinckney at London. The second, regulation of impressment, furnished the burden (aside from routine representations) of Pinckney's light task in the months previous to the outbreak of the war between France and England. The small importance attached to the mission at first, aside from that of properly fulfilling a required formality, is testified by the meagerness of Jefferson's dispatches. Such few letters as were written in the year 1792 and the early months of 1793 confine themselves almost altogether to petty routine claims, or, for example, the purchase of copper for the United States mint, and the hiring of European technicians to superintend the new coinage. Negotiations between the United States and Great Britain in those months were important but not lodged in Pinckney's care.

Pinckney reached London August 3, 1792, and learned that Lord Grenville, Secretary of State for Foreign Affairs, was in the midst of his honeymoon. The new minister was presented to the king by Henry Dundas, Home Secretary, who reported to Grenville: "He is rather a gentlemanlike man, and the king's conversation to him was highly proper." [13]

Very discreetly Pinckney delayed disturbing the delights of Grenville's country sojourns until a more propitious moment. "I am told at the office," he wrote, "that any matter of business which I may have to transact with my Lord Grenville will be immediately communicated to him by their messenger—but I fear that if I were to occasion his leaving home under his present circumstances he might not bring with him that temper of mind in which I hope to meet him at a future day." No one can accuse the mild-tempered [14] South Carolinian of

12. Jefferson to Pinckney, June 11, 1792, *Writings of Jefferson* (ed. Ford), 7, 104.

13. Dundas to Grenville, Aug. 8, 1792, *Dropmore Papers*, 2, 299. Pinckney was received at the Foreign Office by his "old acquaintance and schoolfellow," Burges, who had taken pains first to call on him. Grenville saw him briefly Aug. 4, but was leaving town. Burges introduced him to Dundas. Pinckney to the Secretary of State, Aug. 7, 1792, Dispatches, Eng., *3*.

14. It should be remembered that Pinckney's urbanity had not remained unruffled during his military campaigns. By the resolute method of cutting down its leader with his sword he had, single-handed, quelled an incipient mutiny while captain of infantry in 1776. Pinckney's *Pinckney*, p. 49.

a diplomatic blunder in these the first days of his new career.[15]

The propriety of the king's conversation "to" the American minister was distinctly chilly.

> The only circumstance worth remarking in my conference with the King was that lord North's rope of sand appeared not to have been entirely effaced from his Majesty's memory, which I infer from his mentioning the differing circumstances of the northern and southern parts of our country as tending to produce disunion. I declined entering into any discussion on the subject, observing only that we agreed very well at present and hoped a continuance of the same disposition.

Pinckney faithfully attended the royal levees along with the other members of the diplomatic corps. George III never failed to hold a few moments' conversation with him "on the weather or other topic equally important," but carefully eschewed political subjects. The court and diplomatic corps generally seemed to hold the United States, by virtue of the example of the American Revolution, somewhat responsible for the convulsions brought on Europe by the French upheaval. Consequently Americans were not considered desirable associates. This Pinckney gathered from the foreign ministers with whom he was able to cultivate any degree of intimacy. "At the same time they have been polite enough to make themselves a proper distinction between the mode of conducting the revolutions in the two countries," he recorded.[16]

Pinckney's representations concerning impressments [17] give us a glimpse into the beginning of this notable and insoluble issue. Since the war of American independence there had been little occasion for the press-gang in British ports. But during the Nootka crisis of 1790 a press of seamen occurred to man the new naval armaments intended for a Spanish war. Several American sailors were then taken in British ports. Release of these men was eventually secured, through the intervention of American consuls and of Gouverneur Morris, who was then on an informal mission to the British Foreign Office as the personal agent of President Washington.[18] Some of the men thus reduced to

15. Pinckney to the Secretary of State, Aug. 29, 1792, Dispatches, Eng., 3.

16. Same to same, Dec. 13, 1792, ibid., printed in Trescot's *Diplomatic History*, pp. 86–87, and in Pinckney's *Pinckney*, pp. 103–05.

17. Mahan's classic historical summary of impressments does not mention Pinckney's diplomacy on this subject. See Alfred Thayer Mahan, *Sea Power in Its Relation to the War of 1812* (2 vols. Boston, 1905), *I*, 114–28.

18. *A.S.P., F.R., I*, 124.

servitude found their liberty only after barbarous treatment on board British men-of-war. The expense and inconvenience to the government in liberating the impressed sailors, and possibly the indefensible character of the outrage, had impelled Jefferson to urge the adoption of some arrangement to prevent impressments whenever another European crisis should occur.[19] The question of impressment in this instance was limited to British territorial waters. In the discussion which Morris had with the Duke of Leeds in 1790 Morris had suggested that American sailors be furnished with certificates of citizenship as a protection. Jefferson repelled this proposition and suggested that British press-gangs might be permitted to board an American ship in British port only when the crew of that ship was ascertained, by a previous visit of a strictly limited number of officers, to have more than an agreed proportion of hands to her tonnage. He actually authorized Pinckney to agree to an article of convention on such a basis,[20] a principle which, to any disciple of Mahan, would appear a most supine solution. Jefferson did not attempt to deny the domestic jurisdiction of England within any of her own waters into which American ships might choose to sail; he even admitted the propriety of impressment of surplus crews in case an American captain should refuse to deliver up the men stipulated by the press-captain.

Pinckney, with unusual discernment for a man of his limited European experience, immediately on his arrival foresaw the possibility of England's being involved in the Continental war then raging. Because of this, he believed it desirable to adjust the problem of impressment before any new occasion for sudden expansion of the British navy should occur.[21] Conferences with Lord Grenville on the subject and written representations dragged along without result.[22] When the war with France did in fact begin, impressments commenced anew. They continued with ominous frequency. Soon British captains ventured to take alleged British subjects from the decks of American ships without careful distinction between territorial waters and the high seas. In February 1793, Pinckney was referred by Grenville to Phineas Bond,[23] who was delegated, without powers, to discuss the subject. Bond suggested the old idea of furnishing in the United States certificates of citizenship to American seamen setting forth on the seas.

19. Jefferson to Washington, Feb. 7, 1792, *Writings of Jefferson*, 6, 388.
20. Jefferson to Pinckney, June 11, 1792, *Writings of Jefferson*, 7, 104–07.
21. Pinckney to Jefferson, Aug. 29, 1792, Dispatches, Eng., 3.
22. Same to same, Dec. 13, 1792, Jan. 3, Mar. 13, 1793, ibid.
23. Consul at Philadelphia, then on a vacation in England.

I told him the inconveniences arising from this procedure [reports Pinckney] would be equally felt by both nations, for that we should expect their seamen to be furnished with similar testimonials when they came to our ports to those they expected our mariners would bring to theirs; he asked in what instance it could become necessary (alluding I presume to our not being in the habit of impressing). I answered that unless we could come to some accomodation which might insure our seamen against this oppression measures would be taken to cause the inconvenience to be equally felt on both sides.[24]

Soon afterward Bond was sent back to the United States as a consul-general. Pinckney wrote in April:

I have no hope of obtaining at present any convention respecting seamen, as lord Grenville now says it is necessary for them to make enquiries as to some points in America, which object is given in charge to Mr. Bond.[25] The impressment on the present occasion has not been so detrimental to our trade as it was on former occasions, though several instances of hardship have occurred which I have endeavor'd to remedy but not always with succcss.

Jefferson regarded this failure to be of a "serious nature indeed" but decided "to hazard no further reflection on the subject through the present channel of consequences [sic]." [26]

Pinckney was henceforth reduced to the procedure of protesting all cases of impressment which came to his attention and of supplicating for the immediate release of American seamen concerned. At first his numerous notes to this effect were met with a certain accommodation. Americans, when proved to be such to the satisfaction of the Admiralty, were let go. At first, too, some moderation was manifest as to impressments from American ships. Toward the end of 1793 and in the spring of 1794 Pinckney's applications met with less success. Fewer Americans succeeded in proving their citizenship. Uniformly the answer to the minister's notes was that they had been referred to

24. Pinckney to Jefferson, Mar. 13, 1793, Dispatches, Eng., 3.
25. "You mention that when proposing arrangements for the regulation of impressments . . . you were told that Mr. Bond was to make enquiries here for a final arrangement. He has been long arrived, and we have never heard of any enquiries." Jefferson to Pinckney, Sept. 11, 1793, D.S., Instructions to U.S. Ministers, 2, 16.
26. Jefferson to Pinckney, June 2, 1793, *Writings of Jefferson*, 7, 359.

the Admiralty for decision. Correspondence then passed back and forth with great delay between the various departments—a veritable "circumlocution office." Meanwhile the impressed American sailor might be sent off on a long voyage to the East Indies or exposed to the hazards of warfare against an enemy for whom he bore no enmity. Apparently this mode of procedure was not insupportable to the government. It was tolerated, except for written protests, to the extent that when Jay was sent to England on his special mission in 1794 to prevent war, if possible, the matter of impressment was not mentioned in his comprehensive instructions. Except for Pinckney's protests these unfortunate sailors were abandoned to the atrocious British practice and left to prove their own citizenship as best they could. Many an American boy seeking adventure in a voyage at sea ended it in the forecastle of a British man-of-war.

Through the spring and summer of 1794 and throughout the Jay negotiations (which reached no settlement of the impressment issue), Pinckney peppered the Foreign Office with applications for the release of impressed Americans. His notes, some of them several times repeated, were solemnly referred to the Admiralty with instructions for release "if the men should be proved to be Americans." Months often passed before action was taken, if taken at all. "Transmitted to the Admiralty with the usual letter" is the form of indorsement one reads on the back of such a note.[27] To Pinckney's request that some "permanent arrangement" for the prevention of such injustices be made, Grenville replied curtly that there was no disinclination on the part of his government to accede to any permanent arrangement "which shall not be so open to abuse, as to produce to the Public Service of this Country an Inconvenience far exceeding that of which Mr. Pinckney complains on the part of the American States." [28]

For a short period after the signature of Jay's Treaty the press-gangs were more circumspect. "Mr. Jay and I continue to be treated with great Attention by the Members of the Administration," Pinckney reported on February 2, 1795 (the treaty was signed on November 19, 1794), "and I have lately been more successful than heretofore in obtaining the Liberation of our impressed Mariners." [29] In April of that year he left London as a special plenipotentiary to negotiate a treaty with Spain, turning over affairs of the legation to his sharp-quilled

27. Pinckney to Grenville, Oct. 28, 1794, P.R.O., F.O., 5, 7.
28. Grenville to Pinckney, Mar. 17, 1794, Dispatches, Eng., 3.
29. Pinckney to the Secretary of State, Feb. 2, 1795, ibid.

secretary, William A. Deas, as chargé. Relaxation of impressments now proved to have been only temporary and not practiced at all in the West Indies.[30] Deas continued to send in applications for release, as well as protests at the arbitrary conduct of British cruisers in violation of the maritime principles written into the new treaty.[31] Even the propitiatory Jay after his return to the United States felt impelled to write Grenville a polite private note mildly suggesting that the severity of impressments was greatly injuring the work of conciliation recently accomplished by the treaty.[32]

Though Jefferson had not approved the principle, the practice developed of American sailors using their own initiative to secure certificates of citizenship from the United States consuls abroad, or from a magistrate either in the United States or in foreign countries.[33] On

30. For impressment of 76 Americans at Hispaniola and protest of the American chargé at London, see Deas to Grenville, Nov. 5, Dec. 22, 1795, P.R.O., F.O., 5, 12.

31. For correspondence between Deas and Grenville see P.R.O., F.O., 5, 12.

32. Jay to Grenville, New York, May 1, 1796, P.R.O., F.O., 5, 16.

33. Following are copies of (a) a certificate of citizenship granted by the American consul at London, (b) a certificate of citizenship by voluntary deposition before the lord mayor of London:

(a) "Joshua Johnson, Esq., Consul to the United States of America for the Port of London, etc., etc. Witnesseth, that the Bearer hereof (a description of whose person is on the other side), to wit, *Richard Weaver, a black man,* appears by affidavit made this day by *William Blen,* before *James Robinson, Esq.,* one of His Majesty's Justices of the Peace, and witnessed by *Lieutenant W. I. Stephens,* to be a Subject of the United States of America, as such being liable to be called upon in the service of his country, must not, on any Pretense whatever, be interrupted in his lawful business, by Sea or Land, either by Impress Masters, or any other Officers, Civil or Military. London, *21 July* 1791, JOSHUA JOHNSON." (Note: a printed form, italics and small capitals indicating the words filled in by handwriting.)

(b) "These are to Certify to those whom it may concern *that Captain Samuel Chancery of the Ship Hercules of Portsmouth in New Hampshire* came before me, *Paul Le Mesurier, Lord Mayor of the City* And voluntarily maketh Oath and sayeth, to the best of his Knowledge and Belief, that *Robert Darling* (the description of whose Person is at the Bottom) *is a Native and Citizen of the* United States of America, and that he is actually one of the crew of the American Ship *Hercules* as a *Seaman*—SAM'L CHANCERY. And the said *Robert Darling* Likewise maketh Oath and sayeth, that he is a Native of America, and a Citizen of the United States of America and that to the best of his Knowledge and Belief he was born in *Portsmouth* County, in the State of *New Hampshire,* and that he is one of the Crew of the Ship *Hercules.* ROBERT DARLING. Sworn before me, London July 27, 1794, PAUL LE MESURIER, Mayor. Description: The said *Robert Darling* is about *5* Feet *4* Inches high *brown* Complexion *brown* hair, *and* about *28* years of age." (Note: as in a.) These forms were enclosed in Pinckney to Grenville, Oct. 28, 1794, P.R.O., F.O., 5, 7.

May 28, 1796, Congress enacted a law allowing but not compelling such "protections" to be taken out.[34] After this the Admiralty refused to liberate any American who could not produce such a protection.[35] Jefferson's fear that this would be the case if the policy of issuing certificates should be adopted was thus promptly realized. Nor did a "protection" necessarily protect. There was the suspicion that it might have been fraudulently secured, and it frequently was.[36] Again, a "natural-born" British subject might have become a naturalized American citizen, even if English judges would not admit that possibility.

Pinckney returned to London in April 1796, and immediately took up again the matter of impressments. He continued to apply for release of American citizens who could establish their identity, thus practically [37] acquiescing in the procedure of the Admiralty and only trying to secure quicker justice under the Admiralty's definition of it. In going over his correspondence with the Foreign Office from January 1 to July 1, 1796 (including some letters of Deas), the writer has enumerated fifty cases in which Pinckney or Deas requested the release of American sailors. Such cross-correspondence as is on file at the For-

34. Act of May 28, 1796, *Statutes at Large, 1*, 477.

35. Nepean to Hammond, Admiralty Office, Apr. 2, May 7, 1796, P.R.O., F.O., 5, 16.

36. "I have this day received from Mr Moore, Information that the Seamen who deserted from His Majesty's *Africa* and *Thistle* in Boston Harbour, have entered on Board the *Hunter* and *Washington* East Indiaman, fitting out at New York, and on Board the East India Ships, the *George Washington* and *General Greene* now getting ready for Sea at Providence in Rhode Island: And that the Seamen who deserted from the *Nautilus* are also in the American East India Trade. One of our Seamen who has entered on Board the Ship *General Greene,* gave this Intelligence; His name is Thomas McCartney, who declared half the Crew would be British Sailors. The Crew will be furnished with a Species of Passport declaring the respective Seamen to be native American Citizens. These Passports my Lord are, for the most part, Magisterial Attestations, in some instances having the Solemnity of a Corporate Seal. No sort of Reliance is to be placed upon them, nor, I should presume, will any thing be deemed competent to operate as a protection, short of a Certificate of Birth to be attested by His Majesty's Consuls within the United States." Bond to Grenville, Philadelphia, Nov. 25, 1795. It is significant that the above-quoted extract was conveyed to the Admiralty. See also letter of Admiralty Office to Grenville, May 12, 1795, P.R.O., F.O., 5, 12, transmitting letter of collector and comptroller of port of Glasgow, telling of British seamen "clandestinely employed" on American vessels, including several men who left the village of Dunoon for service on an American ship, the captain of which was offering wages as high as six pounds sterling a month.

37. Pinckney's statement of the case was that "if the seamen impressed should not appear *bona fide* subjects of His Majesty . . . they be released and such measures adopted as to prevent similar conduct in the future." Pinckney to Grenville, May 14, 1796, P.R.O., F.O., 5, 16.

eign Office between that department and the Admiralty shows that in thirty-five of these cases investigation was requested by the Foreign Office. Refusal by the Admiralty to release on ground of insufficient proof is reported in sixteen cases. Liberation in the case of three men is to be noted. Frequently the investigations of the Admiralty were only perfunctory and discontinued on the least excuse. One of the impressed men, for instance, was said by Pinckney to be in the hospital. When the Admiralty "got around" to look up the case the man was found not to be in the hospital as reported. The case was straightway dropped.[38] One wonders whether he had died or had been sent back to his ship.

In another instance one of the several men whose release was requested in the same note was found to be on board a ship that had recently sailed from Plymouth. Investigation was promised upon the return of the war-vessel, but we are left to wonder what was done with the other men whose names were included in the list affected by the forced departure of one of them.[39] On another occasion a man was held because he could not answer to the satisfaction of a British officer questions of geography pertaining to America.[40] Sometimes the captain of the British ship acknowledged the men to be Americans but refused to let them go without instructions from the Admiralty, which he never received.[41] Though there is evidence of fraud in the matter of protection papers and though not infrequently the British seaman, attracted by high wages and better living conditions as well as immunity from war risks, may have deserted into the American merchant marine, there are also several cases recorded, at the beginning of the war at least, where British subjects bound by contract in American crews deserted to enlist on board a man-of-war. The deserter's ship was then distrained to collect his back-wages which the American captain had refused to pay on the breaking of the contract.[42] Some American sailors are recorded by the Admiralty as having accepted the king's bounty and regularly enlisted. They were never released. Enough has been said to show that the system of impressment in British ports tolerated by the United States government was, with

38. Nepean to Burges, Admiralty Office, Mar. 11, 1795, P.R.O., F.O., 5, 12.
39. Same to same, Mar. 10, 1795, ibid.
40. Letter of Capt. Haworth, Kingshead, Mar. 7, 1794, enclosed in letter of Joshua Johnson (American consul at London) to Pinckney, contained in Pinckney to Grenville, Mar. 17, 1794, P.R.O., F.O., 5, 7.
41. Pinckney to Grenville, Oct. 15, 1794, P.R.O., F.O., 5, 7.
42. Pinckney to Grenville, Dec. 31, 1792; to the Secretary of State, Feb. 5, 1793, Dispatches, Eng., 3.

all its qualifications and whatever defense it had from the point of view of military necessity on the part of England, an outrageous enslaving of American citizens. The United States could not secure its rights because it had no navy to enforce them. It could not retaliate by impressment of British sailors, for it had not enough warships on which to put the British subjects against whom the reprisals might be made.

Upon Pinckney's return to London from Madrid he had before him a perfect case of impressment on the high seas with sufficiently explicit documentary evidence to enable him to support it without question of fact. In a note to Grenville shortly before his departure home at the end of his mission Pinckney entered into a lengthy discussion of the principles of impressment, drawing a sharp distinction between impressment within British territorial waters and on the high seas. It might be a right, however impolitic, he said, for Great Britain to require proofs of citizenship from foreigners within her jurisdiction; but when men were impressed on the high seas it was immaterial whether they had such proofs so long as the ship itself was American. There was no right by which a man could be forcibly taken from an American ship on the high seas.

> No article of the existing Treaty [Jay's] requires, neither does any Maxim of the Law of Nations impose upon Americans the hard Condition of not being able to navigate the Seas without taking with them such Proofs of their being Citizens of the United States as may satisfy the Officers of any Power who may judge it expedient to stop and distress their Vessels on this Account. And as it is a fair Argument to illustrate a Position by reversing it, it may be asked what Sensations it would excite here if the Commanders of American armed Vessels should take upon themselves to stop British Vessels on the High Sea and impress into their Service such of the Mariners as had not with them full Proof of their being His Majesty's Subjects.[43]

Grenville denied the validity of any such distinction. He declared that the principle that the jurisdiction of a state over a ship is supreme till the ship enters a foreign port had never been recognized by the British government nor by the best authorities on international law.

> It was unknown to the practice or pretentions of all civilized nations in former times. On the contrary it appears perfectly clear

43. Pinckney to Grenville, June 16, 1796, Dispatches, Eng., *3*.

that the belligerent has a right to visit neutral vessels upon the high seas to take therefrom all goods belonging to such subjects of the enemy (a right inconsistent with every idea of territory) and to take the subjects of the enemy, found on board, as prisoners of war—it has also the right to take its own subjects found on board of a foreign vessel on the high seas, for all the purposes for which they are liable to be taken by any act of its legal power and discretion. . . . [This right Grenville declared was being used cautiously and discreetly. It would not be relinquished.] Instances . . . unquestionably have occurred of seamen being detained as British subjects, who were actually citizens of the United States, but there is little doubt of their being but rare. If any mode can be devised by the mutual concurrence of both countries of identifying *native* [italics inserted] citizens of the United States and thereby exempting them from impressment, His Majesty's Government will most cheerfully accede to it. In the meantime until such an arrangement can be made, it will always be ready to receive with attention every application relating to the impressment of persons alleged to be Americans, and to liberate all such as may be proved of that description.[44]

This was the last act of Pinckney as American minister to the court of St. James's. When he departed the issue of impressment was left clearcut. Repeated efforts of his to secure an arrangement satisfactory to both countries showed that Grenville's professed willingness for any such arrangement was subject to a strict maintenance of the principles set forth in the above quotation. Applications for the release of impressed Americans were made with increasing frequency during the latter part of 1796. Scarcely a day passed without correspondence on the matter between the successor of Pinckney and the Foreign Office.[45] From then on until the War of 1812 any American citizen who had the misfortune to look like an Englishman and who could not prove to the satisfaction of the British Admiralty that he was not one, was likely to be seized from the deck of an American ship whenever that ship ventured from an American harbor, and placed in the hull of a British

44. Grenville to Pinckney, July 13, 1796, P.R.O., F.O., 5, 6.

45. "An account of the Number of Applications which have been made to this Office by Ld. Grenville, for the discharge of Seamen said to be citizens of America, together with the number of persons applied for, and of those discharged, between Aug. 1, 1796, and March 9, 1797: Number of Applications, 31. Number of persons applied for, 254. Number of persons discharged, 83." Dated Admiralty Office, Mar. 9, 1797, P.R.O., F.O., 5, 20.

man-of-war perhaps for the remainder of his natural life. Acquiescence in this atrocious injustice is a real measure of the military and naval strength of the United States in the first twenty-five years of its existence.

After the outbreak of the Anglo-French war in 1793 Pinckney soon received intimations as to what the British policy as to contraband, neutral property, and neutral decks would be.[46] Several weeks before the issue of the famous Provision Order of June 8, 1793,[47] he warned Jefferson to expect it, and received instructions to protest any procedure not sanctioned by the "modern" usage of nations.[48] He himself thought that opposition by the United States should be restricted to nothing more than commercial retaliation.[49] He replied to the order by elaborating the injury caused to neutral shipping and the ill-will which this procedure, not to be supported by any modern principle of international law, would arouse in America.[50] After this perfunctory protest he proceeded to use his best efforts to secure judgment of freight and demurrage to American ships whose cargoes, under the order, were pre-empted for British instead of French grain-bins. To Pinckney's observations on international law Grenville replied that he had directed Hammond to make some explanations on that subject.[51] When later in the year a formal protest was delivered by the American minister,[52] at Jefferson's direction, the Foreign Secretary again shifted the discussion across the Atlantic, and directed Hammond to answer the note in the same temperate and conciliatory terms in which it had been written.[53] Thus the matter was kept in a train of innocuous legal argument while the work of the cruisers went on unmolested. A second Order-in-Council, November 6,[54] of even more unjustifiable nature, applied the Rule of 1756 to American trade with

46. Pinckney to the Sec. of State, Jan. 30, Mar. 13, Apr. 5, 1793, Dispatches, Eng., *3*.

47. "That it shall be lawful to stop and detain all vessels loaded wholly or in part with corn, flour, or meal, bound to any port in France, or any port occupied by the armies of France" and to purchase the said cargoes, with a due allowance to the master of the vessel for freight. *A.S.P., F.R., 1*, 240.

48. Jefferson to Pinckney, May 7, 1793, D.S., Instructions to U.S. Ministers, *1*, 278–81.

49. *A.S.P., F.R., 1*, 241.

50. Ibid.

51. Pinckney to the Sec. of State, Aug. 28, 1793, ibid

52. A copy is enclosed in Pinckney's dispatch of Jan. 28, 1794, Dispatches, Eng., *3*.

53. Grenville to Hammond, Jan. 11, 1794, P.R.O., F.O., 5, 4.

54. "That they shall stop and detain all ships laden with goods the produce of any colony belonging to France, or carrying provisions or other supplies for the use of any such colony, and shall bring the same, with their cargoes, to legal adjudication in our courts of admiralty." *A.S.P., F.R., 1*, 430.

the French colonies, even though a part of the trade had been open before the war. The possibility of this order arousing a dangerous hostility in the United States led to its revocation on January 8, 1794,[55] at which time Great Britain reverted to the principle of the much protested order of June 8. That is, she claimed the right of capture of enemy property on neutral decks, and pre-emption as contraband of foodstuffs bound for Continental France—but allowed immunity to American ships trading with the French West India Islands, except in "naval or military stores" or to a blockaded port.[56] While Pinckney expressed gratification to Grenville at the comparative moderation of the latest order, he was careful not to admit its legality.[57] This question of neutral rights, which had meanwhile helped to produce a war crisis in America, soon passed out of Pinckney's hand when John Jay arrived in England in June 1794. Pinckney therefore cannot be said to have had much to do, aside from the mere function of a reporter, with the famous controversy over the Orders-in-Council.[58]

In an interview with Grenville in November 1793, Pinckney ventured to take up the question of British occupation of American posts on the northern frontier, a subject not delegated to him as one of his duties. The discussion of this, which had been absorbed into the general arguments over the treaty of peace between Hammond and Jefferson, had been in abeyance for over a year and a half. Pinckney now asked Grenville outright whether the posts would be evacuated if the United States fulfilled the treaty of peace. He thus gave an opening which previously had not been presented, because of Jefferson's masterly denial that the United States had ever violated the treaty except when some of the states had been driven to reprisals by previous British violations.[59] Grenville immediately answered that where one party to a treaty had deferred fulfillment of its obligations for some years,

55. Pinckney to the Sec. of State, Jan. 28, 1794, Dispatches, Eng., *3*. J. B. Burges, undersecretary, records in his Foreign Office journal, under date of Dec. 28, 1793, "Mr. Pinckney called; much agitated in consequence of the new instruction to commanders of ships of war and privateers—very anxious to know whether it would be rigorously enforced—insisted strongly on the injustice of such a measure, and on the destructive consequences it must entail on his country, which now would be deprived of every means of exporting its produce, as the Act of Navigation shut them out from our islands, and this new instruction would equally shut them out from those of France; so that nothing but a few inconsiderable markets would be left to them." *Dropmore Papers*, 2, 488.

56. For text of order see *A.S.P., F.R., 1*, 431.

57. Pinckney to the Sec. of State, Jan. 7, 1794, Dispatches, Eng., *3*.

58. For a good statement of this controversy see Mahan, *Sea Power and the War of 1812, 1*, ch. 2.

59. *A.S.P., F.R., 1*, 201.

whereby complete execution could not afterwards be had, neither reason nor the law of nations could expect a strict compliance from the other party. Pinckney interpreted this as refusal ever to give up the posts. His dispatch recording this conversation, when delivered to Congress, made a painful impression, that added to the crisis of March 1794. In a private letter the impressionable Southerner wrote to Jefferson that he considered war pretty certain and asked the Secretary about removing with his family to France, for the sake of his children's education, when hostilities should break out.[60]

War in fact did nearly occur between the United States and England in 1794, but not as a result of the above interview. The trouble was due to a combination of the frontier grievance, sharpened by the hostile conduct of Canadian frontier officials of the crown, and the violations of international law occasioned by the Caribbean captures under the Order-in-Council of November 6. This crisis was met, and war was averted, by Jay's well-known mission of 1794. Pinckney's feelings about the possible significance of Jay's presence in relation to his own diplomatic ability were not pleasant, but he loyally submitted to the superseding of his more important functions.[61]

It seems clear that Pinckney was recognized in London as distinctly less disposed than Jay to make concessions to Great Britain. Count Woronzow, the Russian ambassador, after a talk with Gouverneur Morris in June 1795, reports to Grenville that Morris "n'est pas dans les principes de Pinkney [*sic*], mais bien dans ceux de Monsieur Jay," and Burges, undersecretary, speaks, or reports Morris as speaking, to the same effect.[62]

Pinckney seems to have been consulted by Jay during the negotiation and to have been kept generally abreast of its progress. His dispatches on this subject are meager. He wrote in 1796 that, while Jay had advised with him throughout the negotiation, he himself had not been present at any of the conferences with Grenville and could not share either the merits or the demerits of the treaty.[63] He appreciated, as a just reward for judicious and patriotic conduct during the Jay

60. Pinckney to Jefferson, Nov. 27, 1793, Dispatches, Eng., *3*. His wife died in 1794; Pinckney's *Pinckney*, p. 144.

61. Same to same, June 23, 1794, Dispatches, Eng., *3*, quoted by Trescot, p. 106. Almost identical language is to be found in a letter to his brother, C. C. Pinckney, in Pinckney's *Pinckney*, p. 123.

62. *Dropmore Papers*, *3*, 78, 87—that "Mr. Jay must now be arrived [in America], and would be able to do away the very unfavourable impressions which had been made, and were still making, by Pinckney and Deas."

63. Pinckney to Jefferson, Feb. 26, 1796, Dispatches, Eng., *3*.

negotiations,[64] the appointment as a special plenipotentiary to Spain, where he similarly supplanted the ordinary functions of the resident minister, Short.

Pinckney was the vehicle, in April 1794, before the arrival of Jay, through which the Swedish minister at London conveyed to the United States the famous invitation of Sweden to join the abortive Scandinavian armed neutrality of 1794, a combination repelled by Washington at Hamilton's advice as an "entangling" alliance.[65] That the American minister did not share the confidence of his government in its decision on this question is indicated by a dispatch from London in 1796, which complains that he had not received a "syllable in reply" to this celebrated proposal.[66]

Another outstanding feature of Pinckney's mission, one of more popular interest today, was his connection with Washington's attempt to secure the release of Lafayette from a Prussian prison. Ever since the publication of John Marshall's *Life of Washington* it has been known that the President, acting as a private individual and the friend and military comrade of General Lafayette, tried in vain to induce the King of Prussia to liberate the illustrious and lovable friend of America on condition of his going to the United States. A good many scattered sources suggest that this is a subject worthy of more extended treatment than the limits of this paper allow.[66a] A brief summary of Pinckney's relation to it is sufficient here.

At the time of his voluntary "capture" by the Austrian forces in August 1792, Lafayette was given the treatment of a prisoner of state instead of an émigré, because he very nobly refused to lead an army of invasion under foreign flags into his beloved France.[67] Through Gouverneur Morris, American minister at Paris, and William Short, our resident at The Hague, and through the marquis's brother-in-law, the Vicomte de Noailles, who reached America via London, he importuned Washington to use his influence to get him out on condition of his going to America.[68] Similar requests came from Madame de Lafayette,[69] who was later permitted by the Emperor to join her hus-

64. Same to same, Feb. 23, 1795, ibid.
65. See Chap. 6 of this volume, pp. 170–71.
66. Pinckney to the Sec. of State, Mar. 7, 1796, Dispatches, Eng., 3.
66a. See Chap. 9 of this volume, pp. 209–39.
67. B. Tuckerman, *Life of General Lafayette* (2 vols. London and New York, 1889), 2, 87 ff.
68. Short to Morris, The Hague, Sept. 7, 1792, *A.S.P., F.R., 1,* 341; Pinckney to Washington, Pinckney's *Pinckney,* p. 116.
69. *Writings of Washington* (ed. Ford), *12,* 261; *Writings of Jefferson, 7,* 264.

band in prison. Reluctance to mix either in the political complications of Europe or in the internal convulsions of France, particularly during the existing delicate posture of Franco-American affairs, caused Washington to accept the advice of his agents abroad not to make the matter a subject of formal diplomatic intervention. The predicament of the "unfortunate Lafayette" aroused the sympathy of all patriotic Americans, particularly of his former companions in arms, of whom there was none more affectionate than Washington himself. The pay which Lafayette as an American general had declined to receive was now taken out of the treasury by executive action and placed at his disposal, an act later reinforced by Congressional legislation.[70] Washington determined "as a private citizen" to do his utmost to free Lafayette. Pinckney was the agent to whom the direction of this matter was intrusted. Already Pinckney had "unofficially and expressly in his private capacity" applied to the Prussian minister at London to learn the intentions of the court of Berlin. Gratitude for Lafayette's past services, he assured, would impel the United States to adopt any honorable proceeding to procure permission for the general to go to America. These applications, as well as others by Lafayette's friends, though duly reported to Berlin, all failed. Pinckney then turned to England. Directly after the revocation in January of the order of November 6, when Pinckney imagined it might be agreeable to the British government to confer an obligation on the United States, he requested Grenville to use his influence with an ally in favor of Lafayette. This Grenville politely declined to do.[71] Despairing of success by this sort of informal proceeding, Pinckney countenanced the efforts of Lafayette's friend to effect his escape, as the most likely way to get anything done.[72]

After the subject had been officially and formally sanctioned by a cabinet meeting, it was decided that the President should unofficially and informally undertake a personal intercession with the King of Prussia for Lafayette's release.[73] An informal letter was therefore written by General Washington to that monarch, in "the language of a private gentleman untinctured by the most distant recollection of

70. Hamilton to Randolph, May 31, 1794, enclosed in Randolph to Pinckney, June 8, 1794, Instructions to U.S. Ministers, 2, 99. The amount made payable to Lafayette by the act of Mar. 27, 1794, was 60,449 guilders.

71. Pinckney to the Sec. of State, Jan. 10, 1794, Dispatches, Eng., 3.

72. Same to same, Feb. 28, 1794, ibid.

73. Randolph to Pinckney, Jan. 16, 1794, Instructions to U.S. Ministers, 2, 56–59. For cabinet meeting sanctioning this step, Hamilton, *Works* (ed. J. C. Hamilton), *4*, 505.

his being the President." [74] The direction of the business was given to Pinckney, and James M. Marshall of Virginia, brother of the future chief justice, was selected as the confidential agent to undertake the journey to Prussia. Marshall left London for the Continent in the spring of 1794. In April he met Prince Henry of Prussia at Rheinsberg. Henry was a friend of Lafayette, and apparently willing to further the project with his nephew the king. But the opposition of the Prussian ministry could not be broken down. When Marshall reached Berlin, bearing letters from Henry to the king, he was informed that the illustrious political prisoner had already been transferred to Austria. He returned to London unsuccessful. [75]

In December 1794, Pinckney reported that Lafayette had escaped from Olmütz, [76] his Austrian prison, but had been recaptured. He advised that a power be lodged with some American minister in Europe to secure the famous soldier's liberation, for fear that a European peace might leave him in prison for want of somebody to request his release. [77]

In 1796 Washington considered interposition as a private individual by appeal to the good graces of the Austrian emperor. He sent to Pinckney a personal letter to the Emperor to be presented to the Austrian minister at London should the right occasion arise. [78] But Pinckney had already terminated his diplomatic career before this instruction could be fully acted on. If indeed it was ever sent to Austria, the letter was not answered. [79] Despite the efforts of his American friends Lafayette languished a prisoner until Bonaparte's Italian campaign unlocked the doors of Olmütz.

On his return from Madrid, where his most notable diplomatic work was done, Pinckney stayed only a short while in London. On the completion of the Spanish negotiations he had asked the President to be

74. Pinckney to Mr. Marshall, Mar. 23, 1794, D.S., Dispatches, Eng., *4*, 274–288. See A. J. Beveridge, *The Life of John Marshall* (4 vols. Boston and New York, 1919), *2*, 33.

75. James Marshall to Pinckney, June —, 1794, Dispatches, Eng., *3*.

76. The well-known attempt of Bollman and Huger. See Tuckerman's *Life of General Lafayette*, *2*; the sources are printed out of the Vienna archives in Max Büdinger, "Lafayette in Oesterreich," in vol. 92 of the *Sitzungsberichte der Kaiserliche Akademie der Wissenschaften, Philosophisch-Historische Classe* (Vienna, 1878).

77. Pinckney to the Sec. of State, Dec. 10, 1794, Dispatches, Eng., *3*.

78. Washington to the Emperor, Philadelphia, May 15, 1796, Pinckney's *Pinckney*, p. 119; see also Washington's letter to Pinckney, Feb. 20, 1796, ibid., p. 117.

79. The best account of Lafayette's imprisonment in Austria, and its political effects, is Max Büdinger's "Lafayette in Oesterreich," which presents a detailed study based on documents in the Vienna archives. Büdinger states that Washington's letter was not answered, but does not indicate absolutely that it was ever received.

recalled from the service.[80] After his return to America he is remembered as the unsuccessful Federalist candidate for the vice-presidency in 1796 and as a member of Congress from 1797 to 1801. He then settled down to a long life full of respect and action in his native state of South Carolina and in the southern campaigns of the War of 1812. He lived long enough finally to meet Lafayette on the occasion of the memorable visit to the United States in 1825.

Pinckney's reputation as a diplomatist comes chiefly from the Treaty of San Lorenzo with Spain, which does not concern the subject of this paper. Aside from that one treaty his diplomatic career is not of major importance. But as illustrating the early years of Anglo-American relations, particularly the development of the vexing question of impressment and the attitude of Washington's administration toward it, the London mission is well worth the attention of the American historian.

80. For letter requesting recall, see *Writings of Washington* (ed. Ford), *13*, 169.

6. The United States and the Abortive Armed Neutrality of 1794

ASIDE from the great issues between the belligerents, nothing has been more strongly forced upon international attention by the present war [World War I] than the increasingly difficult position in which neutral states find themselves between the two groups of antagonists reeling at grips across the face of the world. Economic, national, and imperial interests have impelled the great belligerents to form their own systems for the preservation of their lives; only when a neutral is able to present power behind its behests are the mighty combatants of world wars likely to depart enough from their own considerations to give heed to its demands. The history of American neutrality from 1914 to 1917 will remain one of the greatest illustrations of this fact.

On two familiar occasions in the past, neutral nations who have seen their interests injured and unheeded by belligerents in world wars have adopted a joint defense by threat of armed force as a means of obtaining what they deemed their rights, short of actually entering war. Such a combination has been successful according to the degree of force that has been behind it, and according to the degree in which the interests of the united neutrals have coincided.

In the First Armed Neutrality, of 1780–83, to which the United States was sympathetic, the alliance of neutrals to enforce enlightened principles of international law was sufficiently numerous, sufficiently unified in interests, and sufficiently strong to force Great Britain to much greater prudence, and to a mitigation of the severity of her prize laws.[1] It constituted one element in the forces balancing against the United Kingdom that induced British statesmen to come to terms with America.[2] The Second Armed Neutrality, of 1800, including Sweden, Denmark, Russia, and Prussia, was not strong enough to prevent the collapse of Denmark under the guns of Nelson. Skillful British diplomacy playing on the divergent interests of the neutral allies, the

1. Richard Kleen, *Lois et Usages de la Neutralité* (2 vols. Paris, 1898–1900), *1*, 20 ff.
2. C. H. Van Tyne, *The American Revolution, 1776–1783* (New York, 1905), p. 328.

Published in *American Historical Review*, 24, no. 1, 1918.

bombardment of Copenhagen, and the death of the Tsar Paul, shattered that neutral combination before it attained sufficient momentum to influence materially the naval policy of Great Britain.

Not much mention has ever been made of the beginnings of another armed neutrality that threatened British naval control in a manner equally dangerous, in the year 1794. It is interesting to students of American history, because the relation of the United States to it shows how the action of small belligerents in the face of all-powerful opponents is dictated thoroughly by the interests of self-preservation, just as deviations from accepted principles of international law on the part of great belligerents are frequently dictated—and always explained —by the same motives. It is interesting, again, because the decision then taken by the government of the United States to abstain from such an alliance, and to acquiesce in the principal British interpretations of sea law, marks the first conscious and official embarkation on a policy which remained the polestar of American foreign relations until the vastly altered conditions of 1917—the policy of abstention from entangling alliances.

Great Britain's entrance, in February 1793, into the European conflagration precipitated by the French Revolution extended that great conflict of political antagonisms beyond the marches and countermarches of Continental armies. Republican legions of France successfully met the threat of Pillnitz and the manifesto of the Duke of Brunswick, but the regenerated vigor of revolutionary warfare found indomitable opposition in the British sea power and the controlling diplomacy that worked hand in hand with it. To sweep the tricolor from the seas, and by choking the commerce of France so to impede the effectiveness of her armies as to force them to yield to those of the Coalition, was the policy of Great Britain. With the development of this maritime policy neutral nations saw themselves seriously injured by the increasingly arbitrary Orders-in-Council and the wholly one-sided decisions of the admiralty courts. Great Britain did not propose for one minute that the protection of a neutral flag should nullify her naval might.

Though strong, British sea power was not at the beginning of the war omnipotent. The diplomacy of Downing Street was therefore directed in the spring and summer of 1794 toward bolstering by treaties and alliances the naval power of the empire. First fruit of this masterful foreign policy was the treaty with Russia, in which both powers agreed to stop all exports of military supplies or provisions to French ports and frankly acknowledged the purpose of taking "all other measures for injuring the commerce of France" and preventing neutrals from giving protection to it on the high seas. In quick succession there followed a series of measures of like consequence. Spain acceded to a similar arrangement on May 25. The first Orders-in-Council came, June 8, to bring into British harbors all provisions found on board neutral ships bound for French ports, whether these ports were blockaded or not.[3] The Two Sicilies (July 12), Prussia (July 14), Austria (August 30), and Portugal (September 26) acknowledged in treaties with Great Britain the same determination to annihilate the commerce of the new republic.[4] French armies withstood valiantly the blows of Europe armed against them. The reborn vigor that never fails France delivered counterstrokes of more than equal weight. Yet the rulers of the Revolution saw the British naval-diplomatic system engulfing the principal monarchies of Europe, and British fighting vessels everywhere threatening arbitrary control of all other powers.

France by the autumn of 1793 saw herself almost completely encircled by the constricting coils of the power that controls the sea. The diplomatic representatives of Russia and Great Britain had informed the monarchs of Sweden and Denmark that British and Russian fleets would be stationed in the Baltic and North seas to stop all kinds of provisions bound for France under whatever flag.[5] If the plan were carried out successfully, the English had succeeded in blocking the Baltic to France by extending contraband to cover not only naval-store products of that region, so necessary to the French navy, but the great supplies of food that the Swedes and Danes sent through the Sounds to the impoverished republic. The same prohibitions confronted vessels from America. They were forced to land their masts and barrels of tar and pitch on British wharves, and to empty their cargoes of grain into the bins of British warehouses. Except for the Baltic Scandinavian

3. "That it shall be lawful to stop and detain all vessels loaded wholly or in part with corn, flour, or meal, bound to any port of France, or any port occupied by the armies of France, and to send them to such ports as shall be convenient, in order that such corn, meal, or flour may be purchased on behalf of His Majesty's Government, and the ships be released after such purchase, and after a due allowance for freight, or that the masters of such ships, on giving due security, to be approved by the court of admiralty, be permitted to proceed to dispose of their cargoes of corn, meal, or flour, in the ports of any country in amity with His Majesty." *A.S.P., F.R., 1,* 240.

4. For text of these treaties see *A.S.P., F.R., 1,* 243 (for Russia); for Prussia, Austria, Spain, the Two Sicilies, and Portugal, see *Parliamentary History, 30,* 1053–58. Portugal and the Two Sicilies, however, did not accept the provision concerning neutrals.

5. For text of notes see *Annual Register,* 1794, p. 241.

ports, a few Italian harbors, and the cities of the Levant, all Europe and America, as a result of the British system, was closing to the ships of the new republican flag.

Among those nations still upholding the more liberal interpretations of international law lingering from the First Armed Neutrality remained only Sweden, Denmark, feeble Poland (now already slipping into the grasp of the three partitioners), and Turkey. The United States, to be sure, had incorporated these principles in its first treaties and had made formal protest against the Orders-in-Council of June 8; [6] but the protests were fortified only by paragraphs from Pufendorf and Vattel. The relentless pressure of naval power had made them only perfunctory. The British ministry had been careful to feel out the attitude of the American administration toward any such proceeding before the Orders were issued. Alexander Hamilton, the most influential and cogent of the advisers of Washington, for five years had been in confidential communication with the British minister, George Hammond, and with Major George Beckwith, in an informal sense his predecessor. [7] He quietly assured Hammond that he saw the justice behind the Orders-in-Council, though he was not able to answer for the opinions of his colleagues. [8] As a result, the British Foreign Office paid only polite attention to the protests penned so assiduously by Jefferson, Secretary of State. [9] Even along the thinly populated shores of the coast of northern Africa the pressure made itself felt; there lurked the sea-harpies of the Mediterranean, the Barbary pirates, whose corsairs, released by British mediation from a war with Portugal, [10] were free to prey on such French vessels as might slip past hostile cruisers on the voyage to Venice and the Levant. Both in the old and in the new world the remorseless force of the enemy's sea power threatened to strangle the commercial life of France.

With this aggressive diplomatic and naval system threatening to neutralize all the valor of the armies of France, the revolutionary executives strove to achieve some effective opposing combination. There was

---

6. *A.S.P., F.R., 1,* 241, 449–54.

7. The confidential relations of Hamilton with the British representatives at Philadelphia may be seen clearly in the correspondence of those representatives with the Foreign Office. See P.R.O., F.O., 4, 12 for Beckwith correspondence; vols. 13–16 for Hammond correspondence.

8. Hammond to Grenville, Philadelphia, May 17, 1793. P.R.O., F.O., 5, 1. Where there is not specifically mentioned in these notes the name of some other state, in parenthesis, it is to be understood that citations of these volumes of Foreign Office correspondence refer to America.

9. Grenville to Hammond, Jan. 11, 1794. P.R.O., F.O., 5, 4.

10. *A.S.P., F.R., 1,* 288.

one obvious possibility. Encroachments and restrictions on neutral trade struck vitally at the prosperity of the Scandinavian nations, whose flags in wartime obviously would cover great profits, but who depended even in times of peace on the business of the carrying trade. They followed that impulse which is almost an instinct with small nations that have large merchant marines but small fighting navies. The two northern monarchies, whose interests led them to adopt more liberal principles of the law of nations, protested vigorously against the British provision order. Their protest brought nothing but chagrin. Neither kingdom could undertake resistance by force. Sweden, lacking funds to equip a half-dozen ships-of-the-line, had the dangerous Finnish and Pomeranian frontiers and little real strength to guard them. Denmark was clamped in a vice, the jaws of which were the British and Russian navies.

French diplomats, however, saw in the Baltic a chance to offset the system of the English. It consisted in resurrecting the armed neutrality of the previous war. Soon after matters had begun to adjust themselves to British participation in the conflict, a French agent had accompanied to Stockholm the Baron de Staël, Swedish minister in France, in an effort to induce the two powers of the north to unite in a new armed neutrality. But the Regent of Sweden—with an eye always to his threatened frontiers—had desired a permanent alliance; and France, already launched on the successful campaign of 1793, did not regard with much enthusiasm the few equivalents which Sweden, diplomatically and geographically isolated, could offer for such an alliance.[11]

These early negotiations withered away, but the French continued to give sharp attention to the Baltic and to the possibility of concerted action by Sweden and Denmark in the face of England. A French agent, Philippe de Grouvelle, was vested with the powers of minister plenipotentiary in the summer of 1793 and sent to Copenhagen as representative of the French republic. He had instructions to keep Denmark and Sweden united diplomatically in defense of their neutral rights as interpreted by themselves, and if possible to stimulate the two courts to a real joint alliance in favor of France.[12] Grouvelle soon found that France had a common grievance with the Baltic Powers because of the British and Russian notes, above referred to, and he had no difficulty in establishing himself on the most friendly terms

11. Rapport au Comité de Salut Public, Suède et Dannemarck, 16 Floréal, an II (May 5, 1794). Arch. Aff. Etrang., Suède vol. 286, pp. 224–27.

12. Grouvelle au Ministre des Affaires Étrangères, Copenhagen, Sept. 10, 1793. Arch. Aff. Etrang., Dannemarck, vol. 169, p. 245.

with the Count Bernstorff, the royal Danish chancellor.[13] In the face of the monarchs allied against France, Bernstorff did not quite dare to receive Grouvelle as the official representative of the revolutionary French republic.[14] Nevertheless, he had frequent and intimate conferences with him and for all practical purposes Grouvelle had the status and influence of French ambassador. He made arrangements for the quicker and more lucrative disposal of French prizes brought into Norwegian harbors, brought forward proposals for a new commercial treaty, supplied the Committee of Public Safety with such information as he had gleaned from the chancellor concerning the belligerent courts —then, as now, neutral Denmark was a great clearinghouse for European war news, and Bernstorff was best informed of all diplomats— and above all pushed his proposals for joint armed neutrality of Sweden and Denmark.[15]

Bernstorff asserted to Grouvelle that complete confidence and unanimity as to policy prevailed between Denmark and Sweden, but refused to make any definite promises.[16] He said that such a proposal for a joint armament had been made by Denmark to Sweden. It was soon hinted by Ehrenheim, Swedish minister at Copenhagen, that Sweden's delay in preparing any armament to be used in possible cooperation with Denmark was due to poverty—a French subsidy to help Sweden to maintain her armed neutrality would be useful and proper.[17] The French Minister of Foreign Affairs thought such an investment unwise on the ground that commercial privileges offered by France would be sufficient stimulus for such an armed neutrality; the interest of Denmark and Sweden, Grouvelle was instructed,[18] would be sufficient to induce them to combine forces against Russia and England. Grouvelle wrote back that though apparently steps were being taken by the Scandinavians to preserve neutrality by separate action, he did not think such inducements would suffice to maintain a joint alliance.[19]

13. Grouvelle au Ministre des Affaires Étrangères, Hamburg, Aug. 14, 1793. Ibid., vol. 169, p. 213.

14. Same to same. Ibid., pp. 394, 427, 428.

15. Same to same (no. 18), Copenhagen, 11 Nivôse, an II (Dec. 31, 1793). Ibid., p. 476.

16. Grouvelle au Ministre des Affaires Étrangères, Copenhagen, Sept. 3, 1793. Ibid., p. 232.

17. Same to same, Copenhagen, Oct. 1, 1793. Ibid., p. 270.

18. Deforgues, Ministre des Affaires Étrangères, à Grouvelle, Paris, Nov. 13, 1793. Ibid., p. 347.

19. Grouvelle au Ministre des Affaires Étrangères, Copenhagen, Dec. 17, 1793. Ibid., p. 345.

Meanwhile plans were being made in Paris to expand the possibilities of a Baltic armed neutrality into a grandiose combination. There is a memorandum of the plan in the library of the French Ministry of Foreign Affairs. The Committee of Public Safety elaborated the early approaches to Sweden and Grouvelle's diplomacy into an ambitious design to strengthen the European influence of the revolutionary government, already stiffened into some coherence by the victories of 1793. The project was to unite all remaining neutral naval states about the French revolutionary executive in resistance to British sea power. It included Sweden, Denmark, Turkey, Poland, Venice, Genoa, and the United States. Singly these nations saw themselves powerless to enforce what they considered to be principles of fairness toward neutral flags. Together they might be strong enough to revive the power of the armed neutrality of the last war. The foundation of the League, reads this interesting document, was to be "the indefeasible rights and independence of these nations and their immediate interests."

As a foyer for this "counter-coalition," so formidable on paper, and really pregnant with powerful possibilities, the committee selected the Scandinavian courts. The monarchies were to enter a joint defensive alliance to assert the principles of armed neutrality against all naval aggressions. France would offer peculiar commercial advantages to the armed neutrals, and on actual signature of a treaty she would engage to furnish 6,000,000 *livres*, in addition to 500,000 *livres* for each vessel of the line fully equipped and 300,000 *livres* for each frigate.

The committee had drawn up instructions accordingly and had appointed proper diplomatic agents for the affair, when there arrived in Paris a copy of a convention [20] already signed by Sweden and Denmark and setting forth in a timorous way the armed neutrality principles. This treaty, signed secretly on March 27, 1794, was for the duration of the war. The two northern powers agreed to furnish a joint armament of sixteen ships-of-the-line to protect their subjects in the exercise of rights sanctioned by law and indisputably to be enjoyed by independent nations. The Baltic was to be closed to the war vessels of belligerent nations, and to be free, therefore, from rules of war. Faltering protection against illegal interference with their rightful commerce by the

20. "Projet d'Arrêté du Comité de Salut Public," undated. It was never carried out. Adet, former minister to the United States, was nominated. It is indorsed "N'a pas eu lieu." Arch. Aff. Etrang., Dannemarck, vol. 170, p. 85. See also "Rapport au Comité de Salut Public, Suède et Dannemarck," Arch. Aff. Etrang., Suède, vol. 286, p. 225, *verso*. This document enables one to fix the date of the *Projet*.

immense British and Russian naval forces was provided as follows: the neutral allies would make reprisals in concert after all other means of dissuasion had been rejected, and "at the latest, four months after the rejection of their behests, whenever such reprisals should be deemed suitable, the Baltic always excepted." In no specific form were the rights of neutral nations defined; definition was to be covered by the treaty interpretations of the Baltic Powers [21]—the principles of the First Armed Neutrality. The lack of resolute provision for energetic action made the convention at best a weak one. "It is a demonstration of a force and temper which do not exist," wrote the observing Gouverneur Morris from France.[22]

Half-hearted as this instrument may have been, it was a good beginning for the plans then being formulated in Paris. The instructions already drawn up were dropped, for what they aimed to accomplish in the first place had been attained. The Swedes had been indiscreet enough to close the convention door before the French subsidy horse had been led in—unwisely they had asked for money after the treaty had been signed and made known.[23] At one time the committee had decided to advance substantial funds to accelerate the Swedish armament,[24] but Grouvelle wrote that it seemed probable that Sweden herself might afford the initial expenses of armament,[25] and the money chest of the revolutionary executive was notoriously hollow. The advances were never made. The failure of the French subsidy, the threatening presence in the Baltic and North seas of Russian and British fleets, and one other factor smothered the infant armed neutrality in its cradle. With it expired the hopes of including other powers in the "counter-coalition." The other, third, factor in the downfall of this ambitious diplomatic enterprise was the diplomatic mission to England of John Jay, chief justice of the United States.

21. Treaty of Mutual Defense, Liberty, Security, and Commerce, March 27, 1794. P.R.O., F.O., 115, 3; *Annual Register*, 1794, pp. 238–39.

22. "You will observe that time is given the belligerent Powers for repentance and amendment, before any hostile act of resentment by the contracting parties. You will observe, also, that the period specified is sufficient to permit the arrestation of all supplies shipped for this country [France] during the present season. Thus the next autumn and winter are left clear for negotiation, *should the allies be unsuccessful in this campaign*." Morris to Randolph, Sainport, May 31, 1794. *A.S.P., F.R., 1*, 400.

23. Grouvelle à Deforgues, no. 30, Copenhagen, March 28, 1794. Arch. Aff. Etrang., Dannemarck, vol. 70.

24. "Rapport," Arch. Aff. Etrang., Suède, vol. 286, pp. 224–27.

25. See long and interesting dispatch of Grouvelle au Ministre des Affaires Étrangères, Copenhagen, Feb. 18, 1794. Arch. Aff. Etrang., Dannemarck, vol. 170, p. 55.

In the spring of 1794, without the ministry in London being immediately aware of it, owing to the tardiness of winter mail, British-American relations had reached a critical stage. The crisis had been brought about by the several familiar disputes between England and America that in March had suddenly ripened to an ominous condition. First were the old disputes about the northern frontier posts on American soil. British troops still held these strategic points under the ostensible but not real excuse [26] that the United States had first violated the treaty by obstructing the collection of ante-bellum debts to English merchants. With these stood the legacy of minor disputes also left by the treaty. Second, there was the disappointment of the American government at not being able to conclude a commercial treaty with Great Britain, whose navigation laws struck sharply at the now independent states, particularly by excluding their ships from the British West Indies. England at first had been quite content to "sit still" in the agreeable commercial status quo, since American trade still ran in old colonial channels to English wharves; [27] but this commercial situation, so undesirable to the United States, led to American tariff and tonnage duties in favor of American vessels.[28] This bore particularly hard on British trade, because the traffic with England constituted three-fourths of all American commerce and over half of this three-fourths was carried in British ships.[29] A strong movement, developing in Congress and the administration, under the leadership of Madison and Jefferson, to discriminate specifically against the British flag, had only been checked by a sudden decision to establish a permanent British

26. This statement is based on a careful reading of the Canadian correspondence in Ottawa and London, which shows that orders were actually sent to General Haldimand to hold the posts before the very convenient and plausible excuse of American violations of the treaty was discovered. The evidence is too long to be quoted in detail here. Particularly illuminating, however, is the dispatch of Sydney to Haldimand, April 8, 1784 (C.A., Q, 23, 55), sent before the formal exchange of ratifications of the definitive treaty. It should be read in connection with Grenville's argument as stated in Jay to Randolph, London, Sept. 13, 1794. *A.S.P., F.R., 1*, 485–96. See also Edward Channing, *A History of the United States* (6 vols. New York, 1905–25), *4*, 148–49, for an illuminating note.

27. Sheffield, *Observations on the Commerce of the American States* (6th ed. 1784), p. 161; Report of the Privy Council on American Trade, Jan. 28, 1791, in *Collection of Important Papers on Navigation and Trade* (London, 1808), p. 114.

28. Acts of July 4, July 20, 1789; June 20, Aug. 10, 1790. *U.S. Statutes at Large, 1*, 27, 180, 335.

29. The proportion which American commerce to Great Britain bore to the total is ascertained by a comparison of American exports and imports as stated annually from 1790 in *A.S.P., C.N., 1*. For figures for tonnage see: *Collection of Interesting and Important Papers on Navigation and Trade*, app. XXIV.

legation in Philadelphia headed by George Hammond, first British minister to the United States.[30] Soon it became evident that Hammond had no instructions to sign a commercial treaty and that he was trying to couple the evacuation of the frontier posts with the establishment of a "neutral" Indian barrier state that would keep the natives of the great American hinterland north of the Ohio in a British sphere of influence, economic and political. The negotiations as to the border fell into abeyance, and when frontier friction between British officers and "British" Indians, and the Americans, had worked disastrously on the self-control of Lord Dorchester, governor general of Canada, the latter made his notorious and bellicose secret speech to a delegation of Indian tribes, February 10, 1794, in which he prophesied an immediate war with the Americans and sought the alliance of the tomahawk.[31] Intelligence of this unwary utterance soon leaked out. It reached Philadelphia almost simultaneously with the arrival of news from the West Indies of the capture of about three hundred American schooners under the wholly arbitrary Order-in-Council of November 6, 1793, and the barbarous incarceration of their crews and officers.

In late March and April the majority of the American people were for war with Great Britain. The crystallizing "Democratic" party, under the leadership of Madison and the now retired Jefferson, passed an embargo for a month, soon extended for another thirty days, on all shipping in American harbors. Bills for actual sequestration of British property and vigorous discrimination against the British flag specifically, immediately received strong support in Congress. The movement was headed off by Alexander Hamilton, profound leader of the Federalist party, that had formed in contradistinction to the "Democrats" (the division in 1794 was chiefly over the British policy). In a war with England at that particular time, the Federalists forecasted the total collapse of the new government under the Constitution. The new political system, brought into practical operation by Hamilton's genius in establishing American credit, depended for revenues almost wholly on the tariff and tonnage duties collected in American ports. Almost alone this financial means upheld the credit of the federal and the assumed state debts and paid the operating expenses of the govern-

30. See Beckwith to Grenville, March 3, 1791, P.R.O., F.O., 4, 12; P. Colquhoun to Grenville, Aug. 5, 1791, *Dropmore Papers*, 2, 157; Beckwith to Grenville, Philadelphia, July 31, 1791, P.R.O., F.O., 4, 12; Colquhoun to Grenville, July 29, 1791, *Dropmore Papers*, 2, 145; *C.A. Report*, 1890, p. 172.

31. For copy of speech see *Annual Register*, 1794, pp. 250–51; also C.A., Q, 64, 109.

ment itself. By war, suddenly to eliminate three-fourths of American commerce and to endanger the rest to the point of extinction meant to knock away the scaffolding of credit from beneath the new government, and so to precipitate its destruction. A lapse into the pitiful political helplessness of the Confederation would be then inevitable. To avoid this, Hamilton, in close and quiet intimacy with Hammond, used that connection, in a sort of "back-stairs" diplomacy,[32] to thwart the official anti-Anglican character of the negotiations of the Secretary of State, Jefferson. With a group of Federalist senators [33] he now had sufficient influence in the administration to bring about the appointment of Chief Justice John Jay for the peace mission of 1794. In Congress he marshaled sufficient power to block the retaliatory and hostile measures until the results of Jay's mission should be known. Meanwhile the Federalists with vigor supported a bill for raising an army, and Hamilton led the British minister to believe that if Jay did not succeed in getting a certain minimum of moderate concessions, which he outlined in private to him, the existing peaceful relations with England could not endure.[34]

At the very moment when the Danish-Swedish convention of March 27, 1794, was signed, this ominous American war cloud was rising on the other side of the Atlantic. Meanwhile the solidity of the First Coalition was beginning to weaken. Secret agents of the British Foreign Office were reporting that France was seeking to detach Spain by approaches through neutral Denmark.[35] As a matter of fact, the Spanish minister in Copenhagen did have instructions to make overtures looking toward peace.[36] Simultaneously, in view of the greater allurement of the Polish spoil, Prussia's influence on the Rhine was weakening. Among the allies "there was far more of disunion than union." [37]

Though the Swedish-Danish convention had been ratified in secret, and its negotiation was supposed to have been kept in the same secrecy, the whole train of Franco-Scandinavian diplomacy was well and with a fair degree of accuracy known to Lord Grenville. The increasing naval armaments of Denmark had for some time excited the suspicion

32. See evidence cited above, note 7.

33. C. R. King, *Life and Correspondence of Rufus King* (6 vols. New York, 1894–1900), *1*, 516.

34. Hammond to Grenville (no. 15), Philadelphia, April 17, 1794, P.R.O., F.O., 5, 4.

35. Précis of Secret Intelligence from Copenhagen. P.R.O., F.O., Holland, 37, 36.

36. Grouvelle Correspondence, Arch. Aff. Etrang., Dannemarck, vols. 169 and 170.

37. J. H. Rose, *William Pitt and the Great War* (London, 1911), p. 204.

of his representative in Copenhagen, although Count Bernstorff had strongly denied any connection with France,[38] and at Stockholm express assurances were made that no arrangements with Denmark were contemplated.[39] Grouvelle, who was more privy to the chancellor than any other foreigner, was imprudent enough to send his dispatches to Paris by ordinary mail, with only parts of them in cipher—a lack of caution wholly inexcusable, for which he was later roundly censured by the Committee of Public Safety.[40] It was so reckless a procedure as almost to prick the investigator's suspicions as to Grouvelle himself. Spies read nearly all of his correspondence. A concise précis of it is preserved at the British Record Office [41] and tallies perfectly with the original dispatches in the library of the Ministry of Foreign Affairs at Paris. They knew the content of Grouvelle's dispatches at Downing Street almost as soon as at the Quai d'Orsay.

The Swedish minister in London was Laurent von Engeström. He informed Thomas Pinckney, American representative there, on April 28, 1794, that he had instructions not only to communicate a copy of the convention but to invite the accession of the United States to it. Pinckney seemed greatly pleased. He secured a statement to that effect in writing and sent it home the very day. It would be received "with open arms," Engeström understood him to believe.[42] The same day, the Swedish and Danish ministers, "lest their sincerity be suspected," [43] gave a copy of the convention to Lord Grenville. Though nothing was divulged of the overture to Pinckney, Grenville, through the intercepted Grouvelle dispatches, soon learned of it by the same means by which he had already known of the convention itself. Immediately he instructed Hammond, at Philadelphia, to make the utmost exertions to prevent the success of any such proposal. To the American "ministers" he must confidently emphasize the marked difference in circum-

38. D. Hailes (British chargé d'affaires at Copenhagen) to Grenville, Copenhagen, March 24, 1794, cipher, rec'd April 3, 1794. P.R.O., F.O., Denmark, 22, 18.

39. H. G. Spencer (British minister to Sweden) to Grenville, Stockholm, April 18, 1794, cipher, P.R.O., F.O., Sweden, 73, 17; same to same, Stockholm, April 18, 1794, cipher, ibid.

40. Commissionnaire des Affaires Étrangères (Buchot) à Grouvelle, Paris, 4 Prairial, an II. Arch. Aff. Etrang., Dannemarck, vol. 170, p. 16.

41. Précis of Secret Intelligence from Copenhagen. P.R.O., F.O., Holland, 37, 56.

42. Engeström to the Royal Chancellor (Frederick Sparre), London, April 29, 1794. Swedish Royal Archives, Anglica, Engeström's Dispatches. For transcriptions of such Swedish documents as are cited here, I am indebted to Dr. Lydia Wahlström, of Stockholm.

43. Engeström to Ehrenheim (Swedish minister, Copenhagen), May 26, 1794. Ibid.

stances between the position of the United States and the Baltic Powers, laying stress on the point that in return for fair neutrality on the part of the United States, American commerce had been treated in a spirit of fairness (this was written before Grenville had heard of the exploding American wrath against the British naval policy). The American government, wrote Grenville, must be aware of the risks of being drawn into a conflict with England, especially in view of the weak state of the Scandinavian navy.[44] Three weeks later, on June 5, Grenville informed Hammond that he had reason to believe that the Swedish proposal to America had not the sanction of the Danish court, but he urged the closest attention to the matter. It was true that the Engeström note to Pinckney did not have the support of Denmark. Grenville learned this through Grouvelle's dispatches. Shortly after it had been made, Engeström received instructions that Denmark had not acquiesced in the *démarche,* and that any American answer must be considered merely *ad referendum.*[45] Bernstorff's reason for declining to join the invitation—this was still before the news of the British-American crisis was known in Europe—was that he considered the American navy wholly too feeble to cooperate effectively; [46] really the reason was that too much of this adventurous policy on his part would probably result in a quick offensive by the English or Russian fleet, then parading the Baltic [47]—the lot of Holland in 1780 and the fate of Denmark in 1800.

One of the most interesting aspects of British-American diplomacy in this period lies in the relations of time and distance and the precarious schedule of packet-boats. In the days when neither cable nor wireless telegraph existed, the international situation of the world did not vary like a stockbroker's ribbon as the telegraph clicks off each detail of news from the governments of Christendom and other governments; the most important transatlantic intelligence was often long delayed, and often when news finally arrived it came in big consignments instead of in daily driblets. Such was the case in the crisis of 1794. Up till June 10, after the American commissioner, Jay, had actu-

44. Grenville to Hammond, Downing Street, May 14, 1794 (no. 12), cipher. P.R.O., F.O., 5, 5.

45. The Royal Chancellor (Sparre) to Engeström, Stockholm, May 16, 1794. Swedish Royal Archives, Anglica (1794).

46. Grouvelle to Buchot (Minister of Foreign Affairs), no. 41, 9 Prairial, an II (May 29, 1794). Arch. Aff. Etrang., Dannemarck, vols. 170, 180.

47. Ehrenheim to Engeström, Copenhagen, July 8, 1794. Swedish Royal Archives, Anglica (1794).

ally set foot on English soil, Grenville had not received an official word about the critical American situation.[48] On that day, June 10, a great deal of surprising news from North America lay on the desks of the foreign and home secretaries when the dispatches from the Canadian and American mail-packets were opened. American indignation over the captures made under the additional and unprecedented Order-in-Council of November 6, 1793,[49] Dorchester's speech of February 10 to the Indians, the news of imminent hostilities on the frontier,[50] the embargo, the sequestration and nonintercourse bills, the resolution to send Jay, the sober interview between Hamilton and Hammond, the real and actual imminence of war with America—with America, the source of British naval supplies and the largest single customer for British manufactures—made up a budget of information that gave the Secretary for Foreign Affairs considerable pause and food for thought as on the same morning he unsealed a letter from Falmouth bearing the signature of John Jay, and announcing his commission from the President as special envoy to His Majesty.

The news was a complete surprise; up to this time Grenville had dealt with the United States in a leisurely fashion; there had been little uneasiness at Downing Street over the American situation. Now it was apparent, suddenly, that this confidence was wholly misplaced.

In addition to the information received by way of the intercepted French dispatches, Grenville was receiving other secret reports, false indeed, which made the Scandinavian-American possibilities seem more alarming. On June 20, the day of the first conference between Jay and Grenville, came a letter from the British chargé at Berlin, telling of an interview with Count Finckenstein, the famous Prussian Minister of Foreign Affairs, in which the dubious disposition of America had been discussed. Finckenstein confided some American information that, in view of Jefferson's resignation as secretary of state and retirement on January 1, 1794, to Monticello, was as weirdly fantastic as it must have been startling to Grenville. Jefferson, said the Prussian count, was expected soon in Denmark, there to concert measures that

48. Hammond to Grenville, February 20, April 17, May 1, 1794, P.R.O., F.O., 5, 4; Grenville to Hammond, June 5, 1794, cipher, P.R.O., F.O., 115, 3.

49. To "stop and detain all ships laden with goods the produce of any colony belonging to France, or carrying provisions or other supplies for the use of any such colony, and should bring the same, with their cargoes, for legal adjudication in our courts of admiralty." *A.S.P., F.R., 1*, 430.

50. Dorchester to Dundas, Feb. 24, 1794. C.A., Q, 67, 88.

should be followed by the neutral nations.[51] Strangely enough, the Danish chancellor also had a similar notion.[52] A few days later came a letter from Hammond, of May 25, telling of the increasing hostility of the American public due to the news of the occupation of the old Miamis fort [53] by British troops, and enclosing the acrid correspondence between himself and Randolph, Jefferson's Francophile successor.

As if this were not enough, there arrived, at very near this time, one of the curious Francis Drake bulletins, which purported to transmit secret copies of the minutes of the meetings of the Committee of Public Safety, but were really literary productions meant to be perused by and designed to mislead the British Foreign Office.[54] Whether Grenville was wholly duped by these inventions is uncertain, but he expressly asked Drake to get him information about French negotiations with Sweden and Denmark. The "secret" information which Drake furnished professed to relate that in the Committee of Public Safety dispatches had been read from its American agents, under date of April 1, which declared war between the United States and Great Britain inevitable, and stated that immediately afterward a treaty would be concluded between the former and Denmark and Sweden. The French commissioners in America were represented as having requested

51. G. H. Rose to Grenville, Berlin, June 10, 1794, rec'd June 20. P.R.O., F.O., Prussia, 64, 29.

52. Grouvelle au Ministre des Affaires Étrangères, Copenhagen, 22 Prairial, an II (June 11, 1794). Arch. Aff. Etrang., Dannemarck, vol. 170, p. 192. The present writer has not been able wholly to run down the source of this rumor.

53. Near the city of Toledo, Ohio.

54. The validity of the Drake dispatches was first discredited by Mr. J. H. Clapham (*English Historical Review*, January 1897) and by Professor A. Aulard (*Révolution Française*, 1897, vol. 32) on the ground that they do not agree with certain well-established facts in the sources for the history of the Committee of Public Safety. This opinion rested unchallenged until 1914, when M. Albert Mathiez presented an article in defense of the documents, citing sources with which to him they appear to agree ("Histoire Secrète du Comité de Salut Public," *Revue des Questions Historiques*, January 1914). Without being wholly familiar with the sources for the Committee of Public Safety, the writer was soon convinced, by collating the dispatches from Grouvelle from Copenhagen (whence the committee got its information), those from the French commissioners in Philadelphia to the Committee of Public Safety, and the dispatches of Gouverneur Morris, American minister to France, that the Drake information was not true. Very cleverly, just enough truth is put into the dispatches to make them deceiving. For documents see: Turner, "Correspondence of the French Ministers," A.H.A., *Ann. Rept.*, 1903, 2; Arch. Aff. Etrang., États Unis, vols. 40–43, 1793, 1794; and Dannemarck, vols. 169, 170, 1793, 1794; *A.S.P., F.R., 1*, and published works of G. Morris, edited by A. C. Morris (1888) and J. Sparks (1832).

power to conclude preliminaries of a treaty with the United States and to guarantee Congress that the Convention would not treat with the Northern Powers without admitting the United States to any treaty made by them.[55] This last request was said to have been rejected, but the executive was authorized to negotiate with Morris, the American minister, and to report. It was also stated that letters from Stockholm of May 11 represented that court as ready to ratify a treaty with the French republic.[56]

In short, the British ministry in the summer of 1794 stood confronted with all the dangers of the revival of the old Armed Neutrality at a time when—despite the Prussian treaty of April 1794—the coalition against France was already weakening [57] toward the final disintegration of 1795. There was one exception to the situation of 1781: Pitt could count on Catherine the Great to join Britain against the Baltic Powers; [58] and Prussia, now a nominal ally of Great Britain [59] and absorbed in the Polish partition, had no inclination again to become a member of the Baltic combination. But there can be no doubt that the Baltic situation as viewed by the British ministry in June and July 1794, had an appreciable effect on the American negotiations: it would be folly to allow the United States, the greatest foreign customer of Great Britain,[60] at a time when commerce and the entrepôt system were providing the revenue for the French war,[61] to join in a war against England, or in any such system as the policy of the Northern Powers, greased by French diplomacy, seemed to invite. It would serve to divide the energies and diminish the supplies of the British navy, and to weaken the financial sinews of the government in its great struggle with France. Great Britain desired war no more than did the American Federalists. The time had come for some kind of immediate settlement with the United States.

Grenville took immediate steps to relieve the American tension.

55. Bulletin no. 25, Dispatches of Francis Drake. *Dropmore Papers*, 2, 578. The writer has been unable to find any dispatch of April 1 in the French archives, or anything resembling it.

56. Ibid.

57. Rose, *William Pitt and the Great War*, ch. 8.

58. Prussia's treaty of alliance with Great Britain of 1793 provided for measures to induce neutral powers to adopt a harassing attitude toward French commerce.

59. Whitworth to Grenville, St. Petersburg, April 15, 22, 23, 1794. P.R.O., F.O., Russia, 65, 27.

60. See Chatham Papers, bdle. 286, P.R.O., cited above.

61. Alfred Thayer Mahan, *The Influence of Sea Power upon the French Revolution and Empire* (2 vols. Boston, 1892), 2, 18.

Concessions were made which postponed all immediate danger from America and looked toward a conciliatory negotiation. The old policy of procrastinating at the frontier posts until a "neutral" Indian barrier state had been created was abandoned and arrangements made to step across the line to Canadian soil, in the event of a treaty. For his hostile speech to the Indians, a sharp reprimand to Dorchester followed, accompanied by concise instructions to use every means to cultivate a friendly disposition on the part of the United States.[62] In case hostilities had already broken out between frontier units of American and British forces, Grenville and Jay agreed that everything should remain *in statu quo* pending the negotiations.[63] The king issued an Order-in-Council admitting all the American captures made in the West Indies to appeal in English prize courts from the petty and arbitrary admiralty courts of the islands.[64] By this all that Hamilton had stipulated to Hammond, on the eve of Jay's departure, as "absolutely indispensable for an amicable settlement of differences," [65] was granted, and the door opened to a settlement of all points in dispute between the two nations. Grenville even went a step further. The Order-in-Council of June 8, 1793 (that of November 6 had been altered already in January to the sense of June 8), was unostentatiously repealed insofar as it directed the capture and pre-emption of neutral grain-ships bound for France.[66]

From August till November the negotiations between Jay and Grenville went on in leisurely discussion. The main principles necessary for a treaty had been agreed on when the British concessions were made and when Jay had consented to a commission for the adjudication of debts due to British creditors, and for settling the question of French prizes sold in American waters after Washington's prohibition of their sale. Grenville's bargaining after this was very sharp. He attenuated his chaffering until he could hear from Hammond precisely the position of the American administration as to the Baltic Powers.

In Jay's official instructions, made familiar by the publication for the Senate of part of the Jay negotiations, was the following paragraph:

62. This led eventually to Dorchester's resignation. Dorchester to Dundas, Quebec, Sept. 4, 1794. C.A., Q, 69–1, p. 176.

63. Jay to Randolph, London, July 12, 1794, *A.S.P., F.R.*, *1*, 479; Grenville to Hammond, July 15, 1794, P.R.O., F.O., 115, 3.

64. Orders-in-Council, West Indies and America (1786–97), P.R.O.

65. Hammond to Grenville (no. 15), Philadelphia, April 17, 1794. P.R.O., F.O., 5, 4.

66. Instructions to Naval Commanders, approved by the Privy Council, August 6, 1794, P.R.O., C.O., 5, 33; Orders-in-Council, West Indies to America, 1786–97, Privy Council Register, vol. 141, p. 11.

You will have no difficulty in gaining access to the ministers of Russia, Denmark, and Sweden, at the Court of London. The principles of the armed neutrality would abundantly cover our neutral rights. If, therefore, the situation of things with respect to Great Britain should dictate the necessity of taking the precaution of foreign co-operation upon his head; if no prospect of accommodation should be thwarted by the danger of such a measure being known to the British court; and if an entire view of all our political relations shall, in your judgment, permit the step, you will sound those ministers upon the probability of an alliance with their nations to support those principles.[67]

Randolph wrote this paragraph. But Jay assumed a slightly patronizing tone toward an official superior who was really of inferior political stature,[68] and paid attention to the formal instructions of the Secretary of State only when convenient. That Jay might of necessity waive the principle of the armed neutrality, even to the extent of acquiescing in the Order of June 8, was admitted in Hamilton's private letter to him.[69] Hamilton later states his disapproval of any diplomatic union with the Baltic Powers.

At first Jay was intimate with the Danish and Swedish ministers at London. But it soon became their policy to "let him take his way" without making any definite assurances.[70] Denmark was threatened by the Russian fleet patrolling the Baltic. Sweden had to guard its Finnish and Pomeranian frontiers. There was also the English fleet which five years later worked such havoc at Copenhagen. The Armed Neutrality of 1794 was a threat rather than an immediate direct force. Only if political circumstances were opportune did it allow actual reprisals and the closure of the Baltic. Engeström's correspondence with Stockholm shows that while Swedish diplomats considered more initiative advisable as to the United States, the Danish chancellor hesitated. He thought that, if no agreement was reached by Jay with the British court, the Americans would fall naturally into the arms of the Scan-

---

67. Instructions to Jay, May 6, 1794. *A.S.P., F.R., 1,* 473. This was before any news of the Engeström overture to Pinckney could have reached America, and was a mere conjecture of a possible diplomatic lever. Randolph's ignorance of the real state of European politics is shown by his allusion to Russia, then the maritime ally of England.

68. Jay to Randolph, July 30, 1794. *A.S.P., F.R., 1,* 480.

69. Hamilton to Jay, May 6, 1794. Hamilton, *Works, 4,* 551.

70. Engeström to the Royal Chancellor (Sparre), Aug. 12, 1794. Swedish Royal Archives, Anglica (1794).

dinavians and an enlarged armed neutrality, and then would come the best time for real negotiations with them. If a treaty were concluded and concessions were made to the United States not allowed to other neutrals, it would be almost equivalent to a declaration of war by England on Denmark and Sweden.[71] Whatever may have been the conferences with the Scandinavians, of which not a word was ever made known in the official correspondence turned over to the American Senate, Jay by August had turned aside from such cordiality.[72] This was after the first conciliatory concessions had been made to him by the British negotiator. One wonders whether the Federalists could have later put the Jay Treaty through the Senate if *all* the correspondence had been published!

Before Grenville learned from Hammond the real attitude of the American government toward armed neutrality, he was on the point of making much greater concessions in the proposed American treaty than were eventually considered. On September 30, 1794, Jay submitted a draft which, he believed, incorporated most of the principles on which previous conferences had led him to expect agreement. No copy of this draft was conveyed to the Senate with the other drafts and projects of the negotiations turned over to it at the time when the treaty came up for ratification. One can guess the reason. This draft —more important than all the preliminary projects—was not included in the Jay correspondence, and probably was never even read by anyone on this side of the Atlantic,[73] because it compared too unfavorably with the terms of the final treaty itself. A copy, however, is in the British Record Office.[74]

There is no space here to enumerate the favorable terms of the draft of September 30. They were never agreed to because, ten days previously, Grenville had heard from Hammond that Alexander Hamilton said the United States would never accede to the Scandinavian convention. Hammond reported that Hamilton said

> with great seriousness and with every demonstration of sincerity
> . . . that it was the settled policy of this government in every

71. Ehrenheim to Engeström, Copenhagen, July 8, 1794. Ibid.

72. Engeström to the Royal Chancellor (Sparre), Aug. 12, 1794. Swedish Royal Archives, Anglica (1794).

73. It is not included among the duplicates of Jay's correspondence in the Jay manuscripts in the New York Historical Society's collections, nor, of course, in the published works of Jay.

74. P.R.O., F.O., 95, 512.

contingency, even in that of an open contest with Great Britain, to avoid entangling itself with European connections, which would only tend to involve this country where it might have no possible interest, and connect it to a common cause with allies, from whom, in the moment of danger, it could derive no succor. . . . In support of this policy Mr. Hamilton urged many of the arguments advanced in your lordship's despatch, the dissimilitude between the political views as well as between general interests of the United States and those of the Baltic Powers, and the inefficiency of the latter, from their enfeebled condition, either to protect the navigation of the former in Europe or to afford it any active assistance if necessary in its own territory.

Hammond could not find out whether the supposed Swedish propositions had arrived from Pinckney, but from Hamilton's decided manner he believed that the matter had received his attention before, and that what he had stated represented the deliberations of himself and of the American administration.[75] That the Swedish proposal was received with no enthusiasm is indicated by Hamilton's letter of July 8, to Randolph, quoted in his works.[76]

The result of this information in the hands of Grenville was to reduce all his fear of American cooperation with the Baltic Powers. With the latest news from Philadelphia in mind, no reason any longer existed why Grenville should submit to Jay's propositions of maritime law, and, so that the Americans were mollified sufficiently to prevent hostilities or injurious commercial legislation, there was no longer any particular occasion for hurry. Jay, on the other hand, feared that some unforeseen contingency in the maelstrom of European policy might derange the attitude of the British ministry toward the United States. The only concession Grenville would now make was to agree to a joint survey and settlement by commission of the unknown northwestern

75. Hammond to Grenville, no. 28, New York, Aug. 3, 1794, rec'd Sept. 20. P.R.O., F.O., 5, 5. That the matter had received discussion, probably in the Cabinet, is indicated by Hamilton's letter of July 8, 1794 (at about the time the Engeström proposal would have been received in America): "The United States have peculiar advantages from situation, which would thereby be thrown into common stock without an equivalent. The United States had better stand in its own ground."

76. "If a war, on the question of Neutral Rights, should take place, common interest would secure all the co-operation which is practical and occasional arrangements may be made; what has already been done in this respect appears to be sufficient." Hamilton to Randolph, Philadelphia, July 8, 1794. Hamilton, *Works, 4,* 571.

boundary. The other new points of Jay's draft he deemed "insurmount-able obstacles."

Convinced that he could get no better terms and that on the whole those he had were satisfactory, the American envoy signed the treaty which has since been connected with his name. The articles, long familiar in American history, were a triumph of British diplomacy. The only concessions made were the evacuation of the posts, which Grenville had before decided on in order to prevent a disruption of the valuable British-American trade; [77] the admission of American vessels, during the war only, to a direct West Indian trade, which the conditions of war had rendered it impracticable for British ships adequately to maintain; [78] and compensation for captures "made under cover" of the arbitrary Orders-in-Council, without giving up the principle of those orders. The price paid by the Federalists was, to make, by abeyance, a heavy though a regrettably necessary sacrifice of principle in the face of other national interests. Only one real advantage was secured —the evacuation of the frontier posts and the clearance of the last vestige of British control from the soil of the United States. By means of a mixed commission to compensate for spoliation "under cover" of the Orders-in-Council, Pitt secured from America a peaceable acquiescence in British naval policy that reversed completely the position taken by the young republic in all its previous treaties.[79]

77. Consideration on suggestions proposed for the Government of Upper and Lower Canada. P.R.O., C.O., 42, 88, pp. 575–79.

78. Mahan, *Sea Power and French Revolution*, 2, 258. This article was not ratified by the Senate.

79. If the principle of the rule of 1756 was not recognized, it was consented to tacitly—a voluntary relaxation from it having been made, so far as the trade between the United States and the French islands was concerned, by the repeal of the Order of November 6, 1793. Restrictions on American exportations of stipulated West Indian products, of which the voyage had been broken by landing on American soil, would have cut off the carriage of French colonial products, had the article been ratified by the Senate. There was no agreement on the question of foodstuffs as contraband, which the United States was bound by treaties with France, Sweden, and Holland to treat as noncontraband; the practice of Great Britain, who controlled the sea, in pre-empting foodstuffs bound for France was allowed by not being prohibited. In fact, Grenville stated that the treaty was a specific recognition of the British principle in this respect, when a little later the American government questioned additional instructions to British naval commanders of April 25, 1795, to detain all ships laden with provision for France. (Grenville to Bond—*chargé d'affaires* at Philadelphia after Hammond's departure—Nov. 4, 1795, enclosing copy of the instructions, P.R.O., F.O., 115, 4). The principles of free ships, free goods, and the immunity of naval stores from seizure as contraband were wholly lost sight of.

The episode of the abortive renewal in 1794 of the Armed Neutrality and the relations of the United States to it are interesting in two ways. The decision of Hamilton, who in 1794 preponderated in the councils of Washington, not to participate in a European combination, marks the first definite acceptance by the government of the United States of the principle of abstention from foreign entanglements. Though the idea of such a policy may not have been wholly original with Hamilton, it was he who first gave it practical application. It was the proposal of the Scandinavians in the world war of the French Revolution that offered a chance for such a decision, and on the basis of Hamilton's reasoning the new government's policy was first actually oriented in that direction.[80] Two years later it was publicly restated in Washington's Farewell Address, as an American policy of abstention from foreign entanglements; Hamilton's verbal coinage of 1794 was there repeated. In this sense, Alexander Hamilton was the author of one-half of the Monroe Doctrine, just as nearly thirty years later John Quincy Adams was the author of the other half.

Again, the episode has its interest from the ambitious Franco-Scandinavian "neutral counter-coalition," so adventurously constructed in the imagination of French diplomatists. Though the lack of French subsidies to Sweden prevented that power from arming more actively in concert with Denmark against the preponderating naval power of England and Russia, the Jay Treaty administered the final blow to this daring diplomatic conception. Bernstorff constantly insisted to Grouvelle,[81] while the Jay negotiations were proceeding, that it was the intention of the northern allies jointly to invite the accession of the United States. But that was not done, and meanwhile the treaty was signed. "The agreement by which the American agent, Jay, has just terminated the disputes between England and America," wrote Grouvelle from Copenhagen to the Committee of Public Safety after the treaty became known there, "breaks absolutely this *liaison*" (i.e., a possible Scandinavian-American *liaison*).[82] The French design for another armed neutrality quickly expired as the United States, under the guiding reason of Hamilton, acquiesced in the *real* facts of British sea power.

80. The idea, itself, that abstention from European alliances was advisable had occurred to other American political thinkers before Hamilton first put it into operation. See A. B. Hart, *The Monroe Doctrine: An Interpretation* (Boston, 1916), pp. 9–10.

81. Grouvelle au Ministre (des Affaires Étrangères), no. 50, Copenhagen, 27 messidor, an II. Arch. Aff. Etrang., Dannemarck, vol. 170, p. 232.

82. Grouvelle aux Membres du Comité de Salut Public, Déchiffrement, Copenhagen, 3 Nivôse, an III. Ibid., p. 359.

7. Jay's Treaty and the Northwest Boundary Gap

HAD the negotiators of the treaty of peace and independence between the United States and Great Britain in 1782 been accompanied by the staffs of experts so indispensable to twentieth-century peacemakers there probably never would have been any northwest boundary gap. As it was, the peace commissioners, after some debate, agreed to fix the northern boundary on the general principle of the now familiar river-and-lake line from 45 degrees North Latitude on the St. Lawrence to the Lake of the Woods and the Mississippi. There is nothing to indicate that these men ever made use of any other knowledge of the northwestern corner of the United States than was contained in the official British Mitchell's Map of 1755. This showed the territory as far west as the Lake of the Woods, and to that body of water the line was carried with reasonable precision. But over the northwest corner of Mitchell's Map from forty-seven to fifty-two degrees North Latitude is spread an inset map of Labrador and Hudson's Bay. Out from under the inset flows the Mississippi, its source shrouded in mystery. A legend on the main map reads: "The head of the Mississippi is not yet known. It is supposed to arise about the 50th degree of latitude and western bounds of this map." The commissioners complacently projected the line from the northwesternmost corner of the Lake of the Woods due west to the hypothetical Mississippi.[1] Any professor-expert, had there been such in those days of inefficient diplomacy, could have shown the commissioners that such a line was impossible because the Mississippi really rises well to the south of the latitude of the Lake of the Woods, as many maps drawn between 1755 and 1782 indicate with fair accuracy.[2]

The treaty thus left a boundary gap of approximately 175 miles in an air line between the source of the Mississippi and the northwestern-

1. For facsimile of Mitchell's Map, see Channing, *History of the United States, 3*, 361. For discussion of the northern boundary negotiations, 1779–82, ibid., 386; A. J. Hill, in Minnesota Historical Society, *Collections*, 7, 305–17; A. N. Winchell, ibid., *8*, 187–94.

2. For enumeration and description of contemporary maps, see *Statutes, Documents, and Papers respecting the Northern and Western Boundaries of Ontario* (Toronto, 1878), pp. 135–40.

Published in *American Historical Review*, 27, no. 3, 1922.

most corner of the Lake of the Woods. It was not until nine years after
ratification that this fact was discovered and became a matter of diplomatic negotiations. From the first, however, the new boundary line was
the cause of consternation to British subjects in Canada. Immediately
the terms of the preliminary articles of peace were known on the banks
of the St. Lawrence it was apparent that the British diplomatists in
yielding to the extensive territorial claims of their adversaries had
overlooked a matter of great economic consequence to Canada, a geographical detail which might have been adjusted easily had the negotiators known anything about the lands they were dividing. This was
the location of the Grand Portage between Lake Superior and the
navigable portion of Pigeon River, up which stream went the goods
of the Montreal fur merchants to be carried across the height of land
and by way of the Lake of the Woods to the intricate canoe routes of
the virgin fur country of the great territory of the Northwest.

The Canadian fur trade, the prostration of which appeared to be
threatened by fulfilment of the treaty terms and which thus came to
be connected intimately with the boundary question, was the most
profitable single industry of eighteenth-century North America. On
it depended the immediate prosperity of the remaining British continental possessions. For the ten years after the peace of 1783 the business produced furs worth £200,000 sterling annually.[3] Half of this came
from United States territory to the south of the Great Lakes, country
dominated until 1796 by British occupation in violation of Article II [4]
of the treaty of peace. Moreover, furs to the value of £40,000 annually
already were coming in from the Northwest over the Grand Portage,[5]
which portage to their disappointment the fur princes of Montreal discovered to have been ceded to the United States through the ignorance
of the king's peacemakers. At the same time that the traders contemplated the withdrawal of British forces from control of their fur preserves in what was now American territory to the south of the new
boundary line—a withdrawal against which they vigorously pro-

3. "Importance of Skins from Canada, 1788," C.A., Q, 43, 826, from P.R.O., C.O. 42
66; "Report to Grenville on the Fur Trade of Canada, furnished by John Inglis to
Lord Grenville," Mark Lane, May 31, 1790, C.A., Q, 49, 287, from P.R.O., C.O. 42, 72;
"Memoir in regard to the Fur Trade, about 1794," Chatham MSS, bdle. 346. These
three documents are now available in print in the appendix to G. C. Davidson's *The
North West Company* (Berkeley, 1918).

4. That American soil should be evacuated by British troops "with all convenient
speed."

5. Account of the fur trade of Canada furnished by John Inglis, see note 3 above.

tested [6]—it was by no means pleasant to observe that the Grand Portage, artery of the fur trade to the new and unexploited regions of the Northwest and the Rocky Mountains, had been carelessly ceded away.[7]

The first effort to escape the consequences of this loss was to send out explorers to find some other route, wholly within British territory, between the Lake of the Woods and Lake Superior. Under the employ of the North West Company, Umfreville and St. Germain in 1784 did find an alternative route by way of the Kaministiquia River and Lake Nipigon,[8] a passage previously known to old French traders but neither so convenient nor so direct. But it soon became evident that recourse to the new waterway would not be necessary. The British government, acting in the interests of the fur merchants of Canada and London and in behalf of the Indian nations of the Ohio Valley, their former allies who were uneasy at anticipated American dominion over their lands, decided not to fulfill for the time being the terms of the treaty of peace.[9] Orders to the governor general of British North America to refuse delivery of the frontier posts went forth from Whitehall, in fact, the day before George III proclaimed ratification of the treaty and publicly promised to enforce it.[10] Soon thereafter it developed that the United States on its side was unable to carry out faithfully some of the American obligations under the treaty, notably the guaranty of unimpeded collection of ante-bellum debts due to British creditors. In this way the armory of British diplomacy was furnished with a plausible enough excuse for refusing to deliver. As long as these strategic

6. Benjamin Frobisher to Adam Mabane, Montreal, Apr. 19, 1784, C.A., B, 75–2, 75, printed in *M.P.C.*, *20*, 219–22. Compare this letter with that of Haldimand to Captain Robertson, Quebec, May 6, 1784, ibid., p. 226. For direct solicitations of the fur traders to the government, see Benjamin and Joseph Frobisher to Haldimand, Montreal, Oct. 4, 1784, C.A. *Report*, 1890, p. 50; Haldimand to Thomas Townshend, C.A., Q, 21, 220; unsigned letter to Nepean, Detroit, Sept. 1, 1784, *M.P.C.*, *24*, 17.

7. "Observations by Isaac Todd and Simon McTavish," etc., Chatham MSS, bdle. 346, printed in Davidson, p. 278.

8. Benjamin and Joseph Frobisher to Haldimand, Montreal, Oct. 4, 1784, C.A., Q, 24–2, 409; James McGill to Hon. Henry Hamilton, ibid., Q, 25, 111.

9. Evidence on this point has been abundantly found by the present investigator after painstaking examination of the Canadian Archives and of the Colonial Office Papers in the Public Record Office. The correspondence is too voluminous to cite here. Some of it has been presented in McLaughlin's "British Debts and Western Posts," in A.H.A., *Annual Report*, 1894, p. 444. See also Douglas Brymner's comments in his introduction to C.A. *Report*, 1890, p. xxxi.

10. Sydney to Haldimand, Apr. 8, 1785, C.A., Q, 23, 55. The ratification of the treaty was proclaimed by the king on April 9.

positions thus continued to be garrisoned by British troops the fur trade on United States soil went on unrestricted and the North West Company's *voyageurs* used the Grand Portage without hindrance, the nearest American being hundreds of miles away.

The question of the retention of the posts soon developed into that protracted diplomatic contest, familiar to students of the period, which eventually ended by their evacuation in 1796 according to the terms of Jay's Treaty (signed November 19, 1794). Observing that the matter of the frontier boundary had thus passed into a long diplomatic contest the fur traders importuned the government to secure their interests in any final settlement to be reached with the United States: (1) by providing that British traders might freely pass and repass the boundary to trade with the Indians on the American side,[11] and (2) by securing for British subjects liberty of passage through the few miles of United States territory to the southward of Pigeon River over which ran the Grand Portage.[12] It might even be possible, some of them thought, to secure such minor rectification of the boundary in the northwest corner of the United States as would include the Grand Portage within British territory.[13]

Affairs were in this posture when the British minister at Philadelphia, George Hammond, received from Montreal a map proving that the line due west from the Lake of the Woods could never strike the Mississippi. It was evident that a new line would have to be drawn in that part of the country, and England now had a good reason for wishing to change the boundary there. It dawned on Hammond that the necessity for a boundary rectification might be turned to the great profit of his government.[14] At the time, he was competing in an unequal contest with the astute Jefferson in regard to the whole field of questions in dispute between the two governments, the most important of which was the frontier question—which involved the posts. The British min-

11. "Memoir in regard to the Fur Trade, about 1794," see note 3 above.

12. The topography of the country on the north or British bank of the river made a portage there impossible. For map, see J. B. Moore, *International Arbitrations, 6,* pl. 57.

13. Frobisher to Mabane, Apr. 19, 1784, C.A., B, 75–2, 75.

14. Hammond to Grenville, Philadelphia, Feb. 2, 1792: "I trust that this Government [i.e., the United States] will not endeavour to take advantage of this accidental geographical error, which, if not rectified, will not only leave the limits between the two countries undefined, but also render entirely nugatory the eighth article of the treaty, which stipulates that the navigation of the Mississippi from its source to the ocean is to remain free and open to the subjects of the two countries respectively," P.R.O., F.O., 115, 1, printed in *Dropmore Papers, 2, 254.*

ister now introduced the rectification of the northwest boundary gap as another matter to be regulated in any general diplomatic settlement, and he proceeded further to couple the boundary question with that article of the treaty of peace which had guaranteed the free navigation of the Mississippi to the subjects and citizens of both nations.

To appreciate fully Hammond's argument on this point we should keep in mind that the boundary of the United States is fixed by Article II of the treaty, the article which follows immediately after recognition of independence. Six articles then intervene before the eighth, which is the last but one of the whole document. The eighth article reads: "The navigation of the Mississippi, from its source to the ocean, shall remain free and open to the subjects of Great Britain and the citizens of the United States." Hammond argued that the fixing of a boundary from the Lake of the Woods "on a due west course to the River Mississippi" was proof of intention of the negotiators of the treaty to bring the territory of British North America to abut on the river. He then cited the navigation article (which occurs in another part of the treaty and has no textual relationship to the boundary article) to prove that the geographical impossibility of a line due west of the Lake of the Woods to the river would render "nugatory" one of the chief guaranties of the treaty and one of the most valuable ones for Great Britain, for of what use would a guaranty of navigation be if the territory of that power were prevented from touching the river? The boundary, he maintained, should be rectified in such a way as to bring British territory up to the banks of the river and thus to realize the true intention of the men who drew up the treaty. Such a rectification, Hammond presumed to suggest, would be to the interest of the United States in that it would place a British buffer between the nation and Spanish Louisiana.

Observing the map, the reader will notice that the insertion of British territory to act as an appreciable buffer between the United States and the vacant prairies of Spanish Louisiana would have made necessary a long southward extension down the left bank of the Mississippi. This was exactly what Hammond ventured to propose, an extension which would bring a finger of British soil as far south as the "navigable waters" of the river,[15] which become navigable, for other craft than canoes and small boats, below the Falls of St. Anthony near the present city of St. Paul. It was an effort to create a situation out of which, in the give-and-take of the pending general diplomatic settlement, Eng-

15. "Notes of a Conversation with Mr. Hammond, June 3, 1792," Jefferson, *Writings* (Ford ed.), *1*, 193–98.

land might obtain a much desired cession of commercially strategic territory in a little-heard-of part of the North American continent.

It is certain that some English students of colonial affairs were estimating the future importance of the Mississippi Valley as the seat of a great future Anglo-Saxon population which would constitute a market for English manufactures more valuable than the existing fur trade of that valley, a trade certain to be exhausted as soon as the country should be settled. Both Hammond and Simcoe, the first governor of Upper Canada, placed great stress on the advantages to England of establishing a commercial connection with the future population of the Illinois country by way of the navigation system of the St. Lawrence and the Great Lakes. In the words of Simcoe, Upper Canada might become the vestibule of trade between the increasing population of the great Mississippi Valley and England, in the same way in which the Netherlands was then the vestibule of commerce between the German states and England.[16] Hammond, in describing the possibilities of rectification of the boundary gap, wrote to Grenville, the Secretary of State for Foreign Affairs:

> The rapid progress in population and improvement of the settlements formed along the banks of the Mississippi undoubtedly renders the free navigation of that river an object highly desirable, as it will open a new, extensive and unrivalled market for British manufactures, with which the inhabitants of those settlements can be more reasonably and plentifully supplied by the means of water communication with Canada than through the United States.[17]

Such arguments as these, made during the Industrial Revolution when English manufactures were demanding wider markets and when the British ship of state was wafted to a considerable degree by trade winds, did not escape the attention of Pitt's government. We are not surprised to find among the papers of the Prime Minister in 1794 an anonymous memorandum on frontier policy which must have been under his eye during the Jay negotiation. The writer of this document advocated evacuation of the frontier posts in order to reach a peaceable settlement with the United States. Military protection, he held, was not necessary for the fur trade, as could be instanced in the trade about Lake Superior. The great aim which British policy should serve was not protection of a commerce in peltries, bound soon to perish;

16. Simcoe to Dundas, London, June 2, 1791, C.A., Q, 278, 228–55; report of Simcoe to the Lords of Trade, Sept. 1, 1794, ibid., Q, 280–2, 307.

17. Hammond to Grenville, Feb. 2, 1792, see note 14 above.

rather, the Americans should be conciliated and England should encourage the population of the Ohio and Mississippi valleys— territory which would then furnish extensive markets for British manufactures to be supplied by water carriage from Canada.

> The only object Great Britain can have in retaining Canada in a commercial view, is that Canada extends all along the back of America. It will at all times secure to Great Britain a sale of her manufactures and oblige the Government of America to be moderate in their duties, otherwise the goods will be smuggled in upon them. A good understanding must be courted with all the subjects of America that joins Canada. . . . It is our business from every tie of justice, humanity and sound policy to put an end to the Indian war, and to encourage the Back Settlers all in our power. It is from that country that we will be supplied with hemp. The settlers there will never rival us either in shipping or in sailors nor for ages in manufactures. We will have all their trade without any expense of maintaining them. What more would you require? . . . Receive their wheat on moderate terms and they will take our manufactures. Every check on the sale of their wheat, etc., will drive them the sooner to manufactures.[18]

In the light of such considerations the proposal of Hammond to extend a strip of British territory south to the "navigable waters" of the Mississippi assumes no small significance. It was a design the importance of which has since been emphasized by the economic history of the Mississippi Valley. It was not only of economic importance; such a projection of British territory might have been used as an entering wedge for future political connections. Any one familiar with the intrigues between the officials of British North America and the frontier settlements of the American back country knows that such a connection had been plotted frequently in the years between the establishing of American independence and the ratification of Jay's Treaty. Even if economic penetration should not lead eventually to political connection, the commerce with the American West, with the mouth of the Mississippi closed by Spain, was likely to prove of great profit. Finally, as will be shown, it would have worked against future American sovereignty over an important area of the Far West.

18. Chatham MSS, bdle. 344. Unsigned and undated, but indorsed, "Considerations on the propriety of Great Britain abandoning the Indian Posts and coming to a good understanding with America"; see also letter of N. Miller to Alexander Hamilton, Feb. 19, 1792, *Miss. Valley Hist. Rev., 8,* 264–66.

Jefferson was quick to discern Hammond's purpose. The Virginian agreed that there should be no objection to closing the boundary gap, but insisted that it should be done by "as small and unimportant an alteration as might be," such as a line drawn from the most northern source of the Mississippi due north to strike a line extending due west from the Lake of the Woods. The navigation article had nothing to do with the boundary article, he asserted. It concerned the southern boundary of the United States and the secret article of the preliminaries of peace which had contemplated British possession of Florida as a result of a peace between England and Spain, in which case the navigation of the Mississippi would have been most important to Great Britain as a riparian power.[19] In bringing up the subject in this fashion the British minister, Jefferson decided, "showed a desire that such a slice of our Northwest Territory might be cut off for them as would admit them [the English] to the navigation and profit of the Mississippi." [20]

The subject having now been introduced by Hammond, it came up for attention in Washington's Cabinet, but not as a result of the conversation between Hammond and the Secretary of State. On October 31, 1792, a Cabinet meeting was held to consider what reply ought to be made to Spain on the matter of Spanish interference in the execution of a treaty between the United States and the Creek Indians,[21] and on the question of the southwestern boundary then in dispute between the United States and Spain. According to Jefferson's notes of the meeting, he himself favored transferring the whole discussion from Philadelphia to Madrid, thus postponing the question and creating a delay during which new developments might make it possible to avoid a rupture, which delay was "much to be desired, while we had similar points to discuss with Great Britain."

Alexander Hamilton, Secretary of the Treasury, then spoke. He advised peace as a growing period for national strength but anticipated eventual war with Spain and sought an ally—England. To purchase that alliance he proposed among other equivalents the adjusting of the northwest boundary in such a way as to admit England to "some naviga-

19. "Notes of a Conversation with Mr. Hammond, June 3, 1792," see note 15 above.
20. Jefferson to Madison, June 4, 1792, Jefferson, *Writings* (Library ed.), *8*, 364. Hammond's account of this part of the conversation is very brief. He merely states that he emphasized the necessity of ascertaining with precision the respective boundaries, particularly those of the St. Croix [i.e., in Maine] and in the northwest. "Mr. Jefferson acknowledged the truth of this observation, but assured me that this government would readily concur in any reasonable settlement." Hammond to Grenville, June 8, 1792, P.R.O., F.O., 4, 15.
21. *A.S.P., F.R., 1*, 259.

ble part of the Mississippi," and argued that joint possession with Great Britain of the navigation of the Mississippi would be desirable because it would mean joint protection of the same.[22]

How did Alexander Hamilton, who confessedly had not even looked the matter up on a map, come to make a proposal that fell in so neatly with the project for rectification suggested by the British minister at Philadelphia? In other pages the writer has shown the intimacy which existed between Hamilton and Hammond. It amounted to collusion between the two to thwart what Hamilton feared to be the "personal predilections" of "honest" Jefferson in favor of France and his prejudice against England.[23] In pursuit of a perspicuous foreign policy of his own, Hamilton considered peace between England and the United States vitally necessary to the newly engendered American nationality, and he went great lengths to prevent any interruption of Anglo-American commerce, upon which the revenues of his financial system depended. Such would have been his excuse for intriguing with the British minister who was supposed to conduct his negotiations with Jefferson, Secretary of State.

Enjoying as he did close relations with Hamilton, whose advice he considered the most weighty of any of Washington's advisers, Hammond had discussed the boundary rectification with the Secretary of the Treasury more intimately than with the Secretary of State. He wrote Lord Grenville that Hamilton had said in the "last conversation" that undoubtedly the United States government would allow a "free intercourse" with the Indians on the American side of the boundary (a matter to which Hammond had not been inattentive) if the British government would allow the same privilege to Americans trading with the Indians on the British side of the line.[24] In his confidence the British minister then asked Hamilton—who had agreed, in the course of a general conversation on the navigation of the Mississippi, that it was for the interest of the United States to share with Great Britain the defense as well as the enjoyment of that navigation—whether anything contrary to British interests might be expected in the negotiations which were going on between the United States and Spain. Hamilton gave assurances that nothing would be agreed to that was contrary to the British rights of navigation on the river. Hammond then ventured to presume that the United States would have no objections to regulating the northwest boundary so as to afford His Majesty's govern-

22. Jefferson, *Writings, 1,* 237.
23. See Chap. 6, above.
24. Hammond to Grenville, no. 26, Philadelphia, July 3, 1792, P.R.O., F.O., 4, 16.

ment an effective communication with the Mississippi. Here Hamilton stiffened. He would give no assurances but replied that he believed the United States would consent to as liberal an accommodation as would not be detrimental to its own interests. Hammond did not consider this as a rebuff. On the contrary he wrote to Downing Street: "I am of the opinion that this government would consent to such a regulation of the northwest boundary as would afford a free and effectual connection with the Mississippi by means of some of the rivers falling into Lake Superior." [25]

This conversation had occurred in July, over three months before the Cabinet meeting above described. We conclude that at the Cabinet meeting of October 31, Hamilton was seeking official sanction to an overture which for lack of authority he had not been able to make behind the back of Jefferson, some weeks before. We infer that, as a means of erecting an Anglo-American alliance, he wished to take advantage of the English desire to get into the Mississippi. The arguments which he advanced to his colleagues in the administration reflect what had already passed between him and Hammond. Knox, Secretary of War, agreed in general with Hamilton, and Randolph, Attorney General, with Jefferson, who opposed the overtures to England. Fortunately for the future of the American West Hamilton's proposal was dismissed by President Washington with the comment that "the remedy was worse than the disease." [26]

The next stage in the history of the northwest boundary gap is to be noticed in connection with the Jay-Grenville negotiations in London during the summer of 1794. The general negotiation between Hammond and Jefferson, into which Hammond, in 1792, had introduced the northwest boundary, had dragged along slowly until in 1793 the outbreak of the war between France and England monopolized the energies of the Foreign Office and postponed discussion of the boundary until John Jay arrived in England in the summer of 1794 on a mission which was to determine peace or war at a time when the British navy was only too busy in controlling the European situation.

Lord Grenville, following Hammond's emphasis on the importance of the rectification, and doubtless adopting the minister's confidence that the United States would accept it, brought forward the matter as one of the necessary settlements in any general treaty.[27] He made use

25. Hammond to Grenville, no. 27, Philadelphia, July 3, 1792, ibid.
26. "Notes of a Cabinet Meeting, Oct. 31, 1792," Jefferson, *Writings, 1*, 237.
27. In answer to Hammond's communication on the diplomatic importance of the northwest boundary gap, Grenville had written the following to Hammond, Apr. 25,

of Hammond's suggestion that the northwest boundary should be rectified in such a way as to give real effect to the navigation article of the treaty of peace. That article, he asserted, meant to give access to the navigable part of the river *"without passing through foreign territory."* He argued with Jay that because of the impossibility of the line due west from the Lake of the Woods, a wholly new line, now a proper subject for negotiation, might be drawn in that quarter with no necessary reference to the old attempt to fix a boundary. Accordingly he offered to the United States a choice of two lines based on such geographical knowledge of the upper Mississippi country as was afforded by Faden's map of 1793. One of the proposed lines ran due west from Lake Superior, at West Bay, to Red Lake River (represented by Faden as one of the western tributaries of the Mississippi), and thence down that river to its supposed confluence with the Mississippi. This would have moved the American frontier of western Canada south to the latitude of the present city of Duluth. That is, it would have done so had it been itself geographically possible, but in fact it was a line as impossible as the delimitation laid down at Versailles in 1783; Red Lake River does not flow into the Mississippi but into the Red River of the North.[28] Such a line undoubtedly was calculated by Grenville to secure British possession of the Grand Portage, but really it would still have left a northwest boundary gap to be settled. The acceptable alternative to this boundary was described as running due north from the mouth of the St. Croix River to the water communication between Lake Superior and the Lake of the Woods, the communication already followed in the treaty of 1783. It would have left the Grand Portage on American soil but would have extended a wedge of British territory south along the left bank of the Mississippi to an apex located about twenty-five miles below the present city of St. Paul, Minnesota—that is, to the "navigable portion" of the great river below the Falls of St. Anthony. One line would have given to Great Britain undisputed possession of the Grand Portage; the other would have recognized an extension

---

1792: "It will be an object of greatest Importance, at all Events, to secure, if possible, to His Majesty's Subjects in Canada the free and uninterrupted Communication between the Lakes and the Mississippi, either by the Ouisconsing River, which I understand affords great Facility for that Purpose, or by such other Rivers as . . . shall appear more proper." P.R.O., F.O., 115, 1.

28. Although Grenville was one of the best-informed men in England on North America, he was not wholly at home in the geography of the American West, a subject little known at best. See his instructions for Vancouver's celebrated expedition in the Pacific Ocean and the northwest coast of America in 1791. *Report of Provincial Archivist of British Columbia* for 1913, p. 46.

of territory of even greater commercial importance, a trade entrance into the American West and a port on the upper navigable waters of the Mississippi River. In case the latter line were chosen, Grenville had more than provided for the security of British trade over the Grand Portage by introducing into the new treaty a clause by which British subjects were to have freedom of passage "over the several waters, carrying-places, and roads adjacent to the Lakes or connecting with them." [29]

To his eternal credit this is one of the few demands of the British Foreign Minister which John Jay in his anxiety for peace did not accept. The adoption of either of the proposed lines, as Jay pointed out, would have meant the cession of between 30,000 and 35,000 square miles of United States territory. Had he accepted such a limitation, it is difficult to conceive that in the future boundary conventions the United States could have obtained the line of forty-nine degrees North Latitude, west to the Rocky Mountains, and, eventually, to the Pacific Ocean.

Jay showed that on the very map on which Grenville relied for his geographical information several other streams were marked "Mississippi by conjecture," and he contended that it would be only reasonable, in view of admitted uncertainty of geographical knowledge in that quarter, to have a joint survey made which should serve as the basis for future definitive settlement. This proposition, which was far from closing all possibilities of rectification favorable to Great Britain at some future date, Grenville had to accept.[30] The reasonableness of

29. *A.S.P., F.R., 1*, 490–95. All the papers relating to the Jay negotiation are not published here, nor were they submitted to the Senate. In the case of the northwest boundary gap, the unpublished papers of the Foreign Office, which include copies of all notes exchanged (the negotiation took place in writing), and which the writer has examined, add nothing to the material in *Foreign Relations;* neither do the Jay Papers in the library of the New York Historical Society.

30. *A.S.P., F.R., 1*, 490–95. Jay refusing to accept either of the proposed rectifications, Grenville drafted an article providing for an immediate joint survey on the basis of this formula: "Whereas it is a question of difference between the said parties, in case these lines [i.e., the boundary lines of the Treaty of 1783] should be found not to close, whether, according to the true intent and meaning of the 2d and 8th articles of the Treaty of Peace, these lines ought to be closed in such a manner, as that Canada should border on navigable water of the said river—which question it would be premature to discuss and endeavour to settle, while the said Parties remain uninformed of the actual extent and many other material circumstances of the said river," etc. The survey was to measure the depth and channel of the river, particularly "the intervals where it may be found to be navigable." A copy of this draft was secured for the writer by the editor of this *Review* [J. Franklin Jameson], who found it among the private, unprinted, manuscripts of Lord Grenville preserved at Dropmore, England.

Jay's contention is reinforced when one examines the modern map, and finds that the Red Lake River line would have still left a northwest boundary gap, and when one reflects that up to that time there had been no question of the identity of the boundary as far west as the Lake of the Woods, part of which accepted line Grenville, under guise of fashioning an entirely new boundary, was now attempting to rectify.

Though Lord Grenville was not successful in securing British title to a tract of land of incalculable value to the future United States, the treaty which he and John Jay signed provided abundantly for the protection of the British fur trade of the Northwest and for the security of the Grand Portage route. Article III of Jay's Treaty stipulated:

> It is agreed that it shall at all times be free to His Majesty's subjects, and to the citizens of the United States, and also to the Indians dwelling on either side of the said boundary line, freely to pass and repass by land and inland navigation into the respective territories and countries of the two parties on the continent of America (the country within the limits of the Hudson's Bay Company only excepted), and to navigate all the lakes, rivers and waters thereof, and freely to carry on trade and commerce with each other. . . .[31]
>
> The river Mississippi shall . . . according to the treaty of peace, be entirely open to both parties; and it is further agreed, that all ports and places on its eastern side, to whichsoever of the parties belonging, may freely be resorted to and used by both parties, in as ample a manner as any of the Atlantic ports or places of the United States, or any of the ports and places of His Majesty in Great Britain. . . .
>
> [Reciprocal favored-nation privileges were agreed to by the same article, which further provided] that no duty shall ever be laid by either party on peltries brought by land or inland navigation into the said territories respectively, nor shall the Indians passing or

---

Jay refused to consider any article which discussed in any way the question of bringing Canada to the navigable waters of the Mississippi, though he included in his treaty draft of September 30 an article for a joint commission to survey the region of the supposed boundary gap. Article IV of the treaty finally signed provided that "measures shall be taken in concert" for a joint survey, but did not provide the measures at that time. No commission was set up for the purpose, as was done in Article V for the settlement of the disputed northeastern boundary. A definite settlement was in this way postponed.

31. An exception was made in the case of rivers other than the Mississippi which were navigable from the sea.

repassing with their own proper goods and effects of whatever nature, pay for any import or duty whatsoever. But goods in bales,
or other packages unusual among Indians, shall not be considered
as goods belonging *bona fide* to Indians.

Again, free passage across the portages on both sides of the boundary
was stipulated, and goods and traders thus crossing portages and back
into their own territory were to be free from tariffs.

Thus, even though in fulfilment of Jay's Treaty Great Britain finally
evacuated American soil, she secured permanent [32] commercial privileges on the frontier which enabled her to hold the rich fur trade she
had built up among the United States Indians and to secure the use
of the Grand Portage to the Canadian Northwest. More than this,
by the right to use the inland water navigation and to establish warehouses and other facilities for trade anywhere on the east bank of the
Mississippi, equal in privilege to the port privileges extended by the
United States to foreign subjects in Atlantic ports, the way was open
for that future great commerce which sanguine Englishmen hoped
would flow into the American West by way of the Great Lakes, making
Montreal and not New Orleans the future *entrepôt* of the commerce
of the Mississippi Valley.

That these trading privileges were nominally reciprocal [33] did not
make them, to any great extent, advantageous to the United States.
By virtue of their long-standing connections with the Indians within
American territory, British traders were able to cope successfully with
American competition [34] until the War of 1812.[35] Until that time they
had a practical monopoly of the upper Mississippi country.[36] Alexander Hamilton, who became the most powerful advocate before the
public for the ratification of Jay's Treaty, in elucidating Article III
dwelt on the advantages of this reciprocity. Only a small proportion of

32. The first ten articles of the treaty were to be permanent in their operation.
33. As first drafted by Grenville, this article did not even contain reciprocal
privileges for American traders in British territory.
34. Astor's company, which was tied up with Canadian stockholders, carried on
from Mackinaw a considerable fur trade within British territory on the east side of
Lake Huron. See H. M. Chittenden, *The American Fur Trade of the Far West* (3
vols. New York, 1902), *I*, 311.
35. Gallatin to Astor, Aug. 5, 1835, Washington Irving, *Astoria* (2 vols. Philadelphia, 1836), appendix.
36. Pike, in 1805, found only British fur traders in the upper Mississippi country.
They were flying the British flag and distributing British medals to the natives, until
he requested them to stop the practice. Elliott Coues, ed., *The Explorations of Zebulon
Montgomery Pike* (3 vols. New York, 1895), *I*, 247–50.

the Canadian furs had come from American territory, he argued, while now all of Canada would be open to the enterprise of American fur traders.[37] This argument rested on mistaken information. As pointed out above, one-half of the Canadian furs had depended on American territory for their production in the years before Jay's Treaty, while no American traders had resorted to Canada. The nominal reciprocity which was now opened to citizens of the United States to pursue the trade among the Indians dwelling on British soil was to a large degree cut away by the treaty's inhibition to Americans to enter the territory of the Hudson's Bay Company.[38] It was a great boon to the United States when the War of 1812 put an end to this wholly one-sided arrangement.

The limits of the Hudson's Bay Company have a curious connection with the northwest boundary. The charter granted by Charles II to the company in the year 1670 conveyed ownership outright to all the land within the watershed of the streams flowing into Hudson Bay in so far as such territory was not already under the domain of some Christian prince other than the King of England. The watershed of Hudson Bay extends south into the present states of Minnesota and North Dakota. In 1670 this upper portion of the watershed had not been occupied by any other Christian prince, nor had any part of the great Northwest of Canada. Nor for a long time thereafter was it occupied by the Hudson's Bay Company itself, which for a hundred years could not have known the precise southern limits of its charter rights. For a century the company did not venture more than a few miles inland from the shores of the bay, relying on the Indians to bring their furs down the rivers to the factories there. Before the company had occupied any of the great interior described by the royal charter, a Christian prince, the King of France, through the operations and explorations of his subject fur traders and pathfinders, took possession of Canada as far west as the Rocky Mountains, including much of the territory over which the Hudson's Bay Company would have considered that it had legal ownership. Soon the French in peace and war were disputing possession of the

37. "Camillus," no. XII, Hamilton, *Works* (J. C. Hamilton ed.), 7, 277.

38. This possibility did not escape Washington. "All this [Article III] looks very well on paper, but I much question whether in its operation it will not be found to work very much against us. 1st. What are the limits of that Company? . . . 2d. Admitting the fact, will they not, having possession of the trade, and the Indians being in their interest, by every artifice of *their* traders, prevent *ours* from extending themselves into the country, sharing in the profits, and thereby bringing on disputes which may terminate seriously?" Washington to Hamilton, July 13, 1795, Hamilton, *Works* (J. C. Hamilton ed.), 6, 17.

shores of the bay itself. By the Treaty of Utrecht in 1713 France "restored" to England the territory on the shores of Hudson Bay. The King of France did not restore the interior country drained by the Hudson Bay rivers. Of the southern part of this territory he had occupied a great part, just how much nobody precisely knew.[39]

By the terms of Article X of the Treaty of Utrecht an Anglo-French commission was to meet and determine the boundary between New France and the territory of the Hudson's Bay Company. When the commission finally met, in 1719, the English representatives, acting on the behests of the company, claimed a line from Grimmington's Island, off the coast of Labrador (latitude 58° 30′ north) through Lake Mistassine (the source of Rupert's River) thence deflecting southwest to 49° North Latitude, which parallel thenceforth was to be the southern limit of the Hudson's Bay Company's territorial possessions.[40] This claim the French would not accept, and the commission broke up without achieving any result. When New France was ceded to Great Britain, in 1763, the northern limits of the province—that is, the southern boundary of the Hudson's Bay Company's lands—never had been established. Either the charter of 1670 or the undetermined claims of New France had to be taken as the eventual boundary between the new British provinces and the territorial claims of the great corporation, a matter which led later to much Canadian litigation. What interests the investigator of the northwest boundary gap is the fact that contemporary English mapmakers began to consider as the southern limit of western Canada (that is, the boundary between Spanish Louisiana and British North America) the line of 49° North Latitude which had been *claimed* unsuccessfully in 1719 by England on behalf of the Hudson's Bay Company.[41] This cartographical fiction later became the sole precedent for the international boundary of 49°.

The provision of Article IV of Jay's Treaty for a joint survey of the gap was never carried out. The first accurate survey of the upper waters

39. That the King of France did not restore more than the immediate shores of Hudson Bay did not necessarily destroy the English claims to portions of the interior, as some writers against the Hudson's Bay Company would have us believe (Lindsey, *An Investigation of the Unsettled Boundaries of Ontario,* p. 104). It really depends on just how much France could claim as having occupied, for she could not restore what she had never occupied.

40. Petition of the Hudson's Bay Company to Lords of Trade and Plantations, 1714, *Docs. respecting Northern and Western Boundaries of Ontario,* p. 131. For description of accompanying map, ibid., p. 136 i.

41. James White, "Boundary Disputes and Treaties," in *Canada and Her Provinces* (Toronto, 1913), *8,* 838–43; *Docs. respecting Boundaries of Ontario,* pp. 136 f.

of the Mississippi was made in 1797–98 by David Thompson, the distinguished pathfinder and geographer of the North West Company. Thompson designated Turtle Lake (47° 37′ north latitude) as the source,[42] a fact which became known to the world by the publication in 1801 of Alexander Mackenzie's famous *Voyages*.[43] He found the "source" while searching for the precise location of the parallel of 49° north and seeking to locate geographically the North West Company's trading posts in relation to that parallel, the purpose for which he was employed.

Thompson explains in his *Narrative* why the North West Company had this survey made. The motive which he attributes to them can easily be shown to be false, and his explanations on this point give a fatal blow to his *Narrative* as a trustworthy historical source. They show that the old man who wrote, after 1850, the record of events of his youth, fifty years before, unconsciously observed the significance of those events through an imagination stimulated by reflection on the great changes which had taken place in the half-century intervening. He occasionally departed from the skeleton of his old field-notes to embellish his narrative with comments of his own. Thompson declares that the North West Company's desire to learn the precise location of the parallel of 49° north was prompted by the treaty of 1792, which had made that parallel the boundary between the United States and Canada from the Lake of the Woods to the Rocky Mountains. He states that such a line was then adopted to remedy the gap left in 1783. The veteran geographer further declares, in his indignation at Britain's ever conceding such a boundary (49° north by that time had been projected by the Oregon treaty through to the Pacific), that the adoption of the line by the treaty of 1792 was due to the machinations of one Peter Pond,[44] an ubiquitous and quick-tempered American partner of the North West Company who had explored the upper Mississippi as a trader. Pond, who returned to Connecticut, his home, some time after 1790, is asserted by Thompson to have been "at the elbow" of the American commissioners who signed the treaty of 1792. The British diplomatists, on the other hand, were wholly ignorant of the country to the west of Lake Ontario and had no adequate maps. Hence they were duped by the

42. The Lake of the Woods he located at 49° 46′.

43. *Voyages from Montreal on the River St. Lawrence, through the Continent of North America to the Frozen and Pacific Oceans* (London, 1801). See 1902 ed., *1*, xcv–xcvi.

44. For Pond, see "Journal of Peter Pond," Wisconsin Historical Society, *Collections, 18*, 314–54, with editorial introduction; Davidson, *North West Company*, p. 37; C. A. *Report*, 1890, p. 52.

Americans, who got expert advice from Peter Pond.[45] A comparatively recent Canadian writer, among the several who have relied implicitly on Thompson's *Narrative,* lamenting the terms of this treaty, writes that the real reason for the British concessions embodied in the treaty was a "supreme indifference to the territorial interests of British North America which had been so painfully apparent in all the boundary disputes with the United States; for the British commissioners must have had at the time of the negotiations, and for some time before, access to a map of the western country, with remarks upon its character, prepared by Pond himself." [46]

As to the capacity of British negotiators in general in boundary controversies with the United States the present writer feels no call to make comment, but to accuse the Foreign Office of negligence in this instance is to be too severe; there was, of course, never any treaty of 1792. The line of 49° was not established as the international boundary west of the Lake of the Woods until the year 1818.

Dismissing this strange historical figment,[47] why should the North West Company have desired such geographical information, to the

45. David Thompson, *Narrative* (Toronto, 1916), p. 176.

46. Burpee, *Search for the Western Sea* (London, 1908), p. 337. In his old age Thompson got pitifully little reward for his great services to his country. His last years were spent in abject poverty, with little attention to his petitions for relief by the government on account of his sixty years of distinguished services. The harassments of fortune which beset him during these years and his patriotic indignation at the impending danger of loss to Great Britain of the Columbia Basin (and finally its actual loss), into a large portion of which he had been the first white man to penetrate, and which he had claimed for England, can easily account for the confusion of his statements. From 1842 to 1845 Thompson's advice on the geography of the Oregon dispute was sought by officials of the government, and he wrote several reports on his observations of the country. Two of these are important evidence of the absolute untrustworthiness of this ill-treated and indignant old patriot's *ex post facto* accounts of the northwest boundary dispute, for not only do they conflict as to dates and persons and circumstances, but they conflict also with the statements of Thompson noted in the above text, and with each other. Note particularly:

    1. "Statement of David Thompson on the Seventh Article of the Treaty of Ghent" (undated, but apparently included with papers written in 1842–1845), and

    2. "Remarks on the Oregon Boundary" made by David Thompson, June 10, 1845, at Montreal, for Sir James Alexander.

My attention was called to these documents by Mr. T. C. Elliott, of Walla Walla. They are printed in *Report of the Provincial Archivist of British Columbia* for 1913, pp. 114–24.

47. The manuscript of David Thompson's *Narrative* fell into the possession of Mr. Charles Lindsey, who followed it trustfully in *An Investigation of the Unsettled Boundaries of Ontario.* It has been repeated from Lindsey by various Canadian

extent that they were willing to employ a professional geographer to make the survey for them? The records of the company are not available to testify, because the papers of its successor (after the merger of 1821), the Hudson's Bay Company, are not open to historical research; but a book published in 1801 by one of the principal partners in the North West Company affords the clue. This partner was Alexander Mackenzie and the book is none other than his famous *Voyages.* Mackenzie in 1797 had been located at the Grand Portage, and it was he, and William McGillivray, who engaged Thompson for the company. Mackenzie's *Voyages* appeared in London in 1801, but there are indications that the author was at work on this book very soon after Thompson had completed his survey of the upper Mississippi country. In this work, apropos of the northwest boundary gap, Mackenzie declared that if the navigation of the Mississippi were considered of any consequence to Great Britain, "the nearest way to get at it" [48] was from the head of Lake Superior by way of the St. Louis River and the portage to the Mississippi. But the navigation of the Mississippi was only incidental to the real scope of this great pathfinder's plans, which are to be read in some general reflections with which he closes his remarkable book:

> the line of American boundary runs, and it is said to continue through Lake Superior (and through a lake called Long Lake which has no existence), to the Lake of the Woods, in latitude 49.37 North, from whence it is also said to run West to the Mississippi, which it may do, by giving it a good deal of Southing, but not otherwise; as the source of that river does not extend further north than latitude 47.38 North, where it is no more than a small brook; *consequently, if Great Britain retains the right of entering it along the line of division, it must be in a lower latitude, and wherever that may be, the line must be continued West, till it terminates in the Pacific Ocean, to the South of the Columbia.*[49]
> [Italics are the present writer's.]

Mackenzie's great ambition at this time, as is well known,[50] was a merger of the North West and Hudson's Bay companies to control

---

writers, for example, Burpee, *Search for the Western Sea.* It was respected even as late as 1916 in J. B. Tyrrell's excellent edition of Thompson's *Narrative.*

48. Alexander Mackenzie, *Voyages from Montreal* (2 vols. New York, 1902), *1*, xcvi. Mackenzie published a map with his work, the most accurate description of western Canada which had appeared.

49. Ibid., *2*, 343–44.

50. See particularly Joseph Schafer's illuminating article, "British Attitude toward Oregon, 1815–1846," in *A.H.R.*, *16*, 276–78.

the fur trade of British North America as far west as the Pacific Ocean
(to which he had been the first to penetrate overland), including the
basin of the Columbia.[51] The legendary boundary line of 49° North
Latitude, if accepted as the southern boundary of Canada in the west,
would leave on foreign soil several of the posts of the North West
Company west of the Mississippi and, if eventually projected to the
ocean, would shut out the most valuable parts of the Columbia River
basin, as well as much of the fur regions of the Rocky Mountains.
Mackenzie's anxiety about the northwest boundary gap was due to his
desire to obtain an advantageous point of departure, for the projection
through to the Pacific, of the line which some day would have to be
drawn between British North America and Louisiana. He wanted
that line drawn in a latitude far enough south to secure the future of
the fur trade of the Far West.

The boundary rectification contemplated by Hammond and taken
up by Lord Grenville in the Jay negotiations for the sake of the British
fur interests and other commercial interests would have secured the
territorial basis for such far-sighted plans of empire as those imagined
by Mackenzie. If the proposal to extend a wedge of British territory
down to the "navigable" waters of the Mississippi, say to the latitude
of the mouth of the St. Croix, had been accepted by Jay, the future
line between the United States and Canada would in all likelihood
have followed the parallel of 45° north instead of 49°; had Grenville's
alternative line been accepted (the latitude of the present city of
Duluth) it would have been a strong argument for making the future
northern boundary run west along the parallel of about 47° 30′. Either
line was likely to entail the loss, to the future American West, of great
areas of land.

Concerning Jay's refusal to recognize what would have been a cession
of American territory in the northwest corner of the country, the most
distinguished student of western history has observed:

> The modifications which England proposed in 1794 to John Jay
> in the northwestern boundary of the United States from the Lake
> of the Woods to the Mississippi, seemed, doubtless, to him sig-
> nificant chiefly as a matter of principle and as a question of the
> retention or loss of beaver grounds. The historians hardly notice
> the proposals. But they involved, in fact, the ownership of the
> richest and most extensive deposits of iron ore in America, the
> all-important source of a fundamental industry of the United

51. Mackenzie, *Voyages*, 2, 353–55.

States, the occasion for the rise of some of the most influential forces of our time.[52]

Unwittingly Jay was defending more than the territorial basis of the American steel industry. Without realizing it he held in his hand the destiny of a part of Minnesota, of North Dakota, Montana, and the commonwealths of the Pacific Northwest. He was holding for the United States the starting point of the 1818 boundary, which extended the line of 49° to the Rocky Mountains, thus at last eliminating the boundary gap and establishing a basis for the final extension of the international boundary to the Pacific Coast. These future states, which now elect as many United States senators as old New England did and which have incalculably rich natural resources (water power so abundant, for example, as to make it possible to transfer industrial development in the twentieth century from the old northeastern to the new northwestern states), were the invisible stakes for which Jay and Grenville unconsciously played, amidst the immediate problems of a great world war, in those fateful days of 1794. From the twentieth-century point of view the historical student may well see, in the defeat of the Hammond-Grenville rectification project by the patriotic principles of Jefferson and Jay, one of those strokes of good fortune which have so strikingly and abundantly illustrated the boundary diplomacy of the United States. Had the suggestions of the equally patriotic Hamilton been adopted it is not very likely that much of the Pacific Northwest, Montana, and a part of Minnesota and South Dakota as well as all of North Dakota would be in the American Union today.[53]

52. In Professor F. J. Turner's presidential address to the American Historical Association, Dec. 28, 1910, "Social Forces in American History," in *A.H.R.*, *16*, 226.

53. For a history of the northwest boundary, 1803–15, see Dr. Schafer's paper, above cited, note 51; A. J. Hill, in Minnesota Hist. Soc., *Collections*, 7, 317–52, and A. N. Winchell, *8*, 185–212.

8. Alexander Hamilton and the Limitation
of Armaments

THE AMERICAN IDEA of limitation of armaments was first conceived by Alexander Hamilton. Fine-combed as have been the life and times of that great American statesman, his final biography has not yet been written. When this is done, his connection with one of the greatest diplomatic achievements in the nineteenth and twentieth centuries may stand out in proper relief. Not only the incident of Hamilton's statesmanship to be narrated in these pages but various other unrecorded features of his foreign policy so vitally important to the perpetuation of American nationality will be placed before the eyes of the English-reading world. The unused material on the life of Hamilton is to be found in the archives of the British Public Record Office, in the Canada archives at Ottawa, and among the unpublished papers of Baron Grenville, the Foreign Secretary of Great Britain at one of the most critical periods of the Empire's international relations, namely the first years of the great war with France that began in 1793.

Without exception, as far as the writer is aware, the origin of the principle of limitation of armaments on the frontier between the United States and British North America is attributed by historical writers to the negotiations between the two governments which ended in the Treaty of 1818. That treaty, it will be remembered, established the international boundary along the parallel of forty-nine degrees North Latitude from the Lake of the Woods to the Rocky Mountains and adopted the principle of the abolition of naval armaments on the Great Lakes and of any kind of armament along the land frontier throughout its length. For over a hundred years it has testified to the possibility of international peace founded on good will and mutual understanding. A great and beneficent precedent, the Anglo-American Treaty of 1818 has had that tonic effect on the war-weary generations of the old world which comes to one who breathes the clear free air of those lofty ranges whose summits the treaty line itself climbed.

Published in *Pacific Review*, 2, no. 4, 1922.

The principle adopted in 1818 runs back as far as the year 1794 and into the brain of Alexander Hamilton. It was expressed in the negotiations of that year with England which resulted in the famous Jay's Treaty, the first treaty ever submitted to the United States Senate. That the principle, thus as old as American foreign policy itself, was not then adopted was not the fault of the United States.

Hamilton's principle was proposed by John Jay to the British government in the summer of 1794. To place in its proper setting the negotiation of Jay it is necessary to recall certain features of the international relations between Great Britain and the United States in the years intervening between the treaty of independence and the treaty of 1794. The reader is asked to tolerate this digression because it is necessary to explain why the American proposal was refused by Great Britain.

The treaty of peace of 1783 was an acknowledgment by England of independence but by no means of American nationality. There was no American nation in 1783. We read in Article I of the treaty that His Britannic Majesty recognizes the independence of "the United States; viz. New Hampshire, Massachusetts Bay, Rhode Island and Providence Plantations, Connecticut, New York, New Jersey, Pennsylvania, Delaware, Maryland, Virginia, North Carolina, South Carolina, and Georgia." During the weak government under the Articles of Confederation, from 1781 to 1789, the pitiful ineptitude of the American Confederacy impressed foreign as well as domestic observers with the certainty of imminent dissolution. We remember how the sovereign powers of the thirteen states and their jealousies one of the other and of the central government made it impossible for the Congress to collect taxes, execute laws, or compel the observance of treaties. The national spirit which had been successful in war could not cope with the tasks and problems of peace. Bankrupt and disunited, the American people stood face to face with domestic chaos and foreign contumely.

Two articles of the treaty of peace which became the subject of much dispute during these years of states' rights anarchy should be recalled. Article II stipulated that British troops should evacuate American territory "with all convenient speed." Article IV guaranteed to British creditors full payment of debts contracted by Americans before the war. Neither of these articles was fully complied with. It is true that the troops located at New York City and a few other places along the Atlantic Coast were speedily embarked for Europe after the preliminaries of peace had been signed, for it was expected that they would be badly needed there. But British garrisons continued to occupy, after final ratification of the treaty, the military posts along the Canadian frontier. These were on the American side of the boundary, at the northern end of Lake Champlain, on the shore of Lake Ontario, on the Niagara River, and at Detroit and Michilimakinack, Michigan. These strategic points dominated the Great Lakes, as well as the Champlain water route to Canada, and constituted so many *points d'appui* from which British influence could be extended over the hinterlands of the American West. On April 8, 1784, the day before King George III proclaimed ratification of the treaty and publicly commanded his subjects to observe its terms all and singular, secret orders were sent from London to the governor general of Canada to postpone indefinitely the evacuation of these posts. For the next thirteen years British redcoats made daily parade on drill grounds on American soil and the world grew used to the astonishing spectacle of a power which had been defeated in war continuing to occupy the territory of the victor as security, it was asserted, for the proper fulfilment of the treaty terms by the United States.

The real reasons for this continued occupation of the American back country are apparent to him who reads the official correspondence between the Canadian governor general and the Home Office in London. The territory lying between the Great Lakes and the Ohio River and between the Mississippi and western Pennsylvania was yielding to the merchants of Montreal and London at the time the treaty was ratified a fur trade worth half a million dollars annually in values of those days. It was the most profitable single commercial industry in North America and to deliver over into the hands of the Americans the western posts would mean the loss of the business. This was one reason for the retention of the posts. The other was that in the peace treaty the British commissioners had been unable to secure any protection for the interests of their Indian allies, who lived in this same western country, which the American Congress in 1787 organized as the Northwest Territory. The treaty ceded over to the United States all the land south of the boundary without reservation or mention of any rights of the natives. These people, attracted first to the posts as the bases of military operations during the war, continued to flock about them after the peace. Thousands depended for their daily victuals on the bounty of the Canadian Department of Indian Affairs, which maintained its supply houses under the protecting guns of the garrisons. These posts, too, had become the marts of the fur trade. To desert them suddenly, to cut off the supplies to which the savages had been accustomed, to deliver the tribal lands of the Indians over to their enemies meant the end of all control over the native nations. It threatened not only to destroy British trade with them but, as one English officer pointed out, to force them to bite the hand that had fed. Officers who had led Indian raids on the outposts of American backwoods settlements during the war knew all too intimately the horrors of savage warfare to care to see it repeated on Canadian soil.

No reference to any failure on the part of the United States to adhere to the treaty terms was made when the orders were first dispatched from England to hold the posts. In fact, none could be made, for the treaty of that day was still formally unratified. But it soon became evident that Congress was not able to prevent the several states from putting legal impediments in the way of the collection of debts by British creditors. It was useless to appeal to the states to carry out the treaty punctiliously. The interests of property within the state were stronger than the power of Congress outside the state and legislatures were irritated at the continued presence of British troops on American soil. Thus was the armory of British diplomacy furnished with a plausible and convenient excuse for keeping the posts—these positions would be held until the debts were paid. The onus of infraction of the treaty was neatly handed over to the American government, and the valuable furs of the Northwest Territory continued to be shipped down the St. Lawrence instead of being diverted to the Potomac or the Hudson.

It was impossible for Congress to prevent this humiliating situation. John Adams was dispatched to London as American minister. George III received him politely and coldly, but no British minister was sent to the United States. American ships were shut out, as foreigners, from the prosperous trade with the British West Indies. Exasperated at the English Navigation Laws, humiliated by the continued occupation of American territory, some of the states adopted a policy of commercial discrimination against British trade only to find that other states then let it come in free. The trade laws of individual states as well as the protests of the American minister were complacently ignored by the British government. "It will not be an easy matter to bring the American States to act as a nation," wrote the most widely-read publicist in England, Lord Sheffield. "They are not to be feared by us. It must be a long time before they can engage, or will concur, in any material expense. We might as reasonably dread the effects of combinations among the Germans as among the American States and deprecate the resolves of the Diet as those of Congress." And so the posts were held, in defiance of the treaty. In disgust John Adams withdrew from the Court of St. James's.

Peace with England was not accompanied by any peace between the United States and the western Indians who had fought at the side of British regiments. Most of the Six Nations came to terms but the numerous tribes of the Northwest Territory refused to treat with the peace commissioners sent out by Congress. Minority representatives, indeed, signed peace treaties, but the majority of the Indians, united in a loose confederacy under the leadership of the shrewd half-breed Mohawk, Joseph Brant, repudiated these treaties and stood out for the line of the Ohio River as the rightful boundary of their lands. This Congress refused to recognize. Brant made a trip to England to get the active alliance of British forces for the support of his confederacy. Though he received a big grant of money in the form of compensation for the property losses sustained by the Mohawks during the war, he was refused any open aid. But he was encouraged by Lord Sydney, Secretary of State for Home Affairs (a portfolio which then included the administration of Colonial Affairs) to "stick to his rights" as respected the "encroachments" of the Americans. As Brant left London Sydney instructed Lord Dorchester, the governor general at Quebec, not to give the Indians any "open" assistance. Nevertheless it would not be consistent with justice, he was reminded, to leave them to "the mercy of the Americans." "To afford them [the Indians] active assistance would be a measure extremely imprudent, but at the same time it would not become us to refuse them such supplies of ammunition as might enable them to defend themselves."

The effect of such instructions on the commandants of the frontier garrisons may easily be imagined. During their desultory conflict with the levies of frontier militia and their raids on exposed settlements the savages depended on the British posts for munitions and supplies, which though not "openly" given were none the less valuable and effective for their bloody purposes. There was no means of preventing this as long as only the Articles of Confederation continued to bind the government of the United States, nor was any headway made in the task of pacifying the savages by force.

Meanwhile paid informants of the British government, whose reports may now be read in the archives of the Foreign Office, were prophesying the dissolution of the American Union. Intrigues were already underway with prominent citizens of Kentucky, Tennessee, and Vermont, which aimed at detaching the whole American West, including Vermont, from the United States in the event of dissolution, and attaching them to Canada. The posts became breeding places of insidious political intrigue as well as of murderous savage warfare. Such was the situation when the notable political revolution of 1788 resulted in the adoption of the United States Constitution and the creation of a strong national government with George Washington as President and Alexander Hamilton as Secretary of the Treasury and Thomas Jefferson as Secretary of State.

Washington's first motion in the field of foreign affairs was to sound England as to her attitude toward the new administration. Gouverneur Morris, literary stylist of the Constitution, was the "personal agent" who served in this capacity. He had instructions from Washington to inquire whether there were any objections now to fulfilling the articles of the treaty, and whether there were any inclinations for a treaty of commerce with the United States. The American agent was courteously received, and had conferences with both the Secretary for Foreign Affairs, at that time the Duke of Leeds, and with William Pitt, Prime Minister. Morris found that his overtures were listened to more graciously during the Nootka Crisis of 1790, when war between Great Britain and Spain seemed certain, than after the passing of that affair. He concluded that there was no real inclination either to negotiate a treaty of commerce or to evacuate the frontier, except in case England should be embarrassed in such a war as to make it desirable for her to extend favors to the United States.

The Morris mission elicited no adequate response from the Pitt ministry, but the passage of tariff and navigation laws by the first American Congress under the new national government aroused attention as nothing else could. These laws gave a tariff rebate of ten per cent on goods imported in American ships distinguished from foreign vessels and levied much lower tonnage duties on native than on foreign ships. Not specifically aimed at British shipping they hit it heavily, because British vessels far outnumbered all other foreign craft entering American harbors. The laws started a gradual shift of Anglo-American commerce to American bottoms, to the detriment of English shipowners and British sea power. Moreover, a strong movement in Congress had been manifested from the first for specific discrimination against British as distinguished from other foreign shipping. By 1791 this tendency had become so threatening that a minister resident was at last established at Philadelphia for the purpose of heading it off. Of all foreign countries the United States was the biggest market for English manufactures. No government of England in the days of the Industrial Revolution could afford to lose the nation's biggest customer. The navigation laws of Congress thus forced a recognition of American nationality which England had until then been loath to give.

At Downing Street it was well realized that even the presence of a minister at the American capital could not prevent the passage of laws discriminating against British commerce, if the government refused to discuss infractions of the treaty. George Hammond, the new minister, therefore was empowered to discuss *ad referendum* an adjustment of the frontier situation which might involve the evacuation of the posts in exchange for a guaranty by the United States government of the payment to British creditors of private ante-bellum debts. The ministry conceived an ambitious project by which the evacuation, when finally arranged, should not injure British control of the fur trade of the Northwest Territory and of the Indians there. A formal mediation by His Majesty's governor general in Canada was to be proposed between the United States and the hostile Indians, under cover of which was to be erected a "neutral barrier state," nominally independent and under Indian sovereignty and outside the dominion of either the United States or Great Britain. This state was to be composed of a broad belt of territory between the Mississippi and Vermont and north of the Ohio. Under the guise of this "independent" native state the whole Northwest Territory and part of the state of Pennsylvania and New York were to be separated from the sovereignty of the United States. The Americans would be absolutely excluded from the Great Lakes which would remain under exclusively British control. To complete the scheme, rectifications of the boundary of 1783 were to be proposed in the northwest and northeast so as to give Great Britain control respectively of the upper navigable waters of the Mississippi and of the navigation of Lake Champlain. Thus would a scientific frontier be established for British North America. Thus would the fur trade be secure as long as it should last. Thus would England continue to dominate the Indians of the American West and check American expansion north of the Ohio River and west of the Allegheny.

It is needless to say that this design to partition the United States under the pretense of friendly mediation had no chance of succeeding as long as the government should be able to protect its territory by physical resistance, nor as long as a man of General Washington's experience with Indian warfare remained President. Hammond became so persuaded of the impossibility of the mediation project that he never ventured to propose it officially. Even his informal suggestions in that direction to Jefferson and Hamilton were most emphatically repelled.

Meanwhile the British minister had been severely worsted by Jefferson in the long written controversy over the priority of infraction of the treaty. Jefferson's well-reasoned demonstration of the good faith of the American government as to the fulfilment of the treaty had been unanswered for eighteen months when in 1793 war broke out between England and France.

During the long series of campaigns of the United States against the western Indians the tribes had received political tutelage and covert material support from the British authorities in Canada. It was a nightmare of those officials that should the Indians finally be conquered the victorious American troops would next be employed forcibly to take possession of the posts. For this reason it was expedient to stiffen the Indian resistance. It was hoped, too, that a succession of disastrous campaigns, like St. Clair's defeat of 1791, against the confederated tribes, would finally make the mediation project acceptable and the neutral Indian barrier state possible. It consequently became the policy of the British government to delay as long as possible a settlement of the question of the posts, until the final outcome of the American military exertions against the natives should be certain.

The declaration of war by France in 1793 prevented this delay and increased the nervousness of the commanders of the occupied posts. Technically the United States was an ally of France, and even Washington's proclamation of neutrality did not remove the fear that this government would take advantage of England's being involved in an European war to possess itself of its own posts by force. So excited did the governor of Upper Canada and the governor general of British North America become at this prospect that Dorchester secretly made a speech to the Indians in February 1794, predicting war and declaring that soon the King's warriors would unite with their own to draw a new boundary line to the complete satisfaction of both. News of this speech leaked out and was published in Philadelphia simultaneously with that of the notorious Caribbean captures of January 1794. British cruisers, armed with an unpublished Order-in-Council, had swooped down on the unsuspecting American West Indian traffic and brought into prize courts over three hundred Yankee vessels which had been trading with the French Islands. The atrocious interpretation of international law which covered these captures was no more justifiable than Dorchester's bellicose speech to the western savages. Coming as they did at the same time these two incidents produced a crisis in Anglo-American relations.

Into the motives and intrigues of the Federalist Party which led to the mission of John Jay to England as the last means of averting war we cannot go here. Nor have we space to consider the terms of the treaty which bears his name.[1] Suffice it to remark that over ninety-two per cent of the revenue of the United States at that time depended on tariffs levied on imports from England. It was this tariff revenue that enabled Hamilton to establish national credit. And credit was an indispensable support to American nationality in 1794. War with Great Britain meant the destruction of credit and of nationality. Jay's Treaty, which was a written acquiescence in British sea power as the fountainhead of international law for the duration of the war with France, was the necessary price paid for the perpetuation of American nationality at a time when it was vitally imperiled.

Now it is an interesting feature of Jay's instructions that though written by Randolph, Jefferson's successor as Secretary of State, the principles on which they were based had already been outlined in a memorandum by Alexander Hamilton written for the President and entitled "Points to be considered in Mr. Jay's instructions." Hamilton at this time dominated the whole policy of the administration of President Washington. The instructions of Randolph in general follow the principles laid down by the Federalist leader, disagreeable as that task of copying may have been for the Virginian Secretary of State. Jay's negotiation throughout was dominated by Hamilton, and the treaty might much more properly be called "Hamilton's Treaty." Only so far as his instructions represented the ideas of Hamilton did the envoy pay much attention to them.

Manifestly one of the indispensable conditions of the United States to any friendly settlement with Great Britain at this critical time was the evacuation of the posts. Lord Grenville speedily acceded to that demand, and they were relinquished, according to the terms of Jay's Treaty, in 1796. England was not anxious to complicate the European situation by adding the United States to her enemies. Hamilton in outlining Jay's instructions, which were to demand among other things the evacuation of the posts, appears to have kept in mind the possibility that these posts could be removed just across the international water-boundary and still fulfil all strategical demands. From bases on British soil it would be equally easy to intrigue with the Indians in American territory. This, in fact, is precisely what did happen after the evacuation. It must have been with the idea of preventing such a situation that Hamilton laid down the following principles:

1. See my *Jay's Treaty* (rev. ed. Yale University Press, 1962).

A stipulation that in case of war with any Indian tribe, the other party shall furnish no supplies whatever to that tribe, except such, and in such quantity only, as it was accustomed to furnish previous to the war; and the party at war to have the right to keep an agent or agents at posts or settlements of the other party nearest to such Indians, to ascertain the faithful execution of this *stipulation*.

It may be desired, and would it not be for our interest to agree, that neither party shall in time of peace keep up any armed force upon the lakes, nor any fortified places nearer than ———miles to the lakes, except for small guards (the number to be defined) stationed for the security of trading houses.

In effect what Hamilton here proposed was a guaranty that if the Americans should conquer the natives, rendered helpless without British support, the United States would not compete with Great Britain for control of the Great Lakes but would be willing to accept the principle of an absolute limitation of armaments there. This is the origin of the American principle of the limitation of armaments as it later found expression in the Treaty of 1818.

These points outlined in Hamilton's memorandum are thus worded by Randolph in Jay's official instructions:

One of the consequences of holding the posts has been much bloodshed on our frontiers by the Indians, and much expense. The British Government having denied their abetting of the Indians we must of course acquit them. But we have satisfactory proofs (some of which, however, cannot, as you will discover, be used in public) that British agents are guilty of stirring up, and of assisting with arms, ammunition, and warlike instruments, the different tribes of Indians against us. It is incumbent on that Government to restrain those agents; or the forebearance to restrain them cannot be interpreted otherwise than a determination to discountenance them. It is a principle from which the United States will not easily depart, either in their conduct towards other nations, or what they may expect from them, that the Indians dwelling within the territories of one shall not be interferred with by the other.

Having laid down this principle of noninterference with each other's Indians as the basis of adjustment of the frontier question, the instructions proceeded to outline *seriatim* a number of provisions which it was desirable to incorporate in any treaty. The sixteenth of these desirabilities reads:

> In case of an Indian war, none but the usual supplies in peace shall be furnished.

The seventeenth reads:

> In peace, no troops to be kept within a limited distance from the Lakes.

Another interesting feature of the Jay negotiation is that all the papers dealing with it were not submitted to the Senate when that body met to consider ratification. There is, for example, a very important draft of a treaty which John Jay submitted to Lord Grenville on September 30, 1794. This was not given to the Senate. More than that, so far as the writer's investigations have enabled him to determine, it was not even enclosed in Jay's official dispatches to his government and no copy of it is now to be found in the archives of the Department of State. But a copy does exist in the British Public Record Office, and another copy, slightly modified, may be seen among the private un-printed papers of Lord Grenville preserved at the estate of Mr. J. B. Fortescue at Dropmore, England. A perusal of the draft suggests that it was never sent home because it testified to such a diplomatic defeat for Jay; for in the draft Jay had incorporated a lot of desirable pro-visions which Grenville promptly declared "insurmountable obstacles" to a treaty. Jay was forced to abandon them all. Most of the points re-linquished were those of neutral rights as conceived by the United States. But the proposals which concern us here are those which deal with the principle of the limitation of armaments, which Hamilton had outlined in the points for Jay's instructions.

Article II of Jay's draft of September 30 contains the following stipulation:

> Neither of the contracting Parties will form any political con-nextions, nor hold any Treaties with Indians dwelling within the boundaries of the other. They will with good faith endeavour to restrain their respective Indians from war, and the better to pre-vent it, they will make every future Indian war a common cause so far as to prohibit and prevent any supplies of ammunition or arms being given or sold even by Indian traders to the belligerent tribe or tribes or to any individuals of them.

In case it should happen (which God forbid), that war should exist between the said parties, they mutually engage to abstain not only from inviting but also from permitting any Indians to join in it; but on the contrary will reject their offers of aid and receive no assistance from them; nor shall they be allowed under any pretence or in any capacity, to attend or resort to the armies or detachments of either of the said parties.

No armed vessels shall be kept by either of the parties on the lakes and waters thro' which the boundary line between them passes. *It being their earnest desire to render mutual justice, confidence, and goodwill, a sufficient Barrier against encroachment and aggression.* [Italics are the author's.]

Under the influence of these motives they will as soon as circumstances shall render it seasonable, enter into arrangements for diminishing or wholly withdrawing all military force from the Borders.

This proposal here and now, after one hundred and twenty-seven years, is made public for the first time.

Lord Grenville would accept none of the above propositions and Jay thought himself obliged to sign the treaty without them. The motive of Grenville in rejecting such beneficent principles is apparent when one discovers that three days after the signature he instructed Hammond to bring forward again the mediation proposal, if necessary to make it a secret arrangement between himself and Hamilton. "It is particularly desirable," he wrote, "for reasons with which you are not unacquainted that this matter should be adjusted in the manner I have mentioned before the evacuation of the posts." But this dispatch was intercepted by a French cruiser and before duplicates reached Hammond General Wayne's crushing defeat of the Indians had dashed all immediate hopes of any mediation.

The neutral Indian barrier state project, however, did not die the early death which its chances for success would have augured. It recurred in the plans and maps of the Foreign Office at various intervals until the negotiations at Ghent which ended the War of 1812 marked its disappearance. Tecumseh's confederation of 1811 and his notorious relations with the British frontier forts; the alliance of the British military forces with the United States Indians during the War of 1812; the vital importance of the naval control of the Lakes during that conflict; the resurrection at Ghent of the rectification proposal to bring

Canada south to the navigable waters of the Mississippi; all these facts testify that British ambitions in the West did not cease until the end of the War of 1812.

Only in the West can the War of 1812 be called a victory for the United States. For it removed forever the sinister intrigues with American Indians by powers outside the United States and did away with the bitter territorial rivalry which marked the period 1783–1815. The peace of Ghent paved the way for the century of peaceful boundary settlements which have since been such a distinguishing characteristic of Anglo-American diplomacy. It led soon to the ratification of the principle enunciated by Hamilton and elaborated by Jay in 1794, the "earnest desire to render mutual justice, confidence, and goodwill, a sufficient Barrier against encroachment and aggression."

Between the Treaty of 1818 and the Washington Conference of 1921 there is a distinct historical connection. And the student of American history must recognize that the germ of that idea sprang from the brain of Alexander Hamilton.

9. George Washington and Lafayette, the Prisoner in Europe

THE ILLUSTRIOUS FRIEND and soldier of American liberty, General Lafayette, returned in 1784 to the United States and tasted to the full the affectionate adulations of the fellow countrymen of his adoption. He was appropriately fêted and acclaimed in the principal American cities on a scale surpassed only by his better remembered visit one hundred years ago this year [1924].

His fellow countrymen? This question becomes more pertinent as we continue. On the occasion of his 1784 visit two states naturalized him. A special act of the Maryland legislature, after listing in fitting language his disinterested services, declared "that the Marquis de Lafayette and his heirs male forever shall be, and they, and each of them, are hereby deemed, adjudged and taken to be natural-born citizens thereof (i.e., of the State of Maryland), and they and every one of them, conforming to the Constitution and laws of this state, in the enjoyment and exercise of such immunities, rights, and privileges." [1] The legislature of Virginia declared that "the Marquis De La Fayette be henceforth deemed and considered a citizen of this State, and that he shall enjoy all the rights, privileges and immunities thereunto belonging." [2]

The Congress of the United States, until 1788 not vested with power to enact uniform naturalization laws, in a resolution of December 9, 1784, publicly felicitating Lafayette, stated that his uniform and unceasing attachment to this country "has resembled that of a patriotic citizen," and accordingly, "the United States regard him with particular affection, and will not cease to feel an interest in whatever may

1. *Laws of Maryland, 1781–84, 12.* "You and your heirs are made citizens of this State," Washington to Lafayette, Annapolis; Dec. 23, 1784, Jared Sparks, ed., *The Writings of George Washington* (12 vols. Boston, 1834–37), *9*, 82.

2. W. W. Hening, *The Statutes at Large, Being a Collection of All the Laws of Virginia* (13 vols. Richmond, 1810–23), *12*, 30.

Published under the title "The United States and Lafayette" in *Daughters of the American Revolution Magazine, 58,* June, July, August 1924, in honor of the centenary of Lafayette's farewell visit to the United States.

concern his honor and prosperity, and that their best and kindest wishes will always attend him." It is not apparent that Lafayette at this time considered his citizenship in two American states in any more than a complimentary way. One feels that he had no more sense of the obligations and immunities of American citizenship than any illustrious foreign visitor has today in accepting the keys of a city wishing thus to honor him. His contemporary letter to the Count de Vergennes is couched in the style of a loyal subject of the King of France.[3]

When the federal Constitution was ratified in 1788 the citizens of Virignia, Maryland, and the other states became *ipso facto* citizens of the United States. Thus so did Lafayette. It is true that he later became engaged in the service of a foreign prince, a service he discontinued abruptly in 1792. Nothing in the laws of the United States before or during that year prevented an American citizen from so doing, if he desired.[4] It is not at all absurd to argue that, had Lafayette resided in the United States the full fourteen years demanded by the Constitution as qualification for the presidency (and were old enough), it would have been constitutionally possible for him to hold that office, because like Alexander Hamilton he was a citizen of the United States when the instrument was ratified. This notwithstanding the fact that he had not renounced his allegiance to the King of France.

Eight years after his American naturalization Lafayette became a leading figure in the other great revolution of the eighteenth century, as keenly a knight for liberty, as he saw it, in the Old World as he had been its champion in the New. From the beginning an advocate

3. *Mémoires, Correspondance et Manuscrits de Lafayette* (hereinafter cited as *Mémoires*), 2, 98, note 1.

4. The first neutrality proclamation, of April 22, 1793, rendered citizens of the United States liable to punishment or forfeiture under the law of nations, by committing, aiding, or abetting hostilities against a belligerent power, and withdrew from such citizens the protection of the United States. J. B. Moore, *A Digest of International Law* (8 vols. Washington, 1906), 7, 1003. The Virginia statute of October 1783, had provided "that no person whatsoever, having or holding any place or pension from any foreign state or potentate, shall be eligible to any office, legislative, executive, or judiciary *within this commonwealth*" (italics inserted). It provided for expatriation by voluntary statement in writing, but stipulated no act tantamount to expatriation. Hening's *Statutes of Virginia*, 1782–84, *11*, 322. The first act of Congress (I *U.S. Statutes at Large*, 103) to establish a uniform rule of naturalization, Mar. 26, 1790, made no reference to expatriation. The act of Jan. 29, 1795 (ibid., p. 414), required all persons to be naturalized by the United States to forswear former allegiance and to renounce any hereditary title or order of nobility, and repealed the act of 1790. No statutory provision defining expatriation was enacted until much later, the matter being regulated by executive discretion. At the time of Lafayette's case, about to be narrated, there was no precedent of executive action.

of the Rights of Man and a constitutional monarchy, he became the supporter to the bitter end of the French Constitution of 1791, which he considered as satisfactory a crystallization of his political ideas as was at that time practicable. When war broke out with the allied monarchs of Prussia and Austria, Lafayette found himself at the front in command of one of the three armies defending the soil of France. Before he had much opportunity to demonstrate any great military capacity which his experience under Washington might have developed, France, involved in Jacobin intrigues, approached the revolution of August 10. Lafayette, having accepted the constitutional monarchy, went out of his way to oppose the intrigues of the clubs. In turn he became suspect. The triumph of the Jacobins placed him in a position identical to that of many a moderate Russian revolutionist when the Bolsheviki came into power. His life in danger after the intimidated assembly had ordered his arrest on August 19, ought he to submit, in the face of the foreign enemy, to the dictatorship of the Terror? Or ought he to flee the country, like the horde of *émigrés* for whose desertion of the nation he professed the greatest scorn? Lafayette chose the latter course. With twenty-three members of his staff and several orderlies and servants, a company of fifty-three people all told, he left his army and started across the Austrian Netherlands for neutral Dutch territory. "I could have found a high station in the new order of things," he wrote a few days subsequently to the United States minister at The Hague, "without even having meddled with the plot, but my feelings did not even admit of such an idea, I raised an opposition to Jacobin tyranny—but you know the weakness of our *honnêtes gens*. I was abandonned, the Army gave way to clubbish acts. I had nothing left but to leave France." [5] Historians recognize that the Terror saved

5. William Short to the Secretary of State, The Hague, Aug. 31, 1792, D.S., Hague and Spain, 1792, Letters of Wm. Short. The original letter of Lafayette to Short, dated Brussels, Aug. 26, 1792, is in the William Short Papers, *21*, 3650, Library of Congress. Lafayette's explanation of his position to d'Archenholz in his secret letter from prison at Magdeburg, March 27, 1793, is somewhat different. It was written after he had six months to think things over and for the purpose of supplying his friends with arguments in justification of his political conduct, in order to influence the public through the press against his further imprisonment: "J'étais destitué, accusé, c'est-a-dire proscrit. Ma défense eût pu être sanglate, mais elle aurait été inutile, et l'ennemi était à portée d'en profiter. Je voulus l'attaquer pour être tué: mais, n'y prévoyant aucun avantage militaire, je m'arrêtai. Je voulus aller mourir à Paris. Mais je craignis qu'un tel exemple d'ingratitude populaire ne décourageât les futurs promoteurs de la liberté." *Mémoires, 4,* 228. The same document, carefully corrected from the original, is published by J. Thomas (see next note), p. 187. Lafayette's *Mémoires* were worked over by himself and after his death

France from foreign invasion, and Lafayette later may have had some difficulty in reconciling himself [6] to the decision he made, but of the merits of that decision we do not judge here. We are concerned more with its results, which illumine a hitherto obscure but not insignificant chapter of the diplomatic history of the United States.

Lafayette and his party of officers were identified as they crossed the frontier. They were stopped and taken into custody at an outpost of the Austrian army at Rochefort, a village near Liége, a neutral bishopric which had been swept over by the Imperial armies. Protesting against this detention they signed—Lafayette's signature leads the others—a statement to the effect that they were "French citizens," compelled by imperious circumstances to renounce their positions in the French army and hence not to be considered as enemy forces, nor as *émigrés,* but "as foreigners claiming a free passage assured by international law" en route to a neutral country.[7] The Austrian commander ignored this plea. Without explanations, warnings, or requests for passage, Lafayette and his company had ventured into enemy territory and had been taken, well armed and mounted. That there was any violation of international law in detaining them—if indeed international law was at all definite concerning such a case as this—is not seriously to be considered.[8] A commission of the allied monarchs, on which sat an *émigré* representative of the French king, condemned to imprisonment Lafayette and those members of his party who had been members of the Constituent Assembly. They were given over to the custody of the King of Prussia. It soon became evident that Lafayette was being held as a prisoner of state rather than of war, for the allies regarded him as the evil genius of the whole revolutionary

---

by his son. In arranging the papers for publication, the General undoubtedly did more than to "eliminate repetitions and insignificant details," as he explained. M. Thomas has found the original manuscripts of most of Lafayette's prison correspondence and published them in his *Correspondance Inédite.* By publishing considerable material altogether omitted in the *Mémoires,* and by comparing with their originals the text of letters in the *Mémoires,* he demonstrates that Lafayette touched up or deleted, for apologetic purposes, certain details. The Thomas edition of prison correspondence, for the discriminating student, therefore supersedes the *Mémoires.* Thomas's introduction is a valuable psychological analysis of Lafayette's character and career.

6. J. Thomas, ed., *Correspondance inédite de La Fayette, 1793–1801* (Paris, 1903), p. 140. Hereinafter cited as *Correspondance inédite.*

7. Copy of protest in Charavay, *Le Général La Fayette, 1757–1834* (Paris, 1898), p. 331.

8. M. Büdinger, "Lafayette in Oesterreich" in *Sitzungsberichte der Kaiserlichen Akademie der Wissenschaften, Phil.-Hist. Classe, 92,* 231.

movement of two continents. Their thrones would be safer, it appeared to them, if he were kept behind bars. They accordingly decided to hold him as a hostage pending the restoration of the King of France to his legitimate throne, when they would deliver him up to the graces of that monarch.[9]

Lafayette and his three fellow prisoners, Latour Maubourg, Bureau de Pusy and Alexander Lameth,[10] together with their personal servants, were taken by successive marches through Luxembourg, Trèves, and Coblentz to the Prussian fortress of Wesel, in Westphalia. Here they remained from September 18 to December 31, 1792, when they were transported to Magdeburg, about 150 kilometers from Berlin. After exactly one year's imprisonment at Magdeburg they were shifted, January 4, 1794, to Neisse, near the Silesian frontier.[11] The imprisonment has afforded a dramatic theme for historians and no small problem for historical criticism.[12] The documentary material dealing with the episode has been pretty thoroughly worked over by European scholars, insofar as it bears on the facts and circumstances of his sojourn in enemy fortresses, but the relation of the United States to the imprisonment of the benefactor of American liberty has not been so well known.

No sooner did he realize his plight, after the capture at Rochefort, than Lafayette began to consider various hopes and chances of liberation. In the solitude and insalubrity of his several prison cells, his active and impulsive mind raced over the various possible avenues of escape or release. These distressing five years of his life were consumed —so far as any mental exercise can measure such slowly passing time —with the elaboration of various designs for getting back his freedom.

9. Short informally asked the Imperial minister at The Hague what action was contemplated toward Lafayette. "He told me with much frankness and in the same unofficial manner that he was persuaded the Emperor attached no importance to the confinement of M. de Lafayette other than what might be supposed to result from the desire to let the King of France decide on it—not dissembling that it was his opinion that he would be surrendered to the King when restored to the throne." Short to Pinckney, The Hague, Sept. 25, 1792, Short Papers, *21*, 3747. See also Short to the Secretary of State, The Hague, Aug. 31, Sept. 18, Sept. 28, 1792, D.S., Hague and Spain, 1792, Wm. Short.

10. Alexander Lameth, also a member of the Constituent Assembly, and radical political opponent of Lafayette, was detained but later released, after two years' imprisonment, by the King of Prussia in 1794. As to members of Lafayette's party who had served incarceration in the citadel of Antwerp, see *Correspondance inédite*, pp. 110–15.

11. *Correspondance inédite*, p. 111.

12. See note 5 above. See also M. Büdinger's study, "Lafayette in Oesterreich."

The first of these projects was that of bringing about the intervention of the United States in his favor. "We are French citizens," read Lafayette's protest to his Austrian captors August 19, 1792. Under a different citizenship he wrote a week later to William Short, our minister at The Hague, enclosing for publication a copy of the very protest to his Austrian captors in which he and his fellow officers had referred to themselves as French citizens. "You will greatly oblige me, my dear friend, to set out at once for Brussels as soon as this reaches you, and insist upon seeing me. I am an American citizen, an American officer, no longer in the French service. This is your right and I don't doubt of your immediate and urging [*sic*] arrival. God bless you!" [13]

No immediate reply came. Lafayette repeated his appeal more urgently three days later. "You must immediately in the name of the United States, in common with the other American Ministers, and perhaps in common with England interfere in our affair and have us set at liberty—if not our chance is bad—to be sure this conduct of the Austrian Government is equally unjust and impolitic, but it is not [14] . . . a reason, it seems. Depend on it, no time is to be lost. Adieu." [15]

In this direct and human language Lafayette made the first appeal of a naturalized American citizen—if we exclude some of the earliest impressment cases—for relief from arbitrary imprisonment abroad. It was before any legislation had ever defined the status of a citizen engaging in the service of a foreign prince. It was before any executive precedent on the subject. It was at a time when European affairs were in the midst of a most complicated imbroglio of Old World philosophies and political antagonisms in which the United States had no interest except that of maintaining friendly relations with all nations. It was when the newly consolidated nationality, which Lafayette had so ardently applauded in the United States Constitution, was, historically speaking, on trial for its life. It was when the United States demanded above all else, for the success of that vital political experiment, peace and abstention from European political questions. The appeal was made by the one foreigner—if indeed he was a foreigner—most beloved in America, whose disinterested services and lofty principles

13. The original letter in English, dated Brussels, Aug. 26, 1792, is in the Short Papers, *21*, 3650. It is also printed fairly accurately in Sparks, *Life of G. Morris, 1*, 399.

14. Word obliterated in the MS.

15. Lafayette to Short. Nivelles, on setting out for Luxembourg, Aug. 30, 1792, Short Papers, *21*, 3667.

were still very warm in the memories of young American citizens. It was made by a man upon whom the United States within the year had been relying to further its interests by inducing France to persuade Spain to open the Mississippi to the navigation of the United States; in fact the Secretary of State had instructed the *chargé* at Paris to leave American affairs, during his absences, under Lafayette's direction, though the latter was overwhelmed by multitudinous other vital political business of his own.[16] It was made to the diplomatic representatives of a President who loved Lafayette at least as much as he did any living man. This call for help in the black hour of his greatest need, from the old comrade in arms who had never accepted material reward for his great services in securing the independence of that very nation whose assistance he now requested, undoubtedly put to President Washington one of the most embarrassing political problems he ever encountered, particularly so when the plea was reinforced by the moving entreaties of Lafayette's remarkable wife.

The appeal was first made to William Short, upon whom fell the necessity of answering it immediately. As Lafayette had written, no time was to be lost. The weeks and months necessary to refer such a question to Philadelphia for decision would have seen the prisoners far removed from the proximity of an American minister and rust accumulating on their bolts and bars. To take an immediate official step for Lafayette's liberation, without instructions personally to visit the Austrian camp and demand, as a right, to see the prisoner and to obtain the liberation of a man who but a few days before had led an army against his captors, would have required a bold diplomatist. Short felt forced to resort to consoling but empty replies. Though "mortified" at Lafayette's predicament, he wrote him the not very impressive explanation that it was absolutely impossible to quit The Hague at that time because he was daily expecting delayed instructions to proceed to Madrid on an important diplomatic mission.

> This will carry me through Brussels, of course. Should I go immediately, as is highly probable, I will not fail to solicit with much warmth the favor of seeing you, being persuaded it would be refused if claimed as a right. Should my letter expected from America be still delayed I flatter myself I shall have the pleasure of seeing you on neutral territory, for I cannot think you will be long detained. . . . As you urge my coming to see you, it is possible that you may suppose I might if there contribute to

16. For references to this affair, see D.S., Dispatches, France, Wm. Short, *1*.

your obtaining a free passage. Although I cannot flatter myself
that any solicitation on my part could in the smallest degree influence the government of the Austrian Netherlands or add at all
to the reasons of justice which must weigh on them for ceasing
to refuse to you what all persons *not in arms* [italics inserted] have
a right to expect, namely a free and peaceable passage; yet if there
is any way in which I can serve you I hope you will mention it,
and be assured that nobody can feel greater pleasure in doing
you whatever may be really useful to you.[17]

We can imagine the lugubrious smile with which the prisoner must
have read this last unctuous sentence.

By the time Short had received any definite instructions as to his
expected Spanish mission,[18] Lafayette long since had been whisked
away to prison by the Allies and rendered (except for secret correspondence which eluded the vigilance of his guards) incommunicado.
We have observed that he requested a joint intervention of Short and
the other American ministers abroad. Short put the case to Gouverneur
Morris, in Paris, and Thomas Pinckney, in London.

Although this business presents itself at first blush as desperate
as well from the principle on which such a demand could [19]
. . . be presented, as the power that would have to decide on it;
yet there is something so insupportably painful in seeing a person
so long and so disinterestedly devoted to the United States now
for the first time ask their aid and ask it in vain, that I do not
hesitate a moment in communicating to you . . . the urging [sic]
request that he has made. . . . If there is anything within the
scope of practicability which can in any way secure his liberation
it will occur to one or both of you.

Short declared he saw nothing that could be done which presented
"the most glimmering prospect of utility," though he acknowledged
that regard to national character demanded action, if possible, by the
United States minister.[20]

Morris immediately counseled nonintervention. Lafayette, said he,

17. Short to Lafayette, The Hague, Aug. 29, 1792, Short Papers, *21*, 3655.
18. He remained in The Hague until Dec. 18. Short to his brother, Dec. 18, 1792,
ibid., *22*, 3961.
19. Word illegible in badly faded letterpress copy.
20. Short to Pinckney, The Hague, Sept. 7, 1792, Short Papers, *21*, 3689. A similar
letter was addressed to Gouverneur Morris, ibid.

was a French citizen.[21] Pinckney was willing to sign a joint declaration that Lafayette was an American citizen and expressing confidence that he would be protected in rights belonging to such character, but apprised of Morris's reply to Short, he decided that he would not favor any intervention unless the three were unanimously in favor of it.[22] Meanwhile it became evident to Short from his conversation with the Imperial minister at The Hague that there was little likelihood of Lafayette being released by the Allied governments.[23]

News of Lafayette's arrest and imprisonment, and of cross correspondence of the United States ministers abroad on the subject, arrived in Philadelphia by the regular diplomatic channels.[24] Further details, including the sufferings of the prisoners and their change of prisons, arrived in letters from Lafayette's numerous friends in Europe, and

21. G. Morris to Short, Paris, 12 Sept., 1792, *A.S.P.*, *F.R.*, *1*, 342. "Supposing that M. de Lafayette were a natural born subject of America and taken under the circumstances in which he was placed, I do not exactly see how the United States could claim him. He was not in their service. If he had been made a prisoner of war could they claim him as their citizen? If claimed and delivered up would they not be bound to put him to death for having attacked a neutral power, or else by the very act of acquitting him declare war against those who had taken him? Can the United States interfere in an affair of this sort without making themselves parties in the quarrel? But M. de Lafayette is a Frenchman, and it is as a Frenchman that he is taken and is to be treated."

"I had very good reasons to apprehend that our interference at that time would have been injurious to him, but I hope that a moment will soon offer in which something may be done for his relief. In reading my correspondence with Mr. Short, you must consider that I wrote to the French and the Austrian governments, as each would take the liberty to read my letter." Morris to Washington, Paris, Oct. 23, 1792, *A.S.P.*, *F.R.*, *1*, 394. Short thoroughly agreed with Morris. Short to Morris, The Hague, Sept. 18, 1792, Short Papers, *21*, 3715.

22. Pinckney to Short, London, Sept. 21, 1792, ibid., 3726.

23. Short to Pinckney, The Hague, Sept. 25, Oct. 2, Nov. 25, 1792, ibid., *21*, 3473, 3755; *22*, 3899. Part of this correspondence is printed in Jared Sparks, *The Life of Gouverneur Morris* (3 vols. Boston, 1832), *1*, 398–406. "As to our fellow citizen in confinement, and of whom you desire to be fully informed," he wrote to Morris, Dec. 7, "I can only tell you, that the most impenetrable secrecy has been observed in respect to him and his fellow sufferers. It is certain, that he is the individual of all France, that both the Austrians and Prussians hate most cordially. The desire to revenge and determination to punish made them inflict the most flagrant injustice, and the most shameful violation of the *droit de gens*. They are probably sensible of it, and therefore wish to smother the whole business, and the victims also." Short to Morris, The Hague, Dec. 7, 1792; Sparks, *Life of G. Morris, 1*, 403. See also Morris to Short, Paris, 29 Nov., 1792, A. C. Morris, *Diary and Letters of Gouverneur Morris* (2 vols. New York, 1888).

24. Short to the Secretary of State, Aug. 31, Sept. 18, 28, Oct. 12, 19, 1792, D.S., Hague and Spain, Wm. Short, *1*; Morris to same, *A.S.P.*, *F.R.*, *1*, 341, 394.

from Madame de Lafayette herself, who wrote to President Washington requesting him to take steps to secure the liberation of her husband as an American citizen.[25] Members of the party who escaped from the fortress at Antwerp brought additional details to Short, which were duly transmitted to the Secretary of State. Pinckney and Morris were bespoken further, by Lafayette's friends, and by the General himself, who celebrated the Fourth of July, 1793, in his cell at Magdeburg by managing to write a secret letter to Pinckney with appropriate reflections on the American and French Revolutions. The initiative of Gouverneur Morris was meanwhile exerted to the extent of drawing unauthorized, and on his own recognizance, on the credit of the United States to the extent of ten thousand florins, which were deposited at Lafayette's disposal at Magdeburg.[26] The money, despite the extortion of his jailers, served at least to ameliorate the vile prison fare. Gouverneur Morris also personally loaned 100,000 livres to Madame de Lafayette,[27] who had requested him to pledge the credit of the United States to her account to satisfy creditors to whom she felt in honor bound.[28] He assured her that the United States would take care of the needs of herself and husband. The American minister by his personal influence with the Committee of Public Safety seems to have persuaded them out of revenging themselves with the guillotine on the wife and daughters of Lafayette,[29] after the authorities had already wrought a dreadful vengeance by actually decapitating the Marquise's sister, mother, and aged grandmother. Morris also penned for Madame Lafayette a rather abject and humble petition to the King of Prussia for the release of her husband. The document, hitherto supposed to have been undelivered, was duly signed by her and transmitted to that monarch, but in vain.[30] Washington, unsolicited, sent 2310 guilders out of his own pocket to the distressed woman.[31]

25. For her letters of Oct. 8, 1792, and March 13, 1793, see Sparks, *Writings of George Washington, 10*, 315, 324.

26. *Correspondance inédite*, p. 210.

27. Sparks, *Life of G. Morris, 1*, 411.

28. The money was paid back in 1804 in depreciated French currency worth 53,500 livres. For this the scrupulous Morris, who had no affection for Lafayette's ebullient personality, never forgave the General. See A. C. Morris, *Diary and Letters of G. Morris, 2*, 407–12. See Sparks MSS, *89*, in Harvard Library.

29. A. C. Morris, *Diary and Letters of G. Morris, 2*, 63. See also Sparks MSS, *89*.

30. For copy of the letter see *Diary, 2*, 4. The letter was transferred from London by the Prussian minister, Baron von Jacobi-Klöst, who received it from Pinckney. Jacobi-Klöst to the King, London, Jan. 22, 1793. Geheimnis Staatsarchiv, Berlin, *Repositorium* 96, 150 K., 2.

31. Washington to Mme. de Lafayette, Jan. 31, 1793. Sparks, *Writings of George Washington, 10*, 314.

Washington's decision, immediately taken, was to approve the action —or rather lack of action—taken by Morris, Pinckney, and Short. He requested Jefferson as Secretary of State to direct Morris to lose no favorable opportunity to express *informally* the sentiments and wishes of the United States respecting Lafayette. Jefferson's actual instructions, copies of which were sent to all the American ministers abroad, expressed approval of their action and went on to state that "the interest which the President himself, and our citizens in general take in the welfare of this gentleman is great and sincere, and will entirely justify all prudent efforts to serve him." These efforts were to be limited to procuring his liberty by informal solicitations if possible. "But if formal ones shall be necessary, and the moment shall arrive when you shall find that they shall be effectual, you are authorized to signify, through such channels as you shall find suitable, that our government and nation . . . will view his liberation as a mark of consideration and friendship for the United States." [32] There is no evidence that any of the ministers interpreted these instructions to the extent of justifying more than informal inquiries and expressions of interest in Lafayette's fate and a wish to see him liberated.[33] This course received the thorough approbation of the State Department and President. Jefferson, indeed, at this very time had strongly expressed himself against "meddling with the internal affairs of any country, nor with the general affairs of Europe." [34] Thomas Pinckney, in London, held fruitless informal conferences with the Prussian minister in London, only to learn that Lafayette was to be transferred to Austrian custody. He had tried to induce Lord Grenville, the English Secretary of State for Foreign Affairs, to press Great Britain's ally for the prisoner's release. Grenville politely but consistently refused to pursue the matter, concerning which the Opposition, instigated by Lafayette's friends and led by Fitzpatrick and Fox, had begun to bait him. On March 17, 1794, General Fitzpatrick introduced into the Commons a motion that the detention of Lafayette and his fellow prisoners was injurious to the cause of His Majesty and his allies, and beseeched the government to intercede with the court of Berlin for their liberation. His motion

32. T. Jefferson to G. Morris, and other United States ministers abroad, Philadelphia, March 15, 1793. *Writings of Jefferson* (Ford ed.), *6*, 202.

33. For remarkable irregularity of Carmichael's conduct, see note at end of this instalment.

34. T. Jefferson to Mr. Dumas, Philadelphia, March 24, 1793, D.S., Instructions, *1*, 262.

was supported by Fox and Sheridan, but voted down 46–153. Burke let loose a thundering invective against Lafayette. He thought "that the 'illustrious exile' as he was called, though, in fact, the outcast of the world, deserved the fate he had met with . . . England had done la Fayette no injury and was not obliged to do him any service, but to leave him where he was. . . . I would not debauch any humanity by supporting an application like the present, in behalf of such a horrid ruffian." [35]

John Jay, who had a not unfavorable opportunity to present such a request for Lafayette during the general negotiations in 1794, does not appear to have mentioned the matter.[36] Pinckney, despairing of diplomacy, then lent his countenance to a plot to abet Lafayette's escape. This also failed after a most dramatic attempt.[37]

To Madame Lafayette's urgent solicitations for an American mission to demand her husband's release, that he and his family might be taken to the United States, President Washington replied kindly but negatively that her purposes were "perhaps not exactly those which I could pursue; perhaps indeed, not the most likely, under actual circumstances, to obtain our object; but he assured, that I am not inattentive to his condition, nor contenting myself with inactive wishes for his liberation." The letter was drafted, at Washington's request, by Jefferson. The fine hand of the Secretary of State, who did not share the abhorrence which American ministers abroad, particularly Short and Morris, entertained for Jacobin rule, is to be seen in this sentence included in Washington's letter: "My affection to his nation and to himself are unabated, and notwithstanding the line of separation, which has unfortunately drawn between them, I am confident that

35. Hansard, *Parliamentary Debates, 31*, 38 ff. The debates are reported with care by the Prussian minister, Jacobi-Klöst. See his letter of March 18, 1794, in Geheimnis Staatsarchiv, Berlin, *Repositorium* 96, 150 M., *4*, 1792.

36. That Lafayette was uncertain whether his messages reached Jay is indicated by the following passage in the famous letter, written in blood (in French) on his handkerchief, which he smuggled out of Olmütz. A copy is preserved in the private library of Dr. P. M. Keating of Philadelphia, where it was examined for me by Dr. J. Franklin Jameson. "Notwithstanding my requisition, I doubt whether there has been delivered to Mr. Jay the long interrogatory, written from Germany, in French, which I submitted pour ne pas nuire *aux messies (sic)*."

37. See above, pp. 150–51. For Bollman and Huger's well-known attempt at Lafayette's liberation, see below. On Jan. 19, 1796, Hamilton wrote to Washington, introducing Bollman: "I have reason to believe that Mr. Pinckney, among others, encouraged him and as a consequence of it, he hopes for some civil employment under the Government. . . . He brought me letters from Mr. and Mrs. Church [Mrs. Church, of London, was Hamilton's sister-in-law] which speak handsomely of him. I believe they had a chief agency in promoting his undertaking." Hamilton, *Works, 6*, 85.

both have been led on by a pure love of liberty, and a desire to secure public happiness." [38]

Probably Washington would not have added this last sentence had he written the letter himself, but he signed it as drafted by Jefferson, to Madame Lafayette's infinite sorrow. "I thought, indeed, I confess," she wrote to Gouverneur Morris, in a still unpublished letter, "that the succession of events in our country could not be correctly judged at such a distance, but that Mr. Washington would himself write to me, in the month of March, and in answer to my letter written in October, after all which had then taken place, and all that has since passed," that her husband and the Jacobins were animated by the same pure love of liberty and desire to serve public happiness—"this is truly desolating to my heart." [39] The summer and autumn of 1793 passed without further definite information regarding the distinguished prisoner of state. [40]

Meanwhile the Executive confidentially informed "certain members of Congress" of the money which had been advanced to Lafayette and suggested that his unaccepted salary as an American officer be appropriated to cover this expenditure and additional relief. [41] This was eventually done by an Act of March 27, 1794. [42] The sum of $24,424 was duly placed to his credit by the American ministers abroad. [43] It afforded a much needed relief. In January 1794, a Cabinet meeting was held to consider Lafayette's case. The President put the question "whether, in consideration of the eminent services of M. de Lafayette to the United States, it be not advisable for the President in a *private* and *unofficial* character to address the King of Prussia a letter, requesting his release on parole, founded on motives of personal friendship only." [44] The proposed *démarche* was agreed to by the three "Heads of Departments." A letter by Randolph, the new Secretary of State,

38. Washington to the Marchioness de Lafayette, Mar. 16, 1793, *Writings of Washington* (Ford ed.), *12*, 270.

39. Noailles de Lafayette to Gouverneur Morris, July 12, 1793, Sparks MSS, *89*, 21–25, Harvard College Library.

40. "We wish to hear from you on the subject of M. de Lafayette, tho' we know that circumstances do not admit sanguine hopes." Jefferson to T. Pinckney, Germantown, 27 Nov. 1793. D.S., Instructions, *2*, 34.

41. Randolph to Pinckney, Jan. 17, 1794, D.S., Instructions, *2*, 56.

42. *U.S. Statutes at Large, 1*, 351. Curiously enough one bill, which appropriated monies, originated in the Senate. *Annals of Congress*, 1793–95, 505, 522, 526. There is no record of a debate or division.

43. Randolph to Pinckney, June 8, 1794, enclosing letter of Secretary of the Treasury of May 31, 1794. D.S., Instructions, *2*, 41. Same to same, June 5, 1795, ibid., *2*, 1.

44. *Works of Alexander Hamilton* (J. C. Hamilton, ed.), *4*, 505.

immediately sent the necessary instructions to Thomas Pinckney. Financial assistance was not enough, the instructions read, and went on to state:

> The President, under whose eye he moved during the American war, has waited, until this day, to attempt his release; only because no feasible plan had occurred. He has at length written the inclosed letter for this purpose to the King of Prussia on whose will the fate of the Marquis seems to depend.
>
> On the first opening of this subject to the mind, its novelty produced some hesitation. That the Chief Magistrate of the United States should, as such, condescend to ask a personal favor from a crowned head, was inadmissible; and had its possible dangers from the discontent which the French nation might feel at such a solicitude, expressed in a public form, for the enlargment of a man, so obnoxious to them at this moment. Objections of this kind do not apply, against the indulgence of private friendship, exerting itself in a private character. Official station cannot so far absorb social affection, as to forbid a man to gratify the one, by occasionally laying aside the other, to perform certain acts irrelative to public duties.
>
> These sentiments were opposed by the difficulty of framing a letter, which should be the language of a private gentleman, untinctured by the most distant recollection of being the President. I trust, however, that such a letter has been accomplished; and that the only remaining condition is as to the manner and circumstances of its delivery.

Mr. James Marshall of Virginia, brother of the later eminent Chief Justice, was recommended, on Alexander Hamilton's advice, as the proper person to present the letter in question. The individuals proper for Mr. Marshall to approach for the success of the mission and the circumstances under which he should undertake it, were left to Pinckney's discretion. "Success is desirable, not only for the happiness, which will acompany it, but also, because it will obviate the uneasiness of having the request refused. This last idea is of such magnitude that if Mr. Marshall shall clearly discover, that it will be abortive, the letter is to be withheld." [45]

The writer searched in vain among the unpublished Washington Papers and in the State Department archives for the missing letter of the President to the King of Prussia, nor could it be found in the

45. Randolph to T. Pinckney, Philadelphia, Jan. 16, 1794. D.S., Instructions, 2, 56.

Prussian archives. As these paragraphs were being prepared for the printer the letter was located in the Pierpont Morgan Library in New York, recently thrown open to the public. Through the courtesy of the librarian we reproduce the text in a footnote below.[46]

46. The Prussian archives were consulted at my direction but without success by Dr. Konrad Schünemann, to whose assistance I owe copies of such Prussian documents as are hereafter cited. The Washington letter from the Morgan Library is from Washington's copy retained by him in his note book:

Philadelphia Jany. 15th
1794

To His Majesty the
         King of Prussia
Sire,

However unusual it may be for your Majesty to receive an address from a person, who, at the very moment of making it, disclaims the exercise of any public function, and acts as a private individual yet it is believed from your illustrious character, that the motives, which lead me to the measure, will serve as an ample apology.

I cannot longer resist the impulse of friendship, to lay before you, who know so well, how to appreciate its force, my personal and affectionate anxiety for the welfare of M. de la Fayette. Report informs me, that he is under confinement in the dominions of Prussia, and therefore at your disposal.

At an early period of his life—at a season, and on an occasion far remote from the time and causes, which have subjected him to his present condition, he pursued his military career, with so much benefit to my country, and honor to himself, that he acquired a most endearing place in my affections.

A sincere attachment then commenced was strengthened by an intercourse which continued after the return of peace had separated us until more active and interesting scenes served to interrupt it.—Upon the events, which succeeded, I shall be silent; only entreating your Majesty to be persuaded, that as I separate myself, in this letter, from my official station, to render a tribute to your liberality; so I beg to be understood as intending to observe that delicacy, which becomes every man, whose country has, with perfect sincerity, cherished peace and impartiality towards the whole world.

Permit me then to ask and obtain from your Majesty, a favor, in which the most lively sensibility of my fellow-citizens is engaged—the release of M. de la Fayette on his parole. If his word should not be deemed a sufficient pledge, I shall regret, that your Majesty does not entertain the same conviction of his fidelity, as a full experience has impressed upon myself.—But I can never be persuaded of the possibility of his departing from that innocence of conduct, which is always to be expected from a prisoner of war.

This request, unsolicited by, and unknown to him asks the patronage of your Majesty's sensibility; and is dictated by a confidence, that he could not be in the power of any sovereign, who would more delight in indulging a friendship, which cannot acquit itself, without thus endeavoring to deliver him, under your benevolent auspices.—

I pray God to preserve your Majesty in his holy keeping.

Go. Washington.

Equipped by Pinckney with letters of introduction to Prince Henry of Prussia, an old friend of the Marquis, who had already been approached by Lafayette's friends, Marshall set forth for Berlin. The failure of his mission is best described in Marshall's report on the subject, here revealed for the first time:

I delivered your Letter to Prince Henry of Prussia on the 28th of April and at the same time declared my intention of following his Advice in the Business which had been entrusted with me— he appeared highly gratified by the Confidence which was placed in him, and expressed himself in terms of the warmest Admiration of our President and Friendship for M. de Lafayette. Whilst I remain'd with him he wrote a letter to the King his Nephew informing him of the Letter with which I was charged, and urging a Compliance with the request which it contained.

On my departure from Rheinsberg his Royal Highness gave me a Letter to the Minister of State on the same subject who immediately informed me that nothing could be done for M. de Lafayette, as an agreement had actually taken place by which he was to be delivered up to the Austrians and he added that probably the agreement was already executed. He spoke favorably of M. de Lafayette and lamented that it was not in the power of Prussia to comply with the Request of his Friends. As the only chance which remained I endeavored to discover if it were possible to prevail on the Ministry to favor the Escape of Fayette from the Fortress where he was confined. Alvensleben the Minister of State to whom I made the proposal, acknowledged his wish that it could be done but declared to me that it was too late. I could not press the subject further but as the Minister had not said that M. de la Fayette was actually in the hands of the Austrians I wrote requesting permission to see him before that event took place, intending if my request was granted to renew my Proposal. I inclose you the answer of Alvensleben. As Business with him was at an end, I wrote, as I had promised, to give Prince Henry an account of my want of success, and to inquire if he could point out any step by which I could yet be of service to M. de la Fayette, the answer by the Baron Munchausen I inclose you, I cannot very well understand it, but I clearly perceived that Prince Henry could do nothing for Fayette, and as I did not wish to be obliged to converse with him, on what our Government might possibly yet

do to procure his Enlargement, I declined the Invitation to Rheinsberg.[47]

Thus closed the first chapter of Washington's efforts to liberate his
beloved friend. The affair did not end here. The King of Prussia was
wearied and embarrassed at the continued requests which he received
for the release of the prisoners.[48] Lured away from the Rhine by the
Polish partition spoil he was already about to desert the coalition.
King Frederick William, a few weeks before Marshall's trip to Berlin,
had asked the Emperor to take over the custody of the prisoners. To
this the Court of Vienna formally agreed in March 1794.[49] In his new
prison at Olmütz, in Moravia, Lafayette continued feverishly to devise
ways and means of escape. By secret avenues of correspondence developed through "certain hommes magnétisables pour la liberté" he sent
out letters to his friends and former aides-de-camp and to acquaintances
who seemed likely to be able to contribute in some degree in assisting
him. The purpose of much of this correspondence was to furnish arguments for the press [50] and for the parliamentary Opposition in England, to be used in influencing public opinion in his favor. He sent
sympathetic letters to the unfortunate King of Poland and certain of

47. James Marshall to Pinckney, June 1794. D.S., Dispatches, England, 3. Alvensleben's letter to Marshall, inclosed by the latter to Pinckney (ibid.), says that he would
be glad to comply with the request as to Lafayette, but for the fact that the prisoner
had already been delivered over to the Austrians. "I cannot forbear to observe at
the same time, that if during his confinement at Magdebourg anybody had made a
request of that kind, surely it would not have been refused him. What grieved me
the most is to be disappointed of the only occasion I could have to prove my regard
for General Washington."
Münchausen wrote from Rheinsberg, May 9, 1794, that Prince Henry was disappointed that Marshall did not succeed in his quest, that he extends his hospitality,
and that he "will never forget the amiable young gentleman from Virginia."
(Ibid.)
48. Thugut an den Kaiser, Wien, Feb. 25, 1794. M. Büdinger, "Lafayette in Oesterreich," p. 263.
49. Bericht des Cabinetsministeriums an den König Friederich Wilhelm II, 6
März, 1794. Geheimnis Staatsarchiv, Berlin, *Repositorium* 96, 147 T. The King of
Prussia requested the transfer of Lafayette without mentioning his companions.
The Emperor replied he would take over Lafayette *and* the officers arrested with
him. The Prussian council accepted this extension "as being conformable to the
interests" of the King.
50. Lafayette to Archenholz (of Hamburg), Magdeburg, 27 March 1793, *Correspondance inédite*, p. 187. For press propaganda for Lafayette's release, see Charavay's *Lafayette*, pp. 344–52.

his officers, calculated to open the way for a possible escape into that adjacent monarchy.[51]

He even put some reliance on his friendly relations with the Jews in 1790 as affording him an appeal to Jews in Poland, "adroits, intriguants et discrets." [52] Above all other expedients he still placed his hopes in some definite and formal ultimatum by the United States demanding his release as an American citizen.[53]

51. *Correspondance inédite*, p. 262.

52. Lafayette à M. de la Colombe, Magdeburg, 3 Jan. 1794, *Correspondance inédite*, p. 255. This passage is suppressed in the original printed *Mémoires*. See Thomas's comment, ibid., 132. A letter by one Duport was sent from London, Oct. 29, 1792, directed to the Prussian Jewish emissary, Ephraim, with whom Lafayette had had dealings in Paris in 1790. It was turned over by Ephraim to the Minister Schulenberg, Geheimnis Staatsarchiv, Berlin, *Repositorium* 96, 147 G.

53. See his long memoir to his aides-de-camp from Magdeburg, Dec. 10, 1793, the first of which was later repeated from Olmütz in other letters, *Correspondance inédite*, p. 241. Lafayette hoped that the American ministers, including Carmichael, in Spain, would all sign such a formal demand. The mention of Carmichael here must be accompanied by an explanation of that official envoy's curious conduct in regard to Lafayette's imprisonment. Carmichael had been American agent at Berlin early in the American Revolution. He was never received by that Court. During the last years of the Revolution he had vainly sought recognition of the independence of the United States at the Court of Spain. It was through Lafayette's personal influence at that Court in 1783 that Carmichael was at length officially received as *chargé d'affaires* of the United States, in the presence of Lafayette then at the apogee of his youthful glory. (B. Tuckerman, *Life of Lafayette, 1*, 155–56.) Carmichael's lasting gratitude for this apparently knew no bounds. In 1792 he was still at Madrid, as American minister, clumsily negotiating the Mississippi question. He heard of Lafayette's imprisonment and sent to his friend an astonishing letter, which is in the Prussian archives. It was unsealed and addressed to Lafayette in care of Count Schulenberg and was tantamount to a threat of assassination of Schulenberg and the King of Prussia, unless steps were taken for the release of Lafayette. This letter was presented to the King, but of course was never answered. (Bericht des Cabinetsministeriums V, Schulenberg an den König, Nov. 23, 1792, to which a copy of the Carmichael letter is attached. Geheimnis Staatsarchiv, Berlin, *Repositorium* 96, 147 G.) The letter was shown by Schulenberg to the British minister as an example of American impertinence. (Sir Morton Eden to Lord Auckland, Berlin, Nov. 23, 1792, *Dropmore Papers, 2*, 348. For Carmichael's unexplained mysterious relations with Lord St. Helens at Madrid, see ibid., 2, 257, 263.)

These hitherto unknown documents concerning this curious episode are herewith reproduced from the Prussian archives. We refrain from printing the French translations of the German copyist's rendition of Carmichael's original English text, which translations, for the benefit of his master's ignorance of English, accompanied Schulenberg's covering report to the King. Schulenberg's report is here translated. The letter of the *émigré*, Duport, referred to by Schulenberg and also communicated to the King, is too lengthy to print here. Its significance is sufficiently indicated by Schulenberg, viz., that the "Jew Ephraim" turned over to the Prussian ministry

That saintly and indefatigable woman, the Marchioness, left unturned no earthly stone in her efforts to open the doors of her husband's prison. Her letters to the various American ministers to do something for her husband never ceased. In January 1795, after surviving her frightful experience during the Reign of Terror, she managed with the help of James Monroe, the new francophile American minister at Paris, to secure her release from prison and passports allowing her and

---

such confidential letters as were sent him by Lafayette's friends. For Carmichael's early career see above, Chap. 2, pp. 21 ff.

REPORT OF CABINET MINISTER SCHULENBERG
TO THE KING,

November 23, 1792.

I think it my duty to acquaint Your Majesty with the original, and translation, of an anonymous letter written in English and dated the 15th of October, which I have just received in the last mail from Cleves, as well as the enclosure attached to it for the Marquis de la Fayette, signed by the name Carmichael. I vaguely recall having seen here during the American War an American officer by that name, apparently the same who wrote these two letters. I confess that they appear to me to be worthy of nothing but suspicion and that the absurd insults of that hothead in my opinion can excite no serious attention. Meanwhile, I present them very humbly to Your Majesty, submitting to your superior judgment whether you wish any use made of them.

I include at the same time a letter which a French refugee in London, named Duport, has just addressed to Mr. Benjamin Ephraim, which also concerns Monsieur de la Fayette. Mr. Ephraim having asked my permission to enable him merely to acknowledge the receipt of this letter, I felt justified in giving it to him, telling him confidentially nevertheless, to limit himself to that, and to add nothing more [*si non que*] than that he had communicated the letter to me and that I was going to present it to Your Majesty.

Berlin, 23 Novembre 1792   Schulenberg
    To The King.

Original 1.

Sir,   15 October 1792.

I have the honor to inclose to Your Excellency a letter for Mons. de la Fayette; it is open for your perusal. I have never deceived anyone in My life & I am not afraid to annonce my sentiments. I intreat Your Excellency to give your most serious attention to what I write to la Fayette—What would be regarded as nonsense & absurdity in other times is not so at present "les tetes sont exaltées." I would if possible prevent the terrible consequences—I have all in My power. You will know what is intended from other quarters. I earnestly intreat your serious attention to what I whrite and I have the honour with great and sincere respect.

                Your obliged and humble Sert.

Original 2.

My Dear Sir,

You cannot suppose that I the first and most ancient of your American friends

her children to leave France for America.[54] But, resolved personally to interview the Emperor of Austria in behalf of the Marquis, she started on that journey, via Hamburg, which was to result only in the privileges of sharing, with her two daughters, her husband's imprisonment. While en route to Hamburg, Madame de Lafayette, unbeknownst to the Marquis,[55] shrewdly sent her son, George Washington Lafayette, with his tutor, M. Felix Frestel, to the United States, recommended to the friendship and care of President Washington.[56] The voyage of young Lafayette to America was explained to the few people to whom his identity was at first revealed as a trip to his "nouvelle patrie" [57] for the purpose of completing his education and remaining in this country during his father's exile. The unpublished correspondence of

could have heard of what has happened to you without the most violent emotion; you know my attachement to you; you ought to know that I will sacrifice my life and the little fortune which I still possess to assist you to the utmost of my power. I am assured that 4 millions of our Country are as well disposed as Myself, for we love you and we ought to love you if the principles of virtue and honor have any weight with human nature. I know that what I write you, will be seen. I send you this under cover to the Baron de Schulenberg, a minister whom I love and respect and who knows me. I have defeated a project of assination [*sic!*] against the king of Prussia, for asssinations and massacres are not in My Code of Politics unless the necessity is *extreme*. For you My Dear friend I will go greater lengthes than for any person under heaven and I have a few other [?] friends that are determined—Let princes think. We live in a century, ou il n'y a pas de Badinage. Why do you not claim your Title as an American citoyen and abandon forever a Country which has treated you with ingratitudes? My Dear la Fayette with your pleghm you will think me an Enthusiast. I am not . . . I have prepared the means and simple individuals in spite of all precautions, will revenge in sacrificing their Lives every injury every injustice that *others* may practise against you. I have said enough, you will understand me.

I ever am yours affectionately
Carmichael.

A Mons. de la Fayette, Major Generele des armées des Etats Unies de l'Amerique septentrionale.

54. Monroe to the Secretary of State, Paris, Nov. 7, 1794, Jan. 3, 1795. *Writings of J. Monroe*, 2, 107. It is well to note that Monroe, in November 1794, on his own part, officially requested the speedy trial of Thomas Paine, the famous American citizen arrested by the Committee of Public Safety, and his release if found guiltless. Paine was straightway released. He had been naturalized in France, but Monroe considered him still an American citizen. Ibid., 2, 96, 107. Sparks MSS, *89*.

55. His private correspondence proves this.

56. Noailles Lafayette to Washington, undated, in Marie Antoinette Virginie de Lasteyrie, *Life of Madame de Lafayette* (Paris, 1872), p. 317.

57. Felix Frestel à Washington, Boston, 31 aôut, 1795. Washington Papers, *275*, 36670. The Act of Maryland of 1784 had voted citizenship to Lafayette and his heirs male forever.

George Washington Lafayette and of his tutor conclusively show that the real purpose of the voyage was to seek the liberation of his father. It was the hope of the Marchioness that a child's plea might in a personal interview work on the human side of the great man to overcome the political obstacles which hitherto had stood in the way of any official action by the American executive.

Traveling incognito under the name of Motier—the lad's real family name when stripped of his father's title, as the Convention had actually done—the youthful traveler with his companion arrived in Boston in August 1795, and was given hospitality at the home of Joseph Russel. They immediately dispatched letters to the President, informing him of the boy's arrival, pursuant to the desires of his father,[58] and setting forth their professed purposes. They requested Washington's advice, when and where to meet him.[59] The news of their arrival and their intention actually to visit him was most disturbing to the President. Affectionate remembrance of the father and his service to the country, sharpened by the realization of the Marquis's present hard lot, did not blind the General of the American Army to his situation as President of the United States. He desired to be a "friend and father" to his namesake. At the same time the obnoxious light in which the old comrade in arms was viewed by the French government made him think twice before openly receiving the boy.[60] Affairs with France were then in a delicate posture—it was just after Jay's Treaty was made known to the French government. A reception of the man proscribed by the radicals might make more difficult the relations of the United States. On the other hand a failure to extend asylum and friendship to the wandering son of a proven friend of American freedom might stir the Democratic opposition to the President, then at its height.

Washington decided not to receive the two immediately. Preparations already completed for a six weeks' trip away from the Capital offered substantial excuse for delay. He carried his caution to the extent of not himself replying to the letters. They were sent with a note of explanation to George Cabot of Boston, who was requested to set forth to the young Frenchmen the circumstances which prevented their immediate reception. Cabot was directed to express Washington's pa-

58. Probably this would be true, but the fact is that Lafayette at the time knew nothing of his son's departure for America, or his intention to do so.

59. Felix Frestel à George Washington, G. W. Motier Lafayette à George Washington, Boston, 31 aôut, 1795. Washington Papers, *275*, 36670.

60. Washington to George Cabot, private and confidential, Sept. 7, 1795. *Writings of Washington* (Ford ed.), *13*, 100.

ternal personal feelings toward young George, to offer him all necessary
financial assistance and to explain in as kindly manner as possible the
political necessities which complicated their relations. The President
wished that arrangements might be made for entering the Marquis's son
at Harvard.[61]

That the real purpose of these highly cultured young Frenchmen was
not to seek an education in the United States is suggested by Frestel's
explanation to Cabot that the studies now being pursued by "Mr.
Motier" were entirely different from those prescribed in American
universities, and hence it would not be desirable to enter Harvard.
Meanwhile the identity of the pair was becoming known about the
town. The French consul had, in fact, prepared a public reception for
them. It was accordingly decided that G. W. Lafayette and his "mentor"
should depart for New York, near which city La Colombe, a former
aide-de-camp of the Marquis, who had escaped from Antwerp, was
then living in retirement.[62]

At New York M. Frestel, "a very sedate, discreet man," and his charge
delivered letters of introduction to Alexander Hamilton. Hamilton
wrote to Washington, after the two had left for La Colombe's place at
Ramapo (near Hackensack), "On mature reflection, and in sounding
opinion, as far as opportunity and the nature of the case have permitted,
I fully believe the President need be under no embarrassment as to any
good offices his heart may lead him to perform toward this young
man." [63]

Washington thereupon sent all his correspondence concerning young
Lafayette to Hamilton. He asked for further advice. "I am willing . . .
to receive him under any circumstances, or in any manner you may
conceive best; and wish to know what that is." [64] But before Hamilton
replied the President himself decided to receive George and Frestel. He

61. Ibid.

62. G. Cabot to Washington, Brookline, Sept. 16, 1795. Washington Papers, 275,
36705. A paragraph of this long letter is printed in W. C. Ford's edition of the
Writings of Washington, 13, 103 n.

63. "It will not, I am persuaded, displease those in possession of the power of the
country from which he comes, and in ours it will be singularly and generally grateful.
I am even convinced, that the personal and political enemies of the President would
be gratified, should his ideas of the policy of the case restrain him from that conduct
which his friendship to the marquis and the feelings otherwise would dictate. The
youth of this person, joined to the standing of his person, make the way easy."
Hamilton to Washington, N.Y., Oct. 16, 1795. *Works of Hamilton* (J. C. Hamilton,
ed.), *6,* 47.

64. Washington to Hamilton, Philadelphia, Nov. 10, 1785. Ibid., 63.

directed Hamilton to send them on immediately to Philadelphia, unless there should be some powerful reason to prevent it. "The young gentleman must have experienced some unpleasant feelings already from being kept at such a distance from me, and I feel as unpleasantly as he can do, for the same cause." [65] Hamilton now hesitated to do so. "Persons of judgment," he wrote, doubted "whether at the actual crisis it would be prudent to give *publicity* to your protection of him. It seems to be feared, that the factious might use it as a weapon to represent you as a favorer of the anti-revolutionists of France; and it is inferred that it would be inexpedient to furnish at this moment any aliment to their slanders." [66] Washington accordingly reversed his decision. Instead of calling the embarrassing visitors to his home he wrote a kindly note to them, advising that they maintain their incognito until some means could be devised for bringing them forth under more favorable auspices.[67] He now distrusted his own judgment. He feared that his feelings and sentiment might overweigh his obligations to the high office to which he was responsible. The question was doubly troubling. It had two edges, neither of which could be avoided without falling on the other. "On one side I may be charged with countenancing those who have been denounced the enemies of France: on the other, with *not* countenancing the son of a man who is dear to America." This he felt despite the fact that the French minister had declared that the emigration of the two would excite little notice in France. Perplexed and hesitant,[68] he ended by again leaving the whole problem to Hamilton's decision.[69] The latter proceeded to inform the embarrassing travelers as soothingly as possible of the President's attitude. They were not impressed. They appeared hurt. They wanted to see their friend at least once. They would be willing to go to any destination prescribed for them.[70]

This wounded attitude pained the President.[71] The boy was obviously

65. Washington to Hamilton, Philadelphia, Nov. 18, 1795. Ibid., 70.

66. Hamilton to Washington, N.Y., Nov. 19, 1795. Ibid.

67. Washington to G. W. Lafayette, and to Frestel, Philadelphia, Nov. 23, 1795. Washington Papers, *276*, 36830.

68. "I hardly know how to reconcile to my feelings the denial of permitting him to come hither for a few moments . . ." Washington to Hamilton, Philadelphia, Nov. 28, 1795. *Works of Hamilton, 6*, 73.

69. Same to same, Nov. 23, 1795. Ibid., 71.

70. Hamilton to the President of the United States, Nov. 26, 1795. Washington Papers, *276*, 36836.

71. "Have you seen or heard more of young Lafayette? . . . His case gives me pain, and I do not know how to get relieved from it. His sensibility is, I fear,

disappointed at seeing his mission frustrated by what seemed to him an unexplainable attitude of the great man whose name he had been taught from the cradle to revere. "Young Lafayette appears melancholy, and has grown thin," wrote Hamilton. "A letter lately received from his mother, which speaks of something which she wishes him to mention to you (as I learn from his preceptor) has quickened his sensibility, and increased his regret." [72]

On Christmas Day, his sixteenth birthday, young George penned a touching appeal to Washington, to which a brief but effective postscript was added by Frestel. In fact the able manner in which this plaintive letter is worded impels one to wonder for how much more than the postscript the very sedate and discreet M. Frestel was responsible. Our translation of the peculiar French text of this letter follows:

Sir, it would be very difficult for me to express to you the happiness I experienced on receiving the letter which you did me the honor to write.

Respecting, as I ought, because of the confidence I have in your wisdom, the reasons which keep me away from you, I shall only tell you that I ardently long, I assure you, for the moment when they will no longer exist.

The tender and thoughtful attention with which you have been so good as to concern yourself for me and my best friend makes me hope that as soon as they [i.e., the reasons] shall have been removed, I shall be able to fly to you. How happy I shall be then, when I can show you how much I wish to make myself worthy of your kindness, especially in speaking to you about my father—and in behalf of my father, whom you loved and whom you still love now, since you heap favors upon me, who am only his son, without ever having seen me!

I have for the second time received news of my good, dear mother: she was then leaving Hamburg, the 24th of September, for Vienna, to work for the liberation of my father, or to shut herself up with my two sisters in his prison: how I envy their good fortune! Mama writes me that they keep telling her, and that she does not doubt it, that a step on your part with the Emperor will help a great deal. She charges me to speak to you about it. Judge of my grief if I can not even write to her that I have seen you; or to my father, in his prison, that I have spoken to you just once. Ah! Sir, weigh in your wisdom whether there is anything indiscreet in this request, and in your power whether the thing is too difficult: and ask your reputation if it would suffer in any way, even from a useless step in behalf of an unfortunate friend who is still worthy of your esteem. Judge my gratitude by the excess of my happiness, if my request should be listened to by you, and your help should bring back to my sisters and me our father; to my mother the consolation of her life,

---

hurt . . ." Washington to Hamilton, Philadelphia, Dec. 22, 1795. Hamilton, *Works*, 6, 78.

72. Dec. 24, 1795. Ibid., 79.

now that her parents are lost to her; to my country, and to yours, a worthy and true friend. It would be to you, Sir, that we should owe everything if you bring it about that they give him back to us. In addition to all that we already owe to you, consider how sweet and glorious it would be for my father to owe to you liberty, in order that he may again fight for it somewhere before dying for it.

I have the honor to be, with profound respect, Sir,

Your very humble and
very obedient servant
G. W. Motier Lafayete.[73]

This pathetic letter must have been the last straw. For a month Washington was continually uneasy on "account of young LaFayette." On February 13 he again directed Hamilton to send the boy and Frestel to him.[74] After a little delay they arrived at Philadelphia in April 1796. It soon became a matter of public property that the son of Lafayette was living in Washington's family at Mt. Vernon.[75] There is no indica-

73. G. W. Motier Lafayette to George Washington, New York, Dec. 25, 1795. Washington Papers, *276*, 36909.

74. Washington to Hamilton, Philadelphia, Feb. 13, 1796. Washington Papers, *277*, 37002. A personal invitation was sent to G. W. Lafayette on Feb. 28, 1796. Ibid., 37029. The President at this time asked the advice of the Secretary of War, to whom he submitted his correspondence dealing with the Lafayettes, as to whether it would be best to receive the young man publicly or privately. McHenry, who in 1793 had requested for himself an appointment as special envoy to Europe for the release of Lafayette, now counseled against any reception of the son by Washington in a capacity other than that of a private man. James McHenry to Washington, Feb. 13, 1796. Washington Papers, *277*, 37004. For McHenry's request in 1793, Sparks, *Writings of George Washington, 10*, 325.

75. While about to set out for Philadelphia, young Lafayette received from Edward Livingston, chairman of a committee of the House of Representatives, a letter containing a resolution of that body appointing a committee to enquire what means might be taken "to evince the grateful sense entertained by this country for the services of his father." George Washington Lafayette replied courteously from Ramapo, quoting his father's conviction that "the bounty of the United States and the tenderness of my paternal friend do not require to be excited." G. W. Lafayette to Livingston, 28 March, 1796. Washington Papers, *278*, 37118. See also Washington to G. W. Lafayette, Philadelphia, March 31, 1796. Ibid., 37134. Dr. P. M. Keating of Philadelphia has among his Bollman Papers the original copy of the novel *Evelina* on the margins of which Lafayette wrote in invisible ink his messages to Erich Bollman, when they were plotting the famous attempt at his escape from Olmütz. The following passage copied literally for me by Dr. J. Franklin Jameson when he examined those papers, indicates that the phrasing of the younger Lafayette's letter to Livingston did not originate in his youthful mind: "vous souhaittes que j'écrive au general; la bonté des etats unis et la tendresse de mon paternel ami n'ont pas besoin d'être excitees, et c'est parceque je crois inutile que je voudrais l'ecrire et outre que je n'en ai pas les moiens, on ne se chargerait pas d'une lettre destinée a voyager."

tion of the dreadful consequences either in domestic or international affairs which wise and prudent gentlemen had feared might follow the President's generous action.

Before the arrival of G. W. Lafayette at Washington's fireside, the President had firmly withstood the importunities of Lafayette's friends (who were constantly kept stirred to action by the secret prison correspondence emanating from the Marquis himself) soliciting a formal demand of the Austrian government for his liberation. A few days before the coming of the boy and his tutor, Washington had received a visit, which dragged out to an embarrassing length, from Doctor Justus Erich Bollman, the German physician and adventurer who with the American medical student F. M. Huger,[76] of South Carolina, had failed in their well-known attempt forcibly to assist Lafayette's escape at Olmütz in November 1795.[77] Bollman, who had been released from an Austrian prison only on express condition of never returning within the dominions of that empire, wrote at Washington's request a memoir outlining the most efficacious means to secure the desired liberation. He too came to America for the purpose of securing ways and means from Lafayette's revered friend. With him he brought a long letter from Latour Maubourg, Lafayette's companion in prison, with a copy of a note from Lafayette himself, written in the solitude of his cell on a handkerchief with his own blood, stating that Bollman had his full confidence and that reliance might be placed on what he had to suggest as being the mind of the Marquis himself.[78] It contained, amidst his suggestions of plans for liberation, consent, if required, to a promise not to mix in French politics again provided he were released.

Bollman explained Lafayette's continued imprisonment as due to

76. Francis Kinloch requested unavailingly the good offices of the United States to release his nephew, F. K. Huger, a natural born American whose father had been the first American to welcome Lafayette on our shores, who with Bollman suffered a six months' imprisonment as a result of their interferences with Lafayette's custody. T. Pickering to F. M. Kinloch, Sept. 26, 1795. D.S., Domestic Letters, *8*, 412.

77. This interesting incident has been so well worked out by European historians that space does not justify any summary of it. See M. Büdinger, "Lafayette in Oesterreich": E. Charavay, *Le Général La Fayette;* J. Thomas, *Correspondance inédite;* F. Kapp, *Justus Erich Bollman;* K. A. Varnhagen von Ense, *Vermischte Schriften,* 141–271; *Mémoires, Correspondance et Manuscrits de Lafayette,* edited by G. W. Lafayette.

78. Lafayette's letter was not printed in Sparks's reproduction of Maubourg's letter, nor was all of Maubourg's letter itself printed. Latour Maubourg's letter, containing also Lafayette's message, was filed with Bollman's memoir of April 10, 1796, in Washington's papers. See Washington Papers, *278*, 37150, 37154. For printed portions, see Sparks, *Writings of George Washington, 11,* 492.

English malice and revenge and fear of his republican example. England was now (1796) the main ally of Austria against the revived military prowess of the French armies. Hence, ran Bollman's argument, the Emperor could not afford to displease England by acceding to any formal American demand for the prisoner's release as an American citizen. Pinckney's unsuccessful conferences with Grenville had proved the uselessness of hopes from that quarter. Further such overtures, in fact, would be dangerous in that they might occasion a repeated request of the Emperor to keep the General in prison. Bollman suggested that a proper person, for which he himself was represented indirectly as perceiving the unusual set of qualifications demanded, be dispatched by the President to Austria, empowered to connive with the Emperor at the Marquis's escape, thus outwitting English diplomacy.[79] Washington refused to adopt the plan, which was really that of Lafayette and his friends. He revolted, too, at the idea of assisting Bollman to break his parole.[80] Bollman's stay protracted itself, much to Washington's disconcertion, until after young Lafayette's arrival. The latter, as was to be expected, immediately began to press his host to do something more for his father. He adopted the plans of Bollman, which, as we have said, were those of Lafayette. The President rejected these. But, yielding to the pleas of his namesake, he resolved to make one more effort for his friend in need. This was again as "a private person" to send a letter to the Emperor of Austria. In it he would state his wishes and those of his country concerning Lafayette, whose liberation would be looked upon as a "grateful measure." [81] Such a letter was drafted by John Jay and sent to Thomas Pinckney to be delivered through the Imperial minister at London.[82] Whether it was actually received is uncertain. A search in the Austrian archives reveals no trace of it. Nor does the correspondence of Jacobi-Klöst, the Imperial minister. Its fate must be guessed as we narrate the final portion of this humanly interesting chapter of Washingtonian diplomacy.

No attention was paid to Washington's letter, if indeed it was de-

79. J. E. Bollman to Washington, Philadelphia, April 10, 1796. Sparks, *Writings of George Washington, 11,* 497.

80. Washington to Hamilton, Philadelphia, May 8, 1796. *Works of Hamilton, 6,* 119.

81. "Dr. Bollman, who, it is to be feared, will be a troublesome guest among us . . . no mention . . . has come to my knowledge of his going away." Ibid.

82. Washington to Pinckney, Philadelphia, May 22, 1796. *Writings of Washington* (Ford ed.), *13,* 208. For letter to the Emperor, dated May 15, 1796, see Sparks, *Writings of George Washington, 11,* 125. A copy in Washington's own handwriting is in the Pierpont Morgan Library in New York City.

livered. Nothing was done toward Lafayette's release by the Austrian government until Napoleon Bonaparte's triumphant Army of Italy started on the road to Vienna in the spring of 1796. In the negotiations after the armistice of Leoben (April 18, 1797) the release of Lafayette and his companions was made a *sine qua non* by the French Directory. Some complicated haggling with the Vienna government followed, a bickering which was tolerated by Bonaparte and his nominal superiors because of unwillingness to see the apostle of the principles of 1789 return to France at a time when affairs were already hastening toward Fructidor.[83] Though he laid claim to two fatherlands, Lafayette was now indeed a man without a country.

The continental members and ex-members of the Coalition did not want him moving freely about in their domains. He was anathema to the party in power in England, where Pitt imperturbably refused to lift his finger for him. Burke accused him of being responsible for the whole train of misfortunes started by the French Revolution.[84] To George III, to whom he had been formally presented while meditating his first American voyage, and before whom in 1783 he did his best to be presented in an American uniform, Lafayette was *persona summa non grata*. There seemed no asylum for him in the revolutionized Netherlands. Even in the United States political considerations—particularly the critical relations that year with France—made Washington, now retired, anxious that he should not come.[85] Hamilton, in fact, advised him not to come.[86] The upshot of the Franco-Austrian nego-

83. *Correspondance inédite*, pp. 149–61; M. Büdinger, "Lafayette in Oesterreich," pp. 243–55.

84. On Dec. 16, 1796, Wilberforce brought up a motion, after a speech by General Fitzpatrick, that his Majesty use his good offices with his ally, the Emperor, for the liberation of Lafayette. Again it was supported by Fox, Sheridan, and other liberals. Pitt specifically and solemnly denied any obligation, expressed or implied, to the Emperor concerning Lafayette, or any communication on the subject between the two courts. The motion was lost, 50–132. *Hansard*, *32*, 1359. Jacobi-Klöst also sent full reports of this debate to the King of Prussia. See his letter of Dec. 20, 1796, Geheimnis Staatsarchiv, Berlin, *Repositorium* 151 C, vol. VIII, 1796. Gouverneur Morris, whose relations in 1796 with Lord Grenville were semiconfidential, wrote the latter from Vienna privately asking for his intercession for the release of Lafayette, as an act agreeable to America. This followed a further interview between Morris and Thugut. Morris to Grenville, Dec. 21, 1796. A. C. Morris, *Diary and Letters of Gouverneur Morris*, *2*, 239; *Dropmore Papers*, *3*, 289.

85. Washington to Pickering, Oct. 18, 1798. Sparks, *Writings of George Washington*, *11*, 324. Hamilton's advice is referred to in Lafayette to Washington, April 26, 1798. Sparks MSS, *89*.

86. This is revealed in letters written by Lafayette from Holstein, copies of which are now preserved in vol. 89 of the Sparks MSS in Harvard College Library. In a

tiations was an agreement between the Austrian Chancellor, Thugut, and the prisoners of Olmütz that they should be released on condition of never again returning to Imperial territory. To this Lafayette agreed with one qualification, which was accepted: he would not set foot on Imperial soil unless in the service of *either of his countries!* The prisoners were not released however until an informal agreement was reached with the American consul at Hamburg that he would be personally responsible for Lafayette and his "caravan"—to use Thugut's impatient description—leaving that city within eight days. Samuel Williams, the consul, who had no instructions on the subject, gave his personal word of honor to this effect.[87] To this was added the pledge of the ex-consul of the United States, John Parish, a British merchant of that city with whom most of the negotiations were carried on by Thugut's agents.

In the instructions on the subject to the Imperial minister at Hamburg, Thugut stated: "Meanwhile you may observe to him [i.e., to Parish] on this occasion, that His Majesty, having contracted no posi-

letter to Washington of April 26, 1798, Lafayette mentioned the intention of himself and his son George to go to America, leaving in Holstein the Marquise and her daughters, who could not then undergo the rigors of the voyage. This intention is repeated in a letter of May 20, 1798, providing his wife's health would allow him to leave her. In a letter of August 20, 1798, from Witmold, he states, after lengthy comments on the European situation and the French-American controversy: "In a letter from Hamilton wherein he affectionately speaks of my intended departure for America, he seems to be sensible of inconveniences arising from the present unhappy misunderstandings between the two republics." Lafayette comments that "that advice is now useless to discuss," as the state of the Marquise's health, and their involved property affairs, compel him to remain in Europe. In this letter and that of the following September 5, there are references to Lafayette's desire to be the instrument of reconciliation between France and the United States, and of his intended advice to Talleyrand and others, of interest to the student of the X.Y.Z. imbroglio.

87. Samuel Williams to Rufus King, enclosed in King's to Washington of Sept. 6, 1797. Washington Papers, *285*, 38060. Williams states: "It appears to be the wish of his friends that he go by the shortest route to Holland. They expect, perhaps, that he will have leave to enter France and recover his property. I hope so. For, *entre nous,* I would rather that he and his companions were there than in the United States."

A letter from Williams to General Washington, Oct. 5, 1797, speaks of the honor of "embracing our beloved friend, General Lafayette" and the safe arrival of the family at Hamburg. "The General retains his ardent affection and respect for you, Sir, and our Country. Mme. Lafayette's health, the unpleasant state of our affairs with France, and of France herself, may prevent his embarking this fall, for America; but he is still undecided. We all assure him a most affectionate reception there." Ibid., 38111.

tive engagement with the French as to the liberation of the said prisoners, the motive of the particular interest which the United States appears to attach to it has greatly contributed to impel His Majesty to this act of beneficence; finally that His Majesty will always be glad to give to the United States of America, on occasion, real marks of friendship and goodwill." [88]

This gesture, duly acknowledged in the name of the United States by the Englishman Parish,[89] leaves us to guess whether it was occasioned by President Washington's letter as a private gentleman to the Emperor, by some informal conversations on behalf of Lafayette which Gouverneur Morris unsuccessfully had with Thugut in the autumn of 1796, or by the notorious knowledge that the United States had been consistently interested in the fate of Lafayette.[90]

The agreement was duly carried out. After an appropriate reception by the American citizens of Hamburg,[91] Lafayette and his family and fellow prisoners removed to Altona, across the Elbe in Denmark, and thence to Witmold. To that place George Washington Lafayette brought the President's congratulations to his family. The reunited Lafayettes and their numerous relatives and friends spent in Holstein a not unhappy year of exile. After a further sojourn in Holland, whither he

88. Thugut to Buol-Schauenstein, Vienna, Sept. 13, 1797. Printed by Büdinger, p. 288.

89. Parish to Thugut, Aug. 25, 1797. Ibid., p. 286. Though this letter antedates Thugut's it is an answer to Buol's earlier letters to Parish. Parish had been relieved of his office as American consul, following a complaint of the French Directory that he, a British citizen, was unneutral in his conduct as American consul.

90. On March 3, 1795, a resolution was introduced in the House of Representatives by R. G. Harper, that "this House will see with the highest satisfaction any measures which he [the President] may deem expedient to adopt towards effecting the restoration of their said *fellow-citizen* [General de Lafayette—italics inserted] to liberty." In the debate the generous words of the House Resolution of 1784 were recalled and Lafayette's services to America contrasted with the passive attitude of the government in his actual predicament. The resolution was lost 32 to 52. The approaching hour of adjournment *sine die*, the "delicacy" of the subject, and confidence that the Executive had taken all proper steps, were the arguments which prevailed against the resolution. *Annals of Congress*, 1796–97, pp. 2362–67. See R. G. Harper to his constituents, Philadelphia, March 13, 1797. A.H.A., *Annual Report*, 1913, 2, 39.

91. For this negotiation see official correspondence in Büdinger, "Lafayette in Oesterreich, pp. 273–96; *Diary and Letters of G. Morris*, pp. 294–304. The matter was made the subject of only bare mention in one official dispatch of the retired consul, Williams, to the Secretary of State, Sept. 11, 1797 (see D.S., Consular Letters, 1790–1800), but is more fully set forth in Williams's correspondence with the American minister in London, Rufus King. See C. R. King, *Life and Correspondence of Rufus King*, 2, 214, 223–32. For petition to John Quincy Adams, from American residents at Hamburg, for release of Lafayette, see M.H.S., *Proceedings, 46*, 235.

ventured to remove with his family in December 1798, General Lafayette eventually was allowed to return to France after the *coup d'état*
of Brumaire, in 1799.

This hitherto neglected episode of the foreign relations of Washington's administration is worthy of record if only for its portrayal of the
human side of a relationship between two men whose disinterested
services for the success of American independence are unforgettably
enshrined in the memories of the people of America and France. It has
also a political significance most instructive for the student of early
American diplomacy. It is an uncited precedent for executive action in
regard to protection of American citizens—even Lafayettes—who take
service under the colors of foreign princes. It is a previously unrecorded
case of dual citizenship at a time when the international law of citizenship was most uncertain and not at all defined by American law. It may
well be conjectured to have even a more vital meaning. The year 1796
was the year when Washington and Hamilton were crystallizing in their
minds the maxims soon to be expressed in the Farewell Address. Only
two years before they had refused in most positive terms to enter the
Abortive Armed Neutrality of 1794.[92] The problem of foreign entanglements again presented by Lafayette's unusual plea must have had at
least some weight in the formation of a famous principle of the Farewell Address, which has had such ponderous influence in far-reaching
international problems of our own time.

92. See above, Chap. 6, pp. 171–74.

10. Washington's Farewell Address: A Foreign Policy of Independence

THE FAREWELL ADDRESS is often thought of as an expression of abstract ideas of policy looking toward the future, but with little reference to the events of 1796. Its fundamental ideas were, on the contrary, suggested by experience, and very recent and painful experience. To comprehend Washington's point of view and feel the weight of his advice, it is necessary to consider the historical setting, and, for that, to go back to the outbreak of a general European war in February and March 1793.

In the desperate conflict with the allied monarchies of the First Coalition the French Republic expected to find a valuable counterweight in the independent United States, separated from Great Britain by French diplomacy and arms in the previous war. Thoroughly conscious of the naval impotence of the new American nation, France had preferred not to invoke the *casus fœderis* of the treaty of alliance of 1778—the defense of the French West India Islands. A neutral United States promised greater advantages: (1) as a possible transatlantic base of operations against enemy colonies and commerce, (2) as the largest remaining neutral supply of provisions and naval stores, commodities that perhaps might be passed through the British navy under cover of the neutral flag. To finance both of these objects there was the gradually maturing American debt.

President Washington's proclamation of neutrality and the refusal of his government to lend itself to Genêt's projects soon showed France that her ally did not intend to involve itself in the European war by becoming such a base of belligerent naval and military operations. France perforce acquiesced in that decision, being still unwilling to invoke the letter of the alliance. This was because the actual belligerency of the United States which had no navy was worth nothing in itself and had the really great disadvantage of making American shipping immediately liable to capture and confiscation as enemy property. The neutrality of the United States, even though it could not serve as a

Published in *American Historical Review*, *39*, no. 2, 1934.

base for such projects as Genêt attempted, was far more serviceable than American military assistance. The principal object of France was to secure from neutral America provisions for her beleaguered homeland and colonies, imported in American ships under protection of the principles of the commercial treaty of 1778: free ships free goods; provisions and naval stores not contraband; neutral right to trade in noncontraband goods to and between unblockaded enemy ports.

This Franco-American treaty did not bind France's enemy, Great Britain, the principal maritime belligerent. The British had never admitted these "novel" principles. They considered them as exceptional articles in particular treaties binding only between the signatory parties. When hostilities commenced in 1793 Great Britain began seizing enemy property right and left wherever it could be found outside neutral territorial waters, whether in enemy or neutral bottoms. British prize courts under Orders-in-Council began to apply the Rule of 1756, itself an innovation as late as the Seven Years' War. Secretary of State Thomas Jefferson protested in the name of the United States against this practice, which was contrary to the articles written into the Franco-American treaty and all the other European treaties of the United States. But Great Britain was not bound by those treaties.[1] The United States was powerless to challenge the British navy. American credit, newly established, depended primarily on tariff revenue, and tariff revenue depended principally on imports from Great Britain. The collapse of credit at this time would have meant the collapse of the newly established nationality of the United States. Rather than go to war with Great Britain, President Washington took Alexander Hamilton's advice and ratified Jay's Treaty with England which acquiesced in British naval practice for the next twelve years, in effect for the duration of the war.[2] That treaty did not violate the treaties of the United States with France. It recognized a condition which already existed, namely, that the United States could not compel Great Britain to observe the terms of the Franco-American treaty. In 1793 the other maritime powers, which in the War for American Independence had followed principles similar to those of the Franco-American treaty, made treaties with Great Britain agreeing to harass the commerce of France in every possible way. These powers included the old Armed Neutrals of 1780, except Sweden and Denmark. A group of ardent, hateful enemies ringed

1. Great Britain had accepted these principles in the treaty of commerce of 1786 with France, but of course that treaty had ceased to exist with the outbreak of war.
2. I have dwelt in detail upon the significance of this in my *Jay's Treaty* (New York, 1923; rev. ed. New Haven, 1962).

France about by land and sea to close her frontiers, to sweep her commerce from the seas, to take her colonies from her, and to deprive her of naval supplies and of foodstuffs. The neutral United States, the ally of yesteryear, which France herself had brought into the world, stood aloof and acquiesced in this British naval-diplomatic system of strangulation. Thus were frustrated the advantages of neutral carriage which France had relied on from the American treaty of amity and commerce of 1778.

This situation was aggravated in the eyes of French statesmen by Jay's Treaty. If in the face of that document and of British practice the French were still to adhere to the terms of the American treaty, they would have to stand quietly by and watch British cruisers take French property from neutral American ships, confiscate American-owned naval stores as contraband when en route in American vessels to France, and pre-empt (as was the British practice) foodstuffs under similar conditions. Deprived thus by belligerent action of naval stores, foodstuffs, and of the advantages of neutral carriage they would find themselves obliged to abstain from following the British practice; they would have to watch these same goods go unchallenged by French warships into British harbors to feed and strengthen the might of the enemy.

It is not difficult to understand that this seemed unfair to France, and that Jay's Treaty seemed an outrageous, even a treacherous, document, made by an ungrateful nation. But one would be more ready to sympathize with France if her own hands were clean. We must remember that when John Jay signed his famous treaty with Lord Grenville on November 19, 1794, France herself was pursuing and had been pursuing, off and on, since May 9, 1793, a maritime policy of retaliation in practice identical with that of Great Britain in the treatment of neutral shipping, and had been applying it to American ships and cargoes,[3] and that notwithstanding her obligations under her treaty with the

3. The various French laws and decrees affecting neutral commerce were:

May 9, 1793. Law of the National Convention decreeing orders to naval officers and commanders of privateers to bring in "neutral ships laden in whole or in part either with foodstuffs belonging to neutrals and destined to enemy ports, or with goods belonging to the enemy," the former to be purchased at the price they would have commanded at the port of their intended destination, the latter to be confiscated, and an allowance to be fixed by the prize court for freight and detention.

This act was professedly in retaliation for specified British spoliations on neutral ships, and was retroactive to all prizes brought in since the beginning of the war [which implies that some had been brought in before the occasion for "retaliation"]. Compare it with similar provisions of Article I of the British Order-in-Council of June 8, 1793. The law of May 9 was to cease to have effect when the enemy powers should declare free and nonseizable foodstuffs which were neutral property and destined to the ports of the French Republic, as well as merchandise belonging to

United States. As in later European wars (1803–12, and 1914–17) the force of these belligerent retaliations fell heavily on the neutral United States and developed grave diplomatic problems. Unlike the later wars, in this case the United States was protected by the paper and ink of a treaty against such practice on the part of one belligerent. Nevertheless, French spoliations on American shipping rivaled those of Great Britain. French privateers and naval vessels also vied with the British in violence and outrages against neutral crews and passengers.[4]

The French diplomatic commission, headed by Joseph Fauchet, which

---

the French government or French citizens on board neutral ships. *Lois et actes du gouvernement* (Paris, Imprimerie Royale, 1834), 7, 51–52; the laws and decrees referred to here may also be found in J. B. Duvergier's convenient *Collection complète des lois, décrets, ordonnances, règlements, avis du conseil d'état, 1788–1830* (30 vols. 2d ed. Paris, 1834–38), under each date. *A.S.P., F.R., 1,* 377.

May 23, 1793. Law of the National Convention exempting American ships from the operation of the law of May 9, 1793, "conformably to Article XVI [sic] of the treaty of February 6, 1778." [Article XVI deals with the irrelevant matter of restoration of captures made by pirates. Presumably Article XXIII was meant.] *Lois et actes, 8,* 82; *A.S.P., F.R., 1,* 365.

May 28, 1793. Law of the National Convention repealing the law of May 23, 1793, which exempted American ships. *Lois et actes,* 7, 82–83.

July 1, 1793. Law restoring the exemption of American ships, in phraseology identical with that of May 23, 1793. Ibid., 7, 174.

July 27, 1793. Law decreeing the full execution of the law of May 9, 1793, relative to neutral ships loaded with foodstuffs owned by neutrals or with enemy property. Ibid., 7, 241–42.

March 24, 1794 (4 germinal an II). Law decreeing: "The treaties of navigation and of commerce existing between France and nations with whom she is at peace shall be executed according to their form and tenure." Ibid., *8,* 414–15.

Nov. 18, 1794. Decree of the Committee of Public Safety enjoining French naval officers and commanders of privateers to enforce the law of nations and the stipulations of treaties, "conformably to the terms of the decree of the National Convention of July 27, 1793." *A.S.P., F.R., 1,* 689, 752. This decree does not appear in the *Recueil des actes du Comité de salut public,* edited by Alphonse A. Aulard. Jay's Treaty was signed on Nov. 19, 1794.

4. In addition to an undetermined number of captures at sea, Fulwar Skipwith, American claims agent at Paris in October 1794, stated that there were nearly 300 vessels in the ports of France suffering from embargoes (a later list showed that the Bordeaux embargo accounted for 103 cases), spoliations, delays, breaches of contract, nonpayment of purchased cargoes, etc. The United States Court of Claims, which completed adjudication of the French Spoliation Claims for 1793–1800 (responsibility having been assumed by the convention with France of 1800) awarded a total of $7,149,306.10 for 1,853 authentic cases of spoliation. Each case did not, however, represent a particular ship. Congress has appropriated to date only $3,910,860.61, to pay part of these claims. To this may be added $5,000,000 for claims of a special character, assumed by the United States in 1803, in part payment for Louisiana— to wit: embargoes, detention and appropriation of goods in French harbors, money due from the French government for purchases, etc.

in 1794 had succeeded the ruined Genêt in Philadelphia, did not even pretend to reconcile French maritime policy with the obligations of the treaty of commerce of 1778. Nevertheless it claimed for France all the articles of the treaty which were of advantage to her, and requested benevolent interpretations of them. The Committee of Public Safety, in drawing up instructions for these commissioners, anticipated that there would be objections in the United States to the retaliatory French decrees. Admitting deviations from the treaty it became the task of the commissioners to extenuate French policy on the ground of altered circumstances.[5]

Washington and his advisers had foreseen the possible further effect on France of the intended treaty between the United States and Great Britain when John Jay, the Federalist, pro-British diplomatist, departed on his famous mission to London. To mask this mission they sent to France the pro-French Republican senator from Virginia, James Monroe, an old opponent of Jay's diplomacy since 1786, who considered Jay's mission as mischievous and in the Senate voted against his confirmation. Monroe never saw Jay's instructions, possibly was not aware of their real scope.

Like an apostle of the rights of man, Monroe set to work to persuade the French government to observe the treaty of amity and commerce of 1778. The restrictions on private trade in French harbors, the embargoes, the delays in payment for purchased cargoes, had already so jeopardized the American provision supply that the Convention admitted the force of the American remonstrances on every point except free ships free goods.[6] The envoy now argued for the full and entire enforcement of the articles of the treaty. He appealed to old friendship and present interest. He contended that it would be good policy for France to repeal her obnoxious decrees before Great Britain should repeal hers. If she did so, it would combine all America in condemnation of the conduct of the British; if she did not, any later repeal would appear merely to be forced by her enemy. At just this time news arrived[7] of the setting aside, by an Order-in-Council of August 6, 1794, of the British provision order of June 8, 1793—this had been a means in London of easing the English negotiations with Jay. It re-enforced Monroe's argument in Paris. The French law of May 9, 1793, had made

5. *Correspondence of the French Ministers to the United States, 1791–1797,* Frederick J. Turner, ed., A.H.A., *Annual Report,* 1903, 2, 291.

6. *A.S.P., F.R., 1,* 677.

7. See report of Merlin de Douai, brumaire, an III, Arch. Aff. Etrang., Correspondance politique, États Unis, vol. 42, ff. 186–204.

the duration of the "retaliatory" maritime measures contingent upon the repeal by the enemy of his illegal procedure. The Convention now (January 2, 1795) availed itself of this provision to yield to the importunities of the ingratiating James Monroe. "As a grand act of honesty and justice," it wiped out at one stroke all the offensive decrees and enjoined the strict observance of the provisions of the treaty of 1778.[8] Orders were immediately given for the adjudication of all claims arising out of violations of that treaty.

Monroe's triumph was short-lived. Before anything very effective could actually be done about the relief of the claimants the signficance of Jay's Treaty [9] began to be suspected in Paris. In August 1795, the text arrived from Philadelphia. It completely undid Monroe's successes. In 1796 Washington recalled the unhappy minister for not having defended with sufficient vigor the new English treaty.[10] In truth Monroe had repeated to the French government the arguments and defenses sent to him by Secretaries of State Randolph and Pickering. They read well, but one may doubt that his heart was in his words. He thought Jay's Treaty a shameful document.[11] There is evidence suggesting that he had confidential conversations with the French Revolutionary leaders about "the real dispositions of his countrymen," conversa-

8. Law of 13 nivôse, an III, *Bulletin des lois de la République française*, 1ᵉ sér., 3 no. 107; decree of the Committee of Public Safety, 14 nivôse, an III (Jan. 3, 1795), *A.S.P., F.R., 1,* 642 [in English translation; not in Aulard].

9. *Before* the repeal of the retaliatory decrees the committee had asked Monroe about the treaty; and he had conveyed to them information from Jay, to the effect that it contained nothing contrary to the existing treaties of the United States; and had promised that as soon as he might be informed of its contents he would inform the committee. This promise impelled Monroe to refuse to accept from Jay a *confidential* statement of the contents of the treaty. Monroe's *A View of the Conduct of the Executive in the Foreign Affairs of the United States, Connected with the Mission to the French Republic, during the Years 1794, 5, and 6* (Philadelphia, 1797), pp. xvii–xxvii.

10. Monroe's instructions and dispatches are printed in *A.S.P., F.R., 1,* and in his exculpatory *View.* Washington's studied comments on the *View,* written at Mount Vernon on the margin of its pages, are printed in appendix II to Daniel C. Gilman's *James Monroe* (Boston, 1883, 1898). Beverley W. Bond, Jr.'s "The Monroe Mission to France, 1794–1796," in The Johns Hopkins University *Studies in Historical and Political Science,* 25 (1907), 9–103, did not have available the valuable sources in the French Ministry of Foreign Affairs. The various deliberations of committees on Monroe's notes, and relevant reports, quite voluminous, are in Arch. Aff. Etrang., États Unis, vol. 42, particularly ff. 17, 141, 186–204.

11. Monroe to Joseph Jones, Sept. 15, 1795. Calendar, in Division of MSS of the Library of Congress, of the Gouverneur Collection of Monroe Papers, now privately owned. Gilman, p. 62, printed a portion of this letter.

tions which he did not reveal to his own government.[12] He kept up an intimate correspondence with Madison,[13] and other friends of Jefferson, who opposed Jay's Treaty and favored a pro-French policy. He certainly led the French government to believe that any treaty of amity between the United States and Great Britain would never be ratified.[14] When it was known that a treaty had been signed, Monroe repeated this assurance.[15] When Jay's Treaty went through Congress he tried rather lamely to explain its success, and still argued that it would be good policy for the French Republic to observe loyally the terms of its American treaties; the example of that loyalty and the contrasting attitude of the British government would win the good will of the American *people,* from whose eyes the scales of British deception must eventually fall.[16] He led them in Paris to believe that the people would overthrow the administration of President Washington as a result of the treaty, that better things might be expected after the election of 1796.[17] This supposition was re-enforced by advice from the French diplomatic representative in the United States, Fauchet, and his successor Adet, and by Americans in Paris like Monroe's friend, Tom Paine.

After Jay's departure from York Fauchet had become increasingly nervous about the object of the new mission. He sent one of his col-

12. Monroe wrote to the Committee of Public Safety a "non-official letter," Dec. 27, 1794, asking that a member of the committee be deputed to have frank conversations with him concerning any propositions about to be made to the American government "on this subject [i.e., possible propositions] or any other (if you desire) tending to acquaint you [the committee] with the situation and the *real* dispositions of my *countrymen* [italics inserted]. Arch. Aff. Etrang., États Unis, vol. 42, f. 445.

13. Stanislaus Murray Hamilton, ed., *Writings of James Monroe* (7 vols. New York, 1898–1903), 2, passim.

14. Adet to the Committee of Public Safety, 14 thermidor, an III (Aug. 1, 1795), *Corr. Fr. Min.,* p. 762.

15. "I assured them, generally, as I had done before, that I was satisfied the treaty contained in it nothing which could give them uneasiness; but if it did, and especially if it weakened our connexion with France, it would certainly be disapproved in America." Monroe to the Secretary of State, Apr. 14, 1795, *A.S.P., F.R., 1,* 702. He did convey to the Committee on Public Safety Jay's only statement to him about the treaty, that it contained nothing contrary to the treaty stipulations of the United States with other countries.

16. "Exposé sommaire," etc., dated 1796, in the Monroe Collection of MSS, Library of Congress. Internal evidence proves Monroe to be the writer, and one presumes from the same evidence that it was directed to the French government, although I have not found it in the French archives.

17. Monroe to the Minister of Foreign Affairs, Paris, Feb. 17, 1796 (28 pluviôse, an IV), Arch. Aff. Etrang., États Unis, vol. 45, f. 146.

leagues to Paris to warn the Committee of Public Safety that something was in the air, and to say that the other two members of the commission, La Forest and Petry, could not be trusted because they hobnobbed with Alexander Hamilton and other Federalists.[18] When news of the signature of the treaty and rumors of its contents began to leak out, the French minister became very much exasperated. His notes of protest against fancied violations of neutral obligations under the treaty of 1778 took on a more rasping tone, full of intimations of American disloyalty. Fauchet tried by fair means and foul, but in vain, to block the ratification of the treaty by the Senate. He hoped with Secretary Randolph that the President might not sign the ratification, even though the Senate had so advised and consented. His successor Adet, encouraged by the widespread popular protests, labored with the House of Representatives to refuse the appropriations necessary to carry it into effect. When the treaty passed unscathed through the House, Adet's last hope was that the people would overthrow the administration of President Washington in the forthcoming election of 1796.[19] Through the agency of organs of the Republican press which he manipulated and inspired to the extent of his limited financial resources, and by means of the democratic societies which had arisen at the wave of Genêt's wand to applaud the French Revolution, the French minister was working with might and main to that end.[20] He did not know, of course, of the President's determination, long since fixed and presently to be announced, to refuse a third term.

In Paris, American affairs had received less attention than they merited. Before the reorganization of the French government under the constitution of the Year III (1795) the rapidly changing administration of the Foreign Office failed to give methodical attention. French diplomatists at Philadelphia complained bitterly that their dispatches

18. *Corr. Fr. Min.,* pp. 373, 389, 410, 419; Arch. Aff. Etrang., États Unis, vol. 41, ff. 291, 377, 408.

19. *Corr. Fr. Min.,* p. 894. Neither Fauchet and the commissioners, nor their successor Adet, had any actual instructions concerning Jay's Treaty. Once they left Paris, they received scant attention from the Committee of Public Safety.

20. Bernard Faÿ, *L'Esprit révolutionnaire en France et aux États-Unis à la fin du XVIIIᵉ siècle* (Paris, 1925), pp. 254–60. "All these intrigues are sad and displeasing to study when one remembers the sincere enthusiasm which the masses of the American people then testified for France." *Ibid.,* p. 255. John Bach McMaster, *History of the People of the United States* (New York, 1883–1913), 2, ch. 9, is in effect a digest of opposing press and pamphlet comment. The arguments of the Republican press against Jay's Treaty, against Washington, against the Farewell Address, and finally against the candidacy of John Adams, reflect the paragraphs of the political correspondence of the French Foreign Office with its American legation.

went unanswered. For months they waited without instructions. None of them had been told what to do about Jay's Treaty. Fauchet, and his successor Adet, had acted on their own responsibility in their protests against that instrument. The new Directory put the conduct of foreign affairs on a more businesslike basis, under a single minister, Charles Delacroix. He straightway brought in a report concerning the United States. Washington must go, he said. "A friend of France must succeed him in that eminent office." He continued:

> We must raise up the people and at the same time conceal the lever by which we do so . . . I propose to the Executive Directory to authorize me to send orders and instructions to our minister plenipotentiary at Philadelphia to use all the means in his power in the United States to bring about the right kind of revolution (*l'heureuse Révolution*) and Washington's replacement, which, assuring to the Americans their independence, will break off treaties [*sic*] made with England and maintain those which unite them to the French Republic.

As in the case of the Netherlands at that time, France and French agents regarded that political party in the United States which was most useful to their purposes as the "patriot" party. Jefferson, Madison, Monroe, Robert R. Livingston, Senator Tazewell of Virginia, Governor Clinton of New York, and Governor Mifflin of Pennsylvania were patriots. Washington, Hamilton, Jay, Rufus King, and John Adams were aristocrats unfriendly to real liberty. The French Foreign Office looked on the United States as "the Holland of the New World." It hoped for and expected a popular revolution there, on French models, such as did take place in Holland in 1795, to overturn the existing régime of ordered liberty, to cast off the formidable ascendency of President Washington and his Federalist advisers who themselves were esteemed to be beyond the reach of French influence and purpose.[21]

At first the Directory decided on a more positive step to offset Jay's Treaty: to send a special envoy extraordinary to Philadelphia to recall Adet and to announce the end of the Franco-American treaties and then himself to withdraw.[22] Monroe confidentially urged Delacroix against such action: it would please the enemies of both countries. "Left to our-

---

21. To this point there is a remarkable analysis of American politics in relation to French policy, by the undersecretary of the sixth division of the Foreign Office: Memoir on the United States, Florida, and Louisiana, 12 frimaire, an IV (Dec. 3, 1795), Arch. Aff. Etrang., États Unis, vol. 44, ff. 407–17.

22. Report of the Minister of Foreign Affairs to the Executive Directory, 27 nivôse, an IV (Jan. 17, 1796), ibid., vol. 45, ff. 41–53.

selves," he hinted, "everything will I think be satisfactorily arranged and *perhaps in the course of the present year:* and it is always more grateful to make such arrangements ourselves than to be pressed to it." [23]

Delacroix [24] and the Directory took the advice of President Washington's minister to await the President's overthrow. They blamed Washington, Hamilton, and the Federalist Senate, in short the elected government of the people of the United States, against which, according to French agents and correspondents (including Americans in Paris), the people were now in an uproar, from Boston to Savannah. Well they knew that Monroe's hint referred to the approaching presidential election of 1796.[25] They decided to temporize, to protest, to argue (Monroe had advised them not to abandon their claims for redress), pending the new presidential election, to work up "patriot" sentiment against Washington's administration. To this effect they approved instructions to a new minister.[26] Later came news of the success of Jay's Treaty in the House of Representatives. They then decided not to send any new minister after all, but to keep Adet in Philadelphia for a short while at least, and to follow his advice and that of the returned Fauchet to hearten the pro-French "patriots" in America by an unmistakable denunciation of the policy of the executive of the United States, lest by French silence the election should go in Washington's favor.

The inveterate tendency of French policy to stir up the American people against their government had gradually steeled the sympathies of President Washington against the old ally. Though Washington could not know the inner counsels of the French Directory—least of all when he had a minister like Monroe in Paris—the policy of France had been made abundantly apparent by the French diplomatists in Philadelphia. Since Genêt's time they had been openly or covertly attempt-

23. Monroe to the Minister of Foreign Affairs, Paris, Feb. 17, 1796 (28 pluviôse, an IV), ibid., vol. 45, f. 147 [italics inserted]. This highly significant note was not revealed to his own government and is enough to justify Washington's removal of Monroe. Monroe summarized the arguments he had made to Delacroix in a letter to the Secretary of State of Feb. 20, 1796, but made no reference to any written note of his and said nothing about the hint he had given.

24. Delacroix to Monroe, Paris, 1 ventôse, an IV (Feb. 20, 1796), ibid., vol. 45, f. 160.

25. Observations on Mr. Monroe's letter to the Minister of Foreign Affairs, not dated, ibid., vol. 45, f. 148.

26. "Memoir of Political Instructions to the Citizen Vincent, to be sent as Minister Plenipotentiary of the Republic to the United States." *Recueil des actes du Directoire exécutif,* A. Debidour, ed. (Paris, 1910), *1,* 748; 2, 621. Some charges against Vincent's integrity apparently stopped his departure. Later Monroe's protest against the appointment of Mangourit, the former French consul at Charleston during Genêt's obnoxious operations, was effective.

ing to join forces with the anti-Federalist opposition. They had been able to promise themselves much from such strategy because of radical political affinities and because of the memory of French help in the American Revolution. But the French alliance, indispensable as it was to American independence, had always been a great embarrassment to American diplomatists. It was so even during the diplomacy of the Revolution itself, when Vergennes had wavered under the threats of a separate Spanish peace (though his wavering has become known only to scholars in our own day). It was so during the peace negotiations of 1782 in Paris. Experience with it showed the Fathers the danger to independence and sovereignty of any other alliance. Toward the close of the war Congress shrank from committing itself to the Dutch proposal to join the Armed Neutrality. In 1786 John Jay's initialed alliance with Spain (never revealed fully until the twentieth century) collapsed before the opposition of the Southern states who feared for the Mississippi. Soon after, the South united with New England (anxious about its fisheries) [27] and wrote into the Constitution that potent provision that no future treaty could be ratified except by the vote of two-thirds of the senators present in the upper chamber of the national legislature, that Senate in which there must always be exactly two senators from each state. To a certain degree this fixed a constitutional obstacle against European entanglements. More than one delegate supported it for that reason.[28]

The French alliance had become increasingly embarrassing after the French declaration of war on England, February 1, 1793. The proclamation of neutrality was a tangible expression of a sane American policy not of isolation but of diplomatic independence. Washington refused all new foreign alliances. As Hamilton so indiscreetly told the British minister, Hammond, in 1794, he rejected the Swedish invitation to join the second, abortive, Armed Neutrality of 1794. He also turned down Godoy's famous "propositions for the President," of that same year, for a Spanish alliance, as Pinckney too later repelled them in Madrid. In short, the very life-saving French alliance had long since cured the United States of any hankering for more allies.

The first twenty years of American independence had in fact made American statesmen shy of Europe, and they have remained so ever since. Their writings (with the possible exception of James Monroe, whose name after 1823 was to become so inseparably associated with

27. R. Earl McClendon published a useful note on the "Origin of the Two-Thirds Rule in Senate Action upon Treaties," *A.H.R.*, *36* (1931), 768–72.

28. J. Fred Rippy and Angie Debo, "The Historical Background of the American Policy of Isolation," *Smith College Studies in History*, *9* (Apr.–July 1924), 140.

abstention from European politics and wars!) are full of affirmations that it was the true policy of the United States to steer clear of European politics.[29]

Tom Paine had been the first to express this, in 1776: " 'Tis the true interest of America, to steer clear of European contentions, which she never can do, while by her dependance on Britain, she is made the make-weight in the scale of British politics." [30] "I do not love to be entangled in the politics of Europe," wrote John Adams in 1777.[31] In the Virginia ratifying convention in 1788, Madison, speaking for the adoption of the new Federal Constitution asked: "What is the situation of America?" and answered, "She is remote from Europe, and ought not to engage in her politics or wars." [32] Jefferson in France had written in 1787: "I know too that it is a maxim with us, and I think it a wise one, not to entangle ourselves with the affairs of Europe." [33] Again, in 1790: "At such a distance from Europe, and with such an ocean between us, we hope to meddle little in its quarrels or combinations. Its peace and its commerce are what we shall court. . ." [34] Hamilton repeatedly had used words almost identical with essential portions of the text of Washington's Farewell Address of 1796.[35] So had the President, particularly in 1795.[36]

29. Rippy and Debo have collected numerous expressions of abstention from European politics.

30. *Common Sense* (1st ed. Philadelphia, 1776), p. 38.

31. Rippy and Debo, p. 90.

32. *The Writings of James Madison*, Gaillard Hunt, ed. (New York, 1900–10), *5*, 151.

33. *Writings of Thomas Jefferson* (Ford ed.), *4*, 483.

34. To Monsieur de Pinto, New York, Aug. 7, 1790. *The Writings of Thomas Jefferson*, Memorial ed. (Washington, 1903–04), *8*, 74.

35. Over the signature of *Horatius*, arguing for the ratification of Jay's Treaty, Hamilton wrote in 1795: "If you consult your true interest your motto cannot fail to be: 'PEACE AND TRADE WITH ALL NATIONS; beyond our present engagements, POLITICAL CONNECTION WITH NONE.' You ought to spurn from you as the box of Pandora, the fatal heresy of a close alliance, or in the language of *Genet*, a true *family compact*, with France. This would at once make you a mere satellite of France, and entangle you in all the contests, broils, and wars of Europe." The text continues: " 'Tis evident that the controversies of Europe must often grow out of causes and interests foreign to this country. Why then should we, by a close political connection with any power of Europe, expose our peace and interest, as a matter of course, to all the shocks with which their mad rivalship and wicked ambition so frequently convulse the earth? 'T were insanity to embrace such a system." *The Works of Alexander Hamilton*, Henry Cabot Lodge, ed. (New York, 1885–86), *4*, 366–67.

36. To Patrick Henry, Oct. 9, 1795; to Gouverneur Morris, Dec. 22, 1795; *Writings of George Washington* (Ford ed.), *13*, 119, 151. Washington refused to lend his official

If George Washington had retired from the Presidency in the spring of 1793,[37] as he originally intended when he first consulted James Madison about the draft of a valedictory we may presume that he would never have said anything about foreign affairs. There would have been no Farewell Address of the kind that has become so familiar to us—though we cannot say that the policy itself would not soon have been formulated. Certainly Washington's suggestions, and Madison's draft, for a possible valedictory in 1792, did not touch foreign affairs. In the summer of 1796, however, foreign affairs were uppermost in the mind of the Father of His Country. Then unalterably resolved not to serve another term, he prepared to indite a final message to the American people at large.

It was to remove foreign interference in our domestic affairs, to preserve the nation and the people from Europe's distresses, that the retiring first President, with a particular eye to relations with France, marked out for his now private adviser, Alexander Hamilton, the subjects which he would like to include in his final address. In characteristically familiar and felicitous phrases—many of which we may find already expressed in *The Federalist* and other products of his pen—Hamilton wrote out the President's ideas.[38] Of Washington were the trunk and branches of the sturdy tree. The shimmering foliage dancing and shining in the sunlight was Hamilton's. The President edited several drafts before the address was finished. He cast out at least one extraneous thought which Hamilton tried gratuitously to slip in. Despite Hamilton's principal part in the phrasing of the document, and his previous expression of some of the ideas, we may be sure that in the final text the two men were thinking together in absolute unison. The Address was as directly pointed to the diplomatic problems of the time of the French Revolution as were Woodrow Wilson's Fourteen Points to the intricate diplomacy of the World War. President Wilson and Colonel House worked no more intimately together on that document in 1918, drafting and redrafting its clauses, than did President Washington and Colonel Hamilton in 1796, composing and recomposing the paragraphs of the Farewell Address.

---

intercession to assist the release from Austrian and Prussian prisons of his dearest friend, Lafayette, for fear of involving the United States in Europe's wars. See Chap. 9 of this volume, pp. 209–39.

37. I have profited from discussions of President Washington's policies with Frank Louraine of Washington, D.C., particularly on the significance of the Farewell Address in 1796, instead of 1792.

38. Horace Binney in one of the first critical essays in American historiography analyzed the authorship of the document. *An Inquiry into the Formation of Washington's Farewell Address* (Philadelphia, 1859).

The immortal document, ever since a polestar of American foreign policy, represented the crystallization of the experience of remarkably clearheaded men with foreign affairs since the Declaration of Independence. It was given forthwith to the public in a newspaper.[39] It spoke directly to the great and simple audience of the American people. "The name of AMERICAN," it said to them, putting the word into bold type, "which belongs to you in your national capacity, must always exalt the just pride of Patriotism, more than any appelation derived from local discriminations."

We must keep in mind the involvement of the French alliance in American diplomacy and domestic politics as we read the Farewell Address, even as the authors of the document had that constantly before them.

It began thus with an appeal to support the *National Union*. The orthodox phrase Federal Union does not occur in the document, a very significant omission. It continued with a counsel against the practice of party politics, lest the new nation be undermined by internal dissension assisted by foreign intrigue. The first President and his adviser Alexander Hamilton believed that, with the system of checks and balances in the new government, party politics was unnecessary for the preservation of ordered liberty. The rise of an opposition they identified with a faction opposed not only to the policies of the administration but to the new national government itself. They connected this faction with the French government and its agents.

Turning to the subject of foreign affairs, the Address admonished his fellow citizens to steer clear of European alliances and wars. It justified American neutrality whilst the nation, assisted by the advantages of so peculiar a situation, might grow strong enough to command its own fortune. In these words and these counsels the authors of the Address had continually before them the apparition of the life-giving, but the entangling French alliance, and the distant scene of the great wars engulfing Europe. They had behind them the problems solved by Jay's Treaty and by Pinckney's Treaty, thanks to the occupation of Britain and Spain with those troubles in Europe.

The immediate purpose of the Address was to strike a powerful blow against French intermeddling in American affairs.[40] After the victory

---

39. *Claypoole's American Daily Advertiser* (Philadelphia), Sept. 19, 1796.

40. Enclosing the document, Adet reported: "It would be useless to speak to you about it. You will have noticed the lies it contains, the insolent tone that governs it, the immorality which characterizes it. You will have had no difficulty in recognizing the author of a piece extolling ingratitude, showing it as a virtue necessary to the happiness of States, presenting interest as the only counsel which governments

of Jay's Treaty in the House of Representatives it had been Adet's advice, and this was also recommended by the returned Fauchet,[41] that some strong and positive action ought to be taken to make the American ally more amenable to French interests. The people, both of those agents had reported—and reported most voluminously—were in favor of France and opposed to their government, but if France did not call Washington's government to terms, and thus support the action of the "good" people to overthrow it, nothing could be hoped from them. Adet advocated [42] that the French Republic proceed to treat American ships precisely as the United States government allowed its flag to be treated by Great Britain, that is, according to the principles of Jay's Treaty. This was, indeed, what France had been doing up to January 3, 1795, when Monroe secured from the Convention the full and entire recognition of the treaty of 1778. But that "grand act of honesty and justice" had not been enforced since the nature of Jay's Treaty had become suspected in France. Nor was it ever to be. It was to be the United States government itself which was finally to pay—throughout a century of litigation—most of the damages to its citizens wrought by the French spoliations in this war.

Jay's Treaty at last having gone into effect, the French Directory prepared its denunciation of the treachery of Washington's government. As a warning to the American people of worse things to follow if President Washington were continued in office it decided to suspend Adet's functions, and with them formal diplomatic relations with the United States. Characterizing Jay's Treaty as equivalent to an alliance between France's principal enemy and her old, ungrateful ally, it proceeded to invoke against American shipping, as a reprisal for that perfidious treaty, the maritime principles of that document itself.[43] If Jefferson should be elected the plan was to restore relations on the old basis, hoping that a new treaty with France might undo Jay's.[44]

---

ought to follow in the course of their negotiations, putting aside honor and glory. You will have recognized immediately the doctrine of the former Secretary of the Treasury, Hamilton, and the principles of loyalty that have always directed the Philadelphia Government." *Corr. Fr. Min.*, p. 954.

41. See Fauchet's long Memoir on the United States of America, 24 frimaire, an IV (Dec. 15, 1795), Arch. Aff. Etrang., États Unis, vol. 44, ff. 457–529.

42. *Corr. Fr. Min.*, pp. 900–06.

43. The Minister of Foreign Affairs to Adet, 7 fructidor, an IV (Aug. 24, 1796), Arch. Aff. Etrang., États Unis, vol. 46, ff. 144–45. See also drafts and reports associated with these instructions, ibid., ff. 133–40.

44. Same to same, 12 brumaire, an V (Nov. 2, 1796), ibid., ff. 355–58.

To his great satisfaction Adet was able to communicate to the United States government, on October 27, 1796, the text of a decree of the Directory announcing that "All neutral or allied Powers shall, without delay, be notified that the flag of the French republic will treat neutral vessels, either as to confiscation, as to searches, or capture, in the same manner as they shall suffer the English to treat them." [45]

A few weeks later (November 15) he announced the definite suspension of his functions, not, indeed, to indicate a formal rupture between the United States and France, "but as a mark of just discontent, which is to last until the government of the United States returns to sentiments, and to measures, more conformable to the interests of the alliance, and the sworn friendship of the two nations."

It was now the eve of the presidential election of 1796. The several states were choosing their electors. They still had to meet and cast their votes. The precedent had not yet become set which allows the electors no canvas or deliberation among themselves. The French move was studiously calculated to influence the electors to choose Jefferson instead of John Adams.[46] With this in mind, according to his instructions, Adet accompanied his announcement of suspension of his functions with a long and *ex parte* review (with documents) of the whole quarrel between France and the United States over American neutrality. He included a passionate indictment of Jay's Treaty, all under cover of a fervid manifesto to the American people. A summary in English of the contents of this note appeared in the newspapers before the translation of the French original could be prepared in the Department of State. "Let your Government return to itself," wrote Adet, addressing the people rather than the government to which his note was delivered, "and you will still find in Frenchmen faithful friends and generous allies." [47]

To that uncompromising Federalist, Timothy Pickering, old soldier, negotiator of Indian treaties, professional and capable officeholder, and general utility man in Washington's Cabinet, now fell the task of defending the foreign policy laid down in the Farewell Address. Four others had declined the proffered appointment of Secretary of State, with its meager emolument, before he took it. Though Pickering had no special training for the office, he was a facile penman and a sharp-

---

45. Translation of an extract from the resolves of the Directory, of the 14th messidor, an IV (July 2, 1796). *A.S.P., F.R., 1,* 577. This extract is not printed in the proceedings for that date of the *Actes du Directoire exécutif.*

46. *Corr. Fr. Min.,* p. 972.

47. *A.S.P., F.R., 1,* 583.

minded debater. These were the qualifications principally in demand from 1795 to 1800.

Space only forbids us to describe and to analyze Pickering's defense of American neutrality, of Jay's Treaty with England, in short of the foreign policy of George Washington. We may be sure that it was inspired by Alexander Hamilton,[48] the man who inspired Jay's Treaty, and who phrased the Farewell Address. The remarkable public disputation took the form of instruction to Charles C. Pinckney, dated January 16, 1797, who had already sailed to France as successor to the recalled Monroe; but its real purpose, as shown by its immediate release to the press on January 19, 1797,[49] was to serve as a counter-manifesto to Adet's passionate attacks on the administration and his undercover efforts to secure the election of Thomas Jefferson rather than John Adams, the champion of Washington's policies. The historian today who is privileged to read the archives of France and of the United States can have no serious quarrel with Pickering's eloquent rebuttal of French charges of American ingratitude directed against Washington's government, or with his blunt conclusion after a long review that France owed fully as much to the United States as the United States to France in the way of service rendered. The day for finesse had passed. It was time that someone put the truth in this way to the American people, at a moment when foreign diplomacy was again trying to reach over the heads of their government to whip them into European complications. Even then in 1795 and 1796 while French diplomatists were accusing the United States of ingratitude and treachery, they themselves were plotting to re-establish control and tutelage over the American republic by getting Louisiana and West Florida back from Spain, allying France with the southwestern Indians, and tempting the allegiance to the Union of the new western states, to build up thereby a new colonial empire that would be the preponderant power in the New World.[50]

The instructions to C. C. Pinckney,[51] embodying these arguments, rank with Jefferson's rejoinder to Hammond of 1792, with John Quincy Adams's defense of General Jackson's execution of Arbuthnot and Ambrister in 1818, and with Lansing's reply to Austria in 1915 on

48. See Hamilton to Wolcott, Nov. 22, 1796, George Gibbs, *Memoirs of the Administrations of Washington and John Adams, edited from the papers of Oliver Wolcott* (New York, 1846), *1*, 398.

49. It was transmitted to Congress on Jan. 19, 1797, and immediately ordered to be printed. It appeared in the *Aurora* in installments between Jan. 24 and Feb. 3, 1797.

50. Arch. Aff. Etrang., États Unis, vols. 39–42.

51. *A.S.P.*, *F.R.*, *1*, 559–76.

the question of contraband, as one of the greatest defensive documents in the diplomatic history of the United States. Pickering's paper clinched the case for President Washington's foreign policy.

Before the document was printed the presidential electors had elected John Adams President by a majority of one vote and a margin of three votes over Thomas Jefferson, who became Vice President according to the original constitutional provision. Washington's successor fully recognized that the significance of his election lay in the question whether the American people were to govern themselves or be governed by foreign nations.[52] As President he took over Washington's policies, and, to his later vexation, his entire cabinet.

We cannot conclude that Pickering's instructions to Pinckney decided the election. It had been won already. The dispatch was published after the votes of the electors had been announced on the first Wednesday in January, but before they were formally counted on the first Wednesday in February. The document was rather an appeal to the people to support the foreign policy of Washington—and of Hamilton—and an argument to open the door to an escape from the French alliance, by proving, as Hamilton suggested, that the United States had maintained good faith with its engagements; that if the conduct of the other party released it, the release should not be refused, so far as possible without compromising peace. "This idea is very important," Hamilton wrote to Wolcott, of course for Pickering's benefit.[53]

Despite the high hopes which France had placed on Jefferson's election, both John Adams and his close contestant, the new Vice President, Thomas Jefferson, were equally good Americans (albeit of different political philosophy), and, incidentally, almost equally good friends of France. Nor were they unfriendly to each other. Jefferson had gone so far as to authorize his friend Madison to advise electors, in case of a tie, to vote for Adams as a statesman of senior claims to the Presidency.[54] Adet came to sense this relationship before he left. He wrote: [55]

> Mr. Jefferson likes us because he detests England; he seeks to draw near to us because he fears us less than England; but tomorrow he

52. In his Inaugural Address he said: "If the control of an election can be obtained by foreign nations by flattery or menaces, by fraud or violence, by terror, intrigue, or venality, the Government may not be the choice of the American people, but of foreign nations. It may be foreign nations who govern us, and not we, the people, who govern ourselves."

53. Nov. 22, 1796, Gibbs, *1*, 400.

54. Channing, *A History of the United States*, *4*, 173.

55. *Corr. Fr. Min.*, p. 983.

might change his opinion about us if England should cease to inspire his fear. Although Jefferson is the friend of liberty and of science, although he is an admirer of the efforts we have made to cast off our shackles and to clear away the cloud of ignorance which weighs down the human race, Jefferson, I say, is an American, and as such, he cannot sincerely be our friend. An American is the born enemy of all the peoples of Europe.

Such was the historical setting of the famous Farewell Address. Such were the reasons for its pronouncement in 1796, so different a pronouncement from what it would have been if given to the people in 1792. Such was its victory over foreign intrigue within our own country. It did not disown the French alliance, but it taught a patronizing ally that we were an independent and a sovereign nation, and that the French Republic could not use in America the tool that had been so successful with the border satellite states in Europe, the lever of a political opposition to overthrow any government that stood in the way of French policy, purpose, and interest. In Washington's time avoidance of foreign alliances and of foreign entanglement was a question of independence and national sovereignty. What we have generally construed as a policy of "isolation" we ought really to interpret as a policy of vigilant defense and maintenance of sovereign national independence against foreign meddling in our own intimate domestic concerns.

11. John Quincy Adams and George Washington

OVER FORTY YEARS AGO Mr. Worthington C. Ford delivered a paper before this Society entitled "Some Original Documents on the Genesis of the Monroe Doctrine." [1] From the private and public papers of John Quincy Adams he set forth the part which that Secretary of State played in the discussions leading up to the pronouncement of the Monroe Doctrine, both in the diplomatic discussions with Russia and England and in the deliberations of the United States Cabinet preceding the formulation of President Monroe's celebrated message. The *American Historical Review* for July and October 1902 contained a longer essay by Ford, "John Quincy Adams and the Monroe Doctrine." In the latter article he expressed his conclusion that the documents analyzed showed that "the Monroe Doctrine was the work of John Quincy Adams."

Historical scholarship accepted this for a time, but recent careful studies have tended to qualify Ford's conclusion more and more and to give Adams less and less credit for the Monroe Doctrine as a statement of American foreign policy. Governor William A. MacCorkle did not want Massachusetts to pluck a jewel from the diadem of old Virginia, as he put it. In *The Personal Genesis of the Monroe Doctrine*, a little book published in 1923 as a reply to Ford's influential articles, he insisted that it was Monroe who first wanted (in the President's own words) "to make it known that we would view an interference on the part of the European powers and especially an attack on the colonies by them, as an attack on ourselves"; and the Governor stressed the fact that Monroe as President had the final responsibility for decision of policy. In his standard study of the origin of the Monroe Doctrine, Dexter Perkins [2] accepted these qualifications of Ford's earlier judgment. T. R. Schellenberg,[3] in 1934, concluded that Jefferson's mind lay

1. *Proceedings of the Massachusetts Historical Society, 15,* 373–436; issued separately with the title "John Quincy Adams, His Connection with the Monroe Doctrine" (Cambridge, 1902).

2. *The Monroe Doctrine, 1823–1826* (Cambridge, 1927).

3. "Jeffersonian Origins of the Monroe Doctrine," *Hispanic American Historical Review, 14* (February 1934), 1–31.

Read at the February 1944 meeting of the Massachusetts Historical Society. Published in *Proceedings of the Massachusetts Historical Society, 67,* 1941–44.

back of that principle of the Monroe Doctrine that separated Europe
and America into two distinct spheres of policy independent of each
other, and that it was a Frenchman, the Abbé de Pradt, who inspired
Jefferson with that idea; Schellenberg thinks Jefferson more than any
other man the author of the Doctrine. Miss Laura Bornholdt has removed the Abbé de Pradt from the picture.[4] In the most recent general
examination of the subject Professor Arthur P. Whitaker [5] represents
Jefferson and Monroe as the chief architects of the idea of the two
spheres, the separate American system of policy, and the warning to
Europe; Adams, he says, was rather the draftsman than the originator.
Whitaker seems inclined to give Adams less credit than most of the
previous scholars who had appraised the authorship of the Monroe
Doctrine. None of these later writers, however, has given any attention
to John Quincy Adams's associations with American foreign policy in
the eighteenth century.

The Monroe Doctrine as contained in President Monroe's message
to Congress of December 2, 1823, consisted, as everybody knows, of
three principal dicta: (1) no more colonization of the New World by
European powers; (2) abstention of the United States from European
wars and entanglements—only when our rights were attacked or seriously menaced would we resent injuries or take measures for our defense in respect to Europe; (3) as a corollary to the second dictum, nonintervention by Europe in the American Hemisphere. Implicit in the
whole Monroe Doctrine is the concept of separate spheres of policy,
worlds apart, for Europe and for America, the New World versus the
Old.

That John Quincy Adams was the sole author of the first dictum
all scholars agree. That the second dictum, abstention from Europe's
controversies, was expressed by the Fathers of American independence
on various occasions from the Revolution until Washington's Farewell Address in 1796 and thereafter, notably by President Jefferson,
is also agreed; in 1820 Secretary of State Adams repeated it officially
in instructions to the United States minister to Russia declining the invitation of Czar Alexander I to join the Holy Alliance. "The political
system of the United States," he said then, three years before the Monroe Doctrine, "is extra-European. To stand in firm and cautious independence of all entanglement in the European system, has been a

4. "The Abbé de Pradt and the Monroe Doctrine," *Hispanic American Historical
Review*, *24* (May 1944), 201–21.

5. *The United States and the Independence of Latin America, 1800–1830* (Baltimore, 1941).

cardinal point of their policy under every administration of their government from the peace of 1783 to this present day." [6] It will presently be seen that this was not in 1820 a new thought to John Quincy Adams.

It was the supposed danger of European intervention in Latin America in 1823 which produced the third dictum of the Monroe Doctrine: the warning to Europe against intervention in the New World. It is about this new principle that most of the controversy has been centered. In later studies I propose to give this problem of authorship further analysis.[6a] At this time I shall point out a certain very early association of John Quincy Adams with the second dictum, abstention from European political combinations—that is, the foreign policy of George Washington's Farewell Address, later repeated in the Monroe Doctrine—and with the general concept of the two separate spheres, or systems, of policy.[7]

It is necessary first to review Adams's relations with President Washington during the General's lifetime. Adams first met Washington when visiting his father, the Vice President, and family in New York in 1789. A few months later the young law student drafted the address of welcome which the citizens of Newburyport presented to the President on the occasion of his visit to that town. He managed to be on hand at all the official functions which the General attended in the community. Washington remembered the young law student and kept his eye on him thereafter. Doubtless he knew that it was John Quincy Adams who in 1791 wrote the *Letters of Publicola,* reprinted extensively on both sides of the ocean, to refute Tom Paine's advice to the English people to overthrow their government and embody the rights of man in a written constitution like that of France. Later, in 1793, the President took pains to ascertain that it was young Adams who had written the letters of "Columbus" and "Marcellus," widely printed in the American newspapers, defending American neutrality against the purposes of French diplomacy after the great war of the First Coalition began in Europe.

It was in the papers of "Marcellus" that John Quincy Adams had included a passage that is interesting to the student of the Farewell

6. *Writings of John Quincy Adams,* Worthington C. Ford, ed., 7, 49.

6a. See my *John Quincy Adams and the Foundations of American Foreign Policy* (New York, 1949).

7. This paper is based upon Adams's official diplomatic correspondence, now preserved for the most part in the Department of State Records in the National Archives in Washington; on Mr. Ford's edition of the *Writings of John Quincy Adams* (7 vols. New York, 1913–17); and on the *Memoirs of John Quincy Adams,* Charles Francis Adams, ed. (12 vols. Philadelphia, 1874–77).

Address and of the Monroe Doctrine: "as the citizens of a nation at a vast distance from the continent of Europe; of a nation whose happiness consists in a real independence, *disconnected from all European interests and European politics,* it is our duty to remain the peaceful and silent, though sorrowful spectators of the sanguinary scene." [8] And "Columbus" had warned his fellow citizens against the insidious wiles of foreign intrigue:

> of all the dangers which encompass the liberties of a republican State, the intrusion of a foreign influence into the administration of their affairs, is the most alarming, and requires the opposition of the severest caution. . . . The interference of foreigners upon any pretence whatever, in the dissensions of fellow-citizens, must be as inevitably fatal to the liberties of the State, as the admission of strangers to arbitrate upon the domestic differences of man and wife is destructive to the happiness of a private family. . . . If we inquire what is the cause which has been within a quarter of a century, fatal to the Liberties of *Sweden,* of *Geneva,* of *Holland,* and of *Poland,* the answer will be one and the same. It was the association of internal faction, and external power; it was the interference of other nations in their domestic divisions.[9]

The next year, 1794, when a vacancy appeared in the diplomatic service, Washington nominated John Quincy Adams to be minister resident of the United States at The Hague. The Senate unanimously confirmed the nomination. Obviously the Vice President's son was an excellent appointment. He knew Holland from his youth there when his father had been minister. He also knew Europe and its courts. He had fluent command of French and Latin. He could read Dutch, and although he had got rusty in his speaking knowledge of the language, he could soon retrieve it. He was deeply versed in the literature of history and politics as well as in polite letters. He was now a trained lawyer. He knew international law expertly. He had shown a firm grasp of the essentials of American foreign policy as understood by the administration; this he had made evident by his comprehension not only of the problem of neutrality but also of the war crisis with England which had developed subsequently and had resulted in John Jay's mission to London in 1794 as a last resort for peace. He had, in short, an ideal training for diplomacy.

For the United States it was of vital importance to have a representa-

8. *Writings, 1,* 140. The italics are mine.
9. Ibid., 158–60.

tive in Europe capable of grasping the whole international situation thrown up by the French Revolution. Since Jefferson's departure from Paris only one other American diplomat abroad had displayed a perspicacity adequate to understanding and appraising the unprecedented European situation. That was Gouverneur Morris, Jefferson's successor as minister to France. But Morris had involved himself in the plots of Louis XVI and Marie Antoinette against the Revolution. Washington had to recall him, at the request of the French Revolutionary authorities, after he had asked them to withdraw Genêt from the United States for plotting against our government. Morris remained in Europe, with headquarters in London, a favorite at court, his views altogether colored by British policy; in fact he later traveled about the Continent sending in reports to the British Foreign Office.[10] His English prejudices made him of very little further usefulness to his own government. The President did not see fit to appoint him to another diplomatic office, say at The Hague in 1794 instead of Adams, or to the legation at London when that fell vacant in 1796 and went to Rufus King.

James Monroe, whom Washington sent to France to balance Jay's mission to England, was as prejudiced an apostle of the French Revolution as Morris had been an opponent. He openly fraternized with the Revolutionary leaders in a spectacular and embarrassing way. His dispatches showed no unbiased analysis of the European war: they were full of his own fraternal doings, of his gentle urgings to the Committee of Public Safety and the succeeding Directory to observe neutral rights under the American treaty of 1778; they presented sympathetically French animus against Jay's negotiations and treaty. As will be seen, Monroe proved personally disloyal to President Washington as well as disloyal to his positive instructions to defend Jay's Treaty with energy.

In London, John Jay, during his few months' sojourn there, dealt exclusively with his own negotiation. Thomas Pinckney, regular minister to Great Britain since 1792, showed little grasp of the European situation. He concerned himself with protests against British violations of neutral rights and with impressments, and made no particular observation of Continental affairs.[11] Then, at the beginning of 1795, he was off to Madrid on the mission extraordinary that resulted in the

10. A. C. Morris, ed., *The Diary and Letters of Gouverneur Morris*. See also Index entries for Morris in Historical Manuscripts Commission report on *The Manuscripts of J. B. Fortescue, Esq., Preserved at Dropmore, 3* (London, 1899).

11. I have described his activities, from his official dispatches, in "The London Mission of Thomas Pinckney," Chap. 5 of this volume.

notable treaty of that year with Spain. Pinckney's departure left the London legation in care of his inexperienced private secretary, one William Allen Deas, *chargé d'affaires* ad interim. Deas could not be counted on for any adequate analysis of the great picture of European politics. On John Quincy Adams, then, unexpectedly fell the task of reporting to the United States government the wars of the French Revolution.

The new minister's letters from his first legation, where he considered himself paid a good salary—$4,500 a year—for doing nothing at all, were to be of real service to his country in laying the bases of its foreign policy. Suddenly The Hague had become a place of extraordinary significance, particularly for an American diplomat. It was a listening post in the resounding amphitheater of European power politics. It was a perfect testing ground for any ally of the new French Republic with its revolutionary program and propaganda. John Quincy Adams's reports helped to correct the partisan impressions and advice of James Monroe and to strengthen the resolution of the first President, in a very critical period of American foreign relations, not to allow the United States to become, like the Netherlands, a tool of French diplomacy for the purposes of purely European polity.

In his "Columbus" letters in Boston in 1793, John Quincy Adams already had cited the Netherlands as one of the examples of modern history showing how association of internal faction with foreign power was fatal to the liberties of any people. For a century two political factions had contended for supremacy in that ancient republic, buffer state between British sea power and French land power: the Orange Party, which was the party of the hereditary executive, the Stadtholder, and owed its ruling position to alliance with Great Britain and Prussia; and the more liberal Patriot Party, which sought the aid of France to oust its rivals from authority.

When Adams arrived at The Hague in December 1794, the unfortunate Netherlands was the sinking prey of foreign powers. In those portions of the state still defended by unpopular British troops the Patriots were secretly shaping their ranks as fifth columnists (to use a modern phrase) in support of the French invasion. No real Dutch patriots rose to defend the sovereignty and independence of the United Provinces. Seeking their own selfish desires first, the rival political factions perfectly served the purposes of foreign intrigue, hegemony, and, ultimately, annexation and complete loss of independence.

From this legation in The Hague the American minister accurately described, in dispatches to the Secretary of State and in more revealing confidential letters to his father, how the French forces occupied the whole country, expelling the British troops and the Stadtholder's government. He gave due credit to the correct conduct of the army of "liberation" toward the people of the country and their property, whatever their previous political allegiance. He told how democratic societies on Jacobin models sprang up like tulips all over the Low Countries as he had seen them blossom two years before everywhere in the United States. Scarcely a village in the seven provinces but had its political club, and they sent delegates to a central assembly.[12] Small groups of revolutionaries, working behind the scenes, used the Dutch democratic societies as instruments of revolution to supplant the old régime by the Batavian Republic, set up on French models. These groups were the "unseen spring," Adams reported to the Secretary of State, which gave all visible motion to the Revolution, without the "people" knowing how it came to pass.[13] As he wrote these lines, he had in mind the democratic societies that, under the impulse of the French Revolution, had flourished so recently in his own country, where Federalists and Republicans contended with each other, so a French revolutionary government might plausibly conclude, like Orangemen and Patriots, the one a faction apparently partial to British policy, the other seemingly a party of French interest.

French intervention and conquest overthrew the old government of the United Provinces and created the Batavian Republic. The Batavian Republic speedily made a treaty of peace and alliance with the French Republic and changed sides in the war. From her new ally France extracted an indemnity of 100,000,000 florins, together with territorial rectifications, including the cession of Dutch Flanders, and a potential naval base at Flushing. Abruptly the Netherlands found itself the enemy of its former allies, Great Britain and Prussia, and the victim of the latest guarantor of its independence, France. The conquest of the Netherlands was a most portentous demonstration of French power for aggrandizement through the new technique of propaganda and "liberation" as well as by force of arms.

John Quincy Adams soon realized that the correct conduct of the armies of invasion was no assurance of benevolence. On the contrary, it masked an implacable exploitation of the hitherto prosperous provinces for the benefit of France. "The French are still here as conquerors,"

12. John Quincy Adams to the Secretary of State, nos. 47, 48, July 22, 1795. D.S., Dispatches, The Netherlands, *1*.

13. John Quincy Adams to the Secretary of State, no. 25, The Hague, Feb. 15, 1795. *Writings, 1*, 285–91.

he wrote to the Secretary of State in the spring of 1795, "and the substance of independence is not so scrupulously preserved as its forms." [14]
Nominal independence and republican fraternity did not mitigate the
usual consequences of conquest: billeting of troops, requisition of clothing, fuel, and food, the continued support of an army of foreigners, the
forced circulation of depreciated *assignats*. Toward the end of his service at The Hague, in 1797, he reported the net result (for unhappy
Dutchmen) of France's revolutionizing of the country:

> In the course of two years since the establishment of what is called
> their liberty, they have paid nearly twenty per cent upon the whole
> capital of every individual in forced loans, have had their com-
> merce almost entirely suspended, have lost almost all their colo-
> nies, have seen the value of a large portion of the property left
> them depreciate nearly one-half, and have the prospect evidently
> before them of seeing themselves made the victim of both parties,
> whenever a peace shall be concluded. [15]

Such were the reports in John Quincy Adams's official dispatches to
the Secretary of State. It was for his father that he reserved his most
intimate political analyses and reflections. To John Adams he expressed
his hopes and fears for American foreign policy and for the survival
of American nationality in a war which he had correctly seen, from
the moment of his return to Europe, [16] as a titanic duel between France
and England. One by one France was knocking out the Continental
members of the coalition: the Netherlands, Prussia, and Spain fell in
1795; Sardinia would soon have to make its separate peace (1796); Austria's defeat was only a matter of time (1797). Then England would
stand alone. French diplomacy would next try to shut up the ports of
the Continent against all trade with England and close the United
States to England, too, if possible, while France mobilized the naval
power of the European nations for invasion of England and a final
blow against the mistress of the seas. The young minister resident was

14. John Quincy Adams to the Secretary of State, no. 30, The Hague, March 17,
1795. D.S., Dispatches, The Netherlands, *1*.

15. John Quincy Adams to the Secretary of State, no. 94, Feb. 17, 1797. D.S., Dispatches, The Netherlands, *2*.

16. His very first dispatch contained this statement: "At this moment they [the
French] might probably dictate their own terms of Peace to all their enemies except
Great Britain, and it is not improbable that at the opening of the ensuing season,
these two great rival nations will be the only remaining combatants upon the
field." John Quincy Adams to the Secretary of State, no. 1, London, Oct. 22, 1794.
D.S., Dispatches, The Netherlands, *1*.

the first of his countrymen to foresee the Continental System. He realized that the attitude and policy of the United States as it attempted to steer its way between the two mighty combatants would be a matter of life or death for itself, as it had been for the Netherlands. Neutrality and Jay's Treaty with Great Britain were the touchstones of this policy. French diplomacy and the democratic societies would try to destroy both.[17]

> I have several reasons to suppose [he wrote to his father on May 22, 1795] that the policy of the French government at present is to make *use* of the United States, as they are now making use of these Provinces, that is, as an instrument for the benefit of France, as a passive weapon in her hands against her most formidable enemy. . . .
>
> If these conjectures have as much foundation as I apprehend, the whole French influence in America will exert itself with more than usual activity to prevent the ratification of the treaty, and to produce at all events a war between the United States and Great Britain, not assuredly from regard to our interest which they respect as much as they do that of their friends and allies the Hollanders, but because they are sensible of how much importance our commerce is to Great Britain, and suppose that the loss of it would make that nation outrageous for peace, and compel the Minister to make it upon the terms they are disposed to dictate. . . .
>
> If the [Jay] treaty should not be ratified, the French will exert themselves for the purpose of hurrying us into a war, which may hasten their means of making peace, and in which they may be under no obligation of making a common cause with us. Their partizans, perhaps, in declamations or in newspapers will promise wonders from their co-operation; their official characters possibly may employ a great number of what they call *phrases,* but will have no power to contract any substantial engagements; we shall be friends, brothers, allies, fellow-freemen, loaded with all the tenderness of family affections introduced by a political prosopopeia into national concerns, and the final result of the whole matter will be, that all this tender sympathy, this amiable fra-

17. John Quincy Adams to Dr. Thomas Welsh, April 26, 1795, *Writings, I,* 339–40 n.; John Quincy Adams to Abigail Adams, May 16, 1795, ibid., 340 n.; John Quincy Adams to John Adams, May 22, 1795, ibid., 353–63, and Sept. 12, 1795, ibid., 408–17.

ternity, this lovely coalescence of liberty, will leave us the advantage of being sacrificed to their interests, or of purchasing their protection upon the most humiliating and burdensome conditions, and at the same time of being reduced to the condition of glorying in our disgrace, and hailing the instrument of our calamity as the weapon of our deliverance.

I wish that the situation of affairs in America may be such as shall afford a full demonstration, that these are ideas merely visionary, *and above all I wish that we may never have occasion for any political connections in Europe.*

I believe [he again wrote to his father on September 12, 1795] the intention is to draw the United States into it [the European war], merely to make tools of them, in order to procure advantageous terms for others, who would leave us in the well, after using our weight to get themselves out of it. It would be a war in which we should have everything to lose and nothing to gain.

A little wisdom and a little moderation [he wrote to his mother from The Hague on May 16, 1795] is all we want to secure a continuance of the blessings, of which faction, intrigue, private ambition and desperate fortunes have concurred in exertions to deprive us. The government of the United States need not even appeal to the judgment of posterity, whose benedictions will infallibly follow those measures which were the most opposed. The voice of all Europe already pronounces their justification; the nations which have been grappling together with the purpose of mutual destruction, feeble, exhausted, and almost starving, detest on all sides the frantic war they have been waging; those who have had the wisdom to maintain a neutrality have reason more than ever to applaud their policy, and some of them may thank the United States for the example from which it was pursued.[18]

Events in America were clear enough demonstration of the accuracy of Adams's analysis of the external forces of the French Revolution. The popular opposition to Jay's Treaty, the equivocal relation of Secretary of State Randolph to the French legation, leading to his downfall and resignation, and French efforts to stir up a radical opposition either to block Jay's Treaty by withholding the necessary appropriations in

18. *Writings, 1,* 356–62, 409, 340 n. The italics are mine.

the House of Representatives or to defeat Washington for re-election in 1796, or even to overthrow his government by revolution: all this foreign intermeddling showed that French diplomacy was bent on treating the United States as it did the satellite republics which it set up for its own purposes in Europe, under the spell of the principles of the great Revolution. Adams had diagnosed correctly from its European examples the danger of the French Revolution for America. Marching under the cloak of the rights of man, the Republic had launched France again upon a career of conquest and plunder far more formidable than that of Louis XIV. John Quincy Adams saw this with clear eyes [19] and he kept his government's attention continually on it in a way that no other American diplomat could have done.

The French Foreign Office looked upon the United States as "the Holland of the New World." Washington must go, declared the new French Minister of Foreign Affairs under the Directory, Citizen Delacroix:

> A friend of France must succeed him in that eminent office. . . . We must raise up the people and at the same time conceal the lever by which we do so. . . . I propose to the Executive Directory to authorize me to send orders and instructions to our minister plenipotentiary at Philadelphia to use all the means in his power . . . to bring about the right kind of revolution and Washington's replacement, which, assuring to the Americans their independence, will break off treaties made with England and maintain those which unite them to the French Republic.[20]

James Monroe, who as senator had voted against Jay's nomination, and whom Washington by way of ingratiation had sent to France to defend American neutrality while Jay negotiated in England, urged the Directory not to try revolution in America until they should see what happened in the Presidential election of 1796. He was none too loyal to his chief. "Left to ourselves," he slyly hinted to Delacroix,

---

19. "With all the attachment of my countrymen for France I believe [really he *hoped*] they have too much sense and virtue, as well as knowledge of their own interest, to be either persuaded or bullied by her into a war for her benefit, when it has certainly become on her side a war merely of conquest and plunder, provided no new cause of resentment be given them by the future conduct of Britain." John Quincy Adams to John Adams, The Hague, July 21, 1796, *Writings*, 2, 13.

20. See Chap. 10 of this volume, "Washington's Farewell Address: A Foreign Policy of Independence," pp. 240–58.

"everything will I think be satisfactorily arranged and *perhaps in the course of the present year:* and it is always more grateful to make such arrangements ourselves than to be pressed to it." [21] The Directory took Monroe's advice, to await Washington's overthrow in the coming American election. Meanwhile it declared (decree of July 2, 1796) that France would treat American ships precisely as Great Britain did, thus setting aside the maritime principles of the Franco-American treaty of 1778. After communicating the text of this decree, the French minister in Philadelphia announced, in a burning manifesto full of French propaganda, the suspension of diplomatic relations with the United States. These steps were calculated to scare the electorate not to vote for Washington again.

But George Washington did not choose to run again in 1796. He did not want any longer to be buffeted ungratefully in the public prints by "a set of infamous scribblers" who misrepresented and tortured every act of the executive with a view to making it appear odious.[22] Doubtless he questioned whether he could be re-elected. Certainly he could not again have been re-elected unanimously. At any rate, he did not want a third term. He had not desired a second. He had wished to spend his declining years in "the shades of retirement" at beloved Mount Vernon. Already at the end of his first "federal cycle" he had yearned to go home to the banks of the Potomac, and it was then, in 1792, that originally he had prepared to issue a valedictory to his fellow citizens. Only when convinced that his Presidency was necessary to mold national unity while the Constitution took hold on the people and the nation, and that his retirement might blight negotiations under way with Great Britain and Spain for the redemption of the western territory, had he consented to serve a second term. Even so he hoped to be able to resign within a year or two and turn the government over to the Vice President, presumably John Adams. Outbreak of the Anglo-French war in 1793 and the problem of neutrality blighted that hope. At last in 1796 it seemed possible for him to lay down the burden. But he was anxious that his foreign policy should continue under a Federalist successor.

21. Ibid., pp. 248–49. The italics are mine. Before he left the Presidency, Washington recalled Monroe from Paris for not defending Jay's Treaty with the arguments that Secretary of State Pickering had instructed him to employ. He never knew how far Monroe had gone in disloyal insinuations against himself.

22. George Washington to Alexander Hamilton, Mount Vernon, June 26, 1796. *The Writings of George Washington,* John C. Fitzpatrick, ed. (39 vols. Washington, 1931–44), *30,* 101–04.

The Farewell Address to the people of the United States, September 19, 1796, upon announcing his retirement at the end of his second term of office, had a much different content from the document which he would have used in 1792, when the occasion called merely for virtuous consecration of the new Union. In the four years since then a volcanic force had erupted upon the European world. Under Washington's leadership American neutrality and American nationality had barely resisted the tidal wave that swept across the Atlantic, had survived it only at the price of Jay's Treaty and the temporary concession to British sea power. Now in 1796 intervention of the French ally in American domestic politics again threatened neutrality. It was to that danger that Washington pointed his Farewell Address.

Outlined and strictly held to the outline by Washington, but embellished by the phraseology of Alexander Hamilton, whose mind moved in unison with the President's in these matters of statecraft, the Farewell Address invoked the spirit of national unity against the divisions of political and sectional "factions" and the opportunity that "factions" and sections opened to foreign intrigue and interference, presenting a danger to independence itself. From this it proceeded to lay down the great rule of conduct for foreign policy: abstention from the *ordinary* vicissitudes of European politics and the *ordinary* combinations and collisions of European friendships and enmities—in brief, as little *political* connection as possible with foreign nations.

We can say that John Quincy Adams's contributions to the American press and his subsequent letters from The Hague to his father had an appreciable influence upon the mind of the President as he thought over what he desired to say in the Address. The President had read and commended the earlier letters of "Marcellus" and "Columbus." It has already been noted how they led to the younger Adams's appointment in 1794 to the foreign service. John Adams communicated to Washington his son's private letters from The Hague. The President was reading these earlier letters from John Quincy Adams to his father at the very time, in the summer of 1796, he was drafting, with Hamilton's aid, the Farewell Address. In acknowledging four received from Quincy in August 1795, the President wrote to John Adams on August 20: "They contain a great deal of interesting matter, and No. 9 [May 22, 1795] discloses much important information and political insight. Mr. J. Adams, your son, must not think of retiring from the walk of life he is in. His prospects, if he continues in it are fair, and I shall be much mistaken if, in as short a period as can be well expected, he is not found at the head of the diplomatic corps, let the government be administered by whomsoever the people may choose." [23]

Without pausing to comment on this highly authoritative appraisal of John Quincy Adams's abilities and future prospects, let us now compare some of the ideas, even some of the words, of the Farewell Address with the letters of "Marcellus" and of "Columbus" in 1793. In doing so, I shall refer to the text of Washington's original first draft of suggestions for the Address (May 15, 1796) [24] in order to show how John Quincy Adams paralleled Washington's thinking independently of Alexander Hamilton, who certainly agreed with both and thought along similar lines. It is quite possible, indeed likely, that the Vice President showed his son's letters also to Hamilton.

Conspicuous among the admonitions of the Farewell Address are: (1) to exalt patriotically the national words, *America, American, Americans;* (2) to beware of foreign intrigue; (3) to have no political connections with the foreign nations of distant Europe with their different set of primary interests. In all three of these features of the immortal document can be discerned the thought of John Quincy Adams, occasionally suspicious traces of his phraseology.

Observe first the name *America.*

Emphasis on the word *American* is common to the three documents:

John Quincy Adams	Washington's First Draft	The Farewell Address
Is this a condition tolerable to the imagination of *American* [25] freemen? . . . Was it worthy of the generous and heroic self-devotion, which offered the slaughtered thousands of our friends and brethren, as a willing sacrifice at the holy altar of *American* [25] Independence, to be made the miserable	That every citizen would take pride in the name of an American, and act as if he felt the importance of the character by considering that we ourselves are now a distinct Nation the dignity of which will be absorbed, if not annihilated, if we enlist ourselves (further than our obligations may require) under	The name of AMERICAN, which belongs to you, in your national capacity, must always exalt the just pride of Patriotism, more than any appellation derived from local discriminations. With slight shades of difference, you have the same Religeon, Manners, Habits and political Principles. You

23. *Writings, 1,* 408–09 n. "Fair" prospects meant in those days most excellent prospects.

24. See Victor H. Paltsits, *Washington's Farewell Address, in Facsimile, with Transliterations of All the Drafts of Washington, Madison, and Hamilton, together with Their Correspondence and Other Supporting Documents, Edited with a History of Its Origin, Its Reception by the Nation, Rise of the Controversy respecting Its Authorship, and a Bibliography* (New York, New York Public Library, 1935). Horace Binney long since had settled definitely the question of authorship in *An Inquiry into the Formation of Washington's Farewell Address.*

25. The italics are mine.

bubbles of foreign speculation, to be blown like feathers to and fro as the varying breath of foreign influence should be directed: to be bandied about from one nation to another, subservient to the purposes of their mutual resentments, and played with as the passive instruments of their interests and passions? Perish the *American*! [26] whose soul is capable of submitting to such a degrading servitude! Perish the *American*,[26] whose prostituted heart could forsake the genuine purity of our national worship, and offer at a foreign shrine the tribute of his slavish adoration! [27]

the banners of any other Nation whatsoever. [28]

have in a common cause fought and triumphed together. The independence and liberty you possess are the work of joint councils, and joint efforts, of common dangers, sufferings and successes.[29]

Similarly the advice to beware of foreign intrigue is common to the three documents:

John Quincy Adams	*Washington's First Draft*	*The Farewell Address*
Among the nations of antiquity, the *Athenians* were equally distinguished for the freedom of their government, the mildness of their laws, the sagaciousness of their understanding, and the urbanity of their manners. Their Constitution was purely democratic, and their penal laws were few; but the bare appearance of a stranger in the assemblies of the people, they made punishable with death, from a deep and well-grounded conviction, that of all the dangers which	And moreover, that we would guard against the Intriegues of *any* and *every* foreign Nation who shall endeavor to intermingle (however covertly and indirectly) in the internal concerns of our country—or who shall attempt to prescribe rules for our policy with any other power. . . .[30]	Against the insidious wiles of foreign influence (I conjure you to believe me fellow-citizens,) the jealousy of a free people ought to be *constantly* awake; since history and experience prove that foreign influence is one of the most baneful foes of Republican Government. . . .[31]

26. The italics are mine.

27. Letter of "Columbus," Dec. 4, 1793, *Writings, 1,* 159. The letters of "Columbus" stress throughout the words *America, American,* and *Americans,* as an appeal to national pride and exaltation, and as a distinction from state or sectional appellations.

28. Paltsits, *Washington's Farewell Address,* p. 169.

29. Ibid., pp. 142–43.

30. Ibid., p. 169.

31. Ibid., pp. 154–55.

John Quincy Adams
(continued)

encompass the liberties of
a republican State, the intrusion of a foreign influence into the administra-
tion of their affairs, is the
most alarming, and re-
quires the opposition of
the severest caution. . . .
The interference of for-
eigners upon any pretence
whatever, in the dissen-
sions of fellow-citizens,
must be as inevitably fatal
to the liberties of the
State, as the admission of
strangers   to   arbitrate
upon the domestic differ-
ences of man and wife is
destructive to the happi-
ness of a private family.
If the partizans of any
particular faction cease to
rely upon their own tal-
ents and services to sup-
port their influence among
their country men, and
link themselves in union
with an external power,
the principle of self-de-
fence, the instinct of self-
preservation   itself,   will
suggest a similar connec-
tion to their opponents;
whichever of the party
nominally   prevails,   the
whole country is really
enslaved; alternately the
sport of every caprice,
that directs the conduct
of two foreign sovereigns,
alternately the victim of
every base intrigue which
foreign hatred and jeal-
ousy may disguise under
the mask of friendship
and benevolence.[32]

The advice against political connections with foreign powers appears
uniformly throughout the three documents:

John Quincy Adams	*Washington's First Draft*	*The Farewell Address*
. . . as the citizens of a nation at a vast distance from the continent of Europe; of a nation whose	That we may avoid con- necting ourselves with the Politics of any Nation, farther than shall be	The Great rule of conduct for us, in regard to for- eign Nations is in extend- ing our commercial rela-

32. Letter of "Columbus," Dec. 4, 1793, *Writings, 1,* 157–59.

happiness consists in a real independence, disconnected from all European interests and European politics.[33]	found necessary to regulate our own trade; [34]	tions to have with them as little *political* connection as possible. So far as we have already formed engagements let them be fulfilled, with perfect good faith. Here let us stop.[35]

So clearly do the thoughts of the younger Adams, even little traces of his phraseology, appear in the Farewell Address that one may wonder whether Washington may not have had still before him the letters of "Columbus" when he drew up the first draft of that document. Of course this is not to say that John Quincy Adams was unduly responsible for the ideas of the Farewell Address. Until he heard of its pronouncement, he did not even know it was being formulated. Presumably the Address would have been given out, in somewhat the same form, if Adams had never lived, for these ideas already were common to American statesmen and diplomatists of the time.[36] They were the fruit of American diplomatic experience since the Declaration of Independence. Indeed, unbeknownst to Adams, the United States had just declined two offers of European alliance—one from Sweden and Denmark in 1794 for a new Armed Neutrality, and another from Spain in 1795 for a triple alliance with France to guarantee the territories of all in the New World—and it was acutely nervous about its "perpetual alliance" with France. John Quincy Adams shared these principles of foreign policy and validated them from his observation, on the spot, of the wars of the French Revolution. Thus validated, they had reinforced Washington's own opinions and even shaped their expression a little.

Despite his own preference that Washington might serve another term in order to be sure to keep the country out of the European war,[37] John Quincy Adams read with much satisfaction the text of the Farewell Address when finally it reached The Hague. "The reception of the President's address to the people might serve as another indicative to France of the temper of our people," he wrote, for French consumption, to Joseph Pitcairn, United States consul in Paris. "From that let them judge of the success that has attended all their endeavors to tear

33. Letter of "Marcellus," April 24, 1793, *Writings*, *1*, 140.
34. Paltsits, *Washington's Farewell Address*, p. 169.
35. Ibid., p. 155.
36. Cf. my article, "The Background of Washington's Foreign Policy," *Yale Review*, *16* (January 1927), 316–37.
37. John Quincy Adams to Christopher Gore, July 26, 1796, *Writings*, *2*, 13.

our benefactor from our hearts; let them see the issue of all their manœuvres and all their libels; of their Baches and Randolphs in America, as well as their Theremins and their Paines in Europe. . . . Can France possibly believe that Mr. Jefferson, or any other man, would dare to start away from that system of administration which Washington has thus sanctioned, not only by his example, but by his retirement?" [38]

For the benefit of the student of the Monroe Doctrine we may quote the younger Adams once more, in these final weeks of President Washington's administration, on separation from the politics of Europe, although it is only a repetition of what he had already said before the Farewell Address was drafted. Writing to his father after he had read the text of the Address, he said: "The President, indeed, has told us, and I am profoundly convinced of the justice and importance of the advice, that we ought not to involve ourselves at all in the political systems of Europe, but to keep ourselves always distinct and separate from it." [39]

Is it not evident that John Quincy Adams actively shared, indeed independently conceived in his own mind from his diplomatic experience in Europe during the early wars of the French Revolution, the instinctive concept of the Fathers against involvement in the political systems of Europe? Indeed was he not thinking, at this early period, of what later appeared more clearly as the concept of the two separate systems, or spheres, of policy, European and American, that run through the Monroe Doctrine? And ought not historians of the Monroe Doctrine to take this into consideration?

To the President himself Adams had a chance to express himself directly upon the occasion of executing a small personal errand: [40]

> I fervently pray that they [the people] may not only impress all its [the Farewell Address's] admonitions upon their hearts, but that *it may serve as the foundation upon which the whole system of their future policy may rise,* the admiration and example of future time; that your warning voice may upon every great emergency recur to their remembrance with an influence equal to the occa-

38. John Quincy Adams to Joseph Pitcairn, Jan. 31, 1797, *Writings,* 2, 95–96.

39. John Quincy Adams to John Adams, The Hague, Jan. 14, 1797, *Writings,* 2, 88.

40. This concerned investigation into the source of the donation of a sword that had come into Washington's hands from someone in the town of Solingen. See George Washington to John Quincy Adams, Sept. 12, 1796, *Writings of George Washington,* *35,* 207–09.

sion; that it may control the fury of domestic factions and check the encroachments of foreign influence; that it may cement with indissoluble force our national Union, and secure at once our dignity and our peace.[41]

John Quincy Adams at least had helped to inspire the warning voice of 1796. His first diplomatic commission, from the Father of His Country, had enabled him to play a part in laying the foundation of a system of American foreign policy for a century to come.

Adams's European experience had convinced him that neutrality was essential for a continuance of the American constitutional union and even the independence of the United States in that epoch of its history. If the United States preserved its neutrality, its independence, and its union, he wrote to Sylvanus Bourne, United States consul at Amsterdam, it would be thanks to Washington. "At the present moment if our neutrality be still preserved, it will be due to the President alone. Nothing but his weight of character and reputation, combined with his firmness and political intrepidity, could have stood against this torrent that is still tumbling with a fury that resounds even across the Atlantic. He is now pledged, and he is unmoved. If his system of administration now prevails, ten years more will place the United States among the most powerful and opulent nations on earth." [42]

Already Adams was envisioning an American system. "The American [system] will infallibly triumph over the European system eventually," he wrote privately from London to the Secretary of State, Timothy Pickering, "provided it be pursued with the same perseverance." [43]

The rising young diplomat's veneration of Washington contrasted

41. John Quincy Adams to George Washington, Feb. 11, 1797, *Writings*, 2, 119. The italics are mine. Washington wrote to Adams a graceful acknowledgment from Mount Vernon, June 25, 1797: ". . . the approbation of good and Virtuous Men is the most pleasing reward my mind is susceptible of, for any Service it has been in my power to render my Country." *Writings of George Washington*, 35, 476.

42. John Quincy Adams to Sylvanus Bourne, Dec. 24, 1795, *Writings*, *1*, 467. "This, my good friend," Adams continued, "is not the language of a courtier. You and I have known the time when *not to applaud* the man who united all hearts was almost held to be a crime. Should that time return again while he lives, *my* tribute of veneration and gratitude shall again remain silent in my heart. But now, when he does not unite all hearts, when on the contrary a powerful party at home, and a mighty influence from abroad, are joining all their forces to assail his reputation and his character, I think it my duty as an American to avow my sentiments as they concern that man." Ibid., 467–68.

43. John Quincy Adams to Timothy Pickering, *Private*, London, Dec. 22, 1795, *Writings*, *1*, 465. Adams opened himself to Pickering much more than he had done to Randolph.

strongly with his father's final reservations on Washington's place in American history. One wonders what the elder statesman of Quincy may have mused when he learned that his son had christened his first child George Washington Adams,[44] born in Berlin, April 13, 1801, after the Father of His Country had ceased to live in mortal flesh.

> My child was yesterday baptized by the name of George Washington; and may the grace of Almighty God guard his life and enable him, when he is come to manhood, to prove himself worthy of it! I was not induced merely by the public character of that great and good man to show his memory this token of respect. President Washington was, next to my own father, the man upon earth to whom I was indebted for the greatest personal obligations. I knew not whether upon rigorous philosophical principles it be wise to give a great and venerable name to such a lottery-ticket as a new-born infant—but my logical scruples have in this case been overpowered by my instinctive sentiments.[45]

George Washington, whose foreign policy laid the basis for an American system, remained John Quincy Adams's hero of history without reproach or reservation. Adams was deeply affected when the General died. Washington's character, he wrote from Prussia, would to all ages be a model of human virtue untarnished by a single vice. "The loss of such a man is a misfortune to mankind. To our country it is a heavy calamity." [46] His was "one of the greatest names that ever appeared upon earth for the pride and consolation of the human race. I feel it as an inestimable happiness to have been the contemporary and countryman of that man." [47]

44. The tragic death of George Washington Adams in early manhood was the greatest personal affliction which John Quincy Adams had to bear. *Memoirs, 8,* 159–60. For circumstances of the young man's death, April 30, 1829, less than a month after the father vacated the White House, see *Boston Daily Advertiser,* May 4, 1829.

45. John Quincy Adams to Thomas Boylston Adams, quoted, without date, by Dorothie Bobbé in her sprightly (but not always accurate) *Mr. and Mrs. John Quincy Adams* (New York, 1930), p. 113. She explains that she had read the correspondence and private papers of John Quincy and Louisa Catherine Adams, John and Abigail Adams, Thomas Boylston Adams, and Joshua Johnson, among others. Ibid., 303.

46. John Quincy Adams to Joseph Pitcairn, Feb. 4, 1800, *Writings, 2,* 451 n.

47. John Quincy Adams to William Vans Murray, Feb. 11, 1800, *Writings, 2,* 453.

12. The Scuffle in the Rotunda

A Footnote to the Presidency of John Quincy Adams and to the History of Dueling

JOHN QUINCY ADAMS was President during the heyday of dueling in the United States. Gentlemen required apology for an insult or else satisfaction on the "field of honor." Few spirited politicians could afford to let pass anything that smacked of an insult, much less a direct slap in the face. Not to demand satisfaction for an affront, or not to grant it when required by the injured party, could result in social exclusion or ruin a most promising political career. So well established was this American custom and its European background that there were manuals and "codes of honor" for it. The authorities argued that the more polished a society the more sensitive was a gentleman to insult, and what politician or officer of the armed forces of the United States would admit that he was not a gentleman? Practiced pistoleers and frontier bullies and journalistic adventurers could be even more "sensitive" than polished gentlemen; they could and did conjure up insults in order to get rid of a more urbane enemy. They were even quicker to take advantage of a plausible one.

Laws against dueling, like those of Virginia, were of little avail. Public opinion never analyzed the motives of a duelist or the causes of a duel. If a surviving antagonist were indicted for murder no jury would find him guilty even if he had killed the aggrieved party. Distinguished statesmen in both England and the United States—not to mention the greater prevalence of the duello in France and other European countries—felt constrained to meet on the field of honor. William Pitt, George Canning, Lord Castlereagh, and even the Duke of Wellington while Prime Minister had found it necessary to fight duels. In the United States at least four such encounters resulted in national tragedies. Except for Burr's egregious provocation, such affairs seemed to benefit a man rather than injure him politically, if he sur-

Read at the November 1953 meeting of the Massachusetts Historical Society. Published in *Proceedings of the Massachusetts Historical Society, 71,* 1953–57.

vived. Even Burr, taking refuge in the West and South, found favor there. One of his friends had been Andrew Jackson, one of the most celebrated and implacable duelists in the United States, as well as a nervy marksman.

John Quincy Adams did not believe in the duello. He regarded it as a barbarism but for a long time he felt that it was absolutely impractical to try to prohibit it by law. "What influence of fear of punishment," he asked himself, "can be exercised over men who begin by deliberately staking their lives upon a feather?" [1] He did not raise his voice against what Thomas Hart Benton called the most high-toned duel of his experience, the famous meeting between Secretary of State Henry Clay and Senator John Randolph, but he must have passed painful moments while it was being fought out on Virginia soil near the south end of the Falls Bridge.

When President Adams's supporters advanced objections to General Jackson as a candidate for President because of his duels, Duff Green, the most fiery opposition journalist, charged them with rank hypocrisy: at least Jackson had never made profession against the practice, as John Quincy Adams had. "By retaining Mr. Clay [as Secretary of State] Mr. Adams has violated his own professions on the subject of dueling." He cited tellingly—and he could have been still more telling had he remembered the vote of the presidential contest in the House of Representatives in 1825—President Adams's nomination of Judge Andrew Scott for reappointment in the territory of Arkansas after that worthy had challenged and killed Judge Seldon, a brother judge of the same bench. "While his hands were still reeking with blood, Mr. Adams, the *religious Mr. Adams,* the boasted *man of peace,* whose fame is soiled by no work of blood, nominated him to the Senate, to fill, for another term, the bench which he had just polluted!!!" [2]

One wonders that John Quincy Adams himself was never involved in a duel during his long and contentious lifetime. He was given to very frank appraisals—and often to ulcerous judgments—of contemporaries who did not meet his approval. None of the subjects of such descriptions ever challenged him, because he confined his objurgations and epithets to his diary, never printed until long after their deaths and his. But during his Presidency an incident occurred by which his

---

1. *Memoirs of John Quincy Adams, 9,* 500. See also *9,* 503; *10,* 51–52. Although these private opinions were registered in his diary later (1838), at the time of debates in the House of Representatives, they may be said to represent his steady opinion throughout his life.

2. *United States Telegraph,* March 17, 1828.

political enemies sought to bring public opinion to bear upon him and his administration through the unwritten code of the duello. It began at one of the White House receptions on April 2, 1828. Practically anybody of decent appearance and carriage could go to these fortnightly levees or "drawing-rooms." According to the custom it was easy enough to get a card, or even to walk in without an invitation of any kind. The President and Mrs. Adams made no effort themselves to exclude from the "people's palace" persons who were at war with them politically. That was left to the good taste and judgment of the individual concerned.

One such person who did not scruple to attend White House functions, or to bring his visiting relatives to them, was Russell Jarvis. He was editorial scribe of the daily *Telegraph*, which the opposition leaders had combined to set up in Washington to attack the administration, and partner of Duff Green, the President's most vituperative enemy. The jabs and jibes of these devastating journalists had got under Adams's skin, but he succeeded in confining his feelings to his diary. Not so every member of his family.

Jarvis was a thirty-seven year-old New England Democrat born in Boston. As a child he had removed to Claremont, New Hampshire, had graduated from Dartmouth College, and later attended Tapping Reeve's famous law school in Litchfield, Connecticut, where John C. Calhoun had studied after receiving his degree at Yale. Jarvis once had served as editor of the *Boston Patriot*,[3] a pro-Adams paper. A staunch Adams man, he had been secretary to a meeting at Boston that elected delegates to nominate him for the Presidency.[4] Not having received any reward he had gone over to the opposition. On Wednesday evening, April 2, 1828, he and Mrs. Jarvis visited the White House drawing room with a party from Boston, including, among others, his wife's parents, Mr. and Mrs. Thomas Cordis, and two other ladies, whom he personally introduced to Mrs. Adams. After being courteously received they passed on into the East Room. There they found themselves not far from John Adams, 2d, the President's son and private secretary, who was chatting at the moment with the Reverend Caleb Stetson, pastor of the First Parish at Medford, Massachusetts. This church was attended by the Brooks family, to whose daughter Abigail, Mr. and Mrs. Adams's youngest son Charles was engaged.

3. P. P. Degrand to John Quincy Adams, Boston, March 13, 1824, Adams Papers (Massachusetts Historical Society). Quotations from the Adams Papers are by the permission of the Adams Manuscript Trust.
4. Degrand to Adams, Boston, March 17, 1823, Adams Papers.

"Who is that lady?" inquired Mr. Stetson, glancing at the group a few feet away.

"That," responded son John in a voice loud enough to be overheard by the visitors and so intended, "is the wife of one Russell Jarvis. *There is a man who,* if he had any idea of propriety in the conduct of a gentleman, ought not to show his face in this house."

"Take care," warned the clergyman, "he may hear what you say."

"I do not care if he does," replied young Mr. Adams.

The visitors had heard all right. They immediately and politely took their leave of Mrs. Adams and left the house.[5]

The duello was still highly popular in Washington, and there was plausible cause for personal satisfaction. It might also be a most useful incident in an election year. Jarvis checked with Mr. Stetson to identify John Adams, 2d, beyond all doubt as the person whom he had overheard. Then he took time to think over the "insult," perhaps to consult with Duff Green and leaders of the opposition.[6] Here was a wonderful chance to strike at the President, with popular applause, by challenging his son to a duel. If the young man did not accept, or took shelter under his White House employment or relationship, public opinion particularly in southern and western states might brand him as a coward.

Six days after the presidential reception, on April 8, 1828, Jarvis wrote a note to John Adams. It was delivered by Alexander C. McLean, one of the party who had accompanied the ladies in the Jarvis party at the White House levee. McLean was charged to receive any explanations. Young Adams repeated to the intermediary what he had said to Stetson about Jarvis, and contemptuously refused to have any further correspondence.

According to the "code of honor" the next step for a "gentleman" who had received no satisfaction was to return the insult personally and unmistakably so as to provoke a challenge if possible. Jarvis resolved on this recourse.[7] Because the *Telegraph* was the printing organ of the Senate, he had good reason to frequent the Capitol. There he watched for John Adams; we may guess that he did not fail to confer with his employers and political bosses. The President's secretary appeared on Tuesday, April 15, bearing routine messages to the House

5. Testimony in "Case of Russell Jarvis," H. R. Rept. No. 260, 20th Cong., 1st Sess. Hereinafter cited as "Case of Russell Jarvis."

6. Duff Green, in a signed communication to the *U. S. Telegraph,* May 8, 1828, asserted that Jarvis consulted with nobody.

7. ". . . Mr. Jarvis resolved to avail himself of the first opportunity to demand, personally, an explanation; resolved, if it were denied, to inflict such personal indignity as would relieve *him* from the duty of seeking further satisfaction." Duff Green, in *U. S. Telegraph,* May 8, 1828.

of Representatives and the Senate. Having completed his errand to the lower house, he was passing through the Rotunda on his way to the Senate. At that conspicuous place, where members were always coming and going between the House and Senate, Jarvis jumped him.

Precisely what happened in the ensuing fracas is difficult to state with perfect accuracy. Jarvis claimed he pulled John's nose and slapped one side of his face with an open hand without any attempt at bodily injury—the approved provocation to a challenge. He declared later that he was merely requiting John Adams's "insult" to "the ladies." He had no intention, he explained, of violating the rights or dignity of the House of Representatives and was ready to offer any necessary atonement due to that body.[8] John on his part disclaimed any intention of reflecting on the ladies: it was only Jarvis on whom he had commented so pointedly at the White House. He said that, in the Rotunda, Jarvis struck at him and tried to wrest his cane from him. Not succeeding, Jarvis had retreated. John had then turned and ran at him with his cane, but bystanders separated them before he could chastise his assailant.[9]

Of several witnesses to the scuffle, only one, William Emmons of Boston, later supported Jarvis's statement that he pulled John's nose, but that was doubtless Jarvis's intention, whether he succeeded or not. Clement Dorsey, a member of the House from Maryland, who had helped to separate the two antagonists, later testified that Mr. Adams's assailant said: "It is all—it is enough—you know my name—you know the place of my residence."

President Adams drew comfort from Dorsey's later statement to him that John had conducted himself in as manly a spirit as could be.[10]

What was to be done about the incident? No one wanted to play into the hands of the enemy which was provoking it. At first President Adams was inclined to do nothing: to leave it to the Congress to administer censure or punishment for this "outrageous" attack by an "assassin" on the President's personal officer while engaged in his official duties. But both houses of Congress were hostile, dominated by the coalition of Calhoun with the supporters of Andrew Jackson, and warmly sympathetic to the campaign of the Hero of New Orleans for the Presidency. Congress was not likely to do anything at all.

All the Cabinet officers thought that the President ought to hold a Cabinet meeting right away, perhaps send in a message to Congress, in whose purlieus the assault had taken place. A Cabinet meeting took

8. "Case of Russell Jarvis," pp. 12–14.
9. Ibid., pp. 15–20.
10. Adams, *Memoirs*, 7, 508, 519.

place on April 17. The President began by reading the draft of a message to Congress, if such should be called for.

It was Henry Clay, the administration's only qualified duelist, who came to the President's aid and that of his son. No one could question the courage of Clay's honor or his experienced judgment in these affairs. He would avoid personal implications by raising the more serious question of inviolability of the constitutional relationship between the executive and legislative branches of the government. He would invite the responsibility of Congress for redress of the offense. Professing to assume that "personal feelings" might be influencing his chief, the Secretary of State had prepared a draft of his own for a proposed message. It was about the same as the President's—at least so Adams thought—and he adopted it with a few verbal alterations. He then asked his advisers whether he ought after all to send in any message, and if so when.

"At all events," volunteered Clay, "I think the message should be sent, and that immediately."

Attorney General William Wirt was not so sure. "I think there would be more calmness and dignity," he said, "in passing by the transaction without notice."

Clay warmly opposed such silence. "The act is of a most dangerous character as an example," he retorted, and continued solemnly:

> It tends to introduce assassination into the Capitol. It might be practised for the robbery of a confidential message from the Executive to the Legislature. It is indeed too probable that in the present disposition of both houses of Congress they may do nothing to remedy the evil. But there is a duty for the Executive, independently of what Congress may do—to maintain his own dignity and security in the performance of his functions. I understand that both parties in Congress are hesitating what to do about this case, distrustful of each other. . . . I feel sure nothing will be done unless responsibility be put on them—by a message. The very forbearance to send one will be used as an argument for doing nothing. They will refer a motion to a committee. The committee will make a partial report, perverting the facts, giving the wrong to your son's offensive remark. There is now in the House of Representatives no member of weight of character to lead them, in any prepared direction, without some external impulse. Forbearance on the part of the Executive is laudable, but you can carry it to an extreme.

After listening to these views at length (they are recorded in Adams's diary) the other members of the Cabinet, including Wirt, concurred.

Adams feared that some motion or resolution on the subject might have been already offered in the House or Senate, that a communication from him therefore might prejudice its progress, and thus cause an unfavorable effect. But he yielded to the advice of his Cabinet. This time he sent the message not by his son John but by Daniel Brent, chief clerk of the Department of State. Henry Clay went ahead of it to the Capitol to make sure the coast was clear, to decide by what he found there whether the paper should finally be handed in. He ascertained that no motion had yet been offered in the House. Senator Richard M. Johnson of Kentucky told him that none had been brought forward in the Senate either. This proved to be a mistake, and Clay afterwards discovered that Senator Samuel A. Foot of Connecticut had already (April 17) moved for a committee to look into the notorious incident, with power to send for persons and papers (his resolution was tabled next day, on his own motion, the Senate deciding to wait and see what the House would do). Clay directed Brent to present the President's message; he accordingly delivered it to both houses on April 17.[11]

The President mentioned the fact that his private secretary had been "waylaid and assaulted" in the Rotunda by a "person" in the presence of a member of the House who interposed and separated the parties. He thought it proper to communicate the occurrence to Congress so that it might consider in its wisdom any "animadversion" or regulation or legislation to insure security in the official intercourse between President and Congress, and to prevent disorders within the Capitol itself. "In the deliberation of Congress upon this subject," he said, "it is neither expected nor desired that any consequences shall be attached to the private relation in which my secretary stands to me."

The House of Representatives immediately referred the special message to a select committee consisting of four pro-Jackson members, George McDuffie of South Carolina, chairman, Philip P. Barbour of Virginia (brother of the Secretary of War), John Bell of Tennessee, and James W. Ripley of Maine; two administration supporters, Benjamin Gorham of Boston, Massachusetts, and Ralph I. Ingersoll of Connecticut; and one Clinton Democrat, Thomas J. Oakley of New York, supposedly a neutral. In what amounted to a party vote, the Senate voted 24–22 to lay Foot's proposed resolution and the President's message on the table pending action by the House. The only opposition Senator who would admit at this time that Jarvis's attack was entirely

11. Ibid., 7, 508–13.

unjustifiable was the veteran Nathaniel Macon of North Carolina, known as "father of the Congress" because he had served continuously in one house or the other since 1791.

The *National Journal,* the administration paper, referred to the "assault within the Capitol" as an "outrage." The *Telegraph* justified "the pulling of the Prince's nose" and praised "signal chastisement" of the "Royal puppy." [12] As the news spread through the country, like ripples rolling slowly out from a splashing stone, accounts took on either a tinge of scorn for the President's son and ridicule for the father, or of proper indignation and offended dignity—all according to the political affiliations or patronage of the reporting newspapers.

It soon became clear that the opposition did not relish the investigation. The *Telegraph* now asserted that its real purpose was to magnify a personal dispute into an affair of great political importance in order to create popular excitement against General Jackson as candidate for the Presidency. It was also another stratagem—i.e. a red herring—to divert attention from a report which a "certain Paul Prying Committee" was about to make, the opposition committee on retrenchment and reform that was attempting to show up to the electorate the extravagances of the Adams administration.[13]

There was by now a good deal of excitement, particularly in Washington.[14] John's mother, the First Lady, feared for his safety. White House servants attending a street fair had heard a certain Dr. Hagan threaten the President's son with personal violence.[15] The President, who was used to wordy threats of assassination, was not too disturbed on that score, without more positive signs of danger.

Meanwhile Russell Jarvis had sent into the House of Representatives a memorial of his own, to be referred to the committee of investigation.[16] He published the same in his newspaper.

The President's message had put responsibility for any redress of the "outrage" on Congress rather than on himself or any member of his family. "The opposition party will have to do something to manifest their disapprobation of Jarvis's conduct," Senator Bell assured the President, "for the sake of their own credit." This proved to be the case.

12. *National Journal,* April 19, 26, 1828; *U. S. Telegraph,* May 1, 8, 1828.

13. *U. S. Telegraph,* May 1, 1828.

14. "A very extraordinary and unnecessary experiment . . . a storm in a teapot," declared James Hamilton, of South Carolina, in the House of Representatives on May 23, 1828. *National Journal,* May 24, 1828.

15. Adams, *Memoirs,* 7, 513.

16. "Case of Russell Jarvis," pp. 12–14.

The President himself no longer had any confidence Bell was correct, but at least the problem had been shifted off his shoulders and in some measure from the breast of his son. "They brought him [Jarvis] here for the purpose of assassination," he noted in his diary, "and they cannot punish him for laboring in the vocation to which they called him." [17]

The congressional investigators held hearings. They summoned both parties, John and Jarvis. They called witnesses. They allowed Duff Green to appear as attorney for Jarvis and to cross-examine John in great detail.

The committee's report, presented by McDuffie of South Carolina, was really a moral victory for the President. Everybody agreed that Jarvis had followed John Adams out of the Hall of Representatives and assaulted him in the Rotunda. That was all they could agree on. Nobody attempted to conclude just what happened in the scuffle: whether Jarvis really pulled John's nose and slapped his face, or whether John succeeded in chastising his assailant with his cane. "Whatever may have been the cause of provocation," concluded the committee without exception, the assault was an act done in contempt of the authority and dignity of the House. It was a violation of its peculiar privileges. It challenged the immunity of the person selected by the President for taking his official communications to Congress.

A bare majority of the committee agreed the act merited the censure of the House. Another bare majority, differently constructed, agreed that it was not expedient to have any further proceedings in the case. The committee, so to speak, had pronounced the defendant guilty but had refused to suggest punishment.

Philip P. Barbour, champion of states' rights, presented a long and learned minority report arguing that the House did not have any authority to punish: such would be dangerous to rights of the individual.[18]

Almost a week later, on May 23, 1828, Benjamin Gorham of Massachusetts moved in the House an amendment to the committee's report by proposing that the sergeant-at-arms be ordered to bring Jarvis before the bar of the House for reprimand and discharge, and that the Speaker

17. Adams, *Memoirs*, 7, 513–14. "Slander and Assassination are working hand in hand against us. . . . The assault upon your brother . . . was the act of an Assassin. I have myself lived more than three years under threats of assassination, from more than one hand, which I have constantly despised." Adams to Charles Francis Adams, Washington, April 20, 1828, Adams Papers.

18. H. R. Rept. No. 260, 20th Cong., 1st Sess. See also *Register of Debates in Congress*, 4 (1827–28), Pt. 2, 2718–23; *Niles' Weekly Register*, May 24, 1828.

be requested to withhold from the culprit for the remainder of the session and during the next session the courtesies usually extended to the editors of newspapers. Nothing was done except to order the proposed amendment laid upon the table.[19]

The congressional investigation and report had allowed political passion and public opinion to cool down a bit. It is clear that Jarvis had made a tactical mistake in accosting his enemy within the precincts of the Capitol while engaged in official business. It was plain, even to the opposition, that the offense merited censure even if the committee was unwilling to prescribe censure. The need for a duel had evaporated.

On the last day of the session John Long of North Carolina placed on the table of the House the following resolution: *"Resolved; that the Constitution of the United States ought to be amended so as to prevent the practice of dueling."* [20]

The resolution remained inertly on the table when the House adjourned, May 26, 1828. It was not even mentioned in the official *Register of Debates.* Who could word such a constitutional amendment anyway? What prospect was there that it could receive a two-thirds vote of both houses of Congress and be ratified by three-fourths of the states in the Union? Who could guarantee that even if passed it could be enforced?

That very month of May 1828, Dr. Branch A. Archer (later famous in Texas annals), challenged by Mr. Otway Crump at Powhatan, Virginia, killed the latter in a duel at fifteen paces.

The Jarvis-Adams encounter lingered on with fading colors in the public attention during the excessive heat of the election campaign of 1828. But Congress never reverted to the subject when it convened in December 1828, following the election of Andrew Jackson over John Quincy Adams. The scuffle in the Rotunda, though not yet the practice of dueling, passed into the limbo of history.

19. *Register of Debates in Congress, 4,* Pt. 2, 2754–58.
20. *National Journal,* May 27, 1828; *U. S. Telegraph,* May 27, 1828.

13. The Adams Family and Their Manuscripts

IN FELICITATING fond parents upon the birth of a son, it is a nice whimsey to exclaim: "There lies a future President of the United States. Who knows?"

Any boy born in this Republic has a constitutional right to be elected President if he lives to the age of thirty-five years and can get the votes of his fellow citizens. Many a youth or young man, conscious of his heritage of freedom, has deliberately set out to shape his life to the Presidency. Only five—perhaps now six—such people have started out in their early years to make it, and have made it: John Quincy Adams once but not again; Martin Van Buren once and never more; Theodore Roosevelt only once at the suffrage of his countrymen; Woodrow Wilson once and once again; then Franklin Delano Roosevelt once, and again, and again, and again. In only one instance—before 1961 anyway —have the parents successfully planned it that way: that was the case of John Quincy Adams. Perhaps now we shall have to add our fellow Member, John Fitzgerald Kennedy. At any rate President Kennedy is the only chief executive in the history of the United States both of whose parents have lived to see their second son become President, however they may have originally planned. To pursue these pleasant lucubrations further: there have been only two ministers to the Court of St. James's whose sons have become President of our Republic: John Adams and Joseph P. Kennedy. Finally, both progenitors have been men of Massachusetts.

There has been only one President who has lived to see his son also become President. That was John Adams, the son, John Quincy Adams. The Adams manuscripts are the most important of all family records preserved in the United States. They comprise the diaries and letters and other papers of the three Adams statesmen, father, son, and grandson, and their respective families, brothers, sisters, cousins, aunts, and uncles—millions and millions of words. To these formidable autobiographical and epistolary foundations are constantly being added the

Delivered before the Massachusetts Historical Society on Sept. 22, 1961, at the ceremony marking the occasion of publication of the first four volumes of *The Adams Papers*. Published in *Proceedings of the Massachusetts Historical Society, 73, 1961.*

diaries, letters, and other papers of succeeding generations of the family, for who can imagine that the Adamses will ever stop writing, and who would want them to?

We are met here this afternoon to pay our respects to the first three generations of Adams manuscripts and to the massive program of editing and printing them. To use a choice word of the two Presidents Adams, reserved for the greatest of occasions, this event constitutes an *epocha* in American historiography.

No one was more sharply conscious of the necessity of preserving historical records than old John Adams, the original patriot of the Revolution for independence; few were more irregular about the keeping and order of their own papers. Writing to Hezekiah Niles in 1818, a climactic year of the revolutions in Latin America, he mentioned the "real American Revolution." He said:

> To this end, it is greatly to be desired, that young men of letters in all the States, especially in the thirteen original States, would undertake the laborious, but certainly interesting and amusing task, of searching and collecting all the records, pamphlets, newspapers, and even handbills, which in any way contributed to change the temper and views of the people, and compose them into an independent nation.

That indeed has been the principal purpose and task of this Society. John Adams went on to say:

> In this research, the gloriole of individual gentlemen, and of separate States, is of little consequence. The *means and the measures* are the proper objects of investigation. These may be of use to posterity, not only in this nation, but in South America and all other countries.[1]

The publication, now launched, of the Adams manuscripts by the Massachusetts Historical Society and the Harvard University Press, thanks to the financial support of Time, Incorporated, does credit a century and a half later to John Adams's farsighted interest in history, presenting the parts which he and his son and grandson, and their correspondents, official and private, played in the history of our nation.

This most prized collection of our Society embraces the Adams memory of such happenings as the voting of independence by the Continental Congress, the Franco-American alliance, the treaty of peace and independence signed by John Adams and his fellow com-

1. *The Works of John Adams,* ed. C. F. Adams, *10* (Boston, 1856), 283.

missioners at Paris; the foundations of American foreign policy, the Louisiana Purchase, the second treaty of peace with Great Britain signed in
1814 by John Quincy Adams, head of the American peace mission at
Ghent; the Napoleonic invasion of Russia, glimpses of Napoleon himself during the Hundred Days, the framing of the Monroe Doctrine,
the great Transcontinental Treaty of 1819 with Spain, recognition of
the new states of Latin America, the long fight waged by John Quincy
Adams against the "Gag Rule" in the House of Representatives; Manifest Destiny, the annexation of Texas, the War with Mexico; the sectional conflict over slavery; the War for Southern Independence, the
controversy with Great Britain over the building of a Confederate
Navy, the *Alabama* claims and the Geneva Arbitration. In it appear
important letters and data on such statesmen as Washington, Franklin,
Jefferson, Lafayette, Hamilton, Madison, Monroe, Jackson, Polk, Calhoun, Clay, Webster, Seward, Lincoln, Grant, Schurz, Tilden, Hayes,
and European diplomats from Vergennes to Bryce.[2] And something
on every Presidential campaign from Washington to Cleveland, including eight from 1788 to 1872 in which an Adams was a candidate,
either for the Presidency or Vice Presidency.

Why had the Adams manuscripts been so long in coming forth to
the eyes of the honorable community of historians? Because, in the
first place, ever since John Quincy Adams contemplated writing a
history of the United States and editing his patriot father's papers, the
family for a century had furnished its own historians, sufficient unto
themselves, so they believed. The accumulating collection of diaries
and letters, incoming as well as outgoing, served as their private and
exclusive historical quarry. In the Old House at Quincy, John Quincy
Adams, returning from the White House in Washington, first labored
with his son at arranging and editing his father's papers. Soon the fierce
political struggles of his Second Career diverted him from the task,
but Charles Francis Adams finally published (in 1850–56) the ten-
volume edition of the *Works* of John Adams, including *selected* letters
and *selected* passages from his diaries and autobiographies. This ex-
pensive and ill-arranged publication was supported (like the first editions of selected papers of Washington and Jefferson) by an appropriation of Congress to purchase 1,000 copies of the set for $22,500. Until
very recently these volumes have remained the principal source for
biographers of John Adams. Only now are historians, such as Merrill

2. L. H. Butterfield, "The Papers of the Adams Family: Some Account of Their
History," M.H.S., *Proceedings*, *71* (1953–57), 328–56; and "The Adams Papers,"
Daedalus, *86* (1955), 62–71.

Jensen and Stephen G. Kurtz, finding in the unpublished papers of John Adams, recently microfilmed, the yeast that raised the old patriot's public loaf and private dander.

Charles Francis Adams, after his great service as a diplomatist, crowned by his notable work on the Geneva Arbitration Tribunal, like his father John Quincy Adams before him in the case of grandfather John Adams, turned to the task of editing and publishing the famous diary of *his* own famous father, namely John Quincy Adams himself. It appeared in 1874–77 in twelve stout octavo volumes under the title, *Memoirs of John Quincy Adams, Comprising Portions of his Diary from 1795 to 1848.*

It is not too much to say that John Quincy Adams's full diary is the greatest personal record ever set down by an American statesman in the Western Hemisphere. It stretches with very few gaps over seventy years: from November 12, 1779, when he embarked with his father a second time for Europe, to January 4, 1848, in the midst of the Mexican War. The title page of one of his earliest diary booklets contains a quotation from Voltaire: *La mollesse est douce et sa suite est cruelle.* The author lived up to that warning. The holograph diary of some 3,000,000 words is a monument of physical labor and self-discipline.

A detailed critical study of this diary, as printed and as still unprinted, has never been made. It was first of all a record for his own reference, and as such it proved useful in many a controversy. It also served as a release for ulcerous judgments on his political opponents in a time when to say these things out loud might mean a pistol duel. Above all, John Quincy Adams considered it a history of his life, both the outer man and the inner man, for the edification of his descendants. It would not seem that he wrote it for later publication, certainly not in the unstudied form and style in which he put it down. But perhaps one day one of his sons would prepare it for publication, winnowing out the wheat from the chaff.

As for his own appraisal of this record of his life, stated in characteristic Adamsian elevated disillusion and profession of ultimate failure, John Quincy Adams wrote:

> If my intellectual powers had been such as have been sometimes committed by the Creator of man to single individuals of the species, my Diary would have been, next to the Holy Scriptures, the most precious and valuable book ever written by human hands, and I should have been one of the greatest benefactors of my

country and of mankind. I would, by the irresistible power of genius and the irrepressible energy of will and the favor of Almighty God, have banished war and slavery from the face of the earth forever. But the conceptive power of mind was not conferred on me by my Maker, and I have not improved the scanty portion of His gifts as I might and ought to have done.

I should guess that the published portion would measure up in wordage as the smaller half of the whole record, though by far the more important half. Charles Francis Adams included all that he felt to be of historical value illustrative of his father's public life, with copious passages to give an adequate idea of character and personality. Where the editor felt doubtful about the historical value of a passage he included it, even though it seemed personal. But the question remains: on what passages did he feel doubtful, and on what not doubtful? The quick and ready way in which the filial editor did the selection leaves much to be desired. He simply penciled parentheses around the passages to be printed and then turned the manuscript text over to the printer: no editing, no explanation. One can't thus chop across threads of a mingled skein that runs through a life. Much of the man and his personal travail is missing from these printed *Memoirs*. As to the accuracy of the printing, I know of no check that has been made; certainly it must be fallible. Now, the unexpurgated product of the whole loom, public woof and private warp, is to be printed later on in the voluminous series being launched today.

The significance of the *Memoirs* to their editor Charles Francis Adams is attested by a poignant passage from his own unprinted diary: "Yesterday was a memorable day . . . for the reception of the twelfth and last volume of my father's Diary. . . . I am now perfectly ready to go myself."

One thing seems sure about the twelve volumes: financially they must have become a worrisome white elephant for Lippincott, the publisher, for we know of no subvention, from the family or otherwise, that supported them.

In addition to the diary, there is the tremendous quantity of correspondence, public and private, largely out of his own letterbooks, supplemented by a mass of incoming letters on all kinds of subjects from all kinds of people. In contrast to the irregular methods of his father, John Adams, John Quincy Adams kept this correspondence in a most systematic way. Such matter mounted to its greatest quantity during the second Adams's years in Congress and his crusades for the right of petition and the restriction of slavery in the territories—his so-called Second Career.

This material has already had considerable scholarly attention. In 1909 the son of Charles Francis Adams, by name Charles Francis Adams of course, whom we shall call CFA II to distinguish him from CFA I and CFA III, hired Worthington C. Ford away from the Manuscripts Division of the Library of Congress to serve as archivist and editorial consultant of the Adams Family. Ford also acted as Editor of this Society from 1909 to 1929.[3] During his prodigious labors in this building Mr. Ford incidentally published a dozen or so articles of choice or disparate selections drawn from the Adams Manuscripts, which since 1902 had reposed here off this room. Ford's most ambitious project was the editing, in what he estimated would run to twelve volumes, of the *Writings of John Quincy Adams,* presenting selections of his most significant letters public and private, with illustrative footnotes from relevant incoming letters and a moderate selection of John Quincy Adams's other writings. This edition, published by Macmillan between 1913 and 1917, had advanced to seven volumes carrying the selected documents through September 1823, when the publication was discontinued during the First World War. Although its cessation has never been fully explained, it would seem that the exigencies of war and financial uncertainty about further volumes had a good deal to do with it. In due course, it will be resumed and perhaps entirely replaced by a whole new edition of the writings of John Quincy Adams as a part of the great publication now coming up.

Ford's printed volumes as far as published have been of enormous value to students of the period, many of whom, like myself, yearned to look at the documents which Ford saw fit to omit in his effort to condense the publication to practical limits. Curiously enough, and perhaps significantly, Ford never said a word about the provenance of these letters. Maybe it was feared that too much information on this head might lead to too many applications from outside historical scholars for unprinted documents reposing among the family archives. Ford's own discretion as to publication seems to have been greatly

3. In 1929 Mr. Ford retired from the Massachusetts Historical Society on a pension, and accepted the position of European Representative of the Library of Congress, in succession to the author of these remarks. The Second World War and the occupation of France by Nazi Germany suspended the work of the Mission, and Ford died at sea in 1941 while returning home. The editing of the various series selected from the Adams Papers was only a small portion of the total volume of his historical work. A life of Ford with an appraisal of his scholarly activities much needs to be done.

curtailed following the death of Charles Francis Adams II in 1915, the last of the family historians—so far.

We may now look forward to publication in due time in our new enterprise, under the expert editorship of Professor and Mrs. David H. Donald of Princeton, of the diary of the family editor of the first two Adamses, namely that of Charles Francis Adams himself. It stretches over sixty years, 1820–80. It is nearly as voluminous, and certainly more even, if cooler, in literary quality, as if the author were conscious that some day one of *his* sons might publish much of it, at least those portions touching on public affairs. It is a political record foreign and domestic of a tremendous period of American history, notably of the sectional conflict, the Civil War, and the diplomatic aftermath of the war, culminating in the Geneva Arbitration. For the years 1820 to 1847 the diaries of father and son overlap and become an indispensable source to biographers of both statesmen.

The great mass of Charles Francis Adams's correspondence, letter-books and incoming letters, also rivals the corresponding files of John Quincy Adams in value to the historian of his period. This material too will take its place among the future volumes of *The Adams Papers*.

We recall that Charles Francis Adams had four distinguished sons— John Quincy Adams, the Democrat, and the three eminent historians: the incomparable Henry Adams, who of course had access to the Adams Manuscripts but did not make so much use of them as he might have done in his masterly *History,* and his historian brothers Brooks Adams, and Charles Francis Adams II already introduced.

President John Quincy Adams has been said to have had two great careers. His grandson Charles Francis Adams II had three. After a successful military career during the Civil War he had a second spectacular career in railroad management, and finally a notable third career as historian and President of this Society. Following outstanding achievements in the service of Clio, such as his *Three Episodes of Massachusetts History,* his articles on Anglo-American relations during the Civil War, and the short biography of his diplomat father, he took upon himself the task of doing for the diary and papers of Charles Francis Adams I what the latter had done for John Adams and John Quincy Adams. Charles Francis Adams II projected more than that: he planned to supplement this collection with documents copied out of the diplomatic records of the Department of State in Washington, the Foreign Office in London, and the private papers of Lord Palmerston, British Prime Minister during our Civil War, and the Foreign Minister, Lord Russell. He conceived of it as a multivolume work of the magnitude of Nicolay and Hay's ten-volume documentary biography of Abraham Lincoln. He labored at this task until with his increasing years and depleted health the great work broke down under its own massive weight. As a young graduate student, I can remember the old gentleman (whose portrait hangs on the wall of our staircase) moving about in the alcoves of the Society during the last months of his life—I regret I never dared to speak to him.

From what has been said it is evident that for the two Presidents, the Adams historians published or caused to be published (as in the case of Ford's renditions) a major part of their papers which relate to their public life, but for Charles Francis Adams, nothing.

We have noted the fact that in 1902 the Adams Manuscripts had been transferred from the Stone Library in the garden of the Old House at Quincy to the custody—*but not the control or use*—of this Society, where they were impounded for a minimum of fifty years in the Adams Manuscript Trust. After the family historians passed from the scene the more recently co-opted Adams trustees knew less and less about the contents of their trust and were more and more preoccupied with their own busy affairs. They were particularly sensitive to a new school of writers seeking sensational copy to debunk great men by a display of their petty human qualities. Such exhibitionists were prone to exploit human weaknesses rather than strength of character. And who knew what family skeletons might be hidden in the Adams Room! Here was another reason for keeping the collection closed to outsiders.

Ever since the days of Mercy Warren and that journalistic pest Anne Royall, the Adamses, beginning with John Adams and John Quincy Adams, had had a horror of female publicists. Mrs. Royall was the reporter who had annoyed John Quincy Adams in the White House, and is said further—I never could find any good authority for it—once to have followed him down and sat on his clothes and refused to go away until he promised, from the then translucent protection of the Potomac River, to give her an interview when he got back to the White House. When in the age of jazz certain penwomen began to do what amounted to "profiles" of the Adamses it became absolutely impossible for any woman to break through the barrier. As late as our own times even that superlative writer Catherine Drinker Bowen could not use John Adams's papers for her lively volume on *John Adams and the American Revolution*.

When I first began work on John Quincy Adams, the trustees were: Charles Francis Adams III, Secretary of the Navy under President

Hoover and Treasurer of Harvard University, and his cousin Henry Adams II, nephew of the illustrious historian of that name. Henry Adams II in his retirement from business served as the family vigilator over the collection. He was twin brother of John Adams, the recent President of this Society, who rendered such signal service during some very trying years. The spitting image of his great-grandfather John Quincy Adams, Henry Adams II was devoting nearly all his time to the Adams Manuscripts, and trying to carry on the massive enterprise which had weighed down his father, Charles Francis Adams II, the great work on Charles Francis Adams I and the Civil War.

Henry Adams II was rather deaf and had the reputation among some young and impatient scholars of being unreasonable and crotchety. The staff of this Society, who came into contact with him almost daily, did not altogether share this opinion. I certainly never found him really difficult. I worked at a desk there by the window in this great room, then a museum, and he remained watchfully at his desk and typewriter in the exclusive Adams Room, over opposite. When he went out he locked the door of the treasure trove and took the key with him. As I gained his confidence he would leave the key with me, finally leave the door open so I could go in and get whatever I needed, provided I would lock up and put the key in an agreed place when I went out for lunch. Now what do you think of that, for a fellow hailing from what Cotton Mather called "the wrong side of the hedge"?

I can still picture Henry Adams II coming in from Concord of a frosty winter morning, his pale blue eyes running from the cold, rubbing his hands briskly, unlocking the door, opening the window of the inner Adams sanctum and unbolting the iron fireproof and thiefproof shutters one high story up from the ground alleyway. Sometimes he would speak to me, sometimes not. I soon came to feel that this made no difference in his inner friendliness and developing interest in my work and concern for its success. Then he would bring out the volume or volumes of manuscripts for which I was waiting. While I was reading, he would be busy on some concern of his own, answering inquiries, copying passages for scholars, studying Civil War documents for himself, or perhaps wandering around among earlier Adams manuscripts. Sometimes he would get so absorbed in these old family letters that he would almost talk to their authors, certainly to himself: "Confound it! [At least so I remember his words at this distance of time.] Abigail shouldn't have said that!" Or, "the old man should have known better." When I once referred to the "old man," Henry Adams quickly reacted: "In the family we can call him that, but other people shouldn't." He didn't seem to mind, however, when I spoke of "the Old Man Eloquent."

Mr. Adams became a real friend, and we had the pleasure of entertaining him a couple of weekends in New Haven. He was particularly interested in comparing the students of Adams House at Harvard College, where he was a Fellow, with those of Saybrook College at Yale, where I was a Fellow. Once I took him to a picnic of the Saybrook undergraduates, a rollicking occasion on the country greensward, the boys and girls imbued with the sap of Spring, under the thin chaperonage of the Fellows. The antics didn't faze him a bit: on the contrary. I am sure he had once felt, like the Adamses before him (their unprinted manuscripts show it), like the Adamses after him, I presume, and like all of us certainly, the sap of Spring.

It became increasingly evident to Mr. Adams that the papers under his charge were acquiring more and more importance to the world of modern scholarship. The burden of his responsibility as family vigilator became ever more heavy as he tried, singlehandedly, to take care of all the requests and inquiries coming in. I was somewhat shocked to hear him say one day as he came out of his den and turned the key: "I wish Hitler would drop one of his bombs right in the middle of all this!" When I remonstrated, he professed to be serious. If anybody else had suggested such a means of solving his problem, he doubtless would have blown his top.

"What do the historians think of our policy of keeping these papers closed?" he asked me one day. By then I knew him well enough to tell him frankly: "They don't think much of it; they contrast it with unrestricted access to the papers of Washington, Jefferson, Hamilton, Madison, Monroe, and those of many another great American, long since open to scholars, in the Library of Congress, and elsewhere."

I have no doubt that he was discussing this matter with his fellow trustee, "Charlie" Adams, as he called his eminent cousin, Charles Francis Adams III. It was clear that the family could no longer carry the burden of editing and publishing, of caring for the Adams houses in Quincy, the Stone Library there behind the Old House, and the responsibility to scholars and to the nation involved in the custody of the Adams manuscripts here in the Adams Room. The problem of the ancestral houses they solved by turning them over to the city of Quincy and to the United States government as historical monuments. But that did not take care of responsibility for handling and use of these precious manuscripts. Once the faithful Henry should pass from the scene, there would be nobody available in the family to give personal attention to the documents. The family would have either to lock them up altogether or unload them from its own bosom in a way to keep them intact for the whole nation. And the Adamses have always been men of the whole nation.

After the death of Henry Adams II in 1951, two new and young trustees came into the Trust, Mr. Thomas Boylston Adams, President of our Society today, and his cousin Mr. John Quincy Adams. These young men did not profess to be historians but they knew historians and trusted them. They had sensed the high principles, character, and canons of scholarship prevailing in the historical profession in the United States, such as we see embodied in the American Historical Association and its affiliated groups. They called in some professional historical scholars to advise them. The trustees almost stunned their guests by proposing a giant first step, a program of microfilming the entire corpus, every piece and fragment large and small of the Adams manuscripts through the year 1889. It would be a self-sustaining enterprise, supported by subscription of the larger libraries in American cities and universities, strategically located over this whole continental republic. Begun in 1952, this mighty labor, well organized and competently executed, was completed in 1959. Already it has begun to pollenize historical research in this country and abroad. There has developed a veritable cult of Adams history and biography.

Next the new trustees called in a group of scholars to help shape a great decision: publication of the papers of the three Adams statesmen. In 1950 President Harry S. Truman, inspired by the launching of Mr. Julian P. Boyd's marvelous edition of *The Papers of Thomas Jefferson,* had recently given impetus to the work of the National Historical Publications Commission, a quasi-governmental agency, by urging publication of similar complete and scholarly editions of other great Americans' papers in the comprehensive form of Boyd's *Jefferson.* Mr. Truman's proposal had a dynamic effect: practically a publication explosion. First to be set on foot were the papers of Benjamin Franklin (to be noted more particularly), then the Adams Manuscripts, followed by Alexander Hamilton, John Jay, James Madison, Henry Clay, John C. Calhoun, Andrew Johnson, James K. Polk, Woodrow Wilson, and George Catlett Marshall, to cite outstanding projects under way; with plans being formulated for the papers of Albert Gallatin, Henry Laurens, John Marshall, George Mason, William Penn, and Daniel Webster—together with large collections such as the Papers of the Continental Congress, papers on the Ratification of the Constitution,

the Naval Records of the Revolution, etc.[4] These projects are all being
sponsored by universities, historical societies, and various governmental
agencies, some of them assisted by private endowments like the Franklin and Adams enterprises financed by Time, Inc.

First fruits of the Adams enterprise, sponsored by our Society, published by the Belknap Press of Harvard University Press, and supported
by funds from Time, Inc., on behalf of *Life* magazine, are presented to
the public today. It may well be asked why a great publishing firm,
whose business is popular journalism, should put large sums of money
into scholarly enterprises of this kind. The basic reason is that the top
management of that publishing company and the editors of *Life* believe that their readers, though they number in millions, want to see
some of the real stuff of history. *Life,* as you know, has already printed
selections from the documents out of the capacious stores that the
Adams editors have assembled, and more will be printed from time to
time. Our editors must find this deeply heartening. What other scholars
have ever had so wide an audience? What other audience so extensive
has ever had such genuine and meticulously prepared historical materials placed before it?

I am happy to pause here to mention particularly the great publication of the Franklin Papers now going on at Yale, in partnership with
the American Philosophical Society and financed by *Life* magazine,
under the editorship of my distinguished colleague and fellow Corresponding member of this Society, Professor Leonard W. Labaree,
and his associates. Although the Franklin factory in the Sterling
Memorial Library got into gear a little earlier than the Adams shop
here, the latter enterprise with these four volumes has already caught
up with it, but the fourth Franklin volume, now being indexed from
the page proof, will appear later this year, and a fifth volume has
gone to press.

In this noble, growing family of publication of American statesmen
and patriots certainly the Adamses are illustrious companions. We are
happy to pay tribute to them, to their sponsors in print, and to their
capable editor and his associates in a lifetime job for all concerned.

The first step in the publication program was outright conveyance
to the Massachusetts Historical Society in the spring of 1956 of all
the Adams Papers which had been placed on its premises in 1902.
The family was now free of a great burden, and a great responsibility,
with the papers preserved for posterity and made available to anybody

4. National Historical Publications Commission, *Tenth Anniversary* . . . (New
York, 1960).

everywhere, and the Editor equipped with proper place and atmosphere in which to work. All these sequences of the Adams publication occurred, to use Mr. Butterfield's own words, "almost with the speed of a nuclear chain reaction."

What does this great dissemination of Adams Papers, already in microfilm and today beginning to appear in book form, have to reveal to historians that has not already been exhibited in the numerous printed works put forth by the Adams historians and their helpers during more than a century past?

Take the case of John Adams, illustrated by the four volumes published today. He was what we might call in today's parlance the theoretician of the American Revolution and self-government. No man is better entitled to be called the Father of the Revolution. As an analyst of men and measures, and as an exploiter of human springs and motives of government, he might also be called, in the best sense of the appellation, the American Machiavelli. He was sponsor of the balance of power built into three separate branches of government, executive, legislative, and judicial, to protect the liberties of the people. This balance has become the enduring pattern of the American structure of government, state and federal. He was a man of complete honesty and full integrity. But most students of his life and times would concede that with his superlative native ability and literary qualities, there was also an excessive personal pride, egotism, jealousy, and pomposity of character and carriage. Such is the image left by the general histories of the period. The hitherto unprinted diary fragments, and private letters, of the women as well as the men of the Adams family, will throw floods of light on the human qualities of the first President Adams that will soften the public image.

Charles Francis Adams, in editing the *Works* of his patriot grandfather, had cut out such pieces and passages as he thought insignificant or in questionable taste by Victorian standards. The grandson omitted much that is colorful in John Adams's own language and activities, exceedingly important for the biographer who would give us a full portrait of the man as seen by his family and neighbors: reports of village life in Braintree, fishing expeditions, ship-launching festivities, droll stories, and country characters. Mr. Butterfield cites some spicy examples in his scholarly preface in Volume I. John Adams was a devoted farmer whenever he could get the time from public business. But Charles Francis Adams thought that farming was too plebeian an occupation to warrant much reader interest.

There is also in the unpublished letters of John Adams, which we may expect to see in printed form as publication advances beyond the Adams diaries, an amount of new detail on his diplomatic activity, supplemented by his official dispatches—particularly relating to his negotiations in the Netherlands, with occasional digs at Franklin. Perhaps a case might be made for John Adams as more realistic on some political and diplomatic issues than Franklin, and shrewder in his political thinking than his friend Jefferson.

The remarkable correspondence of John Adams with his son the Secretary of State and President, still unprinted, on history, politics, philosophy, science, and religion, will be published for the first time in this great series. John Adams in his long years of retirement read just about everything there was both in the classics and in modern letters. He claimed to be the original Unitarian in Massachusetts: but the son, also a Unitarian, confessed to a smack of orthodoxy. John Quincy Adams thought that all Christian faiths, Protestant or Catholic, were seeking the same destination by different roads. In one of his last letters to his President son, the Elder Statesman John Adams summed up all his long readings and ponderings in a lesson of two indelible words: "Be good!"

Copious as the quantity is of already printed material of the diary and papers of John Quincy Adams, I can testify to the richness of the unprinted papers. Take, for example, the second Adams's correspondence both outgoing and incoming during his years as Secretary of State, as President, and during his long, second career in Congress. They are full of unused material for the political, economic, and social historian, and for the history of science in the United States, that has scarcely been touched except cursorily in the recent biography.

To me as a biographer, the unprinted portions of the diary were most revealing: the neurotic health of Mrs. Adams and incompatibility of temper between the two loving spouses which made their years in the White House so miserable a sojourn; the sudden death of their ill-fated first-born, George Washington Adams, a tragedy which made of John Quincy Adams a veritable American Job; details of the dramatic death of the Old Man Eloquent in the House of Representatives; the circumstances of his national obsequies and burial at Quincy. All these poignant chapters of his extraordinary life would be mostly unknown to the biographer who relied, as early biographers had to rely, on the published documents. And there are the reams of unpublished verse; but here I forbear. No more should be published.

The recent biographies, of *Charles Sumner and the Coming of the Civil War,* by Professor David H. Donald, and of *Charles Francis*

Adams, by my scholarly young colleague Dr. Martin B. Duberman, demonstrate the importance of the third generation of Adams manuscripts to current historical scholarship. Beyond its biographical importance, this great collection of the papers of Charles Francis Adams I presents a rich spread of source material for historians of the Rhodes and Nevins period of American historiography: the antislavery side of the sectional conflict, the breakdown of party lines, the Civil War, and its aftermath of Reconstruction. We may be sure that historians to come will make the most of it.

To come back to our late friend Henry Adams II. I once asked him if he thought there might be presidential timber in present or future generations of the family stock.

He paused to ponder this carefully, as if to make a survey. Then he said: "Yes."

14. Early Diplomatic Missions from Buenos Aires to the United States, 1811-24

I

THE FIRST overt act of revolution against Spanish authority in what is now the Argentine Republic was the deposition of the Spanish Viceroy, governor in the King's name of the Viceroyalty of La Plata, and the deportation of himself and his official associates. This was nominally a protest against the invasion of Spain by Napoleon Bonaparte; the revolutionary *Junta Gubernativa* in Buenos Aires still professed loyalty to the captive king, Ferdinand VII. Actually it was a movement for separation from Spanish sovereignty. Professed allegiance to Ferdinand was a device for evading chastisement by Spanish authority, and for securing British sympathy and even assistance. In the Old World, Great Britain had become the ally of the Spanish patriots, who, through the Council of Regency in Cadiz, under the shelter of British naval guns, conserved and exercised the claims of the Bourbon monarchy recently dethroned by Napoleon. But in distant Buenos Aires they never expected Ferdinand to come back to the throne; that is why they affected to remain his subjects.

Diplomatic reachings for foreign encouragement and assistance followed immediately the events of the 25th of May. The first appeal was to Great Britain. Despite the sympathy of the British minister in Río de Janeiro for the cause of independence in the revolted Spanish provinces, the first diplomatic missions from Buenos Aires [1]—to Lord Strangford in Río, and to the British government in London—were

1. Enrique Ruis Guinazú describes the influence of Strangford on the *emigré* Portuguese court at Río, and his contacts with the Buenos Aires patriots, in his biographical study, based on researches in the British Public Record Office, *Lord Strangford y la revolución de Mayo* (Buenos Aires, 1937). See also Norberto Piñero, *La política internacional Argentina* (Buenos Aires, 1924). The eminent historian of British diplomacy, C. K. Webster, has edited the significant documents illustrating British policy, with a most valuable interpretative introduction, in *Britain and the Independence of Latin America, 1812–1830, Selected Documents from the Foreign*

Published in a paperbound volume by the American Antiquarian Society, 1940. Reprinted from *Proceedings of the American Antiquarian Society, 49,* 1939.

ineffectual because of Great Britain's determined policy to sustain the Spanish nationalists in their struggle against Napoleon and to preserve the old Spanish Empire so that the patriots of the Peninsula might draw support and succor from the royal provinces overseas. The primary object of British diplomacy was to win the titanic European war; a secondary object, however, was—as a price of help to the Spanish nationalists—to keep open the new trade with Spain's hitherto closed overseas dominions.[2]

Their hopes for help from England frustrated by that power's European involvements and commitments, the men of Buenos Aires turned their eyes toward distant North America, whence rumors had arrived of friendly welcome in Washington to a delegation from revolted Venezuela.

In fact, the Supreme Junta of Caracas, in April 1810, still before the Declaration of Independence of that province, had dispatched to the United States two commissioners, Juan Vicente Bolívar and Telésforo de Orea, seeking assistance and alliance; later, in June, a delegation left for London, where they fell in with the agents from Buenos Aires and got the same chilly reception which their colleagues from the South had experienced.[3] Bolívar and Orea reached Washington in May 1810, and offered credentials to Secretary of State Robert Smith, who received them informally and very cordially. He approved the attitude of their provisional government and vouchsafed to them that means would be taken to cultivate friendship and commerce between the United States and Venezuela. As a result, the Secretary of State appointed three "agents for seamen and commerce"[4] of the

Office Archives, published for the Ibero-American Institute of Great Britain (2 vols. New York and London, 1938). The Archivo General de la Nación of the Argentine Republic has published the documents relating to these early missions to England in the first volume of its *Misiones Diplomáticas* (Buenos Aires, 1937). Julian María Rubio y Esteban has described a secret diplomatic mission from the Portuguese Court at Río to the Buenos Aires government, July 17 to Dec. 20, 1810, in "The First Diplomatic Negotiations with the Revolutionary Junta at Buenos Aires," *Hisp. Am. Hist. Rev.,* 4 (1921), 367–444.

2. W. S. Robertson has set forth British policy, with apt quotations from records of the Foreign Office, in "The Beginnings of Spanish-American Diplomacy," in *Essays in American History Dedicated to Frederick Jackson Turner* (New York, 1910), pp. 231–67.

3. The documents from Venezuelan Archives relating to these missions, together with historical articles on them, have been printed by Cristóbal L. Mendoza in the unusually valuable number of the *Boletín de la Academia Nacional de Historia* (Caracas, Venezuela) *18* (Oct.–Dec. 1935), 643–743.

4. Before the Hispanic revolutionary period the United States had appointed

United States: William Shaler, on June 16, 1810, to reside at Vera Cruz; Robert K. Lowry, on June 26, to Caracas; and Joel R. Poinsett, on June 28, to the Port of Buenos Aires. Thus the visit of the Venezuelan envoys begins the first [5] international contacts of Latin American republics with the world outside their own continent.[6] The instructions to these agents of the United States have been quoted many times, but it is worth keeping the essential sentences before us here. To Poinsett (as presumably [7] to the other two agents—*mutatis mutandis*), Robert Smith, Secretary of State for President James Madison, wrote that the possibility, in this crisis, of a separation of the Spanish provinces in America from their old sovereignty had impelled the government to send him to Buenos Aires on a mission of good will and observation.[8]

---

consuls to New Orleans (1798–1803), La Guayra (1800–1807), an agent to Cuba during the American Revolution and a consul there since 1797. The Spanish colonial authorities did not grant them exequaturs as consuls, but tolerated their presence because the necessity of neutral commerce during the Napoleonic wars led Spain to open those colonies to trade from the United States. After 1807, the title "agents for seamen and commerce" was applied to the representative in Havana because the unrecognized title of consul caused too much trouble. These consuls and agents were precursors to those appointed in 1810 to the revolutionary authorities. Roy F. Nichols, "Trade Relations and the Establishment of the United States Consulates in Spanish America, 1779–1809," *Hisp. Am. Hist. Rev., 13* (Aug. 1933), 289–313.

5. They antedated the mission of Simón de Bolívar and Luís López to London, commissioned by the Junta of Caracas of June 2, 1810, who reached London July 12, 1810. Cristóbal L. Mendoza, "Documentos relacionados con la Misión de Bolívar y López Méndez a Londres," *Boletín de la Academia Nacional de Historia* (Caracas), *18*, 643–711.

6. W. S. Robertson, pp. 231–67. Shaler never reached Vera Cruz, but was active in Cuba, and later on the Mexican frontier. Charles Carroll Griffin, *The United States and the Disruption of the Spanish Empire* (Columbia University Press, 1937), 49–55.

7. The instructions to Shaler and Lowry are not preserved, but a later reference by Lowry to his instructions implies they were similar to Poinsett's, and one may presume that Shaler's, written at about the same time, were also similar. Cf. Robertson, p. 250.

8. As a crisis is approaching which must produce great changes in the situation of Spanish America, and may dissolve altogether its colonial relations to Europe, and as the geographical position of the United States, and other obvious considerations, give them an intimate interest in whatever may effect the destiny of that part of the American continent, it is our duty to turn our attention to this important subject, and to take such steps, not incompatible with the neutral character and honest policy of the United States, as the occasion renders proper. With this view, you have been selected to proceed without delay, to Buenos Ayres. You will make it your object, wherever it may be proper, to diffuse the impression that the United States cherish the sincerest good will towards the people of Spanish America as neighbors, as belonging to the same

Poinsett reached Buenos Aires, February 13, 1811, after a stop of several weeks in Río de Janeiro and conference there with the minister of the United States to the Court of Portugal and Brazil, at that capital since 1809, Thomas Sumter, a fellow South Carolinian.

At first the revolutionary leaders at Buenos Aires hesitated to accept Poinsett as an agent of the United States, because he bore no letter of credence to them directly from the President, but misgivings vanished when he explained that his appointment was identical in form to the agents which the United States for some time had maintained in Havana and La Guayra.[9] To fortify their independent position even before they had declared independence to the world, the *Junta* dispatched to President Madison a formal acknowledgment of the acceptance of Poinsett as commercial agent of the United States to regulate commercial treaties as "between nation and nation." [10] Meanwhile, they assured the new agent of their desire to cultivate "the most intimate connection" with the United States, and promised him that its commerce would be placed on the footing of the most-favored-nation. This was done in June 1811, although the customs duties and procedure remained vexatious in the extreme to all nationals.[11] Spokes-

portion of the globe, and as having a mutual interest in cultivating friendly intercourse: that this disposition will exist, whatever may be their internal system or European relation, with respect to which no interference of any sort is pretended: and that, in the event of a political separation from the parent country, and of the establishment of an independent system of National Government, it will coincide with the sentiments and policy of the United States to promote the most friendly relations, and the most liberal intercourse, between the inhabitants of this hemisphere, as having all a common interest, and as lying under a common obligation to maintain that system of peace, justice, and good will, which is the only source of happiness for nations.

Whilst you inculcate these as the principles and dispositions of the United States, it will be no less proper to ascertain those on the other side, not only towards the United States, but in reference to the great nations of Europe, and to the commercial and other connexions with them, respectively: and, generally, to inquire into the state, the characteristics, and the proportions, as to numbers, intelligence, and wealth, of the several parties, the amount of population, the extent and organization of the military force, and the pecuniary resources of the country.

W. R. Manning, *Diplomatic Correspondence of the United States Concerning the Independence of the Latin-American Nations* (Carnegie Endowment for International Peace, New York, 1925), *1*, 6–7.

9. Poinsett to the Secretary of State, Feb. 13, 1811. Poinsett Papers, *1*, 31. Historical Society of Pennsylvania.

10. Manning, *1*, 320.

11. High duties and other barriers to trade with the independent ports of Montevideo and Buenos Aires are described in the letters of Stephen Girard's supercargos

men of the revolutionary *Junta* intimated to him that they intended to declare independence as soon as a revolutionary Congress should meet.[12]

Like most North American representatives after him during this period, Poinsett was an advocate of the revolution. He urged the sending of arms and ammunition from the United States; and he asked in vain for more positive instructions anticipating a declaration of independence, with a letter of credence addressed from the President of the United States to the governments of Buenos Aires, Chile, and Bogotá, all of which he prophesied would become independent.[13] Such credence would have been a recognition forthwith of independence. In fact, President Madison came very close to such a recognition when Secretary of State James Monroe later (April 13, 1811) commissioned Poinsett as consul general of the United States to Buenos Aires, Chile, and Peru, without yet even knowing whether those countries had declared their independence.

It seems quite obvious that Poinsett, who had advised his government to furnish arms to the revolted provinces of the Plata region,

---

in 1810. J. B. McMaster, *The Life and Times of Stephen Girard, Mariner and Merchant* (Philadelphia, 1918), 2, 146–71.

12. Poinsett's first preoccupation in Buenos Aires was Great Britain. He wrote home that the revolutionary groups feared and at the same time courted Great Britain. British policy he sensed as distinctly favorable to them, but prevented by the alliance with Spain from openly encouraging a movement for independence. We know from the investigations of erudite modern scholars (W. S. Robertson and C. K. Webster) that the American agent had sensed the situation not far from correctly. British policy was clearly defined after the alliance with the Spanish national *Junta* against Napoleon: it was to make every effort, by diplomatic suasion or by outright peaceful mediation, to induce the colonies to reconciliation with the mother country, in order that they might maintain relations of commerce, friendship, and communication of succors to Spain in the war against Napoleon. At the same time, Great Britain insisted on profiting by the new trade relations with the Spanish colonies, whose commerce to foreign nations had been opened by the revolt—this trade was a useful sustenance to the British while fighting for the liberation of Spain from the mighty oppressor.

Poinsett discerned a possibility of substituting the influence of the United States for that of Great Britain if the provinces could be brought to declare their independence before the termination of Anglo-Spanish intimacy, which, of course, had resulted from the alliance against Napoleon's invasion of the Peninsula.

13. Dorothy M. Parton, *The Diplomatic Career of Joel Roberts Poinsett* (Catholic University of Washington, 1934), p. 16. Dr. Parton has used the Poinsett Papers in the Historical Society of Pennsylvania, material not now in the State Department. J. Fred Rippy, *Joel R. Poinsett, Versatile American* (Duke University Press, 1935), used and cited the same documents.

must also have encouraged the revolutionists to seek arms and munitions in the United States, as the United States formerly had done in France, and as the Venezuelan agents had recently been doing in Philadelphia.[14] His arrival and suggestions undoubtedly helped to bring about the first mission from Buenos Aires to the United States, but he did not inspire the first appeal to Washington. Shortly before the North American's arrival, the *Junta* had addressed a communication to President Madison:

> The marked proofs which your Excellency has given of your Beneficence and magnanimity towards the Province of Caracas are irrefragable testimonies of the lively Interest which your Excellency takes in the Rights of Humanity. In truth, none are more likely to respect them in others than those who have had the misfortune to see them outraged towards themselves. The perfect conformity of our Political Situation, and of the causes of it, with that of the Noble Caraquans, gives us an equal Right to hope that it will be agreeable to your Excellency, that the United States should tighten with the Provinces on the Rio la Plata the common chain of Nations, by a Cordiality more firm and expressive.[15]

The date of this missive is February 11, 1811. Poinsett landed at Buenos Aires two days later.[16] Less than five months after Poinsett's

14. Poinsett's biographers do not call attention to the fact that voluminous portions of his dispatches remain in cipher, unreadable to date. We may assume that these undeciphered passages are the most important. An allusion in an unciphered letter of June 29, 1811, gives us evidence that he was familiar with the plans and purpose of a mission from Buenos Aires even before the instructions for the same were written: "Sir, this letter will be delivered to you by Don Diego de Saavedra and Don Pedro de Aguirre whose business I mentioned to you in my letter of the 16th of May." Poinsett Papers, *1*, 86. Historical Society of Pennsylvania. The letter of May 16th seems to be missing. Upon his return, Poinsett got his dispatches out of the Department of State and they are now in the Historical Society of Pennsylvania. There are memoranda in the Library of Congress, mostly travel notes.

15. Manning, *1*, 319.

16. Sir, I landed this morning from Rio de Janeiro, and hearing that an American vessel will sail this afternoon for Philadelphia, and being desirous of giving the government all the information I could obtain in so short a time, I waited upon John Larrea, one of the members of the *Junta,* and was by him immediately presented to the *Junta* who were then in sitting. They at once objected to the form of the commission, "it was not directed to them nor signed by the President." I explained to them that it was similar to the commission held by an agent at Havana, and that it bore on the face of it the reasons why it had not been more explicitly worded. They then directed me to enclose my commission in a note to the *Junta* and that I should immediately know their

arrival at Buenos Aires, namely, on June 5, 1811, the Provisional Governing Council (*Junta Gubernativa*) of the United Provinces of the Río de la Plata of South America, "in the name of Ferdinand VII, King of Spain and the Indies," issued full powers, accompanied by detailed instructions, to Don Diego de Saavedra (son of the President of the *Junta*) and Don Pedro de Aguirre (a merchant of Buenos Aires), commissioned to purchase arms in the United States. Saavedra and Aguirre had powers to pledge the public funds of the new government for the purchase of the following articles: 2,000 pairs of pistols of one-ounce caliber; 4,000 carbines, or short cavalry arms with bayonets (*tercerolas*); 8,000 swords; 10,000 guns with cartridges; 1,000,000 flints for the carbines and pistols; to be paid for in Buenos Aires on the presentation of proper documents from the two agents stating that the articles had been bought and shipped on the account and risk of the government. In addition to this, Aguirre and Saavedra had authority to bind the government in the most solemn and legal manner for the payment of up to 30,000 additional guns, carbines, and pistols, when delivered on account and risk of the sellers at Buenos Aires.[17]

Separate instructions confirmed the purposes of the full powers and provided 20,000 pesos for the expenses of their mission. If possible

---

determination. I enclose a copy of their note and my answer by which you will see that they have recognized me as agent for the commerce of the United States . . . it is their determination to declare themselves independent of the mother country the instant they are attacked; in short, all their measures tend to that end . . .

Moreno, a member of the *Junta*, embarked today for London. I do not yet know the object of his mission. I am just informed by a member of the *Junta* that they had written to the President some days previous to my arrival, and that their despatches will be on board the vessel expected to sail this evening.

Joel R. Poinsett to [the Secretary of State], Buenos Aires, Feb. 13, 1811. Poinsett Papers, *1*, 31. Historical Society of Pennsylvania.

The *Junta* in its letter to Madison of February 13, 1811, stated: "Don Josef R Poinsetts [sic] has just presented himself to this *Junta* with a credential signed by the Secy (of State) to be accredited as commercial agent of the U States in this America and this government conformably to the cordial and friendly intentions which it made known to Y E in its official Letter dated yesterday [sic] has decreed his admission to the full exercise of his agency, which it considers as a preliminary to the Treaties between Nation and Nation which will be formed to point out the Rules of a permanent Commerce and of the greatest amity and Union between the two States." Manning, *1*, 320–21.

17. Full powers to Diego de Saavedra and Juan Pedro de Aguirre from "La Junta Provisional gubernativa de las Provincias del Río de la Plata en la América del Sur a nombre del Sr. Don Fernando VII, Rey de España y de la Indias," Buenos Aires, June 5, 1811. A.G.N., S1–A2–A4, No. 9.

they were to ship their procurements on a packet to Buenos Aires or Ensenada de Barragán (a port 40 miles down the estuary from Buenos Aires) or even to Montevideo. In case of the outbreak of war between the United States and Great Britain [18] and the consequent risk of delay to the expedition, they were to avail themselves of letters-patent to fit out a ship to get the purchases to a home port. In addition to procuring the munitions they had instructions to endeavor to send cannon-makers and gunsmiths, with tools and models, for whose services they might promise 3,000 pesos each annually, and also to get apparatus for making gunflints.

A particular injunction of the instructions was not to compromise the government of the United States or any other government. This would require the greatest secrecy as to their names and operations, and the pseudonyms of José Cabrera and Pedro López, with passports accordingly, were provided ready-made for the agents, who represented themselves to be traveling in pursuit of their own commercial business—like our Silas Deane in France in 1776. For delivery to the President they carried a formal letter from the *Junta* frankly revealing their real names and purposes,[19] and recommending the persons of the commissioners and the purpose of the mission, "without a doubt that your Excellency's kindness will generously lend itself to the views and desires of this Government, which will be extremely pleased to comply with what it may have the honor to be asked at any time by your nation." [20]

The envoys left the Plata estuary one of the last days of July for New York on board the cutter *Tigre,* belonging to William G. Miller, a North American trader who soon, on Poinsett's recommendation, was appointed consul of the United States at Buenos Aires. The ship was provided, at the connivance of the revolutionary government, with both Spanish and English papers and flags. Three weeks out from the Plata, they were obliged to put into Río de Janeiro because of damage to their ship by a storm. A dispute with the captain over the expenses of repairs ended by his appropriating 1,043 pesos from their limited funds. One hundred and four days out from Río, they arrived at

18. It is not unlikely that Poinsett may have mentioned this possibility, for he longed to serve his country in such a war.

19. Instrucciones que la Junta Provisional Gubernativa de las Provincias del Río de la Plata en la América del Sur comunica a Dn. Diego de Saavedra y Don Pedro de Aguirre sobre lo que deberan observar en el desempeño de su comisión para la compra de armas y la remisión a esta de los Estados Unidos del Norte, Buenos Aires, junio 5, 1811. A.G.N., S1–A2–A4, No. 9.

20. Manning, *1,* 321.

Philadelphia, in October 1811.[21] At that time commerce was languish-
ing under the nonintercourse measures, and money was tight, at least
for unknown rebel agents from the remote Río de la Plata, with little
cash in hand. They could find no merchant interested in such "speculations" as they proposed. After a delay at Philadelphia, due to the
illness of Aguirre, they reached Washington late in October,[22] and
received an appointment (we do not know what day) for the delivery
of their communications.

James Monroe was now President Madison's Secretary of State. This
"minister" asked the envoys for detailed statements about the political
and economic condition of their country, questions to which they responded with alacrity. They recorded that "two days later" the Secretary assured them in the name of the President "that the United States
of the North would be glad to see the emancipation of their brother
peoples of the South under a liberal constitution, and that he believed
they would continue their glorious career of liberty despite the presence of some risks which perseverance would overcome; that we could
go [*correr*] about the land, and export freely such succors [*auxilios*]
as we pleased, and that desirous of assisting us this [executive] branch
of the Government would for its part dissemble knowledge of any contracts we had made with munitions makers; that assistance could not
go any further than this, since we couldn't be considered otherwise
than one of Spain's old provinces; but if there were anything else in
which the Government could serve us, it would do so with pleasure.
At the same time, Mr. Monroe gave us important warnings and begged
us to let him know ahead of time of our departure." [23]

21. Aguirre to the Junta Gubernativa, Philadelphia, Oct. 19, 1811. A.G.N., S1–
A2–A4, No. 9.

22. José Antonio Cabrera y Pedro López al Secretario Don Jaime Monroe, Georgetown, Oct. 25, 1811. National Archives (Washington) Division of State Department
Archives, series Argentine Republic, Notes, Vol. I, part 1. Feb. 11, 1811 to Oct. 27,
1838.

Luis de Onís, the unrecognized Spanish minister in Washington, noted the presence of suspicious persons, at first believed to be from Cuba, in his dispatches of
Nov. 3, and Nov. 15, 1811 (no. 199), and identifies them as López and Cabrera of
Buenos Aires in his no. 200 of Nov. 20, 1811. They had then returned to Philadelphia
from Washington, "little satisfied apparently with the ostensible reception which
they got from the American Government, although it is very likely that they were
privately received with the sympathy manifested by the President in his speech at
the opening of Congress. They are now in that city and have at their disposal a
considerable sum of gold and silver, which they brought with them from Buenos
Ayres for the objects of their mission, among others the purchase of arms and of
ships to arm." A.H.N., Estado 5637 (Library of Congress facsimiles).

23. Saavedra and Aguirre to the Junta Gubernativa, Philadelphia, Nov. 11, 1811.

The friendly welcome to Saavedra and Aguirre in Washington by President Madison himself contrasts to the chilly reception in London given to Irigoyen by Wellesley, the British Secretary of Foreign Affairs.

The commissioners immediately placed orders for munitions for as much money as they had, with Messrs. Miller and Van Beuren of Philadelphia.[24] Their efforts to order more supplies on credit were unavailing, despite their concert with Telésforo de Orea, the agent in the United States of the Venezuelan government. Manuel Torres, a Venezuelan revolutionist exile of Spanish birth, who had been living in the United States since 1796,[25] the same who in 1822 was to be recognized as the first minister of Venezuela to the United States, suggested that the Provinces of the Plata, and Venezuela, jointly pledge their credit for additional purchases, and also that the United States government might hasten the fulfillment of the purchases by advancing from its own arsenals a delivery of arms, to be replaced out of contracts made by the representatives of Venezuela and Buenos Aires with some reliable dealer.[26] Orea lent himself to the suggestion. Torres then introduced Stephen Girard of Philadelphia to the *porteños* as a substantial merchant in whom the United States might place sufficient confidence to warrant such an operation. They met Girard in Philadelphia, November 30, 1811, and proposed the purchase and shipping without delay against the joint (one-third Venezuelan and two-thirds Argentinian) credit of the "governments" of at least 20,000 muskets and bayonets for the defense of the United Provinces of La Plata and the Kingdom of Chile [*sic*]—"in accordance with the views and desires of their government and in accordance also with the conference which they have had with the envoy of Venezuela, Don Telésforo de Orea." They were anxious to order more muskets, flints, pistols, swords, sabers, etc., as fast as they could be manufactured.

Madison and Monroe dallied with the idea of doing for the United Provinces of the Plata just what the French government had done for

---

A.G.N., S1–A2–A4, No. 9. They do not say whether their communications with Monroe were oral interviews or in writing, but both the context of the dispatches and the circumstances make for the presumption of oral interviews. Dates of the interviews are not recorded.

24. Saavedra and Aguirre to Messrs. Miller and Van Beuren, Philadelphia, Nov. 11, 1811. A.G.N., S1–A2–A4, No. 9.

25. Nicolás García Samudio, *Capítulos de Historia Diplomática* (Bogotá, 1925), p. 45.

26. Telésforo de Orea to José Antonio Cabrera and Pedro López, Washington, Nov. 25, 1811. A.H.N., Estado 5637 (Library of Congress facsimiles), enclosed in Onís's no. 206 to Bardaxi of Nov. 28, 1811. Onís intercepted the letter through the treachery of a postman.

the United States of North America in 1776–78: the extension of secret aid disguised as a commercial transaction. After a consultation with the Attorney General, William Pinkney, Saavedra, Aguirre, and Orea were summoned on the 7th of January 1812, for a conference with the Secretary of State. According to Saavedra and Aguirre, Monroe informed them "that the Government was disposed to sell them the arms, at regular prices, and to satisfy itself with the responsibility for these by the credit of a respectable merchant of the country, that it was moved to do this by its desire for our independence . . ." Elated, the commissioners left the interview requesting to be informed whether Stephen Girard would be acceptable as such a merchant. This information was never forthcoming.[27]

Girard himself was not unwilling to be the Rodrigue Hortalez and Company of North America in this new drama of emancipation, but he required the explicit approval and cooperation of the United States government. When, despite the continued importunities of the South American envoys, the Secretary of State refused to answer a very direct question on the subject, Girard dropped the matter.[28] President Madison would not play the role which Louis XVI's government had assumed toward the revolutionary British colonies in North America in 1776. For this decision there were good reasons of state and vital national interest. We shall not fail to note them presently.

The commissioners, then, had to content themselves with the purchase of such succors as their cash funds could cover; moreover, on January 26, 1812, they unexpectedly received instructions of October 3d not to do more.[29] They left for home as soon as possible on the

27. Saavedra and Aguirre to the Junta Gubernativa, Philadelphia, Feb. 16, 1812. A.G.N., S1–A2–A4, No. 9.

28. "Mr. Diego Saavedra and Mr. Pedro Aguirre, envoys from the Junta of Buenos Aires and Chili, have applied to me to purchase and to ship on account of their respective governments Twenty Thousand muskets with their Bayonettes. Although I am disposed to be serviceable to these gentlemen, yet I do not wish to contract with them, unless I am assured that the shipment alluded to will not be considered as unlawful or disagreeable to the President, etc., etc., of the United States, and that the Government will facilitate me the means of obtaining said muskets, etc., either by selling or lending them to me under such terms and conditions as will be judged reasonable." Girard to Monroe, Dec. 2, 1811. J. B. McMaster, *Life and Times of Stephen Girard*, 2, 168–71.

Saavedra and Aguirre in a note of Jan. 20, 1812, made one last attempt to persuade the government to sanction the proposed operation of Girard. National Archives (Washington) Division of State Department Archives, series Argentine Republic, Notes, *1*, part 1, folio 9.

29. Saavedra and Aguirre to the Junta Gubernativa, Philadelphia, Feb. 16, 1812.

Liberty frigate with 1,000 muskets with bayonets and 362,050 flints, which they brought safely home to the port of Ensenada de Barragán on May 14, 1812.[30]

"The liberality with which we have been considered by the government and inhabitants of the United States," they wrote to Monroe, when embarking from North America, "and their favorable disposition toward the cause we uphold remain graven in our gratitude and respect." [31]

The mission of Saavedra and Aguirre, coupled with the representation of their Venezuelan colleagues, did much to crystallize a policy for President Madison's government, naturally predisposed, as it was —and Jefferson's before him—in favor of the independence of Spain's revolted colonies. After his first interview with the Buenos Aires representatives, Secretary Monroe instructed the United States minister in Russia that "various considerations, which will readily suggest themselves to you, have induced this Government to look with a favorable eye to a Revolution which is now taking place in South America," although a *formal* recognition by the United States of a minister from

A.G.N., S1–A2–A4, No. 9. The instructions may have been due to the crushing defeat sustained by the revolutionists at the Desaguadero, the news of which already had greatly dismayed Saavedra and Aguirre.

30. Aguirre and Saavedra to Supremo Gobierno [of Buenos Aires] and Manuel de Salas to same, Ensenada de Barragán, May 14, 1812. A.G.N., S1–A2–A4, No. 9. These arms must have played a part in the early defense of the Plata region against reconquest.

The commissioners presented to their government on May 19th papers relating to their mission, together with their accounts for approval. The accounts showed expenditures of 29,946 pesos and receipts from the government of 20,000 pesos. An endorsement shows that these accounts were approved, except for two items which were deducted from payment of the balance claimed by Aguirre and Saavedra: 1,043 pesos for money taken by the captain of their boat in Río de Janeiro for repairs, and 4,664 pesos representing a protested note drawn on Mr. Allen of Philadelphia (which note they had apparently purchased on their departure from Buenos Aires) by William Miller on whose ship they had originally sailed from their native land.

As the reader has perceived, the principal source for the first Argentine mission to the United States, as for the others described in this article, consists of such of their papers as remain in the Archivo General de la Nación, in Buenos Aires. José Juan Biedma first described the mission, with some small inaccuracies and omissions, in his brochure *Los Estados Unidos y la independencia Argentina* (Buenos Aires, Imp., Lit. y Encuadernación de G. Kraft, Bartolomé Mitre 724, 1906). He does not cite the source of his information, but it was apparently these same documents now in the Archivo General de la Nación.

31. Saavedra and Aguirre to James Monroe, Secretary of State. National Archives (Washington) Division of State Department Archives, series Argentine Republic, Notes, *1*, pt. 1, 10.

either of the revolted colonies had not been made, "nor has it been urged." [32] To the American minister in France he wrote that "although such recognition in France, England, Denmark and Russia in form has not been made, yet a very friendly and conciliatory answer has been given to them. They have also been informed that the Ministers of the United States in Europe, will be instructed to avail themselves of suitable opportunities to promote their recognition by other powers. You will not fail to attend to this object, which is thought to be equally due to the just claims of our Southern Brethren, to which the United States cannot be indifferent, and to the best interests of this country." [33]

The statement that "Ministers" of Venezuela and Buenos Aires had not been received *formally* implies that they had nevertheless been received, and befriended, informally. The policy pursued by Madison and Monroe in these first contacts with Spain's revolted colonies was tantamount to an unquestionable recognition of belligerency and a very benevolent neutrality. Nevertheless, the South American envoys enjoyed in the United States no more privileges than did the Spanish representative, Luis de Onís, who was not formally received by the United States at this time as minister, although Spanish consuls continued their functions and through them Onís was able to address the government. The United States quite properly had avoided involvement in the contentions of Spanish civil and international strife in Europe, and with equal propriety it had suspended diplomatic relations pending the emergence of a settled and unquestioned government in Spain. Onís meanwhile busied himself buying arms and munitions for the use of Spain against Napoleon in the Peninsula and for the suppression of rebellion in America, and endeavored to frustrate the missions of the revolted provinces to the United States. The fact that in 1811 and 1812 the agents of the colonies were informally re-

32. To John Quincy Adams, Minister to Russia, Nov. 23, 1811. Manning, *1*, 12. It was not accurate to say that formal recognition had not been urged. On Nov. 6, 1811, Orea had delivered to Monroe a copy of the Venezuelan declaration of independence, and requested the recognition of the Confederation of Venezuela as a "free and independent nation," and himself as "agent extraordinary" of that government. On Nov. 27, 1811, in his instructions to the Minister in France (Joel Barlow) cited immediately below, Monroe states that the Venezuelans had "proposed to the President the recognition of their independence and reception of a minister from them." "Documentos relacionados con las misiones de Juan Vicente Bolívar y Telésforo Orea á Washington," *Boletín de la Academia Nacional de Historia* (Caracas), *18* (Oct.–Dec., 1935), 728.

33. To Joel Barlow, Minister to France, Nov. 27, 1811. Manning, *1*, 12.

ceived by the government when Onís was not, that their belligerency was recognized, and that their cause enjoyed the encouragement and assistance of the diplomacy of the United States, speaks for itself, much in contrast with the attitude of Great Britain. If anything more in the way of encouragement and friendly sentiments need have been looked for, short of formal recognition of the independence of these two Spanish provinces (which had not yet themselves declared their independence), it could have been discerned in the expressions of President Madison's message to Congress of November 5, 1811, in which he referred sympathetically to the "scenes" developing in the great "communities" which occupied the southern portion of "our own hemisphere" and pronounced it a national duty to take a "deep interest" in their destinies.[34]

What were the "interests of this country" which made the United States anxious to promote the recognition of the provinces of Venezuela and of Buenos Aires, while still quite properly withholding recognition from either of the contending regimes in Spain itself, where Napoleon and Wellington were locked in their great military duel?

These interests were undoubtedly bound up in the status of Florida and, to a lesser degree, in the disputed borderlands of the Louisiana purchase, that is, Texas; and ultimately in the destiny of Cuba.[35] Less vitally, they were related, as were British interests, to the maintenance

34. The House of Representatives referred the message, together with a copy of the recent Venezuelan declaration of independence, to a special committee of the House of Representatives, which reported (Dec. 10, 1811) a joint resolution which never came to a vote: that the House beheld "with friendly interest, *the establishment of independent sovereignties* by the Spanish provinces in America, consequent upon the actual state of the monarchy to which they belonged; that, as neighbors and inhabitants of the same hemisphere," the United States felt a "great solicitude for their welfare," that when the provinces had attained "the condition of nations, by the *just* exercise of their rights," the Congress would join with the President to establish with them friendly relations and commercial intercourse as sovereign and independent states. Italics inserted. Manning, *1*, 13.

It is significant that Secretary Monroe went out of his way to cite this *proposed* resolution to Orea as evidence of interest of the United States in the cause, and to say that the President had received the Venezuelan declaration of independence "with the interest which so important an event was calculated to excite." W. S. Robertson, p. 255.

Passage of the resolution would have been equivocally close to a formal recognition of independence.

35. The most recent, avowedly polemical, account of Cuban-American relationships at this time is Herminio Portell-Vilá, *Historia de Cuba en sus relaciones con los Estados Unidos y España* (4 vols. Havana, 1938–41), *1*.

of an open trade with the revolted Spanish provinces. The immediate interest of President Madison and Secretary Monroe was Florida.

Madison and his predecessor Jefferson had long since been trying to drive home their imperfect claim to West Florida as a part of the Louisiana cession. The Mobile Act of 1804 had enabled the President to erect a customs district there, but Jefferson, while asserting this act of sovereignty on paper, had carefully avoided a real occupation of the disputed area. He had tried in vain to take advantage of the distresses of Napoleonic times in Europe to secure a recognition of American sovereignty over West Florida, or at least a cession or even a purchase. He had no luck. When the general insurrectionary movement, first against the new Napoleonic dynasty in Spain and then against Spanish sovereignty of any kind in America, showed itself in West Florida as well as in the other continental provinces of Spain, it seemed to present to Jefferson and Madison the opportunity which they had craved.

Jefferson had often said that Spain's strategy of inviting settlers from the United States into her borderlands, supposedly attracting them from their original allegiance, naturalizing them, and making buffer populations out of them, would peaceably solve the Florida question, because these people would remain unalterably American and ultimately gravitate into the republic. In 1810 Jefferson's successor seized this opportunity. He took advantage of, and even encouraged an insurrection of the inhabitants of the Baton Rouge district—preponderantly immigrants from the United States—who wanted annexation. When this happened, he proclaimed (October 27, 1810) the occupation by the United States, under its claim as a part of Louisiana, of all West Florida—from the Iberville to the Perdido Rivers. The actual act of occupation, however, left undisturbed the small Spanish garrison at Mobile, and thus avoided an open conflict with Spain. A remnant of Spanish authority hung by a thread in Mobile. Depressed by the odds against him, the Spanish Governor, Vicente Folch, had made a tentative offer, even before the occupation of Baton Rouge, to turn over his province to the United States in case he were not re-enforced by January 1, 1811 (an offer which he soon withdrew).

The first South American envoys, Juan Vicente Bolívar and Telésforo de Orea, had arrived from Venezuela in May of 1810, seeking recognition and alliance, precisely when Madison's administration was contemplating the interesting developments of an "independence movement" in West Florida. (The envoys from Buenos Aires, as we shall presently note, reached Washington in November 1811, just when

Secretary Monroe was deep in a similar intrigue for the revolution and occupation of East Florida.) It was well known that the example of Venezuela had stimulated insurrection in West Florida.[36] There was, therefore, every reason of self interest, as well as of sentiment, why the United States should receive in a kindly and stimulating way the envoys of republican revolutions in South America. To sympathize with a struggle for independence in South America was to encourage it profitably also in West Florida and presently in East Florida, perhaps even in Cuba.[37] There was little doubt that independence of the adjacent Spanish provinces would be followed by annexation, immediately in the case of West Florida already claimed as a part of the United States, probably soon in the case of East Florida for which the United States had been seeking to exchange its spoliation and and other claims against Spain; Jefferson hoped to take in Cuba, too, before the Napoleonic wars were over. Administration leaders sensed the import of British policy of keeping Spain's sovereignty intact in the New World in order not to weaken her as an ally in the Peninsula, and as a price for open trade with a colonial system hitherto closed to their shipping. Madison feared the possibility both of French influence in West Florida (where Napoleon had sent an agent) and of British intrusion there by way of protection. He did not know that the French minister at Washington, Turreau, had advised his government in 1808 to occupy both Floridas as a means of curbing the United States.[38] British influence was the more feared, there, because of the strategic relationship of Florida to the imminent war with Great Britain.

The British *chargé* at Washington, John Philip Morier, prompted by the unrecognized Spanish envoy, Onís, had protested formally to the United States at the occupation of West Florida.[39] Protest by the representative of a government which was already stirring the Indians of the northwestern territory to war against the United States made Madison only more eager to control Florida, a possible avenue of British attack against the Southwest, and a possible area of conquest

36. I. J. Cox, *The West Florida Question* (Johns Hopkins Press, 1918).

37. From June to Nov. 1811, William Shaler (see above, p. 306) was in Cuba sounding out Creole sentiment and even Spanish authorities on the possibility of annexation to the United States. Any conceivable chance for such a union was frustrated by a rising of Negroes early in 1812 and by the advent of war between the United States and Great Britain. Portell-Vilá, *1*, 166–78.

38. Portell-Vilá, *1*, 151.

39. Morier to Robert Smith, Dec. 15, 1810. Henry Adams, *History of the United States* (New York, 1890), *5*, 315.

from a British ally. The protest of the British *chargé* plus the offer of Folch prompted Madison to the historic special secret message to Congress, which resulted in the notable resolution and act of January 15, 1811.

The resolution recorded the famous "no-transfer" principle, since firmly embedded in the foreign policy of the United States and so closely associated with the Monroe Doctrine as not to be distinguished from it: "considering the influence which the destiny of the territory adjoining the southern border of the United States may have upon their security, tranquillity and commerce, . . . the United States . . . cannot, without serious inquietude, see any part of the said territory pass into the hands of any foreign power." The accompanying act authorized the President to take possession of all or any part of East Florida if an agreement to that effect should be reached with the "local authorities," "or in the event of an attempt to occupy the said territory, or any part thereof, by any foreign government," and to use the army and navy for that purpose.

At the passage of this act, the indignant British *chargé*, after concerting with Onís, counseled his government to occupy Pensacola and New Orleans and to incite a slave insurrection in the southern states of the United States.[40] Madison presumably did not know of this, either.

When the first envoys from Buenos Aires reached Washington in November 1811, Madison's government was engaged, through the intermediary of General George Mathews of Georgia, in covert intrigues with inhabitants of East Florida on the south bank of the St. Mary's River, where immigrants from the United States constituted a preponderating element in a very mixed and rough frontier population. In this way "local authorities" could be called into existence for the purpose of delivering the province over to occupation by the United States army or navy under the terms of the act of January 15, 1811. In Washington, Mathews appears to have received oral instructions from James Monroe to go down there and stir up a revolution like that of Baton Rouge. Military and naval forces had been ordered to the St. Mary's River where Mathews was diligently at work. Having no recorded instructions, this *agent provocateur* could be disavowed—as he later was—in case he should make a false step up the backstairs of Florida occupation, or in case his activities, secretly provoked, should become too seriously embarrassing to the United States government.

40. Portell-Vilá, *1*, 165. See also Onís to Pezuela, Oct. 26, 1812. A.H.N., Estado, leg. 5638.

It is quite understandable that the government and people, particularly of the southern states, looked on the revolution of South American patriots in a friendly light because of a natural affinity of republicanism; but Florida—and beyond Florida, Cuba—make it easy to understand why Madison's government looked with so "favorable an eye" on the revolution taking place in Spanish America, why it received the first envoys with all but formal recognition, why it desired to help promote the recognition by other powers of the independence of Venezuela and of Buenos Aires, even though the provinces of the Plata region, at least, had not yet declared their independence. The weaker Spain's power in America should become, because of her distresses in Europe, the greater would be the advantage of the United States, the closer the republic of the North would be to a definitive and peaceful solution of the Florida Question, and thus to a rounding out of the nation's coastline by the addition of a contiguous old Spanish province, never overlooking the possibility, at least, of eventually annexing the island of Cuba.

II

The War of 1812–15 between the United States and Great Britain interrupted the procession of missions from Buenos Aires to Washington.[41] During the war the United States was desperately busy, at first striving to conquer Canada, and then trying to defend its own territory. It was no longer possible for foreign rebel agents to buy

41. In the Archivo General de la Nación, S1–S2–A4, No. 9, is an unexecuted commission, dated Feb. 7, 1812, to Alvarez Fonte for a mission to the United States never realized "por las sospechas prudentes que sobrevinieron respecto del Extranjero con quien hubo de efectuarse por los Estados Unidos." The foreigner whose good faith was thus suspected at the last moment was one George Ducht, a citizen of the United States, Ducht having agreed, upon liberal terms and every sign of good faith, to facilitate the procurance of arms and munitions. The government of the Provinces, unable to secure credit abroad, prepared to send, upon only thirty hours' notice, Don Antonio Alvarez de Fonte to New York, under strictest secrecy and the pseudonym of "Tom Jones" with 40,000 *pesos de plata* and 9 *tejos de oro* for the purchase of rifles, knapsacks, and cavalry sabers. If later he could arrange credit, he was to contract for more, and to persuade artificers (gunsmiths, swordsmiths, potters, papermakers, printers, cotton and linen spinners and weavers, and mineralogists) to emigrate to Buenos Aires with families, in return for land grants and wages of 60 to 90 pesos [a month?]. The detailed instructions to Fonte, of 17 articles, were never acted on. There are in the *expediente* the notes for a draft of a communication to the Congress of the United States, dated Feb. 12, 1812, which, roughly translated, reads: "Let that republic be reminded of the kindness shown to the Caracans and let it see the equal claims of our own government to promises of protection."

munitions, even if they could get through the British blockade.[42] Such supplies were needed for the defense of the country.

The War of 1812 proved no more fruitful on the southern frontier than to the north. As expected, British forces occupied East Florida,

42. There were, nevertheless, some communications received from Buenos Aires at Washington during the war. Manuel Moreno addressed the President of the United States, from the "Fortaleza de Buenos Aires," July 21, 1813, enclosing certain printed matter to show the state of public affairs in the United Provinces of the Río de la Plata, and the noble efforts and sacrifices with which the inhabitants consecrate themselves for their liberty in common with that of the American continent. National Archives (Washington) Division of State Department Archives, series Argentine Republic, Notes, *1*, pt. 1, 12.

The Supreme Director of the United Provinces of the Río de la Plata, Gervasio Antonio de Posadas, addressed two letters to President Madison, March 9, 1814, translations of which are printed in Manning, *1*, 334. In the first, Posadas declared: "The United Provinces of Río de la Plata aspire to a close and intimate relation with the United States; and it would give me a pleasure if you, according to the known generosity of your character, would permit me to communicate to them the wishes of my countrymen. It gives me great pleasure to have the present opportunity of communicating to you my respects, and most anxious solicitude for a friendly alliance." In the second letter, he says: "The victories of the North, which obliged France to cease oppressing Spain, may enable our enemies, with the assistance of Great Britain, to injure our cause, if some powerful arm does not volunteer her aid. Though humanity and justice are interested in the sacred cause defended by South America, four years of experience have taught this people, that it is not for the interest of the Potentates of Europe to favor the independence of the colonies. Hitherto the greatness of the powers of Europe has been founded on our degradation. Perhaps the preponderance we should give to your influence in the commercial world has not a little influence. It is on you we place our present hopes, who have the happiness to govern the only free people in the world, whose philosophic and patriotic sentiments we are ambitious to imitate. I am sensible the war, in which you are at present engaged, will prevent your giving us that immediate aid that would end our troubles. The people of this country can as yet support their cause with dignity, could they procure a supply of arms and ammunitions. Your Excellency cannot fail of being able to afford us these supplies; and our prompt and ready payment cannot be doubted. Your Excellency may be assured that the Provinces of Río de la Plata will not be ungrateful for such a relief, and will be ready to engage in any treaties of commerce that will be advantageous to the United States. The interest that the inhabitants of said States have generally felt for the success of our cause, convinces me of the happy result of this request."

In the Archivo General de la Nación, in Buenos Aires, there is a draft of a letter of May 30, 1815, to the President of the United States, requesting court action favorable to the release of certain property belonging to the government of Buenos Aires, "also American" (*como Americano también*), in the custody of Manuel Pinto, who was on a British ship, the *Nereide*, when it was captured in Dec. 1813, by an American privateer. The articles were described as "necessary to sustain with honor the common cause of all peoples." I have found no evidence to show that a corresponding document was delivered to its addressee, but a letter from Pinto, dated

at Pensacola, as a base for invasion of the United States. General Andrew Jackson dislodged them (November 8, 1814) after his successful campaign against the Creek Indians, but he had to hurry away to defend New Orleans from Pakenham's invasion. On the eastern extremity of the frontier with East Florida, the military and naval forces of the United States before the outbreak of the war had occupied Amelia Island, in the mouth of the St. Mary's River, taking it over from the "local authorities" *á la Baton Rouge,* according to the terms of the Act of January 15, 1811. After an abortive campaign to extend the occupation to St. Augustine, the invaders retired to Amelia Island. It was deemed expedient to disavow the machinations of General Mathews, rather than make a formal enemy of Spain. Amelia Island itself was evacuated May 16, 1813, in order to be able to present a fairer front at the peace negotiations expected to be conducted under Russian mediation.[43] Throughout the remaining months of the war it afforded a nest to smugglers through whom American citizens illegally traded with the enemy. So the war ended with East Florida clear of American troops, and West Florida formally annexed, despite Spanish protests, to the territory of Mississippi and the State of Louisiana. The fond expectations of the Southern Expansionists to take East Florida from Britain's ally, in any war with Great Britain, had been frustrated.

Before peace had been re-established in the United States in 1815, Wellington's major military efforts in Spain and elsewhere had been completely successful. Napoleon had been driven out of the Peninsula; Ferdinand VII had been brought back to his throne; and England, apparently with a tacit understanding that she would still carry on

London, Aug. 10, 1815, says that he has won his claim for the release of the "neutral goods" upon appeal to the Supreme Court of the United States—the celebrated case of the *Nereide.* Instructions to Pinto direct him to concert with Saavedra (newly appointed agent to London) for the use of the funds forthcoming from the United States after the award of this claim.

43. "You know that to take by force any place in the possession of another nation, whatever our claim to that place may be, is war; and you must be aware that both Russia and Great Britain will feel disposed, if not to support the pretentions of Spain against us, at least to take part against the aggressor." Gallatin to Monroe, May 2, 1813, quoted by Julius W. Pratt, *Expansionists of 1812* (New York, 1925), p. 236. Every student of the subject remains a debtor to Professor Pratt's penetrating work, as well as to the ironic chapters in Henry Adams, *History of the United States During the Administrations of Jefferson and Madison* (New York, 1889–90), these among a voluminous literature. Alfred Hasbrouck has described the military features of this episode, and has presented a map, in "Our Undeclared War with Spain," in *Jour. Am. Military Hist. Foundation,* 2 (Fall, 1938), 115–26.

the trade opened with the colonies during their insurrection,[44] had made a convention with the restored Bourbon monarch to take the most effectual measures to prevent her subjects from furnishing the rebels in Spanish America with military supplies.[45] Freed from pressure in Europe, Ferdinand's forces now suffocated one after another the rebel governments throughout his vast continental domains in Mexico, Central America, northern South America, and the Pacific Coast of that continent. At the beginning of the year 1816, monarchical authority had been restored everywhere except in the provinces of the Río de la Plata, which throughout the Peninsular War had professed, at least in words, allegiance to Ferdinand VII, fondly expecting that he would never be restored to the throne. It was in these first months of 1816 that the great San Martín was drilling his small army in the Cuyo, on the western frontier of the present Argentine, secretly projecting his immortal campaign over the passes of the Andes for the liberation of Chile. At Buenos Aires the stormy Chilean fugitive patriot, José Miguel Carrera, was dreaming of a similar exploit, a dreamer in exile without an army.

Failure to annex Florida during the convulsion in the Spanish peninsula and its repercussion in the Spanish colonies, the subsequent liberation of Spain, the restoration of the Bourbons, the collapse of emancipation over such a great part of America, the reaffirmation of the Anglo-Spanish alliance with the restored monarchy, peace in Europe, and the proclamation of the Holy Alliance; all this put the Florida Question and relations between the United States and Spain in a new light when diplomatic relations were re-established, December 19, 1815, by the reception of Luis de Onís as minister of Ferdinand VII. For one thing, political conditions in Spain were now definitely stabilized, and there was no longer any reason for not resuming diplomatic relations by a recognition of the monarchical regime. Second, Spain's demonstration of force in America and her allies in Europe gave tone to her representations against assistance to her rebelled sub-

---

44. W. S. Robertson, p. 264.

45. Additional articles, of Aug. 28, 1814, to the Anglo-Spanish treaty of alliance of July 5, 1814. In the treaty of alliance it was agreed, pending the formulation without delay of a definitive treaty of commerce, and in the case of foreign nations being permitted to trade with Spanish-American colonies, that British subjects should be admitted to trade in those colonies on the basis of the most-favored and privileged nation. *De facto* British trade continued with the Spanish provinces but British diplomacy was not able to insert into a formal treaty the right to trade with the Spanish colonies. Cf. Jerónimo Becker, *Historia de las relaciones exteriores de España durante el siglo XIX* (Madrid, 1924), *1*, 332–44.

jects in America, or the recognition or encouragement of their cause, even informally as Madison and Monroe had been prone to do in 1811. President Madison formally proclaimed (September 1, 1815) the neutrality of the United States in the war between Spain and her revolted colonies, and Onís was now entitled to satisfaction for any violation of the law of neutrality by the government to which he was accredited. "Unequivocal neutrality," [46] therefore, became the order of the day, and the neutrality laws were amended by the Acts of 1817 and 1818, specifically applying to "colonies," "provinces" or "people" (i.e., the revolted South American communities), as well as to "princes" and "states." Neutrality between the belligerents, of course, did not prohibit (as had been forbidden by the Anglo-Spanish alliance) trade in contraband to either, subject to interception by the enemy. It would, however, forbid extending the hand of annexation to the "local authorities" of adjacent Spanish provinces revolted against their sovereign, like Florida in 1811. Nevertheless, Florida in 1815–21 remained the principal object of the administration's diplomacy, to be acquired in diplomatic negotiations between the United States and Spain, without the use of force.

Until the signature by John Quincy Adams and Luis de Onís of the Transcontinental Treaty of February 22, 1819, and after that until its ratification exactly two years later, the question of the independence of the revolted Spanish provinces and the Florida Question served as counter and foil in a diplomatic duel of continental stakes between the Old World and the New. It began in 1817 when Richard Rush, Acting Secretary of State, refused to entertain Onís's protests over violations of neutrality unless he would negotiate for the cession of Florida and a new boundary line west of the Mississippi.[47] Spain, on her part, tried to make the progress of the Florida negotiations contingent upon nonrecognition by the United States of Buenos Aires and other revolted provinces. The United States in effect threatened Spain with their recognition if she did not yield, but was cautious not to follow up the threat until Florida was safely in the bag. Spain, retreating before President Monroe and his able successor as Secretary of State, the redoubtable John Quincy Adams, appealed to Europe for help. Not until they were sure that there would be no real help from

46. "The part pursued by the Government of the United-States in this contest, has been unequivocal Neutrality." Secretary J. Q. Adams to G. W. Erving, Minister to Spain, Washington, April 20, 1818. Manning, *1*, 61.

47. Richard Rush to Luis de Onís, Department of State, April 20, 1817. *Annals of Congress*, 15th Cong., 1st Sess., *2*, 1931.

Europe did Monroe and Adams push home the charge, by permitting and resolutely justifying, if they did not actually inspire, General Andrew Jackson's punitive pursuit in 1818 of the Seminole Indians over the frontier to their base in Florida; this foreshadowed a forceful occupation of a defenseless and anarchical province if Spain did not relinquish it by negotiation. In 1819 Onís signed away Florida and accepted a fixed boundary from the Gulf of Mexico to the Pacific Ocean, at least saving Texas for his master, but the King delayed ratification of the treaty for two years in an effort to postpone recognition by the United States of the new states to the south.

During this diplomatic duel public sympathy warmed toward brother republican peoples struggling, as the people of the United States themselves had struggled only a generation before, to throw off another yoke of European sovereignty in the New World. In the battle of propaganda, which Onís declared in the press, the agents from South America got the better of it. The voice of the North American people, which had been inarticulate amidst the issues with Great Britain before 1812, now swelled in favor of recognition. New nationalists, with presidential aspirations, like Henry Clay, sensed its import and became its champion.[48] They wanted recognition of the new Hispanic states first, and were sure that Florida would follow easily into the sovereignty of the United States anyway. The President and his Cabinet at times inclined to yield to this pressure for immediate recognition. John Quincy Adams, no less sympathetic to the patriotic cause and certainly realizing its significance for the whole American world, persuaded the administration to go slow, first to secure the interests of the United States, and if possible to avoid war with Spain, perhaps with Europe, too.

The first mission from Buenos Aires after the return of peace in the United States was that of Thomas Taylor, a citizen of the United States who had embarked on a career of privateering under the flag of the United Provinces.[49] He came to fit out privateers. He was provided with a letter of introduction to the President from General Ignacio Alvarez, then the Supreme Chief of the United Provinces. Taylor succeeded in preparing, under the guise of American merchant ships, two vessels, which were armed as privateers after leaving port, and had remarkably successful voyages. In the Archivo General de la Nación at Buenos Aires there is only one letter from Taylor about

48. Griffin, p. 134.
49. Lewis Winkler Bealer, *Los Corsarios de Buenos Aires, 1815–1821, Publicaciones del Instituto de Investigaciones Históricas,* No. 72 (Buenos Aires, 1937).

this mission, of February 8, 1816. It shows, first, that it had the official support and direction of the government of the United Provinces, and second, that Taylor was well pleased with his contacts in the United States at this time.[50]

Taylor went back to the United States as a fellow passenger [51] with the next significant visitor from the far south, the Chilean exile, José Miguel Carrera, who came on his famous self-sustained mission, supported by his own wits and contrivances, to collect arms and to recruit an expedition for the liberation of Chile. The three Carrera brothers were among the remnants of Chilean patriots, including Bernardo O'Higgins, whom the victorious Spanish royalists had driven eastward through the Andes in November 1814. Of these refugees in Mendoza, General San Martín selected the more reliable O'Higgins for Chilean collaborator in his own grand strategy for the liberation of that country. The presence of the Carreras and their rival ambitions interfered with San Martín's own plans. Presently they found themselves under military surveillance and expelled from the Cuyo frontier to Buenos Aires. From the recent months of comradeship with Joel Poinsett [52] in the unsuccessful insurrection in Chile, José Miguel Carrera, like most revolutionists in South America, had shaped a glowing image of the United States as a land of liberty and of help for freedom. He had pictured asylums of refuge there and the outfitting

50. Tomás Taylor al Exmo. Supmo. Director de las Provincias de Río de la Plata, Philadelphia, Feb. 8, 1816. A.G.N., S1–A2–A4, No. 9.
I have the honor to inform your excellency of my safe arrival in these Provinces [sic] on January 16 last, after a voyage of 64 days.
Immediately after disembarking at Annapolis, and eager to put into practice the object of my mission, I proceeded to Baltimore and then to this city. Though I have not yet seen the principal people who are to take part in the negotiation, I can assure your Excellency that, according to present prospects, your intentions will be completely fulfilled, since everything is working out well in this country, which knows our needs and the justice of our cause, and which takes an interest equal to ours in the fate of those peoples. Within a month a vessel ought to be perfectly armed for sea, and I believe I have to do no more than await the arrival of the frigate *Avispa* in these parts in order to go with all the rest. Your Excellency will be apprised of everything immediately.
The newspapers which I am sending will inform you of the latest events in Europe and of the setbacks (*contrastes*) which the system suffers in the points of revolution (*puntos rebolucionados*) in this part of America.
51. William Miller Collier y Guillermo Feliú Cruz, *La primera misión de los Estados Unidos de América en Chile* (Santiago de Chile, 1926), p. 190.
52. Poinsett had gone to Chile after a few months in Buenos Aires. His connection as a consul general did not prevent him from taking a personal part in the Chilean revolution.

of expeditions from the northern republic. After vainly attempting to organize in Buenos Aires a campaign of his own for the liberation of Chile, Don José Miguel pawned his wife's jewels and made his way to the United States on a returning gun-runner, relying on a fund of 5,000 pesos which Poinsett had taken for him to North America.

Carrera arrived at Annapolis, January 17, 1816, on the ship *Expedition,* owned by the Baltimore trader and outfitter of privateers, Henri Didier. Commodore Porter presented him to President Madison this same month of January, later to the Secretary of State, Monroe.[53] Carrera made the acquaintance of many other prominent people during his year's sojourn in the United States. He represented himself as plenipotentiary of the revolutionary government of Chile, and went through the form of securing from two surviving members of the expelled *Junta* of Santiago a mandate to that effect. The good Commodore Porter, then superintendent of the navy yard, and his discreet friend, Poinsett, helped him all they could. It is uncertain whether he ever cashed the 5,000 pesos previously taken for him to the United States by Poinsett, which seems to have been transferred to Halifax; but he managed to borrow $4,000 from John Skinner, postmaster of Baltimore, one of a group of men interested in speculations in munition shipments to South America and in the outfitting of privateers. With this start he managed, on promises to pay upon arrival, to recruit and outfit an expedition for the redemption of Chile, to be achieved by a march overland from Buenos Aires or by an expedition through the Straits of Magellan, as chance should dictate.

The ships, at least the *Clifton* and *Salvaje,* were furnished and loaded by Darcy and Didier of Baltimore. Carrera guaranteed payment for them by the government of Chile.

Carrera sailed from the United States December 5, 1816, on the ship *Clifton,* with some thirty young adventurers, mostly French and North American, followed by others in the brig *Salvaje* and the schooner *Davei.* When he arrived at the Río de la Plata, San Martín had already crossed the Andes and defeated the Spanish forces at Chacabuco, and O'Higgins was ruler of Chile. Carrera's still unpaid adventurers promptly cast their lot with the Buenos Aires government, which bought in the vessels and their supplies (except for the *Salvaje,* which eventually got away around the Horn and reached Chile in

53. Collier y Feliú Cruz, p. 202, notes that they called on Monroe, but did not find him in. A letter from Porter to Monroe three years later recalls that he once presented Carrera to him (Monroe). Porter to Monroe, January 3, 1819. Monroe Papers, XVII-2209, Library of Congress.

May 1817, where the supercargo, Henry Hill, disposed of the warlike stores to General San Martín),[54] and took the people into its service.[55] When Carrera plotted to get away from Buenos Aires for Chile with one of these ships, he was arrested and imprisoned.

Carrera's activities in the United States have never been considered one of the early missions from Buenos Aires which are the subject of this paper. The revolutionary government acknowledged no responsibility for his representations or his debts. Nevertheless, there is in the National Archives of the Argentine Republic the unsigned draft of a

54. Henry Hill, *Recollections of an Octogenerian* (Boston, D. Lothrop, 1884), p. 82.

The voyage of the *Salvaje* (*Savage*) from Buenos Aires to Coquimbo, together with much information about North American trade with revolutionary Chile, is set forth in great detail in the correspondence of the pious Henry Hill, whose manuscript papers are now preserved in the Sterling Memorial Library at Yale University. The *Salvaje* returned to Baltimore with a cargo of copper and specie.

55. The history of this expedition and the final tragic fate of José Miguel Carrera and his brothers have been immortalized in Benjamin Vicuña Mackenna's epic volume *El Ostracismo de los Carreras* (Santiago, 1857, and later editions, including the 1938 edition in the republication of Vicuña Mackenna's works by the University of Chile). Vicuña Mackenna had access to the papers (now preserved in the National Archives of Chile) of Carrera, but not his diary. The later discovery and use of the diary enabled Miguel Varas Velásquez to make certain corrections, particularly of the voyage to the United States, in his *Don José Miguel Carrera en los Estados Unidos* (Santiago de Chile, 1912) first published in *Revista Chilena de Historia y Geografía* (1912), Núm. 7 y 8. William Miller Collier and Guillermo Feliú Cruz have availed themselves of this material and documents in the United States to summarize carefully Carrera's visit to the United States in their *La primera misión de los Estados Unidos de America en Chile*.

Skinner entrusted to his father-in-law, Judge Theodorick Bland, for collection, Carrera's note for $4,000, when Bland went to South America in 1817 as a member of the commission of investigation (Caesar A. Rodney, John Graham, and Bland) to Buenos Aires, Chile, and Peru. (John Skinner to the Supreme Director of the United Provinces, Baltimore, June 5, 1818. A.G.N., S1–A2–A4, No. 8.) Bland tried to collect the note from the Buenos Aires government on the ground that the interposition of that government, and its use of the military munitions and officers procured by Carrera, had prevented them going into the hands and service for whom they were particularly intended (Theodorick Bland to His Excellency Juan Martín de Pueyrredón, Supreme Director of the United Provinces of South America, Buenos Aires, April 4, 1818. Ibid.) I found no evidence of action on this petition. In Chile, Bland applied to the dictator, O'Higgins, for payment of the note to one Richard R. Boughan [Brougham?] who had power of attorney. O'Higgins declared that Carrera had no authorized mission in the United States, notwithstanding the patriotic nature of his activities, and he eventually obliged José M. Carrera's father to pay the note (although the father denied responsibility for it and even questioned its authenticity) presumably out of Don José's patrimony. Archivo Nacional (Santiago de Chile), Varios, Vol. 128, 238.

communication to the President of the United States, dated May 29, 1815, that throws some new light on Carrera's possible relation to the Buenos Aires government. The letter itself, signed by General Alvarez, Supreme Director of the United Provinces of the Río de la Plata— who had manifested some sympathy for Carrera's projects in Buenos Aires—is preserved in the records of the Department of State,[56] in the National Archives at Washington, showing that it was delivered. It states that Alvarez, availing himself of the occasion of Carrera's trip, was appealing for aid in materials of war, for the punctual payment of which the Buenos Aires government would be responsible. "The above mentioned brigadier, Don José Miguel Carrera, will explain verbally to your Excellency our situation and the succours we are most interested in, and I confidently hope for all from your Excellency's generosity." [57]

If the Buenos Aires government denied all responsibility for Carrera's activities in the United States, while appropriating the fruits of them, it was eager to send him back there, with passports for his two brothers, in order to get rid of all three. San Martín visited Don José in prison and offered to send him to the United States on a diplomatic mission if he would desist from further projects in Chile.[58] Carrera resolutely refused, later escaped to Montevideo, engaged in hostilities against Buenos Aires, and eventually met his death before a firing squad, like his two brothers before him. The Carreras were passionate patriots who wanted to see their country free, but would not tolerate its emancipation at any hands but their own.

The European situation had clarified after the year 1815 by the exile of Napoleon and the restoration of legitimate governments everywhere, including that Ferdinand VII to whom the people of Buenos Aires had professed their allegiance. As the historic Congress at Tucumán was assembling, the provisional government decided to send to the United States a secret formal mission in anticipation of a declaration of independence. While Carrera was still in the United States, the Supreme Director of the United Provinces of the Río de la Plata, the same General Alvarez who had provided the Chilean patriot

56. Argentine Republic, Notes, *1*, pt. 1, 24. It is interesting to note the sense in which a clerk in the State Department summarized this note at some later date, in a slip pasted on the document: "May 26, 1815, Buenos Aires. General Alvarez, Pres't. of, writes to the Pres't. of the U.S., that Gen'l. José Miguel Carrera is about visiting the United States and hopes the U.S. will furnish war materials to his country for which Carrera will pay promptly, etc."

57. A.G.N., S1–A2–A4, No. 9.

58. Bartolomé Mitre, *Historia de San Martín* (2d ed. Buenos Aires, 1889), *2*, 92.

with a species of credentials to President Madison, designated one Colonel Martin Thompson as an agent, not yet invested with public character or disposed to exceed the "specific object" of his mission without an understanding beforehand with the United States government.

Thompson's instructions [59] reveal an attempt to play off the United States against Great Britain. They imposed upon him inviolable secrecy as to his voyage and mission, except for complete information about it to the President. He was to make known to the President the state of affairs in Buenos Aires, and the desire of those provinces to tighten their relations with the United States by a "pact of reciprocal interests," which, however, must be ratified by "the authorities of the United Provinces." In the name of the Buenos Aires government, he was to order every kind of material assistance, pledging that government to compensate with all imaginable advantages for the commerce of the United States. "If munitions of war cannot be gotten in any other way," read the instructions, "you may guarantee cash payment for them. Specifically, you will request two, or at least one frigate, to protect the commerce of that nation and to introduce a preponderance of North Americans over British nationals." He was to try to procure from the United States government officers of all classes, promising them attractive distinctions. He was to urge the President to get those European powers without colonies to neutralize the machinations of the other powers, particularly Spain, by taking part in the destiny of the Plata country; and he was to seek to establish secret relations with the patriot government in Mexico. In general, he was to accept any proposal which might help to advance and sustain the cause of the Buenos Aires government.[60]

In a credential presenting Thompson to the President of the United States, General Alvarez bespoke for him full credit and consideration, and offered similar consideration and security to such ministers as the President might send to the United Provinces. The Director mentioned the "well-known circumstances" which hitherto had prevented the United Provinces from establishing with the United States the relations of amity and strict correspondence which reciprocal interest and a common glory ought to have inspired. Evidently he was referring

59. [Alvarez] to James Madison, President of the United States, Buenos Aires, Jan. 16, 1816. A.G.N., S1–A2–A4, No. 9. The English text is in Manning, *1*, 343.

60. Instructions for the Delegate [*diputado*] to the United States, Buenos Aires, Jan. 16, 1816, accompanied by full powers from the "Honorable Junta of Observation." A.G.N., S1–A2–A4, No. 9.

to the failure of the Provinces to declare their independence (perhaps also to the interruption of communication by the War of 1812–15 between the United States and Great Britain), for he went on to say that "a series of extraordinary Events and unexpected changes, which have taken place in our ancient Mother-Country, have constrained us not to make a formal Declaration of Independence: nevertheless our conduct and our Public Papers have sufficiently expressed our Resolution. When this Letter reaches Your Excellency, The General Congress of our Representatives will have met, and I can assure you, without fear of being mistaken, that one of its first acts will be a solemn Declaration of the Independence of these Provinces of the Spanish Monarchy and of all other Foreign Sovereigns or Powers." [61] A separate missive used a more personal tone to Madison: confident as he was of the great desire of his fellow citizens to form a close connection with the United States, he was sending by the "national Colonel Martin Thompson" a specimen of the first arms manufactured in the Provinces of Buenos Aires and Tucumán under the auspices of a free government, as an homage due to the Chief Magistrate of the United States. It was accompanied by a manuscript essay on the new mineral discoveries in those provinces. The Director closed his epistle with what may be hoped to be a prophetic note: "the expressions of the sentiments of a people, who amidst the struggle in which they are engaged to secure their rights, reflect on the natural relations which are one day to unite them with that people over whom you so worthily preside." [62]

Here was a temptation for the United States—if it wished to take its eyes off Florida and dared to challenge the menacing European concert where the Holy Alliance had just been proclaimed—to bind itself prematurely to a new republic, indeed to the whole southern continent. But the advantage of such a consummation was not sufficiently great to compensate for the risks in a possible collision with Great Britain, or with a European coalition, or both, in support of Spain. We now know that Europe was not sufficiently united to support Spain, but Madison's government did not yet know it; besides, it was more interested in Florida. Even if Madison had been prepared to recognize this new mission from the Argentine, he would have been prevented from doing so by the blunders and ineptness of the envoy himself.

Thompson reached New York on May 3, 1816, somewhat indisposed

61. Manning, *1*, 341.

62. National Archives (Washington) Division of State Department Archives, series Argentine Republic, Notes, *1*, pt. 1, 26–28.

in health [63] (it is worth recording this, in view of the sequel). The absence of the President and of the principal cabinet officers from Washington during the summer heat induced him to delay going to Washington until August,[64] at which time he met only subordinate officials. Meanwhile he had occupied himself in contracting directly with a number of officers (French and Polish *emigrés* and some North American veterans of the recent war with England) for services in Buenos Aires, in confabulations with Carrera and his intimates, in marveling at the new spectacle of steamboats (*estímbotes*) and writing long dispatches about them and their possible usefulness in the far south. Bickerings over unimportant matters, and requests for more salary and more secretarial aid, filled up his dispatches. When in November he reached Baltimore again, en route to Washington, he noted [65] that since he was not invested with a public character, and could not transcend the object of his mission without an understanding with the Washington government, this might make it impossible to be received as a deputy of the United Provinces of the Río de la Plata even after their declaration of independence. He wished, therefore, to receive more liberal and expansive instructions, giving him a public rank.[66] When this dispatch reached Buenos Aires, Thompson had already been removed. The reasons given by the Director (now Pueyrredón) were that, in his dealings with the "Polish officers" [67] directly (instead of through the United States government), he had violated his instructions on several scores: first by engaging the officers directly, and second, by thus revealing the nature of his mission; he had further entered into negotiations with shipping firms before reaching an understanding with the Washington government.[68]

Pueyrredón took formal pains to explain to the President that Thompson was being removed for violation of his instructions for

63. Martin Thompson to the Supreme Director of the Provinces of the Río de la Plata, No. 1, New York, May 20, 1816. A.G.N., S1–A2–A4.

64. Martin Thompson to the Supreme Director, No. 4, Philadelphia, Aug. 23, 1816. A.G.N., S1–A2–A4, No. 9.

65. Thompson to the Supreme Director, Baltimore, Nov. 14, 1816. A.G.N., S1–A2–A4, No. 9.

66. Thompson to the Supreme Director, No. 13, Baltimore, Nov. 14, 1816. A.G.N., S1–A2–A4, No. 9.

67. The government nevertheless honored the contracts he had made with such officers, after instructing him to make no more.

68. Draft of a dispatch to Martin Thompson, Buenos Aires, Jan. 10, 1817. A.G.N., S1–A2–A4, No. 9.

having arbitrarily departed from the line of duties marked out for him and because "without having duly estimated the honor of conferring with you he has granted licenses which are in direct contradiction with the said principles [69] [of his instructions]." Presumably this refers to the granting of privateering commissions, which were causing the United States much annoyance because of the well-established protests of Onís at these violations of neutrality.[70]

It had been the principal purpose of Thompson's mission—as revealed so clearly in his instructions—to make the United States government, by and with its own consent and approval, the intermediary of assistance for the United Provinces, and to commit it to direct dealings. Thompson could not have worse mishandled his duty. His letter of dismissal bluntly said that it would not even be necessary for him to return to Buenos Aires.[71] The most decisive comment on his diplomacy is a postscript to a dispatch of his successor: "Thompson is in a hospital, hopelessly crazy." [72]

From now on the operations of the Buenos Aires privateers began to play an important and vexatious part both in the relations between Spain and between the United States and the Provinces. The War of 1812–15 between the United States and Great Britain had left a horde of veteran privateer commanders, crews, and well-adapted vessels idle in North American ports. The revolted provinces of Hispanic America possessed no significant naval forces. The Spanish navy was not large enough to convoy that nation's merchant marine successfully against privateers

69. Pueyrredón to Madison, Jan. 10, 1817. A.G.N., S1–A2–A4, No. 9. The English text is printed in Manning, *1*, 346, where it is misdated Jan. 1, 1817.

After the order for Thompson's removal had already left Buenos Aires, but perhaps before it was received in the United States, he foolishly affixed his name, as "Deputy from the Río de la Plata," jointly with the agents from Venezuela, New Granada, and Mexico, to a commission from "the deputies of free America, resident in the United States of the North, to their compatriot, Gregor MacGregor, General of Brigade, in the services of the United Provinces of New Granada and Venezuela" to take possession of East and West Florida. This commission, dated March 31, 1817, naturally made all its signatories *personae non gratae*, but it was not the cause of Thompson's removal, as asserted by Alberto Palomeque, because Pueyrredón already had revoked his commission three months earlier. Bolívar immediately disavowed the document. For the text, see *Annals of Congress*, 15th Cong., 2d Sess. (1819), *2*, 1612, and *A.S.P., F.R.*, *4*. The Buenos Aires authorities, and Bolívar also, disavowed the commission to MacGregor.

70. For the lengthy correspondence between Onís and the Secretary of State, see *Annals*, 15th Cong., 1st Sess. (1818), *2*, 1899–1943.

71. Draft of Feb. 9, 1817, for instructions to Martin Thompson. A.G.N., S1–A2–A4, No. 9.

72. Manuel H. Aguirre to Pueyrredón, Aug. 17, 1817. A.G.N., S1–A2–A4, No. 9.

as did the British navy during the war with the United States. Quite naturally, therefore, the rebels turned to the use of privateers, and with formidable results, particularly in the case of the United Provinces and Venezuela. These were not shipbuilding countries; they commissioned their first privateers to foreigners appearing in the Plata estuary and on the Spanish Main; later, beginning in 1816, they sent forth by their agents to foreign parts blank letters of marque to commission such foreigners as could be had. The devastating horde of South American privateers was thus practically all foreign, most of them procured in foreign ports, many in the United States.

Investigators have estimated that at least thirty-nine privateers carrying the flag of Buenos Aires—sometimes also that of other revolted countries and even that of Portugal, fraudulently, of course—frequented the ports and waters of the United States. Nine of them had once been privateers under the flag of the United States in the recent war against England. Most of these vessels were puchased in the United States, and fitted out either outside of its jurisdiction, or actually in its territorial waters in violation of the law. Onís's protests against illegal commissioning and equipment of privateers and the sale of their plunder in the United States, constituted a great part of his difficult written exchanges with the Secretary of State. They reiterated the charge that these craft had been armed and equipped within the United States in violation of the law of nations, the treaty of 1795 between Spain and the United States, and the neutrality laws of the United States itself, and that the vessels were commanded and principally manned by the citizens thereof. Despite Adams's laborious defensive replies to Onís, he acknowledged in other documents, the justice of the protests.[73] The neutrality laws allowed the sale of ships to all comers, provided they were not armed within the country;

73. Manning, *1*, 49. "You will remonstrate to them: that the fitting out of privateers in our Ports, to cruize either for or against them [the South American revolted provinces] is prohibited by our Laws; that many such privateers have been fitted out in our Ports (unknown to this Government), and though manned and officered entirely by people of this country they have captured the property of nations with whom we are at peace . . . that the licentious abuse of their flags by these freebooters, of every nation but their own, has an influence unpropitious to the cause of their freedom, and tendency to deter other countries from recognizing them as regular Governments." John Quincy Adams, Secretary of State, to Caesar A. Rodney, John Graham, and Theodorick Bland, Special Commissioners of the United States to South America, Washington, Nov. 21, 1817. Manning, *1*, 47.

In 1805 Spanish authorities in Cuba granted to citizens of the United States letters of marque against Great Britain. Portell-Vilá, p. 144.

and though they forbade American citizens taking commissions or enlisting *within the United States,* it was possible to do so outside the nation's jurisdiction. The remote ungoverned Texan port of Galveston (claimed to be within the United States) and Amelia Island, just outside the national jurisdiction, became rendezvous and markets for these illegally equipped corsair vessels. Both of those places were beyond the immediate control of the Washington government; in fact, the federal forces available for police work were not adequate to patrol the extensive territorial waters proper. Even within waters where some surveillance was possible, like Chesapeake Bay, outfitting and illegal augmentation took place. Where arrests followed, as they occasionally did, it was almost impossible to get juries to convict except in cases of flagrant atrocity. Public opinion was on the side of the privateers.[74] Embarrassments caused by the activities of these craft, and sympathy for them, became a problem for John Quincy Adams in his dealings with new agents from Buenos Aires.

III

General San Martín's grand strategy for the emancipation of Peru and the winning at last of independence throughout the continent was directly responsible for another mission from Buenos Aires. Having crossed the Andes in January 1817, and defeated the royalist army at Chacabuco (February 12, 1817), the General planned his next major move: the delivery of Peru by an invasion from the sea. He suddenly returned unannounced to Buenos Aires and arranged with Pueyrredón, the Supreme Director of the now independent United Provinces (the Declaration of Independence had been voted at Tucumán July 9, 1816), for a mission to the United States to buy or build, fit out, and man a naval squadron to make the long voyage to Valparaiso in order to control the Pacific and to help convoy an army of liberation to the shores of Peru. For this important representation they chose Manuel Hermenejildo de Aguirre, with the honorary title of Commissioner General of War and Marine, as chief of mission, and Gregorio Gómez, captain in the customs service, as second, with the honorary

74. Two scholars have written excellent but not definitive accounts of the privateers of the United Provinces. Theodore S. Currier, *Los corsarios del Río de la Plata* (*Publicaciones del Instituto de Investigaciones Históricas,* No. XLV, Facultad de Filosofía y Letras, Buenos Aires, 1929) exhausts the voluminous published sources in the United States, but does not utilize the materials printed in the Argentine. Lewis Winkler Bealer, *Los corsarios de Buenos Aires,* notes this deficiency but himself does not exhaust the archival material either in the United States or the Argentine.

title of Commissioner of Marine. The envoys sailed from Buenos Aires late in May 1817, equipped with credentials and detailed instructions based on a special contract between General San Martín and Aguirre.

By the terms of this contract, General San Martín, exercising powers conferred on him by the Supreme Director of Chile (Bernardo O'Higgins), named Aguirre as agent of that state to buy or to have constructed in the United States, two 34-gun frigates, according to specifications set forth in detail, and as many other ships of war as he could get, and to send them under the United States flag, fully equipped and armed, to the Río de la Plata en route for Valparaiso For this he was provided with 100,000 pesos cash, and promised 100,000 more in three months. In case Lima should be taken with the aid of these ships, Aguirre was to get a bonus of 100,000 pesos for himself in addition to a salary of 12,000 pesos for the trip and traveling expenses.[75] Pueyrredón jointly guaranteed the contract on behalf of the United Provinces and he also authorized Aguirre to borrow on authority of his government up to 2,000,000 pesos [76] to supplement the 200,000

75. *Convención celebrado entre el Exmo. Señor Capitán General don José de San Martín y el cuidadano de las Provincias Unidas don Manuel H. Aguirre.* Buenos Aires, April 17, 1817. This and related documents (but not all those cited in this essay) are printed by Alberto Palomeque, *Orígines de la diplomacia argentina, Misión Aguirre á Norte América* (Buenos Aires, 1905), 2, 123–28. Palomeque had access to a collection of Aguirre's own papers, containing copies of the contract, and numerous other documents, which were assembled by Aguirre to defend a claim of 52,098 pesos which he presented to the Chilean government after his return from North America (see p. 356, note 124 below). This original *expediente* is now in the possession of Señor Carlos Ibaguren of Buenos Aires, who kindly permitted me to inspect it; but a transcript is also in the Archivo General de la Nación. Practically all these documents are printed in one place or another in Palomeque's imperfectly organized volume. Apparently Palomeque did not use the important but incomplete *expediente* of documents relating to the mission of Aguirre and Gómez which are now preserved in the Archivo General de la Nación, in Buenos Aires, or the much smaller and more fragmentary *expediente,* labeled "Aguirre, 1818," in the Archivo del Ministerio de Relaciones y Culto, in the same city. Some of these, however, are duplicated in the family *expediente* used by Palomeque. Where possible, I here cite Palomeque's printed documents for the reader's convenience, instead of the archival originals; otherwise I cite the latter.

76. In using the words pesos and dollars, I have used them just as they occur in the documents, without being able to know the prevailing rate of exchange for translation into dollar equivalents. I presume a silver peso and silver dollar were then roughly equivalent.

The consul of the United States, at Buenos Aires, Thomas Lloyd Halsey, irresponsibly had led the government of the United Provinces to expect an issue of a 9 per cent loan of 2,000,000 dollars from private sources in the United States, with the assistance of the government of the latter, the same to be negotiated by John Devereux,

pesos provided by Chile.[77] Gómez, on his part, was promised by the Buenos Aires government a contingent bonus of 10,000 pesos similarly, in addition to traveling expenses and the continuance of his regular salary as commissioner of customs, plus an annual supplement of 1,500 pesos during the trip. The envoys received 25 blank privateering commissions from each government, and authority to guarantee exemption from all customs duties in Chilean ports of prizes made within ten months of the date of privateering commissions. Pueyrredón had explained to Madison the removal of Martin Thompson among other reasons for granting certain "licenses" contrary to the sense of his instructions, but he had no hesitation in giving Aguirre and Gómez express instructions to issue the same.

Supplementary instructions from Pueyrredón to Aguirre and Gómez directed them, in case they could not get the frigates, to procure six

---

special agent of the United States, who had left Buenos Aires for the United States with a loan contract signed by Pueyrredón and Thomas Lloyd Halsey, dated Buenos Aires, Jan. 31, 1817. The loan was not to be payable until ten years after the conclusion of the existing war, but optionally before that. The "House of Mr. John Devereux" was to get a six per cent commission for underwriting the loan. "And to the end that these conditions may have all the force and effect necessary for their fulfillment on both sides by means of the signature of the consul of the United States, this document has been respectively signed by us both, and countersigned by the Secretary of the Treasury, in conformity with a copy duly verified, and deposited in the proper office for the uses of official purposes which are or may be required." Buenos Aires, Jan. 31, 1817. [signed] Pueyrredón, Thomas Lloyd Halsey, José Domingo Trillo, acting Secretary of the Treasury. National Archives (Washington), Division of State Department Records, Argentine Republic, Notes. *1*, part 1, 13. See also Manning, *1*, 347, 349, 354. Richard Rush, acting Secretary of State in Washington, promptly repudiated this agreement. Richard Rush to "Señor [———]" Department of State, April 21, 1817. A.G.N., S1–A2–A4, No. 8.

In acknowledging the Secretary's dispatch of April 20, 1817, relating to the agreement, Halsey observed that it was Devereux' project, not his: "My signature to it was merely as his agent in his absence. The United States not allowing any salary to its consular agents in foreign countries, they are obliged to seek their maintenance by commercial or other pursuits, and, therefore, it sometimes happens that the signature as an individual is unintentionally blended with the official capacity . . . I repeatedly explained to them that I could not answer for the success of the proposition." Consul T. L. Halsey to the Secretary of State, Buenos Aires, Nov. 21, 1817. National Archives (Washington), Division of State Department Archives, Buenos Aires, Consular Dispatches, Dec. 9, 1811—Nov., 1817. The body of the proposed contract, above quoted, does not admit of such an excuse of "unintentional blending."

77. On the other hand, O'Higgins promised to "fulfil inviolably and religiously all engagements and commitments which we may make with that nation [the United States]." O'Higgins to Aguirre, Concepción, June 4, 1817. Palomeque, *2*, 124.

corvettes of 25 to 30 guns each, and a listed [78] quantity of guns and ammunition for the armament of other ships in Buenos Aires (the latter purchases to be paid out of the anticipated loan). The Supreme Director added an order to procure two proper sabers and two fine pairs of pistols, suitably ornamented and appropriately engraved, as gifts for San Martín and O'Higgins in gratitude for their services on the memorable day of Chacabuco; also a dozen good quality sabers to be presented on occasion in the future as rewards for valor to deserving officers. Finally, they were to buy "for the use of this government" a good telescope and barometer with thermometer attached.[79]

The credentials which Aguirre carried with him, including letters to the President from Pueyrredón, San Martín, and O'Higgins, have interest because of certain technical questions that he encountered in Washington, and because they describe the essential object of his mission. His formal credentials, signed by Pueyrredón as Supreme Director of the United Provinces of South America, and by Gregorio Tagle, Minister of State, denominate him as "agent of this government near that of the United States of North America, granting to him the privileges, pre-eminences and prerogatives which belong to said title." A letter from General San Martín to the President explained that the Supreme Director of the Government of Chile (O'Higgins) had considered that a principal instrument to secure the liberty of America was the armament in the United States of a squadron destined to the Pacific Ocean.

This squadron, said San Martín,

> united to the forces which are now preparing in the river La Plata, may co-operate in sustaining the ulterior military operations of

78. List No. 1:

Cannon	balls	of	caliber	8	 8,000
"	"	"	"	6	 4,000
"	"	"	"	4	 8,000
"	"	"	"	2	 4,000
Six-inch	shells				 4,000

List No. 2:

Mortars		caliber	18	number of:	24
"		"	12	" "	24
Cannon		"	9	" "	24

79. [Supreme Director] to the Commissioner Don Manuel Aguirre [draft], Buenos Aires, April 30, 1817; unsigned draft of a communication to Don Gregorio Gómez, advising him of his appointment as second to Don Manuel H. de Aguirre in the mission to be sent to North America, April 30, 1817; [Supreme Director] to Gregorio Gómez, May 6, 1817. A.G.N., S1–A2–A4, No. 9.

the army under my command in South America; and, convinced of the advantages which our actual political situation promises, I have crossed the Andes in order to concert in that capital [Buenos Aires], among other things, the guaranty of my Government, and, in compliance with the stipulations between the Supreme Director of Chile and its intimate ally, to carry into effect the plan which has been confided to Don Manuel Aguirre. Your Excellency, who enjoys the honor of presiding over a free people, who contended and shed their blood in a similar cause to that in which the inhabitants of South America are now engaged, will, I hope, deign to extend to the above-named person such protection as is compatible with the actual relations of your Government; and I have the high satisfaction of assuring Your Excellency that the arms of the country under my orders will not fail to give consistency and respect to the promises of both Governments.[80]

This straightforward and purposeful document is, so far as I know, the only letter which the immortal San Martín ever addressed to the immortal James Monroe. It shows that a naval armament which he hoped to get from the United States was a factor in his grand strategic combination. It was not, however, an indispensable factor, for the great commander's resourcefulness would turn in any direction.

Pueyrredón, in a letter presenting Aguirre to Monroe, said that he was deputed to the President "in the character of the agent of this Government" and requested for him "all the protection and consideration required by his *diplomatic rank* and the actual state of our relations.[81] This will be a *new tie,* by which the United States of the North will more effectually secure the gratitude and affection of the free provinces of the South."

80. Don José Francisco de San Martín, General of the Army of the Andes, to James Monroe, President of the United States, Santiago, Chile, April 1, 1817. Note that this letter is antedated to April 1, and at Santiago. Manning, *1,* 352.

81. Italics inserted. The "actual state of our relations" had been described in the first paragraph of the letter: "When the interests of sound policy are in accord with the principles of justice, nothing is more easy or more pleasing than the maintenance of harmony and good understanding between Powers which are connected by close relations. This seems to be exactly the case in which the United States and these provinces stand with respect to each other; a flattering situation, which gives the signal of our success, and forms our best apology." Juan Martín Pueyrredón, Supreme Director of the United Provinces of South America, to James Monroe, President of the United States, April 28, 1817. Manning, *1,* 353. I did not find in Buenos Aires any copies of these communications, of which Manning prints the Department of State translations.

Neither the credentials which Aguirre carried, the contract which served as his instructions, nor the supplementary instructions from Pueyrredón that he carried from Buenos Aires directed him to solicit a recognition of independence. By implication, and in effect, they left it open to the United States to decide what diplomatic rank, if any, the actual situation would justify extending to him.

The envoys arrived in Baltimore, in July 1817, after a swift voyage of fifty-nine days.[82] Aguirre immediately proceeded to Washington, where he presented his credentials to Richard Rush, who was acting as Secretary of State *ad interim*, pending the arrival from London of John Quincy Adams to take over that office. President Monroe was absent from the city on a "good feeling" tour of the country. Rush received the visitor from the distant Río de la Plata in a private and informal but nonetheless warmly sympathetic manner. He did not scruple to say that he believed that the President, in common with the nation at large, cherished the most sincere good will toward all the inhabitants of the American continent, and looked with feelings of great solicitude and kindness upon the struggle in which so many of them were engaged. He made it plain that *the government* of the United States, because of its policy of strict neutrality, and because of its treaty of commerce and amity with Spain, could take no part whatever in this struggle; and he emphasized that this policy of neutrality was the one most likely to be beneficial to the South Americans themselves.[83]

Aguirre, unabashed, asked if the United States government would sell some ships out of its own navy to assist this campaign for the liberation of Peru. Rush, of course, said no; but he explained that neither the laws of the United States nor international law would prevent Aguirre as an individual from purchasing arms and munitions from private individuals, the purchaser taking upon himself the risk of carrying contraband. He was free to buy ships of any size from other private individuals in the seaports of the United States, but he must not arm or in any way equip them for war. As long as he kept his activities and purchases within the sphere of an individual, avoiding any breach of the laws, his conduct would be sanctioned and he himself protected; if the cause of his country could in this way be

82. Palomeque, *1*, 39. One may question the precise dates of departure and arrival as stated by Palomeque, but not the months.

83. "The last idea was pressed the most distinctly, as it was calculated to suggest to the commissioner the best excuse for not recognizing him in his official capacity." Rush's statement of Nov. 22, 1817.

benefited, then the people and government of the United States would be content. According to Rush, Aguirre was quite satisfied with this declaration and the sentiments manifested; he said plainly that he did not expect to be received in his official character, and that since he could have no further business with the government, he would set off the next day for Baltimore and begin his operations "as a merchant" there and in other cities. Rush ended the conversation on a note stressing the advantages of free and popular governments, and was somewhat surprised to hear Aguirre intimate guardedly that the people of Buenos Aires were scarcely fitted to be republicans, or at any rate would not be able to set up a democratic form of government; that "the better sort" were against it; and that conformably to this incapacity they would make an offer to Don Carlos, brother of Ferdinand, to come from Spain to rule over them in the capacity of an "independent King." [84] From this moment the possibility of more monarchies in the New World became an anxiety to Monroe and his advisers.

"This Government says that it is against its interests to become involved in a war with Spain, and all that it can do is to *let me do.*" Aguirre thus summarized this first interview.[85]

84. Richard Rush, Statement in relation to the contents of a Letter of Don Manuel de Aguirre, of 14 Novbre. 1817, Nov. 22, 1817. The National Archives (Washington), Division of State Department Archives, Notes from the Argentine Legation, *1*, Part 1, Feb. 11, 1811, to Oct. 27, 1838. Aguirre made a similar statement to Adams, Dec. 24, 1817, about an offer to Don Carlos. J. Q. Adams, *Memoirs.*

Palomeque, in his study passionately exalting Aguirre as a patriot of the revolution, prints a Spanish translation of Rush's remarks, but omits this last statement.

85. Aguirre to Supreme Director, New York, Aug. 30, 1817. A.G.N., S1–A2–A4, No. 9. In this dispatch Aguirre states that this is the sense of what he had written in an earlier dispatch (not extant in this collection). Bartolomé Mitre, *Historia de Belgrano* (4th ed. Buenos Aires, 1887), *3*, 98, summarizes this earlier dispatch, of July 30, 1817, out of the Secret Archives of the Congress of Tucumán.

Some months later, in a letter to the Supreme Director, without date, Aguirre mentions that in "his first communications" he had described the interview with the Secretary of State *ad interim*, "in which he assured me orally that ships, cannon, arms and ammunition were articles of commerce by the laws of this country and that I would be protected by this Government in the execution of my mission, so long as it appeared as a business deal under neutral flag and in a neutral vessel." (Aguirre to the Supreme Director [1817]. Archivo del Ministerio de Relaciones y Culto (Buenos Aires) Misión Aguirre, 1818.) This agrees substantially with Rush's account of the interview; but in a letter of Nov. 14, 1817, to J. Q. Adams, Aguirre represented Rush to have said that the government could take no "open and direct part" in favor of the Spanish colonies. The National Archives (Washington), Division of State Department Records. Notes from the Argentine Legation, *1*, Part 1, Feb. 11, 1811, to Oct. 27, 1838. Adams referred this letter immediately to Rush, who responded Nov. 22, 1817, with the detailed description of the interview above cited.

With these friendly expressions, even encouragement, from the Department of State, the agents hastened away from Washington to buy or build their cruisers. They soon found that all talk of loans, with or without the sanction of the United States government (which last, of course, was out of question) was foolish. Carrera's unfulfilled promises had ruined the credit of both Chile and of Buenos Aires, and now ships were returning from the Plata with discouraging reports of conditions there.[86] All they could do was to use the 100,000 pesos in hand to contract [87] for the construction, in New York, of two 34-gun frigates, to cost a total of 200,000 pesos; the balance was to be paid before the vessels left the port. They were also able to persuade several privateers to take commissions in the Chilean service and to set out loaded with cargoes of munitions, on their own account and risk, for sale to the government of Buenos Aires or Chile.[88] Optimistically they wrote home that the frigates might be expected to be in Valparaiso the following March, provided that the second 100,000 pesos, promised from the government of Chile, should reach them promptly.

Despite endeavors to disguise the construction of these ships as a private enterprise, it proved impossible to keep the business under cover, if only because of the obvious character of the frigates and the enthusiastic popular interest in them. The Spanish consulate speedily got wind of the truth. While Aguirre was engaged in the execution of formal contracts, "there was presented to him," a copy of the Act of Congress of March 3, 1817, prohibiting, under heavy penalties, all persons from fitting out vessels of this description. Fearful that the frigates could not proceed to their destination, Aguirre, again in Washington, appealed to Secretary Adams for further advice, alluding to his earlier conversation with Rush.[89] Adams referred him to the lawyers. Aguirre then got this legal advice: "The act of preparing and sending out ships armed for war, equipped and manned in a neutral port, is an act of hostility in violation of neutrality and of the laws of this country. The Director of the Customs is empowered by these

86. Aguirre to Pueyrredón, New York, Aug. 17, 1817. A.G.N., S1–A2–A4, No. 9. Same to Supreme Director of Chile, March 18, 1818. Archivo del Ministerio de Relaciones y Culto (Buenos Aires), Misión Aguirre, 1818.

87. According to the depositions secured by the Spanish Consulate (Manning, *3*, 1977), the contractors for the hulls were Messrs. Brown and Chesseman; other contractors supplied rigging, etc.

88. Among these ships were the *Ellen Tooker*, the *Colomb*, the *Araucán*. Aguirre to Pueyrredón, personal, New York, Sept. 12, 1817; Gregorio Gómez to Pueyrredón, New York, Nov. 13, 1817. A.G.N., S1–A2–A4, No. 9.

89. Aguirre to Adams, Nov. 14, 1817. The National Archives (Washington), Division of State Department Archives, Notes from the Argentine Legation, *1*, Part 1, Feb. 11, 1811, to Oct. 27, 1838.

laws to detain and confiscate such ships, the value of their proceeds to be divided between the informer and the Government; and the owner or the person who appears to be such, to be imprisoned for ten years and fined $10,000." Dismayed at this prospect, he determined to risk jail for his country's sake.[90] The construction of the cruisers went forward, and the agents anxiously wrote home imploring that the second 100,000 pesos be sent to them, as promised, so that the frigates could be delivered and put to sea.[91]

Leaving Gómez to watch over the construction of the frigates in New York, Aguirre returned to Washington in late October.

The rising tide of popular sentiment in favor of the revolutionists in South America had already made further impression upon the natural sympathies of President Monroe. He had been an instinctive apostle of the rights of man ever since his participation as a youthful soldier in the revolution of the English colonies in North America and his first diplomatic mission to revolutionary France in 1794–96. We have observed the cordiality with which he had received the first emissaries from the Plata region in 1811, when Secretary of State. His inclination toward recognition, fortified by warming public opinion, had impelled him to appoint, on his own responsibility, a commission of investigation to visit South America, particularly Buenos Aires, to report upon the condition of the United Provinces. Taking advantage of the difficulty of organizing this fact-finding commission, which consisted finally of John Graham, Caesar A. Rodney, and Theodorick Bland, and of family concerns of one of its members, Adams had persuaded the President to delay its departure for several months.[92] The commissioners were still awaiting their departure on the frigate *Congress* when Aguirre reappeared in Washington.

Aguirre called on Secretary Adams on October 29, 1817, and left his commission as "agent" of the United Provinces, signed by Pueyrredón, and another commission as purchasing agent of Chile, signed by O'Higgins. More significantly, he delivered a letter for the President, containing a copy of the Declaration of Independence of July 9, 1816,

90. Aguirre to the Supreme Director, no date [1818]. Archivo del Ministerio de Relaciones y Culto (Buenos Aires) Misión Aguirre, 1818. Printed, with minor errors in Palomeque, *1, 59.*

91. Aguirre to Supreme Director, Baltimore, Nov. 25, 1817. A.G.N., S1–A2–A4, No. 9.

92. Onís to Pizarro, Dec. 2, 1817, A.H.N., Estado, leg. 5642. For the commission see amidst a voluminous literature: Frederick L. Paxson, *The Independence of the South American Republics; a Study in Recognition and Foreign Policy* (Philadelphia, 1916) and Griffin.

and an eloquent statement of the reasons why his countrymen had undertaken their political emancipation at the risk of their lives, their fortunes, and their honor.[93] There is no record of his having asked at this time for a recognition of that independence, although he may have been hoping to be received formally. A formal reception by the President of the "agent" after he had just presented his country's Declaration of Independence, would have been actual recognition.

Already Monroe had announced to the Secretary of State, five days before Aguirre's interview of the 29th, that he was going to put to the Cabinet the question: "whether we should acknowledge the Government of Buenos Aires." We are unable to determine precisely when Aguirre had arrived in Washington, before the 29th, and consequently whether it was his presence that impelled Monroe to consider this important subject. Certainly Aguirre's communication of the 29th must have strengthened this decision.

In a cabinet meeting of October 30, 1817, Monroe presented for discussion the following questions:

> Has the executive power to acknowledge the independence of the new states whose independence is not recognized by the parent country and between which parties war exists?
>
> Is sending a minister equal to recognition?
>
> Is it expedient for the United States to recognize Buenos Aires or other revolted provinces?
>
> What ought to be the future conduct of the U. States towards Spain, considering the evasion practised by her government and amounting to a refusal to make reparation for injuries?
>
> Is it expedient to break up the Amelia Island establishment which is of a piratical and highly mischievous nature?
>
> Is it expedient to act as was accorded in the previous May and suspended, i.e. to send a commission to South America to report on the progress of the revolution and the probability of its success? [94]

Nothing could illustrate better than these queries the interrelationship of the Florida Question, then in negotiation with Spain, and the question of recognition of the new Latin American countries now

93. J. Q. Adams, *Memoirs;* Manning, *1,* 14.

94. J. Q. Adams notes the discussion in a summary way in his *Memoirs* for that date. The questions above quoted are as paraphrased by Griffin, pp. 140–41, from a memorandum of "October, 1817" in the Monroe Papers in the Library of Congress.

centered upon Buenos Aires.[95] The Cabinet decided affirmatively the last two questions. Adams argued successfully against the expediency of acknowledging the independence of Buenos Aires, and urged that the next dispatch from the United States Legation in Madrid be awaited before assuming any new attitude toward Spain; this was also agreed to.[96]

Amelia Island, the subject of the fifth question, had become a port for outlawed slave traders, smugglers, privateers, and pirates, ever since evacuation by the United States in 1813. We have already noted [97] that the Venezuelan and Mexican agents in the United States and the unfortunate Martin Thompson from Buenos Aires had signed a commission on March 31, 1817, to the English adventurer, Gregor MacGregor, empowering him to take possession of East and West Florida in the name of their governments, "for the purpose of carrying into execution, either in whole or in part, an enterprise so interesting to the glorious cause in which we are engaged." MacGregor, with a company of filibusters recruited at Charleston and Savannah, forthwith possessed himself of Amelia Island.[98] It speedily became, like Galveston, a port not only for the privateers of the revolutionary governments of South America, seeking a place to condemn and sell their prizes, but a meeting place for privateers degenerated into pirates, the enemy of any flag, a rendezvous for thieves, thugs, renegades, and rascals of all complexions of race and nationality whose only object was ill-gotten gain, pelf, and plunder. The government decided in this notable Cabinet meeting to wipe out once and for all these pirates' nests. On December 23, 1817, Amelia Island was occupied under a

---

95. "The points upon which the important interests in this country are depending, and upon which the success or failure will affect the interests of the Administration, are the relations with Spain, those with Great Britain, and Indian affairs. The Spanish include those with South America." J. Q. Adams, *Memoirs*, July 28, 1818.

96. Adams, *Memoirs*.

97. See above, p. 334, note 69.

98. There are two outstanding contributions amidst the literature on MacGregor and the second occupation of Amelia Island: T. Frederick Davis, "MacGregor's Invasion of Florida, 1817," in *Florida Historical Society Quarterly*, 7 (July 1928), 3–72; and Rufus Kay Wyllys, "The Filibusters of Amelia Island," in *Georgia Historical Quarterly*, *12* (Dec. 1928), 297–325. MacGregor was closely associated with the Baltimore outfitters of Buenos Aires privateers, particularly John Skinner (who had lent the $4,000 to Carrera). Skinner wrote Adams that he had believed MacGregor when the latter told him he intended to bring about the annexation of Florida to the United States after it had served its purpose of furnishing a depot of supplies for South American revolutionists (*Florida Hist. Soc. Quar.*, 5 [July 1926], 54–57), but this did not deter the government from occupying the island.

strained interpretation of the law of January 15, 1811. It met the immediate protest of Onís, and later, as we shall see, of Aguirre.

The decision to occupy Amelia Island again was considered a decisive reason for finally dispatching to Buenos Aires the frigate *Congress* and the commission of inquiry, to explain the same.[99] Before they embarked, Messrs. Rodney and Bland, on instruction from the Secretary of State, got in touch with Aguirre and explained to him, too, the necessity of this action which meant no alteration of the friendly sentiments of the administration toward the United Provinces. Aguirre at that time readily acknowledged the propriety of the step.[100] In sending this mission particularly, and in dealing with Buenos Aires and the other revolted provinces generally, it was Monroe's idea "to elevate South America as high as we could without a compromitment with the allied powers who may probably, or rather possibly, take the part of Spain. The pulse of the allied powers will be felt while the United States remain free to act." [101] All this was accomplished by executive action before Congress convened on December 1, 1817.[102]

We have stressed the fact that Aguirre carried with him no authority to solicit recognition of independence. Before the meeting of Congress, he made no such request, although naturally he had offered Adams every opportunity to receive him formally as a diplomatic agent. In exercising this restraint he had been wise. Things were not going badly for his cause. He had been warmly received and encouraged to buy his ships—as an individual merchant acting within the law. The

99. J. Q. Adams, *Memoirs*, Oct. 30, 1817.

100. Ibid., Jan. 22, 1818.

101. Griffin, p. 142, citing Monroe to [————], Dec. 2, 1817. Monroe Papers, Library of Congress.

102. In dispatches to his government, Aguirre took credit for having been responsible for the sending of the famous fact-finding commission, aboard the *Congress* (Aguirre to the Supreme Director, Baltimore, Nov. 25, 1817. A.G.N., S1–A2–A4, No. 9). He claimed it was the result of his note of October 29th to Monroe on the reasons for the Declaration of Independence. Argentine historians, including Mitre (*Historia de Belgrano*, 4th ed., *3*, 97–99), have accepted this, stressing the importance of that mission of investigation as a step in bringing about the recognition of the United Provinces by the United States. Of course, Aguirre had nothing to do with it. Monroe had decided on it, on his own initiative, long before the arrival of Aguirre and Gómez, and it was the second occupation of Amelia Island which ended the delay of the commission's departure. As they left, the commissioners carried additional instructions to explain the affair of Amelia Island and to protest against the illegal armament of privateers in ports of the United States, "the licentious abuse of their flags by these craft, of every nation but their own, has an influence unpropitious to the cause of their freedom, and tendency to deter other countries from recognizing them as regular governments." Manning, *1*, 47.

President and his advisers were even debating the possibility of recognizing the government of Buenos Aires. They had dispatched a friendly commission of inquiry to that distant capital to report on the stability of its government. It was the agitation in Congress that misled the agent into premature, undiplomatic, and unauthorized activities.

No sooner had Congress opened than Henry Clay "mounted his South American great horse." [103] Seeking to harass and embarrass the Administration in every way, he and his followers fanned up the first clouds in the Era of Good Feeling by opposing the Spanish and South American policies of Monroe and Adams. First they attacked the neutrality act of March 3, 1817, as inequitable to the patriots—that same neutrality law against which Onís was so bitterly inveighing as unfavorable to Spain. Next they protested against the occupation of Amelia Island as being unfair to the revolutionists (it deprived them of a shelter for privateers illegally fitted out in the United States). Then they began a campaign for the immediate recognition of the independence of the United Provinces.[104] Aguirre's dispatches do not reveal whether he confabulated with the opposition in Congress, but his policy became more aggressive immediately he sensed this situation. In numerous conferences with Adams during December and January,[105] he solicited recognition of independence; he complained of the inequalities, as he termed them, of the neutrality law; he protested the occupation of Amelia Island as an invasion of the common sovereignty over which Spain and her revolted colonies were contending in civil war; he threatened that if the United States did not recognize the independence of the United Provinces the Buenos Aires government might shut off to this country its newly opened trade. Knowing that the House of Representatives had called upon the President for communication of all correspondence relating to the revolted provinces of South America, and hoping it would publish them with a resulting appeal to the public, Aguirre carefully recapitulated his interviews in written notes to the Secretary of State.[106]

All this plagued Adams, but he patiently and skillfully met Aguirre's importunities. He inquired if the request for recognition came from any new instructions; Aguirre said no, it resulted from what had transpired in Congress. The experienced Adams observed that the *ordinary*

103. J. Q. Adams, *Memoirs,* Dec. 6, 1817.
104. *Annals of Congress,* 15th Cong., 1st Sess., *1, 402–650.*
105. Adams, *Memoirs.*
106. Manning, *1, 361–68, 373.*

way to achieve recognition was by a treaty between the parties; did Aguirre have powers to negotiate one? The agent was obliged to say that he had no specific powers; but he asserted that he was so enabled by the general tenor of his credentials. The Secretary asked exactly what portion of the United Provinces was under the control of the Buenos Aires government; how about Montevideo, occupied by Portuguese troops? How about Artigas, who claimed separate authority over the Banda Oriental? When Aguirre intimated that North American trade to Buenos Aires rested on the sufferance of temporary decrees of that government, rather than on a permanent treaty basis, Adams hinted that, in case of a change, the ports of the United States might be closed to the flag of Buenos Aires. Aguirre replied tartly that this would make no difference; the shipping, even the privateers, was all under the flag of the United States, and owned by its citizens. When Aguirre protested about Amelia Island, Adams asked him to put this, too, in writing; if the government of Buenos Aires were to assume a "superintendency" of all Spanish provinces in both of the continents of America, it were well that the United States know this perfectly, in order to govern itself accordingly. At this Aguirre drew back; he admitted that he was not speaking for his government in regard to Florida.[107]

Nothing could have been more undiplomatic than this strategy, or more calculated to prejudice the agent and his government in the eyes of the administration. In protesting about Florida, Aguirre had touched a principal nerve center of North American foreign policy. Right then Monroe was nervous about a possible war with Spain, particularly after the occupation of Amelia Island, and Adams still feared that Spain might find European support. And Aguirre was untactful enough to tell Adams that the possibility of the United States becoming involved in war was no just motive why he should not solicit the recognition of his nation! It is no wonder that Monroe and his advisers, particularly Adams, very definitely decided against any recognition at this time.

Meanwhile Clay's group continued to press the subject on the floor of the House of Representatives. They successfully called for papers connected with the Amelia Island affair. The House requested the communication by the President of all papers relating to the revolted Spanish Provinces. Adams provided an accompanying statement, stressing the fact that Aguirre had no diplomatic title, no powers to treat, and that all his demands for recognition had arisen since the assembly

107. Adams, *Memoirs, 4,* 45.

of Congress. But the notes and credentials of Aguirre were made public, as he doubtless had intended, and circulated before a public ever more sympathetic. When the President requested the necessary appropriation for defraying the expenses of the commission of inquiry which he had sent to South America, Clay attached an amendment appropriating $18,000 for a minister and legation in Buenos Aires; this was vigorously and eloquently debated, and defeated on March 28, 1818, by a vote of 45–115, but Clay's notable speeches, widely circulated in the sober press of that day, popularized the cause of the patriots.

It so happened that the very day after Clay's motion for recognition had been so decisively defeated, namely, on March 29, 1818, Aguirre received from Buenos Aires a letter of Pueyrredón for President Monroe,[108] at last formally requesting recognition of independence. The

108. As long as the United Provinces of Río de la Plata considered the issue of the contest in which, in obedience to honour and justice, they had engaged with the Mother Country, as doubtful, they cautiously abstained from requiring of other Nations to compromit their interests by a formal acknowledgment of their Independence. This manly silence, uninterrupted either by actual reverses or the greatest difficulties and dangers, allowed sufficient time to other Nations to apprize them of their unavailing sacrifices, if, on consideration of their magnanimous resolution, they had deemed it rash or unjust;—but having left us to the exertion of our own efforts, awaiting as it were their result, the time appears at length to have arrived, which authorizes us to claim of the respectable powers of the civilized world a warmer interest in our sufferings and in those eventful scenes, which, contrary to every hope of success are renewed by Spanish vengeance throughout every part of the Continent of Columbia. The favourable impression naturally produced by our conduct in the latter years has had its effect on the public mind in Europe, and the case is perhaps not remote, of the disposition felt by a certain Nation to admit us to a rank with it, and thus secure to it the gratitude of a people whose friendship is not to be despised. We cannot easily persuade ourselves that the United States of North America are willing to renounce the glory of meriting above all others, our gratitude by their formal acknowledgment of our Independence, pointed out as they are by so many circumstances as the first to take this step with honour; if however, motives of interest or policy dictate the necessity of deferring this public testimony of the respect due to our virtues and of the disposition relative to our future destiny, we shall pursue our illustrious career, without losing courage, or estimating any sacrifices too high as the price of our Liberty.

Such, Most Excellent Sir, are my sentiments and those of the worthy People over whom I have the honour to preside, which I entreat of you to submit to the consideration of the Congress, provided that step meet your approbation. I formerly transmitted to you the Manifesto published by the Sovereign Congress of these Provinces on the declaration of their Independence of the Mother Country, the King of Spain his successors and of every other Power whatsoever; and I likewise accompanied it with several other copies to which I request you will be pleased to give the direction which may appear most suitable to you.

South American leader explained that this request had not been made before because of a desire not to engage other nations to compromise their interests by any formal acknowledgment while independence remained doubtful. This letter made it apparent that Aguirre had never had any instructions hitherto to solicit recognition, nor indeed to justify any of the representations which he had been making as if he were a recognized diplomatic official. His unauthorized conduct had just secured the rejection of the request which his government now actually did charge him to present. Perhaps it is because he realized this that he did not personally go to Washington for the purpose: he sent Pueyrredón's letter from New York, where he had received it.

The Government had won a striking victory in the overwhelming defeat of Clay's motion. Adams had easily fended off Aguirre's unauthorized importunities and divined their source. But he was as eager as Clay to recognize the independence of the United Provinces, as soon as it could be done conveniently to the diplomatic interests of the United States. At the end of the session of Congress he wrote to the United States Minister in Spain that the debates in the House of Representatives had shown the great and increasing interest felt in the events of South America:

> The part pursued by the Government of the United States in this contest, has been unequivocal Neutrality. None of the Revolutionary Governments has yet been formally acknowledged; but if that of Buenos Ayres should maintain the stability which it appears to have acquired since the Declaration of Independence of July 9, 1816, it cannot be long before they will demand that acknowledgment of right—and however questionable that right may be now considered; it will deserve very seriously the consideration of the European Powers, as well as of the United States, how long that acknowledgment can rightfully be refused.[109]

The year 1818 was probably the most taxing of all John Quincy Adams's career as a diplomatist. No American Secretary of State had

Juan Martín Pueyrredón, Supreme Director of the United Provinces of South America, to James Monroe, President of the United States, Jan. 14, 1818. Manning, *1*, 370.

Aguirre notified Adams on March 29, 1818, from New York, that he had just received dispatches and was now "specially charged by my Government to promote so far as in me lies, the acknowledgment of its Independence by the United States . . ." Ibid., p. 375.

109. J. Q. Adams to George W. Erving, Washington, April 20, 1818. Manning, *1*, 61.

ever handled a group of problems of more vital importance to the nation since its independence: the negotiations with Spain to secure Florida, and the West on the southern frontier; the negotiations with Great Britain, to secure the West on the northern frontier; the question of the independence of the Latin American states; the attitude of Europe toward the New World, with Great Britain a special question mark, and the Holy Alliance a puzzling menace. These questions called for the broadest experience and deepest understanding. It is fortunate that one of Massachusetts' greatest men, and our nation's greatest Secretary of State, held office at this time.

When Congress rose in April 1818, Adams was most anxious about European, particularly British, attitudes toward the claims of the new American states for recognition. He feared that recognition might bring war with Spain and one or more European powers; he did not yet know the position that Great Britain, Spain's old ally, would really assume in case of a move by the Holy Alliance to assist Spain in restoring her sovereignty in the New World. He had in his desk a copy of a lengthy memoir from the Court of Russia, which supported a proposed mediation by the Holy Allies between Spain and Portugal to settle their territorial differences in South America as a first spectacular step to extend the principles of the Holy Alliance to the New World by cooperating with those two Iberian monarchies to extinguish all insurrection in South America, and incidentally to abolish the slave trade.[110] Recognition by the United States of the independence of the United Provinces of the Río de la Plata in the year 1818—an independence which Adams was persuaded they would shortly be in a position to demand as of right—would have had to be made in the face of this ominous possibility of European intervention to stop it. A premature recognition might precipitate more harm than good, not only to the United States but also to the United Provinces, by bringing all Europe into the war. This was the position of Adams until he was sure of the attitude of the European powers. While pressing Spain for Florida, he spent most of the year 1818 trying to find out, through our representatives at the European capitals, what Europe, notably England, would do; particularly, would it consider recognition of independence by the United States as an act of hostility to Spain, and in case Spain should declare war, in consequence, against the United

110. Russian Memorial on the Negotiation relative to the Question of Río de la Plata, and, in general, of the Pacification of the Colonies; for communication to the interested Courts and to the Cabinets of the Mediating Powers, Moscow, November 1817. Manning, *3*, 1853–59.

States, would any or all of those powers take part with her in it? In directing our ministers in Europe to make these soundings, Adams at the same time instructed them to make it clear that the United States would join in no plan of pacification founded on any other basis than that of the entire independence of the South Americans.[111] Thus the recognition of the United Provinces now involved more than the negotiations between Adams and Onís; it concerned the question of Europe and America in the broadest sense; it seemed a matter of peace or war for the United States. It also included two other subordinate problems: could the Buenos Aires government be persuaded to stop the abuse of its flag by illegal and licentious privateers, even actual pirates? and could the United Provinces, liberated by their heroic struggle from Spanish military control, redeem themselves from internal anarchy?

By the summer of 1818 Adams had become persuaded that the five great European allied powers could not agree on any coercive measures to restore Spanish sovereignty in America, because the real policy of Great Britain was to promote the cause of independence, although to delay acknowledging it, for fear of offending Spain. "They will take special care," noted Adams anent the British government, "that the European Alliance shall take no active measures against the Independents . . . There can be no doubt but this appeal of Spain to the thunder bolts of the Allies will terminate in utter disappointment." [112] This was proven later in the year by the conference of Aix-la-Chapelle, when the proposed mediation failed because England, who had initiated it at the request of Spain, refused to countenance the use of force to carry it into effect. In July the *Congress* came back from Buenos Aires, bringing the commissioners, who were unanimously of the opinion that subjugation of the United Provinces to Spain was impossible, though less certain about the internal stability of the country.[113] Monroe was able to announce to Congress when it reassembled in November 1818, that no forceful intervention by Europe was likely, and that there was "good cause to be satisfied with the course heretofore pursued by the United States . . . and to conclude that it is proper to adhere to it, especially in the present state of affairs." [114] The Secretary of State was nevertheless preparing the way for recognition. While engaged in the final phases of his negotiation with Onís, he

111. Manning, *1*, 63–75, 103, and vols. *1, 2, 3,* passim.
112. J. Q. Adams to Thomas Sumter, Jr., Washington, Aug. 27, 1818. Ibid., *1*, 79.
113. J. Q. Adams to Richard Rush, July 30, 1818. Manning, *1*, 74.
114. Message of Nov. 16, 1818. Manning, *1*, 81.

instructed Richard Rush, Minister in London, stating that it was the President's intention to recognize the government at Buenos Aires at no late date, "should no event occur which will justify a further postponement of that intention," and invited Great Britain to do the same in concert with the United States.[115] Every schoolboy in the United States recalls that Great Britain persistently refused to join the United States in such a recognition.

In anticipating the ultimate recognition of the independence of the United Provinces, we must not lose sight of Aguirre, who had urged it so prematurely and undiplomatically. After the rejection of his ill-timed requests for recognition, his protest at the occupation of Amelia Island, and the retrieving of his credentials from the Secretary of State, he had left Washington late in January for New York, to attend to the completion of the frigates. Adams's complaint that he held no diplomatic title impelled him to ask from the Supreme Director of Chile larger powers and a commission as *chargé d'affaires*.[116] At the same time, he resigned his honorary title of War and Marine Commissioner of Buenos Aires, explaining that he preferred the title of a simple citizen of his country.[117] Presumably this was because, pending his possible elevation to a diplomatic title, he wished to remove from his person any imputation of official character, the better to get around the neutrality laws. In New York he found the frigates finished and anchored. The contractors would not turn them over to him until they were paid, according to their agreement, the second 100,000 pesos. Expenses were mounting up every day. In desperation, Aguirre sent Gómez to Buenos Aires to explain his predicament and to get the second 100,000 pesos sent to him according to the terms of San Martín's contract.[118]

The summer dragged on and no money came from Buenos Aires far away. Agents of the Spanish consulate easily ferreted out the facts about the armed ships. Onís sent in complaints to Adams documented with a formidable number of unexceptionable depositions.[119] Before the Secretary could reply, Aguirre's enemies had procured his arrest

115. Jan. 1, 1819. Manning, *1*, 85.

116. Aguirre to the Supreme Director of Chile. Archivo del Ministerio de Relaciones y Culto (Buenos Aires), Misión Aguirre, 1818.

117. Aguirre to the Secretary of the Department of Government, N.Y., March 17, 1818. Ibid.

118. Aguirre to the Supreme Director of the United Provinces of South America. New York, March 17, 1818; Aguirre to the Supreme Director of the State of Chile, New York, March 18, 1818. Ibid.

119. Onís to the Secretary of State, Bristol, July 27, 1818. Manning, *3*, 1971–77.

for violation of the neutrality law by fitting out armed vessels intended to cruise against a prince with whom the United States remained at peace. He spent only four days in jail before he was released by an order of Judge Livingston on the ground that it had not been proven that the ship was intended for hostile operation or that the guns in its "cargo" were other than articles of commerce.

Onís lamented the money spent in vain on prosecution of a case where justice was impossible.[120] Aguirre on his part was sore at his brief incarceration—although not so indignant as a twentieth-century Argentine writer about the mission [121]—and discouraged at the rapidly accumulating expenses of maintaining the idle ships still unpaid for. He hurried to Washington to see Adams again. He protested his arrest, explained that without protection from the government he could not carry on against the harassments of his enemy, and offered to sell the frigates to the United States government.[122] The proposal was politely declined. Adams explained that since Aguirre had never presented credentials or commission of a public minister, he enjoyed no diplomatic immunity before the laws of the United States. The Secretary not unkindly went out of his way to state that the President was of the opinion that "Buenos Ayres has afforded strong proof of its ability to maintain its Independence, a sentiment which, he is persuaded, will daily gain strength with the powers of Europe, especially should the same career of good fortune continue in its favor. In deciding the question respecting the Independence of Buenos Ayres many circumstances claim attention, in regard to the colonies as well as to the United States, which make it necessary that he should move in it with caution." [123]

Despite the failure of his inopportune excursions into the field of diplomacy, and, notwithstanding all of these harassments and vexations, Aguirre actually sailed away from New York early in September with his two cruisers, the *Horatio,* Captain Joseph Skinner, and the *Curiacio,* Captain Paul Delano, with crews recruited in the United

120. For the indignant report of Onís to his government, see Onís to Pizarro, No. 139 of Aug. 6, 1818, with enclosed statement from the Spanish Consul in New York, Tomás Stoughton. "I think the attached documents are sufficient to persuade Your Excellency of the state of affairs in which we find ourselves and that we cannot hope for justice from these gentry." A.H.N., Estado, legajo 5643.

121. Palomeque.

122. Aguirre to the Secretary of State, Aug. 10, 1818. National Archives (Washington), Division of Department of State Archives, series Argentine Republic, Notes, *1*, pt. 1, fol. 77. J. Q. Adams, *Memoirs*, Aug. 8, 1818.

123. Adams to Aguirre, Washington, Aug. 27, 1818. Manning, *1*, 76.

States. Their armament was shipped to Buenos Aires separately in merchant ships.[124] The promised second 100,000 pesos never arrived, but he somehow borrowed money enough, on notes due upon the arrival of the ships in Buenos Aires, to satisfy temporarily his creditors.[125] The frigates reached the Río de la Plata early in November. After much delay, the *Curiacio* took on its armament and sailed for Chile, where it arrived, June 23, 1819, in time for the new campaign then underway for the liberation of Peru, in which the frigate participated under the name *Independencia*. Captain Skinner of the *Horatio* refused to deliver up his ship in Buenos Aires until he received payment for a note of 69,541 pesos. Before the local authorities could overreach him and seize the ship, he cleared out for Río de Janeiro, where he finally sold the frigate to the Portuguese government to satisfy the debt.[126]

Lima surrendered July 21, 1821, to San Martín, whose army arrived on a fleet commanded by the English Lord Cochrane, under the Chilean flag, but Aguirre never got his bonus. We infer from the latter's papers that Pueyrredón was not content with his conduct in the United States, particularly his inexpedient protests about Florida.[127] He got

124. Pueyrredón to San Martín, Nov. 1818, *Documentos del Archivo de San Martín, 4,* 601, cited by Carlos Ibaguren, *En la penumbra de la historia argentina* (Buenos Aires, 1932).

125. Palomeque, *1,* 122, prints a summary of Aguirre's expense account, itemizing the loans.

126. Diego Barros Arana, *Historia jeneral de Chile* (Santiago, 1893), *12,* 285.

127. On being informed in March 1818, by Messrs. Bland, Graham, and Rodney of the reasons for occupying Amelia Island, Gregorio Tagle, the Secretary of State at Buenos Aires, declared that "the removal of those establishments could not fail to be attended with good consequences to the patriot cause . . . and, therefore, his Government could certainly only see in that measure of the United States the manifestation towards it of the most friendly disposition." Manning, *1,* 386.

Immediately upon Aguirre's return to Buenos Aires, the Supreme Director called upon him (Nov. 10, 1818) for copies of the correspondence initiated by him for recognition of the United Provinces by the United States. In transmitting the documents Aguirre expressed a belief that they might create some doubts, and went to great lengths, and very disingenuously, to explain his protests about the occupation of Florida. He had been notified of it, he declared, by Messrs. Rodney and Bland before they departed on the *Congress* (in Nov. 1817); his belated protest (only after the opposition had raised its voice in Congress) he explained as due to the publication, two months later of the Act of Congress of 1811 (Jan. 15, 1811) under authority of which the occupation took place, and was made more necessary by the threats of Adams and the passionate and shameless way in which he defended the occupation and resented any protest. Aguirre took credit for his protest having caused the government to state in the public newspapers that the "American general" had exceeded his instructions in occupying Florida. Here he is alluding to Andrew Jack-

precious little thanks for his work. The Buenos Aires government took exception to his accounts, in which he claimed that somebody, either the government of Buenos Aires, or that of Chile, owed him personally 52,098.18 pesos. Years later, in 1833, he was paid 24,729.79 pesos by the Argentine government. In this way he drops out of history.[128] As a diplomatist he had not been much of a success, because he exceeded his authority, but he certainly accomplished the real object of his mission: the delivery of the frigates; and the escape of the *Horatio* from Buenos Aires was not his fault.

IV

In this essay we have been describing the early missions from Buenos Aires to the United States, with only incidental mention of the representation of the United States in the Plata region, which is so much better known, thanks to both North and South American historians and voluminous publication of official correspondence. It is my purpose here to touch on this merely enough to make clear the history of the early Buenos Aires missions. It is necessary only to recall that since Poinsett's arrival in February 1811, the United States had maintained there a succession of consuls, and a series of special executive agents in Buenos Aires. We remember that the sending of consuls to that port, as well as to Chile and Venezuela, followed a well-established practice of dispatching similar officials to Spanish colonial posts, New Orleans, Havana, and La Guayra, before the outbreak of the revolutions. Spanish authorities admitted them, from time to time, according to necessities of war, and they functioned informally as "Agents for

son's later penetration of Florida to St. Marks in April 1818, not to Amelia Island. We may be sure that Aguirre's earlier protest about Amelia Island had nothing to do with the government's attitude toward Jackson's invasion; as a matter of fact, we recall that John Quincy Adams rigorously and successfully defended Jackson's action. Aguirre al Secretario de Estado del Gobierno de las Provincias Unidas, Buenos Aires, Jan. 13, 1819. A.G.N., S1–A2–A4, No. 9.

128. Palomeque prints in appendix the *expediente* of documents representing Aguirre's claim, which was passed on by Buenos Aires to the Chilean government, although both governments had guaranteed his debts. Aguirre defended his claim personally in Chile. After examining his accounts a Chilean commission threw out several large items, and claimed that Aguirre really owed Chile 89,937 pesos! He returned to Buenos Aires without satisfaction. In 1832 an Argentine commission found that he was entitled to 24,729 pesos. This was paid to him in 1833 by the Argentine government and charged up to Chile. (I have no record of its ever having been paid by Chile.) Aguirre continued unsuccessfully to press Chile for full payment of his claim until his death in 1843.

Seamen and Commerce," without exequaturs.[129] Poinsett received his commission as Consul General for Buenos Aires, Chile, and Peru when the United Provinces of the Plata still professed allegiance to King Ferdinand, but the local revolutionary government readily recognized him and succeeding consuls and vice-consuls, and such recognition, with exequaturs, continued in practice after the Declaration of Independence of 1816. The government of Buenos Aires, of course, was eager to accept any practice which might imply even in a very strained sense a recognition of its sovereignty.

Poinsett, it will be recalled,[130] at first was a special agent, before he became a consul. Another special agent was Colonel John Devereux, who went out to Buenos Aires on business of his own in 1816.[131] We have noted how he involved the United States consul, Thomas L. Halsey, in an abortive $2,000,000 nine per cent loan agreement with Pueyrredón, later repudiated by the United States.[132] William G. D. Worthington was appointed in 1817, as a special agent in Buenos Aires, Chile, and Peru, to disavow the acts of Devereux, and to report on the revolutionary movement. "The real as well as the ostensible object of your mission," said his instructions, "is to explain the mutual advantage of a commerce with the United States, to promote liberal and stable regulations, and to transmit seasonable information on the subject." [133] In exceeding his own instructions, Worthington soon outdid Devereux, whose indiscretions he had been sent to disavow. With no more authority than the sentence just quoted, he proceeded to draw up with Pueyrredón's government a set of articles which was almost a provisional treaty of amity and commerce.[134]

129. See p. 306, note 4, above.

130. Above, p. 307.

131. Henry Merritt Wriston, *Executive Agents in American Foreign Relations* (Johns Hopkins Press, 1929), p. 414.

132. Above, pp. 337–38, note 76. Probably the repudiation of this loan agreement alienated Halsey from favor in Pueyrredón's eyes. Later, his contacts with the revolted General Artigas, the father of Uruguayan independence, in the *Banda Oriental*, produced an order for his immediate expulsion from Buenos Aires (not however immediately executed) and a request to President Monroe in 1818 for his recall, which was immediately complied with.

133. Wriston, p. 415.

134. "Twenty-four Articles between the United States and the United Provinces of Río de la Plata concluded by Mr. Worthington and Mr. Alvarez on the 1st of January, 1818, at the City of Buenos Aires," constituted an agreement to ameliorate "as far as possible the condition and intercourse of the two countries during the actual war which now exists and still appears likely to continue between the said Provinces and His Catholic Majesty, but not to violate in any manner either ex-

The Buenos Aires authorities naturally looked upon the Worthington agreement as a big step toward acknowledgment of their independence. It is quite understandable that Pueyrredón, who had been careful hitherto not to instruct Aguirre to solicit recognition, should now [135] dispatch to President Monroe a formal request for such, in the letter which arrived, as we have noticed, after the agent Aguirre's unauthorized importunities had been turned aside by Adams, and just after Clay's motion for recognition of the United Provinces had been voted down so decisively in the House of Representatives. The Supreme Director followed this up by arranging for a more adequate and complete diplomatic representation at Washington than that furnished by Aguirre, whose business had been to procure the ships-of-war for San Martín's campaign for the liberation of Peru.

The new appointment of a deputy (*diputado*) in Washington originated with Thomas Taylor, who had made the voyage, above mentioned, to North America in 1816 for the purpose of outfitting and commissioning privateers. His observations of the United States and its people, and their attitude toward the independence of South America, had convinced him that all that was needed to bring this to a head was the impulse of some person of competence and brilliance (*brillo*). For this purpose he recommended General William H. Winder, a citizen of the United States in Baltimore, who, with his entire family, including a buxom wife and six sturdy sons, was a fervent friend of independence and of the privateers. He woud be a splendid advocate of the Cause in North America.[136]

Mention of General William H. Winder does not recall any shining clouds of glory. We remember him as an able and respected Baltimore lawyer who injudiciously accepted a military command in the War of 1812, a responsibility for which he had no experience or talent. He led a brigade at the capture of Fort George, Ontario, in 1813, where General Winfield Scott "fought nine-tenths of the battle," but ten days later he unwittingly walked into the British lines during the dusk of the evening, in the disastrous affair of Stony Creek, and was taken prisoner. We cannot say that the British commander shrewdly gave

---

pressly or by implication the neutral obligations which the United States may owe, according to the law of nations, to the King of Spain and the said Province of Buenos Aires." National Archives (Washington), Division of State Department Archives, series Argentine Republic, W. G. D. Worthington, April 26, 1817–July 9, 1818. Folio 59–61.

135. Jan. 14, 1818. Manning, *1*, 370.

136. Thomas Taylor, Secretario de Estado, al Supremo Director, Buenos Aires, Feb. 19, 1818. A.G.N., S1–A2–A4, No. 8.

him a short parole, in order to get him back in the American army, but unfortunately it did expire just in time to allow him to command the militia forces in front of the British advance on Washington in 1814. There he was routed in one of the greatest exhibitions of military incompetence in all our history. We remember the vivid passages in which Henry Adams described Winder's inglorious day at the battle of Bladensburg, the capture of Washington and the burning of the Capitol that followed. But Taylor's opinion of Winder had been formed not by an historian still unborn but by Winder himself, entertaining his client in the bosom of his family in times of peace, of piping peace made all the more agreeable by the pleasant profits of defending, before sympathetic juries, Baltimore privateers that flew the flag of Buenos Aires and were manned by local boys.

Pueyrredón promptly accepted the nomination. He announced the appointment of Winder in a letter of February 25, 1818, to the President: "The authorized intervention of a person who unites probity, distinction and public esteem with high rank, can do no less than produce results favorable to the reciprocal interests and relations which happily exist between the States over which you so worthily preside, and the provinces under my command." [137] To Winder he forwarded a title of citizenship in Buenos Aires, together with an appointment as Special Deputy of the United Provinces near the government of the United States, for which credentials were enclosed. His only instructions were that he lend his "protection" to the activities of a consul general, Don David Cortez DeForest, the bearer of the papers. A flattering and fulsome letter stated that the exploits of the "hero of Canada" were not unknown along the Río de la Plata! [138] There was no vulgar mention of emolument in dealing with a man of so much *brillo* as Winder of Bladensburg.

David Curtis DeForest, who now steps into the picture, was an adventurous Connecticut Yankee, like John Ledyard before him. Ledyard's journeyings had been to the Northwest Coast, China, Russia, and the distant steppes of Siberia. DeForest, a robust swarthy hulk of a youth, roamed the North and South Atlantic, the great plains of Rio Grande do Sul and the Plata, and the pampas of Patagonia. Born at Huntington, Connecticut, in 1774, he established himself, after a

137. Pueyrredón to the President of the United States, Buenos Aires [Feb. 25, 1818], National Archives (Washington), Records of the Department of State, Argentine Republic, Notes. *1*, pt. 1, fol. 72. This is endorsed "translation to the Secretary, May 7" [1818].

138. Buenos Aires, Feb. 25, 1818. A.G.N., S1–A2–A4, No. 8.

most adventurous career, as a prosperous merchant in Buenos Aires in the days of the Spanish viceroys, when, we are so often given to understand, all commerce was closed to foreigners. His biography [139] reveals that North American ships with the Stars and Stripes were frequenting that port in the very first years of the century.[140] By 1809 the young man had already acquired a competence. In December of that year he was suddenly expelled from the country by the Spanish viceroy Cisneros. Before this he had prudently transferred some of his funds to the United States, an example which many a later resident of Latin America has done well to imitate, before the recent reversal of the trend. After a visit to England, he returned to his home town of Huntington, in 1811, where he promptly married Julia Wooster, one of the belles of Connecticut, then a "blonde sparkling girl of sixteen years," "a golden-haired woman with a skin like roseate snow," to use the sedulously chosen words of the nephew biographer.

The Revolution of May 25, 1810, cleared the way for DeForest's return to Buenos Aires early in 1812. His business prospered again, thanks to favors of the government. By this time he was a citizen there and doing well, too. In the autumn of 1815 he secured an agency

139. J. W. DeForest, a nephew, had access to some business ledgers and correspondence and other papers of DeForest, which he uses in the chapters devoted to him in *The DeForests of Avesnes* (New Haven, 1900). L. Effingham DeForest, a descendant, has kindly furnished me with notes and transcripts from David C. DeForest's accounts and letterbooks which were made for the biographer by Col. George Butler Griffin, the son of one of D. C. DeForest's daughters. L. E. DeForest published two letters of D. C. DeForest, written in 1802 from Montevideo, which narrate his early wanderings in Brazil, and the *Banda Oriental*. See "A Trip Through Brazil in 1802," *Brazil* (N.Y.), Year IX, No. 101, March 1937. Most important of all, I have been privileged to read eight volumes of a personal journal, 1800–18, and nine volumes of letterbooks, 1798–1825, of David C. DeForest. These documents, hitherto unexploited by historians, were in the possession of Frederick Hill of Catskill, N.Y., a great-grandson of DeForest and have been recently acquired by the Sterling Memorial Library of Yale University.

140. In 1807 DeForest suggested to the Department of State the advisability of sending a commercial agent to Buenos Aires. National Archives (Washington), Division of Department of State Archives, Miscellaneous Letters, Oct. 4, 1807. Dr. Lewis Hanke called my attention to this document, which is also in the DeForest letterbooks. In 1811, DeForest tried unsuccessfully for appointment as United States consul to Buenos Aires, or to Rio de Janeiro. DeForest letterbooks.

Charles Lyon Chandler published some notes on "Early River Plate Voyages, 1798–1800" in *A.H.R.*, 23 (July 1918), 816–26, showing that the first recorded vessel flying the flag of the United States in the Plata estuary was the ship *John*, Captain Day, of Philadelphia, which arrived at Montevideo in Nov. 1798. The first at Buenos Aires was the *Palmyra*, admitted to Spanish registry. Chandler lists a number of arrivals at Montevideo and Buenos Aires between 1799 and 1807.

for distributing letters of marque in the United States, and lent his name technically to the ownership of four privateers commissioned to cruise against the commerce of Spain, and fitted out, one by John Jacob Astor of New York, one by George Crowninshield of Salem, one by Thomas Tenant of Baltimore, and one by d'Arcy and Didier of Baltimore.[141] DeForest, records his biographer, netted ten per cent of the sales of prizes taken by these vessels, and it ran into big money. In the spring of 1817, he decided to quit and go home. He sent his wife and four small children ahead of him on the big *Aurora*, Captain Searl, for New Haven. After winding up his business, he followed in February 1818. It was on this occasion that Tagle made him consul general, and bearer of the dispatches to General Winder. Of all this, Aguirre, still in the United States, remained uninformed until apprised by DeForest himself from Baltimore.[142]

DeForest's instructions of February 24, 1818, placed him under the governance of general regulations and obligations of consuls, gave him power to appoint vice-consuls, and stated that until an "ambassador" or other functionary should be dispatched to the United States, he, the consul general, would undertake to secure the recognition of independence by the United States, and promises for succors. He had powers to distribute letters of marque for privateers, and: "In case our corsairs should take some island suitable as a base and to which none of the recognized nations should have any right, the said Consul is empowered to set up such a municipal government there as may seem best to him, taking possession of the island in the name of this government." Finally, he was to concert all his proceedings with General Winder, in whose talents and liberal sentiments much confidence was placed. A supplementary mandate authorized him to treat and negotiate with the chief of any country where it might be convenient to fit out privateers.[143] Nothing was said about a salary for the consul general, or even expenses. Was he not a rich American?

The newly appointed consul general bore a letter from Pueyrredón to President Monroe, stating that in conformity with the articles [144] agreed upon with citizen William G. D. Worthington, the agent of the

141. J. W. DeForest. It may have been in connection with these craft that Tagle made his way to the United States in 1816.

142. Aguirre to DeForest, New York, May 5, 1818. He acknowledged DeForest's of April 30, and stated that he would have been glad to felicitate him earlier upon his appointment as consul general if the Buenos Aires government had notified him. A.G.N., S1–A2–A4, No. 8.

143. Instructions for DeForest as Consul General in the United States. Draft, Buenos Aires, Feb. 24, 1818. A.G.N., S1–A2–A4, No. 8.

144. Article 18 provided for consuls, vice-consuls, and vice-commercial agents of

United States in these provinces, he had nominated citizen David C. DeForest as consul general to the United States, with the powers specified in his commission and instructions respectively.[145] DeForest's credentials were thus based on the unsafe authority of Worthington's unauthorized agreement, and we may presume that the alert John Quincy Adams would not fail to note this, should he find it convenient to do so.

The ink was scarcely dry on DeForest's instructions when Tagle received the special fact-finding commission from the United States, Theodorick Bland, John Graham, and Caesar A. Rodney, who landed at Buenos Aires on February 28, 1818. They found the Secretary ready to accept their representations on everything. He told them that the government thoroughly approved the step which the United States had taken in occupying Amelia Island, and disavowed any authorization on its part to the adventurer, MacGregor. When they represented to him the depredations on the commerce of the United States by the illegal privateers flying the flag of Buenos Aires, and expressed a hope that the government would stop the abuse of its commissions, he replied that hitherto no formal complaint had been made, but his government would afford redress upon representation and proof of the injury.[146] These assurances, of course, did not correspond with the confidential instructions just issued to the newly appointed consul general to the United States.

DeForest was distinctly the ablest person who sought to represent the Buenos Aires government in Washington during these early years of informal contacts, and no less disingenuous than his chief, Gregorio Tagle. His first act was to deliver the papers to Winder, who immediately informed the President of the appointment, and asked what to do about it.[147] During the war with England, Monroe had been Secretary of War, and he and Winder had remained on most friendly terms

---

either party to reside in the territory of the other and to enjoy all the rights and privileges belonging to them by reason of their function. Article 24 pledged both parties to use their best efforts with the Powers to encourage the abolition of the African slave trade!

145. Manning, *1*, 378.

146. It "had taken every possible precaution in its power in such cases; that it had established and promulgated a set of rules and regulations for the governance of its private armed vessels . . . and that it had, in all cases, *as far as practicable,* enjoined and enforced a strict observance of those regulations and the law of nations." Report of Theodorick Bland, Nov. 2, 1818. Manning, *1*, 386. Italics inserted.

147. Winder to Monroe, Baltimore, May 3, 1818. Mary M. Kenway, "Correspondence between General William Winder and President Monroe with References to Proposals Made by the United Provinces of South America," *Hispanic American Historical Review*, *12* (1932), 458–59.

since then, perhaps because of their mutual confidence in each other's military competence, or lack of it. Monroe replied that if Winder took the appointment it would be highly acceptable to the government, particularly to the executive, which would feel free to communicate with him on all subjects interesting to both parties.[148]

Despite the President's encouragement, Winder did not accept the commission, perhaps for the reasons which had led DeForest to suggest to Tagle that a retainer would have been appropriate.[149] Such seems to be the way of lawyers. In declining the honor, he declared that DeForest appeared to have the necessary qualifications, and he promised to aid him with his advice and judgment. He added some lengthy and well-stated comments on the attitude of the United States toward Hispanic America, along the lines of the counsel just received from Monroe, and urged the Buenos Aires government to conserve the advantages of the neutral position of the United States.[150]

On Winder's advice DeForest proceeded immediately to Washington to present his credentials as consul general. The Worthington agreement had preceded his arrival by several weeks. It had greatly displeased the President. "Dismiss him instantly," he ordered the Secretary of State. "Recall him. Dismiss him! Now, to think what recommendations that man had! Dismiss him at once, and send him the notice of his dismission by every possible channel. Send it to Halsey [the Consul], although Halsey himself is recalled. However, the Commissioners, when they arrived there, will have set all right." [151] Naturally this unauthorized document made Monroe's government cautious about dealing with DeForest, lest it thereby sanction the agreement and recognize out of hand the independence of the Buenos Aires government.

On May 7, 1818, the Secretary of State received DeForest, whose credentials rested on this unauthorized instrument.

"Under existing circumstances," Adams explained, after the usual exchange of amenities, "it has not been thought prudent to recognize the Government of Buenos Aires. Further, the supposed treaty which

148. Monroe to Winder, Washington, May 11, 1818, ibid.

149. DeForest to Tagle, Baltimore, May 17, 1818. A.G.N., S1–A2–A4, No. 8.

150. Winder to Tagle, Baltimore, June 5, 1818. A.G.N., S1–A2–A4, No. 8. Winder sent the President a copy of his reply. Winder to Monroe, Baltimore, July 23, 1818, in Johnson Collection of the Monroe Papers, Library of Congress. Miss Mary M. Kenway, in printing this exchange of letters between Monroe and Winder, notes a calendar in the Library of Congress of Monroe Papers still in private hands, which contains a copy of the letter of June 5, 1818, to Tagle.

151. J. Q. Adams, *Memoirs,* March 28, 1818.

Mr. Worthington assumed to make is without any authority and has not been approved by the President. Consequently we cannot receive you formally in your character of Consul General, but you are at liberty to seat yourself down in any part of the United States and to act in your official character in the same manner as if you were received in due form. You may correspond with this Department and you will receive all proper attentions and respect from the Government."

"All the Americans in Buenos Aires think Mr. Worthington's treaty very ridiculous," responded DeForest, "done solely with a view to making himself seem important; but he will doubtless make a similar treaty in Chile."

"Since a Consul from this country has been appointed to Buenos Aires," he observed further, "the Director, Mr. Pueyrredón, thought there would be no difficulty in receiving one here. I myself am a citizen of the United States, and have returned to remain here. I have no intention ever to go back to South America. I didn't ask for my appointment; it was given to me in order to prevent irregularities like those which have been committed by privateers under the flag of Buenos Aires, which the Director highly disapproves. After all, mine is only a mercantile agency. It can't be considered in the same light as one of a political nature. Shall I show you my commission? Or, if I apply in writing for an *exequatur,* shall I receive an answer?"

"It will be unnecessary to write," said the Secretary. "It would be more consistent with delicacy if we understand each other orally. But if you prefer to write, I will answer you to the same effect as what I now tell you."

"I shall accept with pleasure," replied DeForest, "the acknowledgment made, though informal, and hope that the relations of the two countries may, ere long, be placed on a more intimate footing."

"I want to say further," he declared, doubtless referring to Aguirre's ill-advised protests over the occupation of Amelia Island, "that I am confident that the government of South America [152] is not disposed to urge any point which might be disagreeable to this government, and so I shall be studiously cautious not to take any step calculated to embarrass its measures."

152. The phrases "United Provinces of the Río de la Plata," "United Provinces of South America," "Government of South America," etc., were all used with little distinction, to designate the government of Buenos Aires; but Adams, later in December, urged DeForest that a government should have a fixed and appropriate name. He did not recall the various analogous differing terminologies through which the United States of America had confirmed its official name.

"Does your commission interfere with Mr. Aguirre's?" asked Adams.

"No. Mr. Aguirre's commission is merely to procure arms and naval stores, and an armed vessel. He has no authority to ask for the acknowledgment of his government and he knew it was not the wish of the Director to press this government upon that subject. Other persons here have instigated him to do that."

"Will it be all right for me to see the President?" he inquired at the end of the interview.

"I have no doubt it will be," said Adams. "I shall mention your wish to him tomorrow morning. No doubt if you call at the house you will be received." [153]

In this first interview DeForest had masked the real object of his mission: to seek recognition; to give out *letters-of-marque;* to look for a privateering base. He ventured a little further in another conversation the next day. Of course, he did not reveal his instructions to take possession of some island as a base for privateering operations.

"If the Government of Buenos Aires should send an expedition to take Florida," he asked Adams outright, "would the Government of the United States take any measure to prevent it?"

"The same law by which we took possession of Amelia Island applies in such a contingency to all Florida," the Secretary answered emphatically. "It has been in existence ever since 1815 [*sic*], and it expressly provides that no foreign power be permitted to take possession of that province or of any part of it. The United States have a claim upon it for indemnities which have long been due from Spain, and they cannot suffer it should be taken out of their hands by a third party."

"The Government of Buenos Aires had no concern in the late transactions at Amelia Island," DeForest vouchsafed, "and were entirely satisfied with the steps taken there by the United States. But the possession of a port in the Gulf of Mexico would be of great importance to them as a means of annoyance to Spain, and unless they can take Florida they can have no port upon the Gulf to which their privateers can resort."

"Congress passed its law without any intention to injure the interests

153. I have reconstructed this interview from the account in J. Q. Adams's *Memoirs* for that date and from DeForest to Tagle, Baltimore, May 17, 1818, above. For the benefit of the critical student, I wish to explain that remarks above put into quotations, and not found in the *Memoirs,* are taken from DeForest's dispatch. The two accounts do not disagree, but rather supplement each other. DeForest, however, includes all conversation as of the interview of May 7.

of Buenos Aires," replied Adams; "while it remains in force the President is bound to execute it. The Commissioners to South America have been instructed to give every suitable explanation upon that subject. No doubt they have done so at Buenos Aires."

DeForest decided to let his reception as Consul General rest, for the time being at least, upon these conversations with Adams, without any further exchange of notes. He then went to the President's house, where he was received in the most friendly fashion. Monroe assured him that he regretted most sincerely the causes which prevented a formal recognition, and hoped that these would soon be removed. He observed to DeForest (what he wrote in answer to Winder): the world was in such a state that much caution was necessary; all that could be done at this moment was to place relations with Buenos Aires upon an equal footing with Spain.[154]

After these discreet beginnings, DeForest decided to wait until the next session of Congress before doing anything more. Perhaps coached by Aguirre, whom he visited in New York, he had discovered that the great question of South American independence had become much mixed up in the party politics of the United States. He returned to Baltimore and proceeded on a tour of the north and east.[155] At New Haven he seated himself and family down to make their home. On the northwest corner of Church and Elm Streets, fronting the Green, he started to build a pretentious house. By the opening of Congress in November 1818, he was again in Washington, with his attractive young wife, for the winter season. He hoped that the return of the commissioners from Buenos Aires, and the increasing public sympathy for the South American revolutionists, might precipitate a move in Congress for recognition. He conferred with Henry Clay, leader of the opposition.

President Monroe by now had his mind almost made up for recognition. But the divided reports of the commissioners cast much doubt on the stability of the Buenos Aires government. John Quincy Adams felt that this afforded ample reason for going slow. The negotiation with Onís was at last offering some promise of success for the acquisition of Florida and expansion of the western frontier. Another reason impelling Adams to delay action was the mediation then underway

154. DeForest to Tagle, Baltimore, May 17, 1818, above. DeForest, writing even a week later, places the interview with the President as May 9. Adams notes it in his *Memoirs* as May 8, but says nothing of the conversation.

155. DeForest to Tagle, Boston, Aug. 20, 1818.

by the European allies between Spain and her revolted colonies. "It is our true policy to let this experiment fail," he noted, "without attempting to disturb it, which might unnecessarily give offense to the allies; and after it shall have failed, as fail it must, we shall then be at perfect liberty to recognize any of the South American Governments without coming into collision with the allies." [156] Adams resolutely refused, meanwhile, to make any bargain with Spain not to recognize the independence of the revolted colonies as a price for Onís's signature of the treaty that was expected to yield the coveted Florida and a new frontier line through to the other ocean. At the same time, upon Monroe's impulsion, he went through the motions of requesting France and Great Britain to unite with the United States in recognizing the revolted provinces. This would consume time. If accepted, contrary to Adams's expectation, so much the better.

DeForest, after talking with Clay, was now determined to push the government to acknowledge him formally,[157] and to get his representations into writing, so that Congress could call for the record, and it could be thus printed for popular appeal. After a written solicitation to the Secretary of State, he appeared at the Department for a long conference, on December 14, 1818. Again the Secretary explained that the President thought the time had not yet come for such a formal recognition as would be signalized by an exequatur to him as consul general. At the proper time, however, acknowledgment "would not be withheld," although any recognition by the United States would not decide the extent of territory claimed by Buenos Aires, such as the *Banda Oriental,* Santa Fé, and Paraguay, where separatist movements had gained headway.

It was now agreed that the substance of this should be recorded in notes passed between the two men.[158] This was done, and the Secretary added another note protesting against the excesses and irregularities of Buenos Aires privateers and their violation of the neutrality laws.[159] Adams suspected that DeForest himself was commissioning privateers, but could not prove it.[160] We know that he had instructions to do so, and that in the past he had grown rich at that business. Throughout

156. J. Q. Adams, *Memoirs,* Nov. 7, 1818.

157. DeForest to Tagle, Dec. 12, 1818. A.G.N., S1–A2–A4, No. 8. DeForest to Adams, Dec. 9, 1818. Manning, *1,* 515.

158. The interview is recorded by both men, without any substantial discrepancies: in Adams's *Memoirs,* Dec. 14, 1818, and in DeForest to Tagle, Georgetown, Dec. 18, 1818. A.G.N., S1–A2–A4, No. 8.

159. Adams to DeForest, Jan. 1, 1819. Manning, *1,* 88.

160. J. Q. Adams, *Memoirs.*

the rest of his life he remained engaged in claims relating to his privateers and agencies for others.[161]

In the interview of the 14th, DeForest had asked if it would be proper to appear at the President's drawing room. He met no objection. On Christmas Day he and his wife presented themselves.

DeForest was very proud of the impression made by his wife at this *soirée*. He wrote to his little daughter, Pastora, back in Connecticut, that mamma had been the most elegantly dressed woman of all. People had admired her so much that papa was afraid of losing her. "She was called the Buenos Aires beauty, and a great many people thought she was a native of that, your native country. May you excel your mother in everything, my little Darling." [162]

The Spanish minister did not share this pride. He had been horrified to discover himself at the same meeting with such people. A dispatch of his in the Spanish archives dutifully describes his official embarrassment:

Last Wednesday, finding myself at what is called here the Drawing Room, where the President and his wife hold court together, I saw rather a nice looking lady in the *salon* beside one of my daughters next to the fireplace, which is the spot of most distinction at this time of the winter. I noticed that she seemed to feel at home, and that a great many people were paying homage to her. When I asked who that person was, I was told that she was Mrs. Forest, the wife of the Consul General of Buenos Aires, and they pointed out to me, near her, an uncouth, rough-looking man, six feet six [163] in height, saying that he was her husband, a millionaire, who a few years ago was a stable-boy in this country. Without saying anything, I immediately picked up my daughters and went home, with the British Minister following after me— although conceivably the latter might not have been leaving for the same reason. This is the second time that I have encountered such gentry in this court. The first was in the time of the previous President, Mr. Madison, when I met up with the famous Gual, who then called himself Minister of Cartagena and Caracas, but having then shown my disgust to people who could suggest to the

161. His attorney was Judge David Daggett of New Haven. In the Daggett papers at Yale University Library there are a few letters from DeForest about privateering matters. The DeForest letterbooks have more of such matter.

162. Dec. 30, 1818, cited by J. W. DeForest, p. 148, under the date of Dec. 30, 1819.

163. DeForest was actually 5 feet 11½ inches in height, as shown by his military record. DeForest letterbooks.

President that he ought not to return, I didn't see him any more. I don't think this will be the case now, because DeForest enjoys a high degree of protection, above all by Clay's party, and the Government does not care to collide with *him*.[164]

These appreciations are belied by the portrait of DeForest which, with one of his wife, hangs in the Yale Gallery of Fine Arts. Samuel F. B. Morse painted a fine and distinguished gentleman. The "Buenos Aires beauty" appears in the same dress she wore at the President's levée. This portrait makes the husband appear much younger than a second one painted at the same time by Morse, and presented by DeForest to the University of Buenos Aires, on request. It now hangs in the *Museo Nacional* of that capital.

DeForest was waiting for Clay's opposition to manifest itself again in Congress. On January 14, 1819, the House of Representatives passed a resolution requesting information whether any independent government in South America had asked for the recognition of a minister or consul general, and what reply had been made. Adams sent in the correspondence he had exchanged with DeForest and with Lino de Clemente of Venezuela. He explained that the government had refused to have any communication with Clemente because he had been one of those who (with Martin Thompson) had signed the commission to MacGregor to take possession of Amelia Island; as to DeForest, his credentials were imperfect because they rested on Worthington's unauthorized articles; "recognition of him as consul general from the United Provinces of South America could not be granted, either upon the stipulation of supposed articles, which were a nullity, or upon the commission of a credential letter of the Supreme Director, without recognizing thereby the authority from which it emanated as a sovereign and independent Power." Adams made clear his suspicion that DeForest was working with the opposition by pointing out that in the previous May the envoy had declared himself entirely satisfied with his informal reception, but that "shortly after the commencement of the present session of Congress" he had renewed his solicitations.[165]

The Secretary, therefore, preferred to keep DeForest at arm's length. "In this affair everything is insidious and factious," Adams had noted

164. Onís to Casa Irujo, Washington, Dec. 29, 1818. A.H.N., Estado, leg. 5643.

165. Adams to President Monroe, for transmission to the House of Representatives, Washington, Jan. 28, 1819. Manning, *1*, 88. Carlos Calvo printed translations of these documents in his *Anales de la revolución de la América Latina* (Buenos Aires, 1867), *5*, 172–79.

while preparing his statement for Congress to accompany the correspondence. "The call is made for the purpose of baiting the Administration, and especially of fastening upon the Secretary of State the odium of refusing to receive the South American ministers and consuls general. DeForest's notes are cunning and deceptive." [166]

A happy inspiration enabled the shrewd Secretary of State to break up this collusion with Clay. When DeForest next appeared at the Department, Adams deftly reminded him that he was still a citizen of the United States, and hinted that he was liable to prosecution for violation of the neutrality laws.[167]

The hint was enough. It changed DeForest's attitude immediately. He did not care to face a host of lawsuits, the loss of his curiously gotten fortune, perhaps jail itself. He quickly declared himself entirely satisfied with the friendly disposition of the executive, and became straightway convinced, as he told Adams, that the proceedings of Clay, with whom he admitted having talked, and his supporters, had injured rather than aided the cause of South America. He went back to New Haven and finished his house there and never seriously bothered John Quincy Adams any more. Soon afterward the opposition in Congress was conjured by Adams's magnificent diplomatic victory, the Trans-continental Treaty. Spain had yielded Florida and acknowledged a new frontier from the Gulf of Mexico to the Pacific Ocean.

The effect of this triumph was to change Clay's tactics to one of milder opposition to the government. On May 10, 1820, the House of Representatives passed his resolution: "that it is expedient to provide by law a suitable outfit and salary for such Minister or Ministers *as the President, by and with the advice and consent of the Senate, may send to the Governments of South America,* which have established and are maintaining, their independence of Spain." [168]

For two years more Monroe's government postponed recognition. Good pretexts for delay still stood to hand: the confusion of anarchical governments in Buenos Aires, and the continued depredations of irresponsible privateers bearing the flag of that government. These problems eventually cleared up. The European mediation had collapsed. Spain finally ratified the Transcontinental Treaty (February 22, 1821). A semblance of order emerged from chaos on the banks of the Plata. To satisfy complaints of the United States, the government

166. J. Q. Adams, *Memoirs,* Jan. 20, 1819.
167. Ibid., Jan. 22, 1819.
168. Italics inserted.

down there revoked all its commissions to privateers (October 6, 1821). Congress, on February 10, 1821, had passed Clay's resolution of sympathy for the revolted provinces, and endorsed recognition of their independence *whenever the President should decide to act.* Now the way was clear for recognition. On March 8, 1822, President Monroe sent in to an expectant and wholly cooperative Congress a message urging an appropriation to support diplomatic missions to the new states. A bill for that purpose passed almost unanimously, May 4, 1822.

Monroe's message prompted DeForest to the last diplomatic effort of his career. He wrote a letter from New Haven claiming for Buenos Aires the privilege of being the first state to be recognized, with himself as *chargé d'affaires* and consul general. Adams answered that since he was an American citizen he could not serve as *chargé d'affaires;* to be recognized as consul general he would need a new commission wholly unrelated to the unauthorized Worthington agreement.[169] The honor of being first went to Colombia. Her tactful agent, Manuel Torres, long a resident of the United States, never made the mistake of collaborating with the opposition in Congress. He had gained the complete confidence of Monroe and Adams. The President received him as *chargé d'affaires* on June 19, 1822. Next came Mexico (December 12, 1822), the Central American Confederation (September 10, 1823), the Empire of Brazil, now separated from personal union with Portugal (May 26, 1824). Formal diplomatic representatives were appointed to the United Provinces of the Río de la Plata (January 27, 1823), to Chile (January 27, 1823), and Peru (May 2, 1826). The American minister, Caesar A. Rodney,[170] arrived at Buenos Aires before a minister had been sent from that republic to the United States; but on October 7, 1824, President Monroe received General Carlos Alvear as minister from the Buenos Aires government. In a long and intimate conference, speaking in Spanish, the President reviewed the whole of American policy toward recognition of the revolted provinces, and gave an account of the motives and events that had induced him to proclaim the Monroe Doctrine in the previous December. The friendliness and sincerity of the President, and his venerable appearance, made a lasting impression on Alvear, who returned to Buenos Aires with a conviction that the United States was South America's best friend.[171]

169. Adams to DeForest, Washington, May 23, 1822. Manning, *1,* 159.

170. Enrique Loudet, *El Primer Diplomático Norteamericano en la República Argentina* (Publicaciones del Instituto Cultural Argentino-Norteamericano, Buenos Aires, junio 1938).

171. Thomas B. Davis, Jr., *Carlos de Alvear, Man of Revolution: The Diplomatic*

DeForest had already begun in New Haven annual celebrations of the national holiday of the United Provinces, the 25th of May. The first of these was held in 1821, with a dinner and toasts at the County Hotel, and an oration at the County Court House. At seven o'clock in the evening cannon were drawn up in front of DeForest's new mansion, which flew the blue and white flag of Buenos Aires, and a national salute was fired to "a Sister Republic." Later a reception occurred in the DeForest house.[172] This he repeated in 1822.[173]

Of course he had absolutely no authority to request to be recognized as *chargé d'affaires,* as well as consul general. He had received no communication whatsoever from the Buenos Aires government since the establishment of the new Rivadavia government in 1821. That government in 1823 decreed the immediate recall of all outstanding diplomatic or consular commissions. On March 13, Rivadavia wrote to DeForest apprising him of the cessation of his office as consul general in the United States, and instructing him to send home all of his official papers directly to the government, together with any

---

Career of Argentina's First Minister to the United States (Duke University Press, 1955).

172. *Connecticut Herald* (New Haven), May 29, 1821. See also *Columbian Register,* May 26, 1821.

173. Under the heading, "The Independence of Buenos Aires," the *Connecticut Journal* thus described the ceremony:

> On Friday evening of the past week, the birthday of this Sister Republic was suitably commemorated in this city. A large number of the most respectable citizens of New Haven, and gentlemen of both branches of the Legislature, assembled by previous invitation at the elegant mansion of David C. DeForest, who was elected First Consul to the United States by the new government. After the usual congratulations, the company partook of a sumptuous entertainment, and the evening passed with much mutual good feeling, and with the highest gratification which the occasion and the appropriate and elegant preparations could inspire.
>
> The following poem was written for the occasion, and read at the close of the entertainment with unmingled applause. We need not add that it is from the pen of the inimitable Percival:
>
> > Hail to the land of the free and the bold,
> > Where Honour and Justice have planted their throne,
> > Where the hearts of the meanest can never be sold,
> > And Order and Liberty reign there alone.
> > Hail to the souls that can never be slaves,
> > Who boast of the rights they have won by the sword,
> > Who fight for their forefathers' altars and graves
> > And soar, as the eagle, who rescued them, soar'd.

J. W. DeForest, p. 152.

remaining letters of marque with an explanation of the status of any that he had used.[174]

DeForest received this in New Haven on June 15, and immediately notified Adams of the termination of his functions as *"chargé d'affaires* and consul general."* To Rivadavia he replied belatedly that "want of a convenient opportunity" prevented him from acknowledging the notice of his dismissal until September 7. It may be suspected that he was playing for time, hesitating to entrust to ordinary conveyance his official archives, documents so highly compromising to him as a citizen of the United States. He therefore awaited a suitable occasion to send them by a confidential person. In his last letter of September 7, 1823, DeForest said that the notice of March 12 was the only communication received from the government of Buenos Aires since the establishment of the present administration; moreover, that government had not acknowledged receipt of any communications from him, "of which I have made many, most of them in triplicate. Nor does it intimate to me how and when I am to be rewarded for my services during the time I have been in their employ." This farewell epistle, nevertheless, closed on a note of good will: "With my best wishes for the happiness of Buenos Aires, I have the honor to remain . . . David C. De-Forest." [175]

The first recognized minister from Buenos Aires, Carlos Alvear, had instructions to secure DeForest's official archives and bring them home. The latter invited Alvear to New Haven, but the minister did not come. Thereupon DeForest sent to him in New York three packets of unused letters of marque and privateering commissions, and two old surrendered, used commissions, together with the exchanges of notes with John Quincy Adams.[176]

He never forgot his foster-country, the scene of his early adventures, the source of his fortune. His home on the Green in New Haven is remembered for the public celebrations of the 25th of May. In the

---

174. Bernardino Rivadavia al Sr. David C. DeForest, March 13, 1823. *Documentos para la historia Argentina,* XIV, *Correspondencias generales de la Provincia de Buenos Aires relativas a relaciones exteriores,* Emilio Ravignani, editor (Buenos Aires, Facultad de Filosofía y Letras, 1921).

175. DeForest to Rivadavia, New Haven, Sept. 7, 1823. A.G.N., S1–A2–A4, No. 8.

176. DeForest letterbooks. DeForest did not surrender his private letterbooks in which he had entered copies of all his official dispatches. I have not located any letters *received* by DeForest, such as his signed instructions, drafts of which I read in Buenos Aires. Comparison with DeForest's own letterbooks shows that the dispatches from him which accumulated in Buenos Aires, and are now preserved in the Archivo General de la Nación, are fairly complete.

basement of the new house the brawny man from Buenos Aires had placed a marble tablet, engraved on both sides. On one side was an injunction to future owners of the house always to observe with befitting ceremony the anniversary of the 25th of May.[177] On the other side was a legend, like that of a tombstone, recording the names with dates and places of birth, of David Curtis DeForest, his wife, and five children (the last born in New Haven). The "Don," as wondering New Haveners dubbed him, became a benefactor of Yale College. He was able himself to celebrate only one more *veinte-cinco de Mayo*, before he died from a sudden pneumonia on February 22, 1825. The "elegant house" remained fronting the New Haven Green until 1910 when it was torn down to make place for the present County Court House.

V

What may we conclude from such light on this great movement for emancipation as is thrown by a study of the early missions from Buenos Aires to the United States?

177. To the owner of this House.
David C. DeForest,
A native citizen of Huntington in
this state; and at present Consul
General of the United Provinces of
South America, of which Buenos
Ayres is the Capital, where he
resided for many years; and
assisted in establishing its
Independence. greeting.
I have caused this
beautiful building to be erected
for your use, as well as mine; &
have taken much pains to accom
odate you, for which you will
never pay; & being no relative of
mine, I demand; that you assemble
your friends together on every
25th day of May in honor of
the Independence of South
America; it being on that day
in the year 1810. that the
Inhabitants of
Buenos Ayres
established a free Government
New Haven. 1820
David Hoadley, Arch't.
Horace Butler, Mason   D. Ritter, Sculp.

Inevitably the analogy of French policy toward the revolted English colonies of North America suggests itself to the student of the diplomatic history of the United States. In receiving with sympathetic encouragement the agents of the Latin American countries, in opening its ports to their flag, in permitting the export of all kinds of goods, including war materials, the United States recognized the belligerency of the new states, even before formal announcement by the proclamation of neutrality in 1815. It manifested a benevolent patience at the violation of its neutrality laws—public opinion would scarcely have permitted any other attitude on this score—and thereby ran its risks with Spain. This sympathy, stemming from a common ideology, and strengthening that ideology against the restoration of the legitimate monarchical model from Europe, and this source of armament and depot for marine operations, were certainly of significant aid to the cause of emancipation in the remainder of the New World to the south. Here the United States stopped. It did not go as far as France during the North American Revolution; it did not furnish war material from its own arsenals under any guise; it did not, finally, recognize independence before the issue was determined, nor make an alliance with any of the new states to enter the war for the purpose of breaking up the Spanish Empire, as did France in the case of Britain's great colonial war. It stood aside and let the Spanish Empire of Spain fall of its own weight and decrepitude. It allowed its republican example, its lively sympathy, and the succors of its neutrality to stream out to South America within the law of nations.

There was little else that the United States could have done that would have been practical or more helpful. From 1812 to 1815 the nation was at war with Great Britain. After 1815 Europe was restored in force on the formula of legitimacy and avowedly favorable to a restoration of Spanish sovereignty in the New World. Until 1819 it was not possible for John Quincy Adams to know surely whether the Holy Alliance would compel by mediation the return of Spanish legitimacy in America; he looked for first light on this question from Great Britain, and until 1818 Castlereagh kept him in the dark. Until then Adams could not be sure that recognition by the United States of the independence of Buenos Aires would not be regarded by one or more of the European powers as an act of hostility. If by involving itself in the Spanish American revolutions the United States had foolishly gone to war again in these years, immediately after its recent foolish war with Great Britain, it would have corresponded neither with national interests clearly seen nor with the welfare of the revolted provinces emotionally envisioned. On the contrary, as the warm-hearted James Monroe and the cool-headed John Quincy Adams both understood, it would have cut off the one great neutral storehouse and asylum of republicanism available to the revolted communities.

A universally respected British historian, Sir Charles Webster, in a masterly introduction to the very recent publication of selected official documents on *Britain and the Independence of Latin America,* concludes that without British diplomatic aid and the assistance of British volunteers in the patriot armies and navies, independence would have taken longer to achieve and have been more costly to Latin America. This may be true. He further insists that the United States contributed nothing more than the force of its republican example: both the example of its original successful revolution against Great Britain, and the persistent visibility of its healthy republican life during the period under discussion. The same authority concludes—and to this historians of whatever nationality will certainly agree—that their independence was won by the Latin Americans themselves. We beg, however, to challenge his comparison of the policies of Great Britain and of the United States toward Latin America.

If the United States had done no more than by its example to keep republicanism alive in the New World while it was being extinguished in Europe it would have merited well of Latin America; such service in itself far outranks that of British diplomacy on this side of the water. But the United States contributed more than the force of its example. In any comparison of the United States and Great Britain in action and policy vis-à-vis Latin America from 1810 to 1824, certain strong lights appear on the broad highway of history:

1. Against the British mercenaries who served heroically in the cause of liberty in South America we may balance the North American adventurers who manned the privateers of Buenos Aires and other states; the activities of both groups were frowned upon by the laws of their own countries.

2. Great Britain prohibited exports of arms and ammunition to the patriots; the United States allowed it.

3. Great Britain closed her ports to the flag of Buenos Aires and of the other new states; the United States opened its ports to them.

4. Great Britain did not recognize the belligerency of the new states until the very last phase of their struggle left no other choice; the United States recognized their belligerency at once, eleven years before Great Britain did.

5. The efforts of British diplomacy were directed primarily toward

the restoration of Spanish sovereignty over the revolted colonies until the patriots by their own efforts had made this impossible; then Great Britain, as the next best choice, worked for the establishment of independent monarchies in the New World under European princes, and achieved this in the one notable instance of Brazil. North American diplomacy actively endeavored to concert, particularly with Great Britain, a recognition by the principal powers of the independence of the new republics. British diplomacy shrank from such a concert, and finally recognized the independence of those republics only after recognition by the United States, two years earlier, had made it impossible to do otherwise and retain any influence in Latin America. The big test of the essence of policy was when in 1823 George Canning invited the United States to join in a declaration against intervention by Europe in the New World. The United States was willing—if Great Britain would at the same time recognize the independence of the new republics. Even then Great Britain refused to do so. In the last analysis, that is the one supreme fact in any comparison of British policy with that of the United States toward the independence of Latin America. Finally, the Monroe Doctrine, proclaimed as a result of Britain's reluctance to recognize, was not only a hands-off-the-New World sign to Europe, it was a proclamation of faith in republicanism in the New World and distrust of monarchy in the Old World.

The new states won their independence by their own efforts. For this more glory to their history. In the great *epopeya* of emancipation, all the neutral powers were following primarily their own interests, as every sincere and self-respecting nation ought to do within the law; but the national interests of the United States, freed from the diplomacy of the Old World, coincided more closely with those of the new states than did those of Great Britain with its unescapable commitments to the continent of Europe. The benevolently neutral policy of the United States was of more assistance to the revolutionists of South America than could have been its belligerency in a formal alliance, since it lacked control of the sea; that benevolent neutrality, it is submitted, was more helpful to the cause of emancipation than was Britain's partiality to Spain. And the beacon light of successful republicanism held aloft in the New World helped to deter the new states from being guided by British diplomacy into the realms of European monarchical legitimacy, that shadowed vestibule leading back to the power politics of the Old World.

15. Woodrow Wilson and Latin America

To MARK Woodrow Wilson's Centennial there has been little pomp and parade or celebration with shows, games, sports, bells, bonfires, and illuminations from one end of the continent to another, such as old John Adams prescribed for public commemorations like the Fourth of July. It is rather in quiet academic conferences and convocations, in churches, and in meetings of learned societies that we are paying hopeful tribute to one of our most eminent Presidents, founder of the League of Nations. A notable feature of such memorials has been the historians' appraisal and reappraisal, in the midst of a divided, deeply troubled world, of Wilson's personality, character, career, and place in history. One would like to believe that Woodrow Wilson would have it so. Did he not, conscious of some historic destiny, preserve every bit of his personal papers—four tons of them (including the weight of the filing cases)—for scholars to study in future generations? Assiduous investigators have now examined every scrap, plus tons of state papers and other documents. Would Wilson be content with their findings? One hundred years after his birth it would seem that many of them have presented more of an autopsy than an apotheosis of the great Virginian, apostle of world peace.

It is not my purpose to repeat, much less try to add to, the refinements of Woodrow Wilson's lonely personality and obstinate character that have been elaborated so perspicuously by the centennial historians and biographers.[1] Nor shall I deal with Woodrow Wilson and the

---

1. Charles Seymour, "Woodrow Wilson in Perspective," *Foreign Affairs* (Jan. 1956), 175–86; Robert H. Ferrell, "Woodrow Wilson: Man and Statesman," *Review of Politics* (April 1956), 131–45. An interesting section program at the forty-ninth annual meeting of the Mississippi Valley Historical Society, in Pittsburgh, Pa., presided over by Miss Katharine E. Brand, accomplished custodian of the Wilson Papers in the Library of Congress, produced two remarkably perspicuous papers, since printed: John A. Garraty, "Woodrow Wilson: a Study in Personality," *South Atlantic Quarterly* (April 1957); and John M. Blum, "Woodrow Wilson: a Study in Intellect," published in *Confluence* (Winter 1957). Arthur S. Link, who participated in the same program, has given us a realistic picture of *Woodrow Wilson and the*

Chapter in *Wilson's Foreign Policy in Perspective*, ed. by Edward H. Buehrig (Bloomington, Indiana University Press, 1957).

First World War, into which Wilson's moral choice of neutral policy involved the United States instinctively—to use a well-chosen word of Professor Buehrig's—on the right side.[2] Nor am I called on to appraise Woodrow Wilson at the Peace Conference, the supreme effort of his career. It is rather my assignment to deal with a less emphasized feature of President Wilson's foreign policy—his attitude toward Latin America and relations with the republics of the Western Hemisphere before and during the First World War.[3]

Morality, everybody agrees, was the fundamental basis of Woodrow Wilson's life, character, politics, and foreign policy. What, O teachers and O preachers, what is morality? Historians, philosophers, theologians, and sociologists have long struggled with this question. Woodrow Wilson had little difficulty in defining morality. To him it was the Christian religion, as interpreted and articulated by the Presbyterian faith which had been codified during the English Civil War between the forces of representative self-government and absolute monarchy. Morality in politics meant to Wilson self-government as developed out of English constitutional history by the Puritan Revolution of the seventeenth century and the Bill of Rights of 1689, translated by the Declaration of Independence and the Constitution of the United States into an American model of self-government and developing democracy, with the rights of the individual protected by independent courts of law. Wilson believed that the United States had a moral mission to defend, extend, and support Abraham Lincoln's concept of government of the people, by the people, and for the people

---

Progressive Era, 1910–1917 (New York, 1954). This volume contains a valuable selected bibliography of recent writings on Wilson. Professor Link is supplanting Ray Stannard Baker's older "authorized" biography with a new, highly scholarly work of which Volume *1* is entitled *Wilson: The Road to the White House* (Princeton University Press, 1947). I am indebted to him for allowing me to read in typescript the chapters on Woodrow Wilson's Latin American policy from his second volume, entitled *Wilson: The New Freedom* (Princeton University Press, 1956). August Heckscher has an exquisite introduction on Woodrow Wilson's "unshakeable spirit, suffused with inner lights" in his edition of some of Wilson's great speeches, *The Politics of Woodrow Wilson* (New York, 1956). The Woodrow Wilson Foundation, in its annual reports, keeps the reader informed about the progress of Wilsonian research and commemoration.

2. Edward H. Buehrig, *Woodrow Wilson and the Balance of Power* (Indiana University Press, 1955).

3. Adaptations of this theme were expressed in several centennial addresses by the author, including one at Mary Washington College, Fredericksburg, Virginia, Nov. 14, 1956. I have developed the general subject in an earlier publication on *The Latin American Policy of the United States* (New York, 1943).

to the greatest extent possible in peaceful relations with other peoples and nations.[4]

Now, the Latin American republics are independent, but only nominally self-governing on constitutional foundations. Historically there was a great difference between the character of the Anglo-American revolution for independence in North America and the Latin American revolutions for independence in Central and South America a half century later; and also between the constitutional evolution of the United States and that of the several republics (two of them at first monarchies) of Latin America. The uprising of the English colonies in North America was a revolution to preserve a freedom long since won and cherished, known and enjoyed, as "the rights of Englishmen," against a reactionary Crown and Parliament of England. On the other hand, the revolution of the Spanish and Portuguese colonies, inspired by the example of the United States, was a war to secure self-government and individual rights *for the first time.*

The people of the English colonies in North America had back of them generations, even centuries, of experience and education in representative self-government; the scattered Creoles of Latin America, ruling over a large population of semi-infeudated Indian tribes, had no such experience. After they won their independence, they drafted their new constitutions on the model of the United States, only to find that they could not make them function in a stable fashion. They developed a pattern of cycles of revolutions and new constitutions, actually dozens of them in the history of each state (except Cuba, which has had only four, so far), as compared with our own massive but unsuccessful revolution for Southern independence in the United States a century ago. Self-government in a Latin American country would inevitably break down in the course of time; a military dictator, a *caudillo,* would seize power in the name of the people and of public order and take over the government of the nation, sometimes becoming actual proprietor of the republic, even erecting statues to himself. Occasionally the nation, and even the people, would prosper materially under such a dictatorship, thanks to the return of law and public order, and security that invited foreign capital, while the *caudillo* built up an account in gold in European or North American banks against the inevitable popular revolution that some day would overthrow his tyranny, seize his ill-gotten wealth, set up a provisional government, formulate a new constitution, and re-establish representative

4. Harley Notter, *The Origins of the Foreign Policy of Woodrow Wilson* (Johns Hopkins Press, 1937).

and democratic institutions for another try at government of the people, by the people, and for the people.

Such has been the history of every Latin American government *without exception,* and the intermittent dictators have not always been comparatively mild and enlightened rulers like Porfírio Díaz of Mexico, who died a relatively poor man in exile. They have been more likely to be fearsome tyrants such as Rosas of Argentina, bloody Gómez of Venezuela, Machado of Cuba, or Perón of Argentina. Now and again it looked as though a Latin American republic had graduated from the pattern of revolution: Argentina enjoyed over a half-century of democratic self-government between Rosas and Perón; Colombia after 1904 settled down to a half-century of constitutional self-government, only to fall again into a dictator's hands; only Uruguay has sustained during the twentieth century an uninterrupted regime of constitutional democracy. Today a great part of the republics of Latin America are under military government with constitutional guaranties more or less suspended. No student of Latin American history can close his eyes to the historical argument that a government in Latin America is more likely to be changed, or a new constitution formed, by revolution than by fair and free elections after the model of the United States. No student of the subject should be blind to the further fact that despite the general character of their history and government, the Latin American peoples have steadily progressed in economy, material prosperity, and rising culture if not in political stability. And certainly their people are as moral and high-minded as any people, including Woodrow Wilson's countrymen.

This pattern of Latin American political habits was well established by Woodrow Wilson's time, but there is little evidence to suggest that he had known or thought much about peoples and nations to the south or was at all familiar with the Spanish language or literature, or with Latin American history or politics. His political and philosophical preceptors were Burke, Bagehot, and the revered Gladstone, rather than Sarmiento, Martí, and Rodó. I doubt if he had even heard of any of these great Latin American statesmen and moral philosophers. In his five-volume popular *History of the American People*—a work which may be compared in tone and character as well as purpose with Winston Churchill's current *History of the English-Speaking Peoples*—he devotes only ten or twelve pages, framed in facile generalizations, to the Spanish and Portuguese background of discovery, exploration, and conquest. These passages do little more than evoke the spirit of the age in terms of contrast between Spanish "adventure" and English "self-help," between Spanish rule by small groups of *conquistadores* over the vast and disparate spaces of a new world including "quaint and cloistered civilizations" of aborigines, and the unromantic but ardent English adventurers and their "swarming" settlers on the fringes of a continent counterclaimed from sea to sea by the Tudor monarchs. From there the narrative begins to build up the history of the North American people in terms of their English background, their Revolution against King and Parliament, western continental expansion and sectional conflict in the United States, and the development of self-government and democracy. Only incidentally do the Spanish heritage and Latin American independence enter the scene, in connection with the expansion of the United States in conflict with Spain and Mexico.

Woodrow Wilson of Virginia followed the legacy of abolitionist historiography, and the verdict of John Quincy Adams and Abraham Lincoln: he judged the war with Mexico a piece of "inexcusable aggression" on the part of the United States but "fine fighting" on the part of its soldiers. He extolled the Monroe Doctrine, and noted how (as soon as the Civil War in the United States ended) the United States had been the Republic of Mexico's salvation against the European usurper Maximilian and his phantom empire. He praised President Cleveland's insistence, as "best friend" of the Latin American republics, on arbitration of the boundary dispute between Great Britain and Venezuela which came to a head in 1895. He attributed American intervention in Cuba "not to the material aggrandizement of the United States," but rather to "assertion of the right of government to succor those who seemed hopelessly oppressed, to recover the order of its coasts, to free its trade from trammels put upon it by a war to which there seemed no end, to quiet the thoughts of its own people in order that they might turn again without distraction to their own affairs." It was, he further declared, "a war of impulse." Professor Wilson's history terminated with the end of the nineteenth century, without envisaging the new problems of relationships with the nations and peoples of Latin America. Only slowly did he come to regard the Cuban-Spanish-American War—like most North American historians he called it the Spanish-American War—in terms of the new framework of power and politics that was ushering in the twentieth century. Even then he weighed the resulting world picture more in terms of the enhanced potential of the President's role in leadership than its geopolitical significance in the shifting strategy of American defense and diplomacy.

The fervor of Woodrow Wilson's moral background and his almost exclusive preoccupation with the study of English and American history, politics, and literature gave him an inner compulsion to make his presidential dealings with Latin American countries conform to his own patterns of Anglo-American history and political theory. To him revolutions, such frequent occurrences in Latin America, were horrid enemies of self-government, which undermined a developing democracy, wasted the resources of the nation, and invited European intervention to protect foreign nationals—interventions which conceivably could develop into occupations, even protectorates or colonies, *à l'Egypte*. (Such of course, let it be said, would have been the case in independent Latin America, as in Africa, if it had not been for the United States and the Monroe Doctrine.) It followed in Wilson's thought that revolutions, when governments seized power in violation of the constitution of the state and the rights of the individual, were immoral. They should be discouraged; Wilson set his face against them. He seemed not to remember that his own principles of self-government stemmed from revolutions both in England and in America. Or perhaps he believed in revolution only against tyrants or grafters in order to establish honest constitutional governments.

The presidential campaign of 1912 in the United States, which brought Woodrow Wilson into the Presidency, revolved almost exclusively around programs of domestic reform, with no real issue on foreign affairs. To be sure, the platform of the Democratic Party remonstrated against President Taft's patience in dealing with Mexico, vigorously pledged adequate assistance to American citizens and their property abroad, and inveighed against so-called "dollar diplomacy" in the Caribbean and Central America. But these remonstrances were obviously perfunctory; the victorious Democrats would soon be accused of the same shortcomings by the defeated Republicans. Wilson himself made little if any reference to foreign affairs in his campaign speeches, and none whatever to Latin America.[5] "It would be the irony of fate," he remarked to an old Princeton friend a few days before his inauguration, "if my administration had to deal with foreign affairs."

It was Mexico that first imposed itself on President Wilson's attention in the field of foreign relations, and that set the pattern for his Latin American policy. In that neighboring republic a revolution

5. John Wells Davidson has recovered Wilson's campaign speeches, including a great many recorded in shorthand but never fully printed: *A Crossroads of Freedom: The 1912 Campaign Speeches of Woodrow Wilson* (published for the Woodrow Wilson Foundation by Yale University Press, 1956).

against the benevolent dictator, Porfírio Díaz, had produced a short-lived constitutional regime under the mild-mannered Francisco Madero. As Wilson entered the White House, Madero had just been overthrown by a military conspiracy headed by General Victoriano Huerta, who had imprisoned President Madero and Vice President Suárez in the National Palace, and proclaimed himself Provisional President of Mexico. This was certainly not an unprecedented procedure in Latin American history. But Huerta next took a somewhat irregular step. After swearing on a scapulary of the Virgin of Guadalupe and a medal of the Sacred Heart of Jesus, and by the memory of his mother, who had once worn these images on her breast, that he would allow no harm to Madero and Suárez, he did permit them to be molested: he ordered them to be transferred from the palace to the pentitentiary, and while en route under armed guard they were both killed, so it was explained, while attempting to escape. This furtive, bloody action was not an unknown practice, either: the Latin Americans even had a name for it—*ley de la fuga*.

When these political murders—for such is the name for them in English—took place, the foreign missions in Mexico City, including that of the United States, were on the point of recognizing the regime of Huerta, according to international custom, as the constituted authority with which to do business, the only authority, however shocking, immediately capable of protecting the rights of foreigners. European governments followed the advice of their diplomatic representatives and did so, and the usurper got a rump Congress to designate him President following the deaths of the elected President and Vice President, all according to the letter of the Mexican Constitution. Henry Lane Wilson, the United States ambassador, recommended the same action to the Department of State, both under President Taft and under Woodrow Wilson: despite what he lightly termed the "irregularity" of Huerta's removal of Madero and Suárez, recognition of his government was the only way to secure peace and order and the protection of American citizens. H. L. Wilson in fact was privy to the plot by which Huerta had seized power, if he did not actually abet it. President Taft, who had not relished the Huerta murders, had hesitated to recognize the new strong man, but the State Department had delayed advising *de jure* recognition of Huerta's government only as an inducement to secure full pledges for the protection of American citizens and property in Mexico.

President Wilson's reaction to the Mexican murders and the Huerta regime was prompt. He expanded it into a general pronouncement of policy that fitted perfectly his preconceived pattern of Christian morality applied to politics and foreign relations—a doctrine of nonrecognition of revolutionary governments, at least in Latin America. Within a week of his inauguration, on March 11, 1913, he issued his famous "Declaration of Policy in Regard to Latin America," a key document which needs to be quoted in any discussion of Woodrow Wilson and Latin America:

> One of the chief objects of my administration will be to cultivate the friendship and deserve the confidence of our sister republics of Central and South America, and to promote in every proper and honorable way the interests which are common to the peoples of the two continents. I earnestly desire the most cordial understanding and cooperation between the peoples and leaders of America and, therefore, deem it my duty to make this brief statement.
>
> Cooperation is possible only when supported at every turn by the orderly processes of just government based upon law, not upon arbitrary or irregular force. We hold, as I am sure all thoughtful leaders of republican government everywhere hold, that just government rests always upon the consent of the governed, and that there can be no freedom without order based upon law and upon the public conscience and approval. We shall look to make these principles the basis of mutual intercourse, respect and helpfulness between our sister republics and ourselves. We shall lend our influence of every kind to the realization of these principles in fact and practice, knowing that disorder, personal intrigues, and defiance of constitutional rights weaken and discredit government and injure none so much as the people who are unfortunate enough to have their common life and their common affairs so tainted and disturbed. We can have no sympathy with those who seek to seize the power of government to advance their own personal interests or ambition. We are the friends of peace, but we know that there can be no lasting or stable peace in such circumstances. As friends therefore, we shall prefer those who act in the interests of peace and honor, who protect private rights, and respect the restraints of constitutional provision. Mutual respect seems to us the indispensable foundation of friendship between states, as between individuals.
>
> The United States has nothing to seek in Central or South America except the lasting interests of the peoples of the two

continents, the security of governments intended for the people and for no special group or interest, and the development of personal and trade relationships between the two continents which shall redound to the profit and advantage of both and interfere with the rights and liberties of neither.

This policy of not recognizing governments established by unconstitutional methods (Huerta's procedure, aside from the murders, actually did conform with the letter of the Mexican Constitution), or contrary to the will of the people, was a large order indeed. How was the American government to ascertain whether or not a foreign election was conducted in a constitutional manner? How was Washington to decide what was the will of the people in another land? Would it go behind the courts of that country, examine into the nation's history, its politics, its sociology, its cultural anthropology? And even if it were able to do so in the instance of Mexico—which was doubtful how about other peoples and other governments constantly in change all over the globe? It would be a task of inquiry far beyond the capacity of the President of the United States, or any other chief of state, to inquire into and decide, no matter how large his corps of advisers. There were too many nations, too many peoples, too many cultures in the world. Hitherto governments had recognized or refused to recognize revolutionary governments according to their own *raisons d'état* in particular instances only; as a general rule and practice they recognized a government as soon as it had control over the territory of a people or a state and was in a position to carry out its obligations in international law toward foreign governments and nationals. Huerta was initially in this position.

At the beginning of his administration it was impossible for Woodrow Wilson, President of a country whose duty as he conceived it was to carry abroad conscience, ideals, and principles, to choose to recognize the "brute" Huerta. Disgusted at H. L. Wilson's advice, he finally accepted the resignation of that diplomat and relied on the reports of political and journalistic friends like William Bayard Hale, ex-Governor John Lind, and other observers who knew little about Mexican history or political habits, most of whom did not speak Spanish, but who could and did send in startling information, no doubt true, of Huerta's brutal and sodden character. Pursuing his idealistic policy of nonrecognition, the new President became involved in the Tampico incident and entangled in an abortive intervention in Vera Cruz. He overthrew Huerta in the end, only to see Mexico lapse into confusion and counter-confusion, as rival factions swirled in and out of the capital and a real social revolution ravaged the country. Before long he was bogged down in another intervention in northern Mexico, in pursuit of Villa, the bandit leader who killed men, women, and children in provocative raids on Texas towns. He ended by recognizing, in 1917, on the eve of the war with Germany, a military regime labeled "constitutionalist" but not much more moral than Huerta's—that of General Venustiano Carranza. Meanwhile hundreds of millions of dollars' worth of American property had been destroyed in Mexico and hundreds of American citizens had lost their lives.

Wilson's Mexican policy incurred the ill will of the old regime, which was ruined by the social revolution that followed the fall of Huerta; it did not gain the sympathy and friendship of the various revolutionary factions, whose common patriotism was incensed by punitive American interventions; and it involved the United States in distracting difficulties as it became increasingly preoccupied by greater problems arising out of the European war. The President's well-intentioned policy toward Mexico left a legacy of animosity in that country which it took a generation to overcome. And in relation to other areas, such as the Far East, his general nonrecognition policy ended with his administration, even before he left the White House. In China in 1915 he had followed the advice of his ambassador in recognizing Yüan Shih-k'ai's imperial government, set up over the Chinese Republic of 1913, as the government best adapted to the needs of the Chinese people at the time. "When Empire is proclaimed," Secretary Lansing telegraphed to the United States minister in Peking on December 21, 1915, after Yüan Shih-k'ai had raised himself from President to Emperor, "if no serious organized opposition exists and you see no other reason to doubt permanence of new order, you are instructed to recognize new government of China and say that, while the government of the United States may feel a natural sympathy for republican forms of government which fulfill the hopes of people of other countries, we recognize right of every nation to determine form of its government and that the people of China have our good wishes for undisturbed peace and prosperity."

Nevertheless, the inexperience, inconsistencies, and blunders of Woodrow Wilson's dealings with Mexico should not blind us to the essential humanity of his failure. In the face of immense provocation and the temptation to intervene in Mexico to protect the persons and property of United States nationals and other foreigners by a vast extension of the so-called Roosevelt (Theodore) Corollary to the Monroe Doctrine, Wilson (aside from the two punitive expeditions) respected the independence of the neighboring country. Mexico, that tempting cornucopia of wealth, invitingly adjacent to the United States, where already a billion dollars of American capital—and an equal amount of European capital—had been legitimately invested in enterprises great and small, did not suffer the fate of Egypt, Algeria, Morocco, Korea, Czechoslovakia, Rumania, or Poland. It is very doubtful whether public opinion in the United States would have supported such a decisive intervention. Wilson left the destiny of Mexico in the hands of its own people. He became convinced that the Mexican Revolution, politically and socially, represented a great liberating movement in human history, akin to the French Revolution, and he resolved not to let property interests, particularly foreign property interests, and notably American corporate interests, stand in the way of it. Furthermore, Wilson accepted the help of other Latin American countries, by group mediation, in order to extricate himself from his painful involvement with Mexico. That these mediations were unsuccessful does not mean that they were unfruitful, for they set a precedent for constructive inter-American peace efforts in later decades. In this sense—and in a wide moral view—Woodrow Wilson's sorry Mexican policy may not have been in vain.

In Mexico, Wilson refused to recognize a government which had seized power by a barracks revolt and suspended all constitutional guaranties. In the Dominican Republic and Nicaragua, Wilson intervened by force to prevent any overthrow of governments which had been kept in power by the financial protectorate installed by Theodore Roosevelt and stiffened by President Taft, and to secure continuing governments friendly to the purposes of the United States. Wilson strengthened and extended the Dominican protectorate by military occupation and formalized it with a new treaty. In Haiti, following the complete breakdown of law and order in 1915, he established a protectorate on an advanced Dominican model, with added Platt Amendment features, and supplied the reformed republic with a brand new constitution and a government bolstered by the occupation of American marines.

Wilson and his Secretary of State, the evangelical William Jennings Bryan, outdistanced the dollar diplomacy of Taft and Knox, which the Democrats had berated before their triumph of 1912. Bryan would have gone even further. He proposed a grand scheme by which the

United States would assume "safe" Latin American debts owing to European creditors in exchange for Latin American government bonds at $4\frac{1}{4}$ per cent interest, as against the going rate of $5\frac{3}{4}$ per cent for such indebtedness. The saving of $1\frac{1}{2}$ per cent would be put into a sinking fund which would enable the Latin American countries to pay off the debt within a reasonable time. Another advantage, Bryan pointed out to the President, would be that "the plan would give our country such an increased influence . . . that we could prevent revolutions, promote education, and advance stable and just government. . . . We would in the end profit, negatively, by not having to incur expense in guarding our own and other foreign interests there, and positively, by the increase of trade that would come from development and from friendship which would follow the conferring of the benefits named."

The pitfalls hidden in this device, as I have observed elsewhere, were the assumptions that public loans would have to be guarded less carefully than private loans, and that invited borrowing makes debtor governments friendly to creditor governments. And who could tell how long a Latin American government loan would remain "safe"? Wilson rejected Bryan's plan. Yet in a way Bryan's idea became the basis for the expanded and still unstudied dollar diplomacy of the last twenty years, providing low-interest government loans to Latin American countries after they had defaulted on their loans from private sources in the United States.

The fact is that under President Woodrow Wilson, the anti-imperialist, United States interventions reached their apogee in Central America and the Caribbean, in the military occupation of the Dominican Republic, Haiti, and Nicaragua, the development of sanitation and public works in those countries, and the complete control of their domestic and foreign affairs. Bryan would have persisted with Platt Amendment articles in his Nicaragua Canal treaty of 1916 if the Senate would have stood for it; he would also have extended the system to Honduras, if not to Guatemala. Wilson sent marines to Cuba in 1917, invoking the Platt Amendment to "protect life, liberty, and property" against the attempts of General Gómez to overthrow the Menocal government during the First World War. The underlying motive of Woodrow Wilson's whole diplomacy in the Caribbean and Central America, animated as it was by his genuine benevolent desire to better the lot of the peoples concerned, willy-nilly, by introducing North American principles of self-government and fair and free elections, was basically the same as that of Roosevelt and Taft: to remove all justification or pretext for European intervention in countries within the strategic radius of the newly constructed Panama Canal, particularly in case Germany should win the contemporary European war.

At first glance it would seem that Wilson's Latin American policy was not a whit more idealistic than that of his Republican predecessors, notwithstanding the treaty he signed with Colombia making reparation for Theodore Roosevelt's intervention in Panama (never ratified so long as Roosevelt lived). But Wilson looked beyond these interventions into a future in which they would be liquidated and the independence of each country would be mutually guaranteed by an inter-American system of collective security for all the republics of the New World, which would bulwark if not supplant the Monroe Doctrine by Pan-Americanizing it, so to speak. His proposed Pan American Liberty Pact was the most novel and interesting feature of his Latin American policy and the most impressive earnest of his real intentions: it sought to guarantee the territorial integrity and political independence of all the different peoples and nations of Latin America and the United States *under republican forms of government.*

Like most of Wilson's ideas and proposals, domestic and foreign, including the League of Nations, the proposed Pan American Liberty Pact, so to call it, was not his original concept. Other minds passed it along to him from as far back as Simón Bolívar. As late as 1910 a resolution of the Trans-Mississippi Congress called for a joint agreement by the various governments of America for a mutual guaranty of their sovereignty and territorial integrity. James L. Slayden of Texas introduced into the House of Representatives a resolution to this effect on April 23, 1913. Señor Pérez Triana, a former Colombian diplomat steeped in Bolivarian history and a member of the Hague Court of Arbitration, and the philanthropist Andrew Carnegie, who donated the Palace of Justice for the Hague Court, sponsored the idea; Carnegie proposed to Wilson a league of twenty-one American republics as an example to the world. Colonel Edward M. House, Wilson's intimate political adviser, saw a chance for the administration to make a splash in foreign affairs and to give the American people a respite from the continuous fever of domestic legislation; he adroitly strengthened the suggestion in Wilson's mind. House and Wilson began to draft an outline of the proposed treaty in December 1914, after they had got rid of Huerta. As finally presented to the ambassadors of

Argentina, Brazil, and Chile, whose diplomats had shown the most sympathetic interest in the project, the proposed treaty, in four articles, read as follows:

Draft Articles for Proposed Pan-American Treaty

Article I:

That the high contracting parties to this solemn covenant and agreement hereby join one another in a common and mutual guarantee of territorial integrity and of political independence under republican forms of government.

Article II:

To give definitive application to the guarantee set forth in Article I the high contracting parties severally covenant to endeavor forthwith to reach a settlement of all disputes as to boundaries or territories now pending between them by amicable agreement or by means of international arbitration.

Article III:

That the high contracting parties further agree, First, that all questions, of whatever character, arising between any two or more of them which cannot be settled by the ordinary means of diplomatic correspondence shall, before any declaration of war or beginning of hostilities, be first submitted to a permanent international commission for investigation, one year being allowed for such investigation; and, Second, that if the dispute is not settled by investigation, to submit the same to arbitration, provided the question in dispute does not affect the honor, independence, or vital interests of the nations concerned or the interests of third parties.

Article IV:

To the end that domestic tranquility may prevail within their territories the high contracting parties further severally convenant and agree that they will not permit the departure from their respective jurisdictions of any military or naval expedition hostile to the established government of any of the high contracting parties, and that they will prevent the exportation from their respective jurisdictions of arms, ammunition or other munitions of war destined to or for the use of any person or persons notified to be in insurrection or revolt against the established government of any of the high contracting parties.

The Latin American republics were still engaged in too many territorial disputes of their own, Mexico was too unsettled by her revolution, and Caribbean and Central American spirits were too disturbed by Wilson's interventions to bring a quick and general response to this grand idea stemming from Latin American historical tradition.

The negotiations over it dragged along until the breakdown of American neutrality in 1917, then lapsed altogether when the United States entered the First World War.[6] But the big Wilsonian, or let us call it the historical Bolivarian, idea came up again in Woodrow Wilson's and Colonel House's draft for a League of Nations, including non-American as well as American nations, in the famous Article X, the "heart of the covenant," as Wilson termed it:

> The members of the League undertake to respect and preserve as against external aggression the territorial integrity and political independence of all members of the League. In case of any such aggression or in case of any threat or danger of such aggression the [League] Council shall advise upon the means by which this obligation shall be fulfilled.

The immeasurable broadening of Wilson's experience in the World War caused him to leave out of Article X certain features of his projected Latin American covenant. Article X would guarantee political independence and territorial integrity but not necessarily republican government, Wilson's prescription for the New World; there were too many members of the League which were not republics. And Article X did not guarantee against any danger to republican forms of government from *internal* aggression—the moral hub of Wilson's earlier Latin American policy.

In the last year of Wilson's administration, after victory in the World War seemed to have removed any danger of European intervention in Latin America, the President turned his mind to preparing for evacuation of the United States' Caribbean protectorates, beginning with the Dominican Republic—in short, for liquidating United States imperialism. The task was carried forward by his Republican successors, even to the repudiation of the famous corollary of Theodore Roosevelt, and confirmed and baptized by the Good Neighbor policy of Franklin D. Roosevelt and Secretary of State Cordell Hull, and the Latin American doctrine of nonintervention.

What shall we say finally of Woodrow Wilson and Latin America? At first we are tempted to conclude, with many of the critical historians and biographers of the centennial year, that his policy was a historic failure, dramatized by the Mexican imbroglio, and that with the bene-

6. Philip H. Lowry has written an unpublished essay on the proposed Pan American Liberty Pact, as well as a doctoral dissertation on "Woodrow Wilson and Mexico," both now in the Yale University Library.

fit of hindsight the President would not, if he had the opportunity, do it over again the same way. But a second thought teases the mind. Certainly Wilson in his Caribbean policies, notably during the uncertain period of the First World War, was pursuing the vital interests of his country as laid down by his predecessors: to keep the world of Columbus, and particularly the strategic radius of the Panama Canal, free from further European intervention, even at the cost of intervention by the United States. And somehow, despite the fact that Wilson became the greatest interventionist in the history of the United States, the Latin American peoples in retrospect seem to have believed in his good intentions and his moral mission peaceably to extend government of the people, by the people, and for the people throughout the world. During the First World War not a single American republic declared war on the United States—not even Mexico, at the notorious invitation of Germany, or Colombia, at what certainly would have been the most convenient moment in history to do so. Eight republics declared war on Germany. Six eventually severed diplomatic relations with that power. Only six declared themselves strictly neutral.

To be sure, diplomatic practice, both in his own country and elsewhere, including Latin America, has repudiated Wilson's doctrine of nonrecognition; but there has been a large, perhaps a preponderating, portion of public and even of official sentiment in Latin America that shared Wilson's opposition to the recognition of military governments which have overthrown constitutional authority and denied the rights of the individual; witness the Central American regional peace treaties of 1907 and 1921, and the Tobar Doctrine of Wilson's distinguished Ecuadorean contemporary. There are many people in the Latin American republics today who would like to see the United States intervene to restore constitutional governments and individual rights in particular countries, although this is inconceivable under the solemn treaties of nonintervention. But, above all, note the Declaration of the Rights and Duties of Man at Bogotá in 1948, providing for protection of the rights and freedom of the individual through international or collective action. This Declaration states "that it is the continuing desire of the American States that there may be a full exercise of fundamental human rights and duties" within the American States, but "within the limits of their sovereignty and in accordance with their respective constitutional provisions," and "recommending to the governments of America that they encourage the legitimate activities of any authentically democratic persons or groups who are working to spread the knowledge of such rights and duties, thereby strengthening their observance." Certainly there is a Wilsonian smack about such a declaration.

The historian of inter-American relations could agree, I suggest, with the biographers of Woodrow Wilson that he would enthusiastically applaud the present inter-American peace structure and alliance and that Pan Americanism which is officially defined as a "moral union of all the American republics in defense of their common interests based upon the most perfect equality and reciprocal respect for their rights of autonomy, independence and free development." That, in essence, is what Woodrow Wilson was striving for. That is what he attempted to put into practice with his proposed Pan American Liberty Pact. That is what he tried to embody and expand in the League of Nations, which most of the Latin American countries promptly joined, and for which, perhaps, people all over the world of Columbus remember him most signally a hundred years after his birth.

Woodrow Wilson in his day failed in his Latin American policy. He failed in his broader world policy. His own people denied him during his last years. The people and government of the United States repudiated his diplomacy and, after his death, his foreign policy in the period between the two World Wars. But were not the greatest words ever uttered to human ears if not to human understanding: "He who would save his life must first lose it . . ."? Wilson lost his policy and his life with it, but his great moral vision lives on, let us hope with increasing vitality: great international institutions and grand alliances for human freedom are now deeply rooted in Wilsonianism. "Entirely apart from his contribution to a tangible instrument of political idealism whether permanent or fugitive," observes my eminent colleague Charles Seymour, "*Wilson is justified by faith. . . .* Regardless of the ebb and flow of political and historical opinion, he stands forth as among the greatest of all prophets in the cause of international justice and freedom."

Woodrow Wilson's Latin American policy, unreal as it seemed to diplomatists of his day, and even to many able historians and biographers of our day, was really an act of faith bespoken in the name of the people of the United States. The Good Neighbor policy of happier times, of which Wilson was the North American precursor, is an act of faith. The people of the World of Columbus, and the people of the great globe itself, have been striving, through times that try men's souls, to catch up to Woodrow Wilson's faith. Can they do so before our tortured world explodes into space beyond the capture of human thought or faith?

16. The Shifting Strategy of American Defense and Diplomacy

THESE EXAMPLES illustrate a widespread popular conception, or misconception, in the United States, that we do not have a foreign policy, or anyway what we have is not very well thought out, and that the whole thing had better be overhauled, or "streamlined," before it is too late.

The effort of this essay is to show that we do have a foreign policy, to recall its primæval principles, to trace its historical shape, and to point out its present-day design. At the outset, one should bear in mind the distinction between general principles and objectives, defining foreign policy, on the one hand, and on the other hand describing the changing circumstances and situations and specific test cases which those principles and objectives continually encounter in the historically shifting strategy of American defense and diplomacy, particularly in relation to the balance of power.

The fundamental bases of the foreign policy of any state are security for the state and what the state stands for in the world. Every state seeks security first; if it cannot have security, if it cannot be its own sovereign master, it cannot stand for much in this world. In the lack of collective security, its foreign policy must then be subordinated to that of another state. At least so it has been until now in history. After security, the foreign policies of states differ according to what they stand for in the world: divine-right monarchy, republicanism, free trade, mercantilism, democracy, the rights of man, communism, authoritarianism, imperialism (old-fashioned or new-fashioned), freedom of trade, autarchy, international peace, et cetera.

In terms of security, American foreign policy first meant the winning and preservation of our independence as an Atlantic Coast republic in a world of rival colonial empires; afterwards, security to expand through the empty continent of North America to found a transcontinental republic fronting on the two great oceans; then, security for our established domain and for our republican and democratic insti-

Published in *Virginia Quarterly Review*, 24, 1948.

tutions in a world of legitimate divine-right monarchy; next, in a new order of world politics and power ushered in by the twentieth century, security for the whole republican New World against the menace of imperialistic colossi arising and joining in the Old World; finally, security for all free peoples against the new imperialism of today.

The foundations of American foreign policy, in terms first of security, and then of principles which we stood for, had been laid in classic form by the year 1823. They were:

1. Sovereign independence, in order to preserve the rights of English freemen.

2. Continental expansion.

3. Abstention from the ordinary vicissitudes and ordinary combinations and collisions of European politics: first expressed in Washington's neutrality proclamation of 1793, then in the Farewell Address of 1796, and finally in the Monroe Doctrine of 1823. Washington used the qualifying word *ordinary* twice in his Address.

4. Noncolonization principle—no further European colonization on the American continents.

5. No-transfer principle: i.e., opposition to the transfer of colonial dominions in North America from one European sovereign to another: after the revolution of Latin America this was extended to the entire New World, including former colonies now independent. They should not be transferred back to any European sovereignty.

6. Freedom of international trade without discrimination between nationals and foreigners, including freedom of trade with colonial dominions.

7. Self-determination of peoples—as evidenced by our recognition of the revolted republics of Latin America. We hoped and expected that, despite temporary imperial regimes in Mexico and Brazil, these new states would all be republics, based on the rights of man, modeled on the United States.

8. Freedom of the seas for neutral ships in time of war, according to certain dicta of neutral rights, and freedom of navigation of international rivers.

9. The right of expatriation and the wrong of impressment.

10. Nonintervention—as testified first in the Monroe Doctrine, opposing the intervention of European nations to control the destiny of the free nations of Latin America.

11. Implicitly, in all this, never quite articulate, was a feeling of anti-imperialism. If one defines imperialism as dominion over alien people, the United States can scarcely be said to have been an imperial-

istic nation during the nineteenth century. At the cost of a great Civil War it resisted that temptation. The old Manifest Destiny was not imperialism. The new Manifest Destiny and the imperialism of 1898 that went with it have, as we shall see, been liquidated.

Nothing is clearer than that these were the main tenets and objectives of American foreign policy during the eighteenth and nineteenth centuries. No historian disputes their existence, or even their validity. They have remained fairly constant throughout our history despite the shifting strategy of our defense and diplomacy.

We did not immediately consummate all these principles and objectives, but on the whole we were remarkably successful in making most of them prevail as respected ourselves during the nineteenth century, despite the hazard of a paralyzing Civil War—as successful as any other great nation during that period of history, even more successful, it might be argued.

Before the twentieth century our principles did not reach much beyond the New World in the application of our foreign policy. Today they reach out to all the globe in tests of strength.

Our early diplomatic success was due to taking advantage, for the most part unwittingly, of the wars, rivalries, and distresses of the powers of Europe; to the detached and distant position of the United States; and to the fact that the principles and objectives of its foreign policy, just enumerated, were perfectly compatible with the genius and interests of its people. One other significant factor, the most vital of all, must be emphasized, *the favorable balance of power* behind the British balance in Europe and Asia.

From 1815 during the remainder of the nineteenth century the rival powers of Europe and of Asia were balanced fairly evenly behind the supremacy of British sea power. None of them was able to undertake an adventure in the New World without the assistance of the British navy, or at least the acquiescence of Great Britain. Thus no non-American power could hurt the United States or even gainsay its will in North America, except Great Britain. During all that century the two seacoasts of the United States, not to mention the entire New World, lay at the mercy of the British navy. Britain did not choose to collide uncompromisingly with American policy, whether over Florida, Cuba, Texas, Oregon, Mexico, the Isthmus of Central America, or Alaska, if only because of the long, undefended, exposed flank of Empire, presented by Canada.

In a war between the United States and Great Britain, a contingency happily growing more and more unthinkable decade by decade after 1815, Canada must have taken one of three possible positions: (1) loyal participation in the war against the United States—this would have meant the conquest of Canada; (2) neutrality—this would have been tantamount to secession from the British Empire; (3) war against Great Britain. Obviously, none of these choices was agreeable either to Great Britain or to Canada. Thus Canada served, historically, as a hostage for the good conduct of the British navy toward the United States as we expanded from coast to coast to become a great power. To prevent the growth of such a great power in North America adjacent to Canada, British policy relied on diplomacy rather than force. Great Britain encouraged the independence of Texas and California and tried to prevent their annexation to the United States. The British government, at least, hoped for the success of the Southern Confederacy during the Civil War. If successful, British diplomacy would have South Americanized North America. Texas would have been the Uruguay, California the Chile, the Confederate States the Brazil, the remaining United States the Argentina of North America, none of these nations strong enough to disturb the balance of power behind the British navy in this continent as elsewhere all over the world. Needless to say, British policy in balancing North America into a constellation of independent states like South America was unsuccessful. The victory of the North during the Civil War put an end to any such policy— fortunately for the fate of Great Britain; for had Britain balanced North America into a congeries of small nations, whence finally would have come the power from the West to redress the balance in the Old World during the First and Second World Wars of the twentieth century? Is it not a curious commentary on British foreign policy, the policy of the balance of states in all the continents behind an all-powerful British navy, that British diplomacy strove to prevent the growth of a transcontinental Republic in North America while it did nothing to prevent the rise of the German Empire on the continent of Europe?

One should not leave this interesting poise of Anglo-American relations during the nineteenth century without stressing two things. One is the value to mankind of the British Century, 1815–1914, when world peace rested on a balance of power in Europe, Asia, and South America, behind the all-powerful British navy. It was the happiest century that modern history has known, with self-government burgeoning out all over the five continents to enthrone the rights of man. As a people, as a nation, the United States was content with the British Century. During it our foreign policy, so clearly defined, was successful.

The other point I wish to make is that the historian could not have regarded Canada in the hands of any other strong imperialistic power as a hostage. In that case there would have been no undefended frontier. Canada in the possession of France, or of Germany after 1815, or of Russia, would have been regarded as a vestibule of invasion of the United States. The increasing affinity and benevolence of Anglo-American relationships in all their broad walks of liberty has to be constantly kept in mind when we think of Canada the Hostage, the magnetic field of American foreign policy during the nineteenth century.

The happy, isolated position of the United States, secure, if only because of Canada, behind the balance of power held by the British navy, a position in which we grew up uncudgeled to be a transcontinental Republic—I call it the Continental Republic with due respect for the Continental Dominion—in the choicest region on the surface of the globe, with an optimum climate for human welfare and energy, a national estate fronting on the two great oceans; that position began to disintegrate toward the end of the nineteenth century, when an unprecedented phenomenon suddenly took place: the almost simultaneous appearance of three new world powers: the United States, Germany, and Japan.

The advent of one new world power in the international firmament is in itself a spectacle of tremendous significance. It is certain to cause major perturbations in the orbits of the older powers. A triple birth of world powers—that was unknown in history. It unbalanced power in Europe and in Asia.

Two of the new powers confronted the third, the United States, one across either ocean. Each had a formidable army. Each was building a strong navy. Either would soon be in a position to threaten one of our populous sea coasts, if we did not reconstruct the strategy of our defense. Neither had a hostage like Canada alongside the United States to guarantee its benevolence. North America was no longer a safe, isolated landmass. It was becoming an island-continent menaced by new potentials of power. By the same tokens the British Empire was becoming a world-archipelago threatened by hostile continents. The new picture of power and politics caused the United States and Great Britain to look more and more to each other for the security of their own futures. Great Britain was first to feel the significance of the new order of power and began to look for allies. As the old balance began to tremble under these phenomenal impulses, the American outlook on the world began to change, too.

Ever since the completion of the Continental Republic, American opinion had focused increasingly upon the project of an Isthmian canal. The new frame of power and politics of the twentieth century made such a waterway indispensable for national security. Without a canal two new navies would be necessary, one on each ocean. With a canal one navy might suffice, to be passed back and forth through the Isthmus to protect either coast as circumstances might require. Nobody seems to have dreamed, in the early decades of the present century, that the United States might have to fight simultaneously a two-ocean war. It was Germany who loomed up as the principal disturber of the old balance.

Such was the situation when the United States went to war with Spain over the Cuban Question. Behind the Cuban Question lay the Isthmian Question.

The United States emerged from the Spanish-American War a full-fledged world power, protector of Cuba, mistress of the Caribbean, ready to build, control, and fortify a canal across the Isthmus of Central America. The necessary arrangements, diplomatic and engineering, were quickly completed. Great Britain, eager for firm friendship with the United States against the rising menace of Germany, recognized our paramount interest in the future canal and in Central America and the Caribbean. From 1898 until the Second World War, Panama, not Canada, became the pole of American diplomacy toward which the compass needle came back in every major question despite violent fluctuations east and west.

The diplomatic history of the United States should have taught us by 1914 that there was one danger which ought to disturb the sleep of every American diplomatist—the vision of an undivided Europe agglomerated under one power which could be turned against the United States after overpowering or neutralizing Great Britain; more dreadful still the nightmare of a similar great mass of force united in the Far East which could be allied with Europe against the United States and the New World. As we look back on the First World War it would seem that the real motive for our entrance into that conflict should have been a clearly discerned *raison d'état:* to prevent Germany and her allies from overturning the balance of power against us. It should have been perfectly evident that if the Allies won the war, the United States had nothing to lose by their victory, as proved by the previous British Century and, we can add today looking back, as proved also by the actual event of Allied victory in 1918. It should have been obvious, on the other hand, that the United States had much to fear, much to lose, if Germany should win. Our statesmen did not see this as clearly then as we can see it now.

Woodrow Wilson did not shift the strategy of American diplomacy from Panama to Europe expressly to meet the danger that had now threatened our historic security. He did his best up to the very last moment to keep his country out of the holocaust. We would like to believe that he finally brought the United States into the war on the Allied side in order to prevent Germany from upsetting the balance of power against us. There is no satisfactory evidence that he did. It was rather his *choice* of alternatives of neutral policy between the opposing retaliatory systems of the maritime belligerents, rather than his choice of peace or war, which led this peace-loving President into the First World War against his will. Fortunately he took his country into the conflict on the right side, if belatedly, and thus saved the balance of power for the United States and its associates. Had the United States stayed neutral a few months more until after the Russian collapse, Germany would have won the war, would have become the dominant sea power, and would have been in a position to ally herself with Japan to crush the United States and Canada, to possess herself of Latin America and the Atlantic while Japan took over Asia and the Pacific and perhaps Alaska. Our victory in the First World War saved us from that disaster.

Once in the war Wilson shifted the strategy of American diplomacy in a wholly new and untried direction—world peace through collective security in the form of a League of Nations rather than through the "forever discredited" system of the balance of power. But after the military victory, after restoration of a safe balance in Europe, and the establishment of a new balance in the Pacific and Far East, in short, when everything seemed perfectly secure again in North America and in the New World, the United States turned its back on Woodrow Wilson's League of Nations and his plan of collective security.

After the election of 1920 neither Republican nor Democratic Party dared to stand on a League of Nations platform, not till the closing months of the Second World War.

We may appropriately designate as the "Washington Period" the fifteen years of apparently perfect continental security which followed the Washington Conference of 1922. Never did the Western Hemisphere seem safer, a paradise of peace. Perhaps it would be more accurate to call that period the Fool's Paradise of American history.

During the Washington Period, American foreign policy degenerated into five postulates: isolation, anti-imperialism, disarmament, neutrality, pacifism.

Under the shadow of a new European war, Congress, pressed on by a powerful historiography of revision and disillusion, completely repudiated the policy of Woodrow Wilson during the First World War. One by one the new neutrality laws of 1935–37 outlawed the issues of neutral rights which had brought the United States into that conflict. They all but renounced the ancient American "birthright" of Freedom of the Seas.

All these legislative precautions, all this new retrograde strategy of American diplomacy, designed to keep the United States out of the next war, only served the purpose of keeping it out of the previous war, so to speak, a war which had already been fought and won. The neutrality legislation said in effect to Germany and to Japan and to the would-be world power, Italy, that the United States would not go to war to preserve the balance of power in the Old World, that it would not even allow the democratic allies of Western Europe to replenish their depleted forces from the potential arsenal of American supplies. Such was American world power on the eve of Munich, when Hitler overthrew the balance in Europe and we looked on still satisfied at peace in our time.

When Germany overran Western Europe, and made the Tripartite Pact with Japan and Italy, it was apparent that the anti-imperialistic, pacifistic United States now faced the greatest peril of its history, the nightmare of its diplomatists, the prospect of a two-ocean war with a one-ocean navy. Only England stood between us and destruction, until Hitler made the mistake of attacking Russia. If Germany defeated Great Britain and seized the British fleet, the new Alexander could then organize the sea power, air power, and man power of Europe for an irresistible attack on the New World and the United States from the Atlantic, while Japan attacked from the Pacific.

The strategy of American defense and diplomacy shifted again with the change in the balance of power, from Panama as a lifeline of hemisphere security to England as a base for a war of defense to be waged in Europe instead of America to restore the balance. American neutrality, already shaken by the initial impact of the war, broke down completely in 1941, notwithstanding the pledges of both major parties and their candidates, in the national election of 1940, to keep the United States out of the war.

It will be Franklin D. Roosevelt's claim to statesmanship as compared with that of Woodrow Wilson, that, whatever his initial vacillations and his campaign deceptions, he came to see the American *raison d'état,* the vital relation of the United States to the balance of power at the advent of the Second World War. He protected that relation at the risk and fact of a double war, rather than permit Japan to destroy the British Empire in the Pacific while the United States was striving to preserve it for our defense in the Atlantic. Despite Pearl Harbor, the greatest humiliation of American history, for which Roosevelt seems as much responsible as any one, he was right in taking on the double war: with the help of the British Commonwealth we licked Japan left-handed while our right arm was busy together with so many other armies in Europe.

Roosevelt's understanding of the vital interests of the United States in the new shift of the balance of power after the defeat of Germany and Japan was, I suggest, more questionable.

Now, after the Second World War, the geographical basis of American defense and foreign policy is shifting again with the balance of power, shifting back to the north.

Three unexpected political phenomena of victory are: (1) the rise of a new colossus, in the potential supremacy of Russia in the world; (2) the disintegration of the British Empire; (3) the demoralization, at least temporary, of the United States in the Great Let-Down of 1945–47.

These three phenomena have perturbed international politics and the prospect of world peace almost as profoundly as the sudden birth of three new world powers at the advent of the twentieth century. None of them offsets the others: on the contrary they all supplement each other in favor of Russia. What does that bode for the balance of power and the traditional principles of American foreign policy?

There is increasing reason to believe that the leaders of Russia for reasons of domestic policy fear the *friendship* of the Western World, particularly of the United States, much more than they do its enmity. In fact, given the phenomena of victory just mentioned, and the perfect security of Russian frontiers brought about by the complete defeat of Germany and Japan, they do not fear our *enmity* at all. It is we who fear *their* enmity and want their friendship.

We have extended an eager hand of friendship to Russia to grasp, for the rights of man, for the principles of nonintervention, democracy, self-determination, and freedom—freedom of speech, of religion, freedom from fear (including the fear of atomic warfare), freedom (hopefully) from want, from the crushing burden of armaments, freedom of trade, freedom of the international rivers and straits, in short, the things we have traditionally stood for in the world and still stand for. We had hoped that Russia would grasp that hand, for on such a sincere handclasp is the only hope for world peace. But these are not the things that Russia stands for in the world. What she wants rather is the extension of her opposite principles, by revolution if necessary, to the rest of the world: a World Union of Soviet Socialist Republics, that kind of a United Nations.

What is the strategy of American security and defense now that collective security has failed and the balance of power has turned against us?

It consists, I submit, in three lines of defense: a first line, in Europe; a second line, in the New World, south; a third line in the New World, north, along the Arctic Circle, perhaps south of it. That third line may become, at any moment, the first line, in a new Pearl Harbor.

In respect to Europe, the foreign policy of the United States, since Pearl Harbor, would seem to have undergone nothing less than a diplomatic revolution, but, on second historical thought, it is still the problem of maintaining a safe balance of power. Before the Second World War it was the policy of Great Britain first, and of the British Commonwealth of Nations and the United States behind Great Britain, to rest upon a balanced Europe and a balanced Asia. Now that that balance has been lost, by defeat in victory, at Yalta, at Potsdam, and at home in London, Ottawa, and Washington, in the will and morale of our people, we have had to reform our ideas of the balance. We are making a desperate effort short of war itself to encourage not the division but the union of Western Europe in a new balance before the present precarious situation leads to war. We have sluiced money and munitions, to say the least, into Turkey and Greece to hold back the weight of totalitarian power pressing down upon the Dardanelles. If the plug is pulled, so to speak, at the Dardanelles, Soviet power will pour unobstructed through the Near East into Africa, as Japanese power did through the straits of Singapore in 1942, into Micronesia and Australasia, only more devastatingly: on the one hand into Persia and India, on the other hand flowing into Africa to occupy a springboard for a jump across to sedulously prepared ground in South America.

In addition to sustaining Greece and Turkey, the people of the United States have expended eleven billions of dollars worth of economic aid and loans for the peaceful rehabilitation of an exhausted Western Europe, and are preparing to expand twice as much more in a mammoth program, the Marshall Plan, put together by the free governments in consultation, to rehabilitate the economy of those countries 25 per cent above their prewar level as a means of firming them to resist the threat of revolution from within and aggression from without.

If I were a member of Congress, I would have voted for these aids, but with misgivings. I would vote for them because the American people, still not fully recovered from their postwar demoralization and disillusion, are not yet willing to take other measures more resolute in nature. I would have misgivings because such devices are essentially mercenary in character. If history teaches any lesson, it is that no great people has ever been able safely to rely on mercenaries, on foreign legions, on subsidies, to maintain its liberties. They may help but they cannot be a substitute for valor. The hope of the Marshall Plan is that it may transfuse enough health into Western Europe to enable those peoples to regain a consciousness of liberty, and health to defend it. But it cannot be a substitute for our own right arm and resolution. If it does not work, we shall have to fall back on our second line of defense—in South America—and, perhaps simultaneously, on our third and last line of defense in North America. Here I venture to think the line will eventually be drawn; and we had better use what little time there may be gained by the Marshall Plan, resolutely to prepare for the worst, in order that the best may be saved.

These successive lines of defense are also the lines of defense of those other countries which lie behind them, first, second, and third. People may grieve to find their countries a possible battleground between two great potentials of power; they may wish, they may strive, they doubtless will strive to be neutral. But as they do so, they cannot but realize that the battleground, if such it becomes, is one of liberty against slavery in a struggle for the rights of English freemen, for those fundamental freedoms which flowered in the recent British Century. To be neutral in any final Armageddon means surrender of those priceless human rights, of all the long constitutional log of freedom from Magna Charta to the Statute of Westminster and the Charter of the United Nations. It is inconceivable to me that Britons, Canadians, and Americans, nay before them that Swiss, Frenchmen, Belgians, or Dutchmen, should lie down without a struggle and accept the yoke of Moscow in a W.U.S.S.R. Suppose then that these three lines of defense left for Anglo-Saxon liberty did not remain? Suppose that back of the last there were left no final power for the defense of freedom? Where could free men look for life? The Iron Curtain would be an Iron Cover closed down over all the globe, and no man could tell, no man would be permitted to tell, how many centuries must pass before it could be lifted.

17. Fourth Front in the Caribbean

PROF. ARNOLD TOYNBEE—in a recent, 1958, brilliant study of "The Eve of War, 1939"—has called attention to the fact that in 1940 no power was threatened on more than two fronts, east and west, whilst now, 1959, each of the two surviving power groups—U.S.A. and USSR —is threatened on three fronts, east, west and north, "a first-class revolution in international affairs . . . that is not easily grasped or taken into account."

Now suppose the United States should be threatened on all four fronts, including south as well as north, from the Caribbean, as well as the Arctic? Instead of an expansive and friendly ally like Canada stretching for thousands of miles between us and Soviet jet, submarine and missile bases, with a double line of Distant Early Warning trips, we suddenly become exposed to such bases almost within sight of our Southern coastal cities, and right athwart our naval communications from Atlantic to Pacific by the Panama Canal? Would this not tip the balance of power fatally against the United States in the present deadly crisis of power and politics which we call the "cold war"?

Since 1934, the first line of our defense has shifted from Panama to Europe and Asia. In this geopolitical framework, the stratetical paths over the Arctic regions have indeed become of more *immediate* significance than the Caribbean. It has even been argued by some strategists that, in the atomic age, the Panama Canal is no longer a lifeline for the defense of this country; that we could well afford to have it neutralized under an international authority, so great is the danger that one atomic bomb could neutralize—i.e., paralyze—it by knocking it out.

Scarcely anything, short of withdrawal of American forces from Europe and the Asiatic littoral, or the dissolution of NATO [North Atlantic Treaty Organization] or SEATO [Southeast Asia Treaty Organization] would please the Red imperialists more than the neutralization of the Panama Canal or the transfer of its control and defense

Published in *U. S. News & World Report*, Washington, Dec. 28, 1959, under the title "A Way To Stop the Reds in Latin America." Copyright 1959, United States News Publishing Corporation.

to the Republic of Panama, like the Suez Canal to Egypt. It would split our present global strategy into a two-ocean strategy and prevent the Panama Canal's being used by the West as a substitute for a blocked Suez Canal, or to relieve the burden on our flagging railway system in case of war.

The Communist conspiracy is on its toes today in Panama trying to dislodge the United States from control of this still vital American lifeline.

The United States should make it clear to the world that in the Panama Canal Zone it will continue to act *as if it were sovereign,* as, indeed, it has an explicit treaty right so to do, and to stick beyond any cavil to the military defenses of that waterway.

Much more than the Canal, and all that means to American defense, can be lost. If international communism is allowed to jump the Atlantic and set up a rule in a state of the New World, the way it recently tried to leapfrog over Turkey into Syria and Lebanon, it would mean not only effective neutralization of the hemispheric lifeline in a strategic sense, it would create an active fourth front for the defense of the United States. We simply cannot allow that to happen.

Latin American Communists schooled in Moscow have studied just how to set up their system in the Americas. They tried it once already in Guatemala, while the United States stood by with arms folded around the doctrine of nonintervention, awaiting the uncertain action of a conference of foreign ministers which, thanks only to the counterrevolution of Carlos Armas, never had to meet.

When, finally, the diplomatic doctors did an autopsy on the fallen Arbenz regime in Guatemala, they found the disease of international communism to be far more deep-seated than they had suspected. In fact, it still lingers as a cancer in the body politic of honest liberalism, not only in Guatemala but in all the states of Central America and the Caribbean. It is festering now in Cuba, in Panama, in Venezuela where they spat on Vice President Nixon. The cancer is spreading.

What is there, within the inter-American peace system—pledged as it is to the doctrine of nonintervention—to prevent such a disaster in the New World?

Nonintervention is the keystone of the inter-American peace structure, put into place by the Good Neighbor policy. In numerous treaties since 1933—subject to honorable denunciation by any of the parties on one year's and, in some cases, two years' notice—the American republics have declared inadmissible the intervention of any one of them (1933, 1936) or *group of them* (1948) directly or indirectly or for whatever reason, within the internal affairs of another American state.

There is, however, one outstanding exception to this sweeping pledge: *It does not affect existing treaty obligations.* For example, it would not affect the existing treaties of the United States with Panama or Nicaragua by which the United States guarantees the protection of the Panama Canal and the Nicaraguan canal site; it would not affect our treaty with Cuba giving us the naval base at Guantanamo; it would not affect the provisions of the Inter-American Treaty of Reciprocal Assistance, of Rio de Janeiro, of 1947.

The Rio Pact—the first regional alliance of the diplomatic revolution which now binds the United States to defensive alliances today with some 46 countries of the globe—provides for joint intervention, if two-thirds of the American states shall agree to assist in meeting an armed attack against an American state—the group acting within the inherent right of individual or collective self-defense recognized by Article 51 of the Charter of the United Nations. The treaty also provides, Article 6:

> If the inviolability or the integrity of the territory or the sovereignty or political independence of any American state should be affected by an aggression which is not an armed attack, or by an extracontinental or intercontinental conflict, or *by any other fact or situation* that might endanger the peace of America, the Organ of Consultation [of the Organization of American States] shall meet immediately in order to agree on the measures which should be taken for the common defense and for the maintenance of the peace and security of the continent.

The Rio Pact of 1947 is the same bond which brought inter-American diplomatic intervention to stop local wars between Haiti and the Dominican Republic, and between Nicaragua and Costa Rica. It is the same bond and principle which animated the meeting of the ministers of foreign affairs last August, in Santiago de Chile, invoked by four republics, including the United States—that gentle Pan-American huddle which weakly empowered the Inter-American Peace Commission to watch and study military movements in the Caribbean and report to the next (eleventh) Conference of American States at Quito, Ecuador, in February 1960.

This is the same *casus foederis* [a case within the provisions of a treaty] to which appeal had been made, upon the insistence of Panama, in the case of Guatemala in 1954, for a meeting of foreign ministers of American states to consider the crisis of Guatemala, a meeting prevented by Carlos Armas' successful counterrevolution.

Today it is very doubtful whether the Organization of American

States, through its Organ of Consultation, could muster the necessary two-thirds majority of the high contracting parties quickly enough to give a mandate, under the terms of the Rio Pact of 1947, for joint intervention to suppress a Latin-American government gone Communist by infiltration of a popular-front government or capture of a liberal revolution, and thereby threatening the peace and security of the American continent.

It might be tried, but, if it failed, what then?

There remains the Monroe Doctrine, which declares that interposition by any European powers to extend their *system* to any region of this hemisphere is dangerous to our own peace and safety. There remains the inherent right of self-defense, both individual and collective, even if it is not agreed on by a two-thirds majority of American states.

> We owe it [therefore] to candor [pronounced President Monroe in his famous message of Dec. 2, 1823], and to the amicable relations existing between the United States and those [European] powers, to declare that we should consider any attempt on their part *to extend their system to any portion of this Hemisphere*, as dangerous to our peace and safety . . . we could not consider any interposition for the purpose of oppressing [American states] or controlling in any other manner, their destiny, in any other light than as a manifestation of an unfriendly disposition toward the United States [which would induce measures] indispensable to their security.

An important corollary to the Monroe Doctrine since its origin—indeed, a vital dictum of the Doctrine since 1869—prohibits the transfer of any colony in the New World from one European sovereign to another—lest such an occurrence upset the balance of power against the security of the United States in this hemisphere.

This "no transfer" principle has been bound up in the Monroe Doctrine throughout its history. President Grant officially proclaimed it a part of the Doctrine in 1869.

As Hitler's armies were overrunning Western Europe and threatening to take over French, Dutch, and British colonies in the Western Hemisphere—i.e., Guadalupe, Martinique, Bermuda, the Bahamas, Jamaica, Trinidad, British Honduras, the Guianas, Aruba, etc.—a joint resolution of the United States Congress of June 18, 1940, signed by President Franklin D. Roosevelt, implementing the sense of an earlier declaration by a meeting of the foreign ministers of the American republics at Panama in September 1939, at the beginning of the war, stated:

> (1) That the United States would not recognize any transfer, and would not acquiesce in any attempt to transfer, any geographic region of this Hemisphere from one non-American power to another non-American power; and
>
> (2) That if such transfer or attempt to transfer should appear likely, the United States shall, *in addition to other measures,* immediately consult with other American republics to determine upon the steps which should be taken to safeguard their common interests.

Shortly thereafter, a special conference of foreign ministers of the same republics, facing the danger of Nazi conquest of Europe and England, gave a mandate to any one or more American republics, in case of the imminent danger of transfer of colonial territory in the American continents from one European sovereign to another, to step in and act quickly to forestall such a transfer. A special convention provided for an inter-American committee to administer the government of the rescued region, pending its restoration to its inhabitants upon the return of peace.

But the Havana mandate of 1940 looks only to the actual transfer of an existing colony in America from one European sovereign to another European sovereign. It does not explicitly envisage the case of a European sovereign in fact, if not in name, extending its Communist system to a republic of the American system *à la Guatemala*—and will it be *à la Cuba, à la Panama, à la Venezuela?*

The Pact of Rio of 1947 does anticipate such a "fact or situation" endangering the peace and security of any republic of the New World, but it requires a two-thirds vote of the 21 republics to give a mandate to one or more republics to act in time to stop the danger.

It would be nice if there could issue from the eleventh meeting of American states, to meet at Quito, Ecuador, in February 1960, a declaration on the lines of the Act of Havana of 1940, giving a mandate for individual or joint action to prevent the international Communist system of the Old World extending itself to an American state, directly or indirectly, and thereby threatening the peace and security of the American republics.

It is not known whether our Department of State is endeavoring to put such a business on the agenda for the Quito conference. It ought to be a major goal of our government to secure this kind of declaration. Such a proposal, incidentally, would be a touchstone to reveal the degree of Communist power within the various delegations.

However, it is not likely, in the present condition of inter-American relations, that such a declaration would be accepted by even a bare majority of the states—*and the emergency may be upon us even before the meeting at Quito next February*. Already the Cuban dictatorship has announced its intention to buy jet planes from inside the Iron Curtain.

The dilemma of our Latin American policy today is whether, on the one hand, to interpret the inter-American doctrine of nonintervention so as to permit a non-American power to extend its revolutionary system to the New World by capturing a republic in the Caribbean or Central America, now within easy bombing range of the United States and of the Panama Canal; or, on the other hand, to prepare some anti-interventionist action within the framework of the inter-American peace structure that would really prevent the intervention of international communism. That is: Inter-American intervention to prevent non-American intervention, one horn of the dilemma; or the other horn of absolute nonintervention to permit the intervention of international communism to establish its system in the Western Hemisphere.

In 1940, the Congress acted promptly in the face of the danger arising from the war in Europe. Let it now pass an analogous resolution, to make it clear to our friends and enemies, all over the globe, that this government is determined within its inherent right of self-defense, and within the purview of the pristine Monroe Doctrine, and indeed of the Pact of Rio and the inter-American peace structure, not to permit the intervention of international communism to endanger the peace and security of the United States, and of all the republics of this hemisphere—indeed, the balance of power for freedom against slavery in the entire globe.

Such a resolution against the intervention of international communism—couched in the language of the Monroe Doctrine, the Rio Pact, and the nonintervention declarations of Washington (1951) and Caracas (1954), and the recent Declaration No. XI of Santiago (1959)— should provide for the administration of the state thus defended or rescued, by the same inter-American authority and machinery set up in the Havana Convention of 1940 for the provisional administration of European colonies and possessions in America threatened by a transfer of sovereignty.

Thus stipulated, there need be no apprehension on the part of our good neighbors that the United States would be reverting to the old system that characterized the interventions against European imperialist intervention in this hemisphere during the first quarter of our century.

Such a policy would protect the doctrine of nonintervention against the new technique of intervention by international communism, and would do so within the spirit of the inter-American peace and defense treaties. It would not wait for the accomplished fact of a leap of the Communist revolution across the Atlantic to uproot the Monroe Doctrine in the New World, as it has already destroyed the "open door" policy in China. By thus assuming the initiative in the New World, we can also defend the global balance of power on which the peace and security of the United States and of our sister republics of America in the world must depend during the coming decade.

It is too much the practice of the United States, in the continuing world crisis of our time, to let the initiative rest with the enemy, to wait for the blows to fall and only then endeavor to improvise some action to fend them off.

Let something be done now, before it is too late. For example, Congress ought, at the beginning of the next session in January, immediately, on the eve of the Quito Conference, to pass a joint resolution analogous to that of June 18, 1940, explicitly pointed at the present fact or situation.

If the Quito Conference *doesn't* back it up, then the United States, acting under the pristine Monroe Doctrine, must do so. The act of faith known as the Good Neighbor policy, and the freedom of the New World—but, most essentially, the security of the United States and the blessings of liberty invoked in our Constitution—are now at stake.

PROPOSED RESOLUTION [1]

Inter-American Treaty of Reciprocal Assistance, 1947   WHEREAS, the intervention of international communism directly or indirectly in an American republic would constitute a fact or situation threatening the sovereignty and political independence of the states of the entire New World, and

1. This resolution was proposed by members of both houses of Congress, went into committee in each house, but the committee failed to get the green light from the Department of State, either in the Eisenhower Administration or in the Kennedy Administration. The Quito Conference has been repeatedly postponed.

*Monroe
Doctrine,
1823*

WHEREAS, the American continents, by the free and independent position which they have assumed and maintained, have long since ceased to be considered as subjects for future colonization by any European power or powers, and

*Declaration of
Washington,
1951, and
Declaration of
Caracas, 1954*

WHEREAS, the intervention of international communism, directly or indirectly, or however disguised, in any American state, would be in effect such a colonization by a non-American power or powers, and would violate the sovereignty and political independence of an American state, and

*Inter-American
Treaty of Reciprocal
Assistance, and
Monroe Doctrine*

WHEREAS, such a fact or situation extended to any portions of this Hemisphere would be dangerous to the peace and safety of the United States and the American continents, and

WHEREAS, in the rapidly developing contingencies of the atomic age there might not be time to assemble a meeting of the Inter-American Organ of Consultation to provide for joint action to repel the danger, the Senate and House of Representatives of the United States hereby

RESOLVE, that if such a fact or situation should present a sudden emergency, then any one or more of the high contracting parties to the Inter-American Treaty of Reciprocal Assistance would be justified, in the exercise of individual or collective self-defense under Article 51 of the Charter of the United Nations, in taking steps to forestall intervention, domination, control, and colonization by international communism in the New World.

*Act of Havana,
1940, with
Convention of
Havana, 1940*

In case of such defensive measures having been taken by the defending state or states, it or they should report to the Inter-American Organ of Consultation, to the end that an

*Abraham
Lincoln's
Gettysburg
Address, 1863*

emergency committee, after the manner provided by the Convention of Havana of 1940, be set up for the provisional administration of the state thus defended, pending its restoration to a government of the people, by the people, and for the people.

Bibliography of Samuel Flagg Bemis
1913-62

BOOKS (in chronological order)

Jay's Treaty: A Study in Commerce and Diplomacy, New York, Macmillan, 1923. Rev. ed. New Haven, Yale University Press, 1962 (paperbound and hard cover).

Pinchney's Treaty: A Study of America's Advantage from Europe's Distress, 1783–1800, Baltimore, Johns Hopkins Press, 1926.
2nd printing, 1941.
Rev. ed. New Haven, Yale University Press, 1960 (paperbound and hard cover).

Editor and contributor, *The American Secretaries of State and Their Diplomacy,* 10 vols. New York, Knopf, 1927–29.
Reprinted 10 vols. in 5, New York, Pageant Book Co., 1958.

The Hussey-Cumberland Mission and American Independence: An Essay in the Diplomacy of the American Revolution, Princeton, Princeton University Press, 1931.

With Grace Gardner Griffin, *Guide to the Diplomatic History of the United States, 1775–1921,* Washington, Govt. Printing Office, 1935.
Reprinted Gloucester, Mass., Peter Smith, 1959.

The Diplomacy of the American Revolution, New York, Appleton-Century, 1935.
2nd printing, 1937.
3rd ed. Bloomington, Indiana University Press, 1957 (paperbound).

A Diplomatic History of the United States, New York, Holt, 1936.
2nd ed. revised and expanded, 1942.
3rd ed. revised and extended, 1950.
4th ed. revised and extended, 1955.

La Política internacional de los Estados Unidos: interpretaciones, Lancaster, Lancaster Press, 1939. (Lectures delivered as Carnegie visiting lecturer to Latin American countries, 1937–38.)

The Latin American Policy of the United States, New York, Harcourt, Brace,

1943. Spanish translation: *La diplomacia de los Estados Unidos en la América Latina,* México, Fondo de Cultura Económica, 1944.

John Quincy Adams and the Foundations of American Foreign Policy, New York, Knopf, 1949.

The United States as a World Power: A Diplomatic History, 1900–1950, New York, Holt, 1950. (Reprint, with adaptations, of Part III of *Diplomatic History of the United States,* 3rd ed.)

John Quincy Adams and the Union, New York, Knopf, 1956.

A Short History of American Foreign Policy and Diplomacy, New York, Holt, 1959.

American Foreign Policy and the Blessings of Liberty and Other Essays, New Haven, Yale University Press, 1962.

ARTICLES (in chronological order)

"The Settlement of the Yazoo Boundary Dispute: The First Step in Southern Expansion," *Magazine of History, 17* (Oct.–Nov. 1913), 129–40.

"Relations between Vermont Separatists and Great Britain, 1789–1791," *American Historical Review, 21* (April 1916), 547–60.

"The United States and the Abortive Armed Neutrality of 1794," *American Historical Review, 24* (Oct. 1918), 26–47.

"A Proposed Solution of the American Industrial Problem," *Pacific Review, 1* (March 1921), 520–29.

"The Yap Island Controversy," *Pacific Review, 2* (Sept. 1921), 308–28.

"Alexander Hamilton and the Limitation of Armaments," *Pacific Review, 2* (March 1922), 587–602.

"Jay's Treaty and the Northwest Boundary Gap," *American Historical Review, 27* (April 1922), 465–84.

"Shall We Forget the Lusitania?" *The Outlook, 131* (Aug. 30, 1922), 710–13.

"The London Mission of Thomas Pinckney," *American Historical Review, 28* (Jan. 1923), 228–47.

"Professor Channing and the West," *Washington Historical Quarterly, 14* (Jan. 1923), 37–39.

"David Thompson, Explorer: At Last the Fame of the Great Pathfinder Is Resurrected from a Pauper's Grave," *Sunset Magazine, 50,* no. 3 (March 1923), 28–29.

"Captain John Mullan and the Engineers' Problem," *Washington Historical Quarterly, 14* (July 1923), 201–05.

"British Secret Service and the French-American Alliance," *American Historical Review, 29* (April 1924), 474–95.

"The United States and Lafayette," *Daughters of the American Revolution Magazine, 58* (1924), 341–50, 407–14, 481–89.

"Talleyrand and Jaudenes, 1795" (Documents from the Archivo Histórico Nacional at Madrid, brought to the editor by Professor Samuel Flagg Bemis), *American Historical Review, 30* (July 1925), 778–87.

"The Mellon Plan for Settling American Claims against Germany," *Barron's, 6* (Feb. 1, 1926), 6.

"The Effect of Science on History" (Radio talks on science), *The Scientific Monthly, 22* (March 1926), 224–27.

"Payment of the French Loans to the United States, 1777–1795," *Current History, 23* (March 1926), 824–31.

"Settling War Claims," *Barron's, 6* (Dec. 27, 1926).

"The Background of Washington's Foreign Policy," *Yale Review, 16* (Jan. 1927), 316–36.

"The Alien Property Bill and the Senate," *Barron's, 7* (Feb. 14, 1927), 21.

"Communication" (A note regarding maps in *Pinckney's Treaty*), *Hispanic American Historical Review, 7* (Aug. 1927), 386–89.

"Acquisition of Source Material for American History" (From the report of the director of the European mission of the Library of Congress), *Report of the Librarian of Congress for the Fiscal Year Ending June 30, 1929* (Washington, Govt. Printing Office, 1929), 75–96.

"Fields for Research in the Diplomatic History of the United States to 1900," *American Historical Review, 36* (Oct. 1930), 68–75.

"Canada and the Peace Settlement of 1782–3," *Canadian Historical Review, 14* (Sept. 1933), 265–84.

"John Jay," *Dictionary of American Biography*, New York, Scribner's, *10* (1933).

"Washington's Farewell Address: A Foreign Policy of Independence," *American Historical Review, 39* (Jan. 1934), 250–68.

"George Washington and Our Problems of Today" (Reprint of speech given at Morristown, New Jersey), Washington Associates of New Jersey, 1936.

"A Clarifying Foreign Policy," *Yale Review, 25* (Winter 1936), 221–40.

With Lawrence Martin, "Franklin's Red-Line Map Was a Mitchell," *New England Quarterly, 10* (March 1937), 105–11.

"The Rayneval Memoranda of 1782, and Some Comments on the French Historian Doniol," *Proceedings of the American Antiquarian Society, 47* (April 21, 1937–Oct. 20, 1937), 15–92.
Reprint, Worcester, 1938.

"Can We Undo the Great Aberration?" *Amerasia, 1* (April 1937), 59–61.

"Main Trends of American Foreign Policy," in *Before America Decides,* ed. by Frank P. Davison and George S. Viereck, Cambridge, Harvard University Press, 1938.

"Los Estados Unidos y el problema del Pacifico," and "La doctrina Monroe en nuestros días," in *Revista de derecho y ciencias políticas* (Lima), 2 (1938), 780–803, and *Revista de la Universidad de Guayaquil, 9* (enero–abril 1938), 149–79.

"La emancipación de las islas Filipinas," *Revista de derecho y ciencias políticas, 2* (1938), 769–80.

"La nueva reciprocidad," *Revista de la Universidad de Guayaquil, 9* (1938), 179–91. Reprinted with the two addresses above, *Ciclo de conferencias sustentadas por el doctor Samuel Flagg Bemis,* 1938.

"El buen vecino del norte," *Universidad de los Andes, Revista bimestral* (Mérida, Venezuela), *1* (1938), 162–81. With the four articles preceding, reprinted in *La Política internacional de los Estados Unidos.*

"Observaciones y sugestiones acerca de la historia diplomática," *Boletín de la Academia Nacional de la Historia* (Buenos Aires), *12* (1939), 227–30.

"The New Holy Alliance Crosses the Ocean," *Quarterly Journal of Inter-American Relations, 1* (Jan. 1939), 18–24.

"Early Diplomatic Missions from Buenos Aires to the United States, 1811–1824," *Proceedings of the American Antiquarian Society, 49* (April 19, 1939–Oct. 18, 1939), 11–101.
Reprint, Worcester, 1939.

"The Training of Archivists in the United States," *American Archivist, 2* (July 1939), 154–62.

"Política exterior actual de los Estados Unidos," *La Justicia* (México, D.F.), *9* (dic. 1939), 4269–75. Reprinted in *La Política internacional de los Estados Unidos.*

"Papers of David Curtis DeForest and J. W. DeForest," *The Yale University Library Gazette, 14* (April 1940), 62–63.

About 80 small articles in *Dictionary of American History,* New York, Scribner's, 1940.

Unsigned obituary and in memoriam of Worthington C. Ford, *American Historical Review, 46* (April 1941), 1012–14.

"America Faces Her Greatest Crisis," *Social Science, 16* (July 1941), 218–20.

"Walter Lippmann on U.S. Foreign Policy," *Hispanic American Historical Review, 23* (Nov. 1943), 664–67.

"Joseph Vincent Fuller," *Dictionary of American Biography, 21,* Supplement One, New York, Scribner's, 1944.

"La universidad de Yale en la democracia norteamericano," *Cuadernos del Ateneo de la Habana, 1* (1945), 9–20.

"Historia e historiadores en la democracia norteamericano," *Ultra, 17,* no. 103 (marzo 1945), 186–88.

"John Quincy Adams and George Washington," *Massachusetts Historical Society Proceedings, 67* (Oct. 1941–May 1944), 365–84.

"John Quincy Adams and Russia," *Virginia Quarterly Review, 21* (Autumn 1945), 553–68.

"First Gun of a Revisionist Historiography for the Second World War" (Review of *Pearl Harbor; the Story of the Secret War,* by George Morgenstern), *Journal of Modern History, 19* (March 1947), 55–61. See letter by author to editor in *26* (June 1954), 206, correcting misrepresentations by Dr. Harry Elmer Barnes.

"The Shifting Strategy of American Defense and Diplomacy," *Virginia Quarterly Review, 24* (Summer 1948), 321–35.
Revised and printed under same title in *Essays In Honor of George Hubbard Blakeslee,* Worcester, Clark University Publications, 1949, pp. 1–14, and in *Current Readings on International Relations,* Cambridge, Addison-Wesley Press, 1949, pp. 2–12.

"The United States as a World Power," a chapter in *World Political Geography,* New York, Crowell, 1948, pp. 53–64.

"The Memoirs of Cordell Hull" (Review), *Journal of Modern History, 21* (Dec. 1949), 317–20.

"Fanatics for Freedom," *Proceedings of the Eighty-fourth Convocation of the University of the State of New York, Oct. 20, 1950* (Albany).
Also separately printed, and in part reprinted in *Yale Alumni Magazine, 14* (June 1951).

"The Scuffle in the Rotunda: A Footnote to the Presidency of John Quincy Adams and to the History of Dueling," *Massachusetts Historical Society Proceedings, 71* (Oct. 1953—May 1957), 156–66.

"Yalta Papers," *The Americana Annual,* Washington, 1956, pp. 811–13.

"John Quincy Adams, protegé de Washington y precursor de Lincoln con algunas consideraciones historiográficas. Conferencia leída por el Dr. Samuel Flagg Bemis, Profesor de la Universidad de Yale, el día 10 de enero de 1956, en el auditorium de esta Universidad." (Universidad de Santo Tomás de Villanueva) *Noverim, 1* (mayo 1956), 5–17.

"La crisis de los filibusteros: Abraham Lincoln y el proyectado compriso Crittenden," Academia de la Historia de Cuba, La Habana, 1956.

"American Diplomacy," *Encyclopedia Americana,* 1956 ed., *1,* 510.

"Protocol," *Encyclopedia Americana,* 1956 ed., *22,* 690.

"United States Diplomacy," *Encyclopedia Americana,* 1956 ed., *27,* 482.

"Woodrow Wilson and Latin America," *Wilson's Foreign Policy in Perspective,* ed. by Edward H. Buehrig, Bloomington, Indiana University Press, 1957, pp. 105–40.

"Henry Adams, 2nd," *Massachusetts Historical Society Proceedings, 70* (Oct. 1950—May 1953), 279–81.

"La Historia diplomática de los Estados Unidos," *Libro jubilar de Emeterio S. Santovenia,* La Habana, 1957, pp. 43–52.

"The Opinion of Samuel Flagg Bemis" (on basic curriculum for secondary schools), *American Education, The Thirty-second Discussion and Debate Manual, 1958–59,* Columbia, Mo. Lucas Brothers, 1958, *1,* 64.

"A Way to Stop the Reds in Latin America: A Noted Historian Sets a Course for Quick Action by the U.S." *U.S. News and World Report, 47* (Dec. 28, 1959), 77–80.

"John Quincy Adams," *Encyclopaedia Britannica* (forthcoming edition).

"Isolationism," *Encyclopedia Americana,* 1960 ed.

"John Jay," *Encyclopedia Americana,* 1960 ed.

"Jay's Treaty," *Encyclopedia Americana,* 1960 ed.

"Secret Intelligence, 1777: Two Documents" (with annotation by Helen C. Boatfield), *Huntington Library Quarterly, 24* (May 1961), 233–49.

"George Washington and Foreign Policy" (Editorial), *American Historical Review, 67* (Oct. 1961), 278.

"The Adams Family and Their Manuscripts," an address delivered at a ceremony held at the Massachusetts Historical Society, Sept. 22, 1961, marking the publication of the *Diary and Autobiography of John Adams,* first printed in a bulletin of the Society, entitled *The Adams Papers* (Boston, 1962), later to be published in the Society's regular *Proceedings, 73* (1961–   ).

"American Foreign Policy and the Blessings of Liberty," presidential address to the American Historical Association at Washington, D.C., Dec. 9, 1961, printed in *American Historical Review, 67* (Jan. 1962), 291–305.

Note: Not listed here are some 136 reviews in various newspapers and periodicals, popular and scholarly, as well as numerous newspaper articles and editorials.